Knowledge Management Innovations for Interdisciplinary Education:

Organizational Applications

Sheryl Buckley
University of South Africa, South Africa

Maria Jakovljevic
University of Zadar, Croatia

Managing Director:	Lindsay Johnston
Senior Editorial Director:	Heather A. Probst
Book Production Manager:	Sean Woznicki
Development Manager:	Joel Gamon
Development Editor:	Hannah Abelbeck
Assistant Acquisitions Editor:	Kayla Wolfe
Typesetter:	Alyson Zerbe
Cover Design:	Nick Newcomer

Published in the United States of America by
Information Science Reference (an imprint of IGI Global)
701 E. Chocolate Avenue
Hershey PA 17033
Tel: 717-533-8845
Fax: 717-533-8661
E-mail: cust@igi-global.com
Web site: http://www.igi-global.com

Library of Congress Cataloging-in-Publication Data

Knowledge management innovations for interdisciplinary education: organizational applications / Sheryl Beverly Buckley and Maria Jakovljevic, editors.
    p. cm.
 Includes bibliographical references and index.
 ISBN 978-1-4666-1969-2 (hardcover) -- ISBN 978-1-4666-1970-8 (ebook) -- ISBN 978-1-4666-1971-5 (print & perpetual access) 1. Knowledge management. 2. Management--Technological innovations. I. Buckley, Sheryl Beverly, 1959- II. Jakovljevic, Maria, 1950-
 HD30.2.K626 2013
 378.1'07--dc23
                          2012009685

British Cataloguing in Publication Data
A Cataloguing in Publication record for this book is available from the British Library.

All work contributed to this book is new, previously-unpublished material. The views expressed in this book are those of the authors, but not necessarily of the publisher.

This book is dedicated to the rapid advancement of a maturing knowledge management discipline, and our beloved families for their love, support, and courage.

List of Reviewers

Jaflah Aiammary, *University of Bahrain, Bahrain*
Viveca Asproth, *Mid Sweden University, Sweden*
Sunday Babalola, *University of Ibadan, Nigeria*
Mirjana Pejić Bach, *University of Zagreb, Croatia*
Aurélie Aurilla Arntzen Bechina, *College University I Buskerud, Norway*
Roberto Biloslavo, *University of Primorska, Slovenia*
Sheryl Buckley, *University of South Africa, South Africa*
Kristina Crnjar, *University of Rijeka, Croatia*
Marié Cruywagen, *University of Stellenbosch Business School, South Africa*
Alina Dima, *Bucharest Academy of Economic Studies, Romania*
Tiit Elenurm, *Estonian Business School, Estonia*
Paul Giannakopolous, *University of Johannesburg, South Africa*
Ivanka Avelini Holjevac, *University of Rijeka, Croatia*
Ana-Marija Vrtodušić Hrgović, *University of Rijeka, Croatia*
Maria Jakovljevic, *University of Zadar, Croatia*
Aleksandra Krajnovic, *University of Zadar, Croatia*
Ana Martins, *Xi'an Jiatong-Liverpool University, China*
Ellen Martins, *Organisational Diagnostics, South Africa*
Isabel Martins, *University of Glamorgan Business School, UK*
Sari Metso, *Lappeenranta University of Technology, Finland*
Camellia Okpodu, *Norfolk State University, USA*
Noel James Pearse, *Rhodes University, South Africa*
Orlando Petiz, *University of Minho, Portugal*
John Powell, *University of Stellenbosch, South Africa*
Gillian Ragsdell, *Loughborough University, UK*
John Tull, *University of Sydney, Australia*
Geoff Turner, *University of Nicosia, Cyprus*
Hana Urbancova, *Czech University of Life Sciences Prague, Czech Republic*
Neven Vrcek, *University of Zagreb, Croatia*

Table of Contents

Section 1
Knowledge Management, Innovation, and Education

Detailed Table of Contents

Section 1
Knowledge Management, Innovation, and Education

The effectiveness of Knowledge Management (KM) activities is in large part dependent upon employees' attitudes toward knowledge in general and to KM processes in particular. This chapter reports the results of a small-scale (N = 10) interview study of the "ways of knowing and knowledge sharing" of academics in three Slovene universities. The chapter presents an analysis of the responses from in depth, semi-structured interviews concerning the understanding of knowledge, KM processes, required social ecology, and attitude of academics. Responses were classified and tabulated in relation to theories of epistemology and KM and the findings analysed in relation to how they might be used for development of a conceptual KM framework within Higher Education Institutions (HEIs). The conclusion can be drawn that the KM framework within HEIs needs to take into account the bureaucratic and at the same time competitive and individualistic culture of academia.

Chapter 2

In order for education systems to cope with social and economic changes and perform efficiently, innovation is essential. Innovation in education (and particularly in Higher Education systems) has not been regarded as an important issue by policy makers, education stakeholders, and leaders; it seems to be regarded as "nice-to-have" rather than a necessity. Recently, innovation in education has started to gain attention. This includes systemic study of innovation, innovation strategy, and implementation of innovation strategies by policy makers and leaders. Scientific outputs and research findings can be used as input in national-international policies. In order to achieve this goal it is imperative to conduct close studies and for policy-makers to cooperate, ensuring the relevance of topics, and improving communication, dissemination, and implementation of research recommendations. These are the tools needed for leading change, innovation, and implementing new strategies.

Chapter 3

Ana Martins, Xi'an Jiaotong-Liverpool University, China
Isabel Martins, University of Glamorgan, UK
Orlando Petiz, University of Minho, Portugal

The current knowledge economy has brought several challenges to contemporary organisations. There is need for flexibility on the part of key players, namely individual employees as well as organisations as a whole; this flexibility arises from the innovation in both products and services. The complexity of knowledge requires an education that enhances softer skills. The intellectual capacity, creativity, and adaptability of individuals gives rise to greater flexibility. This strengthens the fact that there is a change of paradigm in the way human capital is viewed. Through the human-oriented perspective, knowledge is seen as collective sense making and social practice. The objective of this chapter lies in this context of complexity, change, and adaptation within an economic and social reality based on knowledge. Therefore, the chapter aims to reflect upon Knowledge Management in companies such as universities where tacit knowledge is stored as intellectual capital in the minds of both lecturers and students and to highlight the need to instill the new paradigm which fosters knowledge creation and sharing in universities.

Chapter 4

Maria Jakovljevic, University of Zadar, Croatia

Teachers-engineers in vocational and technical schools have been exposed to constant pressure concerning methods to foster and manage knowledge transfer of Creativity, Invention, and Innovation (CII) skills as learning outcomes. Knowledge management of CII in a technical-vocational educational environment has been a problem and needs improvement in order to engage teachers-engineers and learners in creativity and innovation activities. The purpose of this chapter is to develop a conceptual model for Creativity, Invention, and Innovation (MCII) from a knowledge management perspective in the technical-vocational and interdisciplinary ecologies of practice. This chapter takes the form of a literature study regarding CII multiple knowledge-sharing issues. A methodological framework has been described in the introductory section of this chapter. The background of the study focuses on the general features of CII, highlighting needs and gaps in terms of teachers-engineers' competence in promoting CII as new learning outcomes. The framework for the MCII focuses on the following main themes: theoretical views on CII issues; institutional and international collaboration; the construct of CII intelligence; teachers-engineers' competence; and creative knowledge-sharing climate. The structure and the flow of the conceptual model are presented, followed by discussion, future research directions, and the conclusion.

Chapter 5

  Alina Mihaela Dima, Bucharest Academy of Economic Studies, Romania

In order to overcome the challenges posed by globalization, an increasingly complex business world, and the transition to the knowledge-based economy, both academia and practitioners need to reinforce the importance of knowledge transfer activities between universities and other stakeholders and the development of new forms of transfer activities between academia and the external environment. As businesses, economies, and society in general become more global, and as the pace of change increases, they become more dependent on science and technology, on new and innovative forms of knowledge transfer, which are provided partially by universities. The knowledge in academics is an asset but also a liability. The innovation processes on knowledge management in education through knowledge transfer activities will facilitate the shift from teaching as the transmission of knowledge to teaching as the facilitation of learning. Drawing from the literature on knowledge exchange and foregoing observations, this chapter explores the innovation side of KM in education, based on knowledge transfer partners and activities. As academics continuously evolve collaborative forms of research activity and re-imagine the nature of academic-practitioner exchange and knowledge transfer, this chapter considers key contributions in the area and details important avenues that warrant further research.

Chapter 6

  Tiit Elenurm, Estonian Business School, Estonia

The aim of this chapter is to link knowledge management as a field of education to innovative learning. There are opportunities to apply personal knowledge management and knowledge sharing logic in several related subject fields that enable innovative learning. Raising awareness of business students about their online and face-to-face networking priorities and entrepreneurial orientations are educational tools for managing personal connectivity and for understanding knowledge management challenges linked to innovative learning. The experiential learning cycle is implemented in field projects, which also support cross-cultural learning and highlight real life challenges of knowledge sharing in innovative activities. The assessment of knowledge management prerequisites in different organizations serves as the departure point for knowledge management development visions. The chapter explains that knowledge management learning in business studies is not limited to a separate knowledge management course. Action learning projects can mean innovative learning both for students and managers that learn how to apply external "gatekeepers."

Chapter 7

  Milly Perry, The Open University, Israel

The under-performance in the creation, diffusion, and utilization of new knowledge represents a specific weakness in knowledge transfer from science to technology in the European Union. The extent of this weakness is reflected in the relatively low numbers of citations and patents in scientific work in comparison to the United States. Comparing these numbers indicates to what extent the linkage between patented inventions and science in European Union countries is weak.

This chapter set several objectives. The initial aim of this chapter is to clarify to what extent the eclectic use of terms: "Knowledge Sharing," "Knowledge Transfer," "Technology Transfer," and "Knowledge Management," relate to knowledge era. As these terms do not form an organizing concept and thinking framework, the second goal of this chapter will be to analyze and clarify these concepts. This chapter will describe their place within the Knowledge cycle in order to map their role and interrelation between the terms. Clarification of the roles and interrelationships will crystallize the contribution to Knowledge Management Strategy in university application have led to the conclusion that Knowledge Management is the appropriate organizing concept and framework for laying the foundations of the Knowledge Era Economy.

Chapter 8

Geoff Turner, University of Nicosia, Cyprus
Clemente Minonne, Zurich University of Applied Sciences, Switzerland

Knowledge is now recognized as the most important factor of wealth creation, meaning there is no clearer way to prosperity than assigning priority to learning and knowledge creation. This is of greater significance to educational institutions because they are the primary drivers in the generation, accumulation, and dissemination of knowledge. As such, the value of an educational institution to society will depend on its capacity to create and share knowledge, which is an unremitting cycle of discovery and dissemination, or the conversion of knowledge from implicit to explicit. The source of an institution's value to society lies in its ability to continuously improve that process by developing a strategy for acquiring and effectively and efficiently managing its knowledge base as well as understanding how and why its value is changing. In this chapter, the authors consider how an institution knows whether it is managing its knowledge assets in a sustainable way and whether they have increased or diminished over a certain period by looking at several propositions already in existence. It then proposes its own strategic approach, the Knowledge Management Monitor, to assist in this management process.

Section 2
Knowledge Management, Innovation, and Business

Chapter 9

Ivanka Avelini Holjevac, University of Rijeka, Croatia
Kristina Črnjar, University of Rijeka, Croatia
Ana-Marija Vrtodušić Hrgović, University of Rijeka, Croatia

Knowledge is an infinite resource of hotel enterprises and society as a whole. In hotel enterprises, it serves as a platform for practising sustainable development and gaining competitive advantages. Knowledge-based economic development provides the best opportunities for dealing with a global environment in which rapid and dynamic changes are taking place. Seen as a precondition to success, Knowledge Management (KM) will result in generating value-added in tourism. A survey was conducted in large and mid-sized hotel enterprises to demonstrate their KM level and the contribution of KM in gaining competitive advantages in the Croatian hotel industry. Empirical research was used to establish the level of KM development in the Croatian hotel industry, and to determine the importance of KM in gaining competitive advantages in the hotel industry. In addition to knowledge, quality is a vital factor in gaining competitive advantages in hotel enterprises. Globalized markets and increasingly discerning customers, demanding more and more for their money, are compelling product and service providers to ground their business systems on customer needs. Total Quality Management (TQM)—a new management philosophy—enables the systematic application of these ideas. This chapter looks at several TQM approaches that define the basic elements essential to successful TQM implementation, in particular, the element pertaining to employees. The application of these elements in the Croatian hotel industry is presented through the results of empirical research on a sample of mid-sized and large hotel enterprises.

Chapter 10

Sari Metso, Lappeenranta University of Technology, Finland

Knowledge management theories emphasize the role of knowledge work and knowledge workers in knowledge-intensive organizations. However, technologization has changed the knowledge work environment. Many knowledge workers create, process, and share simplified information in digitalized networks. This complicates the profession-based definitions of knowledge workers. This chapter contributes to the emerging concern about the future trends of knowledge management. First, the chapter suggests that knowledge management models ignore a large group of professionals possessing practical knowledge. These vocational professionals are considered a new target group for knowledge management. Vocational professionals' practical knowledge is worth managing since they operate with organizational core functions. Second, this chapter presents an alternative education-based categorization of workers. The different functions of KM are manifest in the three categories: a diminishing group of workers without professional qualifications, a large group of vocational professionals, and a group of workers with higher education.

Chapter 11

Sladjana Cabrilo, University Educons, Serbia
Leposava Grubic-Nesic, University of Novi Sad, Serbia

Globalization, fast-paced technological, economic, and social changes, and increased competition have affected the current business environment by changing the role of knowledge, innovation, and creativity in work, learning, and everyday life. Although Knowledge Management (KM) is usually explored separately from creativity and innovation, these concepts are closely related and in practice reinforce each other. Linking KM to innovation and creativity management in a holistic fashion has facilitated the examination of the knowledge management impact on innovation performance of organizations. In addition, this practice makes it possible to examine how creativity and invention can be used to increase the efficiency of knowledge management. This chapter focuses on the analysis of the role and importance of creativity, innovation, and invention in knowledge management. In addition, the chapter investigates the role of KM in innovation, and environmental and personal factors, which contribute to creativity, innovation, and invention in KM.

Chapter 12

This chapter discusses the importance of training workers about the intangible assets in a knowledge economy, the nature of intangible assets, how they are different from other assets, and the concepts of a knowledge workforce in a knowledge economy. It is apparent that many organizations are engaging the services of knowledge workers, but such organizations do not provide enabling environments for these workers to be fully productive. This chapter looks at the relevance of training knowledge workers in identifying intangible assets for creating value and enhancing competitiveness and innovation in a knowledge economy. Given that it has always been difficult to gather the prerequisite information to manage such assets and create value from them, the chapter discusses the nature of intangible assets, the characteristics of a knowledge economy, and the role of knowledge workers in a knowledge economy. Training and education of knowledge workers must not be taken for granted. The chapter also discusses how training and education of knowledge workers may enhance their ability in identifying intangible assets in relation to capturing the value of such assets, the transfer of intangible assets to other owners, and the challenges of managing organizational intangible assets. In a knowledge economy, knowledge workers play a central role in managing and evaluating intangible and knowledge-based assets.

Chapter 13

The aim of organizations is efficient management leading to a competitive advantage. In the current knowledge economy, employees, their knowledge, and potential are considered to be an organization's main competitive advantage and the most important asset towards determining performance and success. By introducing modern areas of management, organizations can quickly identify and utilize knowledge, which enables an early application of knowledge in innovations and key processes. Thus, putting them ahead of their competitors and gaining a competitive advantage in the market. This chapter focuses on the impact of applying Business Continuity Management, Knowledge Management, and Knowledge Continuity Management on innovations in organizations and their productivity.

Chapter 14

Breathless announcements of the latest information access devices occupy whole sections of our daily news, itself increasingly accessed online and on-the-go. This reinforces to the manager or educator the conventional wisdom that strategies for developing organisational capabilities inherently involve ever-quicker access and sharing of information—a belief reflected widely in organisational learning and strategy literatures. However, Knowledge Management's role in translating learning into performance-enhancing capabilities remains opaque; "macro" evaluations are too abstract, leading to recent calls for empirical or "micro" studies. Furthermore, while rare breakthroughs attract headlines and research, customers and clients are mostly won or lost in the more mundane interactions of daily work. The evolution of organisational capabilities and how they rely on the medium of knowledge practices can be unpacked using the construct of an organisation's "absorptive capacity," a construct essentially unknown to KM. That construct can be improved by incorporating "tempo" as a crucial design and governance element. Analysing KM practices as supporting absorptive capacity is a new idea that provides both the manager and the educator with implementable recommendations. A detailed case study identifies the four key factors of capability development via KM, highlighting that "slow knowledge"—gearing knowledge processes to the appropriate absorptive capacity framework—can yield more effective organisational outcomes.

Chapter 15

Marié Cruywagen, University of Stellenbosch Business School, South Africa
Juani Swart, University of Bath, UK
Wim Gevers, University of Stellenbosch Business School, South Africa

The ability to provide an organisational context for the creation, sharing, and integration of knowledge, called the knowledge-centric capability, is a key strategic resource of an organisation and an enabler of innovation. This view is informed by dynamic capabilities, which focus on the ability of an organisation to modify and renew its resource base by creating, integrating, recombining, and releasing its resources in order to adapt to current changes or to affect change in its environment. A knowledge-centric capability comprises three core elements that enable innovation. Organisational intent is the resolve of an organisation to provide the context in which knowledge can serve as a strategic resource in the organisation. Knowledge orientation is the way in which an organisation orientates itself towards its knowledge environment in terms of knowledge types and the role of knowledge in the organisation. Enactment includes elements of knowledge coordination, creation, use, and integration. The authors review how the extent to which the three core elements that are present in an organisation could give an indication of the organisation's ability to innovate by comparing these insights with the practices of Fundamo, one of the world's leading specialist mobile financial services companies.

Section 3
Knowledge Management, Innovation, and Technology

Chapter 16

Sheryl Buckley, University of South Africa, South Africa
Paul Giannakopoulos, University of Johannesburg, South Africa

The role of technology in organisations over the past two decades, whether centred on business or education, has varied from performing simple day-to-day tasks to performing highly sophisticated problem-solving tasks. Many organisations have either adjusted their daily routines to accommodate new technology or developed technologies to satisfy their needs. At the same time, the credo "knowledge is power" was changing to one of "knowledge sharing is power." Once this change was recognized, Communities of Practice (CoPs), a special type of community of practitioners sharing knowledge voluntarily, began to play a very important role in Knowledge Management (KM). Such communities relied heavily on technology in order to prosper. One of the greatest advantages of these communities is the sharing of tacit knowledge, in a disciplinary as well as interdisciplinary environment, which is an "ingredient" of innovation and competitive advantage. This chapter will review the ongoing evolution of the tools, types of technology, and innovations that can be used by both online and offline CoPs. It will further address the matter of which technological innovations and tools academics can use to support CoPs and the design of technology used for this purpose.

Chapter 17

    Alina Mihaela Dima, Bucharest Academy of Economic Studies, Romania

Keeping up-to-date with ever-changing technologies and striving to find innovative ways to integrate them into a classroom setting are constant challenges to all educators. Clearly, technology is associated with changes in practice, but the nature of this association is complex and contested. Innovation in education has always been related to technological developments, but it can also be achieved by introducing changes to teaching practices, curricula, and learning activities, all of which can be regarded as activities included in the knowledge management and transfer paradigm.

Chapter 18

    Livio Cricelli, University of Cassino, Italy
    Michele Grimaldi, University of Cassino, Italy
    Musadaq Hanandi, University of Rome, Italy

The principal aims of this chapter are to provide a comprehensive understanding of the main processes for innovative knowledge management in human capital learning and to define a theoretical model that assesses and measures the human capital value contribution to an organization's performance. The chapter aims to explain how technological advancements and innovation facilitate collaboration, support sharing of dynamic contents, and make the learning process easier and more fruitful. Finally, a summary is provided by way of a strategy map, which allows the tracking of the human capital learning process and assessment of ex-post learning performance.

Chapter 19

    Fiona Masterson, National University of Galway, Ireland

Knowledge is created when individuals come together to solve a problem. Project-based learning focuses on solving problems. One aspect of the work of a 21st century design engineer is the requirement to work remotely on design projects. Engineers coming together to design a product face the problem of working remotely, collaborating, creating, and sharing knowledge. This chapter explores the use of wikis in a product design and development class at an Irish university. This chapter begins by giving an introduction to wikis and their use in education. The design project exercise and assessment process is described. The results of a study are provided that indicate that the vast majority of students found wikis to be a good tool for project collaboration. Wikis were found to be an excellent knowledge management tool that facilitates project-based learning.

Foreword

Today, the management of companies and organizations takes place in a new context that has different names, such as information society, knowledge society, and knowledge economy. Each one has its particularities and characteristics, but we regard them as roughly equivalent and henceforth we will only use the term knowledge economy. Dahlmann and Andersson (2000) define knowledge economy as one that encourages its organizations and people to acquire, create, disseminate and use—codified and tacit—knowledge more effectively for greater economic and social development. Moreover, according to the World Bank (Dahlmann & Andersson, 2000), the four pillars of the knowledge economy are the following: 1) An educational and skilled labor force that continuously upgrades and adapts its skills to efficiently create and use knowledge; 2) An effective innovation system of firms, research centers, universities, consultants, and other organizations that keeps up with the knowledge revolution, taps into the growing stock of global knowledge, and assimilates and adapts new knowledge to local needs; 3) An economic incentive and institutional regime that provides good economic policies and institutions, which promote the efficient creation, dissemination, and use of existing knowledge; and 4) A modern and adequate information infrastructure that facilitates the effective communication, dissemination, and processing of information and knowledge.

The book edited by Professor Sheryl Buckley and Professor Maria Jakovljevic focuses on the latest developments within the above described four pillars, but specifically targets educators, professionals, and researchers working in the field of innovation in knowledge management in various disciplines. In order to better understand its contribution, we describe in the next paragraphs the essential features of this new context, emphasizing the key role of knowledge and intellectual capital in the process of wealth creation.

The economy, the queen of social sciences, has among its many definitions the following: Economics is the study of wealth (Samuelson, 1980). In other words, it is the study of the processes of creation and distribution of wealth. Throughout history, the word economy has been accompanied by various qualifiers relating to key factors of wealth creation for each different era of human history. So in succession, we have moved from agrarian economy to industrial economy, and from industrial economy to service economy. More recently and due to the increasing development of information and telecommunication technologies and the processes of internationalization and globalization, knowledge and learning have emerged as the primary sources of wealth creation (Neef, 1998, pp. 1-12). It is for this reason that today's economy receives the name of "knowledge economy" or the alternative denomination of "knowledge-based economy."

This transformation in the very foundations of the economic process, or in the process of wealth creation, poses significant challenges for management and strategic management of enterprises, organizations, and institutions, and also in the management and strategic management of public entities such as cities, regions, and nations. To cope with these challenges in the field of management, new concepts (knowledge, intangibles and intellectual capital), new disciplines (knowledge management, intellectual capital management and organizational learning) as well as new approaches of previous disciplines have emerged. The new disciplines and approaches are closely related to each other and have some similar goals and objectives, but among them, we consider Knowledge Management (KM) and Intellectual Capital Management (ICM) as the most relevant. Indeed, if we define Intellectual Capital as "knowledge and other intellectual assets that produce value now, or are able to produce value in the future," (Viedma, 2007) we realize that this definition relates knowledge and other intellectual assets with wealth creation, and wealth creation, as mentioned previously, has been and remains the ultimate purpose of the economy. In fact, both disciplines, KM and ICM, share the same strategic objectives and focus on creating value or wealth for companies or organizations. The difference between KM and ICM lies in the approach taken, and in the words of Karl Wigg (1997), is the following:

ICM focuses on building and governing intellectual assets from strategic and enterprise governance perspectives with some focus on tactics. KM has tactical and operational perspectives. KM is more detailed and focuses on facilitating and managing knowledge-related activities such as creation, capture, transformation, and use. Its function is to plan, implement, operate, and monitor all the knowledge-related activities and programs required for effective ICM.

Following a different line of thought, Peter Drucker (Neef, 1998, pp. 15-34) came to similar conclusions in his now famous article, "From Capitalism to Knowledge Society." In his article, he describes and discusses the increasing importance of knowledge in the economic progress of mankind, and considers in his description and analysis an historical perspective, which focuses primarily on the last three centuries. In fact, it focuses primarily on the last three centuries because knowledge had previously been seen as applied almost exclusively to the development of the human being considered individually, that was educated mainly on philosophy, literature, and the arts, or on what later on was called "liberal education." In the period between 1750 and 1900, the focus or object of knowledge changed radically, passing from being to doing, or from improving the human being, to improving economic activities. In this sense, Drucker raises for the last three centuries an evolutionary process that began with the industrial revolution, which continues the productivity revolution and that ends today with what he calls the "management" revolution. The era of the industrial revolution was characterized by the application of knowledge to the tools, products, and processes, the time of the productivity revolution by the application of knowledge to the study of work, and finally, the time of the "management" revolution is characterized by the application of knowledge to knowledge itself. The important role of knowledge in this evolutionary process can be summarized using the words of Drucker, which we transcribe below.

The change in the meaning of knowledge that began 250 years ago has transformed society and economy. Formal knowledge is seen as both the key personal resource and the key economic resource. Knowledge is the only meaningful resource today. The traditional "factors of production"—land (i.e. natural resources), labor, and capital—have not disappeared, but they have become secondary. They can be obtained easily, provided there is knowledge. And knowledge in this new meaning is knowledge as a utility, knowledge as the means to obtain social and economic results.

If we focus on the last stage of the evolutionary process outlined above (stage management), we realize that knowledge is now being applied to knowledge. This is the third and perhaps the ultimate step in the transformation of knowledge. Using again the words of Peter Drucker (Neef, 1998, p. 30):

Supplying knowledge to find out how existing knowledge can best be applied to produce results is, in effect, what we mean by management. But knowledge is now also being applied systematically and purposefully to define what new knowledge is needed, whether it is feasible and what has to be done to make knowledge effective. It is being applied, in other words, to Systematic Innovation.

From the paragraphs and the comments just quoted, it is clear that knowledge is conceived in a utilitarian sense that is closely linked with effectiveness and efficiency and is considered the key economic factor, or almost the only economic factor, not only in the current processes but also in the processes of innovation. Even the "management" discipline is defined as a process of knowledge management.

From another point of view and focusing on key agents of wealth creation in the global knowledge economy, we can say without any doubt that firms are the primary agents of wealth creation. This crucial role of firms is highlighted by M. E. Porter (2005) in the following citation:

It is well understood that sound fiscal and monetary policies, a trusted and efficient legal system, a stable set of democratic institutions, and progress on social conditions contribute greatly to a healthy economy. I have found that these factors are necessary for economic development, but far from sufficient. These broader conditions provide the opportunity to create wealth but do not themselves create wealth. Wealth is actually created in the microeconomic level of the economy. Wealth can only be created by firms. The capacity for wealth creation is rooted in the sophistication of the operating practices and strategies of companies, as well as in the quality of the microeconomic business environment in which a nation's companies compete. More than 80 percent of the variation of GDP per capita across countries is accounted for by microeconomic fundamentals. Unless microeconomic capabilities improve, macroeconomic, political, legal, and social reforms will not bear full fruit.

Nevertheless, not all firms contribute to wealth creation but only the excellent or competitive. An excellent or competitive company is the one that achieves long-term extraordinary profits due to the fact that it has a business model with sustainable competitive advantages. Modern theory of strategic management, especially the resources and capabilities paradigm (Grant, 1991; Collins & Montgomery, 1995; Prahalad & Hamel, 1990; Tecce, Pisano, & Shuen, 1997) and the customer driven paradigm (Von Hippel, 2005; Chesbrough, 2006) fully justifies the important role of intangible resources, core competencies, dynamic capabilities, and ultimately core knowledge in the process of creating and sustaining competitive advantages by firms. However, companies today are organized as a network (Quinn, 1992) and in its wealth-creating processes, they use and rely on other companies, organizations, and institutions, some of which are located in the immediate environment (city, region, cluster, etc.) with which to easily share resources and capabilities, and others located in remote environments with which it is harder to share these resources and capabilities, although the difficulty decreases with the progress of new information and telecommunication technologies. When we say resources, we refer mainly to intangible resources and especially tacit knowledge, which are those that are at the root of sustainable competitive advantages.

Therefore, we can say that the firm, and especially the innovative firm, as the main wealth creator agent, needs in the process of wealth creation, the cooperative efforts of other companies (suppliers, customers, etc.), organizations (universities, science parks, technology parks, venture capitalist, incubators, etc.), and institutions (research centers, etc.), which grouped geographically (city, region, cluster, etc.) constitute its essential complement.

In all these enterprises, organizations, and institutions, the role of knowledge that creates value remains central in gaining and sustaining competitive advantages. All these considerations lead us to the simultaneous and coordinated management of knowledge and intellectual capital in firms, organizations, and institutions considered individually or grouped in clusters of cities, regions, or nations, with the ultimate aim of achieving economic and social development.

The book, edited by Professor Sheryl Buckley and Professor Maria Jakovljevic, has succeeded in its aim to provide relevant academic work, being the latest research findings as well as examples of best practices found in organizations concerning innovation in knowledge management with respect to teaching and learning in academia and the business environment. The book's content addresses the crucial issue of knowledge management innovations for interdisciplinary education from different perspectives and in different environments. Therefore, its contribution is highly significant for value creation in the knowledge economy context.

José Maria Viedma Marti
Polytechnic University of Catalonia, Spain

José Maria Viedma Martí *is a Professor of Business Administration at Polytechnic University of Catalonia, President of Intellectual Capital Management Systems, and Founding Partner of M&A Fusiones y Adquisiciones.*

REFERENCES

Chesbrough, H. W. (2006). Open innovation: A new paradigm for understanding industrial innovation. In H. Chesbrough, W. Vanhaverbeke, & J. West (Eds.), *Open Innovation: Researching a New Paradigm*. Oxford, UK: Oxford University Press.

Collins & Montgomery. (1995, July-August). Competing on resources: Strategy in the 1990s. *Harvard Business Review*, 118-128.

Dahlmann, C. J., & Andersson, T. (2000). *Korea and the knowledge-based economy: Making the transition*. Washington, DC: The World Bank.

Grant. (1991). The resource-based theory of competitive advantage: Implications for strategy formulation. *California Management Review, 33*(3), 114-135.

Neef, D. (1998). *The knowledge economy*. London, UK: Butterworth-Heinemann.

Porter, M. E.. (2005). What is competitiveness? *IESE Business School: Anselmo Rubiralta Center for Globalization and Strategy*. Retrieved from http://www.iese.edu/en/ad/AnselmoRubiraltas/Apuntes/Competitividad_en.html

Prahalad, & Hamel. (1990, May-June). The core competence of the corporation. *Harvard Business Review*, 79-91.

Quinn, J. B. (1992). *Intelligent enterprise*. New York, NY: The Free Press.

Samuelson, P. A. (1980). *Economics* (11th ed.). New York, NY: McGraw Hill Book Company.

Tecce, , Pisano, & Shuen. (1997). Dynamic capabilities and strategic management. *Strategic Management Journal, 18*(7), 509–533. doi:10.1002/(SICI)1097-0266(199708)18:7<509::AID-SMJ882>3.0.CO;2-Z

Viedma, J. M. (2007). In search of an intellectual capital comprehensive theory. *Electronic Journal of Knowledge Management, 5*(2), 245–256.

Von Hippel, E. (2005). *Democratizing innovation*. Cambridge, MA: The MIT Press.

Wigg, K. (1997). Expert systems with applications. *Knowledge Management, 13*(1), 1–14.

Preface

When insights and experiences embodied in individuals or organizations are shared among people, when they meet the needs of the people who use them—they can and do change organizational processes and practice for the better. We all want to share and transfer insights and experiences that comprise knowledge, providing that a clear path is set through the management of knowledge as a strategic asset. To succeed, we need knowledge management innovations to transfer our insights and experiences in both organizational and educational settings.

Educators and managers alike recognize the need for a more disciplined approach to knowledge management innovations. Many individuals and organizations still apply the practice of knowledge sharing in a disorganized manner, even when using the most advanced technologies. Many professionals and students are unaware of new perspectives on knowledge sharing that comprise creativity, invention, and innovation processes.

Knowledge management efforts typically focus on organizational objectives such as improved performance, competitive advantage, innovation, the sharing of lessons learned, integration, and continuous improvement of the organization (Knowledge Management, 2012). The four pillars of the knowledge economy—skilled labour force, an effective innovation system, an economic incentive, and adequate information infrastructure are highlighted by World Bank (Dahlman & Andersson, 2000). A broad range of thoughts on knowledge management exists to include techno-centric, organizational, and ecological perspectives. This book covers these perspectives and various knowledge management aspects to include, among others, community of practice, social networks, intellectual capital, and information theory.

This book consists of serious research, conscientious studies, and tumultuous debates. The collective experience that has gone into writing this book has come from many authors, as their writing endeavours are embedded in different cultures and societies. The themes of the book and the abstracts preceding each chapter reflect our awareness of knowledge practitioners' needs. An attempt has been made to indicate how the original approach to identify, create, represent, distribute, and enable the adoption of knowledge can empower students, managers, knowledge workers, and educators to become innovative in all aspects of knowledge sharing, resulting in measurable economic benefits to society as a whole.

The book is intended to serve as a guide to a maturing knowledge management discipline. In fact, the book is one of the few detailed resources available on knowledge management and innovations. The combination of a primary emphasis on theory and practice with applications to interdisciplinary education as well as organizational environments make this book unique among the burgeoning literature on knowledge management.

The book is proposed for both students and practitioners, retaining its appeal as a guide for the educational and organizational professionals, and as a comprehensive introduction for the student at the upper-level undergraduate level. The intended audiences for this book, then, are teachers, researchers, students, and knowledge management professionals, who are interested in understanding and applying knowledge management theory and practice.

One will notice that we are not presenting this book as a research text only, as an academic artefact, but we are instead presenting it as a personal route into a depth of knowledge management and innovation. In addition, knowledge management general points and issues are often illustrated, when appropriate, with reference to specific educational and/or educational contexts.

There are 19 chapters in the book. Each chapter concentrates on a particular point of knowledge management and innovation. The 19 chapters have been organized into three sections: Section 1: "Knowledge Management, Innovation, and Education," Section 2: "Knowledge Management, Innovation, and Business," and Section 3: "Knowledge Management, Innovation, and Technology." This has been done to compartmentalize topics.

Section 1, "Knowledge Management, Innovation, and Education," presents different views of knowledge management in interdisciplinary educational settings: considering academics' attitudes (Chapter 1); analyzing innovation policy in HEI (Chapter 2); reflecting upon organisational flexibility through human capital development (Chapter 3); developing a model for creativity invention and innovation (Chapter 4); getting an insight into the nature of innovation and the intellectual capital of educators and learners (Chapter 5); describing knowledge management and innovative learning (Chapter 6); investigating strategic knowledge management in a university context (Chapter 7); and designing the knowledge management monitor (Chapter 8).

Section 2, "Knowledge Management, Innovation, and Business," presents dedicated chapters that address a wide variety of issues: Total Quality Management (TQM) models in Croatian tourism (Chapter 9); vocational professionals as a new target group for knowledge management (Chapter 10); environmental and personal factors that contribute to creativity and innovation in knowledge management (Chapter 11); the intangible assets in a knowledge economy (Chapter 12); business continuity management, knowledge management, and knowledge continuity management in organizations (Chapter 13); adoption and extension of "absorptive capacity" construct in gearing knowledge processes (Chapter 14); and the knowledge-centric capability in organizations (Chapter 15).

Section 3, "Knowledge Management, Innovation, and Technology," presents topics on: tools, technology, and innovation that academics can use to support communities of practice (Chapter 16); challenges and opportunities for innovation in teaching and learning in an interdisciplinary environment (Chapter 17); technological advancements for the tracking of the human capital learning process and assessment of ex-post learning performance (Chapter 18); and the use of wikis in a product design and development class (Chapter 19).

OVERVIEW OF THE CHAPTERS

Synopses of chapters are described in the following paragraphs.

Chapter 1: Knowledge Management and Higher-Educational Institutions: Challenges and Opportunities

The chapter presents an empirical analysis of the responses from in depth, semi-structured interviews concerning the understanding of knowledge, KM processes, required social ecology, and the attitudes of academics in three Slovene universities. The research results of the study show that the success of KM in HEIs is influenced by four critical factors, namely the mentor, HEI leadership, ICT, and the academic community. ICT is mostly used in the process of KM for knowledge storage and teaching, while the role of the academic community is mainly in promoting the process of negotiation among its members, which can result in new knowledge.

Chapter 2: Innovation in Higher Education in Israel: Public Policy Implications

Innovation in higher education systems has not been regarded as an important issue by policy makers, education stakeholders, and leaders; it seems to be regarded as "nice-to-have" rather than a necessity. Scientific outputs and research findings can be used as input in national-international policies. In order to achieve this goal, it is imperative that researchers and policy-makers cooperate, ensuring the relevance of topics, and improving communication, dissemination, and implementation of research recommendations. These are the tools needed for leading change, innovation, and implementing new strategies.

Chapter 3: Organisational Flexibility through Human Capital Development

The chapter demonstrates that, in the knowledge society, systemic flexibility allows organisations to respond to the dynamic environmental forces of change placed on it. This chapter strengthens the fact that organizational flexibility through human capital development improves quality amongst individual employees in their multi-faceted areas, namely, intellectual capacity, creativity, and adaptability. Universities are the hub where knowledge, the key resource of the new millennia, is created, shared, and stored through the organisation's intellectual capital.

Chapter 4: A Conceptual Model of Creativity, Invention, and Innovation (MCII) for Entrepreneurial Engineers

Teachers-engineers in vocational and technical schools have been exposed to constant pressure concerning methods to foster and manage the knowledge transfer of Creativity, Invention, and Innovation (CII) skills as learning outcomes. This chapter presents a conceptual Model for Creativity, Invention, and Innovation (MCII) from a knowledge management perspective in the technical-vocational and interdisciplinary ecologies of practice. Five major subsystems of MCII are identified, namely: theoretical perspectives on CII; the four dimensions of CII intelligence; joint institutional and international collaboration; teachers' competence in terms of CII; and an appropriate environment for CII.

Chapter 5: Knowledge Transfer: The Innovation Side of Knowledge Management in Education

The innovation processes of knowledge management in education through activities will facilitate the shift from teaching as the transmission of knowledge transfer to teaching as the facilitation of learning. Drawing from the literature on knowledge exchange and foregoing observations, this chapter explores the innovation side of KM in education based on knowledge transfer partners and activities. As academics continuously evolve collaborative forms of research activity and re-imagine the nature of academic-practitioner exchanges and knowledge transfer, this chapter considers key contributions in the area and details important avenues that warrant further research.

Chapter 6: Knowledge Management and Innovative Learning

The chapter explains how knowledge management and innovative learning are integrated by assessing personal orientations of knowledge search and by clarifying networking and knowledge management development priorities. Action learning projects can mean innovative learning for both students and managers learning how to apply external "gatekeepers."

Chapter 7: Strategic Knowledge Management: A University Application

This chapter clarifies the extent of the eclectic use of the terms: "knowledge sharing," "knowledge transfer," "technology transfer," and "knowledge management," related to the knowledge era, and describes their place within the knowledge cycle in order to map their role and interrelation between the terms. Clarification of the roles and interrelationships will crystallize the contribution to the knowledge management strategy, and university applications have led to the conclusion that knowledge management is the appropriate organizing concept and framework for laying the foundations of the knowledge era economy.

Chapter 8: Effective Knowledge Management through Measurement

The value to society of an educational institution is related to its capacity to create and share knowledge, particularly by converting implicit knowledge to explicit knowledge. This requires a strategy for acquiring and effectively and efficiently managing its knowledge base. This chapter considers how an institution knows whether it is managing its knowledge assets in a sustainable way and whether they have increased or diminished over a certain period of time by looking at several propositions already in existence and then discussing the knowledge management monitor to assist in monitoring this process.

Chapter 9: Knowledge Management and Quality in Croatian Tourism

This chapter presents the results of a survey conducted in large and mid-sized hotel enterprises in order to establish the level of KM development and its importance in gaining competitive advantages in the Croatian hotel industry. In addition, this chapter looks at several Total Quality Management (TQM) approaches that define the basic elements essential to successful TQM implementation in the Croatian hotel industry, based on empirical research. Seen as a precondition to success, Knowledge Management (KM) will result in generating added value in tourism.

Chapter 10: A New Perspective on Knowledge Management Research: The Role of Vocational Professionals

This chapter suggests that technologization diminishes the role of knowledge work and knowledge workers in Knowledge Management (KM). Instead, professionals possessing practical knowledge are considered a new target group for KM. Their knowledge is worth managing since they operate with organizational core functions. Based on this idea, the chapter suggests an alternative education-based categorization of workers.

Chapter 11: The Role of Creativity, Innovation, and Invention in Knowledge Management

Since creativity, invention, and innovation concern the process of creating and applying new knowledge, they are at heart of the KM process. This chapter focuses on the analysis of the role and importance of creativity, invention, and innovation in knowledge management. Knowledge management improves innovation management; it fosters individual and group creativity, invention, and innovation. However, creativity and innovativeness could be regarded as the main developers of knowledge processes. An integrated approach to KM, innovation, creativity, and invention, as applied in this chapter, should be applied in organizations to facilitate their future development.

Chapter 12: Educating and Training Organizational Knowledge Workers in Evaluating and Managing Intangible and Knowledge-Based Assets in the Knowledge Economy

The chapter is on the significance of training and educating organizational knowledge workers about intangible assets in a knowledge economy. The chapter also discusses the concept of the "knowledge economy" and its characteristics as well as the nature of intangible assets. The chapter highlights the importance of investing in intangible assets and why knowledge workers should be equipped with relevant skills in managing such assets. Specific areas in which knowledge workers should be trained and educated are recommended.

Chapter 13: The Influence of the Application of Business Continuity Management, Knowledge Management, and Knowledge Continuity Management on the Innovation in Organizations

This chapter identifies the importance of knowledge in the process of innovations and the impact of the implementation on the innovative development that determines an organization's performance. Managers should make business continuity management part of managerial roles in order to achieve the optimal level of business continuity. This chapter focuses on the impact of applying business continuity management, knowledge management, and knowledge continuity management on innovations in organizations and their productivity.

Chapter 14: Slow Knowledge: The Case for Savouring Learning and Innovation

Conflating the innovation capabilities demanded by our hyper-competitive environment with "the need for (KM) speed" is often counter-productive. This chapter presents a longitudinal case study introducing two innovations that help managers and educators to better integrate KM with capability development: adoption of the "Absorptive Capacity" construct from strategic management and extension of that construct to bring into focus the role of "tempo" in knowledge creation that supports effective practice.

Chapter 15: The Role of a Knowledge-Centric Capability in Innovation: A Case Study

Knowledge-centric capability, i.e. the ability to provide an organisational context for the creation, sharing, and integration of knowledge, is a key strategic resource and an enabler of innovation within an organisation. The chapter illustrates that the nature of an organisation's knowledge-centric capability could serve as an indicator of its ability to innovate by exploring the practices of Fundamo, one of the world's leading specialist mobile financial services companies.

Chapter 16: Technology and Tools Supporting CoPs

One of the greatest advantages of Communities of Practice (CoPs) is the sharing of tacit knowledge, in a disciplinary as well as interdisciplinary environment, which is an "ingredient" to innovation and competitive advantage. In the knowledge era, the use of CoPs to create, disseminate, and share knowledge can only be enhanced through the use of technology, which provides the necessary tools for such tasks. This chapter reviews an ongoing evolution of tools, types of technology, and innovations that can be used by online/offline CoPs. The chapter further addresses what technology innovation or tools academics can use to support CoPs and the design of technology to support CoPs.

Chapter 17: Challenges and Opportunities for Innovation in Teaching and Learning in an Interdisciplinary Environment

Although innovation in education has always been related to technological developments, in evaluating the impact of technology-stimulated changes in education, we are facing various major challenges. Recent evidence shows that innovation can also be achieved by introducing changes to teaching practices, curricula, and learning activities, all of which can be regarded as activities included in the knowledge management and transfer paradigm. This chapter underlines that the process of knowledge management becomes the essential point of innovation processes in education, where the educators should play the most important role and facilitate the creation, transfer, and sharing of knowledge.

Chapter 18: Innovation and IT in Knowledge Management to Enhance Learning and Assess Human Capital

This chapter highlights the analysis of the role of knowledge management and knowledge management systems in human capital learning. Additionally, the chapter reflects upon the synchronization among human capital, organization processes, and information technology in education and learning. Finally, this chapter defines a human capital assessment model in order to enhance learning and assess human capital.

Chapter 19: Knowledge Management in Practice: Using Wikis to Facilitate Project-Based Learning

One aspect of the work of a 21st century design engineer is the requirement to work remotely on design projects. Engineers coming together to design a product face the problem of working remotely, collaborating, creating, and sharing knowledge. This chapter explores the use of wikis in a product design and development class at an Irish university. A design project that used wikis is described. The results of a study provided indicate that the vast majority of students found wikis to be a good tool for project collaboration.

The book, *Knowledge Management Innovations for Interdisciplinary Education: Organizational Applications,* is a collection of a broad array of resources that has been written and edited to provide flexibility and depth of knowledge management innovations, strategies and practices.

Maria Jakovljevic
University of Zadar, Croatia

REFERENCES

Dahlman, C. J., & Andersson, T. (2000). *Korea and the knowledge-based economy: Making the transition*. Washington, DC: The World Bank.

Knowledge Management. (2012). *Wikipedia.* Retrieved from http://en.wikipedia.org/wiki/Knowledge_management

Acknowledgment

Editing a book of this nature proved to be a daunting task for a number of reasons: First, forming the editorial team. Here, Maria Jakovljević proved to be the pillar that supported the book structure. Her vast knowledge and experience made the task easier. Second, the quality of submissions was of such a high standard that many times it proved very difficult to choose those studies to be included in the book. A big thank you to those whose papers are included, as well as to those whose work was not included in the book.

The primary aim of this book is to contribute to the further advancement of a maturing knowledge management discipline, disseminate original research and new developments within the discipline, and provide for interesting reading. These chapters represent truly global research, from 17 countries, from Australia to South Africa, England to Finland, and China to USA. The high standard of the book is derived from the independent treble blind peer review process. We would like to thank the 29 reviewers from 16 countries, again spanning the globe, who have critically evaluated the chapters. Special thanks go to José María Viedma Marti from Spain for writing the foreword.

Finally, we hope that the chapters will stimulate further progress in the knowledge management discipline and can give rise to a more global collaborative approach to knowledge management, underpinned by innovation. In a fast changing world, it is only though innovation that we keep ahead of time.

Sheryl Buckley
University of South Africa, South Africa

Section 1
Knowledge Management, Innovation, and Education

Chapter 1
Knowledge Management and Higher–Educational Institutions:
Challenges and Opportunities

Roberto Biloslavo
University of Primorska, Slovenia

Katjusa Gorela
University of Primorska, Slovenia

ABSTRACT

The effectiveness of Knowledge Management (KM) activities is in large part dependent upon employees' attitudes toward knowledge in general and to KM processes in particular. This chapter reports the results of a small-scale (N = 10) interview study of the "ways of knowing and knowledge sharing" of academics in three Slovene universities. The chapter presents an analysis of the responses from in depth, semi-structured interviews concerning the understanding of knowledge, KM processes, required social ecology, and attitude of academics. Responses were classified and tabulated in relation to theories of epistemology and KM and the findings analysed in relation to how they might be used for development of a conceptual KM framework within Higher Education Institutions (HEIs). The conclusion can be drawn that the KM framework within HEIs needs to take into account the bureaucratic and at the same time competitive and individualistic culture of academia.

INTRODUCTION

Higher Educational Institutions (HEIs) operate in a dynamic environment characterized by challenges, which require a rapid and possibly "different" response. HEIs, both public and private, do not compete for students and research budget only within their national boundaries, but also with foreign educational organisations, due to the increasing trend of the internationalization of higher education (de Wit, 2002). Within such a competitive environment, successful HEIs are those who have some kind of competitive advantage. The main source of competitive advantage of HEIs are their staff, their knowledge, and the ability to generate new knowledge, which has to be properly stored and made available through education and publication to the society (Marquardt, 1996).

DOI: 10.4018/978-1-4666-1969-2.ch001

According to a resource-based view of organisations, which argues that the diversity, quality, and inimitability of internal resources provides a better and more enduring basis for defining strategy than the products or services these resources bring about (Barney, 1991; Conner, 1991), knowledge is the critical resource and source of competitive advantage (Grant, 1996). Therefore, it is of crucial importance for HEIs to identify the available knowledge, and to appropriately use it in order to contribute to the development of the organisation, of the individuals within who are the knowledge carriers and of the larger society. On the other hand, creating, acquiring, storing, and applying knowledge represent the main areas of Knowledge Management (KM).

KM has now become an integral part of the overall management process which takes place in an organisation, even though it was just fifteen years ago that KM began to make great headway as a management discourse (Swan & Scarbrough, 2001). There are different definitions of KM in the literature, describing it as a systematic, explicit, and deliberate collection, storage, and application of knowledge to enhance an organisation's performance and recover its investments in intellectual capital (Wiig, 1997); or as a formal process which ensures that staff, technology and business processes together efficiently utilise knowledge and transfer it to the right people at the right time (Duffy, 2001); or as an action in accordance with the strategy of managing human capital (Brooking, 1998). Therefore, it seems that KM implies knowledge itself as well as the management of people who have this knowledge. If the definition of KM is still fluid and open to different concepts, knowledge as a concept is even more loose, ambiguous, and rich (Alvesson & Kärreman, 2001).

KM in HEIs can be considered as a deliberate process through which organisations identify internal knowledge (employees' knowledge) and knowledge existing outside of theirs boundaries (Firestone, 2001) to employ them in generating new knowledge. Geng et al. (2005) argue that within HEIs, academic and operational knowledge are present, where the former is expressed through teaching, research, documentation, publications, conferences, and patents. Operational knowledge, on the other hand, belongs to the employees who perform supportive or other activities in these institutions.

Knowledge management authors and practitioners have put considerable effort into designing a broad range of interventions, both organizational and technological, that are aimed at promoting the effectiveness of KM (e.g., Davenport & Prusak, 1998; Probst, Raub, & Romhardt, 2000). However, in the literature few models of KM related to HEIs can be found while many generic models of KM within for-profit organisations exist (see Butler, et al., 2007; Dufour & Steane, 2007; Kulkarni, et al., 2007; Moffet, et al., 2002; Nonaka & Takeuchi, 1995; Syed-Ikhsan & Rowland, 2004; Xu & Quaddus, 2005). Based on this fact, it can be concluded that KM within the context of HEIs remains an under-researched area.

Previous studies on KM in HEIs mainly dealt with the field of organisational culture (see Gomezelj Omerzel, Biloslavo, & Trnavčevič, 2010; Srikanthan & Dalrymple, 2002), organisational structure, the role of ICT (Jarvenpaa & Staples, 2000; Numprasertchai & Poovarawan, 2008) and the relationship between a supervisor and a PhD student (Ugrin, Odum, & Pearson, 2008). However, they did not address the issue of the attitude and understanding teachers and researchers have about KM and its processes. We believe the knowledge of this issue is a prerequisite for the development of a holistic model of KM in HEIs, which would cover the critical factors for success and provide a basis for the creation of appropriate measures and guidelines for future action. This is the main goal that we want to achieve—through our research, and present in this contribution.

Our main research questions are:

- How do academics understand the process of creating new knowledge in their area of expertise and in teaching and research praxis?
- How do academics evaluate the effectiveness of transfer and application of the existing knowledge within HEIs?
- How do academics see their own role (i.e. individually and as members of teams), the role of ICT and the leadership of HEIs in relation to KM?

A qualitative approach will be used in the research. This will allow an insight into KM within the context of HEIs from the perspective of those who are direct participants. Data gathered from in-depth, semi-structured interviews will allow a more holistic treatment of KM, recognising the existence of more than one reality and/or truth, which could ultimately lead to unexpected insights. The research will be carried out in Slovenia, whose system of higher education shares a lot of common characteristics with higher education systems in other post-transition countries, which, like the EU Member States, decided to implement the Bologna Process. The research will involve a small sample of academics from humanities, social, and natural science at three Slovenian universities.

The chapter is laid out as follows. The introduction is followed by a literature review of the characteristics of knowledge management and its role within the context of HEIs. The empirical research section is focused on research design, analysis, and interpretation of the data collected by semi-structured interviews. The final part is the conclusion, in which the main results of the research are summarised and directions for future research of KM in the context of HEIs are presented.

BACKGROUND

Knowledge

Knowledge is a very broad concept which has been studied by a number of disciplines (e.g. philosophy, psychology, sociology), and therefore, it is not surprising that numerous definitions of knowledge exist in management literature. Knowledge is defined by Nonaka (1994), for example, who says that it is "justified true belief." On the other hand, Tippins (2003) understands it as "information that is relevant, actionable, and linked to meaningful behaviour and is characterised by its tacit elements that are derived from first-hand experience." (p. 340). According to Winterton (2005), knowledge is socially constructed and represents a sum of one's intelligence, that is, their ability to learn, and circumstances or possibilities they have for learning. Whereas Alavi and Leidner (2001, p. 109) say that:

... knowledge is information possessed in the mind of individuals: it is personalized information (which may or may not be new, unique, useful, or accurate) related to facts, procedures, concepts, interpretations, ideas, observations, and judgments.

An individual's knowledge can be classified into different categories according to its content. Zack (1998), for example, divides knowledge into declarative (*know about*), procedural (*know how*), causal (*know why*), conditional (*know when*), and relational knowledge (*know with*), while Lundvall and Johnson (1994) argue that an individual's knowledge falls into one of the following four categories—*know-what* (knowledge about facts), *know-why* (knowledge about scientific facts), *know-who* (knowledge which refers to social relations), and *know-how* (knowledge, which refers to skills). Among well-known and established knowledge classifications is the one developed in the 1960s by Polanyi (1966) and was used a few decades later by Nonaka (1994) as the basis for his theory of organisational knowledge creation. According to this classification, an individual's knowledge comprises two dimensions; explicit and tacit. Explicit knowledge is formal, systematic, and refers to facts and concepts. For example, explicit knowledge can be encoded in forms such as words or images and is consequently more easily transferred from one person to another. An individual's tacit knowledge is difficult to formalise. It is linked to performance and context, which means that it is virtually impossible to encode it, or transfer it to other people (Dyck, et al., 2005). The tacit knowledge dimension includes *know-how*, referring to an individual's technical skills, mindsets, beliefs and points of view that cannot be easily translated into words, but still affect the individual's perception of events and the world (Nonaka, 1994). Although the Cartesian-laden distinction between tacit and explicit knowledge (e.g., Nonaka & Takeuchi, 1995) is widely accepted in theory and practice, it does not give a final definition of the concept of knowledge. Thus, some authors regard the dialectical relationship between tacit and explicit knowledge as a relationship between two distinct categories or typologies of knowledge, while the others see it as two essential aspects (not types) of knowledge which are needed in order to connect knowledge with activity that creates this knowledge (e.g., Blackler, 1995). The latter perspective has inspired a conceptualisation of organisational knowledge debates based on their epistemic nature (Cook & Brown, 1999).

Organisational Knowledge

An organisation is a community of individuals, and when these individuals join an organisation they bring along with them their knowledge, which subsumes their skills, previous experiences and known facts. However, organisational knowledge is more than simply the sum of employees' knowledge, as it consists of everything an organisation has achieved through the learning processes, and it is therefore essential for its operation (Levitt & March, 1988; Nelson & Winter, 1982; Winter, 1996).

Just as an individual's knowledge changes and upgrades through experience and self-reflection, organisational knowledge is also transformed over time and takes on new dimensions. At the organisational level, knowledge is divided according to the degree of articulation into explicit and tacit, and according to the degree of aggregation into individual and collective knowledge (see Blackler, 1995; Lam, 2000; Nonaka & Takeuchi, 1995; Spender, 1996). Individual knowledge is the knowledge held by each employee, whereas collective knowledge represents a set of organisational knowledge stored in rules, procedures, routines and shared norms (Lam, 2000). Walsh and Ungson (1991) believe that collective knowledge is actually the memory of an organisation. Blackler (1995), who takes his the categorisation of knowledge suggested by Collins (1993), divides knowledge into *embrained knowledge*, which depends on an individual's conceptual skills and cognitive abilities, e.g., knowledge and understanding of natural laws; *embodied knowledge*, which is action-oriented and only partly explicit, acquired by doing and rooted in a context; *encultured knowledge*, which refers to the process of achieving shared understandings; *embedded knowledge*, which resides in organisational routines and shared norms; and *encoded knowledge*, which refers to information conveyed by signs and symbols, such as plans and codes of practice.

Since it is difficult to find two organisations with the same previous experiences, we can say that knowledge is a factor which distinguishes one organisation from another and represents a key strategic resource (see Boisot, 1998; Spender, 1996; Nanda, 1996). Accordingly, it should be of interest to organisations to fully exploit the potential of their employees and in this way gain or maintain competitive advantage. This can be easily achieved if an organisational environment is created in a way that prevents the decline of mostly tacit knowledge. This means that the employees are given enough autonomy and the possibility to be creative in their work. Therefore, an organisation should take into account that the creation of new knowledge is not only affected by the diversity of employee experience, but also (and most of all) by "high quality" experiences. A working environment, organised in such a way, will encourage an individual's willingness to create new organisational knowledge and absorb the existing knowledge (Nonaka, 1994).

All this suggests that knowledge is a complex phenomenon and an important organisational resource, which can be, to some extent transformed, extended and effectively used with the help of systematic planning and management; in other words, by applying Knowledge Management (KM).

Knowledge Management

In a global and rapidly changing environment, organisations can only withstand rapid changes and face new challenges if they appropriately use the knowledge available inside and outside their organisational frameworks. This is realised through knowledge management. KM was first introduced in the 1980s (Wiig, 1997), and since then many authors have studied it (Nonaka & Takeuchi, 1995; Moffet, et al., 2002; Syed-Ikhsan & Rowland, 2004; Xu & Quaddus, 2005; Butler, et al., 2007; Dufour & Steane, 2007; Kulkarni, et al., 2007). As in the case of knowledge, numerous definitions can also be found for KM in the literature (Scarbrough, et al., 1999; Cortada & Woods, 1999, 2000; Duke, et al., 1999; Bonner, 2000; Mahota, 2000). Sarvary (1999), for example, defines KM as a deliberate effort to create, store and apply collective knowledge held by an organisation. Wiig (1997) asserts that

the role of KM is "to make the enterprise act as intelligently as possible to secure its viability and overall success and to otherwise realise the best value of its knowledge assets" (p. 1). According to Hackbarth (1998), the purpose of KM in an organisation is to increase its innovation and responsiveness. Generally speaking, we can say that KM is composed of four phases—knowledge creation, knowledge storage, knowledge transfer, and knowledge application (Alavi & Leidner, 1999; Myers, 1996; Wiig, 1999) that invoke people, business processes, and technology.

Knowledge Creation

KM begins with the knowledge creation phase in which interaction takes place between an individual's tacit and explicit spheres of knowledge (Nonaka & von Krogh, 2009), or as Nonaka (1994, p. 15) says "a dialogue between explicit and tacit knowledge which drives the creation of new ideas and concepts," is constantly present. Therefore, his theory suggests that an individual's new knowledge is formed by the conversion between these two knowledge dimensions. Within the creation phase then, there are several processes. In the socialisation process, knowledge is converted from tacit to tacit. In this phase, knowledge is transmitted through dialogue, observation, imitation, and experiences. During the process of externalisation, knowledge is converted from tacit to explicit. In this process, an individual's tacit knowledge and his mindsets are converted into words, metaphors and analogies, and in this way, they are more easily transferred from one person to another. The combination process is about the combination of already existing explicit knowledge. Such knowledge is usually transmitted with the help of documents such as technical manuals, guidebooks, reports, and drawings. The internalisation process converts knowledge from explicit to tacit and this happens when an individual acquires knowledge from written documents, for example, and in this way, they expand their tacit knowledge.

At the end of each process in the creation phase described above, an individual acquires some new knowledge. In order to create new organisational knowledge, each of the four processes play their part in one continuous cycle that moves on an ever higher level. In other words, we are speaking about a spiral process or about a spiral of knowledge where new knowledge is created on an individual level and is then transmitted to a group, then to the organisation, sometimes even surpassing organisational borders (Nonaka, 1994).

In this phase of KM, the employees' motivation and desire to apply new approaches to their work have an important role. In order to achieve this, an organisation should have sufficiently flexible structures and systems, which promote innovative approaches and give sufficient autonomy, build mutual trust and establish appropriate mechanisms for the transmission of newly-created knowledge (Gupta & Govindarajan, 2000).

Knowledge Storage

When the phase of knowledge creation is complete, new knowledge has to be properly stored. This storage phase is very important for a successful KM, since empirical studies show that created knowledge can otherwise be partially and even entirely forgotten (Argote, et al., 1990; Darr, et al., 1995). If an organisation's knowledge is stored properly and made available to employees, they can use it at work and in this way avoid the repetition of the procedures used in the past to lead to this same knowledge. While several decades ago organisational knowledge was stored in printed documents, such as reports and manuals, today knowledge held by an organisation is mainly stored in electronic form and is accessible to members of the organisation through shared Web applications.

Knowledge Transfer

Newly created and stored knowledge should not be an end in itself, however. At this point in KM,

an organisation should arrange for knowledge transfer to the employees. In the transfer phase, cooperation needs to occur between those who already have knowledge and those who do not have it but are willing to get it (Major & Cordey-Hayes, 2002), or as Lee says (2001) it is about "activities of transferring or disseminating knowledge from one person, group or organisation to another" (p. 324). It is in the interests of the organisation to transfer the knowledge to employees in time, so that they can use it at work. However, depending on the type of knowledge that is to be transferred, the particular transfer method used must be considered (Inkpen & Dinur, 1998). Explicit, encoded knowledge is easier to transfer to others, while transfer of tacit knowledge requires cooperation between employees, some kind of shared understanding, and mutual trust (Lam, 2000).

Knowledge does not lose its value when it is transferred. It is just the opposite, knowledge increases when it is being used (Sveiby, 2001). However, its transfer in an organisation does not take place in a natural and obvious way because some employees do not want to share their knowledge with others. The decision to transfer or not to transfer their knowledge to other members of the organisation is to some extent affected by an individual's subjective assessment about the pros and cons of such a decision. People are usually willing to share their knowledge with others if this gives them a sense of fulfilment, enhances their reputation or if they are rewarded publicly (Cabrera & Cabrera, 2002). Some people, however, do not want to transfer their knowledge to colleagues either because they do not see any benefit they would gain by doing this, they do not know how to include this process in their work, or simply because they would rather devote their time to their own tasks that bring them tangible benefits. The reason for knowledge retention may also lie in the fact that employees do not know how to use ICT, which is increasingly more prevalent and facilitates the transfer of knowledge. Impediments to knowledge transfer may also lie in the top management of an organisation that does not, for example, support the introduction of innovations. Finally, in organisations with typical internal competition the reason may also reside in the maintenance of one's own competitive advantage and avoidance of fragility (KPMG, 2000). Once an organisation understands that knowledge transfer is critical for its success, it can employ an array of mechanisms at its disposal to encourage it—e.g. monetary or intangible rewards or efficient and user-friendly ICT (Kerr, 1989; Rapoport, et al., 1983).

Knowledge Application

However, to just have knowledge it is not enough. Knowledge has to be used effectively in the process of new knowledge creation and business operation as well (Alavi & Leidner, 2001). If this is not the case, the reason may lie in the lack of time and possibility to use such knowledge, in the distrust of knowledge source, or in the fear of making mistakes.

Information Communication Technology and KM

A modern organisation can no longer operate successfully and effectively without using appropriate Information and Communication Technology (ICT) to support the majority of its work processes. Among other things, ICT helps to provide information necessary to make decisions and solve problems, to connect remote units, to access various documents, and to facilitate the creation, sharing, and application of organisational knowledge. Therefore, ICT undoubtedly contributes to successful KM since it significantly reduces the time and distance between individuals involved. The benefits brought to the field of organisational knowledge creation by modern technology are the facilitated data collection process, its interpretation, storage, and diffusion.

In considering Nonaka's theory about new knowledge creation phase, we see that ICT is useful in all four processes. In the *socialisation* process it contributes to the communication and integration between individuals (e.g. teleconferencing). In the *externalisation* process where it contributes to the conversion of tacit knowledge into explicit knowledge (e.g. with groupware tools and email). ICT can also be helpful in the *combination* process where new explicit knowledge can be stored in electronic rather than paper form. In the final *internalisation* process of knowledge creation, where explicit knowledge is transferred in practice, an individual has a variety of computer applications at their disposal to improve their decision-making ability (Junnarkar & Brown, 1997).

Despite the substantial progress achieved in the field of ICT and its ability to virtually connect people who are physically remote from one another, it remains particularly suitable for the transfer of knowledge, which can be encoded, i.e. explicit knowledge, but less effective for the transfer of tacit knowledge, which needs a large degree of face-to-face contacts.

HEIs and KM

Reasons for Promoting KM within HEIs

Until recently, the rapid global changes and trends that have affected the operation of most organisations have been considered to be outside the comparatively stable environment in which universities operate. However, this is no longer the case since we are witnesses of great changes and challenges introduced by the so called Bologna Process on the one hand, and the need for a higher level of responsibility of public HEIs to use public funds on the other hand and therefore KM is equally important to HEIs. The necessity of more strict management of public funds is leading governments to apply free-market principles to academic research, emphasising audits and accountability (Ewan & Calvert, 2000; Fuller, 2001; Harvey, et al., 2002). The position of universities has now changed to the extent that they do not compete with each other just in the area of knowledge creation and transfer, but also (and even more so) in the areas of attracting domestic and foreign students and competing for national and foreign funds for research activities. In addition, HEIs are expected at the same time to be stable and reliable (Farjoun, 2010), "innovative, flexible and responsive to change" (Steinkellner & Czerny, 2010, p. 2).

Therefore, higher education institutions have started to use approaches that have previously been the domain of business enterprises only. One of these approaches is KM, which according to Geng et al. (2005) can improve their effectiveness in knowledge generation, storage, and transfer. At the same time, it should be remembered that differences between HEIs and business enterprises still exist since management-related aspects such as control, funding, decision-making, performance appraisal, and motivation are, for the most part, perceived and experienced differently within an academic community (cf. Cohen, et al., 1999). As Ward (1968, p. 584) wrote, education "is an enterprise so wholly dissimilar from those of ordinary business life that an entirely different set of principles must be applied to it throughout." We can conclude that management initiatives, as KM for example, need to be designed and implemented in a way that fits the specificity of the organisations as HEIs are.

The reasons for the promotion of KM within HEIs are therefore many and directly related to the fundamental missions of HEIs; namely, research, education/teaching, and service to society. Despite all this, it is actually surprising that so little has been written about knowledge management in HEIs (Sharimllah Devi, et al., 2007; Kidwell, et al., 2000; Park, et al., 2004). The work of Piccoli et al. (2000) was one of the first which dealt with the scope of KM in HEIs and defined a model consisting of three main processes—knowledge creation which involves the collection of new knowledge and its creation; knowledge transmission where individuals find the knowledge they

need by themselves ("pull" strategy) or where knowledge is provided to them by others ("push" strategy); and storage of knowledge (Piccoli, et al., 2000). Biloslavo and Trnavčevič (2007), on the other hand, argue that a model in accordance with the generic models of KM which comprises the conventional phases of knowledge creation, storage, transfer and application is more suitable for the HEI context.

Knowledge Creation and Sharing within HEIs

HEIs' mission is to create new knowledge and transfer it to other entities from their immediate and broader social contexts. Knowledge generated by HEIs should therefore be useful for them and the society as a whole. Lecturers and researchers employed in HEIs gain new knowledge by studying professional literature, participating in research projects, working in teams, exchanging views via formal and informal meetings, and through their own reflection. Knowledge generated by academics is mostly stored in the form of scientific articles, books, reports and other publications that can be accessed through various online databases (e.g. e-libraries). On the other hand, knowledge generated in HEIs by professional staff is usually stored in the form of manuals, rules, reports, etc. and is available to employees in printed and/or electronic form (e.g. documents on the intranet).

After new knowledge is created, it needs to be shared between employees as to increase its value. However, it often happens that in this process physical and mental barriers arise in an individual, which complicate the process (Tippins, 2003). Liebowitz and Chen (2003) carried out a survey on KM in the public sector and discovered that employees do not want to share their knowledge with others because for them it represents power, or as Wiig (1999, p. 164) says "knowledge possessed by a person is a separator—"knowledge is power...." Thus, even in the academic world there are a lot of people who consider knowledge as a private property and prefer to keep it to themselves (Wind & Main, 1999). Perhaps academics who create new knowledge are not sufficiently aware that though it is true that by transferring their knowledge to others they lose its exclusiveness, they stand to gain reputation, get cited more often and are publicly praised because they have created new and useful knowledge (Teichler, 2004).

Among the reasons why some employees in HEIs do not want to participate actively in the processes of KM are (Tippins, 2003, pp. 341-342):

- Interpretation of knowledge as an important source of differentiation;
- Lack of interest;
- Insufficient knowledge of a particular field or topic (which can complicate the transfer of knowledge between experts from different fields);
- Insufficient formal and informal mutual relations which can be a consequence of the nature of work (e.g. the possibility of performing certain activities outside the HEIs premises) or the infrastructure of the faculty (e.g. lack of common areas for employees);
- Lack of information about who has the knowledge someone needs, or to whom their knowledge has to be transferred;
- Busyness and lack of time;
- Financial reasons (lack of funds).

Effective KM in HEIs is also affected by the use of modern ICT, which is increasingly more important, especially for the entry, storage, retrieval, and distribution of its knowledge (Gill, 2009). Today, ICT is also indispensable for HEIs in teaching and research processes because, for example, it provides access to global databases, e-libraries, electronic meetings, and supports e-learning.

EMPIRICAL RESEARCH

Research Method

In-depth, semi-structured interviews were used to investigate knowledge practices within the HEIs. The need to address informal as well as formal knowledge processes and scholars' attitudes meant that interviewees were asked about their actual working practices, the nature of their work (alone or in communication with others) and social antecedents for effective knowledge generation and transfer.

Participants in the research were selected on the basis of prior research links and personal contacts. No claim is made that the sample used in the study is a structured or a representative sample of Slovene university scholars. The potential problem of sample bias was considered, especially with regard to the use of personal contacts. However, in the area of KM, there was no indication that the chosen HEIs and their scholars had, or did not have, any particular interest in KM. Further, to ensure greater validity of the research the participants are employed at three different Slovene Universities and come from three different research disciplines. According to Kitzinger (1995, p. 300) is "advantageous to bring together a diverse group (for example a range of professions) to maximise exploration of different perspectives within a group setting."

Potential participants were told that interviews would last approximately 1 hour, and that they would be recorded and transcribed for later analysis. Participants were advised that the readership of the transcripts would be limited and discreet. In all 10 academics agreed to participate in the study and the recording of their responses. Given that full details had been given to them about the nature and purpose of the study and that accepted principles for conducting interview-based research had been followed (Merriam, 2009), interviews occurred in a spirit of collegiality and trust. The interview typically lasted 1–1.5 hours and were performed during the period between June 28th and July 14th, 2011, with a digital Dictaphone that according to Nair and Riege (1995) increases the reliability of the research. The transcriptions of the interviews were completed on the same day or on the day after the interview.

Within the research sample scholars from social sciences prevails. We believe that a more balanced sample could contribute to a broader range of views and ideas. However, the sample reflects the fact that colleagues from natural science for various reasons could not or did not want to participate in the interview. In addition we assume that the theme of the research is closer to the research fellows in the humanities and social sciences and that based on their own prior research they are able of the in-depth thinking about knowledge, KM and other related concepts. However, the structure of the sample represents a certain limitation of the study. Table 1 provides an overview of the key features of the research participants.

Findings

The Concept of KM

In discussing the general concept of KM, the study participants were unanimous in defining it as an organisational process, which consists of two basic parts. The first part is to find out existing organisational knowledge, transfer it to organisational employees, and then apply it. The second part is an identification of future organisational knowledge needs and possible ways to develop needed knowledge either internally or by acquiring it externally. The degree of understanding of these basic principles varied across participants.

Participant E says "… we need to somehow manage knowledge… we need to be systematically engaged with it." On the other hand, participant J says "… KM means how … knowledge that exists within an institution… can be created, transferred, and applied in the most efficient way." Meanwhile

Table 1. Demographic profile of participant pool (N = 10)

Participant	Gender	University	Field of Expertise	Academic Title	Age	Employment era at HEI
A	Female	University of Ljubljana	Humanities	Full Professor	35-45	15-20
B	Male	University of Maribor	Social Sciences	Full Professor	45 or more	15-20
C	Male	University of Primorska	Social Sciences	Full Professor	45 or more	20 or more
D	Female	University of Primorska	Social Sciences	Associate Professor	35-45	15-20
E	Female	University of Primorska	Social Sciences	Associate Professor	45 or more	20 or more
F	Male	University of Primorska	Natural Sciences	Assistant Professor	35-45	5-10
G	Female	University of Ljubljana	Humanities	Assistant Professor	25-35	5-10
H	Male	University of Ljubljana	Social Sciences	Assistant Professor	35-45	10-15
I	Male	University of Ljubljana	Social Sciences	Assistant Professor	35-45	5-10
J	Male	University of Primorska	Social Sciences	Lecturer	35-45	5-10

participant F defines KM as "…a process of coding and categorizing knowledge, managing it and making it available to others." Participant F distinguishes among different dimensions and characteristics of knowledge and perceives the problem of transferring tacit knowledge "… um, hidden knowledge… KM deals also with this more informal, more soft, more social part of knowledge transfer …" We can see that the problem of transferring tacit knowledge emphasized by Nonaka (1994) and later on by different authors is perceived also in organisational practice.

Participant H recognises the four phases within KM "… we have four phases. Which one? Knowledge generation, storing, transfer, and um … application." These four phases are confirmed by different authors as for example Alavi and Leidner (2001), Biloslavo and Prevodnik (2010), Butler et al. (2007), Tippins (2003).

Among all study participants only participant B couched KM through its purpose as "… how now, … no, how managers of profit and not-profit organisations day after day apply knowledge to achieve or increase organisational competitive advantage…" KM within HEIs is than seen as a tool for achieving competitive advantage that is in the line with the position of the business enterprises. From that point of view no differences exist between HEIs and business enterprises.

Another important fact that needs to be mentioned in relation to the understanding of KM concepts in general is that the participants in this study predominantly used the knowledge as a resource metaphor (Andriessen, 2008). This metaphor highlights the adding, storing, and sharing of knowledge as well as its quantity. At the same time, it hides non-additiveness and tacitness of knowledge (Andriessen, 2008). This confirms that academics, like others, are tied to the prevalent epistemology, in this case the Western one. They are constrained by their social and historical circumstances and the exigencies of the mode of knowledge production.

The Importance of Academic Discipline for KM

Based on participants' responses we can decipher that knowledge generation within HEIs depends on the academic discipline where this knowledge is generated. Study participants emphasized the difference between social and natural science, where humanities was somehow considered as sub-category of social science. The basic approach to knowledge generation is through research, where individual research work and research work in teams are equally important. In either case, we cannot neglect the importance of informal interpersonal contacts for new knowledge generation.

Three participants particularly emphasized that knowledge generation in higher education depends on the research discipline where this knowledge is generated. Participant E says:

… I would divide between natural and social science. I think in the social science exist too much knowledge reproduction, … we have relatively a very small number of conceptual, new solutions, which are not rooted in existing solutions. [New] solutions are developed from [an] existing one and sometimes perhaps a little step further is done. From that point of view, natural science is much more radical and leaps in development are much bigger. In the laboratory setting at the end something happen[s], which is tangible and demonstrable whereas in social science we can even develop a radically new concept but this is still based on our preconceptions and values … then if I would say take it and bring it to the practice is even more difficult to do. At the same time, the value of our ideas is defined by practice. The practice verifies our concepts, isn't [that so]?

This attitude aligns with the prevailing view of scientific knowledge in the natural sciences as being based upon universal standards and absolute warrant. These universal standards allow scientists to evaluate and interpret their results without the influence of subjective or social values. In other words, scientific knowledge and facts in natural science are value free. Absolute warrant refers to the empirical evidence obtained from scientific experimentation, and it is this, which permits scientists to choose with confidence among competing theories. Consequently, the end result of the scientific enterprise is knowledge about the natural world that is both factual and absolute. Such knowledge is defined in traditional terms as justified, true belief (Nonaka & Takeuchi, 1995). On the other hand, scientific knowledge in social sciences is not composed of empirical facts but of social artefacts; that is to say, constructed facts. These facts are imbued with social values and are the result of negotiation among members of society.

The same idea is shared by participant B, who says that new knowledge generation "... depends on academic discipline; one thing is the natural science another is the social science" and he adds that research represents the main way new knowledge is created at his faculty; however, he emphasises the role of the individual in the process "like in all social science faculties new knowledge is generated through research ... we cannot however forget interrupted research ... um... research that is carrying on for the whole life or for a long period of time ... somebody studies a specific research area for a long time and publishes papers based on that ... in that way he enriches ... expands and supplements existing knowledge based on his own prior knowledge." A similar point of view is shared by participant A, who says that knowledge generation depends on academic discipline and like participant B supports the idea that individual research work is very important in this process "... in humanities we research more or less individually. Sure, we do some teamwork but much less than colleagues in natural science ... um ... new knowledge is generated more or less behind my computer, in my room—as far as I am concerned, and I think that the same thing happens also to my colleagues. Sure sometimes

we put our staff together and we work as a team, in that case new knowledge is generated by the team. However, I believe that primarily what counts is individual research." Here we can see the difference with Nonaka et al. (2000, p. 3) who say that knowledge is generated "through the dynamic interactions among individuals and/ or between individuals and their environments." New knowledge can be then generated also in the loneliness of the individual own thinking and self-reflection.

New Knowledge as a Result of Research

All study participants agree that new knowledge within HEIs is first of all generated through research, which goes on within different projects, as participant G says "The main way for new knowledge generation is still to do research, isn't [it]?" Participant F adds that new knowledge is not only an outcome of the research work done within research projects, but also "...by mentoring undergraduate and postgraduate students." This view is echoed by participant C who says "new knowledge is without question generated by the research ... undergraduate and postgraduate theses, projects, etc." Of the same opinion is participant D, who says, "... each thesis or project contributes a little bit to science ... so we can say that each of them brings at least a small fragment of new knowledge" and she adds, "with each new student that I [am] mentoring I get some new knowledge. At the same time participant D differentiates between entirely new knowledge and new knowledge for institution, "... what we are searching around ... can maybe be considered as a new knowledge for [the] institution ... this knowledge doesn't exist before. It's no new knowledge in the world. When I and my colleagues learn something new we gain some knowledge, which is new for the institution."

Participant H exposes the specificity of knowledge generation within higher education "Okay, we are ... we are anyway in knowledge generating business, so …" and he confirms that the basic way for creating new knowledge is "by writing and publishing papers we generate new knowledge. Basically we do research and publish papers based on it. In that way we generate new knowledge." Participant F also agrees with others that new knowledge is a result of research work but he adds, "new knowledge is created because we need to solve some specific problems." Participant B shares the same point of view and emphasises "… knowledge needs to have some practical purpose," and "even the basic research needs to have as its final goal production of some applicable knowledge … for solving real problems … that is … to be useful in the real world."

The Importance of Informal Contacts for New Knowledge Generation

Besides emphasizing research as the main way for new knowledge generation within HEIs, participants are aware how important communication and interpersonal contacts are in the process. For participant A new knowledge is generated "by observation, by research. I would say we get new knowledge more by observation than by research. It's not only research, speaking in the strict sense, which generates new knowledge, but also observation. I could say new knowledge is not created only by research but also in this very general way—by observing in the largest sense." This corresponds to Bandura's (1977) idea of learning as a passive process that happens by observing others who have more knowledge. However, we need to appreciate and trust these persons. Atkinson (1995, p. 127) points out "Not all knowledge is treated as having equal value. It has different sources, and has different weight attached to it, and may be regarded as more or less warranted." In the case we do not trust the knowledge source (i.e., who has produced knowledge, where it is produced and how it is produced) we do not accept knowledge that we could learn from it.

Participant F also confirms the high importance of informal contacts for new knowledge generation when he says, "we must be careful to not underestimate this informal part of knowledge generation. I don't want to say that is the most important part of the process, as we cannot put it in the papers, however … without these informal conversations everything is senseless. For this reason … we need to socialise, talk, and be close to the right people who can guide you as well as you guide them." This aligns with Nonaka (1994) who says that face-to-face contacts, continuing communication and exchange of experience contribute to new knowledge generation.

Tangible and Intangible Form of Knowledge Storage

Participants say that knowledge created by HEIs is stored in both tangible and intangible form. Two participants give high importance to individual tacit knowledge, which everybody brings in oneself. Because of this, such knowledge is difficult to codify and transfer from person to person. Other participants emphasise knowledge storage in tangible form as papers, books and other publications.

Participant C says that most knowledge is stored within individuals and gives high importance to tacit knowledge "… I think that most knowledge is stored in our heads, most knowledge is intangible, … my experience, my understanding…" about codified explicit knowledge, he says, "… what is in the computer is irrelevant." Participant C places more emphasis on individual memory, which is formed by observation, experience and activity (Alavi & Leidner, 2001). Participant A agrees but also stresses the importance of tangible forms of knowledge storage "… partly I store my knowledge in my brain, however this is delicate, temporary, so what I can I store in my computer or in my library. I can say that I use tangible and intangible form of knowledge storage. Both are important."

All participants agree that knowledge created by HEIs is usually stored "… in journals" as participant H says or as participant G "we are trying to publish as much as possible" or as participant J "… researchers or academics write books and papers …" This is in line with Marquardt (1996) who says that knowledge generated by an organisation (i.e. explicit knowledge) needs to be stored in an appropriate form that allows access to it and in some cases recovering of the content. In the modern organisation, this type of knowledge is usually stored in e-form but may also be in the form of printed documents and manuals (Probst, Raub, & Romhardt, 1999).

The Directions of Knowledge Transfer and the Importance of Interpersonal Relationships

From participants' statements, we can conclude that within HEIs three main directions of knowledge transfer exist; between professors and students, between HEIs and society, and within HEIs themselves. Explicit knowledge is transferred mostly by use of written documents like scientific papers and books. On the other hand, positive interpersonal relationships and observation of colleagues are of critical importance for tacit knowledge transfer.

Participant B differentiates among these three directions of knowledge transfer within HEIs. "The first one is our core purpose, that is the knowledge transfer to students … the second one is the knowledge transfer to the larger society … the last one is the knowledge transfer within the institution." He then adds that at his faculty knowledge transfer is institutionalized "within departments, which unites people from the same research area … through collaboration in R&D projects where we solve some specific scientific problems and … through publications … our own publications and by reading others publication. These are the main ways of knowledge transfer."

Participant A says that knowledge transfer happens mainly through written sources. "Partly knowledge transfer takes place on a completely impersonal basis when you read papers of other academics that you even don't know... this is very important because in that way we can acknowledge ideas and research results of people that are far away from us." She however also recognises that a more personal way of knowledge transfer is present within HEIs. "The other way for knowledge transfer is based on personal contacts when you make acquaintance of somebody at the conference or at the near office so you know him first personally and then professionally by reading his work. I believe both ways are important." Participant A also recognises that tacit knowledge is transferred through collaboration and mutual communication and says "if I can talk with my colleague who follows my research work as well as I follow hers then a kind of tacit knowledge transfer can happen … which is very important as it allows to come to know the *formo menti* of the other researcher as well as to adapt and update our own…." Participant A also believes that observation and imitation are very important for tacit knowledge transfer "Yes, imitation is human. We cannot live without it, as we cannot live without observation … I don't imitate somebody directly, but I look around for good and less good models."

Participant J regards knowledge transfer within HEIs as a process, which takes place "… between older and younger academics" and he also says that when he started his academic career he learned by observing his colleagues "when I started my career I went to the lectures. I went there to see what they are doing so I could repeat that later on." He is of the opinion that this is very useful "yes, I think you need to do this. At least at the very beginning when you are just push[ed] in [the] water to swim." This corresponds to Roberts (2000) who believes that tacit knowledge can be effectively transferred from person to person through a process of demonstration (show-how), which is enabled by face-to-face contact between the source and recipient of knowledge.

Participant C says, "I was present at all lectures of my professors" and stresses the importance of interpersonal relationships "... I think it happens only through conversations or other forms of discussion. More among younger academics because they need to learn more, probably less among older academics because they are more individualist." Also participant H agrees that knowledge transfer happens "... informally. You just know who is good in what and when you need this kind of expertise you go to find him or her."

Participant F says that knowledge transfer between him and his colleagues happens "... when we approach a concrete scientific problem and we divide our work based on our different expertise. For example, we collaborate together in designing the questionnaire. In that way we transfer our knowledge." After Nonaka (1994) a new generation of organisational knowledge begins with the individual and his tacit knowledge. This individual approaches a kind of self-organizing team composed of employees with different expertise. Through dialogue, the team members are able to articulate their beliefs, create concepts and verified their own models and ideas. We can conclude, based on participant F's comments that a similar process also happens within HEIs.

Participant F also says that a considerable amount of knowledge is transferred through written sources but at the same he confirms that informal socialisation is very important for tacit knowledge transfer in stating that "... any knowledge, any hidden knowledge is difficult to write down, so informal conversations are the way for tacit knowledge transfer ... I believe this is the main fuel for development of new contributions to science." Holtman and Courtney (1998) state that knowledge transfer can happen through different knowledge transfer channels, formal or informal, impersonal or personal, each with their own strengths and weaknesses. Formal knowledge transfer channel (e.g. training) usu-

ally bring a greater distribution of knowledge, but can inhibit creativity (Fahey & Prusak, 1998), informal transfer channels (e.g. unscheduled meetings, a chat over a cup of coffee) probably help promote socialization, but on the other hand can also disable wide dissemination (Holtman & Courtney, 1998). Further, because informal transfer channels do not use formal coding of the knowledge, the knowledge recipient may have an inaccurate understanding of knowledge or the knowledge he gets may come from a limited number of knowledge holders (Huysam, et al., 1998). The difference between impersonal and personal knowledge transfer channels is in the context—knowledge that is transferred through impersonal knowledge transfer channels (e. g. knowledge repositories) can be used in different contexts, whereas knowledge that is transferred through personal channels (e.g. apprenticeship) is more context specific (Fahey & Prusak, 1998).

The Role of Mentor

From studying participant responses, we can establish that at the beginning of the academic career colleagues and mentors give direction to the individual and transfer to him or her at least part of their explicit and implicit knowledge.

Participant A is of the opinion that knowledge that is transferred through observation is very important "I think is very important that you have good models, good and bad models. [It] Is better to have more good models; however, the bad one[s] are useful to learn how you must not ... cannot act. Anyhow, learning through the models of your colleagues is very important." A similar point of view is shared by participant G, who adds that a mentor had an important role in his start of academic career "... I need to say that my mentor and some other postgraduate professors had an important role in this part of my life story ...uhm ... I had an opportunity for in depth talks about different topics, I was led by means of questions and interpretation that helped me to get an insight in ... in ... I don't know exactly if how to ask questions, methodological questions or just an understanding of some content dilemma, anyway in these discussions and consultations, in these informal conversations tete-a-tete I have got a lot." This is in line with Bolton (1980, p. 198; in Sands, Parson, & Duane, 1991) who see the figure of mentor "as a guide, a tutor or coach, and a confidant" as well as with Merriam (1983, p. 162; in Sands, Parson, & Duane, 1991) who describes mentoring as "a powerful emotional interaction between an older and younger person, a relationship in which the older member is trusted, loving, and experienced in the guidance of the younger," and she adds "The mentor helps shape the growth and development of the protégé." That such a mentor is very important for the young academic's development is clear to participant F who says "... you are not even conscious how many characteristics you get from that person. You can even take some phraseology from him." This idea fits with Roberts (2000) when he says that knowledge transfer from person to person can happen deliberately or unplanned.

Participant F then adds "... you find yourself ... uhm ... face-to-face with a pile of challenges that you need to solve. You need to learn from these people also many other things—how to go through this story." An individual does not take only expert knowledge from the mentor, but also knowledge about the organisation, its routines, its formal and informal system of leadership; who does what and how (Swap, Leonard, Shields, & Abrams, 2001). Finally, it is during collaboration with their mentor that a protégé can come to know the mentor's important contacts (Geiger, 1992; Pfleeger & Mertz, 1995; Simonetti, Ariss, & Martinez, 1999; Snowden, 1999). For the mentee, this knowledge is important as it helps him to become part of the "team" and get new trustworthy knowledge sources.

Participant J also agrees that a mentor's role is very important for an individual's professional career, especially to consult and encourage the protégé at work "... when I write a PhD thesis with my mentor, uhm ... he consults me, isn't it? The same thing happens when I write a paper, so ... how the paper needs to be structured, what I need to emphasise ... or he stimulates me when I just stop." This point of view is similar to Darling's (1985, p. 42; in Sands, Parson, & Duane, 1991), definition, which says that a mentor is "a person who leads, guides, and advises a person more junior in experience." However, participant J goes further and states "... it is not anymore as it was in the past, when each professor had an assistant. ... it is logical that a professor gives some knowledge to his assistant, isn't it? Uhm... now at my institution we are too much involved in the pedagogical process. So assistants are in the classrooms, they teach. More or less." Of similar opinion is participant D who says that too many young colleagues are lacking a mentor figure and they are left to themselves "...I'm irritated that ...we have not the classical organization of work with professors—head of the course and assistants. Here everybody does everything. If you have a real assistant ... who comes to your lectures so you can work with him or her on preparing exercises, what will be the content of the course etc. ... this is a true mentoring, isn't it? Here when assistants come they are just push[ed] ... in."

For participant B as well, the task of the mentor is mostly to transfer knowledge from him to the assistant and to lead him or her during the work "... professor who is [a] mentor to the assistant needs to give him a direction, isn't it [so]? Individually as also ... Uhmm ...by including him in the pedagogical and research process – professor checks the exercises and gives feedback and in that way transfer[s] knowledge to the assistant." An individual obtains expert knowledge through years of work and experience and he develops through the learning-by-doing process, which most of the time happens under the control of the mentor, who has more knowledge in that specific area (Swap, Leonard, Shields, & Abrams, 2001).

Knowledge as a Market Asset

From the participants' answers, we can infer that HEIs use the knowledge of academics to implement their main missions—teaching and research. Three participants say that their HEIs also sell their knowledge.

Participant J, like all other participants, says that professors use their knowledge within the pedagogical and research process "… you teach your students…, knowledge of the researchers is used to write papers … they do the research and write …." Participant H also says that his faculty uses the knowledge of lecturers and researchers "… we forward our knowledge to students in the pedagogical work, within research we publish papers…" and he adds "…for my institution [it] is very important that we get money from what we know by bringing research or commercial projects." This is similar to the way of thinking by participant G who says that the knowledge of teachers is applied in the pedagogical process, knowledge of researchers in research projects and then he adds that at his faculty "…we do also some additional training for teachers in the elementary and secondary schools…." Market activities are also present in the faculty of participant F as "we offer training… to everybody interested in [it]." Participant C agrees with other participants.

ICT in Support to Explicit Knowledge Storage and Retrieval

Of the ten people included in the research sample, only three had some doubts about the appropriateness of the use of ICT. This is probably associated with their age, the other interviewees are more inclined to use it and they see it primarily as a source for obtaining explicit knowledge and a means to transfer knowledge to students. All participants agree that ICT is only a tool and no substitute for genuine human relationships. They are aware that ICT is highly important but not a guarantee for a better knowledge system or better knowledge-based results.

Participant B is of the opinion that application of ICT within the modern academic environment is essential "… without it work doesn't exist anymore … without ICT you cannot work." For participant G ICT also plays an important role in the pedagogical and research process "… it is very important, it can help you a lot" and like participant H she sees its value mostly in acquiring written documents in order to access sources of explicit knowledge "… we have access to higher number of journals and books…," which is of major importance for HEIs. Participant D agrees that ICT positively impacts the work of academics and says "… it helps you by the way…" and she also sees as its biggest benefit the opportunity to access knowledge bases "… with technology you can search more and you have everything in your palm." Of a similar opinion is participant A who says that ICT really increased the quality of working conditions for employees within HEIs "… it really opened a huge pool of resources and opportunities and I think that life is now very different than it was when I started to work here say, fifteen, seventeen years ago. " ICT does not only enable access to recorded sources of knowledge or allow searching different databases, but it is also appropriate in getting data from projects already concluded, for sharing knowledge or collaborating within virtual-teams (KPMG, 1998a; Alavi & Leidner, 2001, p. 114).

Participant J, like the rest of the participants, agrees that ICT is a great tool for accessing knowledge bases, so too articles and other publications, but he expressed a desire "… that would be possible to access [these] databases, like ProQuest, also from other places, not only from here [from the faculty]. Part of the academics' job happens at their homes so ICT is very important in supporting their collaboration and search for knowledge outside their offices.

Of a somewhat different view is participant E who attributes a dual role to ICT- first, "On the one hand, as a terrorist... because I get 70 emails a day, and different cc..." and then she recognized its importance "... gives me a support, a strong support." Participant C is even more sceptical of the use of ICT, but still says "... ICT is a support ..." and he adds, "to me personally this doesn't bother, but some special benefit from this doesn't exist, I think that this is only a good opportunity to put people on the sidetrack...," the reason for its critical attitude towards ICT he relates to his age, "... I'm somewhat of the second generation and maybe I wrongly understand the matter." This does not match the results of a survey, which was carried out at lower secondary schools within 26 countries, which shows that age barriers are not important obstacles for the use of ICT (Pelgrum, 2001).

E-Learning

Like other HEIs in the world Slovene HEIs are also making use of e-learning and participant F says that at his institution, "E-learning is used, I will not say by all, but by the vast majority of employees." Participant H also says that at his Faculty ICT is widely used for teaching purposes "At my institution practically everything happens on the Internet, all materials are placed on the Internet," which also applies to the institution where participant I is employed and who goes so far as to say "we must put all materials for our courses on the net." Participant J believes that the e-classroom is useful and he uses it primarily to "... put up articles, literature, and other materials." However, he adds that ICT is only "... an addition ..." in the teaching process or in the process of transferring knowledge to students, a point which is shared by all the interviewees. Even participant D positively regards the use of ICT for teaching purposes, and like other interviewees, she believes that it is only an expedient "Certainly, I don't want to have the whole course delivered in that way." Among the advantages of its use she considers especially "we have already done some exercises via e-classroom,

which would not have been feasible otherwise," while she also states its negative side and that is "... [it] request [requires] from me an awful lot of work." She sees the e-classroom as a means for establishing informal contact with students "... we use it for other things, from greeting the new year... to anything up to a 'bouquet of flowers' when the day is sunny."

Unlike participant D, who says that to her e-classroom takes a lot of time, participant G says that she has increasingly used it because "it makes my work easier and I think that makes me even better and more efficient, in this sense, more rational. Certain things I can transfer to the e-classroom, on the forum within it, and so on, which I then [do] not need to do in the classroom." However, participant G like everyone else agrees that "this is a very good complement to the live encounters, but it is not a substitute." Is also true that ICT by data exchange simplifies the transfer of explicit knowledge. However, for the transfer of tacit knowledge face-to-face contact between source of knowledge and its recipient is still needed. Such contact cannot be replaced by any modern technology (Roberts, 2000).

Unlike the other interviewees, participant A does not use ICT to transfer knowledge to students, but admits, "I believe it is interesting, but I did not even try." She adds, as other participants do, "I still believe in the face-to-face contact and I find it very important, but certainly for different reasons this [ICT] could be a useful tool." Even for participant C the use of ICT for knowledge transfer to students "... is too impersonal ..." and adds, "I think that contact between students and teachers should be as personal as possible, when you're in the classroom when you talk with them during office hours ..." the advantage of using e-classroom he sees primarily for the business of the faculty, because "... it is ok to reduce costs ... you don't need to pay part of lecture hours...." Indeed, modern ICT makes education more economically rational as we can codify knowledge at lower cost and transfer it to the general public (Roberts, 2000).

Relationships between Colleagues

All interviewees agree that contacts between lecturers and researchers are important, but only two out of ten respondents look at the academic world as an open and collaborative workplace, while the others believe that it is ruled by competition and an individualistic atmosphere. HEIs' leadership also promotes such an atmosphere by rewarding and promoting academics on the basis of their individual performance, rather than being part of a team.

Participant H believes that relations at the department level "... may be even worse than at the faculty level." And adds that the reason for such relations is a different level of engagement of colleagues "We are [a] somewhat specific department with many members who are research inactive or poorly active and it seems to me that this difference is also seen anyway" but nevertheless describes the general atmosphere among fellow academics as "likely cooperative." Clark (1983; in Gizir, 2010, p. 140), on the other hand, says that increasingly specialized disciplinary fields affect the differentiation between employees within HEIs. This leads to a high degree of professional autonomy where individuals act as separate cell groups.

Similarly, participant A believes that the relations in the academic world are predominantly cooperative "... I think in science, however, we more share than hide information. I think this is because we all know that we do not have much to lose... by sharing information." But adds that it is occasionally possible to feel a degree of rivalry "It exists all over the world!" which for her it is not a bad thing "Competitiveness is essential, no. Cannot be otherwise." She thinks that the area of work influences the competition between colleagues within HEIs "Certainly, if someone would do just exactly what I do, but it's so unlikely, because we

are so different and the space our work, or the area is so endless. If someone is doing exactly the same research as I do, but really exactly the same, and my life would depend on this publication, currently being prepared, probably I would not have told everything to this colleague."

Participant D also acknowledges the importance of a degree of competition and says that it exists amongst her colleagues, "Yes, yes, it needs to be a little, it's okay that between us, we are... that we fight... It is Ok... to a certain degree is healthy, do not!" Similarly considers participant F who says that in the course of his career, he received some form of competition, but he acknowledges that some degree of competition in the HEIs is welcome "... I felt... when we started negotiations for example, who is right who is wrong - then I felt the competition. But I don't say that that was bad in this case." In his view within the academic world there could be even more competition between individuals, but this does not occur, because "... we have the fortune that we need each other, at least those of us who work together."

Participant E says that the higher education system is designed in such a way that it forces individuals to continuously compete "... these formal systems based on points and so on, has its effect, certainly. If I can write an article alone and therefore I get x points, why should I share them with others? And this is encouraging in that direction." Similarly participant C considers this as the systemic cause for the highly competitive academic world, "These matters were always like that, I think we always have had habilitation..." and adds that anyone who wants to create a career in this sphere should be aware of this "... competition... no one can say that doesn't exist, it should be, because everyone who comes in this institution enters in a kind of game and competition is never fair...." This matches words by Gizir & Simsek (2005), who recognise that without common goals, individuals are driven to achieve their own goals and this leads to a strongly individualistic environment. Common goals are of great importance as they contribute to organisational unity, with them employees develop "a feeling of belonging and motivation, and [they] provide a means of justifying the institution to its various publics" (Patterson, 2001; in Gizir, 2010, p. 141). Participant I looks at higher education as competitive or "highly" competitive. He says, unlike other interviewees that the reason for this is primarily financial "... because resources are limited..." This view confirms that academics have a perception of the limited pool of available tangible and intangible resources within higher education. Because of that, only the most brilliant and/or politically skilled they believed can get access to this pool. Anyway this perception runs a competition among academics for the highest amount of available resources.

Interviewees experienced academic environment, not only as competitive, but also as a highly individualistic. Participant D says that "... colleagues exploit their knowledge for themselves..." and adds that they know little about each other "some of your colleagues you come to know only when you need to, when you're in a project team." Participant F believes that "... it goes without saying that the top experts are individualists." Participant C agrees with the view that academia is necessary individualistic "... more or less you have to be individualist... essentially you are quite alone" and adds that "no one can understand you, because in the essence you are, we are specialists...."

Participant E also believes academia is dominated by individualists and says the "... academic world consists of highly educated people, very capable..." and she adds that teamwork in the academic environment is relatively poorly presented "... the study itself, so the path to a doctorate and the later title is actually a very individual. That is to say, you've got highly capable, highly skilled people who are at the same time strong individualists, and this individualism is not only about 'Do

I know my area?' but is also about how much you have been through the whole process of your education pushed in cooperation with others."

Participant G, on the other hand, notes that within his profession changes in the structure of work happen, from mostly individual work to a more team oriented work "... If I speak in terms of our department it undergoes several changes in recent times, in the sense that in the past our older colleagues behaved highly individualistic... we started to link with each other, partly because of the nature of research questions, partly I have to say for pragmatic reasons, because the policy, research and university policy is essentially forcing this cooperation and here we are relatively still at the beginning and somehow we have not been very successful, but at least, I don't know, young staff are increasingly trying to do more teamwork." However, she adds that pushing the team work has both advantages and disadvantages for her and her field of work "... the nature of our science is such that we are somehow significant individualists, each has its [their] own views on certain things and now join[ing] this by force would not make sense and would be just bad for the development of our, our scientific discipline... hm ... at the same time is a challenge that you can discuss things from different angles and form something new from that, in the department we are actually at the beginning."

Individualism can prevent the transfer of knowledge, which otherwise occurs when individuals or groups cooperate with each other. However, such cooperation will occur only if individuals or groups can establish a degree of trust, which usually occurs in an environment where decisions are taken openly, where free access to information is possible and where employees are fairly treated and rewarded. On the other hand, a low level of mutual trust will reduce the frequency of communication and will consequently reduce the willingness to share knowledge (Goh, 2001).

Relationships between Staff and Faculty Leadership

From the responses of interviewees, it can be seen that their attitude towards leadership is more or less neutral, with some slightly critical and only one participant pleased with the relationship between lecturers / researchers and faculty management. The relationship between faculty leadership and staff is satisfactory only to participant F who says "... you can announce yourself to the Dean and Vice Deans for an interview at any time without problems, to all of them. ... Not least to the President of the Board.... You can literally knock on the door or... they are available, they are very open and accessible." He however recognizes that this is not typical for the area of higher education, and sees in this relationship "that is our competitive advantage and I hope we will also continue to maintain [it]."

Participant H assesses the leadership of the faculty as being fairly sensitive to suggestions or requests from the employees, but ads "... but it lasts very long. For example to get one program we need to annoy for a couple of years..." and he sees the reason for this in bureaucratic proceedings, "... we are very bureaucratic organization, it is necessary to justify any additional cost, but... I do not see any reason why something is taking three years when it could be done in two months." Even participant J says that the leadership of the faculty is open to academic staff requests, but adds, "... the last time they said that their doors are open. Other thing is where it's been said sincerely.... I have an experience that they didn't really listen too much to certain matters. "

For participant D there are difficult times for managing faculty "Times are tough... There is increasing on different new obligations. In the past it was, I think easier... it was a little more on the academic level for teachers and for management...." Participant A believes the same in describing the relationship between employees and management at her institution and adds that

"Specificity of this faculty is that it is very, very big...I think it has 7000 students, or something like that...it has about 25 departments, it seems to me that are extremely heterogeneous, and now what that leadership can make for us I really do not know. I always say that I do not see much difference in the difficulty of the function of one prime minister or the Dean at my faculty. I do not know what is worse..." Her attitude to leadership is quite sceptical and she says, "... whatever I do not expect much from the faculty management, and because my expectations are low is also very difficult to disappoint me." Such difficulties in managing HEIs, as described by participants D and A are consistent with Enders (2004), who also says that universities are currently in a complex and delicate situation.

Participant I was (somewhat more) critical of his faculty management, who he believes is not receptive to suggestions or other requests of employees. He explains "I think is not, not even is part of the culture, I think declaratively are open, but they just do not have the operational capacity to work in this way...." Finally, the most critical of faculty leadership is participant C, who says "... if the director or dean have not time, say in one or two months to coordinate a meeting with me, then I have nothing to talk with him... if I call the Dean by phone or I contact him by e-mail and he doesn't respond, then our communication is completed, we don' t have anything more to talk to."

Summary

The study was conducted on a small sample but we believe it contributes to a better understanding of KM processes in HEIs. On the basis of participants' answers to questions relating to the processes of new knowledge creation and transfer in HEIs, we can conclude that the main purpose of HEIs remains the creation and transfer of knowledge. On the other hand, the study discovered that HEIs are becoming much more market-oriented and are attempting to receive additional funds with the aid of their employees' knowledge (see subsection *Knowledge as a Market Asset*). Scholars create new knowledge through research activities, and this knowledge should give answers to questions or needs that arise in either the immediate or broader social environment. The study results show that the participants distinguished between knowledge created in natural sciences and knowledge created in social sciences. The first is gained as a result of experiments and is thus formed on the basis of empirical facts, whereas knowledge created in social sciences is influenced by contextual social values and therefore cannot be completely objective. However, knowledge created at HEIs must first be recognized by the broader academic community before it can it can be accepted as new knowledge in general.

Research participants say that they present their findings in the form of articles, books and/or other publications. This simplifies the transfer of explicit knowledge primarily to students, other academic colleagues and to the general public. Publications also serve as a "deposit" of knowledge or written memory. Tacit knowledge, on the other hand, is typically transferred by observation, usually of older and more experienced colleagues, interaction by means of formal and informal meetings, and by exchanging opinions (see subsection *The Role of Mentor*). The findings also show that the relationship established between the mentee and their mentor plays an important role at the beginning of an individual's academic career. Through regular interaction, the mentor transfers a part of their explicit (professional) and tacit knowledge to the mentee, which, among other things, includes the knowledge about social networks and the principles of the institution's operation. The answers to the research question about relationships in HEIs—relationships between academics and their colleagues, relationships between academics and the management of HEIs, and the academics' attitude towards the use of ICT—led to the conclusion that the academic world is dominated by competition and individualism, which negatively

affects the interaction and limits the transfer of knowledge among colleagues. The relationship between academics and the leadership of the faculty can also be described as relatively poor because the leadership usually either fails to meet the needs and wants of the academic staff or pays little attention to them at all.

Related to the role of ICT in modern HEIs we found that it is predominantly used as a means to access explicit knowledge resources. This enables academics to gain insight into an almost unlimited pool of diverse knowledge. In the teaching process, the e-classroom is becoming increasingly more popular and represents an effective tool for the transfer of knowledge to students. However, the study shows that it has not yet replaced the teacher-student direct relationship (see subsection *E-learning*). At the same time, the e-classroom is mainly regarded as a tool for increasing the efficiency of the teaching process and consequently for reducing labour costs rather than a tool for increasing quality of education.

On the basis of the results, we can conclude that knowledge creation and transfer represent two of the main tasks of HEIs. However, the need to directly enter the market and sell knowledge is becoming increasingly urgent amongst competing HEIs. The priority focus on external relationships in an effort to secure financial resources may also be one reason that HEIs do not dedicate enough attention to relationships with employees. At the same time, higher pressure on economic efficiency and market culture increase already present competition between academics which reduces their willingness to cooperate and consequently the possibility to create new knowledge that HEIs could successfully sell on the market.

FUTURE RESEARCH DIRECTION

In spite of the limited size of the sample, the study raises some questions that provide a solid basis for future research of several issues.

The first issue relates to the relationship between the understanding of the role and scope of university teaching and the understanding of KM and its processes. As stated by Dall'Alba and Sandberg (2006), professional development of individuals does not consist of a gradual increase in volume and complexity of available knowledge and skills but rather a changing of the understanding of the profession's purpose and role. That is to say, conceiving of teaching as primarily a knowledge transfer from teacher to learner is very different from placing emphasis on facilitating the change and personal development of the learner. Based on this, it would be interesting in the future to establish whether the importance and role of KM in HEIs varies depending on the understanding of the role and scope of a university lecturer. To a large extent this is the key to further development of KM using the bottom-up approach.

The second issue relates to the importance of the leadership of HEIs for KM success. As stated in the literature, leadership is one of the key success factors of KM (e.g. Alazmi & Airi, 2003; Art, 2006; Conley & Zheng, 2009). At the same time we found in our research study that leadership at best has a neutral role. This requires understanding the essential role of leadership within HEIs. We can differentiate between leadership responsible for policy development and management, which is responsible for policy execution (Middlehurst, Goreham, & Woodfield, 2009). Therefore, in future research it should be taken into account which of the two views of the role of leadership is held by academic staff as this, we believe, influences the expectations they have regarding KM processes.

The last issue raised by this study is the transfer of knowledge from academics to students and from students to academics (i.e. students as recipients and bearers of knowledge) in the information-based society. Modern ICT has simultaneously changed the characteristics of students and encouraged the development of the extended mind. In other words, while students have developed

strong tendencies for multi-tasking and computer assisted social networking, the accompanying weakness in complex analysis skills is offset by ICT's contribution toward their development of the extended mind (i.e. the expansion of mind into the external world composed of different objects that increase cognitive ability). All this undoubtedly changes the process of knowledge transfer that takes place between lecturers and students, and consequently, the importance and role of KM in higher education. On the other side of the coin, we also need to understand how the use of different knowledge metaphors, for example knowledge as thoughts or feeling, influences the way HEIs think about KM.

CONCLUSION

Based on our findings, it can be concluded that within HEIs KM takes place at the intersection of the four critical factors; namely, the mentor, HEI leadership, ICT and the academic community.

If within companies leadership has a central role for the success of knowledge management, within HEIs this role belongs to the mentor. The role of the mentor is present in the relationship between senior and junior academics as well as in the relationship between academics and students. Apart from transferring tacit knowledge and retaining expertise within the HEI, a mentor can help a mentee to become a recognized and accepted member of the academic community by passing on the HEI's values and improving the mentee's academic networking. In the context of a mentoring relationship, beside a discipline-specific knowledge, an understanding of internal organizational policies, values, and mission is also transferred from the mentor to the mentee. A faculty-faculty mentorship enhances the self-awareness of the mentee, develops his skills of dialogue, creates a space of reflection and refines his quality of thinking. At the same time, the participants in the study emphasized that in the mentor-mentee relationship the knowledge transfer occurs in bothdirections. We can define the mentor-mentee relationship as a form of 'ba' (Nonaka & Konno, 1998), which significantly contributes to the creation of the conditions for new knowledge development.

If the mentor has the key role of generating new knowledge and transferring existing knowledge within HEIs, then leadership's task is to create conditions in which there are no organisational, administrative, financial, or other barriers that would prevent or otherwise inhibit effective tutoring. While this is one of the leadership's tasks, it us certainly not the only one, based on the fact that in the study participants have not seen leadership role as particularly contributing to the KM success. However, as demonstrated by other researchers in profit and not-profit organisations, the leadership and organisational culture are the key factors for successful knowledge management. Therefore, another critical task for HEI leadership is motivating academics to share knowledge, even if the general economic situation makes the higher education sector increasingly competitive and more individualistic than previously. Motivation is also related to the issue of trust between the institution (i.e. leadership) and academics. While motivational issues are directly highlighted by the study participants, the issue of trust is exposed indirectly via the attitude that ICT is a mere tool to reduce costs. Based on Hautala (2011, p. 4) who states, "Academic knowledge creation takes place physically, mentally and/or virtually in interaction, in ba"; we believe that leadership needs to take the central position within the dynamic network of actors pursuing their own individual and sometimes collective interests. From this central position, leaders can promote knowledge sharing by leading by example as well as by properly answering the question "What's in it for me?" In any case, to overcome the individualistic tendency of academics, HEIs' leaders need to optimize the conditions needed for innovation and collaboration among academics (i.e. they need to optimize

ba) by designing and promoting systemic policies and strategies. Without them, KM initiatives will remain unrelated and unfocused.

ICT within HEIs can be divided into three groups:

1. Technology for knowledge codification and storage that includes different types of knowledge repositories and training tools.
2. Communication technology that supports knowledge transfer irrespective of its format, user operating system, or communication protocols.
3. Collaborative technology that enhances person-to-person collaboration and includes knowledge maps, which are pointers to knowledge providers inside or outside an organisation.

Based on the study, among the many possibilities that ICT offers, only knowledge storage and collaborative technology are used within HEIs. The question then becomes 'how can ICT be appplied more widely within HEIs?' Assuming funding is available, HEIs need to design and implement training for their academics and motivate lecturers to adopt ICT as a teaching tool (i.e. to move from a content-centered curricula to a competency-based curricula) that emphasizes how the information will be used rather than what the information is. To further support the use of ICT within HEIs, leadership should encourage a constructivist approach to learning. These learning principles can be fully supported by ICT by enabling learning that is closely connected to context and practice (Duffy & Cunningham, 1996).

The academic community represents the last critical factor for KM success within HEIs. Knowledge does not exist if is not accepted by the academic community. From this point of view, academics are limited in their knowledge creation by the basic episteme that frames their knowledge in historical time and a specific social context. For this reason, it is important to develop a common language that can be shared and understood by academics involved in the creation of new knowledge. At such a point, however, the problem of discipline boundaries emerges. Even if modern social problems are transdisciplinary and inter-disciplinary in nature, academics have difficulty communicating across boundaries because of the different languages they use. Epistemology can be seen as the difference between the so-called hard sciences (i.e. natural sciences) and the soft sciences (social sciences and humanities). The natural sciences are perceived to be rational and objective while the social sciences are perceived as subjective and imbued with social values. KM within HEIs must also consider this perception of the new knowledge generation. Even if it is not possible to plan discourse and interaction, HEIs need to acknowledge what kind of knowledge is created in different groups of academics and be aware of which practical modes of organising the group work are appropriate to support the creation of knowledge. The important point is that group work within HEIs is supported without sacrificing time for individual self-reflection and thinking.

REFERENCES

Alavi, M., & Leidner, D. E. (1999). Knowledge management systems: Issues, challenges, and benefits. *Communications of the Association for Information Systems, 1*(7), 1–37.

Alavi, M., & Leidner, D. E. (2001). Review: Knowledge management and knowledge management systems: Conceptual foundations and research issues. *Management Information Systems Quarterly, 25*(3), 107–136. doi:10.2307/3250961

Alazmi, M., & Zairi, M. (2003). Knowledge management critical success factors. *Total Quality Management, 14*(2), 199–204. doi:10.1080/1478336032000051386

Alvesson, M., & Kärreman, D. (2001). Odd couple: Making sense of the curious concept of knowledge management. *Journal of Management Studies, 38*(7), 995–1018. doi:10.1111/1467-6486.00269

Andriessen, D. G. (2008). Stuff or love? How metaphors direct our efforts to manage knowledge in organisations. *Knowledge Management Research & Practice, 6*, 5–12. doi:10.1057/palgrave.kmrp.8500169

Argote, L., Beckman, S., & Epple, D. (1990). The persistence and transfer of learning in industrial settings. *Management Science, 36*, 1750–1763. doi:10.1287/mnsc.36.2.140

Atkinson, P. (1995). *Medical talk and medical work*. Thousand Oaks, CA: Sage Publications.

Barney, J. B. (1991). Firm resources and sustained competitive advantage. *Journal of Management, 17*(1), 99–120. doi:10.1177/014920639101700108

Bender, S., & Fish, A. (2000). The transfer of knowledge and the retention of expertise: The continuing need for global assignments. *Journal of Knowledge Management, 4*(2), 125–137. doi:10.1108/13673270010372251

Biloslavo, R., & Trnavčevič, A. (2007). Knowledge management audit in a higher educational institution: A case study. *Knowledge and Process Management, 14*(4), 275–286. doi:10.1002/kpm.293

Blackler, F. (1995). Knowledge, knowledge work and organizations: An overview and interpretation. *Organization Studies, 16*(6), 1021–1046. doi:10.1177/017084069501600605

Boisot, M. H. (1998). *Knowledge assets: Securing competitive advantage in the information economy*. Oxford, UK: Oxford University Press.

Bolton, E. B. (1980). A conceptual analysis of the mentor relationship in the career development of women. *Adult Education, 30*, 195–207. doi:10.1177/074171368003000401

Bonner, D. (2000). *Leading knowledge management and learning*. Alexandria, VA: American Society of Training & Development.

Bruno, D., Frederick, A. S., Gary, A. M., & Michael, M. (2005). Learning to build a car: An empirical investigation of organizational learning. *Journal of Management Studies, 42*(2), 387–416. doi:10.1111/j.1467-6486.2005.00501.x

Butler, T., Heavin, C., & O'Donovan, F. (2007). A theoretical model and framework for understanding knowledge management system implementation. *Journal of Organizational and End User Computing, 19*(4), 1–21. doi:10.4018/joeuc.2007100101

Cabrera, À., & Cabreta, E. F. (2002). Knowledge-sharing dilemmas. *Organization Studies, 23*(5), 687–710. doi:10.1177/0170840602235001

Clark, B. R. (1983). *The higher education system: Academic Organization in cross-cultural perspective*. London, UK: University of California Press.

Cohen, W. M., & Levinthal, D. A. (1990). Absorptive capacity: A new perspective on learning and innovation. *Administrative Science Quarterly, 35*, 128–152. doi:10.2307/2393553

Collins, H. M. (1993). The structure of knowledge. *Social Research, 60*(1), 95–116.

Conley, C. A., & Zheng, W. (2009). Factors critical to knowledge management success. *Advances in Developing Human Resources, 11*(3), 334–348. doi:10.1177/1523422309338159

Conner, K. R. (1991). A historical comparison of the resource-based theory and five schools of thought within industrial organization economics: Do we have a new theory of the firm? *Journal of Management, 17*(1), 121–154. doi:10.1177/014920639101700109

Cook, S. D. N., & Brown, J. S. (1999). Bridging epistemologies: The generative dance between organizational knowledge and organizational knowing. *Organization Science, 10*, 381–400. doi:10.1287/orsc.10.4.381

Cortada, J. W., & Woods, J. A. (Eds.). (1999). *The knowledge management yearbook: 1999-2000*. Boston, MA: Butterworth-Heinemann.

Cortada, J. W., & Woods, J. A. (Eds.). (2000). *The knowledge management yearbook: 2000-2001*. Boston, MA: Butterworth-Heinemann.

Dall'Alba, G., & Sandberg, J. (2006). Unveiling professional development: A critical review of stage models. *American Educational Research, 76*(3), 383–412.

Darling, L. A. W. (1985). 'Mentors' and 'mentoring'. *The Journal of Nursing Administration, 15*(3), 42–43.

Darr, E. D., Argote, L., & Epple, D. (1995). The acquisition, transfer and depreciation of knowledge in service organizations: Productivity in franchises. *Management Science, 41*(11), 1650–1713. doi:10.1287/mnsc.41.11.1750

Davenport, T. H., & Prusak, L. (1998). *Working knowledge*. Boston, MA: Harvard Business School Press.

de Wit, H. (2002). *Internationalisation of higher education in the United States of America and Europe*. New York, NY: Greenwood.

Duffy, T., & Cunningham, D. (1996). *Constructivism: Implications for the design and delivery of instruction. Handbook of Research for Educational Telecommunications and Technology* (pp. 170–198). New York, NY: Macmillan.

Dufour, Y., & Steane, P. (2007). Implementing knowledge management: A more robust model. *Journal of Knowledge Management, 11*(6), 66–80. doi:10.1108/13673270710832172

Duke, S., Makey, P., & Kiras, N. (1999). *Knowledge management 1999 report series*. Hull, UK: Butler Group.

Dyck, B., Starke, F. A., Mischke, G. A., & Mauws, M. (2005). Learning to build a car: An empirical investigation of organizational learning. *Journal of Management Studies*, *42*(2), 387–416. doi:10.1111/j.1467-6486.2005.00501.x

Ericsson, K. A. (1996). The acquisition of expert performance: An introduction to some of the issues. In Ericsson, K. A. (Ed.), *The Road to Excellence: The Acquisition of Expert Performance in the Arts and Sciences, Sports, and Games* (pp. 1–50). Hillsdale, NJ: Lawrence Erlbaum Associates.

Fahey, L., & Prusak, L. (1998). The eleven deadliest sins of knowledge management. *California Management Review*, *40*(3), 265–276.

Farjoun, M. (2010). Beyond dualism: Stability and change as a duality. *Academy of Management Review*, *35*(2), 202–225. doi:10.5465/AMR.2010.48463331

Firestone, J. M. (2001). Key issues in knowledge management. *Knowledge and Innovation: Journal of the KMCI*, *1*(3), 8–38.

Geiger, A. H. (1992). Measures for mentors. *Training & Development*, *46*(2), 65–67.

Geng, Q., Townley, C., Huang, K., & Zhang, J. (2005). Comparative knowledge management: A pilot study of Chinese and American universities. *Journal of the American Society for Information Science and Technology*, *56*(10), 1031–1044. doi:10.1002/asi.20194

Gill, A. (2009). Knowledge management initiatives at a small university. *International Journal of Educational Management*, *23*(7), 604–616. doi:10.1108/09513540910990834

Gizir, S., & Simsek, H. (2005). Communication in an academic context. *Higher Education*, *50*(2), 197–221. doi:10.1007/s10734-004-6349-x

Goh, S. C. (2002). Managing effective knowledge transfer: An integrative framework and some practice implications. *Journal of Knowledge Management*, *6*(1), 23–30. doi:10.1108/13673270210417664

Gomezelj Omerzel, D., Biloslavo, R., & Trnavčevič, A. (2010). *Management znanja v visokošolskih zavodih*. Koper, Slovenija: Univerza na Primorskem, Fakulteta za management Koper.

Grant, R. M. (1996). Toward a knowledge-based theory of the firm. *Strategic Management Journal*, *17*, 109–122.

Gupta, A. K., & Govindarajan, V. (2000). Knowledge management's social dimension: Lessons from Nucor steel. *Sloan Management Review*, *41*(1), 71–80.

Hackbarth, G. (1998). The impact of organizational memory on IT systems. In E. Hoadley & I. Benbasat (Eds.), *Proceedings of the Fourth Americas Conference on Information Systems*, (pp. 588-590). ACIS.

Hautala, J. (2011). International academic knowledge creation and ba: A case study from Finland. *Knowledge Management Research & Practice*, *9*, 4–16. doi:10.1057/kmrp.2010.23

Holtman, C., & Courtney, N. (1998). The executive learning ladder: A knowledge creation process grounded in the strategic information systems domain. In E. Hoadley & I. Benbasat (Eds.), *Proceedings of the Fourth Americas Conference on Information Systems*, (pp. 594-597). Baltimore, MD: ACIS.

Huysman, M., Creemers, M., & Derksen, D. (1998). Learning from the environment: Exploring the relation between organizational learning, knowledge management and information/communication technology. In E. Hoadley & I. Benbasat (Eds.), *Proceedings of the Fourth Americas Conference on Information Systems,* (pp. 598-600). Baltimore, MD: ACIS.

Inkpen, A., & Dikur, I. (1998). Knowledge management processes and international joint ventures. *Organization Science, 9*(4), 454–468. doi:10.1287/orsc.9.4.454

Ivari, J., & Linger, H. (1999). Knowledge work as collaborative work: A situated activity theory view. In *Proceedings of the Thirty-Second Annual Hawaii International Conference on Systems Sciences*. Los Alamitos, CA: IEEE Press.

Junnarkar, B., & Brown, C. V. (1997). Re-assessing the enabling role of information technology in KM. *Journal of Knowledge Management, 1*(2), 142–148. doi:10.1108/EUM0000000004589

Kerr, N. L. (1989). Illusions of efficacy: The effects of group size on perceived efficacy in social dilemmas. *Journal of Experimental Social Psychology, 25*(4), 287–313. doi:10.1016/0022-1031(89)90024-3

Kidwell, J. J., Vander Linde, K. M., & Johnson, S. L. (2000). Applying corporate knowledge management practices in higher education. *EDUCAUSE Quarterly, 23*(4), 28–33.

Kitzinger, J. (1995). Introducing focus groups. *British Medical Journal, 311*(29), 299–302. doi:10.1136/bmj.311.7000.299

Klopčič, J. (2006). *Pomen organizacijskega učenja v sodobni organizaciji.* Specialistično delo, Univerza v Ljubljani: Ekonomska fakulteta.

KPMG. (2000). *Knowledge management research report 2000.* KPMG Consulting. Retrieved April 5, 2011, from http://www.providersedge.com/docs/km_articles/KPMG_KM_Research_Report_2000.pdf

Kulkarni, U. R., Ravindran, S., & Freeze, R. (2007). A knowledge management success model: Theoretical development and empirical validation. *Journal of Management Information Systems, 23*(3), 309–347. doi:10.2753/MIS0742-1222230311

Lam, A. (2000). Tacit knowledge, organizational learning and societal institutions: An integrated framework. *Organization Studies, 21*(3), 487–513. doi:10.1177/0170840600213001

Lee, J. (2001). The impact of knowledge sharing, organizational capability and partnership quality on IS outsourcing success. *Information & Management, 38*(5), 323–335. doi:10.1016/S0378-7206(00)00074-4

Levitt, B., & March, J. G. (1988). Organizational learning. *Annual Review of Sociology, 14*, 319–340. doi:10.1146/annurev.so.14.080188.001535

Liebowitz, J., & Chen, Y. (2003). Knowledge sharing proficiencies: The key to knowledge management. In Holsapple, C. W. (Ed.), *Handbook on Knowledge Management 1: Knowledge Matters* (pp. 409–424). Berlin, Germany: Springer.

Lundvall, B. A., & Johnson, B. (1994). The learning economy. *Journal of Industry Studies, 1*, 22–42. doi:10.1080/13662719400000002

Major, E., & Cordey-Hayes, M. (2000). Knowledge translation: a new perspective on knowledge transfer and foresight. *Foresight, 2*(4), 411–423. doi:10.1108/14636680010802762

Malhotra, Y. (2000). *Knowledge management and virtual organizations.* Hershey, PA: IGI Global. doi:10.4018/978-1-87828-973-5

Management Consulting, K. P. M. G. (1998). *Case Study: Building a platform for corporate knowledge*. New York, NY: KPMG Management Consulting.

Marquardt, M. J. (1996). *Building the learning organization: A systems approach to quantum improvement and global success*. New York, NY: McGraw-Hill.

McLean, J. E. (2005, June/July). ICT and knowledge management. *British Journal of Administrative Management*, 17–18.

Merriam, S. (1983). Mentors and protégés: A critical review of the literature. *Adult Education Quarterly*, *33*(3), 161–173.

Merriam, S. B. (2009). *Qualitative research: A guide to design and implementation*. San Francisco, CA: Jossey-Bass.

Middlehurst, R., Goreham, H., & Woodfield, S. (2009). Why research leadership in higher education? Exploring contributions from the UK's leadership foundation for higher education. *Leadership*, *5*(3), 311–329. doi:10.1177/1742715009337763

Moffet, S., McAdam, R., & Parkinson, S. (2002). Developing a model for technology and cultural factors in knowledge management: A factor analysis. *Knowledge and Process Management*, *9*(4), 237–255. doi:10.1002/kpm.152

Myers, P. S. (1996). *Knowledge management and organizational design*. Boston, MA: Butterworth-Heinemann.

Nanda, A. (1996). Resources, capabilities, and competencies. In Moingeon, B., & Edmonson, A. (Eds.), *Organizational Learning and Competitive Advantage* (pp. 93–120). London, UK: Sage. doi:10.4135/9781446250228.n6

Nelson, R. R., & Winter, S. G. (1982). *An evolutionary theory of economic change*. Cambridge, MA: Harvard University Press.

Nonaka, I. (1994). A dynamic theory of organizational knowledge creation. *Organization Science*, *5*(1), 14–37. doi:10.1287/orsc.5.1.14

Nonaka, I. (2007). The knowledge-creating company. *Harvard Business Review*, *85*(7/8), 162–171.

Nonaka, I., & Konno, N. (1998). The concept of 'ba': Building a foundation for knowledge creation. *California Management Review*, *40*(3), 40–54.

Nonaka, I., & Takeuchi, H. (1995). *The knowledge-creating company: How Japanese companies create the dynamics of innovation*. Oxford, UK: Oxford University Press.

Nonaka, I., Toyama, R., & Nagata, A. (2000). A firm as a knowledge-creating entity: A new perspective on the theory of the firm. *Industrial and Corporate Change*, *9*(1), 1–20. doi:10.1093/icc/9.1.1

Nonaka, I., & von Krogh, G. (2009). Tacit knowledge and knowledge conversion: Controversy and advancement in organizational knowledge creation theory. *Organization Science*, *20*(3), 635–652. doi:10.1287/orsc.1080.0412

O'Dell, C., & Grayson, C. J. Jr. (1999). Knowledge transfer: Discover your value proposition. *Strategy and Leadership*, *27*(2), 10–15. doi:10.1108/eb054630

Patterson, G. (2001). The applicability of institutional goals to the university. *Journal of Higher Education Policy and Management*, *23*(2), 159–169. doi:10.1080/13600800120088652

Pelgrum, W. J. (2001). Obstacles to the integration of ICT in education: Results from a worldwide educational assessment. *Computers & Education*, *37*, 163–178. doi:10.1016/S0360-1315(01)00045-8

Pfeffer, J., & Sutton, R. (2000). *The knowing-doing gap*. Boston, MA: Harvard Business School Press.

Pfleeger, S., & Merty, N. (1995). Executive mentoring: What makes it work? *Communications of the American Academy of Management, 38*(1), 63–73.

Piccoli, G., Ahmad, R., & Ives, B. (2000). Knowledge management in academia: A proposed framework. *Information Technology Management, 1,* 229–245. doi:10.1023/A:1019129226227

Polanyi, M. (1958). *Personal knowledge: Towards a post-critical philosophy.* London, UK: Routledge and Kegan Paul.

Polanyi, M. (1966). *The tacit dimension.* Garden City, NY: Doubleday & Company, Inc.

Polanyi, M. (1975). Personal knowledge. In Polanyi, M., & Prosch, H. (Eds.), *Meaning* (pp. 22–45). Chicago, IL: University of Chicago Press.

Probst, G., Raub, S., & Romhardt, K. (1999). *Managing knowledge: Building blocks for success.* New York, NY: John Wiley & Sons.

Rapoport, A., Bornstein, G., & Erev, I. (1989). Intergroup competition for public goods: Effects of unequal resources and relative group size. *Journal of Personality and Social Psychology, 56*(5), 748–756. doi:10.1037/0022-3514.56.5.748

Roberts, J. (2000). From know-how to show-how? Questioning the role of information and communication technologies in knowledge transfer. *Technology Analysis and Strategic Management, 12*(4), 429–443. doi:10.1080/713698499

Sanderlands, L. E., & Stablein, R. E. (1987). The concept of organization mind. In Bachrach, S., & DiTomaso, N. (Eds.), *Research in the Sociology of Organization* (*Vol. 5,* pp. 135–162). Greenwich, CT: JAI Press.

Sarvary, M. (1999). Knowledge management and competition in the consulting industry. *California Management Review, 41,* 95–108.

Scarbrough, H., Swan, J., & Preston, J. (1999). *Knowledge management: A literature review.* London, UK: Institute of Personnel and Development.

Schacter, D. L. (1996). *Searching for memory: The brain, the mind, and the past.* New York, NY: Basic Books.

Sharimllah Devi, R., Chong, S. C., & Lin, B. (2007). Organizational culture and KM processes from the perspective of an institution of higher learning. *Inernational Journal of Management in Education, 1*(1/2), 57–79. doi:10.1504/IJMIE.2007.014377

Simonetti, J. L., Ariss, S., & Martinez, J. (1999). Through the top with mentoring. *Business Horizons, 42*(6), 56–63. doi:10.1016/S0007-6813(99)80039-1

Snowden, D. J. (1999). The paradox of story: Simplicity and complexity in strategy. *Journal of Strategy and Scenario Planning, 1*(5), 24–32.

Spender, J. C. (1992). Strategy theorizing: Expanding the agenda. In Shrivastava, P., Huff, A., & Dutton, J. (Eds.), *Advances in Strategic Management* (pp. 3–32). Greenwich, CT: JAI Press.

Spender, J. C. (1996). Competitive advantage from tacit knowledge? Unpacking the concept and its strategic implications. In Moingeon, B., & Edmonson, A. (Eds.), *Organizational Learning and Competitive Advantage* (pp. 56–73). London, UK: Sage Publications. doi:10.4135/9781446250228.n4

Spender, J. C. (1996a). Making knowledge the basis of a dynamic theory of the firm. *Strategic Management Journal, 17,* 45–62.

Spender, J. C. (1996b). Organizational knowledge, learning and memory: Three concepts in search of a theory. *Journal of Organizational Change Management, 9,* 63–78. doi:10.1108/09534819610156813

Srikanthan, G., & Dalrymple, J. F. (2002). Developing a holistic model for quality in higher education. *Quality in Higher Education, 8*(2), 215–224. doi:10.1080/1353832022000031656

Starbuck, W., & Hedberg, B. (1977). Saving an organization from a stagnating environment. In Thorelli, H. (Ed.), *Strategy + Structure = Performance* (pp. 249–258). Bloomington, IN: University Press.

Starbuck, W. H. (1992). Learning by knowledge-intensive firms. *Journal of Management Studies, 29*(6), 713–740. doi:10.1111/j.1467-6486.1992. tb00686.x

Steinkellner, P. F., & Czerny, E. J. (2010). *Educating managers for a paradox world – Duality and paradoxes in management*. Paper presented at the International Conference on Management Learning Management Makes the World Go Around. Vienna, Austria.

Sveiby, K.-E. (1997). *The new organizational wealth: Managing and measuring knowledge-based assets*. San Francisco, CA: Berret-Koehler.

Sveiby, K.-E. (2001). A knowledge-based theory of the firm to guide in strategy formulation. *Journal of Intellectual Capital, 2*(4), 344–358. doi:10.1108/14691930110409651

Swan, J., & Scarbrough, H. (2001). Knowledge management: Concepts and controversies. *Journal of Management Studies, 38*, 913–921. doi:10.1111/1467-6486.00265

Swap, W., Leonard, D., Shields, M., & Abrams, L. (2001). Using mentoring and storytelling to transfer knowledge in the workplace. *Journal of Management Information Systems, 18*(1), 95–114.

Syed-Ikhsan, S. O. S., & Rowland, F. (2004). Knowledge management in a public organization: A study on the relationship between organizational elements and the performance of knowledge transfer. *Journal of Knowledge Management, 8*(2), 95–111. doi:10.1108/13673270410529145

Taylor, J. (2004). Toward a strategy for internationalisation: Lessons and practice from four universities. *Journal of Studies in International Education, 8*(2), 149–171. doi:10.1177/1028315303260827

Teichler, U. (2004). The changing debate on internationalisation of higher education. *Higher Education, 48*, 5–26. doi:10.1023/B:HIGH.0000033771.69078.41

Tippins, M. J. (2003). Implementing knowledge management in academia: Teaching the teachers. *International Journal of Educational Management, 17*(7), 339–345. doi:10.1108/09513540310501021

Tuomi, I. (1999). Data is more than knowledge: Implications of the reversed hierarchy for knowledge management and organizational memory. In *Proceedings of the Thirty-Second Annual Hawaii International Conference on Systems Sciences*. Los Alamitos, CA: IEEE Computer Society Press.

von Krogh, G. (1998). Care in knowledge creation. *California Management Review, 40*(3), 133–153.

Walsh, J. P., & Ungson, G. R. (1991). Organizational memory. *Academy of Management Review, 16*(1), 57–91.

Ward, L. F. (1968). *Dynamic sociology 2*. New York, NY: Johnson Reprint Corporation.

Wiig, K. M. (1993). *Knowledge management foundations: Thinking about thinking: How people and organizations create, represent, and use knowledge*. Arlington, TX: Schema Press.

Wiig, K. M. (1997). Integrating intellectual capital and knowledge management. *Long Range Planning, 30*(3), 399–405. doi:10.1016/S0024-6301(97)90256-9

Wiig, K. M. (1997). Knowledge management: Where did it come from and where will it go? *Expert Systems with Applications, 13*(1), 1–14. doi:10.1016/S0957-4174(97)00018-3

Wiig, K. M. (1999). What future knowledge management users may expect. *Journal of Knowledge Management, 3*(2), 155–165. doi:10.1108/13673279910275611

Wind, J., & Main, J. (1999). *Diving change*. New York, NY: The Free Press.

Winter, S. G. (1996). Organizing for continuous improvement: Evolutionary theory meets the quality revolution. In Cohen, M. D., & Sproull, L. S. (Eds.), *Organizational Learning* (pp. 460–483). Thousand Oaka, CA: Sage Publications.

Winterton, J. Delamare - Le Deist, F., & Stringfellow, E. (2005). *Typology of knowledge, skills, and competences: Clarification of the concept and prototype.* Retrieved June 13, 2011, from http://www.ecotec.com/europeaninventory/publications/method/cedefop_typology.pdf

Xu, J., & Quaddus, M. (2005). From rhetoric towards a model of practical knowledge management systems. *Journal of Management Development, 24*(4), 291–319. doi:10.1108/02621710510591325

Zack, M. (1998). What knowledge problems can information technology help to solve. In E. Hoadley & I. Benbasat (Eds.), *Proceedings of the Fourth Americas Conferences on Information Systems,* (pp. 644-646). Baltimore, MD: ACIS.

ADDITIONAL READING

Antonelli, C. (2008). The new economics of the university: A knowledge governance approach. *The Journal of Technology Transfer, 33*(1), 1–22. doi:10.1007/s10961-007-9064-9

Bleiklie, I., & Henkel, M. (2005). *Governing knowledge: A study of continuity and change in higher education - A festschrift in honour of Maurice Kogan*. Dordrecht, The Netherlands: Springer.

Busch, P. (2008). *Tacit knowledge in organizational learning*. Hershey, PA: IGI Global. doi:10.4018/978-1-59904-501-6

Cummins, J. N. (2004). Work groups, structural diversity and knowledge sharing in a global organization. *Management Science, 50*(3), 352–364. doi:10.1287/mnsc.1030.0134

Dalkir, K. (2005). *Knowledge management in theory and practice. Oxford, UK: Elsevier.* Butterworth: Heinemann.

Gold, A. H., Malhotra, A., & Segars, A. H. (2001). Knowledge management: An organizational capabilities perspective. *Journal of Management Information Systems, 18*(1), 185–214.

Harrington, H. J., & Voehl, F. (2006). *Knowledge management excellence: the art of excelling in knowledge*. Chico, CA: Paton Press.

Ichijo, K., & Nonaka, I. (2006). *Knowledge creation and management: New challenges for managers*. Oxford, UK: Oxford University Press.

Jonson, A., & Kalling, T. (2007). Challenges to knowledge sharing across national and intra-organizational boundaries: Case studies of IKEA and SCA packaging. *Knowledge Management Research & Practice, 5,* 161–172. doi:10.1057/palgrave.kmrp.8500139

Lytras, M., Russ, M., Meier, R., & Naeve, A. (Eds.). (2008). *Knowledge management strategies: A handbook of applied technologies.* Hershey, PA: IGI Global. doi:10.4018/978-1-59904-603-7

Marginson, S. (2006). Dynamics of national and global competition in higher education. *Higher Education, 52,* 1–39. doi:10.1007/s10734-004-7649-x

Martin, B. (2000). Knowledge management within the context of management: An evolving relationship. *Singapore Management Review, 22*(2), 17–36.

Mayor, E., & Cordey-Hayes, M. (2000). Knowledge translation: A new perspective on knowledge transfer and foresight. *Foresight, 2*(4), 411–423. doi:10.1108/14636680010802762

Mooradian, N. (2005). Tacit knowledge: philosophical roots and role in KM. *Journal of Knowledge Management, 9*(6), 28–38. doi:10.1108/13673270510629990

Newell, S., & Swan, J. (2000). Trust and inter-organizational networking. *Human Relations, 53*(10), 287–328.

Norris, D. M., Mason, J., Robson, R., Lefrere, P., & Collier, G. (2003). A revolution in knowledge sharing. *EDUCAUSE Review, 38*(5), 16–26.

Oltra, V. (2005). Knowledge management effectiveness factors: The role of HRM. *Journal of Knowledge Management, 9*(4), 70–86. doi:10.1108/13673270510610341

Rastogi, P. N. (2002). Knowledge management and intellectual capital as a paradigm of value creation. *Human Systems Management, 21*(4), 229–240.

Ringberg, T., & Reihlen, M. (2008). Towards a socio-cognitive approach to knowledge transfer. *Journal of Management Studies, 45*(5), 912–935. doi:10.1111/j.1467-6486.2007.00757.x

Sandhawalia, B. S., & Dalcher, D. (2011). Developing knowledge management capabilities: A structured approach. *Journal of Knowledge Management, 15*(2), 313–328. doi:10.1108/13673271111119718

Senge, P. M. (1998). Sharing knowledge. *Executive Excellence, 15*(6), 11–12.

Sinclair, N. (2006). *Stealth KM: Winning knowledge management strategies for the public sector.* Burlington, MA: Elsevier.

Suppiah, V., & Sandu, M. S. (2011). Organisational culture's influence on tacit knowledge-sharing behaviour. *Journal of Knowledge Management, 15*(3), 462–477. doi:10.1108/13673271111137439

Tian, J., Nakamori, Y., Xiang, J., & Futatsugi, K. (2006). Knowledge management in academia: Survey, analysis and perspective. *International Journal of Management and Decision Making, 7*(2/3), 275–294. doi:10.1504/IJMDM.2006.009149

Unwin, A. (2007). The professionalism of the higher education teacher: What's ICT got to do with it? *Teaching in Higher Education, 12*(3), 295–308. doi:10.1080/13562510701278641

Watson, S., & Hewett, K. (2006). A multi-theoretical model of knowledge transfer in organizations: Determinants of knowledge contribution and knowledge reuse. *Journal of Management Studies, 43*(2), 141–173. doi:10.1111/j.1467-6486.2006.00586.x

KEY TERMS AND DEFINITIONS

Explicit Knowledge: Knowledge that can be codified in words, drawings and numbers.

Knowledge: The capacity to act developed through formal learning, practical hands-on experience and socialization.

Knowledge Management: A deliberate effort to create, store and apply collective knowledge held by an organisation.

Knowledge Creation: Formation of new knowledge in a specific domain through interactions between explicit and tacit knowledge.

Knowledge Transfer: A deliberate approach to solving practical problems of transferring knowledge from one part of the organization to another.

Leadership: Process of social influence in which one person can enlist the aid and support of others in the accomplishment of a given goal.

Mentoring: A support that one individual can give to another to support his/her development as a whole person.

Organisational Knowledge: Knowledge embedded in computer supported knowledge repositories, organisational practices and organisational culture.

Tacit Knowledge: Knowledge embedded in individual action (i.e., skills, habits and experience) and cognition (i.e., values, perspectives and insights) that is context-specific, difficult to communicate and even more difficult to transfer.

Chapter 2
Innovation in Higher Education in Israel:
Public Policy Implications

Milly Perry
The Open University, Israel & Ben Gurion University, Israel

ABSTRACT

In order for education systems to cope with social and economic changes and perform efficiently, innovation is essential. Innovation in education (and particularly in Higher Education systems) has not been regarded as an important issue by policy makers, education stakeholders, and leaders; it seems to be regarded as "nice-to-have" rather than a necessity. Recently, innovation in education has started to gain attention. This includes systemic study of innovation, innovation strategy, and implementation of innovation strategies by policy makers and leaders. Scientific outputs and research findings can be used as input in national-international policies. In order to achieve this goal it is imperative to conduct close studies and for policy-makers to cooperate, ensuring the relevance of topics, and improving communication, dissemination, and implementation of research recommendations. These are the tools needed for leading change, innovation, and implementing new strategies.

INTRODUCTION

The nature of the knowledge-generating process itself is evolving towards a more network-embedded process, with an increased emphasis on stakeholder partnerships, trans-disciplinary growth, and heterogeneity of all players involved. The concepts and practices of "Open Innovation" are gaining wider acceptance in both the public and private sectors.

This research was carried out using a Grounded Theory approach and tools and could be of interest for policy makers, stakeholders and organizations in the Higher Education industry.

The purpose of this study is to define, map, analyze and quantify the existing (or the lack of) innovation policies in the Higher Education system in Israel. The outcomes of this study can potentially provide insights into interdisciplinary organization innovation application using models

DOI: 10.4018/978-1-4666-1969-2.ch002

(from the business sector) for higher education and the public sector.

The study is meant to capture in a systematic way evidence—based documented data, to understand whether Israeli Higher Education reality is adequate and following the innovative nature of this country as frequently described as "Start-Up Nation" (Senor & Singer, 2009) and an "Economic Miracle."

Do the innovation policies of Higher Education in Israel comply with and supply the needs of this "Start up nation?"

BACKGROUND AND LITERATURE REVIEW: INNOVATION

Definitions of innovation abound throughout the literature. Some define innovation in the context of using economic tools whereas others emphasize engineering, business and management fields, technology expertise, or socialism. Most definitions refer to the notion of doing "old" things in a new way. Some of the terms refer to added value to process or products, implicative aspects of the ideas (Mckeown, 2008), or to the degree of change (mild or incremental/revolutionary). Other definitions relate to "introduction of a new or significantly improved product (good or service), process, or method" and to "systemic innovation" as "any kind of dynamic, system-wide change that is intended to add value to the educational processes and outcomes (OECD, 2008).

Innovation policy, although fashionable, is often misunderstood; it should not be an annex to science and technology policy, as often presented. Innovation—the application of knowledge of all types so as to achieve desired social and economic outcomes—is broader than science and technology, often combining technical, organizational, and other sorts of change (World Bank, 2007).

Innovation is becoming popular in many fields such as policy, business, the public sector, and technology. In a world of globalization, economic crisis, incremental changes and competition, its importance is rising. Even though innovation has traditionally swung into and out of fashion, as Barsh, Capozzi, and Davidson (2008) put it "like short skirts: popular in good times and tossed back into the closet in downturns." Today, as the world descends into one of the sharpest downturns of several decades, policy makers look to innovative and entrepreneurial activities to form a basis for long-term, sustainable production (OECD, 2009).

Literature review and researches in the field of Innovation refer to different types of innovation (Technion Innovation Center website):

- **Management Innovation**: The invention and implementation of a management practice, process, structure, or technique, new to the current state of the art, with the intention of furthering organization goals.
- **Product Innovation:** The production of new and creative solutions to problems by means of a process in which novel and appropriate ideas are generated, implemented, and launched as new or improved products.
- **Process Innovation:** The improvement of an organization's efficiency through high-level coordination of the organization's activities, in a rationalized system of end-to-end processes.
- **Service Innovation:** A novel or significantly improved service or improvement in service procedures, implemented to meet customer demands and needs and increase customer satisfaction.
- **Technological Innovation:** An invention incorporating embryonic technology that is rapidly developing in the general scientific community. Innovation may arouse interest and be well understood by others. This innovation can provide the organization with options for initiating or responding to technological change.

In 1995, Bower and Christensen coined the term Disruptive Innovation to indicate an innovation that creates a new (and unexpected) market by applying a different set of values. Disruptive Innovation is the improving innovation or the evolutionary innovation that adding value or broaden existing markets can totally eliminate market or organizations.

Open innovation is "a way of delegating more innovation management to networks of suppliers and independent specialists that interact with each other to co-create products and services" (Barsh, Capozzi, & Davidson, 2008). Open innovation is not only about sourcing external knowledge ("outside-in"). Companies are looking for ways to generate additional revenue from in-house innovations ("inside-out"), particularly when the technology has future potential but is not part of the firm's core strategy. A similar study such as Neo and Chen (2007) suggest three additional activities for dynamic governance and innovation. According to them, "policy innovation means that new and fresh ideas are experimented with and incorporated into policies, so better and different results may be achieved. Yet it is not just about new ideas and contextual "policy execution that makes Dynamic Governance a reality" (p. 13). This study argues that there are three cognitive learning capabilities fundamental to dynamic governance: *thinking ahead*, *thinking again,* and *thinking across*. *Thinking* ahead is needed to predict the reality required to encourage new policies to take advantage of the new opportunities available. *Thinking again* refers to internal issues, improvements, and problem solving. *Thinking across* deals with external practices, innovations, evaluating, and discovering.

This study focuses on understanding whether these Innovation Policy ideas could be applicable for the Higher Education sector.

KNOWLEDGE MANAGEMENT AND INNOVATION IN HIGHER EDUCATION

Under the title of "2009 is the European year of creativity and innovation," the *Europa Media Newsletter* writes: "The EU has long recognized creative thinking as the key to success in a global economy. Innovation is an essential part …." Europe in its knowledge-based economy, consider innovation as the motor of development in a rapidly changing environment. Europe believes Europeans must learn to embrace change and be receptive of different strategies (EU European Policy Brief).

Policy leaders encourage and emphasis the need for innovation policy. OECD (Organization for Economic Co-operation and Development) reports recognize this need in the academic international world. "Changes in the academic profession appear to bring corporate culture closer to academic culture…the academic having more managerial constraints and the knowledge worker having more of the learning freedom he is used to" (OECD, 2008, p. 146). The UNESCO website (2002), under the title of "Reform and Innovation," declares that, "At the Conference on Higher Education (WCHE), UNESCO's objective was to lay down the fundamental principles for the in-depth reform of higher education systems throughout the world and thus contribute to transforming higher education, in its material and virtual manifestations, into an environment for lifelong learning." In order to implement its policy in Higher Education day-to-day life GUNI (Global University network for Innovation) was established. Its objectives dealt with reinforcing local, regional, and international development and reducing the growing distance between industrialized and developing countries, in the fields of higher education and research.

Knowledge management offers higher education an infrastructure for planning and managing innovation and change. Innovation and change are enhanced by cooperation, collaboration and the transfer of knowledge, as part of the activity of the HEI, while relying on and using information technology. Metcalfe (2006) in research notes that HEIs can develop knowledge management strategy, with a defined policy intended specifically to encourage change and progress. Appropriate management makes it possible for an organization to build its ability to deal with long-term and wide-reaching changes. Accountability, which is repeatedly mentioned as being required from universities, is the added value for organizations that adopt a KM strategy. This can also help educational organizations to create the ability for reflective thinking in all areas of their activity, and provide them with means for substantiating their positions, alongside with an organizational culture which encourages ongoing research and learning (Petrides & Nguyen, 2006).

Community of Practice (CoPs), an important KM tool, is a group of people who share a specific concern, a set of problems, or a passion for a topic, and who deepen their knowledge and expertise in this area by interacting on an ongoing basis (Wenger, McDermott, & Snyder, 2007, p. 8). An earlier term, "clusters," coined by Porter, refers to geographic concentrations of interconnected companies and institutions interested in a particular field. The term emphasizes the importance of agglomeration, and conceptually sets the importance of the region.

The tools of coordination, network and communities are held in a new European initiative: European Institute of Innovation and Technology (EIT), and specifically the formation of Knowledge and Innovation Communities (KICs) are innovative 'webs of excellence' and highly integrated partnerships that bring together education, technology, research, business, and entrepreneurship (EIT Website, 2009). The KICs will be driving effective "translation" between partners in ideas (knowledge), technology, culture, and business models, and will, as expected in the EIT vision, create new business for existing industry and for new endeavors.

This is implementing de facto, CoP's KM ideas for innovation, education, and economic purposes, by creating new culture of collaboration between different stakeholders in a geographic region. Several studies can provide evidence for KM use in the regional aspect. A Netherlands experience, reported by Dammers research (1999), suggests that a regional knowledge center may be used as an 'office,' where innovators can get information about knowledge and knowledge utilization, and serve as a meeting place that facilitates sharing and collaboration.

The regional centers should be supported by a national knowledge center. The purposes of regional centers may be to bring awareness to the quality of knowledge practices, to coach and provide information to regional knowledge managers, to cooperate with national and regional governments, and with consultants and research institutions. Dammers emphasizes that the creation and dissemination of knowledge is affected by knowledge management and facilitation, and also by contextual factors which require more knowledge, intended to defend fundamental views and values, and to adopt innovative ways of thinking and acting. For instance, social trends, the changing of economic tide and policy-changes - "knowledge-managers are supposed to call these factors into attention. This enables the innovators to cope with the opportunities and threats they may generate in the region and beyond (Dammers, 1999).

INNOVATION STRATEGY IN ISRAEL

Ben-Aharon (2000) suggests three levels of activity: The *policy level* includes comprehensive policy process; regarding and prioritizing stockholder's priorities, and evaluation and feedback mechanism. The *policy implementation* level includes policy fields, plan designing, plan evaluation, and comparison. The *innovation level* includes evaluation of subjects and the relationships between them. Ben-Aharon (2000) notes that the policy processes are broken and fragmented, lacking a systematic vision that includes dissection in addition to priorities, for which reason no national priorities are set up.

There are indications that the priorities do not react to the rapid environmental changes. Neither technology nor economy is being suitably adapted. Most priorities are implemented by means of "bottom - up" initiatives that are, at times, random and personally centered. The initiatives are usually good indicators of the measure of power held by the stakeholders and the support they hope to obtain from the finance ministry. Party changes in the government and frequent elections are an important hurdle to strategic planning and long term innovation policy. The Horovitz report (2008), argues that strategic planning and innovation policy is not enough to set strategic plans, rather there is a need for Meta-strategy. "It takes more than a winning strategy to build global competitiveness. It rather requires what may be called a "meta-strategy"—a strategic process, in which nations are capable of transforming their underlying competitiveness strategy, reinventing themselves and their capabilities" (Horovitz & Brodeth, 2008, p. 302).

The OECD outlook for 2008 indicates that "Israel's innovation system is a key drive to economic growth and competitiveness." The report places major importance on "the vibrant business sector"—its innovation and entrepreneurial culture. The government's financial framework for innovation, quality university education, incubators and science industry links, were found to be important components as well. (OECD Science, Technology, and Industry Outlook, 2008b, p. 170). This is coherent with the Innovative culture embedded in Israel "nature" as referred in Senor and Singer (2009) as 'Start-up Nation" which endorse the Israeli so called "Economic Miracle" since Israel resources are intellectual and human rather than nature resources.

Several organizations have presented themselves as innovation leaders, policymaking leaders, or bridges of innovation and policy making in Israel. For example:

- The Samuel Neaman Institute (SNI) aims at "research, identify and evaluate solutions for national problems in the areas of science, technology, education, economics, industry, and social development."
- The Knowledge Center for Innovation at the Technion (KCI) was established with the intention of leading innovation activities in Israel whilst serving as a provoking factor that impacts both research, industry and policymaking activities.
- GAL – EDGE is a Network that promotes institutional infrastructure development and supports technology transfer, business/ marketing skills development, strategic alliances, and barrier reduction.

Since this background of Innovation in Higher education and in Israel has been set, the following paragraphs describe the way that this research was conducted, i.e. Grounded Theory methodology and research methods, the main research questions and issues that were examined.

METHODOLOGY AND RESEARCH METHODS

This study examines an organization-wide policy profile in Israeli Higher Education system regarding Innovation issues. These issues have been examined using the grounded theory methodology that is derived from the philosophy of qualitative research. This methodology is used in the field of science policy and governance that was later validated through a comparison with other existing models.

Research questions were refined during the field research and the significant variables are those that surfaced during data gathering.

The main research questions in this study are:

- To what extent innovation policy exists in Higher Education system in Israel and in interface related policy systems.
- How to inform policy makers of the vital importance of innovation (mainly organizational, process and management innovation, not innovation in an academic discipline as such) as a key to economic growth, so they can benefit from a better understanding of the innovation process.

This is a field research conducted by grounded theory approach in which the theory is based on a systematic analysis of data using the "Constant comparative method" (Sabar Ben-Yehoshua, 1990). Grounded Theory is most accurately described as a research method in which the theory is developed from the data, rather than the other way around. That makes this an inductive approach, meaning that it moves from the specific to the more general. The method of study is essentially based on three elements: concepts, categories and propositions, or what was originally called "hypotheses." However, concepts are the key elements of analysis since the theory is developed from the conceptualization of data, rather than the actual data Moreover, internal and external factors that influence innovation processes, the way policy makers relate to and use innovation and the existence (or lack of) systemic innovation forms and models were examined.

This study was based on the working assumption that higher education appreciates innovation as such and more specifically as a higher education value and part of the academic ethos. This research therefore examines and maps the innovation policy processes that is actually practiced in the daily life of The Israeli Higher Education

System (and other systems, which interface with the HE system).

Forty-one (41) data collection sessions at the information gathering stage included open interviews conducted in Israel and Europe, conference presentations, committees' meetings, and decollations. Several concepts emerged from this process, which sorted into categories defined by sets of criteria. Additional information and written data was collected from reports, planning and policy papers, universities' and stakeholders documents and Internet websites. Vast number of publications have been examined and analyzed. Within the criteria's framework, the various themes and subjects that arose from the interviewees' comments were gathered into general fields, each with a clear central idea. Criteria for distinguishing between the various fields, and defining the "threshold" for assignment to each category were established to ensure each particular expression would be relevant to one category and to differentiate between the various ideas and categories. This research therefore examines and maps the innovation policy processes that is actually practiced in the daily life of Israeli Higher Education System (and other systems, which interface with the HE system).

The following findings are the result of all stages of the "constant comparative method": identifying the preliminary categories, designing the categories, refining criteria, and final design of the categories.

DATA AND FINDINGS: INNOVATION IN HIGHER EDUCATION IN ISRAEL

In order to define to what extent the innovation policy was developed and is currently taking place by Higher Education system in Israel and in interface related policy systems, we summarized documents examinations and interviews data analysis which reveal an overall notation that Israel does not have an explicit or implicit systematic innovation policy in the field of Higher Education at the national level. There are some initiatives and "grassroots" actions at local and at national / sub-national level in varied fields.

The following schema (Figure 1) maps the initiatives in order to illustrate it visually (graphically) followed by contextual explanations.

As the main themes (concepts) emerged, and for the purpose of data demonstrating, a range of policy levels was crystallized. This allows presenting an organisational profile, which enables a visualized perception of the policy implementation status and level (if any) and enhance clear tools for comparison. The profile (status map) composes of seven levels of policy and four Innovation types detailed herewith (see Figure 2):

1. At the basic level is the "non existing issue" stage, evidence that there is no policy or system-wide discussion, plan or policy.

2. Level two relates to some extent of awareness to the innovation Policy issue, with beginnings of bottom-up initiatives, public discussions, infrastructure administrative work.

3. Level three relates to drafts of work- plans, road-maps or policy papers published.

4. The forth level relates to the status of an approved plan by the authorized high level decision makers like minister, prime minister etc.

5. The fifth level relates to an approved policy plan with ad-hoc budget allocation, usually defined as "innovation project."

6. The sixth level relates to an organisational permanent budget allocation and resources (manpower, know-how, implementing steps, tools and process) available for implementing the policy at all system levels.

7. Level seven deals with evaluation of the overall policy plan and resources. Evaluation stage is important for future adaptation, renewal of content, targets and policy vision as well as improvement of the implementing steps.

The analysis of policy implementation level across "Innovation Types" in Higher Education Institutions (e.g. Innovation Centre, Technion.) can reveal, pattern or "snap shot" status of the policy implementing level in relation to the different

Figure 1. National and local actors

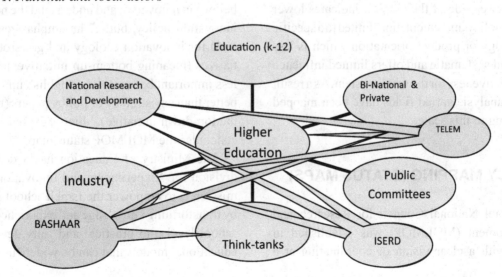

Figure 2. Template for a status map of policy level across "innovation types"

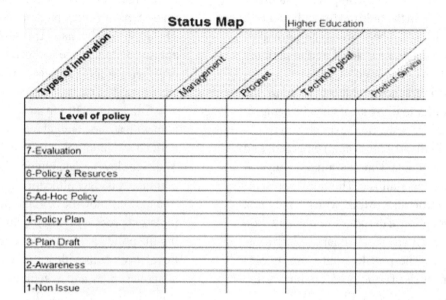

types of innovation (e.g. management, process, technology, products-services). This pattern can provide higher resolution of details. Interpretation of data can suggest that orientation / emphasis on the Left-Upper side of the graph indicates high level of policy implantation done with systemic / generic innovation tools as innovation process or innovation management tools (not specific to a cretin technology or dedicated to specific service or product).

Once the orientations reveal emphasis in the Right-lower side of the graph it indicates lower level of policy implementation limited to a specific technology or product orientation which is less wide and systematic and offers limited influence and effectiveness for the whole system. As a result of this analysis varied fields have been mapped according to this scale.

POLICY MAPPING (STATUS MAPS)

The Israel National Council for Research and Development (MOLMOP) was established in 2004, with a clear vision of coordinating at a national level all the Research and Development stakeholders. The council's mission is to advise the government of Israel with regard to the organization and regulation of civil research and development for a comprehensive national policy, areas of national priority and with regard to the allocation of budgets for its enhancement. None of the diverse committees of The Israel National Council for Research and Development handle Innovation as a policy issue. Though, one of the senior managers clearly declared that he "strongly believe in innovation and understand the need for innovation policy, but…" he emphasizes, "The need for innovation ecology and grassroots initiatives (meaning bottom-up initiatives) are not less important because they establish innovation better than any strategy or policy papers (that are the top-down initiative)." Figure 3 presents and concludes the MOLMOP status map.

The Ministry of Education has a dedicated division for "Experiments and Innovations." Its mission is to empower the Israeli school system by transforming knowledge and experience at the school level into practical and fully developed educational models that can be widely used. Ex-

Figure 3. The Israel national council for research and development (MOLMOP)

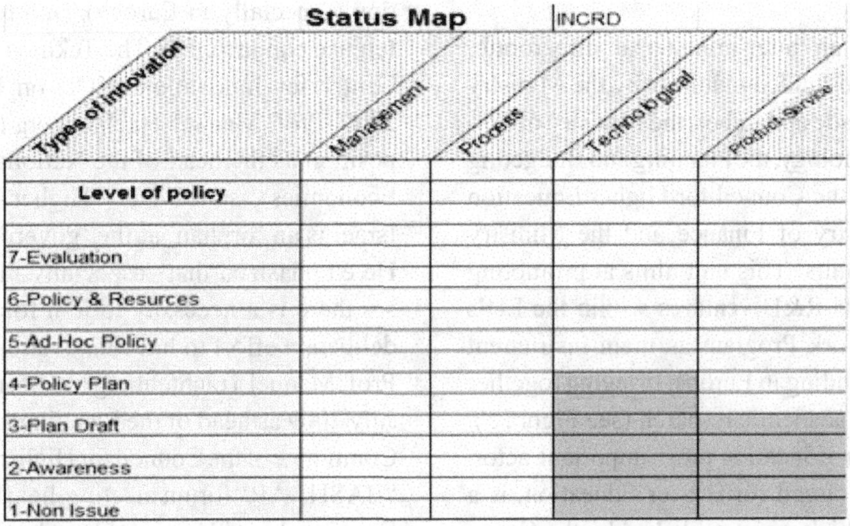

Status Map	INCRD			
Types of innovation	Management	Process	Technological	Product-Service
Level of policy				
7-Evaluation				
6-Policy & Resurces				
5-Ad-Hoc Policy				
4-Policy Plan			▓	
3-Plan Draft			▓	▓
2-Awareness			▓	▓
1-Non Issue			▓	▓

perimental schools are expected to develop models that provide a sound theoretical underpinning method for development, and educational infrastructure needed for successful adaptation by other schools. The models developed are intended to be of outstanding quality so that they can be readily spread throughout the system (see Figure 4).

The Ministry of Industry, Trade, and Labor has an "Encouraging Innovation and Creativity"

policy and a dedicated program (unit) for innovation in Industry. This unit supports innovation process and management methods, provides budget for implementing them in firms and industry factories. Other units support specific technologies and services.

The office runs programs for collaboration with universities, and international collaboration between industries in many countries around the world with a specific national program for en-

Figure 4. Ministry of education

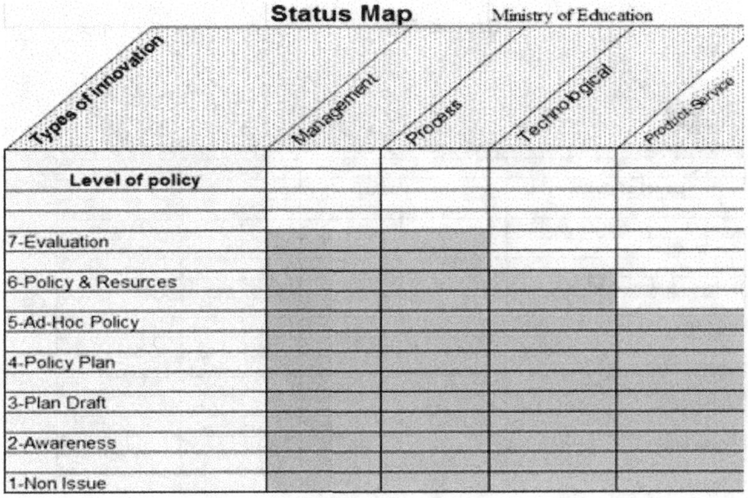

Status Map	Ministry of Education			
Types of innovation	Management	Process	Technological	Product-Service
Level of policy				
7-Evaluation	▓			
6-Policy & Resurces	▓			
5-Ad-Hoc Policy	▓			
4-Policy Plan	▓			
3-Plan Draft	▓			
2-Awareness	▓			
1-Non Issue	▓			

couraging international project academia-industry in Europe.

ISERD is an inter-ministerial directorate, established and funded mutually by the Ministry of Industry, Trade and Labor, the Ministry of Science and Technology, the Planning and Budgeting Committee of the Council for Higher Education and the Ministry of Finance and the Ministry of Foreign Affairs. This unit aims at promoting joint Israeli-EU R&D ventures within the EU's R&D Framework Program as main instrument for research funding in Europe, bringing together industries and academic research (see Figure 5).

The Higher Education most important actor, namely The Council for Higher Education, is a corporation which was established by the Council for Higher Education Law, 1958-5718, with the aim of being the national institution for higher education in Israel. One of its most important missions is to submit to the Government, through the Planning and Budgeting Committee, proposals to develop higher education and for State participation in the budget of the higher education system according to the needs of the society and the country.

The Planning and Budgeting Committee (CHE) established a unit for encouraging international

affairs, Globalization and international collaboration (especially in Europe). In a re-launch conference conducted by The Teknion's Knowledge Center for Innovation (KCI) on February 15th 2009, Prof. Manuel Trachtenberg (in his former position as the head of the National Council for Economics), stated that "Higher Education in Israel is an 'orphan' at the 'government's table.' He emphasized that "especially in times of crises there is a necessity to join forces and make deliberate effort to have innovation as a motto." Prof. Manuel Trachtenberg has been appointed in July 2009 as head of the Planning and Budgeting Committee of the Council for Higher Education. In "BASHAAR" forum meeting, held in 25/12/2009 he pointed out "You would not hear from me any new ideas in this meetings. I am here in order to implement existing ideas and solutions raised by Shochat committee and others." He did not raise Innovation policy or Innovation in any way as one of the system vision or targets. Prof. Trachtenberg did point out that the Council for Higher Education failed to develop any national policy in any field; he declared policy and policy tools would be the main issue for CHE activity in the next years.

Some interviewees note that parts of the "innovation intentions" of CHE are embedded in

Figure 5. The ministry of industry, trade, and labor

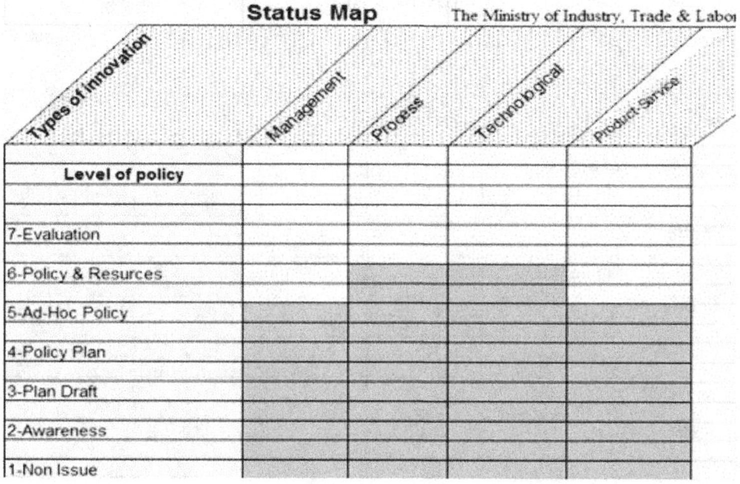

the "financial model" presented to universities and other education organizations in Israel. By this model CHE is delivering its priorities and guideline for the educational activities required.

Few point out that "the day-by-day management do not make any time for innovative ideas."

Others distinguished that "there is no openness for innovation at all….and if it occurs, the 'behavioral reflex' demand budget in order to implant it in the university/college which immediately shut all doors of future interest" (see Figure 6).

The universities are an important parts of Higher Education system. In order to understand the importance of Innovation policy we interviewed academic experts and universities personal. The first notion comes in mind in those interviews are of "University is the ultimate innovation organization."

Universities cherish innovation and have built-in mechanism for analyzing innovative contribution throughout academic peer's reviews and publication process. But this approach relates to the academic product in disciplinary fields; do not consider innovation as important value at the organizational operation administrative and management practices.

In many cases, "administrative/organizational Innovation" interprets in universities into "Technology" or "Information Technology" for teaching and learning. Important as it is, it became the only "Innovation" that Higher Education supports. Most of the budget and effort encourage technologies without any consideration of any "other" innovation type such as new services, new methods, and new process. Technology becomes a synonym for Innovation. This "common conceptual mistake" duplicates in other fields as well. For example, the term R&D is the synonym for "Innovation" in industry and business. It was surprising to find financial support (at The Ministry of Industry, Trade, and Labor) for organizational innovation process and management in traditional Industry that has distinguished between those two terms and intentionally support the latter (see Figure 7).

Experienced personnel, holding former position as decision makers express the notation that "Innovation is very important but cannot be alternative for badly budgeting practice" and "firstly, the system need to focuses on survival. You can't have available mental resource for innovation when you are grasping for air" others note. "Maybe this is the time for innovation; we

Figure 6. Higher education

Status Map Higher Education

Types of innovation / Level of policy	Management	Process	Technological	Product-Service
7-Evaluation				*
6-Policy & Resurces				*
5-Ad-Hoc Policy		^		*
4-Policy Plan		^		*
3-Plan Draft		^		*
2-Awareness		^		*
1-Non Issue		^		*

* refer to the quality assessment initiative we can see as an innovation service
^ refer to the ISEARD unit which involve collaboration in EU projects
refer to the international relation unite in The Council for Higher Education

Figure 7. Presents an analysis of overall policy level

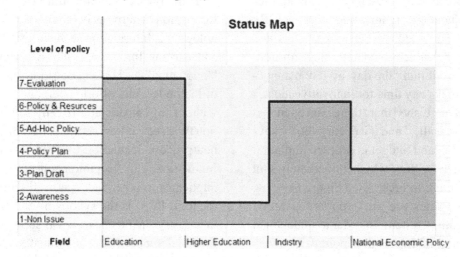

do not have any other path to follow." The expression "innovation is nice to have, it could not replace the 'bread' only the 'butter'" was raised side by side to the notion that "policy is dictated by the Ministry of Finance, no one else is leading Higher Education in Israel."

There are different, sometimes contradicting objectives, in the different fields and vast indication for a blend of policies. While the Ministry of Education emphasizes the importance of learning/ teaching achievement objective, the Horovitz Committee is targeting collaboration with industry. The Ministry of Education allows freedom in curriculum and focuses on teacher training, while the Humanities Fund allots innovation grants, and The Horovitz Committee (2028) deals with stakeholder's engagement.

The Industry Ministry operates its own Innovation Center to promote innovation methods within traditional industry, but the MOLMOP as an integrative body at the national level has not succeeded to integrate all visions and programs or focuses in defined national priorities and the requirement for Meta-Strategy is most obvious.

DISCUSSION AND CONCLUSION

Some of the conclusions of this study are intriguing; some are surprising and a few highlight prevalent notions and circumstances within Israel's Higher Education system.

First and foremost, and contrary to our work assumption, one of the main conclusions of this work is the notion that there is no consensus regarding the importance of Innovation in the Higher education system on the one hand, while on the other hand, most of the interviewees were confident that there is enough Innovation in the academic system altogether. As many interviewees pointed out the academic essence, culture and ethos represent innovation at its best. On the other hand in many cases we can observe that innovation was interpreted immediately in terms of technology Others conclusions that emerge from this research indicate that the Israeli Higher Education system has so far failed to adopt any steps to develop awareness to the importance of Innovation Policy as such. The academic ethos which appreciates innovation in the academic fields of research, that measures and accepts only innovative contribution to the existing body of knowledge, does not apply those tools to its systemic and organizational course of action. Innovation stays at the laboratories but does not enter the corridors of policy makers and management neither as a state-of-mind, nor as an organizational value.

It is vital to stress this lack of awareness to Innovation policy in the higher echelons of management and policy makers, in spite of close connections with policy makers, government officials and others stakeholders in European countries, in the USA and in global community Israel is trying to join. It seems that the new issues concerning policy makers in other countries are not assimilated into the Israeli system. Israel is considered an innovative country, or as coined lately, "A start-up nation" (Senor & Singer, 2009).

This position apparently gives policy makers a reason to "rest on their laurels" and maintain the "comfort zone" of an "Economic Miracle" (Senor & Singer, 2009) than invest in a systematic and strategic effort to preserve this position for the future to come. As pointed out at the beginning of this chapter, there is wide recognition of the importance of innovation but this issue is still being regarded as 'nice-to-have' rather than as a necessity, and it is clearly nowhere near reaching top priority on the agenda of policy makers.

An analysis of the evidence gathered in this study as well as reference literature roughly draw two well-known approaches to describing innovation policy activities:

The Top-down approach may include:

1. National leadership policy commitment and declaration
2. Awareness campaign
3. Globalization—as a tool for Innovation's import mechanism
4. Systematic Think Tanks activities and initiatives
5. Management training
6. Joint operation of government offices where some of the most powerful solutions have to be devised as part of a policy (other than coincidence and circumstance based on individual and personal chemistry).

The Bottom-Up approach may include:

1. Grassroots initiatives
2. Entrepreneurial researchers
3. Academic-like culture and process
4. Open involvement of stakeholders with a view to industry-academia partnership
5. Communities and networks

This dichotomous model appears to lack two other features already recognized at the OECD case study, Widthwise Top-Down (WTD) and the Collaborative and Bottom-Up (CBU). Furthermore, we find this model lacks the dynamic mechanism or "dynamo" which drives the motion in this system. The missing part should bring the system into a spiral shape mode in order to raise its activity to a higher level in any given activity cycle, and to elevate the system from tackling basic issues and solution finding to upper level challenges. This model needs constant fuel injection for its constant operation as well as "a full system cycle" as in "the system theory" which contains evaluation components, systematic planning, feed back channels and thinking outside the box. We believe the main catalyst in this process is the individuals (scholar, manager, researcher), their network impact and their interaction with strategies (INGINEUS European Policy Brief, 2009). This approach is reinforced by the term "Researchers as a policy Entrepreneurs" (Overseas Development Institute, 2009) and led us to the following recommendation.

One of the main obstacles in placing innovation in the right place within policy makers priority is the lack of a systematic development program for middle / high level managers (academic and administrative) in Israel's Higher Education system. The authors suggest that such a program is established as a national priority."

This idea has been specified and developed recently by five Higher Education organizations in Israel and supported by three main Higher Education stakeholders and European experts and

Universities. The program titled IFHEL—Israel's Future Higher Education Leaders—was submitted to an international body for financial support.

The IFHEL development and training program will introduce its participants to the international higher education world as well as to the state of the art of management and transformation in other fields, enabling them to acquire updated management and innovation skills, terminology and understanding. The knowledge derived from the program will enable future HE leaders to meet and lead future challenges the HE system will encounter.

The program should be based on knowledge already existing in knowledge networks and centers operating in Israel as associate partner organizations in relevant fields. These networks and knowledge centers will be active for several years so as to execute their vision and achieve their objectives. In order to be effective and efficient the project will avoid re-inventing the wheel and creating existing knowledge. Rather it will benefit from the existing knowledge and network connections and leverage them by pooling resources, acting in effect as a "network of networks."

To conclude, this study implies that the Higher Education system in Israel needs to develop its strategy towards Innovation. It is vitally important for the system and its actors (stakeholders, universities and colleges) to learn more about innovation and its supporting environment at the global scene in order to improve activities and refresh conceptual ideas and strategies. There is a need to research new patterns and best practice in Europe and other parts of the world, plan and invest efforts in Life Long Learning, Knowledge Management, and organizational learning for change and implementation of innovation as such.

FUTURE RESEARCH

Quantitative and Qualitative research can help higher Education system to focus its efforts and enhance understanding of the way change can take place.

According to Peter Senge's remark, (in Lucas, 2000, p. 276) the challenge of converting the university (and Higher Education system, MP) from a "knowing institution" to a "learning institution" can be realized if the leaders and policy makers in the higher education system understand the need of a permanent mechanism for Innovation.

REFERENCES

Barsh, Capozzi, & Davidson. (2008). Leadership and innovation. *McKinsey Quarterly*. Retrieved from http://www.mckinseyquarterly.com/Leadership_and_innovation_2089

Ben Aharon, N. (2000). *Policy for innovation and creativity in traditional industry*. Jerusalem, Israel: Jerusalem Institute for Israel Study.

Bower, J. L., & Christensen, C. M. (1995). Disruptive technologies: Catching the wave. *Harvard Business Review*. Retrieved from http://www.cc.gatech.edu/~spencer/courses/ethics/misc/bower.pdf

Dammers, E. (1999). *Innovation and learning-Knowledge management and rural innovation*. The Hague, The Netherlands: NRLO. EIT website. (2009). *The European institute of innovation and technology*. Retrieved from http://eit.europa.eu/home.html

European Policy Brief. (2009). *INGINEUS -Impact of networks, globalization, and their interaction with EU strategies*. Geneva, Switzerland: European Research Area.

Horovitz, E., & Brodeth, D. (2008). *Israel 2028 vision and social-economic strategy in the global world*. Jerusalem, Israel: US-Israel Science and Technology Foundation.

INGINEUS. (2011). Impact of networks, globalisation, and their interaction with EU strategies, 2009-2011. Retrieved from http://www.ingineus.eu/getpage.aspx?id=1&sec=1

Mckeown, M. (2008). *The truth about innovation*. Upper Saddle River, NJ: Pearson.

Metcalfe, A. S. (2006). The political economy of knowledge management in higher education. In Metcalfe, A. S. (Ed.), *Knowledge Management and Higher Education: A Critical Analysis* (pp. 1–20). Hershey, PA: IGI Global. doi:10.4018/978-1-59140-509-2.ch001

Neo, B. S., & Chen, G. (2007). *Dynamic governance: Embedding culture, capabilities and change in Singapore*. Singapore: World Scientific. doi:10.1142/9789812771919

OECD. (2008a). *Science, technology and industry outlook*. Paris, France: OECD.

OECD. (2008b). *Higher education to 2030: Demography* (*Vol. 1*). Paris, France: OECD.

OECD. (2009). *The OECD innovation strategy: An interim report*. Paris, France: OECD.

Overseas Development Institute. (2009). *Helping researchers become policy entrepreneur*. London, UK: Overseas Development Institute.

Petrides, L., & Nguyen, L. (2006). Knowledge management trends: Challenges and opportunities for education institutions. In Metcalfe, A. S. (Ed.), *Knowledge Management and Higher Education: A Critical Analysis* (pp. 21–33). Hershey, PA: IGI Global. doi:10.4018/978-1-59140-509-2.ch002

Sabar Ben Yehoshua, N. (1990). *The qualitative research*. Givataim, Israel: Massada.

Senge, P. M. (2000). The academy as learning community: Contradiction in terms or realizable future? In Lucas, A. F. (Ed.), *Leading Academic Change: Essential Roles for Department Chairs* (pp. 215–245). San Francisco, CA: Jossey-Bass.

Senor, D., & Singer, S. (2009). *Start-up nation: The story of Israel's economic miracle*. New York, NY: Hachette Book Group.

Technion Innovation Center. (2012). *Website*. Retrieved from http://ieinnov.technion.ac.il/wps/portal/InnovationCenter/Home/!ut/p/c5/04_SB8K8xLLM9MSSzPy8xBz9C-P0os3hnd0cPE3MfAwODAF8DAyM-3H0OvgNBQIwMvM_1wkA48Kkwg8gY4g-KOBvp9Hfm6qfkF2dpqjo6IiADRPfgM!/dl3/d3/L2dBISEvZ0FBIS9nQSEh/

UNESCO. (2002). *Medium-term strategy: Contribution to peace and human development in an era of globalization through education, the sciences, culture and communication, 2002-2007*. Paris, France: UNESCO.

Wenger, E. C., McDermott, R., & Snyder, W. (2007). *Cultivating communities of practice: A guide to managing knowledge*. Boston, MA: Harvard Business School Press.

World Bank. (2007). *Building knowledge economies, advanced strategies for development*. Washington, DC: The World Bank.

ADDITIONAL READING

Bijker, W. E., & Luciano, D. A. (Eds.). (2009). *Handbook on the socialization of scientific and technological research social sciences and European research capacities (SS-ERC) project*. Rome, Italy: River Press Group.

Janet, E. L., Bercovitz, A., Maryann, P., & Feldman, B. (2007). *Fishing upstream: Firm innovation strategy and university research alliances*. Urbana-Champaign, IL: University of Illinois.

Oates, T. (2008). Going round in circles: Temporal discontinuity as a gross impediment to effective innovation in education and training. *Cambridge Journal of Education, 38*(1), 105–120. doi:10.1080/03057640801890012

Tsipouri, L. J. (2007). *Policy synthesis of EU: Research results*. Athens, Greece: University of Athens.

KEY TERMS AND DEFINITIONS

Management Innovation: The invention and implementation of a management practice, process, structure, or technique, new to the current state of the art, with the intention of furthering organization goals.

Open Innovation: Is a way of delegating more innovation management to networks of suppliers and independent specialists that interact with each other to co-create products and services.

Product Innovation: The production of new and creative solutions to problems by means of a process in which novel and appropriate ideas are generated, implemented, and launched as new or improved products.

Process Innovation: The improvement of an organization's efficiency through high-level coordination of the organization's activities, in a rationalized system of end-to-end processes.

Service Innovation: A novel or significantly improved service or improvement in service procedures, implemented to meet customer demands and needs and increase customer satisfaction.

Technological Innovation: An invention incorporating embryonic technology that is rapidly developing in the general scientific community. Innovation may arouse interest and be well understood by others. This innovation can provide the organization with options for initiating or responding to technological change.

Chapter 3
Organisational Flexibility through Human Capital Development

Ana Martins
Xi'an Jiaotong-Liverpool University, China

Isabel Martins
University of Glamorgan, UK

Orlando Petiz
University of Minho, Portugal

ABSTRACT

The current knowledge economy has brought several challenges to contemporary organisations. There is need for flexibility on the part of key players, namely individual employees as well as organisations as a whole; this flexibility arises from the innovation in both products and services. The complexity of knowledge requires an education that enhances softer skills. The intellectual capacity, creativity, and adaptability of individuals gives rise to greater flexibility. This strengthens the fact that there is a change of paradigm in the way human capital is viewed. Through the human-oriented perspective, knowledge is seen as collective sense making and social practice. The objective of this chapter lies in this context of complexity, change, and adaptation within an economic and social reality based on knowledge. Therefore, the chapter aims to reflect upon Knowledge Management in companies such as universities where tacit knowledge is stored as intellectual capital in the minds of both lecturers and students and to highlight the need to instill the new paradigm which fosters knowledge creation and sharing in universities.

INTRODUCTION

With the Lisbon Agenda set out in 2000, the aim was to make Europe a more competitive and dynamic knowledge-based economy. The Lisbon Agenda is closely linked to globalisation and to the increasing demands placed on all European Union regions indicating the need to restructure, modernise, and generate innovation in knowledge. This means that companies face the need to improve value creation. For the purposes of this chapter, the notion of companies

DOI: 10.4018/978-1-4666-1969-2.ch003

will be extended to Universities. Knowledge in the knowledge economy is the major source of sustainable competitive advantage (Grant, 1996; Nonaka, 1991; Doz & Prahalad, 1991; Bartlett & Goshal, 1989) when viewed as the only "sustainable untapped source of competitive advantage" (McElroy, 2000, p. 195). The Lisbon Agenda is focused both on the knowledge economy and is in harmony with the reforms in higher education undergoing in Europe. Various studies (Caballero, et al., 2008) have been published on this theme looking at the interaction between universities and industry. The main debate is on identifying practices being introduced both at the level of universities and industry in view of their ability to create knowledge and its spillovers in society. However, the debate also focuses upon the role of universities and whether these equip their students with competencies to better prepare them for the labour market. This approach is in line with the Lisbon Agenda as universities are considered to be institutions, per excellence, for both the production and dissemination of knowledge. If universities equip their students with competencies enabling them to face a competitive and sophisticated labour market, they will thus be spilling knowledge over to the entire society. In this way, they will be contributing towards structuring an economy, based on knowledge. The very act of preparing graduates for the market launches tacit knowledge embodied in these graduates, irrespective of any other scientific knowledge they may have. In this respect, Brunner (2009) raises the issue of employability competencies associated with the development of knowledge being essentially linked to developing a combination of tacit and scientific knowledge.

In this regard, higher education, in its 'most noble' mission, sets out to create, develop and transmit knowledge, science, culture and technique thereby preparing citizens to perform activities professionally. Consequently, higher education is considered as both an instrument for social and work integration as well as a variable for economic and social development. This view has been adopted by the International Labour Organisation (ILO), which has also been reflecting on issues, namely, lifelong learning of competencies and employability. For this reason, the concept of employability is prevalent in all discourses and is related to the role of education in the knowledge economy (Bergan, 2009). Furthermore, the ILO maintains that education facilitates technology diffusion, improves employability, and minimises the negative impact of globalisation.

It is in the context of complexity, change, and adaptation in an economic and social reality based on knowledge that the objective of this chapter is situated; therefore, the chapter aims to reflect upon Knowledge Management in companies such as universities where tacit knowledge is stored as intellectual capital in the minds of both lecturers and students.

BACKGROUND

Traditionally, educational economists based their analysis on primary education, which is in line with traditional economic and management theories. However, today with the advent of knowledge economy, these traditional theories are considered have become somewhat outdated. In 2003, therefore, the World Bank challenged this traditional economists' view as a means to develop higher rates of returns by arguing the need for investment in universities and thereby making higher education play a fundamental role in the knowledge economy. Consequently, this means that higher education should undergo a mind shift in order to embrace a new paradigm, i.e. the need for higher education to be closer to industry, and to engage in knowledge production (Kok, 2007). Higher education should remain true to its *raison d'être*—knowledge creation and its quest for truth. This is further corroborated by Kok (2007, p. 184) who highlighted "the development of academic research capacities" is seen as the starting point for the development of human capital and tacit knowledge.

The concept of knowledge has been discussed since the ancient Greeks, hence the plethora of definitions, as Faucher *et al.* (2008) corroborate. In the literature, most of the definitions on knowledge show enormous inconsistencies as highlighted by Faucher *et al.* (2008). Knowledge ranges from scientific information validated through empirical proofs, to a group of perceptions and subjective truths. Drucker maintains that knowledge is now the primary resource of production as opposed to the traditional (land, labour, and capital). Bhardwaj and Monin (2007, p. 73) advocate that "creating and sharing knowledge are intangible activities that can neither be supervised nor forced out of people. This happen when people cooperate voluntarily" which demonstrates the importance of tacit knowledge. The literature on Knowledge Management (KM) is satiated with distinctions between the concepts of knowledge, information and data (Faucher, et al., 2008), designated as the classical, linear, hierarchical model of KM. This is first generation of KM, which is "not about knowledge at all. It's about information—how to capture it, store it, retrieve it, access it and all that stuff…[little more than] a great excuse to sell a lot of information technology under the guise of managing knowledge" (McElroy, 2000, p. 198). Instead, Faucher *et al.* (2008) advocate a non-linear, circular model that includes two further concepts, i.e. wisdom and enlightenment. Drucker (2000) alludes to the distinction between knowledge as a general term to mean wisdom and knowledge to be the base of the current knowledge economy.

The literature on knowledge focuses on the organisational dimension stressing the importance of managing knowledge. The emphasis is on how knowledge is created, administered, and disseminated within the organisations. It is common to see differences drawn between different kinds of knowledge such as tacit and explicit (Nonaka & Takeuchi, 1995). The literature on

KM is saturated with allusions to the concepts of tacit and explicit knowledge. We share the opinion of Mooradian (2005, p. 104) in that "the concept of tacit knowledge as it appears in the literature is vague and ambiguous." Nonaka and Takeuchi (1995) provide a distinction between these two concepts, for them tacit knowledge is personal, context-bound therefore, difficult to communicate, whereas explicit knowledge is transferrable in formal systematic language. In order for tacit knowledge to become explicit knowledge, a change has to occur through a conversion. Tacit knowledge is considered as the most secure form of knowledge and is of strategic importance for the organisation, being inimitable and the main focus for sustainable advantage (Jasimuddin, 2005). Furthermore, tacit knowledge works together with various subsystems in the organisation, such as the social and cultural, intellectual and psychological (Bhardwaj & Monin, 2007). According to Polyani (1958, 1967, 1969) individuals have knowledge, known as tacit knowledge, which is the foundation of explicit knowledge. This tacit knowledge results from a blend of the individual's experience of reality with the influence from the social environment. This leads to the fact that tacit and explicit knowledge are indivisible and this is the context in which organisational learning exists. Polyani further corroborates that tacit knowledge is the point of departure of all knowledge. However, Bhardwaj and Monin (2006) and Takeuchi (1998) maintain that tacit knowledge is essentially subjective; hence its sharing process is difficult.

Tacit knowledge is most relevant to universities. Thus, knowledge as is perceived by intellectuals is highly different to knowledge in the knowledge economy. The 'intellectual' perceives knowledge as that which is written in a book and whilst it is there, it is merely simple data or information. Only once someone has applied this information to compile something does this information become knowledge. The latter, like energy or money is considered a type of energy that exists only while it is executing work. The emergence of the knowledge economy is not part of the intellectual history as it is conceived; instead, it is part of the history of technology that affords a new version to the processes through which humans use it as instruments. While referring to the concept of knowledge, the intellectual refers to something innovative. What matters in the knowledge economy is whether both old and new knowledge is applicable. Indeed, what is relevant is the imagination and the ability of the person that applies it and not the level of sophistication or whether it is current.

There are various epistemological perspectives of KM and this chapter is centred on the human-oriented perspective. This entails practices such as nurturing groups and communities, fostering communication, stimulating new relationships and encouraging contexts enabling these practices to thrive. This perspective concentrates on the learning and development of individuals that is the focus of this chapter. Thus in the process of designing KM courses, lecturers should aim to develop the students' interpersonal and personal capabilities in order to enhance the human-oriented perspective. These capabilities include communication, leading, working in teams, negotiating, solving conflicts, proactivity, creativity, willingness to reflect and learn from experience, perseverance, and trustworthiness.

KNOWLEDGE CREATION AND INTELLECTUAL CAPITAL

Organisations can only create knowledge through individuals (Argyris & Schon, 1978; Bhatt, 2000). Therefore, it is important to highlight Intellectual Capital (IC) in this chapter, as knowledge is created through IC in organisations. IC is related to that which is rational, extensive and created in the mind. IC includes two dimensions, the intangible (tacit) and the tangible (explicit) that are mutually inclusive (Kok, 2007). IC is considered the main force towards achieving innovation and sustain-

able competitive advantage (Marr, et al., 2003). According to Kok (2007) and Marr *et al.* (2003), there are three domains in IC, namely, human capital (know-how, skills, and capabilities), structural or organisational capital (networks, culture, and systems) and relational (customer, relationships with stakeholders). Organisations tend to follow the Newtonian paradigm a consequence thereof demonstrates that in the last 50 years, knowledge creation has been at the level of positivistic science view (Marr, et al., 2003). This chapter will focus on organisational learning theory (Senge, 1990; Fiol & Lyles, 1985; in Rahe, 2009) and the knowledge creation theory (Davenport & Prusak, 1997; Nonaka & Takeuchi, 1995; Polanyi, 1966; in Rahe, 2009). We advocate a new paradigm, wherein knowledge is created according to the interpretative phenomenological viewpoint of autopoietics that stresses the individual thinking (Marr, et al., 2003; Rahe, 2009).

The main objective of KM seems to be to "increase the effectiveness of human capital through knowledge sharing and knowledge synergies and to improve organisational flexibility towards change and innovation" (Rahe, 2009, p. 103). Knowledge as a resource has become of vital importance and, therefore, numerous models have been developed to measure organisational competencies, namely the Skandia Navigator, the Balanced Scorecard, the Centre for Corporate Innovation and Development in Catalonia (CIDEM) Spain and Intellectual Capital Model (ICM). CIDEM developed a more holistic model in that it takes into account issues such as culture and people. Skandia Navigator and Balance Scorecard models tend to be more focused on measuring competencies and performance indicators. Whereas the Intellectual Capital Model Accreditation (ICMA) of organisations is supported through the ICM. Skandia Navigator and the Balanced Scorecard however, tend to follow the paradigm of scientific management model that highlights organisational objectives, thus ignoring the human and individual element within organisations. These models tend to ignore the individual knowledge creation element within organisations because they seem to adopt a "reductionist view of knowledge which is an extension from data and information" (Styre, 2003, p. 32), wherein the Newtonian paradigm is perpetuated. We corroborate with Faucher *et al.* (2008) who highlight a need for a new paradigm that would consider KM with its complexities and holistic meanings. We are also in agreement with the literature that advocates that the complexity theory will enable a better understanding of KM. Therefore, this chapter argues that the complexity theory provides the vehicle to demonstrate how knowledge is created and developed at the level of individuals and higher education.

Contemporary thinking still shows some traces of the Newtonian mechanistic culture in that human beings and organisations are heavily influenced by the Newtonian categories of the machine metaphor. Taylor advocated that every organisation is bound by laws and principles;

individual employees in organisations need to abide by and act in accordance with these rules. These are therefore the key concepts, which guide Newtonian management thinking and thus mechanistic culture. Thus, the culture shift evident from absolute truth to contextualism, from certainty to pluralism, and from accepting complexity, is portrayed in the paradigm shift which, in turn, leads to a new organisational model—the new age management, which can be seen in Table 1.

The two fundamental aspects which link the human being to her/her life world, i.e. the circumstances in which they live, are the emotions and the spiritual side of beings, unlike Computers (ICTs), which lack both these aspects. Therefore, thinking clearly is linked with emotion and spirit—the complexity of self—leads to human creativity and uniqueness. However, computers do not possess selves and therefore no consciousness nor unconsciousness which is the fundamental difference between machines and humans.

Table 1. New age management

Scientific management/ Newtonian paradigm	New Age Management
Managers are seen as the boss – authority personified.	Those individuals who have decision- making roles are seen as leaders and facilitators.
Bureaucrat, solely reliant on rules and regulations, with a view totally focussed inwardly towards the organisation.	Entrepreneur, interested in innovation and creativity.
Believes him/herself to be the only person responsible for everything in the organisation. When things run well claims all merit, but when things turn out wrong blames others.	Has a vision/ awareness of working in teams and therefore the results are shared with others.
Simply focuses on his/her hierarchical boss who is believed to be the client.	Focuses on internal as well as external clients.
Is always the one to make decisions, to have the final say, therefore is the owner of power.	Believes in decision sharing, facilitates group decision-making, never imposes own opinion.
Thinks all subordinates must work for him/her.	Sees him/herself as supplier and is concerned with the team and ensures the teams' needs are met.
Information is all centralized.	Sharing of all information occurs.
Holds the mindset that as manager is always right and someone else is to blame and someone has to lose. Win-lose situation.	A win-win relationship where all team members are winners from the situation.
Power is centralised; subordinates are never prepared.	Power is delegated, ensures others are developed to handle and deal with challenges.
Has the belief to be the only person that has all the information.	Information is shared by everybody and everybody has access to this information.

Source: Authors

Furthermore, companies that want to be sustainable, creative, and innovative will need to develop human and social capitals as these are associated with human beings and not solely in structural capital, among which are machines. Furthermore, a holistic investment in intellectual capital should be striven for, whereas the structures in Newtonian organisations impede the development of spiritual vision because they do not allow for change.

The literature shows that there is a clear connection between Organisational Learning and complexity theory (McElroy, 2000). At the root of complexity theory lie the concepts of innovation and creativity that are the very essence of the existence of universities in order for these to sustain their competitive advantage. In this way Learning Organisations (LO), as Senge postulated, can be considered the turning point for management to reflect on the scientific management structures of Taylor and Fayol because for the first time, through Senge's systemic view, "complexity theory is nothing but systems thinking in practice" (McElroy, 2000, p. 198). Senge paved the way in creating a new mindset and a new paradigm. This led to KM evolving to a second generation of KM that takes into account the creation of knowledge and learning, especially relevant in universities. Furthermore, in this second generation of KM, there seems a need to break away with the dichotomy between practical knowledge and factual knowledge. This is supported by the complexity theory in that organisational learning has evolved and recognised that there should not be a dichotomy between the different types of knowing. Therefore, there should not be a distinction between factual and practical knowledge, i.e. the know-what knowledge and the know-how knowledge.

One of the key concepts of the complexity theory is entropy, which is in simple terms, a state of disorder prevalent in the chaos theory. This state of entropy is irreversible and the bigger the organism the larger the entropy. If we apply this analogy to our globalised economy we can verify that the state of entropy is enormous in organisations such as multinational corporations due to their size as compared to a micro company. We are of the opinion that one of the factors that can 'control' entropy is flexibility, which is supported by focused planning achieved through entrepreneurial leadership. In this context, an important factor is the IC and how it creates knowledge and innovates. As universities are still shackled to the mental models within the Newtonian paradigm of management, knowledge creation is thwarted to a large extent and universities have mostly played the role of knowledge transmitters. However, if universities adopted their true role of knowledge creators, this would diminish entropy and would generate innovative and creative flexibility. Entropy supports individualism that is important for innovation and creativity. Whenever there is control and dictatorial management there can never be creativity. Through entropy, a window opens for creativity and innovation. This individualism is further evident through individual contributions within teamwork with entrepreneurial leaders giving rise to higher levels of creativity and innovation as opposed to the managerial paradigm of controlling individuals, which stifles both innovation and creativity.

Complexity theory provides LOs a theory of how learning happens in organisations. In the literature on KM little has been written about wisdom, this is mainly due to the fact that most of KM literature is essentially concerned with Information or the first generation of KM, as McElroy (2000) supports. "If knowledge is knowing how to do something, wisdom is knowing why, what and how to do something" (Rowley, 2006, p. 254). Furthermore, as was mentioned earlier in this chapter, the concept of wisdom seems to play an important role in knowledge because if one is able to achieve a state of wisdom, this is in line with the systemic thinking as opposed to linear mindsets and processes. Rowley's (2006) argument concerning the concept of wisdom is interesting and adds value to the second generation of KM. The fact that Rowley (2006) places wisdom at the higher level on the pyramid, this hierarchy could illustrate the Newtonian paradigm mindset in that this thinking is linear and hierarchical in nature. Wisdom, however, is viewed as a unique perspective on life that is related to equilibrium and facilitates an understanding of the complex inter-relationships in different contexts (Korac-Kakabadse, et al., 2001). We highlight that this viewpoint on wisdom is linked to the complexity theories and it is opposed to the linear, scientific management theories that seem to be in line with logical positivism.

Within the context of higher education, the concept of knowledge is related to the concept of know-how, that is, knowing how to do something which can be further converted to: knowing how to perform the role of a lecturer/professor, in the case of higher education. This role of knowing how to be a lecturer/professor entails various aspects relevant to the issue of didactics. These include—knowing how to lead the teaching and learning process within the diversity of students; how to transmit various syllabi from a didactic perspective; how to interact with different cohorts collectively and with students (individually); how to design syllabi for specific modules/courses; how to design assessments and also how to assess students through product (exams, tests, and assignments) and through process (attendance, interactive participation, among others). Other important functions include the need to perform the role of lecturer/professor, which includes conducting research, being up to date and being technologically updated, creating academic production (dissertation, theses, articles, and books), creating courses within and out of one's comfort zone. The latter refers to the areas within their conceptual and practical expertise and moving beyond this area is vital. In order to justify the importance inherent in the sharing of know-how, for KM, know what is shared by many and due to its very nature, is difficult to protect. However,

know how is usually made up of practical and collective experiences and is therefore unique and easy to protect contrary to know what which is difficult to protect. Both know how and know what move separately. KM is prevalent in universities, as the definition of knowledge worker includes lecturers and researchers, among others (Drucker, 1994). These institutions are by definition the places which create and diffuse knowledge and wherein institutional IC is stored in the form of individual IC in the minds of the lecturer/professor. The knowledge sharing process is complex in view of it being eminently tacit in nature because it is stored in the minds of individuals. The knowledge that lecturers/professors hold is the purest representation of tacit knowledge (Nonaka & Takeuchi, 1991). This intangible knowledge is rooted in the subjective conclusions and insights of lecturers/professors. Furthermore, it is important that these institutions have the necessary culture, values, and structure to motivate and reward those lecturers/professors who are willing and open to contribute to the transformation of individual IC into institutional IC achieved through sharing knowledge. We highlight that this transformation process could possibly be achieved by moving from the Newtonian paradigm inherent in the bureaucratic structure and dictatorial values (which tend to stress the traditional pedagogies in teaching highlighting automatism, authoritarianism, and unilateralism). This transformation focuses instead on a new paradigm of LOs and complexity theory wherein there is a culture of sharing and learning (the new pedagogy, which considers learning to learn to be fundamental and regards the student as a learner and not as a product but rather a person). From this new pedagogy stems the liberating pedagogy that is inspired on Freire's (2001) autonomous pedagogy that fosters a strong base for adult development. Thus, the lecturer/professor is considered to be the learning facilitator, who nurtures teamwork and collaboration. This fosters individual learning that is advocated in the new paradigm, as we corroborate.

As well as generating, collecting and utilizing knowledge to increase the organisation's progress, knowledge management today also deals with converting and sharing knowledge as discussed in the tacit/explicit knowledge typology (see Table 2).

THE NEED FOR A PARADIGM CHANGE IN UNIVERSITIES

Effective knowledge sharing may never become a reality in higher education as most of these institutions pose a challenge to this process by virtue of their immobility, traditional culture and rigid structure as well as a context being adverse to change. KM presupposes flexibility in management and a high level of interaction among individuals. Therefore, we maintain that systemic flexibility provides an umbrella for the integration of organisational learning, KM, and the complexity theory that can encapsulate all these three aspects (Senge, 1990; Pascale, et al., 2000; Rowley, 2000). Systemic flexibility takes a holistic view (collective knowledge) and factors these perspectives into consideration (Soliman & Spooner, 2000). Therefore, through systemic flexibility the organisation is able to respond to the dynamic forces of change placed on it, at any given moment in time and seeks to become a solution for the problem of knowledge transfer (Jasimuddin, 2008). We further propose that the use of networks and networking enables the organisation to respond in a systemic way that takes into account the complexities of human interaction, development, decision making and knowledge sharing/transfer that exists at every opportunity (Senge, 1990; Beijerse, 1999; Seufert, et al., 1999; Martensson, 2000; Rowley, 2000; Schonstrom, 2005; Jasimuddin, 2008). Therefore, through the strengthening of social capital inherent in networks, the university is able to engage with its environment and can make faster decisions and responses that will ensure its sustainability and generate further growth, whilst developing its knowledge continually (Senge, 1990; Rowley, 2000; Martensson, 2000; Pena, 2002; Schonstrom, 2005; Jasimuddin, 2008; Harlow, 2008). Thus, it is through the concept of flexibility that the university has the capability to meet continual changing needs individually and collectively (Seufert, et al., 1999; Rowley, 2000; Martensson, 2000; Soliman & Spooner, 2000; Pena, 2002; Jasimuddin, 2008).

KM enables the organisation to develop the capabilities with which to capture intellectual knowledge and turn that knowledge into an asset for the university (Beijerse, 1999; Schonstrom, 2005; Seidler & Hartmann, 2008; Harlow, 2008). However, since the nature of tacit knowledge is intangible and is hard to capture and codify, this makes the task of developing it and enhancing it harder because managing knowledge requires controlling, predicting and maintaining stasis, thus preventing it from evolving into something new or greater (Schonstrom, 2005; Soliman & Spooner, 2000; Hall, 2006; Seidler & Hartmann, 2008). In turn, in the first generation of KM, it is counterproductive to the organisations' requirements, because instead of working organically, KM is trying to capture and contain intellectual development and put it in jar with a label on it saying 'preserved' (Senge, 1990; Soliman & Spooner, 2000; Herscel, et al., 2001; Schonstrom, 2005; Hall, 2006; Seidler & Hartmann, 2008). The very act of controlling knowledge prevents it from being innovated, developed and pushed past the boundaries of control and generated into something new (Soliman & Spooner, 2000; Hall, 2006). We would also argue that the subjective quality of the interpretation of codified and explicit knowledge leads to multiple cognitive interpretations and slows down the process of information sharing (Senge, 1990; Seufert, et al., 1999; Soliman & Spooner, 2000; Herscel, et al., 2001; Hall, 2006). This is because it relies heavily on the principle of the knowledge sharer (Seufert, et al., 1999; Seidler & Hartmann, 2008; Harlow, 2008). Therefore, making the task of responding to the new information even harder for the

Table 2. Perspectives and typologies of knowledge (Source: Adapted from Hislop, 2009.)

Perspective/ Typology	Authors	Main Assumptions
Objectivist Perspective of Knowledge	Nonaka & Pelrokorpi (2006), Cook & Brown (1999)	Knowledge can be quantified and measured – explicit. This perspective privileges explicit/objective over implicit/subjective knowledge. It represents the mainstream perspective in KM literature, Knowledge Based Theory of the Firm, an extension of the Resource Based View of the Firm, is linked to this perspective. Knowledge, according to this approach, is regarded as objective and is rooted in Positivism, 'knowledge as truth.'
Subjectivist Perspective of Knowledge	Cook & Brown (1999), Gherardi (2000), Polanyi (1969), Tsoukas 2003)	This perspective is an alternative to the Objectivist Perspective. The Practice-Based Perspective (PBP) is in line with different philosophical perspectives whereas the objective perspective is in tune with positivistic philosophy. Practice-based epistemology views knowledge as something that cannot exist separate from activities that individual people engage in involving the whole body and not just the cognitive processes. This perspective is embedded in practice – the difference between Objectivist and PBP is that knowledge is not separated from people because knowing is inseparable from the human activity. Tacit and explicit are inseparable and this approach rejects the characterisation of knowledge into separate independent parts; instead there is a relationship between tacit and explicit knowledge. These are inseparable and mutually created. Knowledge is embodied in people - all knowing is personal; it is impossible to remove knowledge from people into a fully explicit form. All knowledge has tacit dimensions and is embedded and inseparable from practice as it is socially constructed and culturally embedded. Tacit knowledge is subjective and open to personal interpretation. Knowledge is never totally neutral and unbiased because it is linked to each individual's values and beliefs. Knowledge is contestable and open to dispute. It is not possible to produce objective knowledge as *all* knowledge is subjective. This epistemology presupposes that all knowledge has both facets of tacit and explicit dimensions.
Tacit Knowledge	Gherardi (2000), Newell et al. (2007), Tsoukas (2003)	Represents knowledge that people possess but which is inexpressible. Tacit knowledge incorporates physical and cognitive skills (ability to do mental arithmetic as well as to dance, to weld and to create an advertising slogan) and Cognitive frameworks – i.e. the value systems people possess. Tacit knowledge is Personal, is difficult if not impossible to disembody and codify and may be unconscious.
Explicit Knowledge	Polanyi (1958) and later Nonaka et al (2002)	Explicit knowledge is synonymous with objective knowledge, is viewed as being objective, standing above and separate from individuals and social values and can be codified into a tangible form. There is a tacit-explicit dichotomy which represents two pure and separate forms of knowledge.
Individual Knowledge	Nonaka (1991)	There is another dichotomy, namely between different levels of knowledge, i.e. individual-group/social. Knowledge can only exist at the level of the individual many other authors have a different opinion. Knowledge does exist at the level of the individual but they believe that knowledge can reside in social groups.
Group Knowledge	Lam (1997)	In the dichotomy, individual-group/social knowledge, lies the tacit-explicit knowledge dichotomy. The explicit means it's linked to the individual because it is the conscious knowledge. This is objectified knowledge in the social part. This is linked to explicit group knowledge such as, written rules, company policies, and company routines. The tacit aspect means it's automatic knowledge for the individual and its collective knowledge in the social part. This means knowledge that is not codified, such as informal company routines, stories, etc. At the macro level - group knowledge is linked to national cultural context in determining the nature of organisational knowledge. While at the micro level - group knowledge is evident in communities of practice.

Source: Authors

organisation because it is the process that slows the decision-making (Soliman & Spooner, 2000; Herscel, et al., 2001). Critics of systemic flexibility argue that without structure, organisation systemic flexibility lacks control, direction and is at risk of free flow that no productivity can exist thus arguing that organisations will reach a state of pure chaos (Rowley, 2000). However, as complexity theory proves, the natural state of order will automatically find itself through equilibrium. This is viewed as chaos in an unpredictable order wherein flexibility can arise and be nurtured. Therefore, flexibility can induce more disequilibrium and create further innovation and creativity because change encourages organisations to adapt (Senge, 1990; Pascale, et al., 2000). Furthermore, through knowledge networks and leadership, change can be encouraged thus stimulating more innovation and creativity and new knowledge (Seufert, et al., 1999; Martensson, 2000; Pascale, et al., 2000; Seidler & Hartmann, 2008).

Universities need to create an environment that leads to knowledge sharing in which the organisation's values and structure are regarded as key issues. These will only be successful if supported by leadership. In view of the nature of knowledge, the use of adaptive leadership and specifically champions of knowledge would be an ideal conduit to develop the IC of a university as a way to support and enhance the concept of systemic flexibility (Senge, 1990; Seufert, et al., 1999; Schonstrom, 2005; Jasimuddin, 2008). Furthermore, complexity theory demonstrates that the outdated term of management, as a paradigm, is unsuitable for contemporary organisational needs of because of the global forces they have to deal with due to the increasingly short life cycles of products and services, companies need to act upon these changes in order to speed up the process of adaptation, further creating a turbulent and dynamic environment (Seidler & Hartmann, 2008). The scientific management paradigm which entails control, plan and organise not only contradicts the very essence of knowledge and knowledge

development but it actually confines the organic process (Martensson, 2000; Herscel, et al., 2001; Schonstrom, 2005). Leadership has the capability to encourage, facilitate, and organise the space, to generate face-to-face communication thereby stimulating and generating discussion. This is achieved by using the most simple of techniques, known as continuous feedback and knowledge sharing, as well as through a simple process of talk time. This can be created at any given moment because of the direction and decision making power of the leader (Senge, 1990; Seufert, et al., 1999; Soliman & Spooner, 2000; Schonstrom, 2005; Jasimuddin, 2008). This would require a reduction of hierarchical decision-making and development of high trust, which are left to the leader to determine the suitable course of action (Seufert, et al., 1999). Champions of knowledge are simply the same principle but continually pushing the need to develop, refine and create more knowledge; not only is the leader able to encourage and facilitate this process, but also actually becomes one of the champions of knowledge thus turning into a role model for this process (Soliman & Spooner, 2000; Schonstrom, 2005). The champion of knowledge would promote and insist upon the continual development of the knowledge worker and create a highly skilled workforce, which is able to make decisions and communicate more effectively through networking, as discussed earlier, thus enabling the organisation to respond faster to changing circumstances and needs (Senge, 1990; Seufert, et al., 1999; Soliman & Spooner, 2000; Martensson, 2000; Pena, 2002; Schonstrom, 2005; Seidler & Hartmann, 2008).

Currently there is a real dilemma within universities. They train, teach, and endorse the concepts of KM, organisation learning, complexity theory, and a plethora of new models, concepts, and ideas. However, they are nevertheless an institution based on hierarchical processes and systems with the old paradigm mindset. Therefore, there seems to be an apparent contradiction in that despite teaching and advocating new paradigms of management and mindsets, some university institutions still tend to follow the Newtonian paradigm in their practices as this undermines the very knowledge these universities institutions are encouraging the students to go out and practice within organisations (Beijerse, 1999). If the lecturer's role in the university is to provide knowledge, this then allows for students to transform this knowledge into tacit knowledge. However, the obstacle seems to be whether universities do this or not. Is this not an example of pure hypocrisy in practice; this leads to a dilemma which poses a question as to whether students are able to promote these principles when the very institutions that are teaching them are not applying these principles (Beijerse, 1999). We have proposed the need for knowledge sharing and creation, networking and leadership through the concept of systemic flexibility as being the relevant criteria in an educational establishment and in any other organisation (Senge, 1990; Soliman & Spooner, 2000; Martensson, 2000; Schonstrom, 2005). Furthermore, a prerequisite for any educational institution requires that those who teach the minds of tomorrow's future how to prepare themselves, be the flagships or champions of knowledge themselves (Schonstrom, 2005). We would argue that for survival of educational institutions they need to apply the rhetoric they are keen to promote within the wider community (Beijerse, 1999; Pena, 2002; Schonstrom, 2005). Therefore, what is being proposed is that universities become a knowing organisation rather than a knowledge sharer (Rowley, 2000).

CONCLUSION

Universities are, in essence, institutions that generate and share knowledge. By the same token, a facilitator of knowledge is the embodiment of the knowledge worker. The lecturer/professor/facilitator, as knowledge worker, in addition to sharing and generating knowledge, has the role to stimulate the creation of new knowledge among students. The educator, in addition to transmitting specific content, performs the role of teaching to 'think.' It is not sufficient only to perform the task as teacher but, above all, to create the conditions which allow the student to 'learn critically.' Furthermore, it is the lecturer's/facilitator's responsibility to be constantly updated with recent knowledge in order to gain the competencies to produce and share new knowledge.

Certain scholars support the argument that education is the centre of social strategic investment. It is further highlighted that higher education should achieve four fundamental objectives so as to prepare the individual by developing the person to be in alignment with various contexts, namely: (1) for the labour market; (2) for a productive gainfully employed life and as a member of a democratic society; (3) for personal development; and also (4) towards the developing of a broad framework of knowledge. However, currently the business and economic agenda is focused on the existing dysfunctions between labour market demands and the position that higher education has adopted, seeing that the education system is far from accomplishing its role of developing and training graduates for the labour market. However, what frequently occurs in practice is that personal, social, relational and emotional competencies are not always highly valued in the labour market which, instead, tends to essentially value workplace competencies. Therefore, the current supply of education does not seem to be in total alignment with the labour market and this, in turn, can lead to adverse effects on society. In this way, an issue that should be highlighted is how to prepare the graduate, both for the labour market and for society as a whole. Adjacent to this argument, lies the need to establish a close cooperation between the university and industry. This effective cooperation should be the very essence of both universities and the labour market in order for these to achieve sustainability.

REFERENCES

Alwis, R. S., & Hartmann, E. (2008). The use of tacit knowledge within innovative companies: Knowledge management in innovative enterprises. *Journal of Knowledge Management, 12*(1), 133–147. doi:10.1108/13673270810852449

Argyris, C., & Schon, D. A. (1978). *Organizational learning: A theory of action perspective.* Reading, MA: Addison-Wesley Publishing.

Bartlett, C., & Goshal, S. (1989). *Managing across borders: The transnational solution.* Boston, MA: Harvard Business School Press.

Beijerse, R. (1999). Questions in knowledge management: Defining and conceptualizing a phenomenon. *Journal of Knowledge Management, 3*(2), 94–110. doi:10.1108/13673279910275512

Bergan, S. (2009). Presentación. In Alonso, L. E., Fernández Rodríguez, C. J., & Nyssen, J. M. (Eds.), *El Debate Sobre las Competencias: Una Investigación Qualitativa en Torno a la Educacíon Superior y el Mercado de Trabajo en España.* Madrid, Spain: ANECA.

Bhardwaj, M., & Monin, J. (2006). Tacit to explicit: an interplay shaping organization knowledge. *Journal of Knowledge Management, 10*(3), 72–85. doi:10.1108/13673270610670867

Bhatt, G. D. (2000). Organizing knowledge in the knowledge development cycle. *Journal of Knowledge Management, 4*(1), 15–26. doi:10.1108/13673270010315371

Brunner, J. J. (2009). Prólogo. In Alonso, L. E., Fernández Rodríguez, C. J., & Nyssen, J. M. (Eds.), *El Debate Sobre las Competencias: Una Investigación Qualitativa en Torno a la Educacíon Superior y el Mercado de Trabajo en España.* Madrid, Spain: ANECA.

Caballero, F. G., Piñeiro, G. P., & García-Pintos, A. (2008). Las prácticas en empresas en la universidad española? Cómo son los centros universitários más involucrados? In Neira, (Eds.), *Investigaciones de Economía de la Educación.* Madrid, Spain: AEDE.

Canoy, M., Carvalho, G., Hammarlund, C., Hubert, A., Lerais, F., & Melich, A. (2006). Investing in youth: From childhood to adulthood. *Bureau of European Policy Advisers.* Retrieved 11 October 2006 from http://ec.europa.eu/dgs/policy_advisers/publications/index_en.htm

Cook, S., & Brown, J. (1999). Bridging epistemologies: The generative dance between organisational knowledge and organisational knowing. *Organization Science, 10*(4), 381–400. doi:10.1287/orsc.10.4.381

Doz, Y., & Prahalad, C. (1991). Managing MNC's: A search for a new paradigm. *Strategic Management Journal, 12*(5), 145–164. doi:10.1002/smj.4250120911

Drucker, P. (1994). *Post-capitalist society.* New York, NY: HarperCollins.

Drucker, P. (2000). *Age of discontinuity: Guidelines to our changing society* (3rd ed.). New York, NY: Harper and Row.

Faucher, J.-B. P. L., Everett, A. M., & Lawson, R. (2008). Reconstituting knowledge management. *Journal of Knowledge Management, 12*(3), 3–16. doi:10.1108/13673270810875822

Freire, P. (2001). *Pedagogia de autonomia: Saberes necessários à prática educative* (19th ed.). Rio de Janeiro, Brazil: Páz e Terra.

Gherardi, S. (2000). Practice based theorizing on learning and knowing in organisations. *Organization, 7*(2), 211–233. doi:10.1177/135050840072001

Grant, R. (1996). Towards a knowledge-based theory of the firm. *Strategic Management Journal*, *17*, 109–122.

Hall, M. (2006). Knowledge management and the limits of knowledge codification. *Journal of Knowledge Management*, *10*(3), 117–126. doi:10.1108/13673270610670894

Harlow, H. (2008). The effects of tacit knowledge on a firm's performance. *Journal of Knowledge Management*, *12*(1), 148–163. doi:10.1108/13673270810852458

Herschel, R. T., Nemati, H., & Steiger, D. (2001). Tacit to explicit knowledge conversion: knowledge protocols. *Journal of Knowledge Management*, *5*(1), 107–116. doi:10.1108/13673270110384455

Hislop, D. (2009). *Knowledge Management in Organisations*. 2nd ed., Oxford, Oxford University Press.

Jasimuddin, S. M. (2008). A holistic view of knowledge management strategy. *Journal of Knowledge Management*, *12*(2), 57–66. doi:10.1108/13673270810859514

Jasimuddin, S. M., Klein, J. H., & Connell, C. (2005). The paradox of using tacit and explicit knowledge: Strategies to face dilemmas. *Management Decision*, *43*(1), 102–112. doi:10.1108/00251740510572515

Kok, A. (2007). Intellectual capital management as part of knowledge management initiatives at institutions of higher education. *Journal of Knowledge Management*, *5*(2), 181–192.

Korac-Kakabadse, M., Korac-Kakabadse, A., & Kouzim, A. (2001). Leadership renewal: Towards the philosophy of wisdom. *International Review of Administrative Sciences*, *67*(2), 207–227. doi:10.1177/0020852301672002

Lam, A., & Lambermont-Ford, J. (2010). Knowledge sharing in organisational contexts: A motivation based perspective. *Journal of Knowledge Management*, *14*(1), 51–66. doi:10.1108/13673271011015561

Marr, B., Gupta, O., Pike, S., & Roos, G. (2003). Intellectual capital and knowledge management effectiveness. *Management Decision*, *1*(8), 771–781. doi:10.1108/00251740310496288

Martensson, M. (2000). A critical review of knowledge management as a management tool. *Journal of Knowledge Management*, *4*(3), 204–216. doi:10.1108/13673270010350002

Matos, F., Lopes, A., Rodrigues, S., & Matos, N. (2010). Why intellectual capital management accreditation is a tool for organizational development? *Electronic Journal of Knowledge Management*, *8*(2), 235–244.

McElroy, M. W. (2000). Integrating complexity theory: Knowledge management and organisational learning. *Journal of Knowledge Management*, *4*(3), 195–203. doi:10.1108/13673270010377652

Mooradian, N. (2005). Tacit knowledge: Philosophical roots and role in KM. *Journal of Knowledge Management*, *9*(6), 104–113. doi:10.1108/13673270510629990

Newell, G., Scarbrough, H., Bresnen, M., Edelman, L., & Swan, J. (2000). Sharing knowledge across projects: Limits to ICT led projects review. *Management Learning Practices*, *37*, 167–185. doi:10.1177/1350507606063441

Newell, S., David, G., & Chand, D. (2007). An analysis of trust among globally distributed work teams in and organisational setting. *Knowledge and Process Management*, *14*(3), 158–168. doi:10.1002/kpm.284

Nonaka, I. (1991). The knowledge-creating economy. *Harvard Business Review*, *69*(6), 96–104.

Nonaka, I., & Peltokorpi, V. (2006). Objectivity and subjectivity in knowledge management: A review of top twenty articles. *Knowledge and Process Management, 13*(2), 73–82. doi:10.1002/kpm.251

Nonaka, I., & Takeuchi, H. (1995). *The knowledge creating company: How Japanese companies created the dynamics of innovation.* Oxford, NY: Oxford University Press.

Pascale, R. T., Millemann, M., & Gioja, L. (2000). *Surfing the edge of chaos.* New York, NY: Random House.

Pena, I. (2002). Knowledge networks as part of an integrated knowledge management approach. *Journal of Knowledge Management, 6*(5), 469–478. doi:10.1108/13673270210450423

Polyani, M. (1958). *Personal knowledge: Towards a post-critical philosophy.* London, UK: Routledge and Kogan Paul Ltd.

Polyani, M. (1967). *The tacit dimension.* London, UK: Routledge and Kogan Paul Ltd.

Polyani, M. (1969). *Knowing and being.* London, UK: Routledge and Kogan Paul Ltd.

Rahe, M. (2009). Subjectivity and cognition in knowledge management. *Journal of Knowledge Management, 13*(3), 102–117. doi:10.1108/13673270910962905

Rowley, J. (2000). From learning organisation to knowledge entrepreneur. *Journal of Knowledge Management, 4*(1), 7–15. doi:10.1108/13673270010315362

Rowley, J. (2006). Where is the wisdom that we have lost in knowledge? *The Journal of Documentation, 62*(2), 251–270. doi:10.1108/00220410610650332

Schonstrom, M. (2005). Creating knowledge networks: Lessons from practice. *Journal of Knowledge Management, 9*(6), 17–29. doi:10.1108/13673270510629936

Senge, P. (1990). *The fifth discipline: The art and practice of the learning organisation.* New York, NY: Doubleday.

Seufert, A., Krogh, G. V., & Bach, A. (1999). Towards knowledge networking. *Journal of Knowledge Management, 3*(3), 180–190. doi:10.1108/13673279910288608

Soliman, F., & Spooner, K. (2000). Strategies for implementing knowledge management: Role of human resource management. *Journal of Knowledge Management, 4*(4), 337–345. doi:10.1108/13673270010379894

Styre, A. (2003). Knowledge management beyond codification: Knowing as practice/concept. *Journal of Knowledge Management, 7*(5), 32–40. doi:10.1108/13673270310505368

Takeuchi, H. (1998). Beyond knowledge management: Lessons from Japan. *Monash Mt. Eliza Business Journal, 1*(1).

Tsoukas, H. (1996). The firm as a distributed knowledge system: A constructionist approach. *Strategic Management Journal, 17*, 11–25.

KEY TERMS AND DEFINITIONS

Competencies: A group of skills which include personal, social, relational technical and emotional and prepare individuals for the labour market and for their continuous employability.

Complexity: Theory of complexity provides the vehicle to demonstrate how knowledge is created and developed at the level of individuals.

Flexibility: Improves quality amongst individuals in their multi-faceted areas, namely, intellectual capacity, creativity and adaptability. Systemic flexibility allows organisation to respond to the dynamic forces of change placed on it, at any given moment in time and seeks to become a solution for the problem of knowledge transfer. Flexibility can induce more disequilibrium and create further innovation and creativity because change encourages organisations to adapt.

Innovation: Is the process of creating something new such as knowledge, products and services. Innovation leads to sustainable competitive advantage.

Intellectual Capital: Is related to that which is rational, extensive and created in the mind. IC includes two dimensions, the intangible (tacit) and the tangible (explicit) that are mutually inclusive IC is considered the main force towards achieving innovation and sustainable competitive advantage There are three domains in IC, namely, human capital (know-how, skills and capabilities), structural or organisational capital (networks, culture and systems) and relational (customer, relationships with stakeholders).

Knowledge Management: Takes into account the creation of knowledge and learning. Second generation of KM, has broken away from the dichotomy between practical and factual knowledge, i.e. the know-what knowledge and the know-how knowledge. Organisations recognise that there should not be a dichotomy between the different types of knowing. KM presupposes flexibility in management and a high level of interaction among individuals.

Learning and Development: An instrument for social and work integration as well as a variable for economic and social development which includes lifelong learning of competencies.

Wisdom: The awareness of knowing why, what and how to do something.

Chapter 4

A Conceptual Model of Creativity, Invention, and Innovation (MCII) for Entrepreneurial Engineers

Maria Jakovljevic
University of Zadar, Croatia

ABSTRACT

Teachers-engineers in vocational and technical schools have been exposed to constant pressure concerning methods to foster and manage knowledge transfer of Creativity, Invention, and Innovation (CII) skills as learning outcomes. Knowledge management of CII in a technical-vocational educational environment has been a problem and needs improvement in order to engage teachers-engineers and learners in creativity and innovation activities. The purpose of this chapter is to develop a conceptual model for Creativity, Invention, and Innovation (MCII) from a knowledge management perspective in the technical-vocational and interdisciplinary ecologies of practice. This chapter takes the form of a literature study regarding CII multiple knowledge-sharing issues. A methodological framework has been described in the introductory section of this chapter. The background of the study focuses on the general features of CII, highlighting needs and gaps in terms of teachers-engineers' competence in promoting CII as new learning outcomes. The framework for the MCII focuses on the following main themes: theoretical views on CII issues; institutional and international collaboration; the construct of CII intelligence; teachers-engineers' competence; and creative knowledge-sharing climate. The structure and the flow of the conceptual model are presented, followed by discussion, future research directions, and the conclusion.

INTRODUCTION

With the rapid progress of globalisation and technology, Creativity, Invention, and Innovation (CII) are becoming major driving forces of competitive achievements of industry sectors as well as educational institutions. There are few records in current literature of how to produce strong ties with industry through business creativity support (for example, Badran, 2007), as well as designing a creative and innovative environment within current organisational and educational settings

DOI: 10.4018/978-1-4666-1969-2.ch004

in Croatia (Šajeva, 2010; Martinka, 2006). The problem, therefore, relates in large measure to a missing link between businesses and schools.

In view of increased global competition and its focus on quality products and services, there is a need for schools to be innovative through producing professionals, for example, entrepreneurs or engineers who reflect highly innovative behaviour (Baum & Locke, 2004). In this sense, we aim to capture the challenge and excitement of entrepreneurial companies and their inspiring leaders who provide employees with an opportunity to understand the underpinnings of innovation (Tierney, Farmer, & Graen, 1999; Cardon, 2008). Effective learning means engaging and knowledge sharing in real-world environments; however, teachers-engineers in the technical-vocational setting in Croatia have no adequate support to sustain entrepreneurship initiatives. Only few companies foster innovations and stimulate entrepreneurship among employees in Croatia (Svoboda, 2006).

In order to create effective creative experiences, teachers-engineers have to be prepared. Educating teachers on CII issues is a starting point for the preparation of future innovators. Teachers as innovators have to be acquainted with emotions and feelings (Frigda, 1988; Russell & Barrett, 1999) as well as with analytical, creative, and practical intelligence discussed by Grigorenko and Sternberg (2001) which are beneficial in creative endeavours.

Teachers-engineers raise the performance expectations of learners and seek to transform learners' personal values and their concepts of CII in order to inspire them to higher levels of creative desires and aspirations. This, however, seldom leads to a viable commercial creation, as teachers are isolated from organisational institutions and other community stakeholders.

Teachers-engineers do not have sufficient pedagogical education on facilitating, sharing, transferring, and managing knowledge of CII, in the technical-vocational educational environment in Croatia, and they need to develop novel insight into the knowledge management of CII. Adequately managing knowledge of these exceptional capabilities offers entrance to an individuals' ability to generate new knowledge, which can be made available to learners, institutions, and society as a whole. Thus, the full scope of teachers-engineers' competence in terms of facilitating CII as learning outcomes is an issue to be clarified.

Teachers-engineers lack knowledge related to psychosocial aspects and skills in creating an appropriate climate for CII. In addition, there are unknown aspects of multicultural knowledge exchange between educators through international institutional collaborations. The problem is determining what changes have to be made in the 'educational system' of teachers-engineers to enhance their role in the knowledge management of innovation and invention skills as learning outcomes.

Our aim is to respond to these teaching issues by introducing some CII features in an original way and illustrating their logical connections in the form of a conceptual model. The model is based on wide theoretical perspectives highlighting international collaboration as its starting point in order to engage teachers-engineers so that they are motivated and productive in terms of facilitating CII as learning outcomes. The model could help the teachers-engineers to enhance their CII personal construct and knowledge management of CII, taking into account its novel structure and flow.

This study has been shaped in the form of a project named CroSA that was envisioned through collaboration between the University in Zadar, Croatia, and the University of Johannesburg, South Africa. The collaboration has been extended to include the technical and vocational schools in Zadar County and the chambers of commerce in Zadar and Johannesburg, thus relating to a technical-vocational educational context, which includes entrepreneurial characteristics and the interdisciplinary nature of CII knowledge management.

CroSA includes the network of stakeholders (teachers-engineers, business partners, educators) aiming to develop teachers-engineers' entrepreneurial capabilities and competence in terms of their future ability to facilitate CII as learning outcomes. Thus, the CroSA project is a CII knowledge driver that provides multiple pathways of cross-cultural knowledge acquisition through joint international and institutional collaboration.

The proposed Model of Creativity, Invention, and Innovation (MCII), in synergy with the Continuous Professional Teacher Development (CPTD) framework, serves as a basis for the implementation of innovation training procedures, along with courses on how to write business plans, obtain venture finance and effectively manage innovative operations. The model is still in the preparation phase in terms of human and funding resources and near application in technical and vocational schools. The results of its effectiveness are beyond the scope of this chapter.

The main objective of this chapter is to focus on the multiple aspects of CII taking into account institutional and international collaboration with the goal of building teacher-engineer's enthusiasm for knowledge exchange relating to CII, as well as entrepreneurship mobility within schools. For this purpose a conceptual (MCII) has to be constructed based on current theoretical perspectives, the CPTD model and examples of good practice.

The chapter covers the following key topics in response to the main objective:

- In-depth analysis of CII features and dimensions relevant to entrepreneurial and interdisciplinary education
- In-depth analysis of theoretical perspectives, environmental and psychosocial features in order to facilitate effective CII knowledge exchange
- Multi-layered analysis of institutional and international collaboration on knowledge aspects of CII issues

- In-depth analysis of teachers' competence and creativity climate in CII knowledge transfer and sharing
- The development of a conceptual model that is culturally and contextually sensitive and that can be adjusted accordingly.

This chapter takes the form of a literature study of theoretical perspectives on CII issues with examples of good practice that lead to the development of a conceptual MCII for entrepreneurial education from a knowledge management perspective. It encompasses human aspects and the network of collaborations, dimensions of CII intelligence, environmental and psychosocial features and the learning climate for CII. The application for educational practice is reflected through fresh insight into the multiple components of the MCII and CII learning outcomes that are still in a stage of research within the CroSA project and the Croatian qualifications framework (2009). The results of the study are applicable to interdisciplinary education in view of the homological essence of knowledge transfer (Mende, 2006).

The next section provides background knowledge on the factors within the current practice of CII that need to be taken into account in developing the framework for the conceptual model.

BACKGROUND OF CREATIVITY, INVENTION, AND INNOVATION FROM A KNOWLEDGE MANAGEMENT PERSPECTIVE

It is now necessary to extensively define the elements of CII and their flow with respect to knowledge management; as well as, to detect the needs and gaps in teacher competence that still need to be addressed.

Defining Creativity, Invention, and Innovation

"*Creativity* can be expressed as the ability to make something new, whether a thought or idea, an object, a product or a process, a work of art or performance, or an interpretation" (Morrison & Johnston, 2006). Creativity does not come only from the internal and spontaneous sources of an individual. It comes from interaction, a network of social relationships, communication, a society atmosphere and similar factors (Guilford, 1950; Srića, 1992). Creativity constructs new tools and new learning outcomes—new embodiments of knowledge. It constructs new relationships, rules, communities of practice, and new connections—new social practices (Knight, 2002).

Srića (1992) illustrates *creativity* through five principles: a mental box, codes, buckles, associations, and questions. Codes serve to open mental boxes with different contents. Buckles serve to connect the contents of two or more mental boxes. When the contents of one mental box remind us of the contents of another mental box, we call this an association. Questions serve to design the whole process of searching and development of ideas. A creative idea starts with an association, something what we see, hear, feel, and think about. Creativity is based on unusual associations that allow us to open mental boxes that usually do not fit together.

Invention is a creative event and an original act of imagination that can be controlled. Invention means the combination of earlier existing knowledge in a new way in order to reach novel knowledge, something that did not exist before. Invention comes from different directions and knowledge bases: from empirical to theoretical research, from sudden accidental ideas to logical and provable discoveries (Srića, 1992; Johnson, 1975, 1992).

Innovation is the successful implementation of creative ideas within an organisation (Amabile, 1983) that requires medium to long-term commitment of time and resources (Badran, 2007).

Innovation provides the success and competitive advantages within an organisation (Woodman, Sawyer, & Griffin, 1993).

Educators have no clear line of sight regarding the knowledge flow from creativity, invention to innovation.

The Knowledge Flow from Creativity, Invention, and Innovation

Creativity seems to involve synthetic, analytical, and practical aspects of intelligence: synthetic to come up with ideas, analytical to evaluate the quality of those ideas, and practical to formulate a way of effectively communicating those ideas and persuading people of their value (Sternberg & Lubart, 1999). An inventive idea seldom fulfils the well-known five routes to awaken innate creativity: identification, information gathering, idea generation, idea evaluation and modification, and idea implementation (Zhou, & George, 2003).

Few teachers and learners in institutions of higher education have experienced teaching, learning, and managing knowledge with regard to inventive skills that refer to creating new ventures, markets, or products with new technologies. Invention creates opportunities for knowledge exchange in organisational and educational environments.

In an educational setting there are misunderstandings concerning the flow from creativity, invention and to innovation, their order and how these concepts are linked. These concepts are interrelated and usually the act of creation starts from a creative or inventive idea and continues to its application in the form of a process, product, or service.

In conclusion, invention is a creative idea and innovation is a process, an application of the idea through a product, process or service (Dobre, 2005). Invention without realisation through innovation means little or nothing (Brooks, 1982; Roberts, 2007; Dobre, 2005).

With the goal of fostering CII skills and the knowledge of learners, it is not only important to define CII, but also to identify and analyse the current state of teacher competence. Teacher competences, needs, and gaps will be discussed in the next section.

Teachers' Competences: Needs and Gaps

Owing to the misfortunes of policies, social and cultural uncertainty, the education system in Croatia for teachers-engineers' exhibit gaps regarding competences in line with facilitating and assessing new learning outcomes, such as creativity, invention and innovation, which have been researched further within the Croatian qualification framework (2009). Teachers-engineers exploit variations between widespread learning outcomes (factual knowledge, theoretical knowledge, social skills, cognitive skills, responsibility, and independence), individualising instruction and assessment as much as possible.

Practice indicates that teachers-engineers in technical and vocational schools in Croatia attend pedagogical courses as a part of their in-service training; they are, however, not sufficiently trained in terms of the facilitation of CII skills and knowledge, to learners. The products that come from teachers-engineers' entrepreneurial classrooms seldom pass the innovation barrier, which include the technological development, patenting and commercialisation stages. These realities create a poor perception of entrepreneurship education and so we need to search for new opportunities in order to build a new CII mentality.

To nurture CII and ensure application in a classroom environment, it is essential for educators to have a range of creative knowledge and skills all working together over a long span of time within and across grade levels and disciplines (Hope, 2010). The teacher's interpersonal competence, psycho-professional competences, and cultural competencies (Weisberg, 1986; Struyven & De Meyst, 2010; Keengwe, 2010) are necessary to facilitate the creative and innovative skills of learners. "Whereas, some competences are clearly present in the institutions' policies and practices (e.g. teacher as guide to learning and development, teacher as subject expert), others are poorly represented (e.g. teacher as partner of external parties and as a member of the educational community" (Struyven & De Meyst, 2010, and a teacher as a practically experienced entrepreneur).

Evident factors in reconsidering the competences of teachers-engineers are the perspectives of emotional intelligence, multicultural and international collaboration, which have been overlooked and rarely included through in-service training. Factors in engineering education are associated with a corresponding transdisciplinary knowledge environment, technological creativity, and business creativity support that can produce highly skilled, creative, and innovative engineers (Badran, 2007).

With the rapid progress of globalisation and technology, new learning outcomes, such as the skills of creativity and innovation, are becoming the major driving forces of competitive achievements in any society. This will be discussed in the following section.

Knowledge Empowerment: Creativity and Innovation as Learning Outcomes

Technology teachers in Croatia, who are exposed to the new Croatian qualifications framework, have been partially acquainted to facilitate creativity and innovation as new learning outcomes that are necessary for economic, social, and cultural endeavours (Croatian Qualification Framework, 2009). Perceptions of the 'educational system' as constraining creativity have been remarked on by a young, relatively inexperienced lecturer and also expressed by highly experienced professors (Kleiman, 2008).

Awareness of the need for a fresh approach is reflected in the standards and guidelines for quality assurance in the European Higher Education Area (ENQA, March 2005), which aim to develop learning outcomes with an emphasis on higher order thinking skills, including creativity and innovation. Furthermore, the Dearing Report (Dearing, 1997) indicates the need for technology in order to prepare this kind of creative and innovative workforce.

Creativity has been difficult to define in terms of quantification and it is unclear as an explicit learning outcome in the academic curriculum (McGoldrick, 2002; Knight, 2002). The term creativity is not related only to entrepreneurial creativity; it covers creativity in general and the creativity of teachers-engineers related to a technical-vocational context.

Creativity can be evaluated only over a long period of time and its management must take into account only long-term estimations (Srića, 1992, p. 69). The time set for learning tasks cannot be measured in terms of learning outcomes such as creativity and innovation. Thus, it is necessary to take into account self-assessment and group evaluation of creative work as well as measuring innovation through technology (Tovar, 2010).

These current perspectives on CII issues, as well as teachers-engineers' competence gaps in terms of facilitating new learning outcomes, provide a basis for the MCII framework.

SOLUTIONS AND RECOMMENDATIONS: FRAMEWORK FOR THE MODEL OF CREATIVITY, INVENTION, AND INNOVATION

This section gives more attention to the detailed framework for the intended MCII model through researching current theory and practice on knowledge exchange within technical-vocational and entrepreneurial education; recognising the set of guiding principles of a continuous professional teacher development framework; highlighting the dimensions of CII intelligence; encouraging the effectiveness of multicultural knowledge ex-

change within and between institutions, including international collaboration; as well as, involving the major components of teachers-engineers' competence necessary for enhancing the facilitation of a classroom's project dynamics and creating an appropriate climate for CII.

In order to ultimately equip teachers with the knowledge, skills, attitudes, and values necessary to improve their learners' CII, they need an understanding of different theoretical perspectives.

Theoretical Perspectives as a Basis for the Conceptual Model

This section explores multiple theoretical views on CII issues and the continuous professional teacher development CPTD model, in order to understand the theoretical stance on which a conceptual model has been based.

Theoretical Views on Creativity, Invention, and Innovation

A multiplicity of perspectives and theories exist that illuminate the importance of CII in an educational setting. Cognitive and practical apprenticeship indicate that effective learning means engaging in an authentic activity of a particular culture and knowledge-sharing between experts and novice learners through observation of practice (Collins, Hawkins, & Carver, 1991; Brown, Collins, & Duguid, 1989). Social learning theory (Bandura, 1975) focuses on gaining competence and developing meaning, rather than on creating innovations and inventions in school environments. Game theory suggests that when uncertainty about the future emerges, social actors increasingly weigh private benefits (Parkhe, 1993; Shubik, 1975). As uncertainty regarding the future prevails in developing countries and their education systems, it is possible that teachers will take note of the private benefits of knowledge-sharing and the practice of innovation.

Current theoretical views on creativity highlight two forms of thinking: convergent thinking (an exact logic for one solution of a problem) and divergent thinking (De Bono, 1990; Srića, 1992). Divergent thinking is like an architect approach when ideas are sketched and analysed and the best solution is taken. There are many divergent solutions; the cut-off is determined by time and imagination (Srića, 1992).

A theory of thinking supports vertical (step-by-step approach; a rational way of finding a solution to a problem; dividing a problem into parts) and lateral thinking (spontaneous associative thinking; intuition and subconscious thinking; precognitive knowledge; a vision) (De Bono, 1990). To enhance creativity it is important to find a balance between lateral and vertical thinking, where vertical thinking follows lateral. The biggest problem for inventive thinking is that vertical knowledge blocks lateral knowledge (Srića, 1992). The human inclination towards fragmented knowledge, caused also by information-processing incapability, is an obstacle to innovative practice (Jakovljevic, 2002).

Reinforcement theory (Zhang, Shu, Xu, & Malter, 2010) proposes that an individuals' behaviour is shaped by the presence of pleasurable consequences (rewards) and the absence of aversive ones (punishments). Consistent with the reinforcement theory, rewarding a contribution to a creative work influences the probability of innovative behaviour reoccurring. Rewarding creative and innovative work has been well supported in literature (Drucker, 1985; Holsappie, 1987).

Motivational compensation, the financial and nonfinancial nature of compensation stimulates innovation in people (Svoboda, 2006). Tidd and Bessant (2009) indicate the need for models of rewarding innovation through examples of good practice within big companies (for example, supporting a certain percentage of work on projects or research into interesting ideas).

The development of a well-structured theory is still in its infant stages and it is a long way from having a well-formed theory on CII issues in place. In addition, there is a need for the theory to explore how communities act and function when their primary purpose is not competence or knowledge but innovation (West, 2003; Werner, Ankiewicz, De Swardt, & Jakovljevic, 2012).

It is imperative to determine how these theoretical views and perspectives relate to teachers who are initiating, monitoring and leading creative work, inventive events and innovative processes. Continuous Professional Teacher Development (CPTD) could provide an answer and be the starting point in CII endeavours.

Continuous Professional Teacher Development as a Basis for the Model of Creativity, Invention, and Innovation

The existing problem is that technology teachers do not have the specific guidance to direct their practical and theoretical knowledge and experiences regarding CII as new learning outcomes. In this study, we start with technology teachers or teachers-engineers because of the nature of the CroSA project and the expertise of stakeholders. The Continuous Professional Teacher Development (CPTD) model for technology teachers developed in the South African educational environment will be adapted for teachers-engineers in technical and vocational schools in Zadar County, Croatia (Werner, Ankiewicz, De Swardt, & Jakovljevic, 2012)..

A CPTD model should include teachers' theoretical, practical and reflective experiences, taking into account their social and cultural backgrounds, as well as teamwork in a constructive training environment (Jakovljevic, 2007; Werner, et al., 2012). A well-planned CPTD could enhance teachers' school, discipline and pedagogic knowledge, skills, values and attitudes, as well as their personal subject construct.

A diversity of perspectives on CPTD exists in different educational systems (Jakovljevic, 2007). According to Cavan (2007) multiple partnerships in CPTD are working; for example, at Sheffield Hallam University, teachers are involved in projects in schools, which determine their portfolios for the allocation of credits. The projects are guided by a network of advisers, subject associations and mentors within 'in-school CPTD' and are extended through conferences and journals. Stein, McRobbie and Ginns (1999) provide an illustration of CPTD in Australian schools, which highlight the need for teachers' prior knowledge and beliefs with respect to teaching and learning (Werner, et al., 2012). Teachers-engineers in technical and vocational schools in Croatia can be trained to instil an innovative spirit into the minds of learners based on the CPTD criteria (Werner, et al., 2012). This will allow the teacher to create an appropriate environment for the enrichment of a creative climate for knowledge-sharing.

Learners differ not only in their expression, practice, and knowledge of creativity, but also in their ability to use creativity in their cognitive processes. This will be discussed in the section to follow.

The Construct of Creativity-Invention-Innovation Intelligence

Teachers and learners need a new approach that ensures that CII processes are brought together in a synergetic form. This synergy shapes a new construct of CII intelligence focusing on the four primary dimensions. The creativity-related competencies encompassed by CII intelligence can contribute to the efficient use and management of creativity in everyday classrooms situations. CII intelligence is defined through its four primary dimensions that are described in the following paragraphs:

1. **Estimation and communication of creativity, invention, and innovation:** The first dimension encompasses the ability to assess and express one's own creative ideas accurately, be aware of an inner creative force, appraise the creativity of others, and be empathetic in terms of the creative dilemmas of other people. Learners and teachers differ in their ability to accurately perceive, appraise, and express their own creative ideas and ideas experienced by other people.

2. **Practice of creativity, invention, and innovation processes:** The second dimension encompasses individual differences in the ability to use creative ideas to facilitate cognitive processes. CII intelligence provides learners with the capability to use creative processes in synergy with thinking processes to contribute to effective information processing and knowledge exchange. A learner with low CII intelligence is unable to convince someone of what he or she is doing in a productive manner.

3. **Knowledge of creativity, invention, and innovation:** The third dimension of CII intelligence relates to individual differences in their understanding and reasoning about creativity, innovation, and particularly invention. Individuals with a high CII intelligence (Zhou & George, 2003) have a good understanding of invention and innovation processes and the causes and consequences of the creative behaviour experienced by themselves and by others. Armed with this knowledge, such individuals are able to take advantage of creative ideas without being unduly influenced by temporary and extreme infertile ideas that are short-lived.

4. **Management of creativity, invention, and innovation:** The fourth dimension of CII intelligence is related to the fact that people try to manage or control their creative processes. While creative reactions are functional in that they provide meaning, unmanaged creative ideas can interfere with effective information processing. Managing the creative process of learners is also critically important for teachers as they have a role to play of both sensing and signalling

where creative attention should be focused. Thus, CII intelligence enables teachers and learners not only to use creative ideas but also to manage them.

As would be expected, the four dimensions of CII intelligence are related to one another. They are linked together and treated as an integrated and coherent whole. The teacher possessing all four dimensions of CII intelligence has the opportunity to communicate with the entrepreneurial environment that can trigger 'knowledge fermentation,' and therefore, through knowledge sharing and transfer of these factors, increase the teacher-human capital. Learners' CII knowledge and skills can be accessed through self-assessment, portfolios of their work (Gardner, 1999), selected response items, records of class participation and portfolios of the engineering design process.

While we have included the construct of CII intelligence in the conceptual model, it remains an empirical question as to how teachers-engineers' CII construct can be improved through appropriate training. Teachers-engineers can be trained not only how to estimate and communicate their creative ideas, but also how to practise and manage them.

In today's fast-paced, driven world, innovation is both a desired trait and a necessity for survival. This could be achieved through joint institutional and international collaboration.

Joint Institutional and International Collaboration

Two elements for fostering creativity in entrepreneurial education have been identified and discussed in the next section: interdisciplinary sharing and knowledge transfer of CII, as well as, the various links between the network of stakeholders namely: entrepreneurs, government bodies, and educational institutions.

Interdisciplinary Sharing and Transferring Knowledge of Creativity, Invention, and Innovation

Teachers who face contextual barriers struggle to share and translate innovative knowledge obtained from colleagues in different fields. An innovative practice in one discipline could be transferred to another discipline through homological transfer (Mende, 2006).

In the organisational learning process, a person's sense of innovation, spirit of cooperation and sense of character often have heightened importance (Allam, 2008; Scott & Bruce, 1994). Organisational learning is categorised by three stages: individual learning, solving problems in a team setting and solving problems by interacting with an external environment (Yeo, 2005). Merely sharing and transferring knowledge in institutions is not enough if it is not effectively applied to solving problems and delivering products and services (Choi, Lee, & Yoo, 2010) across international collaboration. These aspects are frequently overlooked in technical-vocational education and may have disastrous effects on the quality of fostering CII.

It is possible to form a group of scientists to act as 'knowledge intermediaries' or brokers by sharing knowledge across disciplines and institutions. As Meso and Smith (2000) propose for organisations, teachers can be organised into interdisciplinary teams that may interact formally or informally.

In the next section we move to discuss the network of stakeholders who are concerned in supporting innovative practice in educational institutions.

The Network of Stakeholders: Entrepreneurs, Government Bodies, and Educational Institutions

There is a missing link between entrepreneurs, government bodies, and educational institutions in developing countries such as Croatia. All stakeholders involved (learners, teachers at high schools and education departments, entrepreneurs, and government officials) are interested in creating value through innovative products or services. CII knowledge-sharing issues could unite all parties' efforts within and between institutions (Boswell & Bondreau, 2001) where the proposed CPTD model plays a role (Ankiewicz & De Swardt, 2002).

Multiple networks (educational institutions, government and business bodies) encompass the body of individual and collective learning that ensure the creation of new CII knowledge, enhancing the school and/or institution's knowledge base. The effective use of networks and scattered individual knowledge of innovation can increase the school's capital, mobilising the enthusiasm for innovation and entrepreneurship of the teachers and learners. Through this network, teachers-engineers can be taught how to advance the spirit of entrepreneurship and innovation among learners. It is necessary, however, to initiate new communication dialogues on all levels between teachers, their colleagues, business partners and learners. Enhancing the potential of teachers and learners through promoting entrepreneurship could further improve their interest in innovation; if entrepreneurs have a passion for innovation that may aid their creative efforts and persistency (Baum, et al., 2004; Morrison, et al., 2006).

An international collaboration feature has been added to this network of stakeholders, so that the focus of knowledge generation and transfer related to CII has a wider scope. Collaborating with South African institutions through the CroSA project means building alliances (Parkhe, 1993; Simonin, 1999), forming joint ventures, and establishing knowledge links with educational and business partners. An external or an internal source is subject to perceptual filters (norms, values, and procedures) that positively influence knowledge acquisition (McNabb, 2007).

This leads to a discussion of teachers' competence that comprises emotional intelligence, leadership skills and entrepreneurial project management skills, amongst many other features.

Teacher's Competence in Terms of Promoting the Features of Creativity, Invention, and Innovation

Emotional Intelligence and Leadership Skills

Emotional intelligence is the management of the emotions of oneself and the emotions of others (Goleman, 1998; George, 2000; Mayer, Salovay, & Caruso, 2000). Emotional intelligence involves the following features: praising and expressing emotion, awareness of verbally and nonverbally expressed emotions, regulation of emotions in the self and others, utilising emotions to provide flexibility in planning, creativity in thinking, motivation, and the ability to redirect attention (Mayer, et al., 2000). According to Zhou and George (2003) and Woodman, Sawyer, and Griffin (1993) engaging in creativity in organisations inevitably creates tension, conflict and emotionally charged debates. This is happening in technical-vocational classrooms.

It seems that self-awareness and intellectual stimulation can influence emotional intelligence (MacKenzie, Podsakoff, & Rich, 2001). Goleman (1998) suggests that emotional intelligence is indeed a trainable skill. In addition, positive emotions may enhance entrepreneurial creativity, which can aid in the recognition of new opportunities (Drucker, 1985; Morrison, et al., 2006). Not only do teachers, as leaders, have to show emotional intelligence; learners too should be trained to control their emotions, which will contribute to innovation and invention outcomes and improve their entrepreneurial creativity.

Research on creativity (Lubart, 2001; Drazin, Glynn, & Kazanjian, 1999) indicates the responsibility of leaders in an organization to support creative ideas (Zhou & George, 2003), however, teachers' responsibilities for creative work and innovation has been unclear. Good leadership can streamline the innovation process, set performance expectations and lead to inspirational motivation. Leadership is "intrinsically an emotional process, where leaders display emotion and attempt to evoke emotion in their members" (Dasborough & Ashkanasy, 2002, p. 615).

Thus, leading a group of people is an emotional process; showing and evoking emotions in project team members (Dasborough & Ashkanasy, 2002, p. 615) is appropriate for an innovation group as a means of raising levels of optimism and enthusiasm for innovation (Aranson, Reilly, & Lynn, 2006). The authors Scott and Bruce (1994) showed that a high-quality communication exchange between a leader and his or her employees was positively related to the innovative behaviour exhibited by the employees.

Teachers can employ various methods and techniques to capture, develop, embrace, and harness innovation.

Teacher Creativity Empowerment Skills to Unlock Creative Inspiration

The potential for creativity resides in all of us (Zhou & George, 2003). The teacher has to recognise the particular times of day that are especially conducive to focus on creative work. The appropriate time, familiar objects, surroundings and other stimuli are associative triggers for innovative states of mind, but these differ among learners. Thus, teachers also have to understand diverse individual requirements in order to achieve the mental alertness necessary for focused creative work. People are most creative primarily via intrinsic motivation (Amabile, 1983; Tierney, Farmer, & Graen, 1999).

Furthermore, it is necessary to pay attention to key elements to unlock creative inspiration, such as: discipline, routine for creative work, one's own efficiency/construction system and spontaneity (McGuinness, 2011; Allam, 2008). Innovation is a product of the heart and brain, so when people realize that they are not forced to follow rigid routines their CII intelligence rises astoundingly.

In developing inspiration for learners' creative work, it is necessary to prepare a plan with a self-questioning approach, for example: What is the role of routines and systems in your creative work? How do you leave room for spontaneity? How can one recognise an idea? How can one give a credit for inventing an idea?

The teacher-engineer can support a project team of learners so that they present an innovative idea in front of internal or external judges. If an idea is given the green light, it is immediately rewarded financially. If an idea has not been successful, it is placed into an innovation box so that others can use it in shaping new ideas or building on old ones. Some ideas can be streamlined for further research and some ideas are discarded.

Innovative teachers motivate learners to pursue entrepreneurship within their profession and to harness "functional" creativity within an entrepreneurial initiative. Thus, there is a need to explain how teachers act and function with innovative learners when their primary purpose is not competence or knowledge, but innovation.

In order to unlock creative inspiration, teachers must be familiar with project type work, as projects are equated with creativity and innovation (Akgun, et al., 2007; Bis, 2009).

Entrepreneurial Project Management Skills: Knowledge Exchange within Innovative Projects Teams

Innovations prosper within group work, because the complexity of tasks is overwhelming for the cognitive capabilities of an individual (Prester, 2010; Tidd & Bessant, 2009). Group innovation shows that innovation does not occur accidentally (Hoegl, Ernst, & Proserpio, 2007, p. 163). Sometimes an individual can produce more results than a group (Aranson, Reilly, & Lynn, 2006, p. 241).

Multidisciplinary teams have been on the rise, who can solve problems from different perspectives (Svoboda, 2006). A project team should be like a symphony orchestra; team players are playing in a dynamic environment and a plan of play is written during the exercise (Srića, 1992). Management, therefore, may choose organisational forms such as project teams (Felin, Zenger, & Tomsik, 2009).

Project teams are not always solutions, as there may be personal disagreements, weak engagement, and poor management of the innovation process. In this sense, teachers-engineers need superior project management skills. In addition, success depends on resources and the strategies of innovation, research and development (Prester, 2010). The right choice of team members must be made and the roles and tasks of members must be clear (Akgun, Byrne, Lynn, & Keskin, 2007; Morgenson, Reider, & Campion, 2005); for example, an innovation champion is a person or group energetic and enthusiastic enough to inspire and keep the spark of innovation going within his team. Furthermore, a leader must be motivated and have technical knowledge, an innovation sponsor, a technological keeper or communicator (Prester, 2010).

Allowing individuals to self-select projects they see as opportunities either to accumulate or to create knowledge is vital for the knowledge economy (Felin, Zenger, & Tomsik, 2009). A person can see the world from a different perspective, feel part of a live eco-system, listen to, adjust and feel comfortable in dialogues, and use intuition in synergy (Martinka, 2006). Thus, a network of a variety of knowledge interactions (Simonin, 1999) can minimise the high percentage of project failure (Tidd, Bessant, & Pavitt, 2005).

Having discussed the key features of how to how to support projects for innovations, we now turn to an environment of a creative climate.

An Appropriate Environment for the Enrichment of a Creative Climate through Knowledge-Sharing

Environmental Stimulants and Inhibitors of the Creative Knowledge-Sharing Climate

Researchers indicate (for example, Srića, 1992; Dobre, 2005) that the development of an innovation climate should not rely on sudden inspiration or fortunate surroundings. Instead, an innovation environment is continually created if teachers and learners are ready to disclaim old rules, habits, and traditions within the school's overall innovative climate.

The Work Environment Inventory (WEI) and environmental stimulants for creativity developed by Amabile and Gryskiewicz (1989) could be applied to motivate teachers-engineers. The WEI includes aspects such as freedom, challenges, resources, supervisor, co-workers, recognition, unity and co-operation, and support for creativity. Teachers-engineers' motivation for innovative work depends on organised creative work, the right climate and techniques for creative thinking. A creative climate is easier to change and it includes repetitive forms of behaviour, attitudes, and feelings that characterise life in the institution (Akkermans, 2008).

The creative climate also depends on micro- and macro-factors. Macro-factors of creativity are political, as are economic factors, the level of democracy and freedom of thought, stability of the legal system and the legislature, and the quality of infrastructure (communication, scientific, financial, transport, educational) (Dobre, 2005, p. 23). Dobre (2005) mentions micro-factors necessary for a creative climate such as motivation for creative thinking and work, quality of innovation potential, leadership within the organisation or institution and the application of modern techniques in the organisational and school environment. Micro-factors help, stimulate, and make it easier for individuals to be creative in an organisation or school; macro-factors of creativity provide opportunities for individuals to develop optimal creative capabilities and realise their potential with the help of a healthy economic and social environment (Dobre, 2005).

There are nine 'environmental obstacles' that inhibit creativity, namely an inappropriate reward system, lack of freedom, organisational disinterest, poor project management, inappropriate evaluation processes, insufficient resources, time constraints, overemphasis on the status quo, and competition (Amabile, et al., 1989).

Good communication, risk-taking, and a free learning atmosphere that includes trial-and-error brainstorming can stimulate the development of a creative environment. Methods to create an innovative knowledge-sharing classroom are essential to achieve this creative environment and will be described in the following section.

An Innovative Knowledge-Sharing Classroom: A Personal Creativity-Innovation Plan

"[A genius] does not know himself how he has come by his ideas, and he has not the power to devise the like at pleasure or in accordance with a plan" (Rothenberg & Hausman, 1976, p. 38). Innovative inspiration cannot be planned for a meeting and can hardly happen during management meetings. These ideas still prevail in educational environments.

An innovative classroom is a secure environment with an innovative teacher where the biggest enemies to creativity (fear of critics, ridicule,

and retrenchment) have been removed. In an innovative classroom learners should develop a 'personal innovation plan' aimed at achieving a better understanding of themselves and of how to recognise and drive their own creativity through self-awareness in future project team and business settings.

An innovative classroom involves learners in new operational ideas, new ways to perform tasks, new product-specific technologies, new manufacturing processes and new marketing-specific products and processes. In an innovative classroom, teachers can plan many activities, for example, introducing and practising creative thinking with the class, developing an invention idea, brainstorming for creative solutions, practising the critical parts of creative thinking, completing and naming the invention and generating marketing activities (Bis, 2009). Many creative knowledge-sharing techniques are used in an innovative classroom, such as free association, comparison, analysis with a list of activities, question lists, peculiar questions, and imitation of ideas, breaking up ideas into parts, group, or individual ideas.

In an innovative classroom, learners could examine both 'entrepreneurial' (start-up and growth) companies and larger global organisations with 'intrapreneurial' departments, projects, and 'spin-outs.' They could chart the lifecycle and time-line of the typical innovative start-up project teams or organisations and explore innovation at each stage of development from product design, development through to manufacturing, financing, marketing, and sales.

An innovative classroom depends on a wider knowledge-sharing environment in schools. These schools could be known as 'intelligent learning factories' that present a new innovative environment and an ideal place for the fulfilment of the CII cycle within project teams.

Schools as "Intelligent Learning Factories": A New Environment for Knowledge Management

Researchers propose that information sophistication and integration lead to an intercreative society (Srića, 1992; Machlup, 1981). An intercreative society is a disciplined society where control of supervision has been transferred to people with the ability to obtain information and undertake qualitative analysis (Srića, 1992). An intercreative society has schools, which are intelligent factories. Intelligent factories have laboratories with the purpose to research ideas. An idea becomes an invention if it is functional in laboratory conditions.

Thus, schools are transforming themselves into intelligent factories. An example is a vocational school in Zadar County that collaborates in the CroSA project. The school has started an entrepreneurial venture in its workshops by designing and manufacturing furniture. Teachers-engineers have formed innovative project teams within the school that design, develop, and sell their product or service.

The above are some key aspects of the technical-vocational educational environment that may influence the motivation of teachers-engineers to undertake multiple knowledge exchange activities in ascertaining the driving influence on the CII climate. Having discussed CII teaching issues, we now turn to a conceptual model for facilitating creativity, invention, and innovation that is in line with the theme set out in the introduction.

A Conceptual Model for Creativity, Invention, and Innovation

Based on the theoretical framework, an MCII model has been created that provides a logical structure and the flow of the issues previously identified in theory and practice. The components within the model may help teachers-engineers to deliver a positive psychological contract and entrepreneurial projects within wide international and institutional knowledge exchange environment. The model provides a wide perspective necessary for the design of teachers-engineers' knowledge exchange, as well as the facilitation of new learning outcomes within entrepreneurial educational settings (see Figure 1).

The Structure and the Flow of the Conceptual Model for Facilitating Creativity, Invention, and Innovation

The conceptual model for entrepreneurial education from a knowledge management perspective consists of five major subsystems with their corresponding components, namely:

a. **The subsystem of theoretical perspectives on CII as a basis for the conceptual model** (game theory, theories on thinking and creativity, social-learning theory, reinforcement theory, cognitive and practical apprenticeship, the CPTD model)

b. **The subsystem of the four dimensions of CII intelligence** (estimation and communication; practice of CII processes; knowledge and management of CII)

c. **The subsystem of joint institutional and international collaboration** (departments of education at two universities; chambers of commerce; technical and vocational high schools; business/industry)

d. **The subsystem of teachers' competence in terms of promoting knowledge sharing of CII features in interdisciplinary education** (emotional intelligence, leadership skills, creativity empowerment skills, entrepreneurial project management skills).

e. **The subsystem of an appropriate environment for the enrichment of a creative climate through knowledge sharing** (creative climate, stimulants and inhibitors of creativity, innovative knowledge-sharing classroom, schools as intelligent learning factories)

The components of subsystems contain corresponding sub-features as indicated in this chapter. The philosophy of innovative theories and practice underpins these components to ensure their integration and an ordered flow. These subsystems and components work in a synergy which could positively influence teachers-engineers' competence in order to build up CII learning outcomes within entrepreneurial education. Cross-cultural collaboration could lead to the empowerment of teachers-engineers' creativity, an enhanced creative climate, teachers-engineers' innovative knowledge-culture and entrepreneur mobility (see Figure 1).

CONCLUSION AND FUTURE RESEARCH DIRECTIONS

The MCII model provides a holistic view of the CII knowledge sharing in the context of collaboration between educational, business and institutions

Figure 1. Conceptual model of creativity, invention, and innovation for entrepreneurial education from a knowledge management perspective

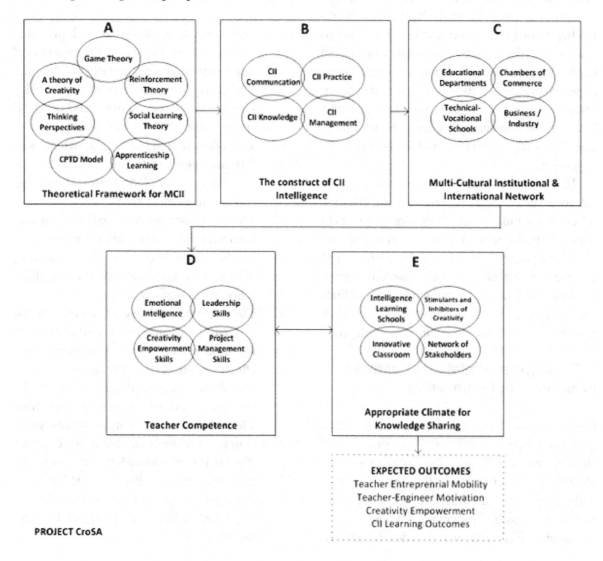

placed in different geographic, cultural, and social environments that aid in the recognition of new opportunities and survival in global competition. Knowledge management of CII aspects and outcomes will benefit from this joint international collaboration and a network of stakeholders. In addition, CII intelligence, while relatively new to scholarly literature, can manifest itself in an ensemble with the effective use and management of creativity in everyday life.

In this sense teacher-engineer competence plays a crucial role, namely:

a. In terms of innovation knowledge culture dealing with the systems of values, beliefs and norms based on the acknowledgement of the importance of knowledge innovation;

b. In terms of CII intelligence based on the four crucial dimensions that determine the success of fostering invention and innovation progression; and

c. In terms of professional knowledge of newer methodologies of teaching, such as the project-entrepreneurial approach in order to facilitate CII skills.

The CroSA project, with the CPTD as its basis and the MCII as its product, allows for expansion of the socio-cultural context through international cross-cultural sharing of knowledge and experience with other people, which could empower teachers-engineers particularly in terms of new learning outcomes. These facts pose intriguing challenges and opportunities for teachers-engineers' educational systems.

Through the CroSA project and the MCII we are developing a coordinated and integrated knowledge environment and the result of this process is an enhanced knowledge-sharing of innovation and invention. Through the MCII and the CroSA project we can build a macro-culture through innovation, cultivate an innovative environment, influence policies and programmes and train teachers-engineers in terms of CII knowledge management.

The MCII with its construct of CII intelligence within the CroSA project has been an attempt at fostering and sharing CII knowledge among teachers and business partners across cultures. The MCII and an adapted CPTD model form the starting point, aimed at near practical applications in vocational and technical schools in Zadar County. The true quality of the MCII is impossible to accurately assess *a priori*, and can only be understood fully after engaging in international collaboration, real world observations, and the results of teacher-engineer's in-service training.

Future research should focus on CII as learning outcomes in interdisciplinary education. Further research opportunities exist in terms of deepening the study of CII intelligence and its dimensions. In addition, it is necessary to investigate the application of the MCII and its influence on the emotional intelligence of learners and teachers. Learning outcomes such as creativity, innovation, critical thinking etc need careful investigation and measurable performance indicators.

ACKNOWLEDGMENT

Special thanks to Marko Jakovljevic of the Flamewave group for his in-depth comments and thoughtful criticisms that have been invaluable.

REFERENCES

Akgun, A. E., Byrne, J. C., Lynn, G. S., & Keskin, H. (2007). Team stressors, management support, and project and process outcomes in new development projects. *Techinnovation*, *27*(10), 628–639. doi:10.1016/j.technovation.2007.02.008

Akkermans, H. (2008). *Organizational climate as an intervening variable between leadership behaviour and innovative productivity: An exploratory study*. Retrieved 15 May, 2011, from http:77www.s-d.be/assets/Thesissen-HR-Award-2009/HUBrusselHnsAkkermans.pdf

Allam, C. (2008). *Creative activity and its impact on student learning – Issues of implementation learning and teaching services*. Sheffield, UK: University of Sheffield.

Amabile, T. M. (1983). *The social psychology of creativity*. New York, NY: Basic Books. doi:10.1007/978-1-4612-5533-8

Amabile, T. M., & Gryskiewicz, N. D. (1989). The creative environment scales: Work environment inventory. *Creativity Research Journal, 2*, 231–253. doi:10.1080/10400418909534321

Ankiewicz, P. J., & De Swardt, A. E. (2002). *Aspects to be taken into account when compiling a learning programme to support effective facilitation of technology education*. Paper presented at the National Conference for Technology Teachers. Durban, South Africa.

Aranson, Z. H., Reilly, R. R., & Lynn, G. S. (2006). The impact of leader personality on new product development teamwork and performance: The moderating role of uncertainty. *Journal of Engineering and Technology Management, 23*(3), 221–247. doi:10.1016/j.jengtecman.2006.06.003

Badran, I. (2007). Enhancing creativity and innovation in engineering education. *European Journal of Engineering Education, 32*(5), 573–585. doi:10.1080/03043790701433061

Bandura, A. (1977). *Social learning theory*. Englewood Cliffs, NJ: Prentice-Hall.

Baum, J. R. (2003*). Entrepreneurs' start-up cognitions and behaviours: Dreams, surprises, shortages, and fast zigzags*. Paper presented at the Babson-Kauffman Entrepreneurship Research Conference. Wellesley, MA.

Baum, J. R., & Locke, E. A. (2004). The relationship of entrepreneurial traits, skill, and motivation to subsequent venture growth. *The Journal of Applied Psychology, 89*(4), 587–598. doi:10.1037/0021-9010.89.4.587

Bis, R. (2009). Financing innovation: A project finance approach to funding patentable innovation. *Intellectual Property & Technology Law Journal, 21*(11), 23–45.

Boswell, W. R., & Bondreau, J. W. (2001). How leading companies create, measure and achieve strategic results through 'line of sight'. *Measurement Decision, 39*(10), 851–859. doi:10.1108/EUM0000000006525

Brooks, H. (1982). *Social and technological innovation*. New York, NY: Pergamon Press.

Brown, J. S., Collins, A., & Duguid, P. (1989). Situated cognition and the culture of learning. *Educational Researcher, 18*(1), 32–42.

Cardon, M. (2008). Is passion contagious? The transference of entrepreneurial passion to employees. *Human Resource Management Review, 18*, 77–86. doi:10.1016/j.hrmr.2008.04.001

Cavan, S. (2007). *Networking with other parties – Developing strategic partnerships*. Paper presented at the International Conference in Educator Lifelong Learning, Kwazulu-Natal Education. Durban, South Africa.

Choi, S. Y., Lee, H., & Yoo, Y. (2010). The impact of information technology and tran active memory systems on knowledge sharing, application, and team performance: A field study. *Management Information Systems Quarterly, 34*(4), 855–870.

Collins, A., Hawkins, J., & Carver, S. (1991). A cognitive apprenticeship for disadvantaged students. In Means, B. (Ed.), *Teaching Advanced Skills to Disadvantaged Students* (pp. 216–243). San Francisco, CA: Jossey-Bass.

Dasborough, M. T., & Ashkanasy, N. M. (2002). Emotion and attribution of intentionality in leader–member relationships. *The Leadership Quarterly, 13*, 615–634. doi:10.1016/S1048-9843(02)00147-9

De Bono, E. (1990). *Lateral thinking for management*. London, UK: Penguin Books.

Dobre, R. (2005). *Inovacije, tehnološke promjene i strategije*. Šibenik, Croatia: Školska knjiga.

Drazin, R., Glynn, M. A., & Kazanjian, R. K. (1999). Multilevel theorizing about creativity in organizations: A sense making perspective. *Academy of Management Review, 24*, 286–307.

Drucker, P. (1985). The discipline of innovation. *Harvard Business Review, 5*(6), 25–45.

Felin, T., Zenger, T. R., & Tomsik, J. (2009). The knowledge economy, emerging organizational forms, missing micro foundations, and key considerations for managing human capital. *Human Resource Management, 48*(4), 555–570. doi:10.1002/hrm.20299

Frigda, N. H. (1988). The laws of emotion. *The American Psychologist, 43*, 349–358. doi:10.1037/0003-066X.43.5.349

Gardner, H. (1999, November 5). Multiple intelligences. *Atlantic Monthly*.

George, J. M. (2000). Emotions and leadership: The role of emotional intelligence. *Human Relations, 53*, 1027–1055. doi:10.1177/0018726700538001

Goleman, D. (1998). *Working with emotional intelligence*. London, UK: Bloomsbury Publishing.

Government of Croatia. (2009). *Croatian qualifications framework*. Zagreb, Croatia: Government of the Republic of Croatia, Ministry of Science, Education, and Sports.

Grigorenko, E. L., & Sternberg, R. J. (2001). Analytical, creative, and practical intelligence as predictors of self–reported adaptive functioning: A case study in Russia. *Intelligence, 29*, 57–73. doi:10.1016/S0160-2896(00)00043-X

Guilford, J. P. (1950). Creativity research: Past, present, and future. *The American Psychologist, 5*, 444–454. doi:10.1037/h0063487

Hoegl, M., Ernst, H., & Proserpio, P. (2007). How teamwork matters more as team member dispersion increases? *Journal of Product Innovation Management, 24*(2), 156–165. doi:10.1111/j.1540-5885.2007.00240.x

Holsappie, C. (1987). *Knowledge management organization and the information society*. London, UK: Taylor & Francis.

Hope, S. (2010). Symposium: Teaching creativity, creativity, content, and policy. *Arts Education Policy Review, 111*, 39–47. doi:10.1080/10632910903455736

Jakovljevic, M. (2002). *An instructional model for teaching complex thinking through web page design*. Unpublished Doctoral Dissertation. Johannesburg, South Africa: Rand Afrikaans University.

Jakovljevic, M. (2007). *CPTD report. Unpublished article*. Johannesburg, South Africa: University of Johannesburg.

Johnson, B. (1992). Institutional learning. In Lundvall, B.-A. (Ed.), *National Systems of Innovation – Towards a Theory of Innovation and Interactive Learning* (pp. 23–44). London, UK: Pinter Publishers.

Johnson, P. S. (1975). *The economic invention and innovation*. London, UK: Martin Robertson & Company.

Keengwe, J. (2010). Fostering cross cultural competence in preservice teachers through multicultural education experiences. *Early Childhood Education Journal, 38*(3), 197–204. doi:10.1007/s10643-010-0401-5

Kleiman, P. (2008). Towards transformation: Conceptions of creativity in higher education. *Educational Media International, 45*(3), 177–194.

Knight, P. (2002). *The idea of a creative curriculum*. Retrieved February 4, 2011, from http://www.palatine.ac.uk/files/999.pdf

Lubart, T. I. (2001). Models of the creative process: Past, present, and future. *Creativity Research Journal*, *13*, 295–308. doi:10.1207/ S15326934CRJ1334_07

Machlup, F. (1981). *Knowledge and knowledge production*. Princeton, NJ: Princeton University Press.

MacKenzie, S. B., Podsakoff, N. P., & Rich, G. A. (2001). Transformational and transactional leadership and salesperson performance. *Journal of the Academy of Marketing Science*, *29*(2), 115–134. doi:10.1177/03079459994506

Martinka, V. (2006). *Inovacije članak: Praksa inoviranja*. Retrieved July 2011, from http://www. quantum21.net

Mayer, J. D., Salovey, P., & Caruso, D. (2000). Models of emotional intelligence. In Sternberg, R. (Ed.), *Handbook of Human Intelligence* (pp. 396–420). New York, NY: Cambridge University Press.

McGoldrick, C. (2002). Creativity and curriculum design: What academics think? York, UK: LTSN Generic Centre. Retrieved May 2011, from http:// www.palatine.ac.uk/files/1038.pdf

McGuinness, M. (2011). *RSS creativity, routines, systems, spontaneity*. Retrieved 10 August 2011, from http://the99percent.com/tips/6127/rss-creativity-routines-systems-spontaneity

McNabb, D. E. (2007). *Knowledge management in the public sector: A blueprint for innovation in government*. New York, NY: M.E. Sharpe, Inc.

Mende, J. (2006). *Using inference trees to detect reasoning errors in expository reports*. Paper presented at the Teaching and Learning Conference, CLTD. Johannesburg, South Africa.

Meso, P., & Smith, R. (2000). A resource-based view of organizational knowledge management systems. *Journal of Knowledge Management*, *4*(3), 224–234. doi:10.1108/13673270010350020

Morgenson, F. P., Reider, M. H., & Campion, M. A. (2005). Selecting individuals in team settings: The importance of social skills, personality characteristics and team performance. *Personnel Psychology*, *58*, 583–611. doi:10.1111/j.1744-6570.2005.655.x

Morrison, A., & Johnston, B. (2006). Personal creativity for entrepreneurship: Teaching and learning strategies. *Active Learning in Higher Education*, *4*, 145–158. doi:10.1177/1469787403004002003

Parkhe, A. (1993). Strategic alliances structuring: A game theoretic and transaction cost examination of infirm cooperation. *Academy of Management Journal*, *38*(4), 794–829. doi:10.2307/256759

Prester, J. (2010). *Management of innovations*. Zagreb, Croatia: Sinergija, nakladništvo, d o.o.

Report, D. (2007). *Dearing*. Retrieved May 2011, from http://www.bbc.co.uk/news/special// politics97/news/07/0723

Roberts, E. (2007). Managing invention and innovation. *Research Technology Management*, *50*, 35–54.

Rothenberg, A., & Hausman, C. R. (1976). *The creativity question*. Durham, NC: Duke University Press.

Russell, J. A., & Barrett, L. F. (1999). Core affect, prototypical emotional episodes, and other things called emotion: Dissecting the elephant. *Journal of Personality and Social Psychology*, *76*(5), 805–819. doi:10.1037/0022-3514.76.5.805

Šajeva, S. (2010). The analysis of key elements of socio-technical knowledge management system. *Ekonomika IR Vadyba*, *15*, 765–775.

Scott, S. G., & Bruce, R. A. (1994). Determinants of innovative behaviour: A path model of individual innovation in the workplace. *Academy of Management Journal*, *37*, 580–607. doi:10.2307/256701

Shubik, M. (1975). *Games for society, business, and war: Toward a theory of gaming*. New York, NY: Elsevier.

Simonin, B. L. (1999). Ambiguity and the process of knowledge transfer in strategic alliances. *Strategic Management Journal, 20*(7), 595–623. doi:10.1002/(SICI)1097-0266(199907)20:7<595::AID-SMJ47>3.0.CO;2-5

Srića, V. (1992). *Upravljanje kreativnošću*. Zagreb, Croatia: Školska knjiga.

Stein, S. J., McRobbie, C. J., & Ginns, I. (1999). *A model for the professional development of teachers in design and technology*. Paper presented at the Annual Conference of the Australian Association for Research in Education, New Zealand Association for Research in Education. Melbourne, Australia.

Sternberg, R. J., & Lubart, T. I. (1999). The concepts of creativity: Prospects and paradigms. In Sternberg, R. J. (Ed.), *The Handbook of Creativity* (pp. 3–15). Cambridge, UK: Cambridge University Press.

Struyven, K., & De Meyst, M. (2010). Competence-based teacher education: Illusion or reality? An assessment of the implementation status in Flanders from teachers' and students' points of view. *Teaching and Teacher Education, 26*(8), 1495–1510. doi:10.1016/j.tate.2010.05.006

Svoboda, R. (2006). *Inovacije: Inovativnost - uvažavanje kreativnosti svih zaposlenika*. Retrieved December 2006, from http://www.quantum21.net

Tidd, J., & Bessant,, J. (2009). *Managing innovation*. West Sussex, UK: John Wiley & Sons.

Tidd, J., Bessant, J., & Pavitt, K. (2005). *Managing innovations*. West Sussex, UK: Wiley.

Tierney, P., Farmer, S. M., & Graen, G. B. (1999). An examination of leadership and employee creativity: The relevance of traits and relationships. *Personnel Psychology, 52*, 591–620. doi:10.1111/j.1744-6570.1999.tb00173.x

Tovar, J. J. (2010). How to measure innovation? New evidence of the technology growth linkage. *UK Research in Economics, 64*, 81–96.

Weisberg, R. W. (1986). *Creativity genius and other myths*. New York, NY: Freman.

Werner, R., Ankiewicz, P. J., De Swardt, E., & Jakovljevic, M. (2012). *A theoretical framework for continuing professional teacher development (CPTD)*. Johannesburg, South Africa: University of Johannesburg.

West, M. A. (2003). Innovation implementation in work teams. In Paulus, P. B., & Nijstad, B. A. (Eds.), *Group Creativity*. Oxford, UK: Oxford University Press. doi:10.1093/acprof:oso/9780195147308.003.0012

Woodman, R. W., Sawyer, J. E., & Griffin, R. W. (1993). Toward a theory of organizational creativity. *Academy of Management Review, 18*, 293–321.

Yeo, R. K. (2005). Revisiting the roots of learning organization: A synthesis of the learning organization literature. *The Learning Organization, 12*(4), 368–382. doi:10.1108/09696470510599145

Zhang, H., Xu, S. J., & Malter, A. J. (2010). Managing knowledge for innovation: The role of cooperation, competition and alliance nationality. *Journal of International Marketing, 18*(4), 74–94. doi:10.1509/jimk.18.4.74

Zhou, J., & George, J. M. (2003). Awakening employee creativity: The role of leader emotional intelligence. *The Leadership Quarterly, 14*, 545–568. doi:10.1016/S1048-9843(03)00051-1

ADDITIONAL READING

Barron, F., & Harrington, D. M. (1981). Creativity, intelligence, and personality. *Annual Review of Psychology, 32*, 439–476. doi:10.1146/annurev. ps.32.020181.002255

Baum, J. R., Locke, E. A., & Smith, K. G. (2001). A multidimensional model of venture growth. *Academy of Management Journal, 44*(2), 292–303. doi:10.2307/3069456

Cha, S. H., Pingry, D. E., & Thatcher, M. E. (2008). Managing the knowledge supply chain: An organizational learning model of information technology offshore outsourcing. *Management Information Systems Quarterly, 32*(2), 281–306.

Chen, C. K., Jiang, B. C., & Hsu, K. Y. (2005). An empirical study of industrial engineering and management curriculum reform in fostering students' creativity. *European Journal of Engineering Education, 30*, 191–202. doi:10.1080/03043790500087423

Clegg, P. (2007). Creativity and critical thinking in the globalised university. *European Journal of Engineering Education, 32*(5), 573–585.

Drucker, P. F. (1985). *Innovation and entrepreneurship: Practice and principles.* New York, NY: Harper and Row, Publishers.

Durcikova, A., & Gray, P. (2009). How knowledge validation processes affect knowledge contribution. *Journal of Management Information Systems, 25*(4), 81–107. doi:10.2753/MIS0742-1222250403

Eisenstein, N. (1985). Effects of contractual, endogenous, or unexpected rewards on high and low interest preschoolers. *The Psychological Record, 35*, 29–39.

ENQA. (2005). *Standards and guidelines for quality assurance in the European higher education area.* ENQA.

Laat, M., & Broer, W. (2004). COPs for COPs: Managing and creating knowledge through networked expertise. In Hildreth, P. M., & Kimble, C. (Eds.), *Knowledge Networks: Innovation through Communities of Practice* (pp. 58–69). Hershey, PA: IGI Global.

Lave, J., & Wenger, E. (1991). *Situated learning: Legitimate peripheral participation.* Cambridge, UK: Cambridge University Press.

Mahbouk, K. C., Portillo, M. B., Liu, Y., & Chandraratna, S. (2004). Measuring and enhancing creativity. *European Journal of Engineering Education, 29*, 29–436.

Matson, E., Priusak, L., & McKinsey, Q. (2010). Boosting the productivity of knowledge workers. *Business Source Complete, 4.*

Mayer, J. D., & Geher, G. (1996). Emotional intelligence and the identification of emotion. *Intelligence, 22*, 89–113. doi:10.1016/S0160-2896(96)90011-2

Mayer, J. D., & Salovey, P. (1997). What is emotional intelligence? In Salovey, P., & Sluyter, D. (Eds.), *Emotional Development and Emotional Intelligence: Educational Implications* (pp. 3–34). New York, NY: Basic Books.

McWilliama, E., Hearnb, G., & Hasemanb, B. (2008). Transdisciplinarity for creative futures: What barriers and opportunities? *Innovations in Education and Teaching International, 45*(3), 219–226.

Mumford, M. D., & Gustafson, S. B. (1988). Creativity syndrome: Integration, application, and innovation. *Psychological Bulletin, 103*(1), 27–43. doi:10.1037/0033-2909.103.1.27

Mumford, M. D., & Licuanan, B. (2004). Leading for innovation: Conclusions, issues, and directions. *The Leadership Quarterly, 15*(1), 163–171. doi:10.1016/j.leaqua.2003.12.010

Mumford, M. D., Mobley, M. I., Uhlman, C. E., Reiter-Palmon, R., & Doares, L. M. (1991). Process analytic models of creative capacities. *Creativity Research Journal*, *4*, 91–122. doi:10.1080/10400419109534380

Radosevic, S. (2002). Regional innovation systems in central and eastern Europe: Determinants, organizers and alignments. *The Journal of Technology Transfer*, *27*(1), 87–96. doi:10.1023/A:1013152721632

Sawhney, M., & Prandelli, E. (2000). Communities of creation: Managing distributed innovation in turbulent markets. *California Management Review*, *42*(4), 24–54.

Tippins, M. J. (2003). Implementing knowledge management in academia: Teaching the teachers. *International Journal of Educational Management*, *17*(6-7), 339–345. doi:10.1108/09513540310501021

Wenger, E. (1998). *Communities of practice: Learning, meaning and identity*. Cambridge, UK: Cambridge University Press.

Wonga, S. C., & Ladkin, A. (2008). Exploring the relationship between employee creativity and job-related motivators in the Hong Kong hotel industry international. *Journal of Hospitality Management*, *27*, 426–437. doi:10.1016/j.ijhm.2008.01.001

KEY TERMS AND DEFINITIONS

CII Learning Outcomes: Creativity, invention and innovation are new learning outcomes proposed in the Croatian and European qualification framework.

CroSA Project: A project based on international and multi-institutional collaboration between educational, business and government institutions in Croatia and South Africa.

Construct of Creativity-Invention-Innovation Intelligence: A construct with four dimensions: estimation and communication, process, knowledge of CII, and management of CII features.

CPTD Model: A theoretical framework for continuous teacher professional development.

Entrepreneurial Projects: A teacher-engineer forms an interdisciplinary team around an original idea shaped within an entrepreneurial climate.

MCII Model: A model with five subsystems that is aimed at empowering teachers-engineers and learners in terms of CII features.

Multiple Networks: Cross-cultural collaboration with multiple stakeholders such as teachers, learners, government officers, entrepreneurs and business partners.

Teachers-Engineers: Teachers in technical and vocational schools trained as engineers with some form of pedagogical education, but lacking entrepreneurial capabilities.

Chapter 5
Knowledge Transfer:
The Innovation Side of Knowledge Management in Education

Alina Mihaela Dima
Bucharest Academy of Economic Studies, Romania

ABSTRACT

In order to overcome the challenges posed by globalization, an increasingly complex business world, and the transition to the knowledge-based economy, both academia and practitioners need to reinforce the importance of knowledge transfer activities between universities and other stakeholders and the development of new forms of transfer activities between academia and the external environment. As businesses, economies, and society in general become more global, and as the pace of change increases, they become more dependent on science and technology, on new and innovative forms of knowledge transfer, which are provided partially by universities. The knowledge in academics is an asset but also a liability. The innovation processes on knowledge management in education through knowledge transfer activities will facilitate the shift from teaching as the transmission of knowledge to teaching as the facilitation of learning. Drawing from the literature on knowledge exchange and foregoing observations, this chapter explores the innovation side of KM in education, based on knowledge transfer partners and activities. As academics continuously evolve collaborative forms of research activity and re-imagine the nature of academic-practitioner exchange and knowledge transfer, this chapter considers key contributions in the area and details important avenues that warrant further research.

INTRODUCTION

The term "knowledge management" is unknown to the classical education science (Hameyer & Strittmatter, 2001). Quality management, marketing, evaluation, organization development, etc. have become important features within the education system that gets increasingly dominated by competition and other dogmas of market economy. Schools are no longer only regarded as "organizations for learning" but "learning organizations" as well.

Knowledge management is closely connected to the concept of the "learning organization." This is based on the willingness and ability of organiza-

DOI: 10.4018/978-1-4666-1969-2.ch005

tion members to learn and apply the knowledge acquired to develop it into new knowledge. Each individual's continuous learning process delivers an important element for the knowledge collected in an organization, but a "learning organization" is more than the sum of the learning activities and achievements of all organization members. It also consists of the continuous interaction with its environment (and transfer partners: other universities, business environment, other public bodies, alumni associations, etc.), the integration into a cultural network and all individual experiences. In this way, new knowledge is created which can successfully be integrated in the already existing system. Knowledge management has to make sure that within a company or university this systemic knowledge based on a common context is kept vital and enriched over time to create an "intelligent organization" that can rely on an independent "collective mind" (Weick & Roberts, 1993; Willke, 1998). Universities and schools need organizational intelligence as well to successfully complete their tasks.

At the beginning, knowledge management in schools is project management. Projects are a form of cooperation in the business world that enables the solving of complex problems and tasks. They are of limited range with a clearly defined beginning and end, pursue specific innovative goals, and take certain risks. Projects are usually granted major importance within an organization (Litke, 1995).

In the last few decades, the economies of the developed countries became knowledge dependent. Knowledge turned into the key driver of sustainable economic growth and productivity. Therefore, economies of the developed countries are becoming increasingly dependent on knowledge producers. An important amount of knowledge is created and provided by universities and research centers. In order to benefit from this knowledge and to use it to increase the common welfare of citizens, the results of research need to be transferred from the university to its

stakeholders (Vinig & Rijsbergen, 2008). This process is known as knowledge transfer. Some authors use the terms "Knowledge Sharing" and "Knowledge Exchange" as synonyms for "Knowledge Transfer."

As different authors suggested, managing knowledge means to create an environment within the organization to facilitate the creation, transfer or sharing of knowledge (Bratianu & Vasilache, 2009). The most discussed activity in the process of knowledge management today is knowledge sharing (Al-Alawi, Al-Marzooqi, & Mohammed, 2007). Why this importance of knowledge sharing activities? Knowledge abounds in organizations, but its existence does not guarantee its use. And thus knowledge sharing leads to faster knowledge connection with portions of the organization that can greatly benefit from this new knowledge (Davenport & Prusak, 2000). Knowledge management determines the improvement of knowledge sharing.

The challenges to be faced in implementing Knowledge Management are many, but universities need to cope with them if they want to succeed in business environment where the consumers' preferences are changing more rapidly than in the past and existing knowledge becomes obsolete after short time life cycles. The knowledge transfer becomes the essential issue and the innovation side is highly related to the definition of transfer partners and activities to ensure its effectiveness.

Several authors (Argote & Ingram, 2000; Duan, et al., 2010; Hubig & Jonen, 2006) define the knowledge transfer as a process by which one individual or organization transmits its experience to another and systematically organized information and skills are exchanged between entities. Authors argue that there are some factors, which facilitate and some other factors, which might hinder knowledge transfer. In the category of facilitators can be included determinants such as: commercial resources of a university, research and teaching experience, the stock of technology, whether it is private or public university, the personnel's background, organizational culture, effectiveness of the public relations activity, the presence of a business incubator and science park, agreements with other universities, NGOs and private enterprises, membership in social networks, social connectedness, etc. (Santoro & Bierly, 2006; Santoro & Gopalakrishnan, 2000; Vinig & Rijsbergen, 2008). Among the hindrances we can mention the emotional issues, "academic arrogance" (scientists' attitude towards business partners, who are "too practice oriented" and therefore might impair the quality of research results), uncertainty of the scientific outcome, a poor marketing of the university, bad reputation of the partner, short term orientation, communication problems, too strong theoretical orientation, financial restrictions (Goldfarb & Henrekson, 2003; Hubig & Jonen, 2006; Ndonzuau, et al., 2002).

Knowledge transfer is classified according to different criteria. We can differentiate between personal and technology transfer (Geuna & Muscio, 2008; Hubig & Jonen, 2006). The first group summarizes the transfer of knowledge in form of well-educated graduates to the labor market, in forms of practitioners delivering presentations within academic courses, in form of scholarships granted by organizations to students, prizes and awards for outstanding results, training programs offered by professors to employees etc. In the category of technology transfer fall joint research programs with the private sector, other public institutions and NGOs, publishing research results, consulting services etc. Next, we can differentiate between knowledge outflow and knowledge inflow. Knowledge produced by the university and transferred to its stakeholders represents the outflow, while knowledge captured by universities from other entities represents the knowledge inflow. Considering the role played by universities in the development of the society a balance between the outflow and inflow of knowledge should be. Knowledge can be transferred through

formal and informal channels (Agrawal, 2001; Link, et al., 2007). The researchers note a shift from the informal processes to formal ones, once the importance of knowledge transfer increased in universities and there were established specialized departments in order to manage this task.

Especially in the last ten years it can be observed the emergence of a large number of papers which examine knowledge transfer activities between universities and business sector (Agrawal, 2001; Geuna & Muscio, 2008; Hubig & Jonen, 2006; Santoro & Gopalakrishnan, 2000; Yusuf, 2008). Less attention was paid to knowledge transfer between universities and other important stakeholders such as students, alumni, society, public institutionsk, etc. In the context of globalization, the perspective that gains importance in considering universities is that of various stakeholders (formal or informal). Business environment represents the main transfer partner because of the financial issues but also because of the technological side involved in the relationship. However, new and innovative forms of transfer appeared during time, mostly determined by the social commitment and corporate social responsibility developed by business community but also academic environment.

The innovation processes on knowledge management in education will facilitate the shift from teaching as the transmission of knowledge to teaching as the facilitation of learning. Based on the literature related on knowledge management, this chapter explores the nature of innovation in education and emergent issues in knowledge management development, knowledge transfer and transfer partners of universities. As in academics continuously evolve collaborative forms of research activity and re-imagine the nature of academic-practitioner exchange and knowledge transfer, this chapter considers key contributions in the area and details important avenues that warrant further research.

KNOWLEDGE TRANSFER ACTIVITIES

Knowledge transfer (one aspect of Knowledge Management) has always existed in one form or another. Examples include on-the-job peer discussions, formal apprenticeship, corporate libraries, professional training, and mentoring programs. However, since the late twentieth century, additional technology has been applied to this task, such as knowledge bases, expert systems, and knowledge repositories. Knowledge Management System attempt to manage the process of creation or identification, accumulation, and application of knowledge or intellectual capital across an organization (Murthy, 2007).

Duan et al. (2010) argue that there are four levels of knowledge transfer: the individual level, the intra-organizational level, the inter-organizational level and the multinational level.

The present chapter will focus on the knowledge transfer at inter-organizational level, namely between universities and its stakeholders. From the perspective of the university, there have been identified four main categories of transfer partners: business environment, public bodies (other universities, international associations, high schools, etc.), students, and third parties (alumni, society, non-governmental organizations, etc.). The innovative part of knowledge management in education is related to development of new partners (such as international associations, non-governmental bodies, etc) but mostly to the development of new and evolved forms of knowledge transfer (research projects, academic social responsibility) as compared with traditional ones that become more and more rare (traditional lecturing, agreements with public bodies, etc.). The new and innovative forms of knowledge transfer allow the shift from teaching as the transmission of knowledge to teaching as the facilitation of learning as they are presented in the Table 1. This change of paradigm implies that the focus is placed on the learner's perspective, and that we view learning not as the end result

of teaching, but as a continuous process which is inevitably unfinished (Brown & Duguid, 1992). An indicator of this shift can be seen in Table 1 in the form of the involvement of university in the life-long learning process of individuals, be they employees or students or simply part of a community. Moreover, the authors cited above make some powerful statements regarding the success of the learning process, which have broad implications for our study of knowledge transfer activities. Firstly, they believe that even if the knowledge intended to be transferred was not received, we cannot regard this as an absence of learning, something is always learnt from an interaction. Secondly, knowledge transfer activities should not be regarded as discrete, point-like intersections, but viewed as a whole, as a history of multiple interactions that influence each other. These beliefs have informed our search for knowledge transfer activities and the way they have to be analyzed in terms of efficiency and innovativeness and this will be discussed in the next sections.

Transfer Activities with Business Environment

In the specialized literature knowledge transfer between universities and business environment has been researched mainly from the perspective of joint research projects. We want to broaden this area of transfer by introducing in our chapter several other activities such as: training offered by university experts to employees by means of post-graduate courses (these might be tailored in order to meet the specific training needs of a company), various educational activities (guest speakers from companies, scholarship programs for students with outstanding results, and jointly supervised master thesis and PhDs, internship programs), joint use of technical infrastructure, consulting services, etc.

Working with business environment or industry can involve collaboration through joint research, contract research, and consulting. Joint

Table 1. Knowledge transfer activities and indicators*

Knowledge Transfer Activity	Indicators
Knowledge transfer with business environment	Joint- research projects financed by business environment
	Students internship in companies
	Visiting lecturers from business environment
	Grants from business environment towards university
	Projects financed by business environment conducted within the university
	Post-graduate courses for employees
	Scholarships granted by business environment to students with outstanding results
Knowledge transfer with public bodies (universities, international associations, high schools, etc.)	Agreements concluded with foreign universities
	Membership in international academic networks
	Joint projects with high schools
	Research projects financed by national public institutions
	Research projects financed by international public institutions
	Scientific output
Knowledge transfer with students	International exchange programs for students
	Facilities in the students campus
	Joint projects with students organizations
	Scholarships granted by university
	Project contests for students within the university
	Summer schools organized by the university
Knowledge transfer with third parties (alumni, society, non-governmental organizations, etc.)	Professional and social networks for alumni
	Social and cultural projects
	Ecological initiatives under social responsibility policy
	Joint projects with non-governmental organizations

*Table 1 presents the transfer activities between universities and external environment.
Source: the author's analysis

(or collaborative) research among academic and industry researchers is widespread (Perkmann & Walsh, 2007). Contract research refers to industry commissioned applied research carried out by university researchers. Consulting involves application-oriented research or advice, commissioned and funded by industry, and provided by academics (Perkmann & Walsh, 2008).

However, interactions between universities and industry take multiple forms (Cohen, et al., 2002) and channels of cooperation range from inter-organizational relationships (e.g. joint research or contract research) to spin-off companies, to IP transfer including patenting and licensing

(Bercovitz & Feldman, 2006; Bonaccorsi & Piccaluga, 1994; Carayol, 2003; Cohen, et al., 2002; D'Este & Patel, 2007; Schartinger, et al., 2002).

Transfer Activities with Third Parties (Alumni, Society, Non-Governmental Organizations, etc.)

The role that universities play goes beyond the mere impact they have on the economic environment. Universities significantly affect the local community (Wright, et al., 2008) and the society through social and cultural projects (arts exhibition, movies gala, charity activities, concerts, and presentations), ecological initiatives (recycling projects, promoting alternatives means of transportation, organizing ecological programs and trainings, etc.), joint projects with non-governmental organizations and alumni associations.

School as an institution has to fulfill a lot of functions. Among many others are the tasks of qualification, socialization, integration, selection, legitimating, and emancipation to mention just a few. Additional functions, for example social or compensation functions are gaining importance due to changing patterns in society.

Knowledge exchange can also be problematic in educational settings, as teachers often do not find an adequate way to transfer it to their colleagues. Many teachers find it difficult to accept knowledge from their colleagues and feel resentments instead of readily accepting advanced knowledge by others in a certain field. On the other hand, there are many teachers that are willing to cooperate and share their knowledge with their colleagues. This happens mainly in the context of informal networks or groups whose members trust each other and communicate (Kirchhoff, 2001). What works well within these groups, however, can often not be translated into a larger context. These social subgroups sometimes develop a specific language and style other members of the organization are not familiar with. Therefore, a transfer of knowledge is more difficult even if everybody involved is prepared to cooperate. Teachers and other school staff tend to reject knowledge that was not created within their own organization (Roehl, 2000).

Transfer Activities with Students

Despite the fact that students are the main beneficiaries of educational services, one can note the lack of research regarding the knowledge transfer activities between universities and students. After doing a longitudinal study of the relevant literature based on 135 articles published from 1980 to 2004, Liu (2007) discovered that only about 1.5% were related to the study of knowledge transfer activities involving students and universities and these were not related to the science of education. In trying to explain the lack of focus given to this topic, Johannesson (2006) was contended that this is only an evidence of a lack of customer focus in universities regarding the transfer of knowledge. However, some authors suggest that the customer metaphor might not be appropriate when treating the subject of knowledge transfer between student and university because their roles change as their relationship progresses (at first, the university is seen as the provider of knowledge and the student is the receiver and by the end the roles are switched) and the customer paradigm hides one side of this relationship (Svensson & Wood, 2007). Consequently, there could be another explanation to this research gap represented by the fact that some authors regard the university as a knowledge building community and focus on the social process of producing and continually improving ideas of value to a community (Bereiter, et al., 1997; Scardamalia & Bereiter, 2003; Hong, et al., 2010).

In spite of the poor treatment of the subject, we have identified several indicators used to ascertain the intensity of the transfer: joint projects with students' organizations, summer schools, conferences and other kinds of projects organized for students in the institutional framework of a university, access to scientific databases and libraries, etc. Whereas the transfer of knowledge towards and from students stands for the core function of a university, the delivery of knowledge to society aims mainly at cultural exchange (Hubig & Jonen, 2006) and is embedded in various collaborations on cultural, ecological and social topics.

Transfer Activities with Public Bodies (Universities, International Associations, High Schools, etc.)

An important role within the knowledge transfer process is assigned to collaboration with other public bodies, like foreign universities, international associations, high schools. This collaboration might occur in form of agreements and joined projects with other universities, joint research and publishing activity with other research institutes (e.g. Ministry of Education and Research), projects carried out with high schools, teachers, and pupils, etc.

The following section will provide an insightful perspective of knowledge transfer with business environment and knowledge transfer with the students.

KNOWLEDGE TRANSFER WITH BUSINESS ENVIRONMENT

The Context of Academia-Business Collaboration

Knowledge transfer between academic institutions and the business sector is understood as "any activities aimed at transferring knowledge or technology that may help either the company or the academic institute—depending on the direction of transfer—to further pursue its activities" (Arvanitis, et al., 2008, p. 1866).

New opportunities for knowledge creation and transfer are emerging. Research grounded in practitioner experience, the involvement of business schools in industry problem solving and role of the business school as a hub facilitating the commercialization of academic knowledge exemplify these new opportunities (Harrington & Kearney, 2011).

The interaction between business sector and science represents a main concern for economic policy makers, since in the knowledge economy science exerts a major influence on innovation, which is one of the main sources of competitive advantage.

In recent years there has been much hope that moves towards a knowledge economy will reignite economies of developed countries and provide them with a new source of competitive advantage on the global stage. Simultaneously businesses aim to exploit and use knowledge to enhance competitiveness (Easterby & Prieto, 2009).

External and financial pressures, debate on the entrepreneurial university, growth of corporate universities and new sources of revenue in the form of new product offerings, industry academic partnerships in research and business development and international student development are evident.

Demands from industry, cost, and revenue pressures on third level institutes, attention given to the "translation" or management practice gap and increased competition in the education "marketplace" are leading to the emergence of practice-based learning (Brennan, 2005).

Policy-makers in a number of countries are promoting such developments by encouraging collaboration between academia and industry (Mowery & Nelson, 2004) providing monetary incentives to facilitate their commercial involvement (Lach & Schankerman, 2008).

Universities are increasingly being called upon to contribute to economic development and competitiveness (Feller, 1990) and policy-makers have implemented measures aimed at increasing the rate of commercialization of university technology. These measures range from laws governing Intellectual Property (IP) arising from public research, government funding for university technology transfer offices and promotion of translational research and public-private research partnerships (Mowery & Sampat, 2005; Siegel, et al., 2007; Zerhouni, 2003).

In addition, many universities have formal policies for encouraging their academic staff to pursue industry assignments for a specified share of their time (Perkmann & Walsh, 2008).

In related studies, academic respondents express significant support for industry collaboration in terms of the benefits related to their research (Lee, 2000). Benefits from industry cooperation include securing funds for graduate students, accessing laboratory equipment, gaining insights applicable to academic research, and supplementing research monies (Mansfield, 1995), acquiring additional research funds and learning (Meyer-Krahmer & Schmoch, 1998), enhancing prestige and reputation, publishing ideas freely (Glaser & Bero, 2005) and providing new impulses for research but that personal remuneration is not seen as important (Baldini, et al., 2007).

The literature on dynamic capabilities and their role in organizational learning (Easterby & Prieto, 2009; Eisenhardt & Martin, 2000) provides a context within which future models of knowledge exchange between academia and practice may be linked. Further, there is increasing awareness and support for the idea that knowledge transfer emanating from university business collaboration leads to economic growth, often through the commercialization of science in the form of patents, licenses and university spin-outs (Sainsbury, 2007; Lambert, 2003).

Despite extensive research into the area of management involving the historical study of the role of knowledge in business through conceptualizations such as the learning organization and knowledge management, there continues to be much debate about how knowledge is created and transferred both internally in organizations, across organizational networks and through management education. It also raises issues as to how universities build quality assurance into new offerings they make resulting from practitioner interaction.

As various authors observe, historically, knowledge has always been managed, at least implicitly. However, effective and active knowledge management requires new perspectives and techniques and touches on almost all facets of an organization (Dalkir, 2005).

The next section discusses the challenges and opportunities for knowledge transfer between academia and business community reflecting mutual benefits but also constraints determined by traditional mission of the university, limited applied research, financial issues, communication difficulties, or conflicts between stakeholders.

Challenges and Opportunities for Knowledge Transfer

In their contribution, Kieser and Leiner (2009) write of academia and practice as closed self referential systems with the need for greater attention to transfer knowledge and learning from research studies concerning practitioner/research communities of practice, networks and collaborations. This point is reinforced by Hodgkinson and Rousseau (2009) suggesting that developing deep partnerships between academics and practitioners supported by appropriate training in theory and research methods can yield outcomes that meet the twin imperatives of high quality scholarship and social usefulness. The leveraging of the distinct competencies of researchers and practitioners provides opportunities for better grounding and greater understanding of complex problem.

There are many papers supporting the partnership between academia and business environment through different forms and collaborations.

Fincham and Clark (2009) point to how the process of management education, with its interaction of practice and theory, leads to new knowledge in terms of heightened critical awareness among practitioners who are viewed as "consumers of management ideas" and may lead to new and innovative "forms and types of engagement." In an analysis of the publishing and patenting activities of the most research-intensive US universities, Owen-Smith (2003) finds there is convergence towards a 'hybrid system' linking scientific and technological success. Specifically, he shows that academic success drives technological invention while advantages in technological invention are driven by organizational learning relating to procedures and organizational arrangements for identifying, protecting, and managing IP.

At the same time, the emergence of practice-based learning creates potential for a reframing of conventional approaches to training and human resource development. Taking a human resource perspective, Argote (2000) points to how knowledge transfer is enabled by effective human resource management acting as a driver of firm-level competitive advantage. Increased recognition of practice will allow organizations to develop their own management education, even to corporate university level, and to provide this both to their own workforce and to that of other organizations. There will be the opportunity for a reappraisal of what constitutes the creation of business knowledge as greater research is conducted into how it is situated historically, culturally and socially from the perspective of practice (Marshall, 2008). Finally, focus on individual development may shift towards the study of informal collective interaction in practice (Gold, et al., 2007).

According to Hodgkinson and Rousseau (2009), an active approach to knowledge exchange including learner practice, problem identification and the taking account of context in module design leads to innovations in management practice, taking the issue from Kieser and Leiner (2009) who argue that management education is narrow, over specialized and "does not provide students with the ability to relate to realistic management problem solving situations."

The growing involvement of universities in technology transfer and commercialization raises questions about their nature and mission (McKelvey & Holmén, 2009). Advocates of the 'triple helix' theory claim that universities have embraced economic and social development as a new mission, in addition to their traditional missions of teaching and research (Etzkowitz, 1998). In embracing this new task, universities are becoming part of a coherent system that includes industry and government and underpins innovation and economic progress (Etzkowitz & Leydesdorff, 2000). Implicit in this view is that the role of academics is shifting. Rather than concentrating on 'blue-skies' research, academics are seen increasingly to be eager to bridge the worlds of science and technology, in an entrepreneurial way, by commercializing the technologies that emerge from their research (Clark, 1998; Etzkowitz, 2003; Shane, 2004).

Further, there are voices stating that, in order to counterbalance the public underfinancing many universities show the tendency of commercialization of the research results and this might jeopardize the fundamental long-term research and teaching objectives of a university and negatively impact on scientific quality (Stephan, 2001; Tijssen, 2004). Others argue that universities and industry are converging towards a hybrid order where the differences between scholarly and commercial logics are becoming blurred (Owen-Smith, 2003).

On the other hand, in the USA there is evidence that projects conducted by universities and financed by private enterprises can meet the needs of both parties, if a long-term perspective is adopted by both entities. Nevertheless, European universities are lagging behind in this aspect (Arvanitis, et al., 2008). This might be traced back to the time when universities were isolated in their ivory tower, being disconnected from practice and to the traditional European paradigm of university's scope and mission in society, as opposed to the concept of entrepreneurial university (Bratianu, 2004).

Knowledge sharing in particular is inhibited by communication difficulties rooted in language (Roos & von Krogh, 2002). Conflict may also ensue from difficulties apportioning rewards among partners and from a related unwillingness of those managing within traditional academic/practitioner context to engage in the relatively risky behavior in entering such a partnership. Alferoff and Knights (2009) conceptualize knowledge exchange in terms of actor networks. Mitigating factors against the success of such networks include the perception of their activities being peripheral to those of the business school, inability of the research outputs to gain publication in peer reviewed journals and a low impact of membership of networks on career development.

Scarborough and Knights (2009) question the extent to which practicing managers are willing to implement the findings of academic research, even where they have had involvement in the research design and administration. Kieser and Leiner (2009) suggest that lack of knowledge transfer relates to the self-referential nature of different social systems inhabited by researchers and management practitioners. Viewed critically it can be argued they fail to imagine scenarios other than those of the traditional classroom and the existing systems of academic publishing in refereed journals.

Knowledge exchange is mediated by institutional context, social networks, and technological artifacts. Knowledge is constantly embedded and disembedded in organizational contexts with managers and policy makers often playing a backstage role more concerned with day-to-day activity than knowledge exchange. It is for this reason that "many knowledge management systems rarely succeed; simply codifying knowledge into a system does not make it practically usable for people in a different time and place" (Scarborough, 2008). Willem and Scarborough (2006) provide empirical evidence of political structures influencing the type of knowledge transferred and the degree of transfer. Applying these insights to a business school context raises questions regarding how knowledge creation occurs.

A number of authors (Krimsky, 2003; Noble, 1977; Slaughter & Leslie, 1997) have criticized by underlining the potentially detrimental effects of 'entrepreneurial' science on the long-term production of scientific knowledge, suggesting that academic science is becoming an instrument manipulated by industry Many universities

appear to have become 'knowledge businesses' which are focused not so much on generating a public good for a national audience but providing services to specific stakeholders (McKelvey & Holmén, 2009; Vallas & Kleinman, 2008). The perceived risks include a shift in scientific research from basic research towards more applied topics and less academic freedom (Behrens & Gray, 2001; Blumenthal, et al., 1986), lower levels of research productivity among academics (Agrawal & Henderson, 2002) and a slowing-down of open knowledge diffusion (Nelson, 2004; Rosell & Agrawal, 2009).

Possible solutions to overcome the shortcoming of university and business cooperation and facilitate knowledge exchange include: improved communication between stakeholders (Kieser & Leiner, 2009), building of common standards, shared systems and shared applications of knowledge between organizations (Ciborra & Andreu, 2001) or growth of associations dedicated to professionalizing management practice act as a bridge to overcome the rigor-relevance gap and rewards academically rigorous research emanating from a practical context while simultaneously generating successful practitioner academic knowledge exchange.

Where communication takes place successfully across stakeholder boundaries, fragmented perspectives can be integrated into a more holistic, gestalt of the challenge under consideration (Van de Ven & Johnson, 2006). Equally, a challenge to future partnerships seeking to improve knowledge exchange is the development of what is conceptualized as a language mutually intelligible to both partners. Ultimately, it is aspired that tension and creative conflict between stakeholders leads to the surfacing of biases, motivations, and interests of all parties and thus contributing to the research process and the consequent development of greater mutual understanding (Van de Ven & Johnson, 2006). One successful example of this process is shown to exist at the FEXIS programme (Huff & Huff, 2001) where research collaboration and knowledge exchange between researchers and practitioners meet the dual criteria of rigor and relevance.

KNOWLEDGE TRANSFER WITH STUDENTS

Teachers everywhere extend knowledge in finished form to learners. They lecture, write, make homework assignments, compose examples and cases, use research results, and in many other ways launch knowledge toward learners. According to Cohen (2008), teachers' knowledge is an essential asset in such work, for the more they know the greater their resources for helping learners. Yet equally learned teachers extend or transfer knowledge in very different ways. Some try to unpack knowledge in order to render it accessible. They use metaphors, analogies, and other intellectual inventions, as well as drawing pictures, making diagrams, and using apparatus in efforts to present and re-present ideas to learners. Teachers who work in such ways try to extend knowledge so that it will be open to learners—that is, they will be able to find varied routes into it, and paths through it, thus increasing the connections learners may make.

However, if teachers' knowledge is an essential asset in their work, it also is a liability. For the more accomplished teachers are in a field, the more finished their knowledge is. They find it convenient and even elegant to extend knowledge in polished and highly compressed form. Such finished material often nicely represents teachers' intellectual accomplishments, but it usually is quite remote from learners' tentative and often puzzling formulations. Because they do not unpack knowledge, teachers who work in this way limit the routes by which students gain access to it and the paths they can find through it.

The innovation processes on knowledge management will facilitate the shift from teaching as the transmission of knowledge to teaching as the facilitation of learning (Price, et al., 2005). This shift is related to changes in technology in complex ways and the new role signifies a shift in the locus of control over student learning. While teachers continue to occupy a powerful position, through making judgments about what counts as worthwhile knowledge and through grading students' work, students are potentially gaining power in a number of ways not least of all in the control of the presentation of the learning environment through the combination of technologies and media (Crook, 2002).

Though teachers extend knowledge in dramatically different ways, knowledge is not a neutral material that teachers transmit. It must be construed somehow to be taught or learned, and teachers construe it in radically different ways. Some treat it as though it was established, objective facts and procedures, while others treat knowledge as though it was contested and constructed. Such differences have an enormous influence on the material teachers launch toward learners. Teachers' conceptions of knowledge also differ in the ways that they compose them. Knowledge in most fields comprises several elements: distinctive methods of inquiry and operations; special terminology; approaches to problem setting; and means of defending results.

However, if all elements play some part in knowing a field, teachers and investigators assign them radically different roles and weights. Some give pride of place to terminology and methods of inquiry while others focus extensively on the defense of results. Some focus only on one or two elements while others try to balance all four. Such compositional variations add up to different conceptions of what it means to know a field, and thus to very different versions of the knowledge that teachers extend to learners (Cohen, 2008).

According to Blumberg (2009), there are four different types of knowledge: (a) factual, (b) conceptual, (c) procedural, and (d) meta-cognitive. By being systematic and seeking to enhance the students' acquisition of knowledge in all four areas, instructors will help students develop a better mastery of the content of the course and retain their learning better. Instructors might even check to see that the students have opportunities to use content that employs as many types of knowledge as possible. Not all the content in courses may require procedural knowledge; but it should require factual, conceptual, and meta-cognitive knowledge. Curricula, on the other hand, should have all four types of knowledge embedded in them. Instructors, as facilitators of learning should consider all type of knowledge in the process of teaching and extend to learners. Many instructors do not provide enough opportunities for students to employ their meta-cognitive knowledge about the discipline. Through the deliberate inclusion of objectives and teaching and learning activities requiring students to engage with content by the application of meta-cognitive knowledge, instructors encourage the students to reflect on their own learning and thinking processes. As students gain experience with the four types of knowledge, they should increase their ability to remember and apply the content and improve their critical thinking skills and thus facilitate learning. Assessment exercises that involve the different types of knowledge can also identify specific aspects that the students have not yet mastered.

Knowledge is increasingly being embedded into the systems that are supporting, if not driving industry, while the need is to sharpen the methods of "thinking," so that the embedded knowledge can be effectively and quickly harnessed for carrying out tasks. The needs of training are therefore, not so much for repetitively physical activity or 'hands-on' experience, which in any case cannot be simulated in the University outside industry, but for training the mind so as to develop training 'skills' in thinking and acting. According to Murthy (2007), the required skill set is the following: (1) basic knowledge of the relevant area, including allied subjects; (2) ability to quickly gather and internalize knowledge; (3) ability to perceive and understand situations that need knowledgeable

response; (4) ability to evolve appropriate and effective responses to deal with such situations.

CONCLUSION

In order to get benefits from transfer of knowledge, academic communities should collaborate with various institutions and bodies from external environment to provide a practice-based perspective in leadership education and training. In the longer-term there is a need to focus attention on stimulating awareness of the relationship between management practitioners at all levels and the wider research community. Main conclusions of the chapter reflect that the challenge of developing relevant actionable knowledge that prepares and enthuses university students not just to observe, but to lead and drive business activity must address the academic-practitioner interface. Management education should be constructed to reflect both academic and practitioner perspectives, by balancing in-class training, rooted in academic knowledge, with the experiential knowledge of business leaders and greater attention and investment needs to be made to better understand this dynamic (Kelliher, et al., 2010).

As we underlined in this chapter, in terms of knowledge, there are nascent signs of new modes of creation emanating from business school transition, from relevant partnerships between academia and external environment, from new collaborative forms of research activity that would re-imagine the nature of academic-practitioner exchange and knowledge transfer.

Inhibiting factors comprising institutional forces, such as the traditional university view of research, the interests of various stakeholders often mitigate against such change. Given the context, research seeking to investigate deeper impact factors in university/external environment collaboration that inhibit and enable the generation of economically useful research output might prove salient. This could be undertaken with specific emphasis on the application of design science, actor network theory, or practice-based perspectives.

From the perspective of knowledge transfer, future research might explore challenges to the uncovering of such skills and their incorporation into theoretical frameworks that allow their use in business schools. The topic may be approached from the role of the individual, as in the focus of much strategy-as-practice research. Alternatively, an approach taking the level of collective interaction (Gold, et al., 2007) may also be taken. Future research might explore the underlying power structures at play in such collaboration and perhaps uncover a mechanism to improve knowledge transfer. In this regard, while Ciborra and Andreu (2001) argue the need to build common standards and a language to enable knowledge transfer within a community, the implication in the term "build" implies a control over emergent properties of the community. They argue that inter-organizational knowledge exchange is facilitated by the building of common standards, shared systems, and shared applications of knowledge between organizations.

However, an efficient learning process will involve the transfer of four types of knowledge, that is, factual, conceptual, procedural, and meta-cognitive. Instructors need to plan how students will practice engaging with content that requires these different types of knowledge and not assume that they will learn the conceptual or procedural knowledge by attending lectures or demonstrations. When instructors ask students to reflect on their own learning processes and to assess their learning progress, thus using meta-cognitive knowledge, students will learn the content of the course better.

Kieser and Leiner (2009) sustain that academia and practice are "self referential systems" with the need to transfer knowledge from research studies concerning practitioner/research communities of practice, networks, and collaborations. Criticizing the traditional linear models of knowledge diffusion between business research institutions and companies, Alferoff and Knights (2009) conceptualize knowledge exchange in terms of actor networks. In this context, there is a conceptual shift from a simple linear process where events happen sequentially to a complex process where there are multiple paths with no optimum mechanism for knowledge exchange. There is room for the development of more sophisticated theory (Scarborough, 2008) capable of describing and analyzing the more complex knowledge transfer process of the network structures involved in such projects. Nonetheless challenges remain. Authors (Mitev & Venters, 2009; Gibbons, 2008) underline the inherent conflict and political nature of knowledge transfer even where planned collaboration (Baldridge, et al., 2004) is in place.

Such developments bring about changes in the way teaching and learning is dealt with in higher education. Innovations in technology, which initiated changing demands in education, have been used to argue that there is a need to reassess and revisit the roles and practices of educators, to accommodate "more flexible learning, for the growth in university services, and for more cost-effective delivery of higher education in an increasingly competitive environment" (Price, et al., 2005).

As in academics continuously evolve collaborative forms of research activity and re-imagine the nature of academic-practitioner exchange and knowledge transfer, this chapter considers key contributions in the area and details important avenues that warrant further research.

REFERENCES

Agrawal, A. (2001). University-to-industry knowledge transfer: Literature review and unanswered questions. *International Journal of Management Reviews*, 3(4), 285–302. doi:10.1111/1468-2370.00069

Agrawal, A., & Henderson, R. M. (2002). Putting patents in context: Exploring knowledge transfer from MIT. *Management Science, 48*(1), 44–60. doi:10.1287/mnsc.48.1.44.14279

Al-Alawi, A. I., Al-Marzooqi, N. Y., & Mohammed, Y. F. (2007). Organizational culture and knowledge sharing: Critical success factors. *Journal of Knowledge Management, 11*(2), 22–42. doi:10.1108/13673270710738898

Alferoff, C., & Knights, D. (2009). Making and mending your nets: Managing relevance, participation and uncertainty in academic-practitioner knowledge networks. *British Journal of Management, 20*(18), 125–140. doi:10.1111/j.1467-8551.2007.00556.x

Argote, L., & Ingram, P. (2000). Knowledge transfer: A basis for competitive advantage in firms. *Organizational Behavior and Human Decision Processes, 82*(1), 150–169. doi:10.1006/obhd.2000.2893

Arvanitis, S., Kubli, U., & Woerter, M. (2008). University-industry knowledge and technology transfer in Switzerland: What university scientists think about co-operation with private enterprises. *Research Policy, 37*, 1865–1883. doi:10.1016/j.respol.2008.07.005

Behrens, T. R., & Gray, D. O. (2001). Unintended consequences of cooperative research: Impact of industry sponsorship on climate for academic freedom and other graduate student outcome. *Research Policy, 30*(2), 179–199. doi:10.1016/S0048-7333(99)00112-2

Bercovitz, J., & Feldman, M. (2006). Entrepreneurial universities and technology transfer: A conceptual framework for understanding knowledge-based economic development. *The Journal of Technology Transfer, 31*(1), 175–188. doi:10.1007/s10961-005-5029-z

Bereiter, C., Scardamalia, M., Cassells, C., & Hewitt, J. (1997). Postmodernism, knowledge building, and elementary science. *The Elementary School Journal, 97*, 329–340. doi:10.1086/461869

Blumberg, P. (2009). Maximizing learning through course alignment and experience with different types of knowledge. *Innovative Higher Education, 34*, 93–103. doi:10.1007/s10755-009-9095-2

Blumenthal, D., Gluck, M., Louis, K. S., Stoto, M. A., & Wise, D. (1986). University-industry research relationships in biotechnology - Implications for the university. *Science, 232*(4756), 1361–1366. doi:10.1126/science.3715452

Bonaccorsi, A., & Piccaluga, A. (1994). A theoretical framework for the evaluation of university-industry relationships. *R & D Management, 24*(3), 229–247. doi:10.1111/j.1467-9310.1994.tb00876.x

Bratianu, C. (2004, May). Entrepreneurial dimensions in the Romanian higher education: Letters from the Black Sea. *International Journal of the Black Sea Universities Network*, 34-37.

Brătianu, C., & Lefter, V. (2001). *Management strategic universitar*. Bucureşti, Romania: Editura Rao.

Bratianu, C., & Vasilache, S. (2009). Implementing innovation and knowledge management in the Romanian economy. In *Proceedings of the Fourth International KMO Conference*. Taipei, Taiwan: KMO.

Brennan, L. (2005). *Integrating work base learning into higher education: A guide to good practice*. Boston, MA: University Vocational Awards Council.

Brown, J., & Duguid, P. (1992). *Stolen knowledge: Educational technology publications*. Retrieved from http://tech-head.com/learning.htm

Carayol, N. (2003). Objectives, agreements and matching in science-industry collaborations: Reassembling the pieces of the puzzle. *Research Policy*, *32*(6), 887–908. doi:10.1016/S0048-7333(02)00108-7

Ciborra, C., & Andreu, R. (2001). Sharing knowledge across boundaries. *Journal of Information Technology*, *16*(2), 73–81. doi:10.1080/02683960110055103

Clark, B. R. (1998). *Creating entrepreneurial universities: Organizational pathways of transformation*. New York, NY: Pergamon.

Cohen, W. M. (2008). Knowledge and teaching. *Oxford Review of Education*, *34*(3), 357–378. doi:10.1080/03054980802116972

Cohen, W. M., Nelson, R. R., & Walsh, J. P. (2002). Links and impacts: The influence of public research on industrial R&D. *Management Science*, *48*(1), 1–23. doi:10.1287/mnsc.48.1.1.14273

D'Este, P., & Patel, P. (2007). University-industry linkages in the UK: What are the factors determining the variety of interactions with industry? *Research Policy*, *36*(9), 1295–1313. doi:10.1016/j.respol.2007.05.002

Dalkir, K. (2005). *Knowledge management in theory and practice*. Oxford, UK: Elsevier.

Davenport, T., & Prusak, L. (2000). *Working knowledge – How organization manage what they know*. Boston, MA: Harvard Business Scholl Press.

Duan, Y., Nie, W., & Coakes, E. (2010). Identifying key factors affecting transnational knowledge transfer. *Information & Management*, *47*(7-8), 356–363. doi:10.1016/j.im.2010.08.003

Easterby-Smith, M., & Prieto, I. (2009). Dynamic capabilities and knowledge management: An integrative role for learning. *British Journal of Management*, *19*(3), 235–249. doi:10.1111/j.1467-8551.2007.00543.x

Eisenhardt, K., & Martin, J. (2000). Dynamic capabilities: What are they. *Strategic Management Journal*, *21*(10), 1105–1121. doi:10.1002/1097-0266(200010/11)21:10/11<1105::AID-SMJ133>3.0.CO;2-E

Etzkowitz, H. (1998). The norms of entrepreneurial science: Cognitive effects of the new university-industry linkages. *Research Policy*, *27*(8), 823–833. doi:10.1016/S0048-7333(98)00093-6

Etzkowitz, H. (2003). Research groups as 'quasi-firms': The invention of the entrepreneurial university. *Research Policy*, *32*(1), 109–121. doi:10.1016/S0048-7333(02)00009-4

Etzkowitz, H., & Leydesdorff, L. (2000). The dynamics of innovation: From national systems and 'mode two' to a triple helix of university, industry and government relations. *Research Policy*, *29*(22), 109–123. doi:10.1016/S0048-7333(99)00055-4

Feller, I. (1990). Universities as engines of R&D-based economic growth: They think they can. *Research Policy*, *19*(4), 335–348. doi:10.1016/0048-7333(90)90017-Z

Field, A. (2005). *Discovering statistics using SPSS* (2nd ed.). Thousand Oaks, CA: Sage Publications.

Fincham, R., & Clark, T. (2009). Introduction to point counterpoint on rigour and relevance in management studies: Can we bridge the rigour relevance gap. *Journal of Management Studies*, *46*(3), 510–515. doi:10.1111/j.1467-6486.2009.00834.x

Geuna, A., & Muscio, A. (2008). *The governance of university knowledge transfer*. SPRU Electronic Working Paper Series, Paper no. 173. SPRU.

Gibbons, M. (2008). *Why is knowledge translation important: Grounding the conversation*. Retrieved from http://www.ncddr.org/kt/products/focus/focus21

Glaser, B., & Bero, L. (2005). Attitudes of academic and clinical researchers toward financial ties in research: A systematic review. *Science and Engineering Ethics, 11*(4), 553–573. doi:10.1007/s11948-005-0026-z

Gold, J., Thorpe, R., Woodall, J., & Sadler-Smith, E. (2007). Continuing professional development in the legal profession: A practice based perspective. *Management Learning, 38*(2), 235–250. doi:10.1177/1350507607075777

Goldfarb, B., & Henrekson, M. (2003). Bottom-up versus top-down policies towards the commercialization of university intellectual property. *Research Policy, 4*(32), 639–658. doi:10.1016/S0048-7333(02)00034-3

Hameyer, U., & Strittmatter, A. (2001). Wissensmanagement – Die neue Selbstverständlichkeit. *Journal für Schulentwicklung, 1,* 4–5.

Harrington, D., & Kearney, A. (2010). The business school in transition: New opportunities in management development, knowledge transfer and knowledge creation. *Journal of European Industrial Training, 35*(2), 116–134. doi:10.1108/03090591111109334

Harvard Business School. (2009). *Annual report 2009*. Retrieved from http://www.hbs.edu/about/annualreport/2009/download2009/annual-2009.pdf

Ho, R. (2006). *Handbook of univariate and multivariate data analysis and interpretation with SPSS*. New York, NY: Taylor & Francis Group. doi:10.1201/9781420011111

Hodgkinson, G. P., & Rousseau, D. (2009). Bridging the rigour relevance gap in management studies: Its already happening. *Journal of Management Studies, 46*(3), 534–546. doi:10.1111/j.1467-6486.2009.00832.x

Hong, H. O., Chen, F. C., Chai, C. S., & Chan, W. C. (2010). Teacher-education students' views about knowledge building theory and practice. *Instructional Science Journal*. Retrieved from http://www.cl.ncu.edu.tw/papers/ChenFC/Teachereducation%20students%27views%20about%20knowledge.pdf

Hubig, L., & Jonen, A. (2006). *Hindrances, benefits and measurement of knowledge transfer in universities - Should be done more in the light of corporate social responsibility?* Retrieved from http://ssrn.com/abstract=939390, retrieved 25.10.2010.

Johannesson, C. (2006). *University strategies for knowledge transfer and commercialization - An overview based on peer reviews at 24 Swedish universities. Vinnova Report 17*. Vinnova.

Kieser, A., & Leiner, L. (2009). Why the rigour relevance gap in management research is unbridgeable. *Journal of Management Studies, 46*(3), 516–533. doi:10.1111/j.1467-6486.2009.00831.x

Kirchhoff, D. (2001). Wissensmanagement ist mehr als das Umgehen mit Informationen. *Journal für Schulentwicklung, 1,* 36–41.

Krimsky, S. (2003). *Science in the private interest: Has the lure of profits corrupted the virtue of biomedical research?* Lanham, UK: Rowman & Littlefield.

Lach, S., & Schankerman, M. (2008). Incentives and invention in universities. *The Rand Journal of Economics, 39*(2), 403–433. doi:10.1111/j.0741-6261.2008.00020.x

Lambert, R. (2003). *Lambert review of university-business collaboration*. London, UK: HM Treasury.

Lee, Y. S. (1996). Technology transfer and the research university: A search for the boundaries of university-industry collaboration. *Research Policy*, *25*(6), 843–863. doi:10.1016/0048-7333(95)00857-8

Lee, Y. S. (2000). The sustainability of university-industry research collaboration: An empirical assessment. *The Journal of Technology Transfer*, *25*(2), 111–133. doi:10.1023/A:1007895322042

Link, A., Siegel, D., & Bozeman, B. (2007). An empirical analysis of the propensity of academics to engage in informal university technology transfer. *Industrial and Corporate Change*, *4*(16), 641–655. doi:10.1093/icc/dtm020

Litke, H.-D. (1995). *Projektmanagement: Methoden, techniken, verhaltensweisen*. München, Germany: Hanser.

Liu, T. L. (2007). Knowledge transfer: Past research and future directions. *Business Review (Federal Reserve Bank of Philadelphia)*, *7*(1), 273–281.

Mansfield, E. (1995). Academic research underlying industrial innovations: Sources, characteristics, and financing. *The Review of Economics and Statistics*, *77*(1), 55–65. doi:10.2307/2109992

Marshall, N. (2008). Cognitive and practice based theories of organizational knowledge and learning: Incompatible or complementary. *Management Learning*, *39*(4), 413–435. doi:10.1177/1350507608093712

McKelvey, M., & Holmén, M. (Eds.). (2009). *Learning to compete in European universities: From social institution to knowledge business*. Cheltenham, UK: Edward Elgar.

Meyer-Krahmer, F., & Schmoch, U. (1998). Science-based technologies: University-industry interactions in four fields. *Research Policy*, *27*(8), 835–851. doi:10.1016/S0048-7333(98)00094-8

Mitev, N., & Venters, W. (2009). Reflexive evaluation of an academic industry research collaboration: Can mode two research be achieved? *Journal of Management Studies*, *46*(5), 733–754. doi:10.1111/j.1467-6486.2009.00846.x

Mowery, D. C., & Nelson, R. R. (Eds.). (2004). *Ivory tower and industrial innovation: University-industry technology before and after the Bayh-Dole act*. Palo Alto, CA: Stanford University Press.

Mowery, D. C., & Sampat, B. N. (2005). The Bayh-Dole act of 1980 and university–industry technology transfer: A model for other OECD governments? *The Journal of Technology Transfer*, *30*(1/2), 115–127.

Murthy, K. V. B. (2007). *Re-engineering higher education - The knowledge management system*. Retrieved from http://ssrn.com/abstract=1073742

Ndonzuau, F., Pirnay, F., & Surlemont, B. (2002). A stage model of academic spin-off creation. *Technovation*, *22*, 281–289. doi:10.1016/S0166-4972(01)00019-0

Nelson, R. R. (2004). The market economy, and the scientific commons. *Research Policy*, *33*(3), 455–471. doi:10.1016/j.respol.2003.09.008

Noble, D. F. (1977). *America by design: Science, technology, and the rise of 37 corporate capitalism*. New York, NY: Knopf.

Owen-Smith, J., & Powell, W. W. (2003). To patent or not: Faculty decisions and institutional success at technology transfer. *The Journal of Technology Transfer*, *26*(1), 99–114. doi:10.1023/A:1007892413701

Perkmann, M., & Walsh, K. (2007). University-industry relationships and open innovation: Towards a research agenda. *International Journal of Management Reviews*, *9*(4), 259–280. doi:10.1111/j.1468-2370.2007.00225.x

Perkmann, M., & Walsh, K. (2008). Engaging the scholar: Three forms of academic consulting and their impact on universities and industry. *Research Policy*, *37*(10), 1884–1891. doi:10.1016/j.respol.2008.07.009

Price, S., Oliver, M., Fartunova, M., Jones, C., Van der Meij, H., Mjelstad, S., … Wasson, B. (2005). *Review of the impact of technology-enhanced learning on roles and practices in higher education*. Kaleidoscope project deliverable 30-02-01-F. Kaleidoscope.

Roehl, H. (2000). *Instrumente der wissensorganization*. Wiesbaden, Germany: Gabler.

Roos, J., & von Krogh, G. (2002). The new language lab – Parts 1 and 2. In Little, S., Quintas, P., & Ray, P. (Eds.), *Managing Knowledge: An Essential Reader*. London, UK: Sage.

Rosell, C., & Agrawal, A. (2009). Have university knowledge flows narrowed? Evidence from patent data. *Research Policy*, *38*(1), 1–13. doi:10.1016/j.respol.2008.07.014

Sainsbury, L. (2007). *Race to the top: Sainsbury review of science and innovation*. London, UK: HM Treasury.

Santoro, M., & Bierly, P. E. (2006). Facilitators of knowledge transfer in university-industry collaborations: A knowledge-based perspective. *IEEE Transactions on Engineering Management*, *53*(4), 495–507. doi:10.1109/TEM.2006.883707

Santoro, M., & Gopalakrishnan, S. (2000). The institutionalization of knowledge transfer activities within industry–university collaborative ventures. *Journal of Engineering and Technology Management*, *17*, 299–319. doi:10.1016/S0923-4748(00)00027-8

Scarborough, H. (2008). *The evolution of business knowledge*. Oxford, UK: Oxford University Press.

Scarborough, H., & Knights, D. (2009). *In search of relevance*. Organisation Studies.

Scardamalia, M., & Bereiter, C. (2003). Knowledge building. In Guthrie, J. W. (Ed.), *Encyclopedia of Education* (2nd ed., pp. 1370–1373). New York, NY: Macmillan Reference.

Schartinger, D., Rammer, C., Fischer, M. M., & Fröhlich, J. (2002). Knowledge interactions between universities and industry in Austria: Sectoral patterns and determinants. *Research Policy*, *31*(3), 303–328. doi:10.1016/S0048-7333(01)00111-1

Shane, S. A. (2004). *Academic entrepreneurship: University spinoffs and wealth creation*. Cheltenham, UK: Edward Elgar.

Siegel, D. S., Wright, M., & Lockett, A. (2007). The rise of entrepreneurial activity at universities: Organizational and societal implications. *Industrial and Corporate Change*, *16*(4), 489–504. doi:10.1093/icc/dtm015

Slaughter, S., & Leslie, L. L. (1997). *Academic capitalism: Politics, policies and the entrepreneurial university*. Baltimore, MD: Johns Hopkins University Press.

Stephan, P. E. (2001). Educational implications of university-industry technology transfer. *The Journal of Technology Transfer*, *26*, 199–205. doi:10.1023/A:1011164806068

Svensson, G., & Wood, G. (2007). Are university students really customers? When illusion may lead to delusion for all! *International Journal of Educational Management*, *21*(1), 17–28. doi:10.1108/09513540710716795

Tijssen, R. J. W. (2004). Is the commercialization of scientific research affecting the production of public knowledge? Global trends in the output of corporate research articles. *Research Policy*, *33*, 709–733. doi:10.1016/j.respol.2003.11.002

Vallas, S. P., & Kleinman, L. (2008). Contradiction, convergence and the knowledge economy: The confluence of academic and commercial biotechnology. *Socio-economic Review, 6*(2), 283–311. doi:10.1093/ser/mwl035

Van de Ven, A., & Johnson, P. (2006). Knowledge for theory and practice. *Academy of Management Review, 31*(4), 802–821. doi:10.5465/AMR.2006.22527385

Vinig, T., & Rijsbergen, P. (2008). *Determinants of university technology transfer - Comparative study of US, Europe, and Australian universities.* Retrieved from http://ssrn.com/abstract=1324601

Weick, K., & Roberts, K. (1993). Collective mind in organizations: Heedful interrelating on flight decks. *American Quarterly, 38,* 357–381.

Willem, A., & Scarborough, H. (2006). Social capital and political bias in knowledge sharing: An exploratory study. *Human Relations, 59*(10), 1343–1370. doi:10.1177/0018726706071527

Willke, H. (1998). *Systemisches wissensmanagement.* Stuttgart, Germany: Lucius & Lucius.

Wright, M., Clarysse, B., Lockett, A., & Knockaert, M. (2008). Mid-range universities' linkages with industry: Knowledge types and the role of intermediaries. *Research Policy, 37,* 1205–1223. doi:10.1016/j.respol.2008.04.021

Yusuf, S. (2008). Intermediating knowledge exchange between universities and businesses. *Research Policy, 37,* 1167–1174. doi:10.1016/j.respol.2008.04.011

Zerhouni, E. (2003). The NIH roadmap. *Science, 302*(5642), 63–72. doi:10.1126/science.1091867

ADDITIONAL READING

Aronowitz, S. (2000). *The knowledge factory: Dismantling the corporate university and creating true higher learning.* Boston, MA: Beacon Press.

Baldridge, J. V., Julius, D. J., & Pfeffer, J. (2000). Power failure in administrative environments. *Academic Leadership.* Retrieved from http://www.academicleadership.org

Bicknell, A., Francis-Smythe, J., & Arthur, J. (2010). Knowledge transfer: De-constructing the entrepreneurial academic. *International Journal of Entrepreneurial Behaviour & Research, 16*(6), 485–501. doi:10.1108/13552551011082461

Bliemel, F., & Fassott, G. (2001). Marketing für universitäten. In Tscheulin, D. K., & Helmig, B. (Eds.), *Branchenspezifisches Marketing* (pp. 265–286). Wiesbaden, Germany: Gabler Verlag.

Bratianu, C. (2011). Universities as knowledge-intensive learning organizations. In Eardley, A., & Uden, L. (Eds.), *Innovative Knowledge Management: Concepts for Organizational Creativity and Collaborative Design* (pp. 1–17). Hershey, PA: IGI Global.

Bratianu, C., & Murakawa, H. (2004). Strategic thinking. *Transactions of JWRI, 33*(1), 79–89.

Burcea, M., & Marinescu, P. (2011). Students' perceptions on corporate social responsibility at the academic level. *Amfiteatru Economic, 13*(29), 207–220.

Löscher, A. (2004). *Developments in university autonomy in England.* Retrieved from http://www2.huberlin.de/gbz/downloads/pdf/University_Autonomy_Loescher.pdf

Mellow, G. O., & Woolis, D. D. (2010). Teetering between eras: Higher education in a global, knowledge networked world. *Horizon, 18*(4), 308–319. doi:10.1108/10748121011082617

Neave, G. (2002). Anything goes: How the accommodation of Europe's universities to European integration integrates an inspiring number of contradictions. *Tertiary Education and Management*, *8*(3), 178–191. doi:10.1080/13583883.2002.9967078

Nelles, N., & Vorley, T. (2010). From policy to practice: engaging and embedding the third mission in contemporary universities. *The International Journal of Sociology and Social Policy*, *30*(7/8), 341–353. doi:10.1108/01443331011060706

Nicolescu, L., & Dima, A. M. (2010). The quality of educational services: Institutional case study from the Romanian higher education. *Transilvanian Review of Administrative Sciences*, *28*, 100–108.

Nicolescu, L., & Păun, C. (2009). Relating higher education with the labour market – Graduates' expectations and employers' requirements. *Tertiary Education and Management*, *15*(1), 17–33. doi:10.1080/13583880802700024

Petruzzellis, L., & Romanazzi, S. (2010). Educational value: How students choose university: Evidence from an Italian university. *International Journal of Educational Management*, *24*(2), 139–158. doi:10.1108/09513541011020954

Readings, B. (1996). *The university in ruins*. Boston, MA: Harvard University Press.

Russell, M. (2005). Marketing education: A review of service quality perceptions among international students. *International Journal of Contemporary Hospitality Management*, *17*(1), 65–77. doi:10.1108/09596110510577680

Vasilache, S., & Prejmerean, M. C. (2006). *Is the university marketable? Strategies which sell careers*. Paper presented at the ASE, Marketing and Development Conference. Bucharest, Romania.

Woods, N. (1999). Good governance in international organization. *Global Governance*, *5*(1), 39–61.

Zhou, C. (2008). Emergence of the entrepreneurial university in evolution of the triple helix: The case of Northeastern University in China. *Journal of Technology Management in China*, *3*(1), 109–126. doi:10.1108/17468770810851539

KEY TERMS AND DEFINITIONS

Knowledge in Education: The constitutive elements are: factual, conceptual, procedural and meta-cognitive.

Knowledge Management: Willingness and ability of organization to organize all type of knowledge and use it in the most efficient way for the organization performance.

Knowledge Transfer: A process by which one individual or organization transmits its experience to another and systematically organized information and skills are exchanged between entities for the mutual benefit.

Knowledge Transfer Academia/Business: Any activities aimed at transferring knowledge or technology that may help either the company or the academic institute—depending on the direction of transfer—to further pursue its activities.

Learning Organization: The sum of the learning activities and achievements of all organization members based on continuous interaction with its environment.

University Knowledge Transfer: The inflow and outflow of knowledge between universities and its transfer partners.

Chapter 6
Knowledge Management and Innovative Learning

Tiit Elenurm
Estonian Business School, Estonia

ABSTRACT

The aim of this chapter is to link knowledge management as a field of education to innovative learning. There are opportunities to apply personal knowledge management and knowledge sharing logic in several related subject fields that enable innovative learning. Raising awareness of business students about their online and face-to-face networking priorities and entrepreneurial orientations are educational tools for managing personal connectivity and for understanding knowledge management challenges linked to innovative learning. The experiential learning cycle is implemented in field projects, which also support cross-cultural learning and highlight real life challenges of knowledge sharing in innovative activities. The assessment of knowledge management prerequisites in different organizations serves as the departure point for knowledge management development visions. The chapter explains that knowledge management learning in business studies is not limited to a separate knowledge management course. Action learning projects can mean innovative learning both for students and managers that learn how to apply external "gatekeepers."

INTRODUCTION

The innovative learning vision was popularized by the Club of Rome three decades ago. Innovative learning is the alternative to learning by shock, which destroys the equilibrium of the social system and is also an alternative to normative learning, which is guided by traditions and reproduces the *status quo*. During recent decades, mankind has witnessed many situations where learning by shock has dominated over anticipation, for instance in the recent global financial and economic crisis. Innovative learning is based on two processes: anticipation of future changes and participation in problem solving based on the new information (Botkin, et al., 1979). In innovative learning, anticipation and participation are not limited to individual learning behaviour, but should be applied in small groups and also in organizations and social institutions. Knowledge management tools support anticipation and participation inside an organisation or in a wider learning community.

DOI: 10.4018/978-1-4666-1969-2.ch006

Knowledge management is also related to normative learning as it enables sharing and reusing earlier knowledge, which is relevant for further action. In a crisis situation knowledge management should help to overcome shock and act smartly and rapidly.

Educational institutions face the challenge of not only preparing students for managing knowledge in organizations but also for personal knowledge management in order to cope with the information overload and to be competitive in new fields of knowledge work. Knowledge-based enterprises face the challenge of anticipating future market and technology trends. Organizations need more active participation of their members in searching for and sharing knowledge that is relevant to their learning and growth perspectives. The objectives of this chapter are:

- To examine the synergies between innovative learning and knowledge management;
- To explain the role of personal knowledge management for linking innovative learning and knowledge sharing;
- To identify and explain innovative educational practices that enable knowledge management and innovative learning in business education and in training and development programmes for organizations.

This chapter at first highlights the background for understanding synergies between innovative learning and knowledge management. Crucial knowledge management concepts are discussed in order to explain their implications for innovative learning. Subsequently, the role of personal knowledge management in linking innovative thinking and knowledge sharing is explained. This theoretical background serves as a point of departure for analyzing five educational and training practices that have been used by the author for enhancing innovative learning.

BACKGROUND

Knowledge Management as an Enabler of Innovative Learning

Davenport and Prusak (1998) have described knowledge as a fluid mix of framed experience, contextual information, and expert insight that provides a framework for evaluating and incorporating new experience and information. This description is especially relevant in situations, where established traditions or procedures are challenged by new ideas but innovators still have only limited explicit and systematic knowledge to prove the effectiveness of the proposed innovation. The relationship between tacit and explicit knowledge (Nonaka & Takeuchi, 1995) has been among central issues in the knowledge management discourse. The SECI (socialization – externalization – combination – internalization) model of these authors introduced the spiral of knowledge conversions as the way to create and apply new knowledge. Socialization, face to face communication and joint work experience are crucial for undertanding tacit knowledge of other people. Tacit knowledge is difficult to transfer to another person by means of text or verbalizing it. It is grounded in the experience of experts who often know more than they are able to express without special tools that support externalization. Explicit knowldedge is clearly structured written or online text, audio or video presentation that can be easily disseminated without personal involvement of the expert who was the original source of this knowledge. Innovative ideas are often created by combining different knowledge sources, through the spiralling of tacit knowledge and explicit knowledge conversion.

In Nonaka and Konno (1998) online neworking benefits are mainly linked to the phase of combining already externalized ideas. Contemporary online social networks such as Facebook or LinkedIn, however, enable some forms of socialization between people that often do not share the same physical space for face-to-face networking. The Internet has enabled information monitoring and search, but it does not necessarily mean that individuals, teams and organizations are prepared to combine new knowledge sources in the way that enables innovative learning. We have modified the SECI scheme of Nonaka and Takeuchi (1995) in order to highlight some challenging innovative learning issues that have to be addressed in the spiral of knowledge conversions (Figure 1). Questions that we have added to four areas of knowledge conversion reflect issues that have been raised by students in our courses for studying business in virtual networks. Similar issues have also been raised by managers, when we have consulted enteprises, where young leaders see innovation and international networking as business development priorities.

Young innovative leaders learn about new ideas when socializing with their staff, but they also often search for innovative ideas in global networks. In order to promote a start-up enterprise that has globalization ambitions, online externalization of the advantages of their technologies and services has become an essential skill. The digital user generation produces new ways of working and communicating (Tapscott, 2009) but easy access to a wide variety of knowledge sources does not necessarily produce the systemic combination that would lead to a new understanding and wisdom (Carr, 2010). This contradiction creates challenges both for academic institutions and businesses that are focused on innovative learning. The anticipation of innovative business opportunties assumes systematic monitoring and combining new knowledge sources. Real participation, however, depends on internalization of new solutions through joint vision, action and reflection.

The traditional domain of higher education has been science-based theoretical thinking but business education has also focused on the externalization of lessons learnt from success stories of experienced business people. Transferring the skill to ride a bicycle is often used as an example of a tacit knowledge for common people. Negotiation skills, especially for copying with conflicting or hidden interests of partners in a stressful situation, is an example from the field of business education, where tacit knowledge is needed. The combination of different knowledge sources is an important challenge for management and entrepreneurship studies, which by their nature have interdisciplinary ambitions. Socialization is supported by training methods that rely on group work exercises.

MBA programmes and in-house management training programmes can both enable knowledge sharing between participants that already have business experience if they are ready to reflect on their experience. Mintzberg (2004) has, however, considered the focus of MBA programmes on financial analysis as obsessive since it happens at the expense of leadership and management learning and does not explain the importance of informal communication. Combining more and less formalized knowledge sources in business studies assumes the understanding of the limitations of codifying tacit knowledge in financial reports and business plans. Codified knowledge that is not understood by representatives of other professions or disciplines complicates participation in knowledge sharing. Disciplinary borders may help to disseminate established knowledge in structured and efficient ways but innovative learning and creation of new knowledge are enabled by practical field projects and other interdisciplinary and experiential learning methods. The internalization of knowledge means integrating it with values and priorities that guide action. Knowledge that students do not link with their practical experience or future prospects is "washed out of their mind" soon after an exam. Such knowledge is not internalized.

Figure 1. SECI model and innovative learning challenges

	Tacit	Tacit	
Tacit			Explicit
	Socialization How to share time between face-to-face and online networking? Creating new contacts or nurturing existing contacts? Focus on limited number of strong ties or on large number of weak ties? Emotional ties versus business interests?	**Externalization** How to externalize your knowledge online and on paper in formats that match users' pre-knowledge and actions? How to link open innovation opportunities and intellectual property protection?	
Tacit	**Internalization** How to make difference between viral buzzwords, theoretical and experience-based knowledge? How to integrate value-based and fact-based knowledge? How to manage risks of testing new idas in action?	**Combination** How to find and monitor new knowledge sources? How to assess relevance of available knowledge sources? How to identify links and contradictions between different knowledge sources?	Explicit
	Explicit	Explicit	

Experiential learning as the process of acquiring knowledge through the transformation of experience in the learning cycle of experiencing, reflecting, thinking, and acting (Kolb & Kolb, 2005) is an educational approach that tries to link the identification of new business opportunities to exploiting the opportunity that was considered to be the best when using the knowledge that was available when starting the action and later learning from after action feedback. Experiential learning includes reviewing learning outcomes and re-defining learning priorities in each cycle. Experiential learning can also make use of fail-ure as a learning experience in order to redesign how business planning is taught by focusing on divergent thinking (Honig, 2004). Reflecting on reasons for success and failure, the values and interpretations of stakeholders involved in business are essential for gaining new personal knowledge in such a learning process. Experiential learning can mean learning by shock if the risk analysis is missing and factors leading to a serious failure are not anticipated. Personal knowledge management skills help to acquire pre-knowledge and to develop supportive networks in order to diminish failure risks.

Personal Knowledge Management and Knowledge Sharing

Peter Drucker (1999) has been among the first management thinkers to highlight the importance of managing oneself as a knowledge worker in the emerging knowledge economy. He stressed that knowledge workers have to understand not only their own strengths and the value of their knowledge, but also the need to take into consideration the learning and communication style of their boss. They have to be able to teach their boss in their own field of expertise. Personal knowledge management skills enable not only the personal growth and advancement of individuals, but also support external information awareness, internal knowledge dissemination, organizational focus on the core business and continuous innovation in organizations (Cheong & Tsui, 2010). Personal knowledge management helps to anticipate future trends in the business environment and technology that are not visible in the everyday work environment of an employee and to understand early signals from markets. In addition to anticipation, personal knowledge management can support also participation as the other key process of innovative learning. Participation in networks across organizational borders can enhance the ability of an employee to introduce the best practices and new ideas to colleagues.

Davenport (2010) explains the core of personal knowledge management by describing capabilities that are essential for creating, sharing, and applying knowledge. These capabilities include searching for knowledge and capturing knowledge in such a way that others can easily benefit from this, for instance tagging personal documents that can be then accessed by others. Prusak and Cranefield (2010) have stressed the importance of four foundational practices of the personal knowledge management:

- Scanning and reinventing;
- Vetting and filtering;
- Investing in networks;
- Getting out of the office.

Scanning and reinventing means not only searching for ideas globally, but also selecting, analysing and assimilating the right ideas that match local needs. Students should be aware of who created the information in addition to how and why it was created and communicated in order to assess the reliability of information sources, including Internet sources such as Wikipedia. Academic educators often blame Wikipedia for the low quality of information used by students, but it would be more constructive to deal with Wikipedia as with one of many Internet-based gateways that can be used for identifying primary information sources and for finding the texts of their original authors.

Vetting and filtering is a skill that is generally not taught in academia (Prusak & Cranefield, 2010) although in a world of information overload and diversity of knowledge sources, learning to evaluate the quality of information and deciding which knowledge sources to trust has become more complex. Traditional measures of cognitive authority such as a respected publishing house and author affiliation are often difficult to apply in the Internet.

Castells (1996) has explained factors that lead to the rise of the network society. Networking has become an especially important business model under the influence of Internet-based learning communities and collaborative innovation networks (Gloor, 2006) that help to overcome distance and time obstacles in business co-operation. Internet-based social networking tools such as Facebook can be used for developing business networks that co-create new business ideas and visions. Snowden (2005) stated that while traditional knowledge management in organizations tries to force people to share knowledge with colleagues they do not necessarily want to work with, social knowledge networking is more about mutually directed relationships and much more communitarian. Wolfe *et al.* (2010) pointed out that dominant technology-driven applications for virtual communication have change cycles of five years (for instance MSN "generation" giving way to Facebook "generation"). Such a technological innovation pace reduces the traditional concept of generation change based on the biological cycle of about twenty years and as a result, even today's technologically competent managers may miss the communication tools and trends of new employees after five years if they are not engaged in continuous learning. Glow (2010) presents his ideas and the Google experience of designing crowd-sourced learning paths, where learning communities use social bookmarking and Twitter lists to disseminate learning resources of experts. The aim is to tear down the boundaries between experts and learners and to empower all learners to be experts in some field, at least experts in defining the problems they need to solve.

Online networking has the potential to create ties, although often weak, with a larger number of people than face to face contacts. Using weak ties for knowledge acquisition in diverse networks, rather than limiting knowledge sources to close friends and family proved to be advantageous for finding a job already before the Internet age (Granovetter, 1974). The Internet offers many career-related networking opportunities to professionals in addition to LinkedIn. Online networking assumes not only information scanning and filtering skills but also participation by sharing one's own knowledge with other networkers. Wenger (2002) stressed the role of peripheral participation in communities of practice in order to develop competencies that are needed for networking. Online networking offers opportunities for cognitive diversity that enables innovative learning but it can also lead to communities, where like-minded persons repeat and reinforce the narrow-minded views of each other. Kolb (2008) analyzed geophysical, technical, interpersonal, cultural, and other dimensions of connectivity for learning and explained that individuals must connect with

others to gain knowledge. However, they have to clarify what is the requisite connectivity for them and at least some of the time be disconnected for individual reflection.

Getting out of your office in the business education context means internship and field projects in enterprises and international mobility of students. Mostert (2007) suggests getting out of your comfort zone as a way to creative ideas. Field projects do not mean that students only acquire experience inside the organization they are trying to help. They can be more useful for their client organization if they are able to combine online knowledge sources with the evidence from direct contacts in the marketplace. That is especially valuable if students come from foreign countries that are potential export destinations for the field project enterprise. New tasks in new environments and in new teams help one to overcome rigid ways of thinking and to apply innovative learning.

When looking for synergy between knowledge management, including personal knowledge management, and preparing students for innovative learning, five desirable learning outcomes can be proposed:

1. Learners are aware of their orientations that serve as a point of departure for understanding their personal knowledge management priorities that are linked to innovative learning.

2. Learners know how to manage their connectivity and participation in social networks and how to find the right balance between online and face-to-face learning.

3. Learners have skills for scanning and filtering information that can lead to discovering and implementing innovative ideas.

4. Learners accomplish experiential learning cycles that highlight real life challenges of knowledge sharing and innovative activities.

5. Learners understand knowledge management prerequisites in different organizations

and are prepared to participate in implementing innovations in knowledge management.

We will give an overview of some training methods and educational practices that we have used for attaining these learning outcomes.

LINKING KNOWLEDGE MANAGEMENT AND INNOVATIVE LEARNING IN BUSINESS EDUCATION AND TRAINING

Understanding Implications of Personal Orientations on Knowledge Search and Sharing

Knowledge management focuses on accessing the right knowledge at the right time and in the right format. Peter Drucker (1985) stressed that innovation and risk-taking are more entrepreneurial than managerial challenges. In the context of business education, self-assessment of entrepreneurial orientations of students can serve as a point of departure for specifying their personal knowledge management priorities. Entrepreneurship researchers have developed the entrepreneurial orientation construct that integrates five dimensions: innovation, pro-activeness, risk-taking, autonomy and competitive aggressiveness (Lumpkin & Dess, 1996). The construct of the single entrepreneurial orientation however does not address some crucial choices that influence knowledge search and sharing by entrepreneurs. The construct of a single entrepreneurial orientation has been further developed by differentiating three entrepreneurial orientations: imitative entrepreneurship, individual innovative entrepreneurship and co-creative entrepreneurship (Elenurm, et al., 2007). Following this differentiated approach to entrepreneurial orientations, we have created self-assessment tool consisting of fifteen questions covering guiding principles and knowledge sources in these main phases of the entrepreneurial process: business opportunity identification, business idea development and implementation. Sources of entrepreneurial ideas, interaction, and knowledge sharing with customers and partners and risk management in the entrepreneurial activity are reflected in the questionnaire. Students, executives and entrepreneurs have been asked to compare under each question statements that correspond to imitative, individual innovative and co-creative orientation and to choose only one statement that is most suitable for describing his/her preferences in the role of an entrepreneur.

From 2005 to 2010 our self-assessment tool was used by 1075 respondents during academic courses and special training sessions for entrepreneurs. 32% of them (98 females and 245 males) had practical entrepreneurship experience. 40% of self-assessment tool users gave priority to statements that correspond to the co-creative entrepreneurial orientation that encourages knowledge sharing in networks and open innovation for developing new business ideas. Open innovation assumes the use of purposive inflows and outflows of knowledge to accelerate internal innovation and simultaneously to expand markets for external use of innovation (Chesbrough, et al., 2006). Individual innovative orientation in the total business creation and development process was supported by 35% and imitative orientation by 25% of respondents in our research. Consistent individual innovators have to focus on protecting their innovative ideas. As a result, their opportunities to rely on open innovation and networking practices are more limited.

What are implications of three entrepreneurial orientations for personal knowledge management and innovative learning? Followers of the imitative orientation could benefit from scanning and filtering these best business practices in more advanced market economies that can easily be transferred to a less advanced business environment. Analysing best practices at the business opportunity identification stage may help one to find solutions that can be combined in a new way at the business development stage. However, innovative orientation and co-creation are necessary for innovative learning by anticipating future trends that lead to radically new business solutions. When comparing choices of statements that correspond to these orientations we can see that at the stage of business opportunity identification more than 46% of respondents preferred statements that represent co-creative entrepreneurial orientation, whereas at the later stage of business development this percentage has diminished to 42% and at the implementation stage to 34%. At the stage of implementation and commercialisation, the individual innovative orientation tends to dominate over the co-creative orientation. It is also reflected in low support for the "open book" approach to disseminating financial information (13% support this). The "open book" approach enables more active knowledge sharing, but it can also increase the risk of competitors undermining the competitive advantage of the entrepreneur if they receive information about the resources and the financial situation of the venture.

When setting up an enterprise, the situation may develop where an entrepreneur encourages other people to develop new ideas collectively and tries to combine good business solutions of partners at the business opportunity identification stage. Then, however, if he does not disclose business information to the earlier contributors or insists on owning the innovation individually at the implementation stage, this may lead to conflicts of interest and diminish further knowledge sharing opportunities.

Respondents that already had acquired entrepreneurship experience were more ready to share even negative information with customers (42%) than inexperienced respondents (30.8%). Although younger respondents are more enthusiastic about innovative entrepreneurship than older experienced entrepreneurs, they often lack skills for anticipating potential problems and for involving employees and customers to the innovative learning in the process of creating and developing a new venture. In the globalizing world,

new entrepreneurs face a crucial choice between entrepreneurial orientations as the departure point for searching and applying business knowledge. Should they start their first business by imitating some well-established business idea? Will they trust their own individual creativity or need creative business partners for innovative learning? Is international networking and co-creation their way to innovation and business success? In-house training sessions have demonstrated that clarifying entrepreneurial orientations of staff members is also important for managers who are interested in encouraging internal entrepreneurship in their organisations and in finding employees who are more interested in proving their knowledge in innovative development projects.

BUSINESS OPPORTUNITIES IN VIRTUAL NETWORKING

Business students tend to have more time and technical skills for communication via Facebook, Twitter, MySpace, Orkut, and other online networking environments than the majority of their professors. Keeping in touch with old classmates and friends or hobbies are, however, for students more usual reasons to spend time online than a systematic approach to developing their virtual network for finding new business opportunities.

Estonian Business School offers the elective course *Business opportunities in virtual networks,* which helps students to clarify their virtual networking priorities as part of the personal knowledge management strategy. "Global village" (McLuhan, 1962), networking society (Castells, 1996), and small world (Uzzi, et al., 2007) concepts are explained and new trends in developing virtual networks are analyzed. The "global village" metaphor explains that virtual networking tools to some extent enable similar connectivity between people all around a globe to that which occurred in a small village in a traditional society. The key challenge is to find the right communities and to build new and meaningful contacts. The small world concept draws attention to the role of networkers that are able to link different communities and in this way to shorten the virtual distance between other people. The main learning focus is on searching for new networking opportunities in teams that students create when discussing their networking experience, the present connectivity, and future priorities of using virtual networking tools. The author of this chapter has run the course 1-2 times a year since 2006.

Building trust as a prerequisite of business co-operation and related knowledge sharing is an important discussion topic during the course. In order to follow the co-creative entrepreneurial orientation, participants of the network should accept interdependence, help each other and be able to overcome tensions between individuality and community. Mutual trust and rules for sharing sensitive business information such as business ideas and contacts have to be established and followed by members of the virtual community. Collective trust is based on shared norms and mutually recognized co-operation principles in a group or community, where members deepen their knowledge and expertise in a common field or topic by interacting on an ongoing basis (Wenger, et al., 2002). During the course, these tools to enhance trust in virtual communities are compared with trust creation in face-to-face business contacts.

Content analysis of student homework that was used as the input for further teamwork in classroom about social and business networking experiences of participants has highlighted the following main patterns of networking practices among students (Elenurm, 2007):

- Being continuously involved with close friends, virtual networking as a way to nurture core and significant ties during international mobility of students;

- "Do it yourself" technically oriented communities of practice;

- News search for finding professional job offers, promoting oneself as a potential employee;

- Sharing professional knowledge with colleagues working in the same field and/or having the same educational background;

- Entertainment-focused networking: sharing music, photos, and videos, playing games.

When comparing virtual networking priorities of students in 2007-2010 some trends towards acquiring new knowledge in their field of business and studies can be observed but active online knowledge sharing is more often demonstrated by students involved in music sharing or in a community for a technical hobby. Younger full-time students are generally well informed about social networking opportunities but often do not have strategic priorities for choosing virtual networks, which could enhance their personal business-related knowledge or link them to entrepreneurs in other countries in order to search for new business opportunities for co-creative entrepreneurship. Distance learning students, who are older and already have entrepreneurial experience, tend to lack the time and experience of online social networking. During the course, however, they discover business opportunities in using social software and become more positive about investing their time in virtual networking. The joint learning process of students, who represent both the Facebook "generation" and the pre-Facebook "generations," has given practical evidence of reverse mentoring, where the younger generation gives advice and coaches older group members in applying the new tools of virtual networking. The experience of Deloitte and other knowledge-based organizations has demonstrated that reverse mentoring is also valuable for innovative learning inside business organizations as a social exchange tool for keeping older employees engaged and younger employees committed (Chaudhuri & Ghosh, 2011). Such practice, however, assumes that both older and younger employees understand their personal knowledge management gaps.

E-Learning as a Learning Community Tool

E-learning can introduce students to knowledge management practices and challenges and especially to the role of tacit and explicit knowledge if e-learning is applied in the blended learning framework (Osguthorpe & Graham, 2003). The blended learning process combines online learning with face to face communication and teamwork in the classroom and in practical field project settings. Blended learning can assist students in acquiring knowledge management skills and involve them in scanning, filtering and developing creative ideas in the learning processes, which are not limited to the time and space of one blended course. Personal knowledge management assumes that one finds the right balance between open and closed learning communities and that one encourages students to search for additional new information from online sources that are not incorporated into the ready-made e-learning courseware.

In order to train students to scan, vet, and filter information in a learning community, tasks to search for and upload relevant publication and website overviews to e-learning discussion forums is a good point of departure for e-learning. When conducting knowledge management and international business courses at the Estonian Business School, we consider it essential to train students to attach the correct metadata to their overview, which allows them to assess the reliability of each knowledge source and to add key words and other types of tags that describe the relevance of their knowledge source for different stakeholders in

organizations. We encourage students to rate the contributions of other students in their individual learning and in their innovative learning of organizations where they are involved in field projects. In additional to virtual discussion forums, wikis, and clearly structured knowledge bases are tools for re-using reviews as a learning input for the next groups of students. The best contributions of students are included in the knowledge base of the course and can be re-used by students in the next learning cycle. New students are, however, not supposed to repeat earlier contributions, but are encouraged to study the contributions of earlier students before searching for new information in order "not to reinvent the wheel."

E-learning enables cross-border knowledge sharing, where students in one country, for instance, comment on reviews of students from another country about knowledge sources that describe business opportunities in their country. We have used such knowledge sharing between students studying the international business opportunities of the Baltic region. The student groups were located in Tallinn, Helsinki and Budapest. It is, however, not easy to align the time schedules of courses arranged in different universities in order to offer feedback from other students at the right time in their learning cycle.

An important contribution of the blended learning process involves helping students to reflect on the impact of synchronous and asynchronous, face-to-face and online, text-based and richer communication tools on business interactions. That process also reveals cultural differences in using explicit knowledge that can be interpreted without the personal involvement of the knowledge provider and tacit knowledge that has to be shared through socialization.

International Student Teams for Experiential Learning in Field Projects for Innovative Enterprises

Cross-cultural teamwork serves as a tool for developing personal knowledge management skills in the "global village." It is essential for understanding the perspectives and worldviews of people with a different background and knowledge base. Values are the key determinants of a culture (Hofstede, 2001). Understanding the implications of values on knowledge searching and sharing behaviours in an intercultural environment can be developed in experiential learning cycles arranged for international student teams.

We conduct courses, where student teams act as gatekeepers that combine international business information, and search potential business contacts for small and medium-sized enterprises mainly by using Internet sources but also personal networks in homelands of their members. "Gatekeeper" is used here as a metaphor for an external group that understands the information needs and knowledge gaps of Small and Medium-Sized Enterprises (SME) and is able to monitor, select and present international business information that is relevant for SME internationalisation. An essential principle during the course is action learning. The action-learning concept developed by Revans (1980) represents a problem-based approach to learning, where co-learners co-operate as members of small groups whose goal is to complete a task and achieve learning through the process of problem solving and reflection. Action research is a process, where preparing and implementing changes is linked to the promotion of learning and collaboration between all participants of the process, but where research results that are applicable in other contexts are also produced (Leitch, 2007). Action learning is applied in our projects by combining overviews of meetings with entrepreneurs and changes in preliminary tasks, cases that train students to understand possible knowledge gaps of entrepreneurs, analysis

of mid-term and final project reports of teams, reflective team discussions and feedback from representatives of enterprises. (Elenurm, 2008). Experience of the Estonian Business School starting from 2006 indicates that the positive impact of student teams both for their own experiential learning and personal knowledge development and for innovative learning of client organizations is highest in projects for innovative start-ups that need creativity to position and possibly re-define their products or services for foreign clients.

Multiple sources of knowledge were used in projects by creating synergy between e-learning and information scanning via the Internet, using online surveys and networks in student's home country, facilitating the development of international teams in a classroom setting through face to face group work and case discussions in addition to knowledge sharing between SMEs and international teams of students outside the classroom. Additional individual tasks for searching and reviewing Internet sources relevant to different stakeholders interested in business opportunities that can be linked to the Baltic countries were used in order to promote business information search skills. The project work results were assessed by the SMEs and by the tutor on the basis of the written reports and oral presentations.

Company projects also functioned as an action learning processes for students in the context of understanding the limitations of management practices, including knowledge management in small organizations. Students learned how to search for additional information and how to attain a mutual understanding of the realistic scope of their task within the team and during meetings with the representative of the SME. Students had to meet the enterprise representative and were encouraged to re-negotiate the preliminary written task if they are able to find better match between knowledge represented in the team and needs of the entrepreneur. Many students did not have any experience of making appointments with busy entrepreneurs-managers before these projects.

Students learned that SME managers are sometimes slow to answer e-mails and tend to change their priorities without timely notice. Quite often entrepreneurs and SME managers did not inform their subordinates enough about the projects and did not delegate the role of SME information disseminator if they themselves happened to go abroad on a business trip. The action research process revealed that even if the management of daily operations has been decentralized, the team approach and empowering subordinates to share business knowledge is used less in development projects that involve outsiders. In some enterprises, the dissemination of information to students and the mandate of the student team to conduct meaningful information exchange with potential business partners were limited by the strict rules safeguarding the company's business secrets.

During their project work, regular inter-team knowledge sharing has been useful for creating synergy between students representing information sources from different countries. Wenger (2002) stresses the role of peripheral participation in order to develop competencies that are needed in a community of practice. Earlier at WebCT and in recent years in Moodle e-learning discussion forums, motivated students can experience peripheral participation by offering to other teams additional innovative ideas for their projects after studying their progress reports.

Efficient communication with busy entrepreneurs was often hindered when the first face-to-face meeting with entrepreneurs occurred too late, but also due to asking the entrepreneur to answer too many irrelevant questions as a result of insufficient preparatory study of Internet sources. Students from some South European countries were often eager to discuss the preliminary task and ideas at some length before deciding on their input for a specific subtask. They preferred to go to the first meeting with the entrepreneur without sufficiently studying the information that was available at the company website or from other online sources. Informal face-to-face communica-

tion is a good way to reveal tacit knowledge, but the Estonian entrepreneurs assumed more active scanning of the information that had been made available in Internet before devoting their time to deeper face-to-face discussions with students. Virtual scanning of information before the face-to-face meeting has usually been a higher priority for students from Germany and Nordic countries.

Five dimensions of national culture: individualism/collectivism, masculinity/femininity, power distance, uncertainty avoidance, and long-term short-term orientation studied by Hofstede (2001) serve as a framework for interpreting some differences of information processing and knowledge sharing between team members in the action learning process. Hofstede and his new team members have (Hofstede, et al., 2010) analysed in their publications the implications of five dimensions on several aspects of intercultural cooperation, including educational institutions and workplaces. The individualism/collectivism dimension influences the readiness to share knowledge in teams. Extreme individualism is reflected in the reluctance to be engaged in a project where the outcome depends on the efforts of other team members. Extremely high collectivism can lead to conformism, where team members do not propose new ideas that may be criticised by others.

Uncertainty avoidance, in the knowledge acquisition and transfer context, means that experts are eager to get exact formal descriptions of their tasks (Thiessen, et al., 2007). Students from countries that are high on uncertainty avoidance scale have often insisted to having a better-structured task with the final instruction and much more background information in the preliminary written task as the departure point for their action learning process. Demanding from SMEs more comprehensive pre-information in a unified format, although helpful for diminishing uncertainty for the team, would have, however, been in conflict with the emergent nature of the action research and diminished the role of innovative learning in the process of co-defining the worthwhile practical task through conversations between students and SME representatives. In fact, training skills for identifying the real problem and finding relevant business information was an essential part of the gatekeeper role. Students from China and from other more collectivistic and relatively high power distance countries have assumed that a team leader appointed by the facilitating lecturer could make the knowledge sharing easier. They felt uncomfortable in the situation, where team leader's role was not pre-defined and could only emerge in the teamwork process. Until roles in the team were not clear, they were reluctant to express individual creative ideas but after the team had clarified roles and tasks of their members, students from China have often applied more efforts to collect information for fulfilling their task than students form more individualistic cultures.

Ideas of student teams that were considered valuable by entrepreneurs were usually related to improving the SME website, presenting an amended SME profile to potential foreign clients and using e-commerce opportunities for international business. Some student teams managed to identify gaps in the available product information and offered new ideas about re-packaging services. Information for creating new international business contacts was, however, most often identified as the most valuable contribution of the student team from the point of view of the entrepreneur.

Limited pre-knowledge about skills and sector-specific networking readiness of international Erasmus exchange students before they are involved to field projects and start to co-operate with innovative entrepreneurs complicates formation of international student teams. One option could be to involve in some mode of peripheral participation in the gatekeeper network these foreign students that have participated in the course earlier and have already left for their home country. They could be motivated to continue to act as external online experts for new cross-border project teams after they have returned to their home university. In order to increase the continuity of the learning

process, one solution is to disseminate information about potential company projects to future Erasmus exchange students already before they arrive in Estonia and are asked to join a project team. This would assume linking the course to a broader online Erasmus exchange student community.

International student teams had to analyze the knowledge gaps of their client entrepreneurs and present a self-reflection of their teamwork experience. The written peer review included the assessment of the general contribution of other students and also the specification of how often each team member participated in knowledge sharing, to what extent he/she was a source of creative ideas, to what extent he/she defended his/her views in discussions and expressed positive feelings in communication. The reflection on the teamwork and possible difficulties in communication with the entrepreneur and his team supported the experiential learning cycles in order to highlight the real life challenges of knowledge sharing and initiating changes in entrepreneurial organizations.

Applying international student teams in the role of "gatekeepers" for growing SMEs should not be seen only as a learning exercise for students. Applying the knowledge of team members that have diversified international backgrounds can also facilitate the organizational learning in entrepreneurial start-ups. The ability to set a task for an international team and implement results that are produced by the student team reflects the readiness of organizations to involve external experts to support their innovative learning and growth processes. Such readiness is linked to the learning and growth perspective of the balanced scorecard. The balance scorecard concept of Kaplan and Norton (1996) has been used as a strategically oriented measurement tool by many organizations during the recent decade. Organizations limit their innovative learning and growth potential if they only measure the reskilling, empowerment, and alignment of their permanent staff. Enterprises that are interested in finding and monitoring new knowledge sources will benefit from new information and ideas offered by outsiders even if these are not experienced consultants. Small start-up enterprises are often too busy to monitor all relevant knowledge sources, and at the same time, they do not have resources for engaging expensive management consultants. In order to benefit from external knowledge providers they should, however, at first assess to what extent they are ready for information sharing with external teams and to anticipate their needs for finding and monitoring additional knowledge sources.

Innovative learning assumes consensus building in the action team and anticipation of potential problems before the action that leads to the new experience. In Figure 2, we have pointed out enablers of innovative learning in the experiential learning cycle that we have tried to create in our action learning projects.

We have involved international teams with diversified knowledge sources and pre-knowledge in joint field experience. Reflective observations have been facilitated not only by the progress reports of the team, but also in creative thinking sessions where teams can offer new ideas to each other. Abstract concept formation has been supported to some extent by discussing future development scenarios of the Baltic region, but the existing project work format has been too limited for developing radical innovations. At the same time, the limited scale and length of projects diminish the risk of the all-embracing failure for all stakeholders involved in the experiential learning cycle. The risk of ending up in learning through shock instead of innovative learning would be higher if all team members have full time jobs and long-term engagement in the same enterprise without alternative career options.

Figure 2. Enablers of innovative learning in the experiential learning cycle

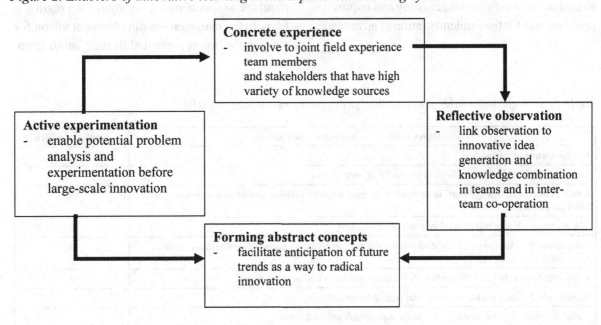

Priorities for Knowledge Management Innovations

Master-level knowledge management courses have to prepare students for introducing innovative knowledge management practices. When searching for and suggesting new knowledge management tools to decision makers in their organizations, students should be able to assess how prepared an organization is for knowledge management initiatives and which knowledge management prerequisites are already in place. Cruywagen *et al.* (2008) have pointed out that "one size does not fit all" and advocated the "best fit" approach that addresses the contextual differences of organisations. Studying knowledge management prerequisites in organisations supports the best fit approach by clarifying the situation that serves as a point of departure for a new knowledge management development initiative. One knowledge management development challenge is how to avoid the premature and formal use of knowledge management technologies that are not supported by organizational learning. A shared understanding of the existing and required prerequisites for the implementation of advanced

knowledge management solutions is needed for innovative learning in organizations.

We have analysed the priorities and potential fields for knowledge management development with the help of a list of statements that reflect some essential knowledge management practices and tools related to these practices. In the process of running knowledge management training courses for master's students since 2001, we have asked participants to rank knowledge management prerequisites according to their importance to the organizations they work for. Respondents were asked to provide supporting arguments for their evaluation of the importance of the knowledge management prerequisites. Table 1 presents a list of short formulations of the knowledge management prerequisites that we have used.

The list in Table 1 reflects soft and hard prerequisites for socialization and codification. The principles essential for personal knowledge management and the tools for applying information technology based networking are included. During knowledge management courses teams of students had to use knowledge management prerequisite assessments as an input for creating a knowledge management development vision for an organisation represented in their small team.

Table 1. Average knowledge management prerequisites rankings in 2010

Prerequisites of efficient knowledge management	Ranking in 2010
Free circulation of information	2
Employees are able to combine different sources of information	4
Virtual databases/knowledge bases, Intranet and colleagues are more valuable sources of information than paper documents	9
The information search and retrieval system is used efficiently	8
Information about the competencies of all members of the organization is accessible on electronic *yellow pages (staff accounting cards)*	10
Employees have recognized fields where their expert knowledge can support others	3
Special virtual project workrooms have been created for project teams	7
Virtual information processing and knowledge sharing tools are used actively	6
Promoting information sharing between colleagues is linked to bonus schemes	5
Trust between employees as a basis for knowledge sharing	1

Students were also encouraged to add their own prerequisites to the original checklist or to propose amendments to prerequisite specifications. During recent years, additional prerequisite proposals of participants are most often linked to using social software tools to be involved in broader professional networks. Readiness to co-operate in the value chain has been suggested as a prerequisite for inter-organisational knowledge management. At the same time, inside the organisation the need for regular personal contacts has been pointed out.

From 2006-2010, the highest placed prerequisite on average has been: *employees have recognised fields where their expert knowledge can support others*. It was followed by: *virtual information processing and knowledge sharing tools are used actively*. *Free circulation of information* has received high rankings not only during the years 2001-2003, but also during 2007-2010. However, during the economic boom in 2006, *free circulation of information, the ability to combine different sources of information* and *the promotion of information sharing between colleagues by using bonus schemes* received relatively low rankings. *Trust between employees* was, on average, the third placed prerequisite in 2006-2009. However, it had topped the ranking list during the economic crises. In some written comments by participants, trust is interpreted as the main prerequisite that enables an individual and an organization to learn from past mistakes. Internal competition inside an organisation, especially in the situation of crises and downsizing, is seen as a factor that inhibits trust and knowledge sharing. A*ctive use of virtual information processing and knowledge sharing tools* has had volatile rankings. Group discussions have demonstrated divergent views about this prerequisite depending on the business sector and existing infrastructure. Some participants link the active use of virtual tools mainly to the human factor and see changing attitudes and the readiness of personnel as a high priority for their organizations, while others

believe that active use is mainly enhanced by developing information technology software and hardware. Master's students from subsidiaries of international corporations link the active use of virtual knowledge sharing tools to a strong corporate culture and the promotion of younger employees to managerial positions. *Considering virtual databases/knowledge bases and colleagues more valuable information sources than paper documents* has received lower ratings during the recent years. Written comments have pointed out that the digitalization of documents is now a normal practice in many organisations and for this reason it has lost its high ranking. *Virtual project workrooms* and *the provision of information about the competencies of all members or organisations in electronic format* have received low ranking during the whole observed period from 2001 to 2010. It can be explained by the domination of small and medium-sized enterprise representatives among course participants. At the same time, the principle that *employees have recognized fields where their expert knowledge can support others* has gained higher popularity. Observing this principle in an organization increases personal knowledge management opportunities. However, it is evident that the application of this principle in organizations is not seen as a function of a knowledge base of personal competencies, but rather an issue of leadership, division of labour and performance assessment. The need to have more regular feedback from the boss was stressed by several participants in their written arguments. These tools link individual and organizational learning.

Change trends of the rankings of knowledge management prerequisites from 2001 to 2010 demonstrates not only the increasing role of the virtual knowledge sharing tools, but also the desire to clarify and value the expert knowledge of employees in organizations. Evangelista *et al.* (2010) have studied a cluster of high technology SMEs in Southern Italy and concluded that wider external knowledge management enabling inter-firm collaboration should have higher priority than internal knowledge management that is restricted by organizational borders. Our action learning indicates that open innovation and related knowledge management initiatives can succeed if virtual tools for knowledge sharing are used in the situation where such prerequisites of knowledge management as understanding and recognizing the expertise of all members of an organisation, free circulation of information and trust between employees are in place. In recent economic crises years, students in master's programmes tended to give higher priority to receiving a clear answer to the question: "Where is the space in my organisation for my expert knowledge?" In order to align connectivity in virtual social networks, inter-organizational learning communities and knowledge sharing inside organizational borders with personal knowledge management, the space metaphor has a crucial role.

"Open space" is a spatial metaphor that has gained popularity as a result of Harrison Owen introducing in 1985, the open space technology to run self-organizing knowledge sharing and knowledge creation meetings for groups of any size. Open space technology is a tool for creativity and innovative learning. Owen (2008) employs several metaphoric expressions in his user guide, such as "creating and holding time and space" and "opening the village marketplace." Open space technology empowers all participants to raise issues and questions they would like to discuss with any interested participants in order to find new ideas. Participants may freely move from one discussion group to another. Open space technology follows "the law of two feet": if participants find themselves in a situation where they are neither learning nor contributing in a group, they can move somewhere where they can learn and contribute. There are also four key principles: "whoever comes is the right people"; "whatever happens is the only thing that could have happened"; "whenever it starts is the right time," "when it's over it's over" Open space has appeared as a powerful but controversial metaphor in the knowledge sharing and innovative learning context (Elenurm, 2010). In terms of safeguarding their intellectual capital in a competitive environment, organizations tend to draw borders between the knowledge space they are eager to control and the knowledge space they agree to share with outsiders. Organizations also try to capture knowledge of individual experts inside the organization. Experts do not always accept sharing all their knowledge, as they want to retain their unique expert status. It is difficult to share and hide knowledge simultaneously.

The ranking of knowledge management prerequisites in organizations helps one to understand the role of cultural values, trust, and motivation compared to the role of information technology applications for developing knowledge management processes in different situations. It helps students to anticipate knowledge management development trends in organizations and to prepare themselves for participation in these innovative activities by highlighting their own personal knowledge management needs. Some master's students who hold a managerial role have involved other team members in ranking knowledge management prerequisites and such a participative approach has clarified knowledge management priorities for their organisations. Our management training and consultancy activities in organizations have revealed situations, where the main challenge of innovative learning is "thinking out of the box" and searching for new ideas. There are, however, more organizations where the main challenge is not a lack of fresh ideas, but rather the involvement of all stakeholders in combining and fine-tuning these ideas in some physical or virtual space and in supporting authors in implementing their ideas.

FUTURE RESEARCH DIRECTIONS

We have given an overview of five training and development tools that link knowledge management and innovative learning. Future research directions for developing these tools can combine action research, which is part of the experiential learning cycle, with surveys of students, entrepreneurs and other stakeholder groups involved in using these tools. Research on co-creative entrepreneurship would benefit from studying entrepreneurial ventures that are inspired by knowledge sharing in communities of practice. That would reveal synergies and potential tensions between co-operation, individual initiative and competition, which are natural features of the market economy.

The landscape of online social networks is rapidly changing and it is hard to predict if Facebook and Twitter will have the same dominant role as they have today in five years. Studying changing trends in using social software allows one to anticipate the positive and negative implications of their virtual connectivity for the academic learning environment and for knowledge sharing in business organizations and in communities of practice. Higher education should not ignore these trends but become more capable of reflecting new online social and business networking tools in their learning process. At least academics in the field of business and social sciences could conduct more research that allows the integration of new e-learning applications and these forms of virtual connectivity that are managed by the learners themselves.

Experiential learning cycles that apply to the field projects of student teams could have more impact on developing personal knowledge management and innovative learning if such project work is not limited to a course offered by one academic department. A capstone course that involves universities from several countries in offering innovative project work and joint mentoring of students in field projects will be a way to enforce the international scope of knowledge sharing. Partner universities that offer business, technological and art education would bring interdisciplinary synergy to cross-cultural teamwork and increase probability of finding innovative

ideas in the action learning process. Following this direction, however, assumes that one leaves the academic ivory towers and overcomes time allocation and information hoarding obstacles in order to involve academics in communities of practice (Buckley & Du Toit, 2010). Promoting interdisciplinary and cross-border action research is a potential shared domain of interest for such communities.

The learning community and knowledge base re-using approach where students rate and develop each other's homework contributions is more focused on knowledge sharing skills than traditional e-learning methods, where the assignments of students are individual and the instructor does not disclose individual results to other students. There is, however, some reluctance among students to rate knowledge contributions of their friends in a fair manner. Instead of assessing the relevance and quality of the knowledge content, their ratings tend to reflect their network of relations in the student community, especially in high collectivism cultures. Experimenting with knowledge sharing tools and procedures that will allow such rating bias to be overcome is an essential priority for aligning the community of practice approaches and the fair grading of individual students.

The action learning processes disclosed conflicts between basic information technology centred and people-centred assumptions, which appeared as a challenge in the organisational learning for creating and implementing knowledge management development visions. Young managers and other categories of employees both in large and small organisations are looking for recognition of the value of their personal expertise as a prerequisite for a more active contribution to knowledge sharing. A longitudinal research for understanding the factors that support or inhibit the implementation in their organization knowledge management development visions, created during the knowledge management course, is a research direction for revealing contradictions between the personal knowledge management and knowledge management practices in organizations.

The authors of the balanced scorecard concept Robert Kaplan and David Norton together with Bjarne Rugelsjoen (2010) have developed the balanced scorecard application for managing strategic alliances. Measuring the readiness of partners to apply external knowledge sources is a future research direction that could support inter-organizational innovative learning.

CONCLUSION

Business schools should train bachelor-level students in the basic skills that are crucial for managing their personal knowledge, for aligning their career visions and possible entrepreneurial orientations with knowledge acquisition and sharing priorities. Awareness of personal knowledge acquisition priorities is a point of departure for life-long learning, and the role of the academic environment in shaping these priorities contributes more to the personal growth and career prospects of students than does teaching theories that students consider irrelevant for their future. The attitudes of students that are wrong or narrow-minded can be changed in innovative and experiential learning processes. Innovative learning means that students anticipate how theories taught will be useful for their future activities and also participate in finding practical applications for new concepts.

Universities have great potential for increasing the connectivity of students both in face-to-face communities and in virtual networks. In order to accomplish this role, the university curriculum should help students to better understand time management and knowledge sharing implications of their networking practices. Choosing between networking opportunities in a smart way is a tool for anticipating emerging technology and market trends and for participating in communities of practice in order to facilitate inter-organizational innovative learning.

Understanding the knowledge sharing potential and challenges in international teamwork is essential for preparing students for international networking and cross-border project work in the "global village." The main barrier to applying the creative synergy of the cross-cultural teams in innovative solutions that can be implemented in a SME is not limited analytical skills, but rather the lack of the real time cross-cultural communication competence within the teams.

The next stage in the innovative learning process is to empower master's-level students to develop knowledge management practices in their organizations depending on several contextual factors such as the role of knowledge as a competitive advantage and the value of expert knowledge, the business sector and the scale of the activity, domestic or international ownership, and involvement in international value chains and networks. Studying and discussing perceptions of knowledge management prerequisites in the action-learning framework is not only a tool for training and understanding the motivation factors of the stakeholders involved, but also a practical way for shaping the participative culture and developing human resources for innovative learning in organizations.

REFERENCES

Botkin, J., Elmandjira, M., & Malitza, M. (1979). *No limits to learning: Bridging the human gap: Report to the club of Rome*. New York, NY: Pergamon Press.

Buckley, S., & Du Toit, A. (2010). Academics leave your ivory tower: Form communities of practice. *Educational Studies, 36*(5), 493–503. doi:10.1080/03055690903425532

Carr, N. (2010). *The shallows: What the internet is doing to our brains*. New York, NY: W.W Norton & Company.

Castells, M. (1996). *The rise of the network society.* Oxford, UK: Blackwell.

Chaudhuri, S., & Ghosh, R. (2011). Reverse mentoring: A social exchange tool for keeping the boomers engaged and millennials committed. *Human Resource Development Review.* Retrieved October 30, 2011 from http://hrd.sagepub.com/content/early/2011/08/20/1534484311417562

Cheong, R., & Tsui, E. (2010). Exploring the linkages between personal knowledge management and organizational learning. In Pauleen, D., & Gorman, G. E. (Eds.), *Personal Knowledege Management* (pp. 189–227). Surrey, UK: Gower.

Chesbrough, H., West, J., & Vanhaverbeke, W. (2006). *Open innovation: Researching a new paradigm.* Oxford, UK: Oxford University Press.

Cruywagen, M., Swart, J., & Gevers, W. (2008). One size does not fit all – Towards a typology of knowledge-centric organizations. *Electronic Journal of Knowledge Management*, 6(2), 101–110.

Davenport, T. (2010). Personal knowledge management and knowledge worker capabilities. In Pauleen, D., & Gorman, G. E. (Eds.), *Personal Knowledege Management* (pp. 167–188). Surrey, UK: Gower.

Davenport, T., & Prusak, L. (1998). *Working knowledge.* Boston, MA: Harvard Business School Press.

Drucker, P. (1999). Managing oneself. *Harvard Business Review*, 77(2), 65–74.

Drucker, P. F. (1985). *Innovation and entrepreneurship: Practice and principle.* New York, NY: Harper Business.

Elenurm, T. (2007). Entrepreneurial knowledge sharing about business opportunities in virtual networks. In B. Martins & D. Remenyi (Eds.), *Proceedings of the 8th European Conference on Knowledge Management,* (pp. 285-290). Reading, UK: Academic Conferences.

Elenurm, T. (2008). Applying cross-cultural student teams for supporting international networking of Estonian enterprises. *Baltic Journal of Management*, 3(2), 145–158. doi:10.1108/17465260810875488

Elenurm, T. (2010). Knowledge as open space. *Electronic Journal of Knowledge Management*, 8(2), 181–266.

Elenurm, T., Ennulo, J., & Laar, J. (2007). Structures of motivation and entrepreneurial orientation in students as the basis for differentiated approaches in developing human resources for future business initiatives. *EBS Review*, 23(2), 50–61.

Evangelista, P., Esposito, E., Lauro, V., & Raffa, M. (2010). The adoption of knowledge management systems in small firms. *Electronic Journal of Knowledge Management*, 8(1), 33–42.

Gloor, P. (2006). *Swarm creativity: Competitive advantage through collaborative innovative networks.* Oxford, UK: Oxford University Press.

Glow, J. (2010). *What problem are we really trying to solve?* In N. Paine & E. Masie (Eds.), *Learning Perspectives 2010.* Retrieved July 28, 2011 from http://www.learning2010.com/ebook

Granovetter, M. (1974). *Getting a job: A study of contacts and careers.* Chicago, IL: The University of Chicago Press.

Hofstede, G. (2001). *Culture's consequences: Comparing values, behaviours, institutions and organizations across cultures* (2nd ed.). Thousand Oaks, CA: Sage Publications.

Hofstede, G., Hofstede, G. J., & Minkov, M. (2010). *Cultures and organizations: Software of the mind: Intercultural cooperation and its importance for survival*. New York, NY: McGraw-Hill.

Honig, B. (2004). Entrepreneurship education: Toward ad model of contingency-based business planning. *Academy of Management Learning & Education*, *3*(3), 258–273. doi:10.5465/AMLE.2004.14242112

Kaplan, R. S., & Norton, D. P. (1996). *The balanced scorecard: From strategy to action*. Boston, MA: Harvard Business School Press.

Kaplan, R. S., Norton, D. P., & Rugelsjoen, B. (2010). Managing alliances with the balanced scorecard. *Harvard Business Review*, 114–120.

Kolb, A. Y., & Kolb, D. A. (2005). Learning styles and learning spaces: Enhancing experiential learning in higher education. *Academy of Management Learning & Education*, *4*(2), 193–212. doi:10.5465/AMLE.2005.17268566

Kolb, D. G. (2008). Exploring the connectivity metaphor: Attributes dimensions and duality. *Organization Studies*, *29*(1), 127–144. doi:10.1177/0170840607084574

Leitch, C. (2007). An action research approach to entrepreneurship. In Neergard, H., & Ulhøi, J. P. (Eds.), *Handbook of Qualitative Research Methods in Entrepreneurship* (pp. 144–169). Cheltenham, UK: Edward Elgar.

Lumpkin, G. T., & Dess, G. G. (1996). Clarifying the entrepreneurial orientation construct and linking it to performance. *Academy of Management Review*, *21*(1), 135–172.

McLuhan, M. (1962). *The Gutenberg galaxy*. London, UK: Routledge & Kegan Paul.

Mintzberg, H. (2004). *Managers, not MBAs: A hard look at the soft practice of managing and management development*. San Francisco, CA: Berrett-Koehler.

Mostert, N. (2007). Diversity of the mind as the key to successful creativity at Unilever. *Creativity and Innovation Management*, *16*(1), 93–100. doi:10.1111/j.1467-8691.2007.00422.x

Nonaka, I., & Konno, N. (1998). The concept of "ba": Building a foundation for knowledge creation. *California Management Review*, *40*(3), 673–684.

Nonaka, I., & Takeuchi, H. (1995). *The knowledge-creating company*. Oxford, UK: Oxford University Press.

Osguthorpe, R. T., & Graham, C. R. (2003). Blended learning environments, definitions and directions. *The Quarterly Review of Distance Education*, *4*(3), 227–233.

Owen, H. (2008). *Open space technology: A user's guide* (3rd ed.). San Francisco, CA: Berrett-Koehler.

Prusak, L., & Granefield, J. (2010). Managing your own knowledge: A personal perspective. In Pauleen, D., & Gorman, G. E. (Eds.), *Personal Knowledege Management* (pp. 99–113). Surrey, UK: Gower.

Revans, R. (1980). *Action learning*. London, UK: Blond & Briggs.

Snowden, D. (2005). From atomism to networks in social systems. *The Learning Organization*, *12*(6), 552–562. doi:10.1108/09696470510626757

Tapscott, D. (2009). *Grown up digital*. New York, NY: McGraw-Hill.

Thiessen, M. S. W., Hindriks, P. H. J., & Essers, C. (2007). Research and development knowledge transfer across national cultures. In Pauleen, D. (Ed.), *Cross-Cultural Perspectives of Knowledge Management* (pp. 219–243). Westport, CT: Libraries Unlimited.

Uzzi, B., Amaral, L. A., & Reed-Tsochas, F. (2007). Small-world networks and management science research: A review. *European Management Review*, *4*, 77–91. doi:10.1057/palgrave.emr.1500078

Wenger, E., McDermott, R., & Snyder, W. (2002). *Cultivating communities of practice*. Boston, MA: Harvard Business School Press.

Wolfe, J., Naylor, T., & Drueke, J. (2010). The role of the academic reference librarian in the learning commons. *DigitalCommons@University of Nebraska – Lincoln*, *50*(2), 107-113. Retrieved October 28, 2011 from http://digitalcommons.unl.edu/libraryscience/221

ADDITIONAL READING

Argyris, C., & Schon, D. (1978). *Organizational learning: A theory of action perspective*. New York, NY: Addison-Wesley.

Audretsch, D. B., Falck, O., Heblich, S., & Lederer, A. (Eds.). (2011). *Handbook of research on innovation and entrepreneurship*. Cheltenham, UK: Edward Elgar.

Avram, G. (2005). At the crossroads of knowledge management with social software. In D. Remenyi (Ed.), *Proceedings of the 6th European Conference on Knowledge Management*, (pp. 49-58). Reading, UK: Academic Conferences.

Barney, J. B. (1991). Firm resources and sustained competitive advantage. *Journal of Management*, *17*(1), 99–120. doi:10.1177/014920639101700108

Bessant, J., & Venables, T. (2008). *Creating wealth from knowledge: Meeting the innovation challenge*. Northampton, MA: Edward Elgar Publishing.

Bettoni, M., Andenmatten, S., & Matheu, R. (2006). Knowledge cooperation in online communities: A duality of participation and cultivation. In P. Feher (Ed.), *Proceedings of the 7th European Conference on Knowledge Management*, (pp. 36-42). Reading, UK: Academic Conferences.

Breschi, S., & Malerba, F. (Eds.). (2005). *Clusters, networks, and innovation*. Oxford, UK: Oxford University Press.

Buckley, S., & Giannakopoulos, A. (2010). Sharing knowledge in a knowledge city using CoPs. In S. Rodrigues (Ed.), *Proceedings of the 2nd European Conference on Intellectual Capital*, (pp. 144-151). Reading, UK: Academic Publishing.

Castiaux, A. (2006). Knowledge building in innovation networks: The impact of collaborative tools. In P. Feher (Ed.), *Proceedings of the 7th European Conference on Knowledge Management*, (pp. 99-107). Reading, UK: Academic Conferences.

Corbett, A. C. (2006). Experiential learning within the process of opportunity identification and exploitation. *Entrepreneurship Theory and Practice*, *29*(4), 473–491. doi:10.1111/j.1540-6520.2005.00094.x

Galaskiewicz, J. (2007). Has a network theory of organizational behaviour lived up its promises. *Management and Organization Review*, *3*(1), 1–18. doi:10.1111/j.1740-8784.2007.00057.x

Georgiadou, E., Siakas, K., & Berki, E. (2006). Knowledge creation and sharing through student-lecturer collaborative group coursework. In P. Feher (Ed.), *Proceedings of the 7th European Conference on Knowledge Management*, (pp. 678-702). Reading, UK: Academic Conferences.

Heinonen, J., & Poikkijoki, S.-A. (2006). An entrepreneurial-directed approach to entrepreneurship education: Mission impossible? *Journal of Management Development, 25*(1), 80–94. doi:10.1108/02621710610637981

Jashapara, A. (2004). *Knowledge management: An integrated approach*. Harlow, UK: Pearson Education.

Kim, W. C., & Mauborgne, R. (2005). *Blue ocean strategy: How to create uncontested market space and make competition irrelevant*. Boston, MA: Harvard Business School Press.

Lobato, J. (2006). Alternative perspectives of the transfer of learning: History, issues, and challenges for future research. *Journal of the Learning Sciences, 15*(4), 431–449. doi:10.1207/s15327809jls1504_1

Love, E. D., Fong, P. S. W., & Irani, Z. (2005). *Management of knowledge in project environments*. Oxford, UK: Elsevier Butterworth-Heinemann.

Lumpkin, G. T., & Lichtenstein, B. B. (2005). The role of organizational learning in the opportunity-recognition process. *Entrepreneurship Theory and Practice, 29*(4), 451–471. doi:10.1111/j.1540-6520.2005.00093.x

McKenzie, J., & Winkelen, C. (2004). *Understanding the knowledgeable organization: Nurturing knowledge competence*. London, UK: Thomson Learning.

Nonaka, I. (1994). The dynamic theory of organizational knowledge creation. *Organization Science, 5*(1), 14–37. doi:10.1287/orsc.5.1.14

Owston, R. D., Garrison, D. R., & Cook, K. (2006). Blended learning at Canadian universities: Issues and practices. In C. J. Bonk, C. R. Graham, & Pfeiffe (Eds.), *The Handbook of Blended Learning: Global Perspectives, Local Designs,* (pp. 338-350). San Francisco, CA: Pfeiffer Publishing.

Prahalad, C. K., & Hamel, G. (1990). The core competence of the corporation. *Harvard Business Review, 68*(3), 79–91.

Rae, D. (2007). *Entrepreneurship: From opportunity to action*. New York, NY: Palgrave Macmillan.

Revans, R. (1980). *Action learning*. London, UK: Blond & Briggs.

Rice, J., & Rice, B. (2005). The applicability of the SECI model to multi-organisational endeavours: An integrative review. *International Journal of Organizational Behaviour, 9*(8), 671–682.

Snowden, D., & Boone, M. (2007). A leader's framework for decision making. *Harvard Business Review, 85*(11), 68–76.

Sveiby, K. E. (1997). *The new organizational wealth – Managing & measuring knowledge-based assets*. San Francisco, CA: Berrett-Koehler.

Valkokari, K., & Helander, N. (2007). Knowledge management in different types of strategic SME networks. *Management Research News, 30*(8), 597–608. doi:10.1108/01409170710773724

Weick, K. (1985). Cosmos vs. chaos: Sense and nonsense in electronic contexts. *Organizational Dynamics, 14*(2), 50–64.

Wong, K. Y., & Aspinwall, E. (2005). An empirical study of the important factors for knowledge management adoption in the SME sector. *Journal of Knowledge Management, 9*(3), 64–82. doi:10.1108/13673270510602773

KEY TERMS AND DEFINITIONS

Experiential Learning Cycle: A four-stage cycle that combines gaining experience, observation and reflection, forming new concepts and testing them in new situations.

Innovative Learning: Anticipating future changes for finding innovative ideas and involving stakeholders to participate in the problem solving based on the new information.

Knowledge: In learning by doing, knowledge is fluid mix of framed experience, contextual information and expert insight that provides a framework for evaluating and incorporating new experiences and information.

Knowledge Management: Systematic and deliberate management of creation, acquisition, sharing, application and renewal of tacit and explicit knowledge for improving the core competence of an organization.

Personal Knowledge Management: Managing personal connectivity in networks for scanning, filtering, evaluating and sharing new knowledge that enables self-development and professional growth.

SECI: The spiral of knowledge conversions that proceeds through socialization, externalization, combination and internalization of knowledge.

Virtual Networking: Networking that is continuously practiced in online communities without face to face contacts in a physical space.

Chapter 7
Strategic Knowledge Management:
A University Application

Milly Perry
The Open University, Israel

ABSTRACT

The under-performance in the creation, diffusion, and utilization of new knowledge represents a specific weakness in knowledge transfer from science to technology in the European Union. The extent of this weakness is reflected in the relatively low numbers of citations and patents in scientific work in comparison to the United States. Comparing these numbers indicates to what extent the linkage between patented inventions and science in European Union countries is weak.

This chapter set several objectives. The initial aim of this chapter is to clarify to what extent the eclectic use of terms: "Knowledge Sharing," "Knowledge Transfer," "Technology Transfer," and "Knowledge Management," relate to knowledge era. As these terms do not form an organizing concept and thinking framework, the second goal of this chapter will be to analyze and clarify these concepts. This chapter will describe their place within the Knowledge cycle in order to map their role and interrelation between the terms.

Clarification of the roles and interrelationships will crystallize the contribution to Knowledge Management Strategy in university application have led to the conclusion that Knowledge Management is the appropriate organizing concept and framework for laying the foundations of the Knowledge Era Economy.

The European Union is at a crossroads where only decisive policy actions will ensure that the route towards increased long-term economic growth and prosperity is the one that is followed [...] this probably reflects an under-performance in the creation, diffusion, and utilization of new knowledge over recent years (European Commission, 2007).

DOI: 10.4018/978-1-4666-1969-2.ch007

INTRODUCTION: THE GAP

In Europe, as in other parts of the world, there is a deep understanding of the importance of knowledge and innovation in science. Policy-makers understand the need to bring knowledge to the forefront not only in words but also in decisive actions. In addition to policy-makers, others have also recognized the problem. According to Giligen (2007), European OECD economies are suffering from sclerosis: the therapy is expected from science, according to The European Union's policy (Lisbon Agenda) and its Seventh Framework Program (FP7) for the funding of research and technological development in Europe.

This need for "therapy" is also reflected by the ministers of the OECD countries who have asked the OECD to develop "a broad-ranging innovation Strategy to build on existing work, address remaining knowledge gaps, and above all provide a cross-disciplinary mutually-reinforcing package of policy elements and recommendations to boost innovation performance" (OECD Innovation and Growth, 2007).

Furthermore, the European Cooperation in Science and Technology Research (COST) has established some targeted actions for "understanding investment in research, development, and innovation, which are a major driver of long-term economic performance." There is also full understanding that policy-makers in Europe have "an urgent need for evidence-based policy recommendations to promote appropriate strategies for the governance, incentives, and conduct of scientific research and of knowledge transfer between public and private entities" (STRIKE, 2007). The main objective of this STRIKE action is "to improve and accelerate the understanding of the process of scientific and technological development and of importance of the transfer of scientific and technological developments to markets and into economic development" (STRIKE, 2007).

Once the challenge is crystal clear and well recognized, it would appear that we are half way towards the solution. The big question we are facing is: What would be the right steps, the right strategic program for enhancing and sustaining knowledge, innovation, global business, and growth?

One approach is to improve outcomes, to some extent, by enhancing application of well-known management strategies even though this would be "more of the same." An alternative method would be to crystallize an appropriate strategy for a knowledge-based economy. Although not many policy makers and countries have adopted an innovative and more challenging approach, this would seem to be the right solution. Every new MBA graduate knows that the owner of a car factory should manage car components as the most important resource of the business. If one owns a bank or insurance company one should concentrate on managing money resources. Why then does the knowledge-based economy not deal with knowledge as its most important resource? Why do knowledge organizations (universities, research centers, governments, etc.) keep on managing "bricks and walls," "car components," budget, and manpower?

Is it feasible for science policy leaders to expect to build a knowledge-era without proper infrastructure, foundations, and in-depth understanding of the adequate culture, tools, and process for driving forward knowledge processes?

Is it reasonable to expect to pick ripe fruits of knowledge as a result of a large scale inter and intra-organizational cooperation (patents) while striving to advance new business and jobs (economic prosperity) out of thin air? We expect a willingness to cooperate and to collaborate among people and organizations without setting up a sharing culture.

To bridge the gap of using old management strategies in a knowledge era we should look for more adequate management tools. Over the last decade, fresh management approaches have been implemented in global organizations and technological companies worldwide. Policy makers and public opinion leaders are committed to lending an attentive ear to these fresh approaches. Listening closely to these best practices can contribute towards increasing benefit for society, enhancing knowledge concepts and frameworks as an infrastructure for communicating and collaborating with a wide variety of stakeholders to establish knowledge-base economy.

LITERATURE REVIEW: SETTING OUT THE DETAILS

The scientific literature related to science policy as well as professional literature related to management and knowledge economy presents many complementary terms and concepts. There are many definitions for each of these terms, some of them overlap, and some have double meaning, while others are too vague to have any meaning. We would argue that in order to draw a roadmap for the knowledge era there is a need to straighten up the big picture so that the details towards increasing long-term economic growth can be set out. This insight of the "big picture" can create the "broad-ranging innovation Strategy to [...] provide a cross-disciplinary mutually-reinforcing package of policy elements and recommendations to boost innovation performance" more effective and efficient (OECD Innovation and Growth, 2007).

KNOWLEDGE SHARING

The knowledge cycle consistently spirals through a number of actions relating to knowledge. At the beginning of the knowledge cycle, we can identify creation of new knowledge, knowledge identification, knowledge preservation, sharing, transferring, of knowledge. In addition, we can identify knowledge adoption, implementation, commercialization, and acquisition of knowl-

edge, which then spirals through additional new knowledge cycles.

This analysis will focus in several terms which are related to chapter main them. The main them is related to the "transferring mode" or "mobility mode" of knowledge (knowledge sharing, knowledge transfer, and technology transfer) in order to clear our arguments and illustrate main ideas. In an initials stage of the knowledge cycle we can identify "Knowledge Sharing" which usually refers to the knowledge within the organization:

Knowledge creation => Knowledge identification => Knowledge preservation => Knowledge sharing / Transferring => Knowledge adoption => Knowledge implementation => Knowledge commercialization / technology => Knowledge acquisition => Knowledge creation.

The meaning of "Knowledge Sharing" is to voluntarily spread and disseminate one's understanding, comprehension, and experience. Knowledge Sharing refers to knowledge streaming from one part of the organization to another. The term "Knowledge Sharing" is part of Knowledge Management since the 1990s. The common definition of "knowledge sharing" focuses on inter-organizational knowledge but the full concept is wider and includes organizational environment interface as well.

Knowledge sharing is a complex action because knowledge is embedded in people, processes, and networks. The more we encourage sharing of knowledge or information between members of an organization, the better served would be both the revelation of tacit knowledge and the explicit know-how, thus adopting, adapting, and applying of knowledge in a way that would help clients, partners and peers work more effectively. Important knowledge in organizations is usually not visible (tacit knowledge) and often not identified.

KNOWLEDGE TRANSFER

In Organizational development and organizational learning the term "Knowledge Transfer" in often used in the same sense as "Knowledge Sharing." In contrast, the term Knowledge transfer has a much wider meaning in the economic literature. These close meanings can partly be explained by their proximity in the knowledge cycle.

One can identify this in the organizational environment interface as follows:

Knowledge creation => Knowledge identification => Knowledge preservation => Knowledge sharing / Transferring => Knowledge adoption => Knowledge implementation => Knowledge commercialization / technology => Knowledge acquisition => Knowledge creation.

Knowledge Transfer refers to the way the university is committed to society and its role within its economy fabric as providing research outcomes to the market. In the past universities were useful to society but not critical: They served the elite without threatening it, and they were able to respond to popular demands and political needs. Furthermore, they contributed to national economic growth and security (Tadmor, 2003). Traditional academic disciplines are pursuing understanding and truth regardless of the usage aspect. More recent scholarship is engaging ways in which academics and practitioners co-produce knowledge interactively in order to reduce the gap between knowledge and action Unfortunately since the last decade knowledge transfer is becoming a synonym for commercialization processes and a wider sense of the knowledge transfer activities are often neglected especially in the public discourse and policy-makers' communications. This reality emerge scholars opposition to this narrow interpretation as contradictory to the academic ethos and freedom.

The United Kingdom office of Science and Technology (2005) refers to "knowledge transfer" within the framework of knowledge driven economy, as transferring good ideas, research results and skills between universities, other research organizations, business and the wider community in order to enable innovative new products and services to be developed. Knowledge transfer focuses on the adoption of knowledge by moving it via some type of channel from person-to-person, group-to-group, and organization-to-organization.

The National Science Foundation (NSF, 2007) defines "Knowledge Transfer" as the deliberate process of exchanging useful information from one part of the knowledge system to another, often across sectors or disciplines." Knowledge transfer is conceived as a direct, two-way interaction between the university and its external communities, involving the development, exchange, and application of knowledge and expertise for mutual benefit. Knowledge transfer disseminates and implements new knowledge from the university to society. In the wider community, public sector and services, the knowledge transfer processes involve improving human capital by recruiting trained people to the work place, life-long-learning programs for employees, providing solutions and innovative services for overcoming society challenges.

Knowledge transfer is a wide concept, inherent in the university culture and academic ethos. Part of the process is done by scholars advising public and private sectors, bringing in new technologies, new ways of operation and new approaches. As governments increase science investments, there is a need to improve and strengthen the link between society and research. Knowledge transfer is considered as a tool for public funds' return on their investment in university's research and teaching activities. The university establishes a relationship with industry, the public sector, and other stakeholders, thereby creating learning opportunities for students and researchers alike which are highly relevant to their profession's real-life experience. These relationships between academia and the private sector are not obvious and not easy to establish.

TECHNOLOGY TRANSFER

Technology is essentially knowledge. Technology transfer is an individual example of knowledge transfer. The term implies commercializing technology application, usually by patents, licensing, spin-off creation, and engaging in science parks. "University-to-Industry" is often used as a synonym for Technology transfer. This relationship addresses the emerging need to commercialize research output in order to enhance economic progress and a country's competitiveness, through which the university rewards society for its financial support.

Another definition of technology transfer relates to enhancing the economic and social impact of universities, developing innovation and new technologies, and helping industrial renewal and breakthrough (Hatakenaka, 2005). Others see universities play a key public role in developing and contributing to commercial progress in a variety of issues within society (Etzkowitz, 2002). All these terms refer to the same issue. Technology transfer is the process of transferring scientific findings from one organization to another for the purpose of further development and commercialization.

AUTM's website (The Association of University Technology Managers) defines typical components of the process as "identifying and protecting new technologies through patents and copyrights." Other sub-processes are within commercialization are licensing, forming start-up companies for earning royalties and revenues as well as recognition, federal regulation fulfillment and attracting talented faculty.

Technology Transfer refers to the stage in which university's knowledge is leveraged to commercialize technology. One can identify this at the end of the Knowledge cycle in the organizational-environment interface as follows:

Knowledge creation => Knowledge identification => Knowledge preservation => Knowledge sharing / Transferring => Knowledge adoption => Knowledge implementation => Knowledge commercialization / technology => Knowledge acquisition => Knowledge creation.

Communities, nations, and geographic regions are increasingly linking their standards to effective knowledge creation and use, thus rendering effective, efficient, and timely knowledge transfer and adoption increasingly important. According to Gibson (2001), this is one of the reasons why knowledge management and technology transfer/commercialization is being extensively covered in academic, government, and business conferences nationally and globally.

Technology Transfer is becoming a major focus of management and involves a range of organizational, informational, and behavioral challenges for getting knowledge (ideas and products) from research to process and market.

Giligen calls "Technology Transfer": "the shift of hardware and software to 'human ware' because people and not folders are carrying the required knowledge and know-how from science to business" (Giligen, 2007). This process seems a particularly difficult type of communication because it requires bridging deep gaps in organizational cultures between Academia and Business purposes in terms of the pace and way things are done.

Technology Transfer is the "packaging knowledge" process. Emphasizing outcomes of complex processes without recognizing the importance of taking necessary preliminary steps seems to pull the carpet from underneath the feet of the whole process and the attempt to manage these processes is thus systematically impaired.

KNOWLEDGE MANAGEMENT

"Knowledge management" is a concept that was coined as an advanced management concept, which deals with the most important of all organizational resources—knowledge. Financial organizations, computer companies, and high-tech corporations recognized the tremendous importance of knowledge and believed that developing and investing in it are the critical stages for the organization's success. Unlike the traditional assets of an organization, the quality of an organization's knowledge is evidence of its future ability to earn profits, competitive edge and maintain an ongoing relative advantage that distinguishes the organization from its competitors. Organizations that understand the importance of knowledge learn to identify, map, nurture, and preserve it. Managing knowledge is different from managing other resources; it requires a different kind of thinking: thinking about thinking (meta-cognition) and breaking out of standard management frameworks. Unlike tangible resources, knowledge is very difficult to capture and define, not to mention manage. The concept "knowledge-rich organization" is generally applied to hi-tech organizations even though the ultimate knowledge organization has existed for centuries and it is none other than the university and research centers. Universities, by their very essence, were intended to meet exactly the needs that the prophets of knowledge management spoke of in the 1990s.

Knowledge Management is a management strategy and thinking framework which has been an established discipline since 1995 with a body of academic courses and both professional and academic journals dedicated to it. Most large companies have resources dedicated to Knowledge Management, often as a part of "Information Technology" or "Human Resource Management" departments, strategic planning, and sometimes reporting directly to the head of the organization. Knowledge Management is a multi-billion dollar worldwide market.

Figure 1 is a simplified model of Knowledge Management Process (Perry, 2002).

Knowledge Management is a strategy for achieving organizational vision and objectives, for enhancing sustainability, survival, or market-leadership using knowledge, innovation and organizational learning. Knowledge Management is taking into account organizational environment demands and circumstances. Knowledge Management programs are typically tied to organizational objectives and are intended to achieve specific outcomes which can include, improved performance, competitive advantage innovation, transfer of "lesson learned" (for example between projects) and the general development of collaborative practices. These invite varied leaning opportunities to create new knowledge as well as Knowledge Transfer and sharing. Examples include on-the-job peer discussions, formal apprenticeship, discussion forums, corporate libraries, professional training, and mentoring programs. However, with technology becoming more widespread in recent years, adaptations of technology such as knowledge bases, expert systems, sharing enhancement tools have been introduced to facilitate Knowledge Management process and culture.

One of Knowledge Management's common tools is the CoP. "Community of Practice" is a professional term from the field of knowledge management. This is a new organizational framework created in knowledge-based organizations, which changes the manner in which information flows in the organization and the way in which learning and change occur. Within the Community of Knowledge, people are connected through informal ties of shared knowledge, experience, and enthusiasm for cooperative work. The community gathers for several reasons: in order to build a foundation for meeting with colleagues and networking on the basis of mutual interests, in response to changes external to the organization or to new challenges. Unrelated to the circumstances of such community gatherings, members of the community share knowledge without boundaries and barriers, creating new methods for learning new subjects and making use of innovative approaches to solving problems and improving the organization. Examples include the World Bank, the automotive industry, the United States government and the hi-tech industry (Wenger & Snyder, 2000).

Figure 1. Knowledge management process

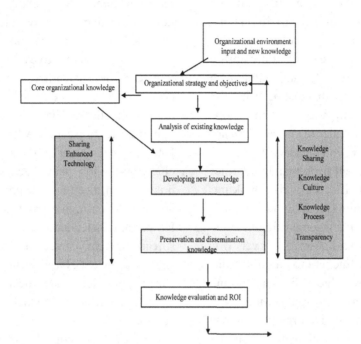

There is a huge debate regarding the extent to which one can really "manage" knowledge. Some would say, "knowledge is not manageable at all," but there is fundamental consent about the need to manage a "Knowledge environment" in a methodological and systematic way in order to gain all the advantages mentioned above. Furthermore, Knowledge Management deals with Knowledge cycle as a whole, not only with selected components, viewing the big picture as a complex of systems and connected global networks in the organization and its environment:

Knowledge creation => Knowledge identification => Knowledge preservation => Knowledge sharing / Transferring => Knowledge adoption => Knowledge implementation => Knowledge commercialization / technology => Knowledge acquisition => Knowledge creation.

ROADMAP FOR THE BIG PICTURE

As is the case in other domains, the application of Knowledge Management principles and techniques should be holistic. This application should fuse human and culture issues with intra- and inter-organisational business processes and require the extensive use of IT tools. Approaching the challenge of technology transfer as a complex social exercise rather than a mechanistic process, whereby technologies are protected through patents and copyrights, could pave the way not only for a better understanding of what is involved but also of how to communicate the outcomes.

Knowledge management is a management strategy; it was not formatted for a specific organizational goal, as Technology Transfer or other targets. Its aim is, generally speaking, to improve the organizational performance and ensure its sustainability and competitive edge in the long run. However, as a management strategy that emerged from within the global competition circumstances and responded to the knowledge era's changing needs, pace and technological tools, it is only reasonable to assume that knowledge organizations will adopt it as an adequate strategy or at least consider it as a preferred working tool.

"Organizations that manage to incorporate elements of 'softer' values such as sense of community, knowledge sharing and idealism into their business model, will perform better in the network economy than organizations with business models that are based solely on economic rationalism" (Jansen, Steenbakkers, & Jegers, 2007, pp. 9).

In the OECD's own words, "Education systems are not always very effective at accumulating knowledge and putting research and innovation to good use." For that reason, the OECD carries out Knowledge Management Projects, which promotes Knowledge Management as "a way of pooling knowledge and experience among educators" (OECD Directorate for Education, 2007).

KNOWLEDGE MANAGEMENT IN HIGHER EDUCATION

The reality of knowledge organization these days has also been expressed elsewhere: "In many institutions of higher education, there is no organized knowledge management system in place or even an understanding that such a system could be useful if not necessary. Since higher education is about the creation, transformation, and transmission of knowledge, such an oversight is striking" (Serban & Luan, 2002).

Research universities were the cradle for many types of technical knowledge that have been created and developed by knowledge companies in the 21st century. This observation demonstrate the paradox that universities lack the consistent ability to use that knowledge as well as Knowledge Management tools for organizational innovation, and for cooperating between society and economy

that value learning and research and are keen to use knowledge as an innovative engine for economy.

Knowledge Management has driven and set the foundation for more flexible organizational structures that better suit knowledge workers, global markets in our "flat world" (Friedman, 2006). Knowledge Management programs attempt to facilitate the process of creation and identification of new knowledge, dissemination and implementation. For example after researchers enter a new subfield or focuses on a specific niche, this information would be known only to them and their students. Once a collaboration opportunity on this issue arises, the university's staff will not be able to help, because they would be unaware of such knowledge. Knowledge Management support in accumulation and application of knowledge across an organization is frequently linked to the idea of the learning organization and strives for innovation and change in the organizations functioned and structure. The university has its own knowledge accumulation mechanisms such as: faculty seminars, colloquiums, and students input- but are these enough?

A lot of senior personnel's knowledge is not shared because no one drives them to do so; neither is knowledge about teaching methods and technologies, knowledge about ways in which the curriculum is developed, know-how regarding internal processes that can be more efficient and less time consuming. Knowledge Management ideas seems somehow obvious, but reality avidness show that without systematic actions sharing culture and process are not to materialize by themselves.

Knowledge management offers a systematic and strategic approach to managing complex organizations. This system sets up an infrastructure that makes it possible to integrate interactions and complex structures, occurring on different, even separate, levels in the organization and its environment (Senge, 1990). Knowledge management requires locating and identifying all of the concealed and open knowledge assets of a university so that they can be used to attain the university's goals. For this purpose, it utilizes organizational agents (who do what), organizational environment agents and networks, technologies, actions, processes, products, and values that result from them, including all of the interactions between them.

A CASE STUDY

Identifying and mapping the university's knowledge regarding experts and expertise is vital: Knowledge (not only information) about funds specifications, expertise in applying and winning regional funds, federal and governmental financing opportunities. Knowledge regarding international research projects management skills and experience, collaboration with big companies and industry. All these are examples of important university's information that would be very valuable to share and transfer within the university.

Other valuable actions that can take place in a systematic Knowledge Management framework within universities include: (1) nurturing new scholars in the department and sharing existing knowledge regarding the teaching process, technology enhancing tools and organizational internal processes; (2) establishing "organizational pipes" to facilitate flow of insights and "success stories" regarding knowledge transfer process, and researchers' role in this process; (3) disseminating important contact points in governmental offices, projects and community to pave research collaboration channels; (4) providing entrepreneurial education and skills for researchers and business support for spin-offs.

Usually Knowledge Management actions use technological tools for better knowledge dissemination. Technologies such as knowledge bases and expert systems for gathering information about possible collaborations with industry or past experience of some years ago can help initiate old-new contact. For example, see "KnowledgeRICH" in Leeds University, which is a free service, connecting the technological needs of industry to our expert network of over 1,000 commercially experienced technical experts within the region's ten universities.

A database about organizational contacts with a specific organization or company can open doors for cooperation regarding expected and future customer or beta-site for technology, knowledge or products. Help desks, corporate intranets and extranets, Content Management, wikis and Document Management drive personal learning process, and organizational learning process, which require new knowledge from outside, change behavior respecting approaching innovation with openness and transparency. Knowledge Management strategy encourage and support learning process such as recommended in the OECD reports: "improving intangible skills such as entrepreneurship abilities, communication skills, adaptability [...] learning strategies and self concept" (OECD Innovation and Growth, 2007, p. 5).

"Communities of Practice," can enable organizational practices for researchers' interests (not academic fields) such as in the case of experienced entrepreneur researchers meeting newcomers. This can enable acquisition of new knowledge from the university business and academic environment, nurturing new networks connections by meeting venture capital investors and industry R&D directors. Networks involve colleagues, consultants or others interests groups from the community can facilitate process understanding and maintaining a new and vital culture of sharing, innovation and will open new opportunity for "out of the box" collaboration and better understanding of end user's needs.

Sharing best practices and disseminating insights gained from one unit or organization to the others and from one expert to newcomers can contribute to more effective processes and a sense of sharing culture (OECD Innovation and Growth, 2007).

University's Yellow Page directories for accessing key personnel regarding a specific issue or needed know-how or gaining insights can contribute a great deal to establishing new "knowledge pipes" in the university. These tools can activate the flow of existing knowledge for the benefit of knowledge workers and the organization as whole.

In order to set up Knowledge Management infrastructure many organizations (and universities) have generated new roles and responsibilities, an early example of which was the CKO—Chief Knowledge Officer.

Let us imagine university X trying to commercialize a specific patent in a local biotech company named "Bio-KM." The company decides to play a "tough game" and maintains intensive negotiations with other universities, across the country that has a less mature patent. The Technology Transfer Officer is not aware of this "implicit organizational knowledge":

The faculty emeritus dean has been sitting on Bio-KM's board of directors for the past ten years and Bio-KM's founder is the biggest donator (two years ago he inaugurated a new lab in his late mother's name). One of the senior business school faculties is setting Bio-KM's strategy for academia co-operating and the university is purchasing lab materials for thousands of dollars every year from "Bio-KM." Furthermore, in the past there were joint ventures between the two organizations that resulted in sending graduates to work in industry, and it appeared that one of the inventor's doctoral students had his internship at the same Bio-KM's lab and took part in successful commercialization process (but he is out of the country doing his post-doc, so who would know!). Do you think this is surrealistic picture? Think again.

Now think how the negotiation might have run with all the above knowledge in the hands of the Technology Transfer Officer?

Can the mentioned university X argue its implements and develop knowledge management strategy and policy in which makes it possible for

the university to build its ability to deal with long-term, wide-reaching needs? (Metcalfe, 2006). Is this university using its existing knowledge to bring its knowledge assets to the market? or can it ensure accountability, which is repeatedly mentioned as a demand made of universities?

Does this university used its added value that accrues to organizations that adopt the knowledge management strategy, which can also help educational organizations create the ability for reflective thinking in all areas of their activity (in Technology Transfer as well. M.P). Knowledge Management can provide university with the means for substantiating their positions and with an organizational culture that encourages ongoing research and learning (Petrides & Nguyen, 2006). In this case, study the answer is probably not.

CONCLUSION

Historically, the higher education system was the first knowledge economy, but today it is no longer alone; it is but one knowledge industry among many. Despite the fact that boundaries between industrial and academic research have been blurred and facilitate joint research that goes beyond the boundaries of institution, nation, and discipline, we have not yet witnessed the change so keenly expected. Policy leaders should use this knowledge advantage in universities and research centers for creating a common language and communicating tool with the industry, which adopts knowledge strategy quicker then universities, realizing its tremendous value for their business sustainability.

Higher education systems needs to take action to rationally manage both internal and external knowledge, to structure and organize orderly, consolidated learning procedures (some of which, as noted, exist and are based on the academic culture) into an active, smoothly functioning mechanism, which regularly examines the position of the university vis-a-vis its goals, environment and future.

Knowledge management offers higher education and industry an infrastructure for planning and managing innovation and change powered by cooperation, collaboration, and dissemination of knowledge, as part of the organization's activity, while relying on and using information technology and supporting cooperation.

Therapy for the "sclerosis" and means for "promoting appropriate strategies for the governance, incentives, and conduct of scientific research and of the knowledge transfer between public and private entities" (STRIKE, 2007; Giligen, 2007) can be achieved, but there is a need to change the management tools and strategy used by government and universities. Change is recognize as a challenge at the organization level, but highly appreciated as a "way of life" in the world we are living in.

In their book, *Dynamic Governance: Embedding Culture, Capabilities and Change in Singapore*, Neo and Chen (2007, p. 1) observe that, "In a world of uncertainty and change, current achievements are no guarantee for future survival. Even if the initial chosen set of principles, policies, and practices are good, static efficiency and governance would eventually lead to stagnation and decay.

No amount of careful planning can assure a government of continual relevance and effectiveness if there is no capacity for learning, innovation and change in the face of ever new challenges in a volatile and unpredictable global environment."

These quote describe the essence and most important values and practice of Knowledge Management. By implementing Knowledge Management strategy, we embed the habit to learn and change in the very way people are acting as well as in the way they are thinking. In a world of rapid, increasing globalization and unrelenting technological advancements "if bureaucratic public institutions can evolve and embed the culture and capabilities that enable continuous learning and change, their contributions to a country's

socio-economic progress and prosperity would be enormous" (Neo & Chen, 2007, p. 1).

Universities and governments, the world over, must adapt to daunting social and educational challenges, in which technology is playing a bigger role than ever before—both in inducing changes as well as in providing the means to cope with them. Implementing Knowledge Management as the right and adequate management strategy for the knowledge-era could contribute a great deal to "ensure that the route towards increased long-term economic growth and prosperity is the one that is followed" (European Commission, 2007).

RECOMMENDATION FOR FURTHER RESEARCH

Further studies should focuses in more detailed case study of successful implementation of Knowledge Management strategy in higher Education organization in order to illustrate the linkage between university success as quantitive variables

REFERENCES

AUTM. (2012). *The association of university technology managers website*. Retrieved from http://www.autm.net

Bijker, W. E., & Luciano, D. A. (Eds.). (2009). *Handbook on the socialization of scientific and technological research social sciences and European research capacities (SS-ERC) project*. Geneva, Switzerland: FP6.

Elkin-Koren, N. (2007). *The ramifications of technology transfer based on intellectual property licensing*. Haifa, Israel: S. Neaman Institute.

Etzkowitz, H. (2002). *The rise of the entrepreneurial university*. New York, NY: Science Policy Institute. doi:10.4324/9780203216675

Friedman, T. L. (2006). *The world is flat: A brief history of the twenty-first century*. New York, NY: Farrar, Straus and Giroux.

Gibson, D. (2001). Paper. In *Proceedings of the 34th Annual Hawaii International Conference on System Sciences (HICSS-34)*. HICSS.

Giligen, P. W. (2007). *The ideal technology incubator workshop in Warsaw, Poland*. Retrieved from http://science24.com/resources/paper/9512/NST2B_Gilgen.P.pdf

Hatakenaka, S. (2005). *Development of third stream activities lessons from international experience*. New York, NY: Higher Education Policy Institute.

Jansen, W., Steenbakkers, W., & Jagers, H. (2007). *New business models for the knowledge economy*. New York, NY: Gower Publisher.

Metcalfe, A. S. (2006). The political economy of knowledge management in higher education. In Metcalfe, A. S. (Ed.), *Knowledge Management and Higher Education: A Critical Analysis* (pp. 1–20). Hershey, PA: IGI Global. doi:10.4018/978-1-59140-509-2.ch001

Neo, B. S., & Chen, G. (2007). *Dynamic governance: Embedding culture, capabilities and change in Singapore*. Singapore: World Scientific. doi:10.1142/9789812771919

NSF. (2007). *Knowledge transfer activities in connection with nanoscale science and engineering. Final Report*. Washington, DC: National Science Foundation.

OECD. (2007). *Innovation and growth: Rational for an innovation strategy*. OECD Publication.

OECD. (2007). *Higher education and region: Globally competitive locally engaged*. OECD Publication.

OECD Directorate for Education. (2007). *Research and knowledge management*. Retrieved from http://www.oecd.org/about/0,3347,en_2649_39263301_1_1_1_1_1,00.html

Perry, M. (2002). *Knowledge management processes in university*. M.A Thesis. Tel Aviv, Israel: Tel Aviv University.

Perry, M., & Shoham, S. (2007). *Knowledge management as a mechanism for large-scale technological and organizational change management in Israeli Universities*. Unpublished.

Petrides, L., & Nguyen, L. (2006). Knowledge management trends: Challenges and opportunities for education institutions. In Metcalfe, A. S. (Ed.), *Knowledge Management and Higher Education: A Critical Analysis* (pp. 21–33). Hershey, PA: IGI Global. doi:10.4018/978-1-59140-509-2.ch002

Ricarda. (2007). *Intellectual capital reporting for regional cluster and networking initiatives: Developing and application of a methodology*. Ricarda.

Senge, P. M. (1990). *The fifth discipline: The art and practice of the learning organization*. London, UK: Random House.

Senge, P. M. (2000). The academy as learning community: Contradiction in terms or realizable future? In Lucas, A. F. (Eds.), *Leading Academic Change: Essential Roles for Department Chairs* (pp. 215–245). San Francisco, CA: Jossey-Bass.

Serban, A. M., & Luan, J. (Eds.). (2002). *Knowledge management: Building a competitive advantage in higher education*. San Francisco, CA: Jossey Bass.

STRIKE. (2012). *Website*. Retrieved from http://www.cost.esf.org/index.php?id=1095

Tadmor, Z. (2003). *The triad research university model or a post 20th century research university model. Haifa, Israel: The S. Neaman Institute of Advance Studies in Science and Technology. European Commission. (2007). Towards a European research area science*. Paris, France: European Commission.

Wenger, E. C., & Snyder, W. M. (2000). Communities of practice: The organizational frontier. *Harvard Business Review, 78*(1), 139–145.

ADDITIONAL READING

Asian Development Bank. (2008). *Regional knowledge and partnership networks for poverty reduction and inclusive growth*. Korea: Asian Development Bank.

Emad, G., & Roth, W. M. (2009). Policy as boundary object: A new way to look at educational policy design and implementation. In *Vocations and Learning* (pp. 19–35). London, UK: Springer. doi:10.1007/s12186-008-9015-0

Overseas Development Institute. (2009). *Helping researchers become policy entrepreneur. Briefing paper*. London, UK: Overseas Development Institute.

KEY TERMS AND DEFINITIONS

Knowledge Management: Is a management strategy and thinking framework which has been an established discipline since 1995 with a body of academic courses and both professional and academic journals dedicated to it. Most large companies have resources dedicated to Knowledge Management, often as a part of "Information Technology" or "Human Resource Management" departments, strategic planning and sometimes reporting directly to the head of the organization.

Knowledge Sharing: Is to voluntarily spread and disseminate one's understanding, comprehension and experience. Knowledge Sharing refers to knowledge streaming from one part of the organization to another.

Knowledge Transfer: Refers to the way the university is committed to society and its role within its economy fabric as providing education and research outcomes to the market.

Technology Transfer: Is an individual example of knowledge transfer. The term implies commercializing technology application, usually by patents, licensing, spin-off creation and engaging in science parks. "University-to-Industry" is often used as a synonym for Technology transfer.

Chapter 8
Effective Knowledge Management through Measurement

Geoff Turner
University of Nicosia, Cyprus

Clemente Minonne
Zurich University of Applied Sciences, Switzerland

ABSTRACT

Knowledge is now recognized as the most important factor of wealth creation, meaning there is no clearer way to prosperity than assigning priority to learning and knowledge creation. This is of greater significance to educational institutions because they are the primary drivers in the generation, accumulation, and dissemination of knowledge. As such, the value of an educational institution to society will depend on its capacity to create and share knowledge, which is an unremitting cycle of discovery and dissemination, or the conversion of knowledge from implicit to explicit. The source of an institution's value to society lies in its ability to continuously improve that process by developing a strategy for acquiring and effectively and efficiently managing its knowledge base as well as understanding how and why its value is changing. In this chapter, the authors consider how an institution knows whether it is managing its knowledge assets in a sustainable way and whether they have increased or diminished over a certain period by looking at several propositions already in existence. It then proposes its own strategic approach, the Knowledge Management Monitor, to assist in this management process.

INTRODUCTION

Any organization's, and in particular an educational institution's, intellectual capital—employees' knowledge, brainpower, know-how, and processes, as well as their ability to continuously improve those processes—is a source of value and competitive advantage. To become knowledge driven, and therefore better able to foster innovation, all institutions need to undertake a journey of discovery that begins with an understanding of what knowledge is needed to achieve their aims and objectives and what knowledge resides in the institution, which allows for the creation of a shopping list of the knowledge that is missing.

DOI: 10.4018/978-1-4666-1969-2.ch008

While the shopping is underway the journey carries on with the development of a strategy for managing an institution's knowledge base, continues by exploring the most efficient and effective ways of managing this knowledge on a daily basis, and comes to an end when the institution learns how to recognize the impact of intellectual capital, and the effective management of its knowledge base, on its value. Will the journey ever end? Probably, but once completed a new journey will begin. More importantly, how will an educational institution know that it is travelling in the right direction insofar as its accumulation and use of knowledge is concerned?

Well, this is really about effective management. In this, measurement is a key device because it provides the information that decision-makers require to accurately monitor those issues related to an institution's aims and objectives including performance against its knowledge management plans. Measurement also provides data that allows managers, and others, to ask the right questions and make the right decisions based on objective information. So, how do we measure the outcomes of an institution's knowledge management practices? How can an institution tell whether it is managing its knowledge assets in a sustainable and strategically competitive way and whether they have increased or diminished over a certain period? It certainly is not easy but it is achievable. What is needed are a set of performance reporting tools that demonstrate achievement in this compelling competitive activity.

Ideally, these tools will have a financial[1] base making it possible to explain what knowledge is valuable, show how the acquisition and dissemination process is being effectively managed and identify where an institution may be missing the boat. Ostensibly, this is often considered a whim but Martin (2000) insists that the measurement of knowledge related outcomes is important. He acknowledges that any attempt to do so is fraught with danger, yet understands that there are probably greater risks in doing nothing. Decidedly

then, the management of knowledge poses an interesting challenge and, given its relevance to their very existence, one that educational institutions ought to address as a matter of priority. Who will provide the necessary information to facilitate this management activity?

Management accountants are the specialists responsible for providing information vital for operating and strategic decisions and for motivating and evaluating organizational performance. Therefore, they ought to provide a germane solution to this challenge. Using their skill in converting relevant data into information, they are able to evaluate how an institution's knowledge management objectives might be achieved by quantifying the impact of each alternative available to the decision-maker. This ought to ensure that if not the best, then at least better decisions about action are made (Chapman, 1997). The strength of accounting information is that it allows an easy comparison and trade-off of the various relevant areas that are impacted by the decision at hand. As such, using the science of accounting to identify ways to assist in directing, controlling, evaluating, and reporting regularly on the knowledge collection and transformation processes in an institution seems to be the most appropriate path to tread.

The accounting for, and reporting on, employee knowledge and skills pose the following three principal challenges. First, there is a need for better tools to manage an institution's investment in people skills. Second, there is a need for some form of indicator that is capable of differentiating between institutions in which the knowledge base is appreciating and those in which it is depreciating. Third, there is increasingly a need to measure, over the long-term, an institution's return on its investment in people. To meet these challenges, management accountants must have an understanding of how the knowledge and skills embodied in human resources are linked to the overall strategic objectives of the institution, how they contribute to the success of the institution and how they compare to the knowledge and skill base of other institutions. As such, it is considered necessary that senior managers, who have a comprehensive picture of the organization's vision and priorities, are involved in developing these performance measures.

In this chapter, our objective is to present a methodology that will provide an opportunity to meet these challenges and, in so doing, position accounting for the knowledge and skill base of an institution not only as an important management tool but also as a component in its performance reporting activities. Such an objective is shared by the OECD (1996) which has recognized that improvement in the information and decision-making systems that shape human capital acquisition and utilization is a key factor in enhancing any organization's competitiveness and, quite obviously, none more so than an educational institution. Indeed, Roslender and Dyson (1992) argue that sustainable organizations will be those that are best able to marry the pursuit of commercial success[2] with the fulfillment of employees. They are convinced that the provision of relevant information on the stock of employees' knowledge and skills will be critical to the effective management of knowledge. This information, they say, will be dissimilar to that traditionally produced by accountants for it needs to be more congruous with a strategic emphasis. Without such information, effective decision-making related to the management of knowledge is likely to be the exception rather than the rule.

The implications are unequivocal. The construction of a germane model that develops relevant measures to establish a quantum and identify changes in the stock of institutional knowledge should go some way towards meeting this objective. The concepts and tools presented in this chapter are not intended to be perfect but simply represent just one information booth on Puxty's (1993) long road by suggesting ways in which this may be achieved.

MANAGING KNOWLEDGE

Before embarking on the journey to develop an effective measurement model, it is important to have a clear understanding of what knowledge management entails. The perceptions of other authors already appear in other chapters of this book but we consider it necessary to do the same, albeit briefly, to provide the basis for our measurement rationale. Even so, doing this may still deliver a blurred picture because there are many and varied interpretations of, and suggestions for distinguishing between, *information* and *knowledge* let alone the terms tacit, implicit, and explicit, which create ongoing confusion in the subject of knowledge management.

Our Understanding of Knowledge

Some authors appear to try to avoid the epistemological debate on the definition of knowledge by comparing data, information, and knowledge. For the record, it is generally accepted that there is a logical transition from data to knowledge. Data represents a fact, or statement of event, with no connection to anything else. To move from data to information there has to be an understanding of a meaningful relationship of some sort (Zack, 1999). Then knowledge represents an understanding of the patterns produced by the information. Alavi and Leidner (2001) do not agree with this, saying that such a hierarchy is inaccurate because the distinguishing factor between these three concepts is not found in any of structure, content, interpretability, or usefulness. They believe that knowledge is simply information processed in the minds of individuals and that it is personalized information related to facts, procedures, concepts, interpretations, ideas, observations, and judgments. Others, such as Tuomi (1999), provide an alternative perspective by suggesting that this hierarchy needs to be regarded inversely because knowledge must exist before information can be formulated and data can be measured to form even more information.

Dahlbom and Mathiassen (1993) add a fourth concept, competence, to the three already mentioned and suggest that each should be regarded from an equal perspective because they refer to different levels of human activity. Taking this one step further, Kakabadse, Kakabadse, and Kouzmin (2003) add some additional concepts to our understanding of the transition from data to knowledge. They propose an extended chain of knowledge flow that looks like this:

Data ➔ *Information* ➔ *Realization* ➔ *Action/ reflection* ➔ *Wisdom*

Their interpretation of knowledge is expressed as *justified true belief*, which is what people believe and value based on the meaningful and organized accumulation of information through experience, communication, or inference. This accumulation of information requires action to obtain. Finally, by arguing that through action and reflection it is also possible to gain wisdom, which is essentially systemic yet a uniquely human state that looks to give us understanding about which there has previously been none (Ackoff, 1989), they propose that realization is information put to productive use.

This *justified true belief* interpretation of knowledge corresponds to the one also used by Sveiby (1997) and goes back to Polanyi's (1958) original work. This is an epistemological position that is acknowledged to have grown out of Plato's discourses (Meno, Phaedo, and Theaetetus) and has been particularly adopted by Western philosophy (Nonaka & Takeuchi, 1995). In one of the most comprehensive taxonomies of knowledge models (Kakabadse, et al., 2003), Plato's concept was debated from the time of Aristotle, one of his students, through Descartes' continental rationalism, to the German philosophy of Kant, Marx, and Hegel, and Locke's British empiricism, and on to twentieth-century philosophers such as

Dewey, Husserl, Sartre, Wittgenstein, Habermas, and Tsoukas.

The implication of all this is that knowledge itself is a very hazy, multifaceted concept with many different characterizations. But we need to move on and so, taking all of the preceding discussion into account, we have adapted a general working definition of *knowledge* from Davenport and Prusak (2000, p. 5), which says:

Knowledge is a fluid mix of framed experience, values, contextual information, and expert insight that provides a framework for evaluating and incorporating new experiences and information. It originates, and is applied, in the minds of knowers. In organizations it often becomes embedded, not only in documents or repositories but also in organizational routines, processes, practices and norms.

So far, we have only sought to get a better understanding of the complexity surrounding this word *knowledge* and find a useful definition that will provide the foundation for our work. We know that it is, unfortunately, not quite that simple as there are some important components that are likely to play havoc with our task of finding appropriate measurement concepts and tools for assessing knowledge management performance. These components are the tacit, implicit, and explicit dimensions that are identified, with some conflicting differentiation, in the literature. Generally, discussion on the components of knowledge is between the tacit and explicit dimensions but, following the introduction by some authors of the implicit dimension, it appears questionable whether that is sufficient. At times, the two dimensions, namely tacit and implicit, are confusingly used interchangeably and so they need to be differentiated[3] more precisely.

Using the investigative work of Nickols (2000) and Wilson (2002) we propose to use the following perception for each of the three dimensions in the development of our concepts and tools:

- **Tacit** knowledge is *not expressible* and in a practical sense cannot be made directly explicit, that is codified into rules and formulations (e.g. the way a lecturer interacts or communicates during a class, or simply the way grandpa used to tell stories). In other words tacit knowledge is about an individual's aptitude for doing things or even cognitively thinking about things.

- **Implicit** knowledge *is expressible* and by applying appropriate knowledge management practices has the chance to be made explicit. Thus, implicit knowledge may be converted into explicit knowledge in a direct way. This conversion process is usually achieved through the dissemination, application, absorption, or interpretation of explicit knowledge, which is exactly what we are doing whilst writing these sentences!

- **Explicit** knowledge is *expressed implicit knowledge*. There is plenty of evidence from the theoretical literature as well as from practice, to suggest that the two terms *explicit knowledge* and *information* have exactly the same meaning. In other words, explicit knowledge should be regarded as implicit knowledge, which has been expressed and thus become information. In this context, the management of explicit knowledge is understood to be the management of knowledge-objects typically held as information in an institution's information base or systems in the form of data records or documents (Tenkasi & Boland, 1996). As such, one could say that the chief purpose of information systems is to help employees communicate knowledge, not simply to store it. The problem appears to be that viewing knowledge as an object impacts on how it should be managed and leads people to focus on databases and other storage devices, which Allee (1997) argues is wrong. In her view, and one with which we are inclined to agree, the focus should be on identifying, organizing, and collecting knowledge and, of course, measuring it.

Without considering the difference between the terms tacit and implicit knowledge, it is important to understand that knowledge creation within an institution centers on the crucial presumption that human knowledge is created and enlarged by means of social interaction. It is only through this interaction that individuals' domain knowledge is capable of being converted into the collective, structural and procedural knowledge of an institution (Turner & Jackson-Cox, 2002). Nevertheless, individuals' *domain* knowledge and institutional *implicit* knowledge are collected and disseminated in different ways, requiring different processes to manage them. This distinction is important because it is the latter that is central to our development of concepts and tools and no consideration is given to individual-oriented knowledge management practices in this chapter.

Knowledge Management Practice

Knowledge and information are among the most important sources of success and, importantly in this era, competitive advantage that an educational institution can have. In no other sphere do employee know-how, innovative capabilities and skills play such a predominant role in defining the productive power of an organization (Quinn, 1992). It is the combination of these attributes in its employees that give an institution its distinctive character and they are, as Coff (1997) observed, the strategic assets of every educational institution. As such, it is the human elements of an institution that are capable of learning, changing, innovating and providing the creative thrust which, if properly motivated, will ensure its sustainability.

Knowledge has advantageous attributes distinct from the attributes of other assets. Generally, it grows with use. The creation and application of new knowledge leads to even greater knowledge, as well as to a motivation to acquire more (Becker & Gerhart, 1996). Knowledge may be shared without being depleted. In fact sharing may be expected to result in increased feedback, acquisition of new knowledge, and modifications and adjustments to current knowledge. With knowledge being such an important factor in the success of institutions, it is critical that senior management devotes a reasonable amount of attention to it. Indeed, executives must be capable of answering the question: *How will managing and using knowledge more productively make us more effective and more successful?*

There is no definitive answer to that question because each institution has a unique vision and strategy. Nevertheless, the extensive library of scholarly and practitioner contributions in the area of knowledge management will help to provide an answer. They cover a wide variety of topics and offer a number of theoretical perspectives that generally have, as a principal characteristic, the management of knowledge related assets. Although portrayed in many different ways, knowledge management generally refers to how institutions analyze and manage knowledge as an institutional resource—in other words, how they create, disseminate, and measure their knowledge related assets and outcomes. Contemporary literature still reflects the individuality of these elements to a certain extent, despite many scholars and practitioners conducting their research, or implementing new knowledge management practices, by looking at the combined effect of these three elements and thus taking a more unified approach.

Two widely recognized practitioners, Tom Davenport and Larry Prusak, have contributed much in the area of managing knowledge assets. Probably their most valuable contribution was their explanation of the various elements of knowledge and where they typically reside in an institution by drawing on the importance of codification, or the transferring of implicit knowledge into explicit

knowledge, of knowledge-objects (Davenport & Prusak, 2000). This, of course, is representative of the system-oriented perspective of knowledge management.

Taking this one-step further, Hansen, Nohria, and Tierney (1999) explored the system-oriented and the human-oriented knowledge management divide by investigating the practices of major consulting firms. It was clear from their study that the currency of knowledge-object oriented strategies is codification, meaning the transfer of implicit knowledge into information systems to produce knowledge assets in an explicit form. Personalization, on the other hand, represents an implicit knowledge oriented strategy, where people-to-people knowledge transfer or exchange, usually through collaboration, is emphasized. Generally, these firms were focusing on one or other of the two strategies and using the other in a supporting role and they did not try to use both approaches to an equal degree in an integrative way.

This disconnection suggests that a system-oriented perspective is the responsibility of the Information Technology department and the human-oriented perspective belongs in the Human Resources department but, in truth, isolating knowledge management in functional departments produces a real risk of losing its strategically competitive benefits (Hansen & Nohria, 2004). Despite the singular use of one strategy or the other, organizational knowledge management really does relate simultaneously to both and allows organizations to build on what they perceive as the most strategically valuable factors: external structure, internal structure, or employee competence. It is the possibility of such an integrative view that appears to be of interest to practitioners, as it will enable them to define and implement new practices for managing the implicit knowledge and explicit knowledge-objects of institutions (Minonne, 2009).

Institutional knowledge management also relates simultaneously to both kinds of knowledge, implicit and explicit, which even though he has made a clear distinction between them, Takeuchi (1998) admits are not totally separate but are mutually complementary. In this regard, his main argument is that knowledge management is more about knowledge creation and less about knowledge management. Knowledge, he says, can only be created and not managed. Interestingly, this position returns us to Polanyi's (1958) understanding of knowledge—that it was *justified true belief*—in that while one may be able to manage related organizational processes like community building and knowledge exchange, one cannot manage knowledge itself (von Krogh, Ichijo, & Nonaka, 2000). The objection is that a legitimate interest in knowledge creation, which in Takeuchi's (1998) mind is the cornerstone of institutional knowledge management, has been reduced to an over-emphasis on information systems (*i.e.* seeing and handling knowledge as an object) or on financial measurement tools for intangible assets. Nevertheless, it is the processes of knowledge creation and knowledge dissemination, as well as the degree of effectiveness of these processes, which underpins the value of an educational institution.

Therefore, it seems that knowledge management practices need to relate simultaneously to three dimensions: the creation, management, and measurement of knowledge assets. Collectively, these three dimensions will generate a mix of various strategic directions from which an educational institution may choose to ensure that it creates value and remains competitive in its chosen market place. The practice of creating value from knowledge requires institutions to focus. O'Dell (1998) suggests there are three reasons why this is critical. First, focus ensures that valuable resources are applied to high payoff areas. There are only so many resources available to spend on managing knowledge. With a clearer insight into what is important, institutions may have a better chance of reaping valuable rewards. Second, focus helps ensure that the right knowledge is being acquired and transferred as well as allowing people to see

a clear reason for this activity. Third, focus makes it easier to get the attention of senior management and subsequent funding.

The Need for Measurement

The most important thing about knowledge, once it has been acquired or created, is putting it to proper use. For this to happen, institutions must have the capability to understand the nature of knowledge as a strategic asset (Teece, 1998). This exemplifies the need for knowledge management, which requires a useful framework that will allow managers to better understand the extent of their current stock of institutional knowledge and then, once having decided what changes are needed to develop a sustainable competitive advantage, to monitor the processes they initiate to implement those changes with appropriate performance measurement metrics.

What is more, there is a strong feeling among both academics and practitioners that if we cannot measure knowledge assets, or the outcomes of knowledge management related practices, we shall not be able to manage either (Globerson, Globerson, & Frampton, 1991). This has been a management truism for more than two decades now yet achieving it is not a simple task. There are many things that we first need to consider, the most important of which is to understand exactly what it is we are planning to manage and how we shall go about doing it. This first step, which represents the translation of institutional strategy into contextual knowledge management targets, is the precursor to the creation of an effective measurement system.

If management requires measurement this is an essential task but it can only be undertaken once an organization has clearly established the strategy-structure-process parameters to ensure it accesses, creates, and embeds the knowledge that it needs. So that we have a better understanding of these parameters, which is necessary before it is possible to develop a relevant model for measuring the effects of knowledge management practices, consideration of how such an approach may help an educational institution more effectively manage its most relevant source of success and competitive advantage is necessary.

Earlier we suggested that knowledge creation within an institution centers on the crucial presumption that human based knowledge is created and enlarged by means of social interaction. Based on Nonaka and Takeuchi's (1995) work, it is easy to conclude that it is this interaction that converts individuals' knowledge into collective, structural and procedural, that is implicit, knowledge within an institution. On the other hand, knowledge management transforms these intellectual assets into enduring value by identifying the knowledge that enhances the institution's esteem in society. In coordination with an institution's strategic objectives, knowledge management provides support in exploring, innovating, disseminating, and automating institutional knowledge (Minonne, 2008). Such an integrative approach to knowledge management embraces four forms of integration, namely *cultural*, *organizational*, *procedural*, and *methodical* integration, and as such enhances an institution's capability for productivity, quality, and innovation gains.

To understand the success or otherwise of an institution's activities in each of the four forms of integration, it is essential to find key indicators that measure performance. Generally, these fall into two groups. The first is *effectiveness* (for example, quality improvement or innovation gains) and the second is *efficiency* (for example, productivity increase through improved internal processes). An insight of Minonne's (2008) study is that organizations having a knowledge management strategy, and actively managing it, focus particularly on the efficiency dimension as it can be operationalized more easily than the effectiveness dimension expressed, for example, in new knowledge creation.

Of course, effectiveness is often confused with efficiency and this is mostly reflected in strategic objectives. As institutions strive to achieve their goals they may become more efficient but their effectiveness does not always improve. In other words, it is possible to be both effective and efficient but rarely does it happen at the same time. Unfortunately, sometimes the price of greater efficiency is less effectiveness. When setting knowledge management targets efficiency is about speed and cost whereas effectiveness is about quality and purpose. Effectiveness comes from taking the time to stop and evaluate and should therefore be the first considered when setting knowledge management targets from strategy.

The importance of knowledge management in positioning an institution for growth and sustainability requires identification, quantification, reporting and participating in the coordination of the various knowledge elements in that institution. More than a decade ago IFAC (1998) highlighted the need for better tools to monitor investment in knowledge assets such as people skills, information bases and technological capabilities. This requires past and future oriented information, both financial and non-financial information, and both numerical and textual information. Clearly then, the targets to be monitored should be measurable. Furthermore, effective performance measures are dynamic and so, apart from being subject to change at any time, will not be appropriate in every situation. At all times, however, they will always be congruent with institutional objectives, easily understood by all employees and promote intended behavior within the institution (Turner, 2000). Therefore, knowledge management targets need to be measurable. This requires the development of extensive quantitative, mainly operational and financial, and qualitative measurements in support of knowledge management strategy. A quantitative approach to measurement promises a more sustainable information base compared to a qualitative one. If, for whatever reason, a quantitative assessment is not a realistic option, a qualitative approach to performance measurement is a better option than no measurement at all.

The choice of knowledge management performance measures in any institution is a difficult one that will inevitably be tied to strategic direction. Furthermore, justification of the expenditures involved in knowledge management activities, by describing the benefits in quantifiable terms using relevant key performance indicators, is the most significant challenge for all institutions.

MEASURING PERFORMANCE

Progress toward thinking about the knowledge aspects of an educational institution will require an operationally useful framework within which a broader range of data concerning the knowledge resources of the institution may be collected and analyzed. In keeping with the notion of a strategic involvement, this effort should not be confined to one functional area but should be fully articulated with the financial and operational functions of the institution in a unified whole. This epitomizes a fundamental touchstone of strategic management in that it will integrate knowledge management issues into the business plan.

No institution can have a clear view of its direction and its future without fully taking into account the impact of knowledge assets on any strategic vision and the potential impact, in turn, of such strategic vision on its knowledge assets. In this regard, institutions need to demonstrate the linkages between their core processes, the resultant knowledge management choices and policies, and the impact on performance.

This may be best achieved by moving from vague, subjective terms to the more specific, objective language of numbers. That said, in the absence of a more useful measurement system, some institutions are likely to rely on the vaguer, qualitative forms of measurement rather than no form of measurement at all. By using consistent, relevant data that is quantified where appropriate and compared with benchmarks and historical information where this is available, management

will be able to reinforce their accountability in this ever increasing sphere of influence over institutional performance. Clearly, a new, vibrant way to account for knowledge assets is wanted.

Historically, performance indicators fall into conceptually different categories. There are those that examine the results of a particular objective and others that measure management of the means or determinants to success. The mix of factors used to gain that success will vary, often significantly, among institutions. Consequently, while indicators of results may be similar, those of determinants almost certainly will not which makes it extremely difficult, if not impossible, to design a completely generic system for measuring the performance of an educational institution's knowledge management practices (Turner, 2005). Indeed, a custom solution is needed for almost every institution.

In that respect, Fitz-Enz (1995) suggests there are five key underlying principles that should form the basis of developing a measurement system relating to an organization's human resources, the prime knowledge assets of an educational institution. First, the effectiveness and efficiency of any function should be measured by some combination of cost, time, quantity, quality, or human reaction indices. Second, a measurement system promotes productivity by focusing attention on the important issues, tasks, and objectives. Third, performance should be measured at both individual and team levels. Fourth, managers ought to be measured by the effectiveness and efficiency of the units they manage, and fifth, that the ultimate measurement is not efficiency but effectiveness. The last of these is probably the most important as it should ensure that all the resources of an institution, *i.e.* human, physical and financial, are directed toward achieving its strategic objectives.

Using these principles, the performance measurement system should help senior managers evaluate how their objectives might be achieved by identifying each available alternative and the impact each of those alternatives will have on their institution. Nevertheless, the accounting for, and reporting of, knowledge management in an educational institution poses three principal challenges:

- First, there is a need for better tools to manage an institution's investment in its knowledge assets.
- Second, there is a need to measure, over the long-term, an institution's return on its investment in knowledge assets.
- Third, there is a need for some form of common indicator that is capable of differentiating between institutions in which the knowledge base is appreciating and those in which it is depreciating.

Developing a Performance Measurement System

With a greater awareness of the four forms of knowledge management integration allied to the managing and leveraging of human-oriented and system-oriented knowledge management practices, and an appreciation of the optimum proportion of each, educational institutions should be better placed to create a performance measurement system that accounts for the management of their knowledge assets. A few preliminary suggestions have already been made to assist in the development of an institution's knowledge management performance reporting model. Fundamentally, key performance indicators that measure the effectiveness and the efficiency of an institution's knowledge management initiatives in each of the four forms of integration are required. Ideally, these key performance indicators should be quantitative wherever possible but qualitative indicators are better than no indicator at all. Bontis (1998) suggests the use of monetary values wherever possible but says that institutions should never be afraid of developing customized indices and metrics if that is all they can do.

Our position is that an effective measurement system to assess the effects of knowledge man-

agement practices must include critical success factors, a mix of financial and non-financial data, and a balance between the four forms of integration. Institutions require appropriate, relevant, and effective forms of performance measurement, which should be congruent with their objectives as well as easily understood by all employees and should promote intended behavior within the institution. Those that are unwilling, or unable, to develop effective measuring and reporting systems are likely to suffer from falling service quality, lower productivity growth and a reduced ability to compete because they will be less successful in acquiring and using relevant knowledge resources.

Key performance indicators that are developed to assess the progress of institutions in this compelling activity need to be aligned with one or another of the four forms of integration and may be either qualitative or quantitative in nature. At present, in most educational institutions, there is no synchronized approach to measuring the effects of knowledge management practices despite this being considered a foundation for effective strategy development and management decision making. We acknowledge that there is no unique solution to this dilemma. Over many years, authors have proffered a variety of suggestions about the development of suitable key performance indicators for the management of knowledge assets (see, for example, Arora, 2002; Edvinsson & Malone, 1997; Fitz-Enz, 1995; Lev, 2001; Neely, 2002; Sveiby, 1997; Turner, 1996) but they have often been focused on operational, rather than strategic aspects of knowledge management. Nevertheless, we push forward with our solution, which is intended to provide a fundamental paradigm shift from the traditional operational approach to a strategic involvement in knowledge management.

Later in this chapter we shall introduce our model, the *Knowledge Management Monitor* (KM²), which was first developed for commercial organizations (Minonne & Turner, 2009) and was inspired by another strategic management concept, Kaplan and Norton's (1996) balanced scorecard.

Their model is more than a measurement system. It is a management system designed to channel the energies, abilities, and knowledge held by people throughout the institution toward achieving long-term strategic goals. Therefore, it is with our model for KM² promotes a balance between the four forms of integration, which is considered the prime consideration in fully understanding an institution's knowledge management performance.

Intangibles, and in particular intelligence, have always been the true source of an educational institution's competitive advantage. Knowledge, especially operational knowledge, has a limited shelf life and, while it is necessary to manage it effectively, alone it is not sufficient to create a competitive edge. Strategic knowledge and the effective management and measurement of an institution's initiatives, on the other hand, are the key to exploiting current competitive advantages and creating new ones. This change in emphasis requires a transformation in the nature of an institution's knowledge management system, which we believe will be well served by KM².

EVALUATING KNOWLEDGE MANAGEMENT PERFORMANCE

Modern day strategic planning should be an exercise in interpolation rather than extrapolation. This means that institutions start with an image of what they want to look like in the future, which is highlighted in their vision statement. Then they decide on the changes required to develop that image from their current state for inclusion in their mission statement. If this process takes a static view of the future then the level of implementation is decided first and the control system, intended to identify actual deviations from plans, the causes of the deviations and the appropriate actions to remedy the situation, is put in place afterwards. On the other hand, and this is the perspective we choose to take, the image of the future is constantly changing, like the scenery along the road being travelled, and this requires an altogether different view of the control system. The tracking and checking-up characteristics of the control system remain but, rather than being concerned with what has already happened, they look forward by continually tracking how the future is changing. In much the same way as a global positioning system, the control system is updated frequently to correspond to the shifting reality.

The control system for the effective implementation of knowledge management strategy needs to measure current performance and guide the institution toward its changing image of the future. To do this effectively a system should include four compulsory elements before control may be fully established. These elements are a predetermined set of *targets*, a means of *measuring current activity*, a means of *comparing current activity* with each target, and a means of *correcting deviations* from the targets. These targets may be scientifically calculated or set arbitrarily using reasonable or totally unreasonable expectations, good or bad. In general, they should be stated explicitly and for this reason quantitative statements are preferred although not necessary. The control system merely provides a means by which activity is directed toward achievement of the targets. As an institution's knowledge management strategy takes on a more formidable look and character, the degree of control improves up to the point where quantitative metrics of *effectiveness* and *efficiency* have been established to guide the institution toward its ever-changing image of the future. Therefore, it is clear that unless suitable ways and means are found to track and check-up on the development and implementation of an appropriate knowledge management strategy it will be hard to move forward with any confidence.

Quite some time ago, Handy (1996) made it clear that managing the knowledge and skills of its employees was a key organizational challenge, yet little progress appears to have been made in cementing integrative knowledge management in the psyche of commercial organizations, let alone educational institutions. Why? Simply because the ability to measure and validate the impact of knowledge management activities remains elusive. How do we know that? We have learned this from our own consulting experiences and a field study conducted in the German spoken region of Europe (Minonne, 2008) where nearly 40% of those participants whose organization is active in knowledge management admitted to being unable to judge their performance because they have few or no measurement criteria and lack the appropriate skills to develop them. In a similar survey conducted in North America (Martin & Bourke, 2009), 43% of respondents indicated that their inability to capture and validate data was the primary barrier their organization had to overcome if they were to understand the organizational impact of knowledge management.

Key indicators that measure the performance of knowledge management integration are needed. They have to measure both *effectiveness* and *efficiency*. As we have mentioned previously, many of those organizations having, and actively executing, a knowledge management strategy tend to focus on the efficiency dimension because it can be evaluated more easily than the effectiveness dimension. Yet this attitude is fraught with danger because, as with many other operational aspects in organizations, the management of knowledge has to be effective before it will provide efficiency gains.

It is for these reasons, and because their model is built on the understanding that cause and effect leads to strategic success, that KM^2 utilizes the underlying principles of Kaplan and Norton's (1996) balanced scorecard concept. This cause and effect hypothesis is fundamental to understanding the metrics that the balanced scorecard prescribes and so it is with KM^2, which promotes an understanding of cause and effect linking the four forms of integration. This is considered essential in the effective measurement of knowledge management performance. It will do so by providing structured information about an institution's

knowledge resources: how they are valued, how they are nurtured and how they contribute to the sustainability of an educational institution.

The Need for Knowledge Management Performance Measures

With all that we have said so far, we hope we have made it abundantly clear that educational institutions are unreservedly dependent on knowledge since it is a fundamental ingredient in everything they do. In every way, the foundation of their strategic success relies on the effective management of their knowledge assets and for this to be successful there needs to be an effective way of assessing performance. Knowledge management and particularly its performance measurement dimension has thus become the most important economic task for educational institutions.

They need to establish a set of key performance indicators that assess their institution's performance in implementing an integrative knowledge management strategy. In doing so, they should resist the temptation to focus only on what is easily measurable, which generally is the *efficiency* dimension of activities and costs (Pfeffer, 1997). Rather, they should focus on measuring outcomes that meet real institutional needs such as innovation and technological development from an educational perspective, research, employee attitudes, experience, learning, and tenure and turnover, which are more likely to represent knowledge management *effectiveness* rather than *efficiency*. While numerous performance indicators may be developed, each is only useful if it allows for the evaluation of ongoing performance toward achieving strategic objectives. As such, it is considered necessary that senior managers who have a comprehensive picture of the institution's vision and priorities are involved in developing the key performance indicators.

Every performance indicator, whether it is used to simply clarify the current position, guide the implementation of a knowledge management strategy, check the effectiveness of a knowledge management strategy, or track changes in the image of the future, will affect actions and decisions. Choosing the right measures is critical to success but the road to good indicators is littered with pitfalls. Many seem right and are easy to measure but have subtle, counterproductive consequences. Others are more difficult to measure but focus the organization on those decisions and actions that are critical to success.

In this setting, the task is to consider ways of assessing performance in each of the four forms of integration, which are *cultural*, *organizational*, *methodical* and *procedural*, in a way that will enable an institution to assess its position in terms of an effective knowledge management strategy. The performance indicators used to assess the progress of institutions in this compelling strategic activity of integrative knowledge management need to be aligned with one or another of these forms of integration. With all of this in mind, work begins on the creation of a prospective control framework, using the KM², for educational institutions.

Monitoring Knowledge Management Progress with the KM² Model

In the development of all control frameworks, or measurement systems, the task of measuring social phenomena is often considered impossible or, at best, fraught with difficulty. All measurement systems rely on proxies, such as monetary units or other indicators that often bear little resemblance to the actual events being reported. As such, Arora (2002) suggests that it is possible to effectively implement knowledge management by developing and applying a knowledge management index based on the balanced scorecard concept.

Arora's index is a single number that incorporates key parameters for assessing knowledge management performance in each of the internal processes, customers, learning and growth, and financial perspectives of the balanced scorecard. Each parameter is weighted according to its importance in achieving the institution's knowledge management strategy and as such the basis of the index will change as often as there are changes in knowledge management strategy. Nevertheless, it represents a balanced consideration of the impact of knowledge management, which is a similar view to that we have taken in the development of KM². The key difference is that Arora's index reflects the progress of knowledge management across the four perspectives of the balanced scorecard whereas KM², depicted in Figure 1, has its focus on the four forms of integration discussed earlier.

The first task in building a working model based on the KM² framework is to define strategic objectives, establish initiatives, and construct targets across the four forms of integration. Then, to monitor and measure it is necessary to develop metrics for performance against each of the targets. These will become the key performance indicators that will guide the effective implementation of an integrative knowledge management strategy.

We begin by creating some exemplary strategic objectives, initiatives, and targets that are not attributable to any particular institution but simply based on the authors' wide academic and research experience. These are provided in Figure 2 where they are aligned to each of the four forms of integration. Using this information, a prototype set of key performance indicators to identify the cause and effect of implementing a knowledge management strategy are developed. The measures may be either *qualitative* or *quantitative*. Qualitative measures are typically judgment based and are used when the item to be measured, or the attribute of interest, does not lend itself to precise or quantifiable measurement. Indeed, they provide an awareness of what is happening in sense of the direction, rather than the speed, of change. Quantitative measures are usually integer-based and there are two further divisions: *financial* and *non-financial*.

Figure 3 provides some prototype key performance indicators for each of the proposed knowledge management targets included in Figure 2.

Figure 1. The knowledge management monitor

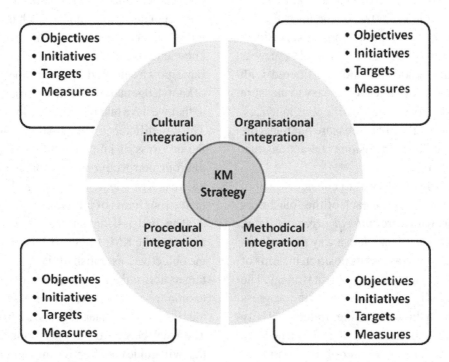

They represent a cross-section of qualitative and quantitative measures and financial and non-financial measures. As intended, KM² promotes an understanding of cause and effect linking the four forms of integration while at the same time using this collective information as a predictor for the future, which has largely been achieved with the example key performance indicators put forward.

Importantly, one of the targets in the *methodical integration* quadrant of KM² was to understand the year-on-year increase, although at times poor management may lead to a decrease, in the stock of knowledge assets. We have suggested some key performance indicators for that target including one that is intended to provide the quantitative indication of the change in the stock of knowledge assets in monetary terms that Bontis (1998) recommends. Is it possible to do this? We believe it is but it will require a sea-change in the mindset of many who might be asked to implement our suggestions. Here they are!

Valuing Institutional Knowledge

KM² really remains unfinished unless we can find a way to value the knowledge embodied in an institution. This will provide the information on employee wealth that Roslender and Dyson (1992) conclude is a vital ingredient in effective knowledge management.

The first task is to consider the most appropriate measurement base to be used in the valuation of knowledge embodied in an institution. This will essentially be a choice from two - market based or cost based measures. It is generally accepted that the price of anything in an open market represents its true value at any given point in time. Is there really a market for knowledge? Other than individual agreements on prices for specific items of intellectual property, such as manuscripts or patents, there is no obvious market for collective institutional knowledge. Our only choice, it would seem, is to use a cost based measurement system.

Figure 2. Selected objectives, initiatives, and targets

	OBJECTIVES	INITIATIVES	TARGETS
CULTURAL INTEGRATION	Knowledge management (KM) is an integral part of institutional culture	Conduct community building by establishing communities of practice (CoP)	Active CoP within each academic department and administrative function and cross-functional CoPs at points of interaction
	KM enables collaboration between experienced and inexperienced personnel	Establish a godparent scheme	All employees with less than five years service to have an experienced godparent
	KM encourages and facilitates the exchange of institutional knowledge	Create an institution-wide job-rotation scheme	An internal job rotation frequency of 2 years for administrative staff
ORGANISATIONAL INTEGRATION	KM defines the institutional structure	Create a process-oriented institutional structure throughout the value-chain	Process-oriented institution structure established and implemented in three years
	KM supports inter-departmental collaboration	Create a KM team made up of representatives from each School and each administrative function	Year-on-year increase in employee satisfaction with inter-departmental collaboration
	KM supports the collaboration between faculty, administrators and managers	Redefine job specifications to diminish hierarchies and cultivate a team ethos within each institutional group	Year-on-year increase in employee perception of managerial collaboration
METHODICAL INTEGRATION	KM practices are integrated into knowledge-intensive work processes	Create knowledge maps of the institution to clarify the knowledge-intensive processes and support them with appropriate KM methods	Annually, identify at least five new KM initiatives that enhance the institution's knowledge assets
	KM supports an integrative (synchronised) approach to managing implicit and explicit knowledge assets	Identify and synchronise initiatives related to KM as well as those related to information management	Year-on-year increase in the number of synchronised activities
	KM supports the exploration, innovation, dissemination and automation of knowledge	Create and execute a KM strategy using an integrated model	Year-on-year increase in the stock of knowledge assets
PROCEDURAL INTEGRATION	KM supports the establishment of continuous internal processes	Analyse and codify key process models and their interfaces to optimise knowledge and information exchange at those points	Year-on-year increase in the number of implemented value adding continuous internal processes
	KM supports the reduction of work processing time	Conduct an audit of the speed of internal processes and initiate KM practices to make them faster	Year-on-year improvement in the speed of internal processes
	KM supports the avoidance of work redundancy	Identify redundant work activities and eliminate them by applying useful KM practices	Elimination of 40% of redundant work activities within five years

Nevertheless, this option is preferred for other reasons. First, the value of something is normally at least equal to the amount one is prepared to pay for it[4]. This amount will change from time to time and the basis of valuation should reflect these changes. Second, once the required cost amounts have been established, they may be applied to all institutions irrespective of their structure, size and nature of operations. Since it is our intention that KM[2] be useful for all forms of institution, it seems more appropriate to proceed with a model that uses cost-based measures as its foundation.

Despite individuals being significant sources, conduits and generators of knowledge, an institution's knowledge base is not just simply the sum of the individual value of employees' explicit, or domain, knowledge (Howells, 1996). Social interaction converts the domain knowledge of individuals into collective structural and procedural, or implicit, knowledge within the institution

Figure 3. Indicative key performance indicators

	TARGETS	KEY PERFORMANCE INDICATOR
CULTURAL INTEGRATION	Active CoP within each academic department and administrative function and cross-functional CoPs at points of interaction	Number of CoPs actively producing new knowledge management initiatives at a functional or cross-functional level
	All employees with less than five years service to have an experienced godparent	Percentage of employees with less than five years service who have a godparent and percentage of experienced employees who act as a godparent
	An internal job rotation frequency of 2 years for administrative staff	Percentage of employees engaged in a planned two year job rotation scheme
ORGANISATIONAL INTEGRATION	Process-oriented institution structure established and implemented in three years	Percentage of required changes satisfactorily implemented
	Year-on-year increase in employee satisfaction with inter-departmental collaboration	Continuously updated on-line employee satisfaction survey, based on a Likert scale, producing an average satisfaction rating
	Year-on-year increase in employee perception of managerial collaboration	Continuously updated on-line employee satisfaction survey, based on a Likert scale, producing an average perception rating
METHODICAL INTEGRATION	Annually, identify at least five new KM initiatives that enhance the institution's knowledge assets	Maintain a register of new KM initiatives implemented identifying the projected and actual present value of the initiative
	Year-on-year increase in the number of synchronised activities	Maintain a register of new synchronised activities implemented identifying the projected and actual present value of each activity
	Year-on-year increase in the stock of knowledge assets	The return on investment in information systems, value-added by KM initiatives and the average of, weighted according to institutional significance, the length of employee service, the level of education, the value of organisational knowledge
PROCEDURAL INTEGRATION	Year-on-year increase in the number of implemented value adding continuous internal processes	Maintain a register of new value adding continuous internal processes implemented identifying the projected and actual present value of each initiative
	Year-on-year improvement in the speed of internal processes	Year-on-year change in processing time for a basket of institutional transactions
	Elimination of 40% of redundant work activities within five years	Cumulative percentage of identified redundant work practices successfully eliminated

(Nonaka & Takeuchi, 1995) thereby creating new knowledge. From an institutional perspective, this form of knowledge has a more permanent dimension and the institution may build its future success around it.

The first step in measuring the wealth of knowledge embodied in an institution is to understand the composition of domain knowledge for each employee and then calculate its value. These individual employee values may then be aggregated to ascertain the total value of domain knowledge within the institution. The second step is to assess the value of implicit knowledge for the institution as a whole. Combining the values determined in each of these steps will provide a value, to the institution, of its knowledge base. Furthermore, it will also be possible to understand how the value of institutional knowledge is created, grown, and even lost.

Let us include an important qualification at this point. Since there is no precise way of knowing what the true value of knowledge is, either to an individual or to an institution, the model devised here can provide no more than an approximation of the value of institutional knowledge. It is important to bear in mind that the more sophisticated the model the more expensive it will be to apply and attempting to achieve a greater degree of precision may not prove cost effective. The aim is, therefore, to provide a practical measurement model, for which the required inputs may be obtained at a reasonable cost, in order to ensure that the value of knowledge will not be neglected in any decision-making process.

Domain Knowledge

Domain knowledge comprises three elements: *formal* education, *post-secondary* education and *professional* training. While it is obvious that it is not possible to have a post-secondary education without having first had a general education, each will be considered exclusive of the other. A similar situation generally prevails with each level of post-secondary education and a consistent approach will be taken there. This is similar to valuing other assets that rely on the existence of something else but are acquired separately.

Since a cost based measurement system has been proposed as the basis of the valuation of organizational knowledge, Dobija (1998) provides a useful starting point for attempting to value each of these elements of domain knowledge. He proposes using the costs associated with attaining a particular level of education as the basis for establishing a pragmatic value of knowledge. One of the difficulties associated with valuing education is that it may only be acquired over a period of years. Estimating the value of each level of education must therefore take into account the opportunity cost of capital invested in that education over its duration. Accordingly, the capitalized value of

costs is proposed as a surrogate measure for the value of the knowledge acquired from a particular level of education. This may be calculated using the following formula:

$$K = c \left[\frac{(1+r)^n - 1}{r} \right],$$

where:
$K =$ *the value of knowledge*
$c =$ *cost of acquiring knowledge in each time period*
$r =$ *a long – run rate of return on investment*
$n =$ *the number of years of education*

The cost of acquiring knowledge[5] varies depending on whether formal education, post-secondary education or subsequent professional training is being considered. In each case it is appropriate to take into account both the visible costs, irrespective of who pays them, and the opportunity costs. How do we determine these costs? Institutions will know how to arrive at the respective costs that are relevant in their environment. Here, so that we can provide a more effective explanation of our proposal, we have included some hypothetical values, expressed in dollars, as this seems to be the most widespread currency name, in our discussion. These well-founded values have their origin in a specific situation in just one corner of our global village that would not be relevant to all of our readers. However, their use makes for a better understanding of how to measure institutional knowledge assets. So, here we go!

An annual standard cost for formal education and post-secondary education of $9,230 and $27,544, respectively, is used. Additional professional training for employees is usually provided by a specialist provider outside the workplace. In addition to the payment of a fee to the course provider[6], the institution will continue to pay the salary or wages of the employee during the period of training. Taking both of these elements into account, a daily standard cost of $704 is used.

The French have a saying: *plus ça change, plus c'est la même chose*—the more things change, the more they stay the same. By carefully scrutinizing the past and the changes it has brought, it may be possible to anticipate the future. In that sense, a key to the development of a valuation model is a long-run rate of return on an investment over time. The question that arises is whether a nominal rate of interest or a real rate of interest should be used in any calculation. The solution lies in the nature of the costs being used as the basis for determining the value of knowledge assets. If the valuation is based on historical costs, then it is appropriate to use the nominal rate of interest for it includes a premium to account for the effects of inflation. However, if the valuation is based on current costs then a real rate of interest is more relevant. Since the calculations use a set of standard costs and these are easier to determine using current data, a real long-run rate of return will be used in all calculations.

A nominal long-run rate of return, which will vary from country to country, may be easily obtained from the Internet. Just how long is long-run? The definition of long-run is arbitrary with periods ranging between 10 and 30 years having some acceptance in differing circumstances. In our case, we chose the middle road, which is a period of twenty years. Since a real long-run rate of return is required, it is necessary to adjust the nominal rate for the effects of inflation. Here, changes in the consumer price index[7] have been used to determine annual inflation rates. Using interest rate data and consumer price indices from the same environment as the cost data above, an annual rate of return over the 20-year period of 5.34% has been determined. This real long-run rate of return will be used in all of our relevant calculations.

Using these parameters in the above equation the value on completion of each level that is attributable to formal education and post-secondary education may be calculated. For example, to calculate the value of a school leaver's formal education just prior to entering university the following data is entered in the equation: $c = \$9,230$, $r = 5.34\%$ and $n = 12$. The value of this level of knowledge, that is K, is calculated to be $149,840. Similarly, the value of a full-time undergraduate degree of three years duration, at its successful conclusion, is determined by entering the following data into the equation: $c = \$27,544$, $r = 5.34\%$ and $n = 3$. The value of this level of knowledge, that is K, is calculated to be $87,123. Similar calculations are conducted for each level of knowledge[8] and the results are provided in Figure 4.

The value of domain knowledge acquired through subsequent professional training must be treated somewhat differently. The knowledge acquired from the attendance at a training program lasting one day may be put into use immediately upon returning to the workplace the following day. Moreover, training that has been received over a period of years could, theoretically, be replaced in a few weeks as long as the volume of such training is normally in the region of a few days each year. Therefore, it would reasonable to assume in this case that there is no accumulation of cost over time. Dobija's (1998) proposal to use the future value of education costs incurred over time as the basis for valuing the knowledge acquired may therefore be deemed irrelevant in the case of formal training programs. What does remain relevant, however, is the notion that the value of something is at least equivalent to the amount one is prepared to pay. Accordingly, the knowledge value of each day of formal training, both to the recipient and to the institution, is equivalent to its cost, which was earlier established to be $704. Naturally, if there has been inflation or deflation, the original annual cost of education must be changed to the new current cost. The value of each employee's domain knowledge, from whichever source, would then have to be recalculated to discover the effect on the value of institutional knowledge.

Figure 4. Attributed value of domain knowledge

LEVEL OF EDUCATION	YEARS IN EACH CATEGORY OF EDUCATION	VALUE OF DOMAIN KNOWLEDGE
FORMAL EDUCATION		
School leaver pre matriculation	11	$133,482
School leaver at matriculation	12	$149,840
POST-SECONDARY EDUCATION		
Apprentice	3	$87,123
Diploma	2	$56,559
Undergraduate degree	3	$87,123
Honours degree	4	$119,319
Masters degree	2	$56,559
Doctorate	5	$153,235
FORMAL TRAINING		
Additional per day of formal training		$704

Depletion of Domain Knowledge

Like most other assets, the value of domain knowledge diminishes over time though the nature and rate of depletion may be expected to vary for different types of knowledge (Becker, 1993). Since a formal education is intended to provide the recipient with lifetime skills, its benefits may reasonably be expected to remain with an individual forever. From an institution's point of view, the value of knowledge acquired from that formal education, though not diminishing in what it provides year-on-year, has less potential value where, for example, it is only available to the institution for a maximum of 15 years rather than 48 years.

In the case of a post-matriculation school leaver who joins an institution immediately on leaving school, the institution could look forward to the possibility of benefiting from the knowledge acquired from that education for a maximum period of 47 years. Since the value of knowledge attributable to a person of that standing, see Table 3, is expected to be of equal benefit to the institution in each of those 47 years, it may be considered equivalent to the institution acquiring an annuity of $8,761 for 47 years. This is calculated using the predetermined real long-run rate of return of 5.34% as the discount rate[9]. After one year's employment, and assuming there has been no change in the current annual cost of a formal education, the value of that employee's knowledge to the institution would be the present value of that annuity for 46 years at 5.34%, that is $149,076. The first year's depletion would therefore be $764. In other words, as the years pass, the period of the annuity is reduced and what is lost is the present value of the final year of the previous annuity. That is, the depletion for the first year is the present value of $8,761 receivable in 47 years time. Should, after two years and not having received any additional training, the employee leave the institution and not be replaced then the value of knowledge lost to the institution is the present value of an annuity of $8,761 for 45 years at 5.34%, that is $148,276[10].

This is different from the more professionally oriented post-secondary education and training received before or after joining an institution. For this form of knowledge there is, in addition to the above, an element of obsolescence. Instead of simply depleting the value of knowledge acquired by the institution over the potential period of employment, it ought to be depleted over the length of time it is expected to provide a benefit to the institution. This will vary depending on the nature of the education and training received. Some forms of knowledge may indeed provide a benefit over the potential period of employment. Others may only provide a benefit during the time a person occupies a certain position in the institution while the benefit period of specific training programs may be a function of the expected state of technology. Clearly, because of the diversity of knowledge gained in this way, the most appropriate number of years over which to amortize these types of knowledge may differ not only for different types of programs but also for different institutions and different jobs within institutions.

What is required is a method, as simple as is reasonably consistent with reality, which takes into account the shorter period that an institution will benefit from this form of knowledge and the value of money over time. In a study conducted by Flamholtz (1985, pp. 285-288), a useful life of approximately fourteen years was established for a group of employees within a single institution. This supports a contention that some part of any knowledge that is acquired by an individual is retained by them and is of use to them and their

institution over many years. It seems appropriate then, from an institution's perspective, to deplete the value of employee domain knowledge acquired from professionally oriented education over a fifteen-year period. Training programs are somewhat different in that they are generally tailored to specific issues that are likely to become obsolete much sooner. For that reason, a shorter period of five years has been chosen as the period of depletion.

Calculations may be completed in a similar manner to that proposed earlier for depletion of an employee's domain knowledge attributable to a formal education. For example, to an institution, the value of knowledge attributable to a person who has just completed an undergraduate degree, see Table 3, would be the equivalent of acquiring an annuity of $8,588 for fifteen years using the predetermined real long-run rate of return of 5.34% as the discount rate. One year after completing the degree, and assuming there has been no change in the current annual cost of that education, the value of that element of the employee's knowledge to the institution would be the present value of that annuity for fourteen years at 5.34%, that is $83,188. The first year's depletion would therefore be $3,935. Similarly, in the fifth year the amount of depletion would be $4,846 and in the tenth year, $6,285. The same rationale may be applied to the depletion of the investment in ongoing formal training programs.

Implicit Knowledge

Institutional implicit knowledge and individual domain knowledge are complementary to each other. Earlier, it was stated that institutional implicit knowledge is created and enlarged by converting the domain knowledge of individuals by means of social interaction within the institution. This was identified as a crucial process in the quest to achieve a sustainable competitive advantage. As such, it is important that some form of measurement is developed to facilitate an assessment of an institution's performance in growing its implicit knowledge.

This form of synergy is difficult to measure. Dodd (1955), however, has developed a model, the *diffusion* or *contagion* model, which is of use. He proposed that the rate at which rumors or information spread through a population is congruous with the frequency of contact between those who have received the information and those who have not. Since this may be likened to the process by which implicit knowledge is disseminated throughout an institution, his model is applied in the search for an acceptable method of determining the value of an institution's implicit knowledge. In its simplest form, Dodd assumes that the instantaneous spread of rumors or information is proportional to both the number of people who have received the information and to the number who have not. Bishir and Drewes (1970, p. 436) expanded the model so that it facilitates the calculation of a value for the constant α. The expanded equation is:

$$\alpha t = \ln y_t - \ln (1-y_t) - \ln y_0 + \ln (1-y_0)$$

If it is assumed that at the end of the available years of employment[11] the maximum amount of institutional implicit knowledge has been absorbed by an employee, it is possible to substitute values for y_t, $(1-y_t)$, y_0 and $(1-y_0)$. The preferred situation is for there to be a value of one for y_{48} and zero for $(1-y_{48})$. Since it is not possible to calculate a value for $ln(0)$, a slightly lower exit value of 0.98, for y_{48}, has been chosen resulting in a value for $(1-y_{48})$ of 0.02. Furthermore, this is congruent with the view that a new starter acquires a small amount of institutional implicit knowledge during the course of employment interviews and induction training received immediately on joining the institution. Therefore, the value of y_0 would be minimal rather than zero. Consequently, a starting point of 0.02 has been assumed for developing the model. Solving the equation, the value of the activity coefficient constant is 0.16216.

A further rationalization of Dodd's original formula after the incorporation of Bishir and Drewes' input provides the basis for calculating a rate (ψ), based on the efflux of time, for the acquisition of institutional implicit knowledge by each employee in the institution. This is represented by the following equation, which we have used to calculate the cumulative rate of acquisition of institutional implicit knowledge held by an individual employee after each year of service (see Figure 5 for a selection of rates).

$$\psi = \frac{0.02e^{\alpha t}}{1 - 0.02(1 - e^{\alpha t})}$$

where :

$t = $ *actual years of service for an employee*

$\alpha = $ *the activity coefficient already calculate*

Even though employees may spend a regular amount of time throughout their working lives sharing knowledge, the acquisition of implicit knowledge does not have to follow the same path. During the first few years of employment, implicit knowledge would accrue at a slower rate than normal. It is also likely that in the latter years of an employee's working life, the acquisition of implicit knowledge would also slow[12]. Using an analogy, when putting together a jigsaw puzzle, the initial pieces are difficult to place. As the assembly progresses the ability to place other pieces improves until there are only a small number of pieces remaining. These do not always fall into place quite so readily. The acquisition of implicit knowledge may be considered in the same light. Figure 6 shows that the calculated cumulative rate of diffusion, or the acquisition of institutional implicit knowledge by an individual employee, exhibits similar tendencies and may therefore be considered a reliable formula for establishing the rate at which implicit knowledge is acquired.

Figure 5. Selected rates of acquisition of implicit knowledge

Years of service	Cumulative rate of acquisition
1	0.02344
2	0.02745
3	0.03213
4	0.03757
5	0.04390
10	0.09362
15	0.18856
20	0.34330
25	0.54046
30	0.72571
35	0.85616
40	0.93051
45	0.96787
46	0.97255
47	0.97656
48	0.98000

All that remains is to determine the basis of valuing the implicit knowledge in the workforce. Previously it was decided that cost based measures should be used as the basis for establishing a pragmatic value of knowledge. Since this form of institutional knowledge is acquired through social interaction, or the sharing of employee experience, the only cost relevant to the institution is the cost of labor for the time spent by its employees on this activity.

To start, it is necessary to consider how much time is spent during the working day in sharing knowledge within the institution. It is unlikely that any records will exist to provide concrete evidence of the time spent by employees on this activity. This being the case, securing an answer requires a rational assessment that will centre on the question of what may be considered reasonable—10%, 15%, or 20%. Undoubtedly, it will vary from one institution to another but, more importantly, it will almost certainly differ for different job specifications within an institution and employee behavior according to the institution's culture. While this is an important element that needs careful consideration, at this point in the development of the model any reasonable assumption will suffice. 12½%, or the equivalent of one hour out of each eight-hour day, will be assumed.

In a similar way to calculating the cost of various elements of domain knowledge, we have used a well-founded hypothetical value for the average annual cost to the institution for each employee, which is $45,872. If 12½% of each employee's time is spent growing the implicit knowledge of an institution, the cost to the institution each year is $5,734 per employee. Earlier, acquisition of institutional implicit knowledge by each employee was assumed to occur over a maximum period of employment of 48 years. Therefore, for each employee, the maximum value to an institution of implicit knowledge is equivalent to the present value of $5,734 for each of 48 years. Using the same real long-run rate of return of 5.34% that was incorporated, where appropriate, in all other calculations, the present value of a working lifetime's implicit knowledge is estimated to be $98,539.

From this point, the value of an institution's implicit knowledge may be determined in three steps. First, multiply this amount by the cumulative rate of acquisition of institutional implicit knowledge for each year of service (see Figure 7 for some selected calculations). Second, multiply the product by the number of employees with that length of service. Third, aggregate all of the values determined in the second step. The result should provide, in most cases, a reasonable indication of

Figure 6. Cumulated rate of diffusion

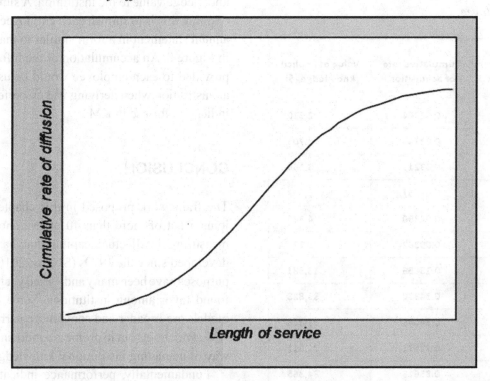

the value of implicit knowledge resident within the institution.

Using the Explicit Knowledge Database

The methods and models put forward in this chapter require access to a wide range of data that is acquired from several sources. Extensive use of current rather than historical data implies that it must be updated on a regular basis. Furthermore, the frequent use of a number of formulae, although not unduly complex, would suggest that electronic processing is the best way to convert the data into useable information.

All of the employee data, such as salary, level of education, time spent on training, length of service and remaining years of service, that are necessary to determine the value of institutional knowledge should be contained in the employees' database. The common data, such as employment related costs, current education and training costs, long-term interest rates, annual inflation rates and

expected maximum length of service, should be regularly imported into the section of the explicit knowledge database reserved for institutional data.

The institution's information system, having been provided with the appropriate algorithms, should then be capable of automatically updating the value to the institution of employees' knowledge every time there is a change to the relevant data in either the employee database or the common database. A further advantage in using the institution's information system, instead of an independent database or spreadsheet, is that on each occasion there is a change in the underlying data the system is capable of providing an immediate analysis by each of the causal elements, such as new employees, departing employees, increase in formal qualifications, formal training programs, inflation, depletion, and continuity of employment, of the variation in the value of institutional knowledge.

More than 30 years ago, Toffler (1980) believed that people would come to see the

Figure 7. Selected values of implicit knowledge per employee

Years of service	Cumulative rate of acquisition	Value of implicit knowledge ($)
1	0.02344	2,310
2	0.02745	2,705
3	0.03213	3,166
4	0.03757	3,702
5	0.04390	4,326
10	0.09362	9,225
15	0.18856	18,581
20	0.34330	33,828
25	0.54046	53,256
30	0.72571	71,511
35	0.85616	84,365
40	0.93051	91,692
45	0.96787	95,373
46	0.97255	95,834
47	0.97656	96,229
48	0.98000	96,568

organization that provided their livelihood as a vehicle through which they were able to grow. In educational institutions that has been the case for even longer, especially for faculty members who see the continual acquisition of new knowledge as part of their everyday working lives. At the same time, institutions are increasingly seeking to differentiate themselves through the quality of their research and educational programs[13]. Since these goals complement each other, it is in an institution's best interests to encourage the aspirations of their employees. Hauser and Katz (1998) believe a valuable way of achieving this is to show their employees how they provide

knowledge value to the institution. A simple way of doing this is to furnish each employee with an annual statement in a form similar to that shown in Figure 8. An accumulation of the information provided to each employee would be useful for an institution when deriving its key performance indicators for use in KM^2.

CONCLUSION

The framework proposed in this chapter, KM^2, joins a list of more than 40 other concepts for measuring intellectual capital that have been developed since the 1970s (Sveiby, 2010). Their purposes have been many and varied yet few have found favor among institutions. Some of these models are broader and some more narrow than KM^2, which sets out to promote a more integrated way of managing institutional knowledge.

Fundamentally, performance indicators that measure *effectiveness* and *efficiency* of an institution's knowledge management initiatives need to be aligned with one or another of the four forms of integration, which are *cultural, organizational, methodical,* and *procedural*. The model put forward in this chapter, KM^2, aims to do just that and is only the beginning of Puxty's (1993) long road in search of a planning, control and performance measurement system that accounts for the human element of an institution's intellectual assets. In the quest to enhance knowledge management in educational institutions, a prerequisite for survival in the long run, our model has concentrated on seeking to fill the void of performance indicators that account for the integrative management of an institution's knowledge assets. At the same time, the need to provide information on value of employee knowledge resident in the institution has also been recognized and articulated in this chapter.

Unfortunately, all measures can be manipulated. Those proposed in our KM^2 are no different in that respect. The value of knowledge may be

Figure 8. Employee's knowledge value to the organization

THE VALUE OF YOUR KNOWLEDGE TO THE INSTITUTION	
Name:	Middle Age
Date of birth:	10th January 1966
Years of service:	15 years
Qualifications:	BSc, MBA
	$
Formal knowledge (education and training)	
Knowledge value at 1st January, 2010	165,971
Adjustment to convert this amount its current value	7,000
	172,971
Increases in knowledge value in the year:	
Formal qualifications	–
Training programs	3,520
	176,491
Decrease due to the efflux of time	14,226
Knowledge value at 31st December, 2010	158,745
Knowledge from being part of the team	
Knowledge value at 31st December, 2010	18,581

increased by providing more training or taking on more employees and since that valuation is based on the cost of acquisition rather than use-value, an institution may acquire inappropriate knowledge and skills. Such acquisitions are likely to have an adverse effect on some other area of institutional performance. For reasons such as this, KM² uses the balanced scorecard concept because it facilitates an understanding of cause-and-effect relationships. Nevertheless, in concert with the objectives of this chapter, KM² is intended to provide a practical framework for providing information on an institution's knowledge and skills: how they are created, how they are nurtured, how they are valued, and how they contribute to institutional success and sustainability.

It is doubtful whether any one person could be an authority on all the concepts and issues addressed in this chapter and some of our proposals may well be challenged. Furthermore, over many years, authors have proffered a variety of suggestions about the development of suitable key performance indicators for the management of knowledge assets but they have often been focused on the operational, rather than the strategic, aspects of knowledge management. In the framework proposed in this chapter the focus is on forward-looking strategic aspects that are embedded in the institution's vision, which provides the standard against which knowledge management is measured. At the same time, use of the models is related to economy[14]. Good economy means good resource management, which in an educational institution is so much more than simply an investment in monetary capital – how they manage talent and accumulated knowledge is far more important.

The road ahead is winding, with many hazards. Further investigation is needed on two aspects. First, we need to have a more comprehensive understanding of the extent of strategic and operational knowledge management in institutional life. Second, we need to investigate why the models developed through research and application are, in the main, rejected by management.

Unfortunately, experience is showing us that refining beliefs is not quite as easy as it sounds. Human beings become very comfortable with the particular set of beliefs that have got them where they are. In other words, they become much attached to the personal paradigms that have served them so well in the past. It is only a preparedness to ask the really difficult questions that allows people to confront the possibility that those paradigms typically have a use-by date. After all, no system, no framework, no model, however effective, will remain current indefinitely. The certain truths of yesterday become the unquestioned myths of today.

We are confident that the discussion in this chapter provides ample reason for accepting the need to critically challenge the currently prevailing myths concerning the management of knowledge in educational institutions and subsequently measuring the performance of that management. We have used deductive reasoning supported by the views of knowledge management practitioners to provide a framework to help with the process of critique. Our proposals require a meaningful change in the performance measurement practices of an institution. We are certain that this change may only be achieved by the transformation of those who comprise the institution and such personal transformations are only ever achieved through a process of learning.

REFERENCES

Ackoff, R. L. (1989). From data to wisdom. *Journal of Applied Systems Analysis, 16*(1), 3–9.

Alavi, M., & Leidner, D. E. (2001). Review: Knowledge management and knowledge management systems: Conceptual foundations and research issues. *Management Information Systems Quarterly, 25*(1), 107–136. doi:10.2307/3250961

Allee, V. (1997). *The knowledge evolution: Expanding organizational intelligence*. Newton, MA: Butterworth-Heinemann.

Arora, R. (2002). Implementing KM: A balanced scorecard approach. *Journal of Knowledge Management, 6*(3), 240–249. doi:10.1108/13673270210434340

Baxter, W. T. (1971). *Depreciation*. London, UK: Sweet & Maxwell.

Becker, B., & Gerhart, B. (1996). The impact of human resource management on organizational performance: Progress and prospects. *Academy of Management Journal, 39*(4), 779–801. doi:10.2307/256712

Becker, G. S. (1993). *Human capital: A theoretical and empirical analysis, with special reference to education* (3rd ed.). Chicago, IL: The University of Chicago Press.

Bishir, J. W., & Drewes, D. W. (1970). *Mathematics in the behavioural and social sciences*. New York, NY: Harcourt, Brace & World Inc.

Bontis, N. (1998). Intellectual capital: An exploratory study that develops measures and models. *Management Decision, 36*(2), 63–76. doi:10.1108/00251749810204142

Chapman, C. S. (1997). Reflections on a contingent view of accounting. *Accounting, Organizations and Society, 22*(2), 189–205. doi:10.1016/S0361-3682(97)00001-9

Coff, R. W. (1997). Human assets and management dilemmas: Coping with the hazards on the road to resource-based theory. *Academy of Management Review, 22*(2), 374–402.

Dahlbom, B., & Mathiassen, L. (1993). *Computers in context: The philosophy and practice of system design*. Oxford, UK: Blackwell Publishers.

Davenport, T. H., & Prusak, L. (2000). *Working knowledge: How organizations manage what they know*. Boston, MA: Harvard Business School Press.

Dobija, M. (1998). How to place human resources into the balance sheet. *Journal of Human Resource Costing and Accounting, 3*(1), 83–92. doi:10.1108/eb029044

Dodd, S. C. (1955). Diffusion is predictable: Testing probability models for laws of interaction. *American Sociological Review, 20*(4), 392–401. doi:10.2307/2092736

Edvinsson, L., & Malone, M. S. (1997). *Intellectual capital: Realizing your company's true value by finding its hidden brainpower*. New York, NY: Harper-Collins.

Fitz-Enz, J. (1995). *How to measure human resources management* (2nd ed.). New York, NY: McGraw-Hill.

Flamholtz, E. G. (1985). *Human resource accounting* (2nd ed.). San Francisco, CA: Jossey-Bass.

Globerson, A., Globerson, S., & Frampton, J. (1991). *You can't manage what you don't measure*. Aldershot, UK: Avebury.

Handy, C. (1996, December). Intelligence – Capitalism's most potent asset. *HR Monthly*, 8–11.

Hansen, M. T., & Nohria, N. (2004). How to build collaborative advantage. *MIT Sloan Management Review, 46*(1), 22–30.

Hansen, M. T., Nohria, N., & Tierney, T. (1999, March-April). What's your strategy for managing knowledge? *Harvard Business Review*, 106–116.

Hauser, J., & Katz, G. (1998). Metrics: You are what you measure. *European Management Journal, 16*(5), 517–528. doi:10.1016/S0263-2373(98)00029-2

Howells, J. (1996). Tacit knowledge, innovation and technology transfer. *Technology Analysis and Strategic Management, 8*(2), 91–106. doi:10.1080/09537329608524237

IFAC. (1998). *The measurement and management of intellectual capital: An introduction*. New York, NY: IFAC Publishing.

Kakabadse, N. K., Kakabadse, A., & Kouzmin, A. (2003). Reviewing the knowledge management literature: Towards a taxonomy. *Journal of Knowledge Management, 7*(4), 75–91. doi:10.1108/13673270310492967

Kaplan, R. S., & Norton, D. P. (1996). *Translating strategy into action: The balanced scorecard*. Boston, MA: Harvard Business School Press.

Lev, B. (2001). *Intangibles: Management, measurement and reporting*. Washington, DC: Brooking Institute Press.

Martin, B. (2000). Knowledge management within the context of management: An evolving relationship. *Singapore Management Review, 22*(2), 17–36.

Martin, K., & Bourke, J. (2009). *Integrated talent management: Improving business results through visibility and alignment*. Boston, MA: Aberdeen Group.

Minonne, C. (2007). *Towards an integrative approach for managing implicit and explicit knowledge: An exploratory study in Switzerland*. Unpublished Doctoral Dissertation. Adelaide, Australia: University of South Australia.

Minonne, C. (2008, November-December). Wissens-management: Wie lautet das erfolgsrezept. *Wissensmanagement Magazin*, 48-49.

Minonne, C. (2009). *Strategic knowledge management: An integrative approach*. Saarbrücken, Germany: SVH Verlag.

Minonne, C., & Turner, G. (2009). Evaluating knowledge management performance. *Electronic Journal of Knowledge Management*, 7(5), 583–592.

Neely, A. (2002). *Business performance measurement*. London, UK: Economist Books. doi:10.1017/CBO9780511753695

Nickols, F. W. (2000). The knowledge in knowledge management. In Cortada, J. W., & Woods, J. A. (Eds.), *The Knowledge Management Yearbook 2000-2001* (pp. 12–21). Boston, MA: Butterworth-Heinemann.

Nonaka, I., & Takeuchi, H. (1995). *The knowledge creating company: How Japanese companies create the dynamics of innovation*. Oxford, UK: Oxford University Press.

O'Dell, C. (1998). *If only we knew what we know: The transfer of internal knowledge and best practice*. New York, NY: The Free Press.

OECD. (1996). *Measuring what people know: Human capital accounting for the knowledge economy*. Paris, France: OECD Publishing.

Pfeffer, J. (1997). Pitfalls on the road to measurement: The dangerous liaison of human resources with the ideas of accounting and finance. *Human Resource Management*, 36(3), 357–365. doi:10.1002/(SICI)1099-050X(199723)36:3<357::AID-HRM7>3.0.CO;2-V

Polanyi, M. (1958). *Personal knowledge: Towards a post-critical philosophy*. London, UK: Routledge and Kegan Paul Ltd.

Puxty, A. G. (1993). *The social and organizational context of management accounting*. London, UK: Academic Press.

Quinn, J. B. (1992). *Intelligent enterprise: A knowledge and service based paradigm for industry*. New York, NY: The Free Press.

Roslender, R., & Dyson, J. R. (1992). Accounting for the worth of employees: A new look at an old problem. *The British Accounting Review*, 24(4), 311–329. doi:10.1016/S0890-8389(05)80040-X

Sveiby, K.-E. (1997). *The new organizational wealth: Managing and measuring knowledge-based assets*. San Francisco, CA: Berrett-Koehler.

Sveiby, K.-E. (2010). *Methods for measuring intangible assets*. Retrieved July 25, 2011, from http://www.sveiby.com/articles/Intangible-Methods.htm

Takeuchi, H. (1998). Beyond knowledge management: Lessons from Japan. *Monash Mt-Eliza Business Journal*, 1(1), 21–30.

Teece, D. J. (1998). Research directions for knowledge management. *California Management Review*, 40(3), 289–292.

Tenkasi, R. V., & Boland, R. J. (1996). Exploring knowledge diversity in knowledge intensive firms: A new role for information systems. *Journal of Organizational Change Management*, 9(1), 79–91. doi:10.1108/09534819610107330

Toffler, A. (1980). *The third wave*. New York, NY: Morrow.

Tuomi, I. (1999). *Corporate knowledge: Theory and practice of intelligent organizations*. Helsinki, Finland: Metaxis.

Turner, G. (1996). Human resource accounting: Whim or wisdom? *Journal of Human Resource Costing and Accounting*, 1(1), 63–73. doi:10.1108/eb029023

Turner, G. (2000). Using human resource accounting to bring balance to the balanced scorecard. *Journal of Human Resource Costing and Accounting, 5*(2), 31–44. doi:10.1108/eb029067

Turner, G. (2005). Accounting for human resources: Quo vadis? *International Journal of Environmental, Cultural. Economic and Social Sustainability, 1*(3), 11–17.

Turner, G., & Jackson-Cox, J. (2002). If management requires measurement how may we cope with knowledge? *Singapore Management Review, 24*(3), 101–111.

von Krogh, G., Ichijo, K., & Nonaka, I. (2000). *Enabling knowledge creation: How to unlock the mystery of tacit knowledge and release the power of innovation.* Oxford, UK: Oxford University Press.

Wilson, T. D. (2002). The nonsense of "knowledge management". *Information Research, 8*(1).

Zack, M. H. (1999). Developing a knowledge strategy. *California Management Review, 41*(3), 125–145.

ADDITIONAL READING

Casselman, R. M., & Sampson, D. (2004). *Moving beyond tacit and explicit: Four dimensions of knowledge.* Melbourne, Australia: Intellectual Property Research Institute of Australia.

Chaudhry, A. S. (2003). What difference does it make: Measuring returns of knowledge management. In Coakes, E. (Ed.), *Knowledge Management: Current Issues and Challenges* (pp. 52–65). Hershey, PA: IGI Global.

Dalkir, K. (2005). *Knowledge management in theory and practice.* Burlington, MA: Elsevier Butterworth-Heinemann.

Easterby-Smith, M., & Lyles, M. A. (Eds.). (2005). *The Blackwell handbook of organizational learning and knowledge management.* Oxford, UK: Blackwell Publishing Ltd.

Fink, K. (2009). Knowledge measurement barriers: Results from a case study. In *Proceedings of AMCIS 2009.* AMCIS.

Foss, N. J., & Michailova, S. (Eds.). (2009). *Knowledge governance: Processes and perspectives.* Oxford, UK: Oxford University Press.

Gao, F., Li, M., & Nakamori, Y. (2002). Systems thinking on knowledge and its management: Systems methodology for knowledge management. *Journal of Knowledge Management, 6*(1), 7–17. doi:10.1108/13673270210417646

Gillies, V., & Lucey, H. (Eds.). (2007). *Power, knowledge and the academy: The institutional is political.* Basingstoke, UK: Palgrave MacMillan. doi:10.1057/9780230287013

Girard, J. P., & McIntyre, S. (2010). Knowledge management modeling in public sector organizations: A case study. *International Journal of Public Sector Management, 23*(1), 71–77. doi:10.1108/09513551011012330

Gorman, M. E. (2002). Types of knowledge and their roles in technology transfer. *The Journal of Technology Transfer, 27*(3), 219–231. doi:10.1023/A:1015672119590

Heisig, P. (2009). Harmonisation of knowledge management – Comparing 160 KM frameworks around the globe. *Journal of Knowledge Management, 13*(4), 4–31. doi:10.1108/13673270910971798

Hildreth, P. J., & Kimble, C. (2002). The duality of knowledge. *Information Research, 8*(1).

Huang, M.-J., Chen, M.-Y., & Yieh, K. (2007). Comparing with your main competitor: The single most important task of knowledge management performance measurement. *Journal of Information Science*, *33*(4), 416–434. doi:10.1177/0165551506076217

Jensen, M. B., Johnson, B., Lorenz, E., & Lundvall, B.-A. (2007). Forms of knowledge and modes of innovation. *Research Policy*, *36*(5), 680–693. doi:10.1016/j.respol.2007.01.006

Jimes, C., & Lucardie, L. (2003). Reconsidering the tacit-explicit distinction – A move toward functional (tacit) knowledge management. *Electronic Journal of Knowledge Management*, *1*(1), 23–32.

Johnson, B., Lorenz, E., & Lundvall, B.-A. (2002). Why all this fuss about codified and tacit knowledge? *Industrial and Corporate Change*, *11*(2), 245–262. doi:10.1093/icc/11.2.245

Kannan, G., & Aulbur, W. G. (2004). Intellectual capital: Measurement effectiveness. *Journal of Intellectual Capital*, *5*(3), 389–413. doi:10.1108/14691930410550363

Kelly, A. (2004). *The intellectual capital of schools – Measuring and managing knowledge, responsibility and reward: Lessons from the commercial sector*. Dordrecht, The Netherlands: Kluwer Academic Publishers.

Kidwell, J. J., van der Linde, K. M., & Johnson, S. L. (2000). Applying corporate knowledge management practices in higher education. *EDUCAUSE Quarterly*, *23*(4), 28–33.

Kok, A. (2006). *Intellectual capital as part of knowledge management initiatives at institutions of higher education*. Johannesburg, South Africa: University of Johannesburg.

Lee, H.-Y., & Roth, G. L. (2009). A conceptual framework for examining knowledge management in higher education contexts. *New Horizons in Adult Education and Human Resource Development*, *23*(4), 22–37.

Little, S., & Ray, T. (Eds.). (2005). *Managing knowledge: An essential reader* (2nd ed.). London, UK: Sage Publications Limited.

Lytras, M., Russ, M., Mayer, R., & Nave, A. (Eds.). (2008). *Knowledge management strategies: A handbook of applied technologies*. Hershey, PA: IGI Publishing. doi:10.4018/978-1-59904-603-7

Metcalfe, A. S. (Ed.). (2006). *Knowledge management and higher education: A critical analysis*. Hershey, PA: IGI Global.

Mutch, A. (2008). *Managing knowledge and information in organizations: A literacy approach*. New York, NY: Routledge.

Nie, K., Ma, T., & Nakamori, Y. (2007). Building a taxonomy to understanding knowledge management. *Electronic Journal of Knowledge Management*, *5*(4), 453–466.

Patriotta, G. (2004). On studying organizational knowledge. *Knowledge Management Research and Practice*, *2*(1), 3–12. doi:10.1057/palgrave.kmrp.8500017

Pozzali, A., & Viale, R. (2007). Cognition, types of "tacit knowledge" and technology transfer. In Topol, R., & Walliser, B. (Eds.), *Cognitive Economics: New Trends* (pp. 205–224). Amsterdam, The Netherlands: Elsevier.

Rodgers, W., & Housel, T. J. (2009). Measures for organizations engaged in a knowledge economy. *Journal of Intellectual Capital*, *10*(3), 341–353. doi:10.1108/14691930910977770

Russ, M., Jones, J. K., & Fineman, R. (2006). Toward a taxonomy of knowledge-based strategies: Early findings. *International Journal of Knowledge and Learning*, *2*(1/2), 1–40. doi:10.1504/IJKL.2006.009677

von Krogh, G., Roos, J., & Kleine, D. (Eds.). (2009). *Knowing in firms: Understanding, managing and measuring knowledge*. London, UK: Sage Publications Limited.

Wu, L.-C., Ong, C.-S., & Hsu, Y.-W. (2008). Knowledge-based organization evaluation. *Decision Support Systems*, *45*(3), 541–549. doi:10.1016/j.dss.2007.06.013

KEY TERMS AND DEFINITIONS

Explicit Knowledge: Implicit knowledge that has been articulated, codified and stored in any way such that it is possible for it to be transmitted to others.

Implicit Knowledge: An individual's knowledge that remains undocumented in any form yet provides an instinctive understanding of situations.

Information: A collection of facts, or statements of events, among which there is a coherent and meaningful relationship of some sort.

Knowledge Assets: Explicit and implicit knowledge regarding the effective utilization of processes, technologies, services, products and markets that enable an educational institution to generate income.

Knowledge: Awareness, familiarity, or understanding acquired through observation, experience, or education.

Management: The judicious organization, coordination and use of the resources available to an educational institution to achieve defined objectives in accordance with certain ideals.

Performance: The progress over time toward some specified objectives.

ENDNOTES

[1] While this may be fundamentally true, customised indices and other metrics may be equally useful.

[2] Such a statement may seem an aberration when talking about an educational institution; however, it is very much a reality in the 21st century.

[3] This distinction also became apparent from interviewees' answers during some field research first reported in Minonne (2007). The single term *tacit* was used in the interview questions to see whether this differentiation was also recognised by practitioners.

[4] Even if a market-based measure were to be used to value institutional knowledge, it is worth remembering that the market value of an institution as a whole is determined by the amount that a purchaser will pay for it.

[5] In all cases, no distinction is made between the quality of graduands. While some will always be better than others, the granting of an award assumes a certain level of knowledge common to all.

[6] Where the training is conducted within the organisation, the cost, per participant, of running the programme should be substituted for the external provider's fee.

[7] This may be called something else in many countries, but it effectively represents changes in the cost of living, which we feel is appropriate in this instance.

[8] Of course, in some countries, the length of time taken to acquire a certain level of education will vary and so it becomes just a matter of making new calculations using relevant cost data and the appropriate number of years.

[9] The real long-run rate of return continues to be used because the amount of the annuity will be recalculated at least annually or, more appropriately, each time there is a

change in the cost base. It may be argued that a different discount rate, perhaps one that is determined by reference to the organisation's Weighted Average Cost of Capital (WACC), should be used. There are two reasons why this rate has been chosen. First, because all the calculations are based on current costs, no premium need be included in the discount rate for the effects of inflation. The WACC inevitably does this. Second, the organisation only benefits from the use of the knowledge and skills of its employees. It does not, and will never, own them as it owns other assets.

[10] See Baxter (1971, pp. 81-87) for a discussion on the theory.

[11] The available years of employment are 48 if calculated from leaving school at age 17 to retirement at an expected age 65, although of course this is unlikely to be the case for very much longer.

[12] Becker (1993), referring to on-the-job training, suggests this is the situation.

[13] The increasing reliance by prospective students and their families on league tables to judge the all-around performance of educational institutions reinforces this point of view.

[14] Use of the word *economy* here reflects a deeper meaning than the one carelessly used in everyday parlance.

Section 2
Knowledge Management, Innovation, and Business

Chapter 9
Knowledge Management and Quality in Croatian Tourism

Ivanka Avelini Holjevac
University of Rijeka, Croatia

Kristina Črnjar
University of Rijeka, Croatia

Ana-Marija Vrtodušić Hrgović
University of Rijeka, Croatia

ABSTRACT

Knowledge is an infinite resource of hotel enterprises and society as a whole. In hotel enterprises, it serves as a platform for practising sustainable development and gaining competitive advantages. Knowledge-based economic development provides the best opportunities for dealing with a global environment in which rapid and dynamic changes are taking place. Seen as a precondition to success, Knowledge Management (KM) will result in generating value-added in tourism. A survey was conducted in large and mid-sized hotel enterprises to demonstrate their KM level and the contribution of KM in gaining competitive advantages in the Croatian hotel industry. Empirical research was used to establish the level of KM development in the Croatian hotel industry, and to determine the importance of KM in gaining competitive advantages in the hotel industry. In addition to knowledge, quality is a vital factor in gaining competitive advantages in hotel enterprises. Globalized markets and increasingly discerning customers, demanding more and more for their money, are compelling product and service providers to ground their business systems on customer needs. Total Quality Management (TQM)—a new management philosophy—enables the systematic application of these ideas. This chapter looks at several TQM approaches that define the basic elements essential to successful TQM implementation, in particular, the element pertaining to employees. The application of these elements in the Croatian hotel industry is presented through the results of empirical research on a sample of mid-sized and large hotel enterprises.

DOI: 10.4018/978-1-4666-1969-2.ch009

INTRODUCTION

The long-term success and sustainability of tourism will be linked to the ability of a destination and its stakeholders to foster innovation in its everyday business. Organizations and companies in tourism are under constant pressure from global competition. They have to improve constantly the quality of their products and services. Factors that will influence innovation in tourism include the economic competence of stakeholders, clustering of resources, including the tourism product, knowledge, and skills, understanding the tourism network and the relationship between stakeholders, entrepreneurial capacity, the involvement of local government in the innovation process, and the effective production and distribution of knowledge throughout the tourism network. An innovation policy in tourism should seek to promote coherence and synergy effects throughout the tourism industry and encourage greater cooperation between state and regional levels, and between municipalities and the business community. Knowledge will become the single unlimited resource of society and the base on which businesses and industries can build sustainable operations and gain competitive advantages.

The difference between new forms of tourism and tourism in the past is reflected primarily in the input of activities related to education. Lifelong learning is needed to achieve sustainable tourism development. This education should be available to all stakeholders and should focus on understanding the connection between people and the environment.

In a knowledge-based economy, Knowledge Management (KM) emerges as a new tool for and new approach to Total Quality Management (TQM). The connection between the two is primarily seen through the great importance of human capital and, in particular, the development and education of employees as a prerequisite for achieving competitiveness and fostering innovation.

TQM differs in many ways from conventional management, and it is seen as a new challenge to many companies, around the world, striving to achieve business excellence. Although TQM was developed primarily in manufacturing companies, the advantages it provides were soon recognized, leading to its application in the service sector. Hotel enterprises soon realized the value and power of quality. Defined as understanding and meeting the needs, wants and expectations of guests, quality is today a unique force, driving and guiding hotel enterprises to provide services that will not only match guest expectations, but exceed them as well.

When it comes to implementing TQM, a variety of approaches can be used. All approaches, however, contain common elements that are essential to TQM implementation. These are the management commitment and leadership, customer-orientation, continuous improvement, employee involvement and management by facts. This chapter focuses on employees and their role in the process of TQM implementation, with emphasize on education and training, and presenting the current situation in the Croatian hotel industry.

BACKGROUND

Knowledge Management (KM) implies the systematic management of knowledge needed to accomplish business objectives and achieve sustainable development, as well as carry out related processes, to ensure competitive ability and business excellence on the global market (Črnjar, 2010). KM has emerged as a response to changes in the innovation process, among other things. Innovation is seen as the integration of knowledge with action, in the sense of blending the specialist knowledge of a range of groups into specific outcomes of either product or process change. Implementation is thus seen as an integral element of innovation (Leonard-Barton, 1998).

While investment in technology, equipment, and processes is very important, it is not enough. It cannot ensure growth and advantages over competitors, if there is little or no investment in people. An organization must continuously take action to stimulate and support learning. In that way, it can emphasize the necessity of lifelong learning. Employees will have a positive attitude towards learning and see it as a chance for improvement and not as a threat.

Additionally, TQM application and success depend upon employees, teamwork, job satisfaction, and investment in developing new knowledge. TQM is the way of life of an organization committed to customer satisfaction through improvement (Dahlgaard, Kristensen, & Kanji, 1998, p. 17). It is an approach to improving the competitiveness, effectiveness, and flexibility of a whole organization. It is essentially a way of planning, organizing, and understanding each activity, and depends on each individual at each level (Oakland, 1995, p. 22). Investment in training and education, that is, investment in knowledge, is an indispensable element of quality management. As TQM approaches have confirmed, factors of vital importance to success are the knowledge possessed by each employee, teamwork, and personal involvement in the overall process.

According to Kanji, the TQM is based on five principles: Leadership, Delight the customer, Continuous improvement, Management by facts, People-based management (Kanji, 2002, p. 3). With the exception of Leadership, which is the fundamental principle, each of these principles is realized through the application of two concepts. People-based management is accomplished through the concepts of Teamwork and Internal Customers. These concepts confirm that, in addition to standards, technology and processes, people are essential in achieving quality.

People need to be motivated to do quality work. The only way to do this is to set clear objectives (telling them what they need to do and what they need to achieve), define processes (telling them how to do a job), provide feedback (telling them how well or how poorly they have done a job), and ensure continuous learning. Employee participation refers not only to their involvement in, but also to their responsibility for, finding ways of continuous improvement on both an individual and team basis. Accordingly, employees need to be empowered to make decisions and initiate action for improvements within their sphere of activity (Skoko, 2000, p. 111). Tenner and De Toro also emphasize the importance of employees in their approach to TQM which is build on three fundamental principles of total quality: Focus on customers—internal and external; Focus on improving work processes to produce consistent, acceptable outputs; and Focus on utilizing the talents of those with whom we work (Tenner & De Toro, 1992, p. 32). Employee involvement, a fundamental TQM principle, begins with active leadership. To improve their performance, employees across all levels are enabled to resolve problems, improve processes, and achieve customer satisfaction. Along with these principles, supporting elements are necessary for successful TQM implementation. One of them is related to education and training that provides employees with information about the enterprise's mission, vision, objectives, and strategies, and enables them to acquire the skilled needed in making improvements and resolving problems. Furthermore, communications are also essential in successful TQM implementation, considering the necessity of communicating the need for change to all employees, as well as reward and recognition awarded to those employees who have effectively applied the quality programme. Besides these, there are other TQM approaches that put emphasis on employees and their role in the successful implementation of TQM (Besterfield, et al., 1999; ISO 9000, 2000; Claver, Tari, & Molina, 2003).

Knowledge represents an important resource, and in accordance with that, it should be managed. KM can be seen as both a medium and outcome of innovation processes in tourism. KM will involve various processes take seek to capitalize on knowledge, which will become a key resource in generating value-added in companies in tourism. Accordingly, KM initiatives will gather and bring together key knowledge and knowledge sources located within companies, as well as outside of companies. Thus, KM may be presented as the perfect medium for the networked, interactive, and knowledge-driven nature of the innovation process (Scarbrough, 2003, p. 508). On the other hand, projects and initiatives developed within a KM framework result in innovations in themselves. These innovations typically involve finding new ways of enhancing the efficiency of processes, development, the design of new work processes and systems, etc. Considering how knowledge represents an enterprise's intangible assets, identifying, developing, gathering, and sharing knowledge is, in itself, a challenge that calls for innovative solutions. Innovations represent a crucial factor in achieving long-term success, a fact confirmed by business excellence models that can be used as frameworks for introducing TQM. For example, "Nurturing Creativity and Innovation" is one of the basic concepts on which the EFQM Excellence Model is based. The concept refers to the need to develop and engage with networks and engaging all stakeholders as potential sources of creativity and innovation (EFQM, 2010, p. 7). Innovation should lead the organization to new dimensions of performance and it is built on the accumulated knowledge of the organization and its people. Therefore, the ability to rapidly disseminate and capitalize on this knowledge is critical to driving organizational innovation (Baldrige National Quality Program, 2007, p. 3).

In the tourism and hotel industry, knowledge, together with human capital as its major provider, is becoming a prime factor in achieving sustainability and competitiveness on the global market. This is not only about generating knowledge, but also about the opportunities the industry has in integrating this new knowledge into its products, services and processes, and propagating it among people through education, training, and information. The importance of worker knowledge, competencies, and skills is becoming all the greater, because of the specific features of the hotel industry, the characteristics of the products and services it offers, and the very customers that consume these services. (Vujić, Črnjar, & Maškarin, 2009) Pursuant to the above, it is easy to conclude that Human Capital Management (together with HRM) will become a key element and support in managing knowledge and making innovations in tourism.

Human Capital Management is a weakness of the hotel industry and tourism as a whole, as well as its great challenge. Several reasons make Human Capital Management such an important challenge to the (international) hotel industry: The hotel industry is affected by high labour turnover, which is, more often than not, the result of ineffective Human Capital Management and inadequate reward policies, in particular. The hotel industry has difficulties in attracting highly trained professionals because of poor career development policies. The hotel industry is badly perceived by most people, who are reluctant to seek employment there. Study programs and syllabuses (that is, educational and training) fail to meet the needs of the hotel industry. In other words, challenges emerge with regard to recruiting staff, retaining the existing staff, the industry's image, training, and employee management. Human capital will represent a major threat to expansion in tourism and the hotel industry. The lack of sufficiently educated staff and competent managers may have a dramatic effect on the ability of the hotel industry to develop at an accelerated pace. In a given destination, there will a lack of sufficiently qualified employees relative to the growth of tourism demand. All the above confirms the fact that Human Capital Management in the hotel industry represents a key development factor and a vital success factor (Črnjar, 2005, pp. 251-265).

With the development of knowledge-based economies, the functions, processes, and roles typical of Human Resource Management (HRM) will change. While keeping some traditional functions and processes, it will develop new ones that will focus on involving all stakeholders (employees, suppliers, manufacturers, and customers) in the value creation chain. The role of Human Capital Management in the innovation process is evident in the flow of knowledge and the flow of people. This will cause some processes and functions to have a greater impact on the innovation process. Three vital HRM processes are the recruitment method, the reward strategy, and employee career development. Practising HRM can influence intersection by promoting or inhabiting knowledge sharing and by shaping the skills and attitudes of individuals. Human Capital Management will also take on other, new roles that will provide greater support to the KM process, such as human capital coordinator, rapid development specialist, relationship builder, and KM facilitator (Lengnick-Hall, 2002, pp. 34-35). All these factors have a vital impact on TQM, KM and innovation.

KM is a continuous process. It includes processes such as knowledge identification, creation, acquisition, development, collection, storage, use, dissemination, and transfer. The constant new flow of information and data emphasizes the need for managing knowledge and continuous learning, and acquiring new skills and competencies. KM implementation in organizations and companies in the field of tourism should be systematic and developed as a strategy, using tools and techniques that are available. The goal should be the accelerated collection of existing knowledge and experiences and their dissemination within the organization. KM should be embedded in daily operations to ensure a continuous flow of new knowledge as a basis for creating new products and services.

KM and quality management are derived one from the other and are closely tied. The next section focuses on their interconnection and their importance in enhancing the competitiveness of the Croatian hotel industry.

KNOWLEDGE AND QUALITY: A BASIS FOR ENHANCING THE COMPETITIVENESS OF CROATIA'S HOTEL INDUSTRY

Tourism and the hotel industry are labour intensive activities that focus on providing services. Trained, motivated, and satisfied employees are a key precondition to providing quality services. A vital element in the development of Croatian tourism, the hotel industry will need to grow based on sustainable development and business efficiency. Quality and knowledge, being the only infinite resources of any hotel enterprise or any society, will need to become a platform for gaining competitive advantages for hotel enterprises.

The importance and interconnection of quality and knowledge have prompted two empirical studies in the Croatian hotel industry. The first pertains to the level of quality systems application, and the second on the development of KM strategies in enhancing the competitiveness of the hotel industry. Research was conducted on a sample of large and mid-sized hotel enterprises in Croatia. The classification criterion was based on the Accounting Act (Official Gazette, 109/07).

Empirical research concerning the level of quality systems application in the Croatian hotel industry was conducted in 2009. At the time of research, of the 13 hotel enterprises possessing the ISO 9001 certificate, large and mid-sized hotel enterprises accounted for up to 70 percent. In addition, large and mid-sized hotel enterprises accounted for 83 percent of total revenue realized and 74 percent of the total assets of Group I 55.1 "Hotels and similar accommodation." Previously announced questionnaires were sent by post and e-mail. Target respondents were quality managers and, alternatively, Board members and hotel operations managers, and in some hotel enterprises, financial managers, human resource managers and marketing managers, considered as being the most knowledgeable of the existing state of quality system development in their respective enterprises.

Thirteen (54 percent) out of a total of 24 large hotel enterprises, and 18 (24 percent) out of a total of 75 mid-sized hotel enterprises, filled out and returned the questionnaire. The hotel enterprises (large and mid-sized) participating in the study accounted for 40 percent of total revenue, 38 percent of the total assets of Group I 55.1, and 39 percent of the total number of persons employed in 2008 (FINA, 2010). The questionnaire consisted of two parts, the first part pertaining to general and financial data about the hotel enterprises and the second concerning the application of quality systems in hotel enterprises. In addition to establishing the level of quality systems application in hotel enterprises, the questionnaire aimed to identify the reasons for introducing a quality system, when and how the system was implemented, the obstacles that needed to be overcome, and the advantages gained from its application.

The survey also looked at the extent to which employees are involved in implementing quality systems, through activities such as education and training, the reward system, teamwork and empowerment.

Results show that (Vrtodušić Hrgović, 2010):

- 94 percent of the total number of respondents invest in education and training for their employees,
- 74 percent of the total number of respondents use teamwork,
- 71 percent of the total number of respondents has a developed system for rewarding their best employees,
- 58 percent of the total number of respondents involves their employees in defining objectives in their respective departments.

Results indicate that almost all enterprises invest in training and education, and this confirms their heightened awareness of the importance of continuous education as the most important form of managing and developing human resources. Investment in training and education has inten-

sified over the last decade. Modern enterprises are dedicating more and more of their resources (money, time, information, energy, etc.) to educating and continuously training their employees. Management is increasingly aware of the fact that continuous employee education and training is one of the most efficient ways of gaining competitive advantages; it is fundamental precondition to market competition for customer favour and trust (Bahtijarević Šiber, 1999, p. 717).

Results also demonstrate that almost two thirds of surveyed hotel enterprises use teamwork and a reward system as activities that help to achieve and improve quality. These results reveal that hotel enterprises are aware of the importance of reward systems as a major factor in motivating employees. For reward systems to have a motivational effect, clear standards of work execution and performance need to be in place, and employees must understand and accept the method of assessing performance, as well as the method of rewarding and evaluation (Bahtijarević Šiber, 1999, p. 616). The reward systems of the majority of hotel enterprises include promotions (84 percent) and financial rewards (77 percent), while more than half of the hotel enterprises (55 percent) reward their employees through public recognition. Paid vacations as a form of reward are less frequent (26 percent), as are other forms of reward, such as lifelong learning and training (16 percent) (Vrtodušić Hrgović, 2010). Organizing employees into teams, with quality improvement as the common objective, helps to improve communication between and within departments and to create ground for introducing change. People are an inexhaustible source of ideas and innovation, and their expertise, experiences, knowledge and cooperation should be exploited to the satisfaction of all stakeholders.

Only in a minority of enterprises (only 58 percent) are employees involved in defining the objectives of their respective departments. Seeing how employee involvement is one of a major intangible work incentive, hotel enterprises should seek to encourage this activity to a greater extent. Participation is the degree to which employees are involved in decision processes regarding vital aspects of work and operations in an organization. It is a process through which organizations seek to involve employees in the decision process and in problem resolution, while tapping into the potential of employees to facilitate the organization in fulfilling its objectives (Bahtijarević Šiber, 1999, p. 682). In this way, employees take responsibility for their work, and the more involved they feel, the greater their wish to perform better. In TQM, employees need to be empowered for the jobs they perform and for the jobs they know best. This makes it easier for them to bring about changes that, in turn, will result in improvements. Employee empowerment does not lessen the role of managers. Instead, it enables employees to make their contribution towards achieving higher levels of quality. Beside the research related to the level of TQM implementation in Croatian hotel industry, and as a part of that the level of employee involvement in that process, the research concerning the implementation of KM strategies also been conducted.

This empirical research was conducted in 2010. The questionnaire consisted of three parts. The first part focused on competitiveness and HRM in the hotel industry, the second on KM in the hotel industry, and the third on knowledge as a strategic resource in the hotel enterprise. The final version of the questionnaire was published on-line. Target respondents were HR managers. Out of the total number of hotel enterprises, 72 percent filled out and returned the questionnaire.

The research sample was targeted, and its size corresponded to the total number of large and mid-sized hotel enterprises in Primorsko-Goranska County and Istria County. Viewed at a national level, the research encompassed 47 percent of Croatia's large hotel enterprises (of the 26 enterprises operating in Croatia, five are located in Primorsko-Goranska County and seven in Istria County) and 25 percent of Croatia's mid-sized

hotel enterprises (of the 74 enterprises operating in Croatia, 12 are located in Primorsko-Goranska County and 6 in Istria County). At the national level, the total number of employees in the group "Hotels and similar accommodation" amounts to 32,463 employees, of which Primorsko-Goranska County (5,056) and Istria County (7,692) account for 39.27 percent. These two counties account for up to 45.61 percent of business in the Croatian hotel industry. At the national level, turnover in hotels amounted to 8,045,876 thousand HRK. In Primorsko-Goranska County, this turnover amounted to 1,293,203 thousand HRK and in Istria County to 2,379,060 thousand HRK (Croatian Bureau of Statistics Tourism, 2009; Croatian Bureau of Statistics Hospitality, 2009).

Previous studies have shown that KM strategies in tourism enterprises are still rare and that KM development and implementation is progressing at a slow pace. In practice, we see the implementation of individual projects that are generally aimed at resolving a single current problem. There is a need to develop a KM framework, which will enable KM to be implemented in tourism organizations and enterprises. The aim of introducing KM is to achieve quality and facilitate innovation in tourism.

The effect of various aspects on gaining competitive advantages in Croatian hotel enterprise is analysed and rated in Figure 1. The degree of influence was measured on a scale of 1 to 5, with 1 signifying "entirely unimportant" and 5, "extremely important."

Respondents have rated the influence of individual aspects on gaining competitive advantages in hotel enterprises with scores ranging from 4.06 to 4.72. These high scores indicate that all aspects listed are largely important in gaining competitiveness. The results displayed in Table 1 show that *buildings and grounds* has the lowest level of influence on the competitive ability of hotel enterprises, while *flexibility (an enterprise's ability to adjust to market conditions)* and *service quality* have the highest average score. This means

Figure 1. The degree of influence of various aspects on gaining competitive advantages in hotel enterprises (Črnjar, 2010)

Ranking	Statements (variables)	Mean	Stand. deviation
1.	Flexibility (an enterprise's ability to adjust to market conditions)	4.72	0.461
2.	**Product and service quality**	**4.72**	**0.461**
3.	**Knowledge, skills and competencies of employees**	**4.67**	**0.594**
4.	An enterprise's development strategy	4.61	0.608
5.	Quality of business contacts	4.44	0.616
6.	Financial stability	4.39	0.778
7.	An enterprise's reputation on the market	4.39	0.850
8.	Legislation in the profession	4.39	0.698
9.	Public infrastructure	4.39	0.698
10.	**Knowledge management strategy**	**4.39**	**0.608**
11.	Technology and technological processes	4.33	0.485
12.	Brand (trademark)	4.33	0.686
13.	Diversity of products and services provided	4.28	0.752
14.	Level of development of demand	4.22	0.548
15.	Building and grounds	4.06	0.873
16.	Competitive environment	4.06	0.725

that flexibility and quality are of vital importance in helping enterprises in the hotel industry gain competitive advantages. The *strategic development of an enterprise* and *the knowledge, skills and competencies of employees* are also aspects that have a high level of importance. While the importance of a KM strategy in gaining competitive advantages received a relatively high score (4.39), it is ranked only tenth among aspects that help in enhancing competitive ability. This is derived from the fact that a developed KM strategy is not present in most hotel enterprises and, hence, is not perceived as being importance. While *the knowledge, skills, and competencies of employees* (ranked third) is seen as an aspect of vital importance in gaining competitiveness, it is not perceived as a matter that needs to be "managed" or whose management should be structured in the form of a prescribed KM strategy. Standard deviation values illustrate the spread of data from the arithmetical mean for each individual variable. The standard deviation for all variables is less than 1, indicating a small spread of data about the mean value.

Analysis of the existence of KM strategies, used as a holistic approach to achieving total quality in Croatian hotel enterprises, suggests that the introduction of KM strategies in Croatia's hotel industry is evolving at a very slow pace. Most 'strategies' are not really strategies, but are rather more like projects or initiatives. To obtain information on the level of KM development in hotel enterprises in which KM does exist, albeit in an incomplete form, respondents were asked to select the description of KM strategies that corresponds the most with the strategy of their hotel enterprise. KM evolution in enterprises was illustrated through a number of levels (Skyrme et al., 2010; Collinson & Parcell, 2005):

- **Level 1:** There is no KM strategy in place. Few employees see knowledge as being important to the organization.
- **Level 2:** There is no KM strategy in place. Most people see knowledge sharing as being important to the enterprise's performance.

- **Level 3:** There is no framework for a formulated KM strategy. There are initiatives that focus on managing employee knowledge.
- **Level 4:** While a KM strategy does exist, it is not yet integrated into the business strategy, though this is being considered.
- **Level 5:** A KM strategy is a component part of business and development strategies.

Figure 2 illustrates KM development in large and mid-sized hotel enterprises.

Figure 2 demonstrates that in 33 percent of enterprises there is no framework for a formal KM strategy, while in 28 percent, there is no KM strategy whatsoever (out of this number, 11 percent of enterprises are at Level 1 of KM development, and 17 percent at Level 2). KM strategies are a component part of the business strategies of 22 percent of hotel enterprises in the sample, while in 17 percent of enterprises, KM strategies do exist but are not yet integrated into business strategies, though this is being considered.

There is no development of KM strategies in tourism. Instead, all initiatives in that direction are about educational programs and projects. As a rule, hotel enterprises introduce KM programs and initiatives as a way of cutting operation costs, gaining competitive advantages, and adjusting quickly to change in the environment. Other reasons for implementing KM programs and initiatives (such as educating the mentors in hotel enterprises, communities of practice, e-learning) include enhancing the effectiveness of HRM, attracting the best employees, and developing new products and services. In an industry in which human resources and knowledge, that is, intangible assets, are of the utmost importance, KM has yet to become fully functional. Despite their low level of KM maturity, hotel enterprises show awareness of the importance of KM in accomplishing the objectives of the enterprises' business and development strategies. They are also aware of the extent to which the level of KM development contributes to achieving business excellence and enhancing the competitive ability of the hotel industry (Črnjar, 2010).

The development of innovation in the tourism industry will largely depend upon the development of KM and quality management. In most cases,

Figure 2. Levels of KM maturity in hotel enterprises (Črnjar, 2010)

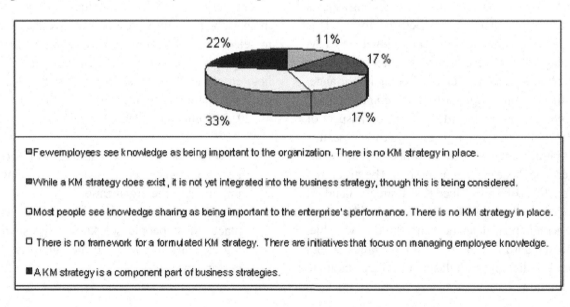

□ Few employees see knowledge as being important to the organization. There is no KM strategy in place.

■ While a KM strategy does exist, it is not yet integrated into the business strategy, though this is being considered.

□ Most people see knowledge sharing as being important to the enterprise's performance. There is no KM strategy in place.

□ There is no framework for a formulated KM strategy. There are initiatives that focus on managing employee knowledge.

■ A KM strategy is a component part of business strategies.

the introduction and realization of innovations in tourism is slow. Issues affecting the development of KM, quality and innovations in tourism are discussed in the following section.

ISSUES AFFECTING THE DEVELOPMENT OF KNOWLEDGE MANAGEMENT, QUALITY, AND INNOVATIONS IN TOURISM

In comparison with other areas, the development of KM in tourism is slow. Until recently, most tourism-related research and publications of this research were of a descriptive nature (European KM Forum, 2009; OECD, 2009; Davenport & Prusak, 1998; etc.). Research was often launched *ad hoc* and at the individual level, with short-term objectives and sparse funding. Typically, a large number of small and mid-sized tourism enterprises are not well disposed towards research and, accordingly, fail to exploit the results of research. As the importance of tourism and its share in a country's GDP continue to grow, the need for in-depth research has been recognized.

There are three key issues affecting the development of innovations in tourism:

- The first key issue refers to the poor cooperation existing between research institutions and tourism organizations. This is especially characteristic of Croatian tourism. Namely, despite numerous associations, ministries, congresses, etc., no efforts are being made to systematically link businesses and research institutions, resulting in a number of studies that have failed to be implemented in business practice.
- The second concerns inadequate syllabuses developed by educational institutions in tourism. Universities, which the majority of young people attend, are slow to introduce changes, in particular, in adjusting syllabuses to the needs of the tourism in-

dustry. They are usually not in touch with information on what kind of knowledge and skills are needed for future tourism development.
- The third refers to the lack of funds allocated to KM and to the development and training of employees, at the company level and at the national level as a whole. As a rule, investment in KM systems, projects, and initiatives typically involves substantial funds, as well as substantial employee participation. Because the results of such initiatives are generally not visible in the short run and are not easy to quantify, there is a reluctance to invest in this segment the limited funds available in the tourism sector. Providing education to people across all levels of society is a precondition to bringing about sustainable development and implementing KM. This is particularly true in tourism, an industry that depends heavily on human capital. Developing a well-designed education system that is abreast of new development trends is vital to regions and countries that count on tourism as a major driver of growth. The only way to improve existing knowledge and discover new knowledge is through continuous investment in educating human capital. A considerable number of companies in tourism still see such investment as costs, while companies working in a knowledge economy see education as an asset.

For education and training to be effective, however, it must be planned in a systematic and objective manner to provide the right sort of learning experience. Education and training must be continuous to meet not only changes in technology but also changes in the environment in which an organization operates, its structure, and perhaps most important of all the people who work there (Oakland, 2003, p. 319).

Only those who are continuously learning can make progress. Hence, continuous learning is one of the phases of the quality cycle. Organized learning is a component part of TQM, because there can be no advancements or development without learning new techniques and methods (Avelini Holjevac, 2002, p. 79).

Organizations need to take continuous action in encouraging and supporting learning to create employees who accept the necessity of lifelong learning. These employees see demands for developing skills as an opportunity, rather than a threat. Today there is much talk about the Learning Organization. In the broadest terms, a Learning Organization is a social system whose members have learned conscious, communal processes for continually generating, retaining and leveraging individual and collective learning to improve the performance of the organizational system in ways that are important to all stakeholders, and continually monitoring and improving performance. An organization's ability to learn must be greater and faster than the changes taking places in its environment. Today's organizations are still mostly task-based, while the dynamic competitive environment calls for them to transform into value-based organizations (Harung, 1996). Task-based organizations are characterised by command-and-control hierarchies in which a small number of top managers are responsible for making decisions and developing policies. On the other hand, value-based organizations have broader frameworks and as they develop so does the emphasis on value. Empowering employees is one of the features of a value-based organization (Harung, 1996). Our research has shown that hotel enterprises need to work on this, because their employees are not empowered to any significant extent that would enable them to have an effect on their own performance. This feature can be found in only 58 percent of surveyed hotel enterprises (Vrtodušić Hrgović, 2010). While the situation concerning teamwork

and reward systems is somewhat better than that in the area of empowerment, certain improvements are required here as well. It is important to note that every single employee needs to learn in order to perform better. Attention should also focus on the broader application of reward systems that are a vital factor in motivating employees.

In tourism practise, the transfer of knowledge and research results is a serious problem. Because knowledge transfer needs to be carried out as efficiently and quickly as possible, it requires the close cooperation of the knowledge provider and knowledge recipient. The successful transfer of knowledge in tourism will depend upon two conditions. First, research institutions (knowledge providers) need to provide the results of research in a form that will enable organisations and other stakeholders in tourism to incorporate them directly into product and service development. Second, organizations at the receiving end need to have a development plan and should be able to articulate the problem to be solved through research. Our survey has shown that synergy between knowledge providers and recipients is extremely poor in tourism and, in particular, in the hotel industry. As high as 50 percent of mid-sized and large hotel enterprises responded that they did not know whether the research results of research institutions could be applied directly to their businesses, while 44.4 percent gave a negative response (Črnjar, 2010).

For knowledge to become an exclusive resource of global sustainable development and to be managed efficiently, it is necessary to formulate, design, and operationalize a science-based KM strategy. However, such a strategy can neither be devised nor put into action without well-trained human resources, an appropriate organization structure and business culture, a well-developed research infrastructure, and contemporary research and educational institutions (Črnjar & Črnjar, 2009, p. 341).

FUTURE RESEARCH DIRECTIONS

Education and training are essential for TQM to succeed. The survey conducted in the Croatian hotel industry has shown that hotel enterprises do invest in education and training. Further research should focus on a more-detailed analysis of these investments, from a variety of perspectives. For example, what is the share of investment in employee education and training in the overall costs of employees, and how does it compare with best practises? What is the employee pattern of employees that take part in education? How much time do they spend in education? Have the objectives of, and responsibilities for, education and training been established? Have the needs for education and training been specified?

In the future, research concerning KM and the innovation process in tourism will need to centre on an array of thematic areas. First, it should take a closer look at the new role of HRM in the innovation process, and it should identify influences. Second, it should focus on developing a KM framework for hotel enterprises, which would serve as a platform for introducing KM strategies to bring together all key elements needed to achieve greater quality. Research should also address the issue of how to bring together existing projects into one single strategy to enable business objectives to be accomplished more efficiently. Creating knowledge networks and communities of practice in tourism is a special area of research in which it is necessary to identify processes, tools, and ways of transferring knowledge and generating new knowledge.

CONCLUSION

One of the largest and most important industries in the world, tourism covers a wide range of phenomena and relationships that emerge during tourist travels. Activities and relationships within tourism affect the economic, social, environmental, and cultural aspects of life. For a great many countries, including Croatia, tourism is a vital source of income and contributes significantly to their economies at the local, national, sub-regional, and regional levels. Clearly, the hotel industry is one of tourism's most prominent elements.

In today's business conditions, quality is seen as a major precondition to the survival and development of hotel industry. This chapter emphasizes the importance of employees, employee education and employee involvement as preconditions to successfully implementing TQM and, in turn, strengthening competitive positions on the market. To ensure that the performance of employees is aligned with the needs, wants and expectations of guests, enterprises need to invest in employee training and education, encourage teamwork, create reward systems for top employees, as well as empower employees and give them more responsibility. Research conducted on a sample of large and mid-sized hotel enterprises demonstrates that they are highly aware of the importance of investing in employee education and training, and suggests that there are still many underutilized opportunities for involving employees in processes that affect their sphere of work.

In a knowledge-based economy, emphasis will be placed upon knowledge management. The management of knowledge and human capital is emerging as a primary resource of the innovation process, a resource that can, ultimately, contribute significantly to sustainable tourism development and the successful management of hotel enterprises. Human capital management in the knowledge-based economy acquires new roles and importance. Unfortunately, KM strategies in Croatian tourism are still in their initial stage. Considering that the competitiveness of tourism is based on KM, this disadvantage gives rise to a series of questions and problems.

REFERENCES

Avelini Holjevac, I. (2002). *Upravljanje kvalitetom u turizmu i hotelskoj industriji*. Opatija, Croatia: Fakultet za Menadžment u Turizmu i Ugostiteljstvu.

Bahtijarević Šiber, F. (1999). *Management ljudskih potencijala*. Zagreb, Croatia: Golden Marketing.

Baldrige National Quality Program. (2007). *Criteria for performance excellence*. Gaithersburg, MD: Baldrige National Quality Program.

Besterfield, D. H., Besterfiell-Michna, C., Besterfield, G. H., & Besterfield-Sacre, M. (1999). *Total quality management*. Upper Saddle River, NJ: Prentice Hall.

Claver, E., & Tari, J. J. (2003). Levels of quality management in certified firms. *Total Quality Management and Business Excellence*, *14*(9), 981–998. doi:10.1080/1478336032000151439

Collinson, C., & Parcell, G. (2005). *Learning to fly – Practical KM from leading and learning organizations*. Oxford, UK: Capstone Publishing Limited.

Črnjar, K. (2005). Faktori produktivnosti rada u hotelskoj indistriji Hrvatske. *Tourism and Hospitality Management*, *11*(1), 251–265.

Črnjar, K. (2010). *Strategija upravljanja znanjem u funkciji konkurentnosti hotelske industrije*. Doctoral Dissertation. Rijeka, Croatia: Sveučilište u Rijeci.

Črnjar, M., & Črnjar, K. (2009). *Menadžment održivog razvoja: Ekonomija, ekologija, zaštita okoliša*. Opatija, Croatia: Fakultet za Menadžment u Turizmu i Ugostiteljstvu.

DZS. (2009a). *Državni zavod za statistiku: Turizam u 2009*. Retroeved frp, http://www.dzs.hr/Hrv_Eng/publication/2010/SI-1408.pdf

DZS. (2009b). *Državni zavod za statistiku: Ugostiteljstvo u 2009*. Retrieved from http://www.dzs.hr/Hrv_Eng/publication/2010/SI-1427.pdf

EFQM. (2009). *EFQM transition guide*. Brussels, Belgium: EFQM.

FINA. (2010). *Financijski pokazatelji za sve poduzetnike: Sve djelatnosti i razred I 55109*. Rijeka, Croatia: FINA.

Harung, H. S. (1996). A world-leading learning organization: A case study of Tomra Systems, Oslo, Norway. *The Learning Organization*, *3*(4), 22–34. doi:10.1108/09696479610126716

ISO. (2000). *Quality management systems – Requirements*. Geneva, Switzerland: ISO. *ISO*, *9000*, 2000.

Kanji, G. K. (2002). *Measuring business excellence*. London, UK: Routledge-Taylor Francis Group.

Lengnick-Hall, M. L., & Lengnick-Hall, C. A. (2002). *Human resource management in the knowledge economy*. San Francisco, CA: Berrett-Koehle Publishers.

Leonard-Barton, D. (1998). Implementation as mutual adaptation of technology and organization. *Research Policy*, *17*, 251–267. doi:10.1016/0048-7333(88)90006-6

Oakland, J. S. (1995). *Total quality management - The route to improving performance*. Oxford, UK: Elsevier Butteworth Heinemann Ltd. Oakland, J. S. (2003). *Total quality management-Text with cases*. Oxford, UK: Elsevier Butteworth-Heinemann Ltd.

Scarbrough, H. (2003). Knowledge management, HRM and the innovation process. *International Journal of Manpower*, *24*(5), 501–516. doi:10.1108/01437720310491053

Skoko, H. (2000). *Upravljanje kvalitetom*. Zagreb, Croatia: Sinergija.

Skyrme, D. J., et al. (2010). *Knowledge management: Approaches and policies*. Retrieved June 1, 2010, from http://www.skyme.com

Tenner, A. R., & DeToro, I. J. (1992). *Total quality management-Three steps to continuous improvement*. Reading, MA: Addison-Wsley Publishing Company, Inc. Deming Prize Committee. (2007). *The guide for the deming application prize*. Tokyo, Japan: The Deming Prize Committee.

Vrtodušić Hrgović, A. M. (2010). *Upravljanje potpunom kvalitetom i poslovna izvrsnost u hotelskoj industriji Hrvatske. Doctoral Disseration*. Rijeka, Croatia: Sveučilište u Rijeci.

Vujić, V., Črnjar, K., & Maškarin, H. (2009). *Knowledge and education of human resources in the Croatian hospitality industry*. Paper presented at the 4th International Scientific Conference: Planning for the Future, Learning from the Past. Rhodes Island, Greece.

ADDITIONAL READING

Abdullah, M. M. B., Uli, J., & Tari, J. J. (2009). The relationship of performance with soft factors and quality improvement. *Total Quality Management and Business Excellence, 20*(7), 735–748. doi:10.1080/14783360903037051

Bouncken, R. B., & Pyo, S. (2002). *Knowledge management in hospitality and tourism*. Oxford, UK: The Haworth Hospitality Press.

Črnjar, K., Dlačić, J., & Fatur- Krmpotić, I. (2009). *Importance of knowledge management and employees in achiving a costomer-oriented organization*. Paper presented at the International Scientific Conference Knowledge and Business Challenge of Globalization. Celje, Slovenia.

Evans, C. (2003). *Managing for knowledge – HRs strategic role*. Oxford, UK: Elsevier Butteworth-Heinemann Ltd.

Jennex, M. E. (2008). *Knowledge management: Concepts, methodologies, tools and applications*. Hershey, PA: IGI Global.

Lambert, G., & Ouedraogo, N. (2008). Empirical investigation of ISO 9001 quality management systems' impact on organisation learning and process performance. *Total Quality Management and Business Excellence, 19*(9-10), 1071–1085.

Skyrme, D. (2003). *Measuring knowledge and Intellectual capital*. London, UK: Optima Publisihing.

Ugboro, I. O., & Obeng, K. (2000). Top management leadership, employee empowerment, job satisfaction, and customer satisfaction in TQM organizations: An empirical study. *Journal of Quality Management, 5*(4), 247–272. doi:10.1016/S1084-8568(01)00023-2

Vujić, V. (2008). *Menadžment ljudskog kapitala*. Opatija, Croatia: Fakultet za Turistički i Hotelski Menadžment.

Vujić, V. (Ed.). (2010). *Knowledge management and human development in tourism*. Opatija, Croatia: Univeristy of Rijeka.

KEY TERMS AND DEFINITIONS

Innovation: Creating and applying new ideas.

Knowledge: Using and connecting information and data with the human potential in organizations, such as human skills, ideas, intuition, motivation and employee loyalty.

Knowledge Management: The systematic management of knowledge needed to achieve business objectives and sustainable development, as well as related processes, to gain competitiveness and business excellence on the global market.

Knowledge Management Strategy: Is the identification of key knowledge (knowledge that can be used to create added value) in organization and implementation of business initiatives for managing and developing this type of asset (key knowledge is a resource) in order to improve organization's performance (business excellence – productivity, adaptability, image, innovativeness).

Quality: Fulfilling customer requirements.

Total Quality Management: An approach to management that focuses on customers (internal and external) and their satisfaction through employee involvement and continuous improvement.

Tourism: Includes activities coming out of travelling and staying of people away from home not longer than a year, for the purpose of pleasure and travelling.

Chapter 10
A New Perspective on Knowledge Management Research:
The Role of Vocational Professionals

Sari Metso
Lappeenranta University of Technology, Finland

ABSTRACT

Knowledge management theories emphasize the role of knowledge work and knowledge workers in knowledge-intensive organizations. However, technologization has changed the knowledge work environment. Many knowledge workers create, process, and share simplified information in digitalized networks. This complicates the profession-based definitions of knowledge workers. This chapter contributes to the emerging concern about the future trends of knowledge management. First, the chapter suggests that knowledge management models ignore a large group of professionals possessing practical knowledge. These vocational professionals are considered a new target group for knowledge management. Vocational professionals' practical knowledge is worth managing since they operate with organizational core functions. Second, this chapter presents an alternative education-based categorization of workers. The different functions of KM are manifest in the three categories: a diminishing group of workers without professional qualifications, a large group of vocational professionals, and a group of workers with higher education.

INTRODUCTION

The term Knowledge Management (KM) has experienced inflation. It has been used in various contexts and for mixed purposes. The established insight is that the KM function includes knowledge creation, sharing, and utilization in organizations.

The development of technological devices helps to fulfill this function. Modern KM can be seen as a general management tool with multiple meanings and vague definitions of both knowledge and management (Alvesson, Kärreman, & Swan, 2002). Contemporary KM is related to organizations and people with theoretical and expert knowledge

DOI: 10.4018/978-1-4666-1969-2.ch010

achieved through higher education. For modern organizations, the most important resource is human capital including knowledge and education instead of capital and technology (Drucker, 2000). Organizations that are able to make their investments in human capital visible and prove to profit from it are appreciated by highly educated individuals both as investors and as potential labor. In this context, human capital can be seen as a factor of production and knowledge workers are considered entrepreneurs within an enterprise. Hence, knowledge workers face uncertainty in the labor market. The literature defines knowledge-intensive organizations as firms where highly educated workers are predominantly represented and work is considered intellectual (Alvesson, 2001). The products of these firms are supposed to be of high quality as a result of remarkable expertise.

The traditional insights related to KM, knowledge work, and knowledge workers are increasingly criticized. The changing environment of knowledge work questions the central role of workers with higher education and specialized expertise in KM models. Technologization has drained the contents of knowledge work. As a consequence, the traditional subject groups of KM research seem to lose their relevance. It is also difficult to define knowledge work according to professions since technological applications are widely used throughout organizations. The mission of this chapter is to contribute to KM research by suggesting a new target group: vocational professionals. This group of workers possesses concrete and relevant knowledge about the core functions and processes of organizations. The contemporary definitions of KM, knowledge work, and knowledge workers are briefly discussed; however, it is beyond the scope of this chapter to provide a thorough discussion of these definitions. Finally, the chapter presents an alternative categorization of the labor force based on education instead of the traditional profession-based labeling.

BACKGROUND

It is argued that knowledge workers are an expanding group of labor. Many rich countries strongly advocate higher education (Alvesson, 2004). Knowledge workers are seen as a significant group in modern organizations (Drucker, 2000; Pyöriä, 2005). The definitions of knowledge workers are discussed widely, but the problem is their ambiguity and difficulty to apply them in practice. In general, knowledge workers are considered highly educated labor receiving, processing, and creating new knowledge with the help of information technology. These tasks are associated with special skills and competency. Generally, knowledge workers are expected to use intellectual abilities and make decisions. They are assumed to have autonomy, as well as a high hierarchical position, and they perform non-routine tasks (Pyöriä, 2005).

There are various definitions describing knowledge work. However, Pyöriä (2005) found some common characteristics in his review of knowledge work concepts, such as higher education, advanced skills, and utilizing information technology in the informational labor process. Modern knowledge work is part of the information society characterized as a complex, increasingly specialized multifactor field under continuous change. Information creation, processing, and sharing are important factors of production in this environment. Knowledge work, its output, and knowledge workers are defined through their information-intensiveness. Knowledge workers are dealing with processes instead of distinct tasks (Pyöriä, 2005). Communication systems, such as wireless mobile networks, social networks, the Internet, the Web, and audiovisual systems, have an important role in facilitating these tasks.

The impact of the above-mentioned definitions on KM theory is obvious. Contemporary KM models emphasize the managing of highly educated knowledge workers. The literature considers the modern and future global economy knowledge-intensive (Borg, 2001; Powell & Snellman, 2004; Sinha & Van de Ven, 2005). Consequently, many organizations categorize themselves as knowledge-intensive. Most KM models assume technology to be a necessary tool in creating, processing, and sharing knowledge (Demarest, 1997; Grover & Davenport, 2001; Sher & Lee, 2004; Tseng, 2008; Wild & Griggs, 2008). Hence, knowledge is reduced to simple and unified information for easy access and communication. This chapter suggests that the focus of KM research should be shifted from knowledge workers towards professionals performing practical jobs, i.e., towards vocational professionals. Practical jobs include practical activities that are non-academic and totally related to a specific trade, occupation or vocation (Davies & Ryan, 2011). The concept "practical" is related to actual doing or using something or to a person who is skilled in manual tasks (Oxford Dictionaries Online). Practical jobs are more concrete than abstract. However, "practical job" is not accurate enough a term to distinguish jobs requiring highly educated, skilled, and competent workers from jobs that require non-academic skilled and competent workers. To elaborate on this distinction the chapter introduces the term "vocational professional." This chapter relates the word "vocational" to an occupation or employment. It is often used in conjunction with work that requires a specialized skill, training, or a knowledge set, such as auto mechanics (BusinessDictionary.com). It is also related to an occupation or employment in the context of vocational training (Oxford Dictionaries Online). Furthermore, it is directed at a particular occupation and its skills (Oxford Dictionaries Online). These definitions suggest that "vocational" refers to non-academic occupations acquired, e.g. through vocational education and training. According to BusinessDictionary.com, the word "professional" has two definitions: "1. Person formally certified by a professional body of belonging to a specific profession by virtue of

having completed a required course of studies and/or practice. And whose competence can usually be measured against an established set of standards. 2. Person who has achieved an acclaimed level of proficiency in a calling or trade." The word "professional" can also be defined as a person engaged or qualified in a profession (Oxford Dictionaries Online). This chapter defines vocational professional as a person with specialized non-academic skills, training, or knowledge required by a specific trade, occupation, or vocation. Hence, employers both recognize and require vocational professionals' skills and knowledge.

This chapter questions the widely accepted importance of knowledge workers to organizations. Emphasizing the role of knowledge workers includes concentration on the theoretical and abstract knowledge provided by higher education. This knowledge is characterized by conceptualization, abstractization, and interpretation (Albrecht, Romney, Lowry, & Moody, 2009). Managing knowledge that is acquired from authentic situations and experiences provides organizations with new aspects that may result in competitive advantage. This type of knowledge is known as practical or procedural knowledge (Albrecht, et al., 2009; Mascha, 2001). Matsuo and Kusumi (2002) define procedural knowledge as knowledge of a method or skill. It is knowledge of how to use methods or strategies in specific situations (knowing how). According to Albrecht et al. (2009) procedural knowledge is personal and tacit. Mascha (2001) also relates procedural knowledge and how to- knowledge. This knowledge is necessary in skillful decision-making. Practical knowledge is expressed through action in specific situations, i.e., it is embodied knowledge (Rix & Lièvre, 2008).

A short review of the KM literature helps understand modern KM. According to Davenport and Prusak (1998) there are built-in knowledge markets in organizations. A knowledge market consists of knowledge buyers (seekers) who need knowledge for problem solving, knowledge sellers who are known to possess knowledge about a process or subject and knowledge brokers (usually managers) who connect buyers and sellers. This is clearly the environment where traditionally defined knowledge workers are assumed to operate. Knowledge generation is systematic and occurs through acquisition, dedicated resources (units or groups generating knowledge), fusion, adaptation, and knowledge networking. After generation, the knowledge is codified and coordinated for easy access and sensible use in an organization. Technology is considered helpful in codifying knowledge, but it is emphasized that KM needs to be more than mere technology.

Davenport and Prusak (1998) considered talking and listening crucial for knowledge transfer. McAdam and McCreedy (1999) also advocated socially constructed knowledge besides scientific knowledge. This requires time, a common language, formal and informal occasions, and transferring forms suitable for the organization. Davenport and Prusak (1998) recognized that KM is present in every job within an organization although the grass root level is not included in KM models emphasizing knowledge-intensive organizations and professions. KM projects are seen as practical rather than abstract and philosophical. This chapter expands the focus of KM research to more practical professions opening new perspectives and facilitating profitable KM projects.

Demarest (1997) suggested that it is crucial for organizations to recognize commercial knowledge (different from scientific or philosophical knowledge) and its role in successful competition. According to Demarest (1997), the process of knowledge production includes construction, dissemination, use, and embodiment within the so-called knowledge economies of organizations. Commercial knowledge is social in the sense that it is created and shared in a network consisting of people and a technological device. Knowledge workers are considered an important group in producing, sharing, and trading commercial knowledge. Commercial knowledge is focused on

improving performance. It is constantly changing and partial.

Chase (1997) found in his KM survey that organizations report knowledge-based problems creating substantial costs. This suggests that the strategies and KM theories of organizations do not meet in practice. According to Chase (1997) the costs are due to insufficient knowledge distribution in organizations, i.e. critical knowledge is accumulated in few employees. This may reflect a situation where knowledge is owned by highly educated knowledge workers ignoring the importance of practical knowledge about organizational functions. From this viewpoint, the problem is not the lack of knowledge but the inability to use existing knowledge efficiently and to generate it from different sources.

Hedlund (1994) built a KM model based on interaction between explicit and tacit knowledge at four levels: the individual, the small group, the organization, and the inter-organizational. The model emphasizes dialogue between individuals and organizational levels in order to increase competitiveness. The interdependence of people and technology is based on combinations and temporary pools of people. The model recognizes the importance of "lower" level employees in the dialogue. However, the focus is on the experienced middle level seniors. The word *middle* refers to employees with specific competences, not necessarily to middle management. This chapter takes into account professionals who perform practical tasks and recognizes the value of their knowledge. Knowledge acquired from authentic work situations, direct contacts with customers, and interaction with other reference groups may produce new ideas and improve the central procedures of organizations.

The traditional KM literature faces increasing criticism. Heaton and Taylor (2002) questioned KM models where knowledge creation, processing, and utilization are based on the interaction of tacit and explicit knowledge. According to them organizations are dependent on highly skilled technical and professional communities of work. There are several communities within an organization, each creating specific knowledge that may not be useful to other communities. Then, the challenge for KM is to manage the collection of communities in order to profit from existing knowledge. Knowledge is not seen as individual property that has to be transferred from tacit to explicit and conveyed further. According to Heaton and Taylor (2002), knowledge is situated due to the various local practices of organizations and increasing importance of professional work. Situated knowledge can be defined as a collective and distributed activity (between humans and non-humans) located in time and space (Gherardi, 2009). Situated knowledge is located in communities of people, and it travels across these communities (Tsoukas, 2002).

Davenport, Prusak, and Strong (2008) recognized that organizations are not very effective in managing human ideas, insights, and expertise as a consequence of excessive concentration on technology or KM actions that fail to take into account the entire structure of an organization. They suggested that KM has to become more pragmatic in order to make job functions and work processes more productive. This chapter advocates a more fundamental change in the focus of KM research. Organizations can acquire relevant knowledge by widening the range of knowledge sources towards practical jobs. The next section discusses and justifies the importance of vocational professionals' knowledge in order to relate this group of workers to KM research.

VOCATIONAL PROFESSIONALS' CONTRIBUTION TO KM RESEARCH

Competition in almost all industries is relatively even in terms of technology, expertise, and management. It is difficult to create competitive advantage in these circumstances. The main theme of this chapter is that educated and experienced individuals who work with practical tasks, i.e., the vocational professionals, have valuable knowledge. This knowledge includes customer needs, other reference groups, competitors, and bottlenecks creating problems in crucial processes. The top management may ignore this type of knowledge or have different ideas about organizational functions. Managers need to listen to the vocational professionals, gather feedback systematically, and give space to reflect on authentic situations. This practical aspect of KM may help organizations to survive intense competition. Furthermore, it can contribute to lower personnel turnover and increased commitment to work. It requires attention from the top management and a shift of focus from traditional knowledge workers to the vocational professionals. Their practical and real-time knowledge can be refined and used throughout the organization.

Practical knowledge does not exclude the theoretical aspect of KM. Vocational professionals need both theoretical and practical knowledge in order to perform successfully. Management of practical knowledge may occur through normal feedback and discussions with workers or among groups of people, e.g., in regular workplace meetings. Practical knowledge is often dispersed in organizations, and it might be difficult for managers to understand it as a valuable asset. Obviously, the change of the key subject group of KM requires new tools.

Another central theme in this chapter is the transformation of the knowledge work environment and hence, the change in the tasks knowledge workers face. As discussed above, KM models consider technology crucial for organizations in order to create, store, and share knowledge. The use of technological devices puts some limits on the form of knowledge. It has to be in a simple and digitalized form in order to be processed and transferred. Are knowledge workers in this environment able to capture the essence of knowledge that is vital for organizations?

Changing Characteristics of Knowledge Work call for a Shift of Focus in KM

The traditional definition of knowledge work is challenged because of rapid technological development and increased use of technology-based applications in organizations. According to some recent studies by authors such as Berardi (2007) and Pyöriä (2005) modern knowledge work occurs in a digitalized network environment. In this environment knowledge work requires specific knowledge that is narrow in scope. Berardi (2007) described the main characteristics of the digitalized network as follows: Communication is switched on and off in the network when needed without antecedent or subsequent actions. A single communicative action is unique in terms of its extent, scope, and duration. Furthermore, meaning is created by each moment of communication. Digitalization requires simplified information in order to transfer and recombine it at high speeds. Knowledge workers face various sets of information simultaneously and are expected to process them at once. In other words, knowledge work is highly flexible and involves fragmentation through discontinuous work performance (Berardi, 2007). The contents of exchange in the network are abstract and reduced to transferring signs.

Pyöriä (2005) referred to the same phenomenon by suggesting that knowledge work requires symbolic and interactive abilities. Liu (2004) also emphasized network interaction with humans in different departments, industries, regions, and across the world. According to Liu (2004), knowledge work is interactive between sciences. It is characterized by rapid learning. Yet another way to define the present knowledge work environment is to see it as a space of flows where flows of information are produced, transferred, and processed (Castells, 2010). According to this viewpoint, the electronic networks have created a new form of a globally functioning assembly line where immaterial production can be spread

as the need arises. This means that (digitalized) information flows are transferred flexibly through the electronic networks where information is needed. The coordination of work occurs within the network. Pyöriä (2005) discussed the complexity of the contemporary economy creating flows of information. Managing and coordinating this type of economy is far from straightforward.

Difficulties in defining knowledge and, knowledge work, as well as labeling knowledge-intensive professions into specific categories have been recognized (Alvesson, 2001, Pyöriä, 2005). It is not easy to understand what KM is and who are considered knowledge workers. Knowledge workers employed by knowledge-intensive firms may perform tasks that do not require theoretical knowledge or specific experience acquired through higher education (Alvesson, 2001). In many organizations defined as knowledge-intensive people are working in a group where they have well-specified tasks. This leaves little space for using talents and expertise. Diehl, Grabill, and Hart-Davidson (2008) examined the "invisibility" of knowledge work. It is difficult to perceive knowledge work and make it visible to others, which hampers KM actions. As discussed above, changes in the knowledge work environment affect the contents of work. The above discussion suggests that KM needs to consider practical aspects.

The contemporary knowledge work environment is characterized by digitalized networks where simplified and abstract information is transferred with high speed. This requires rapid learning abilities and interaction. Technology is widely used on all organizational levels making profession-based knowledge work definitions difficult. Furthermore, transferring digitalized information does not necessarily require higher education or substantial work experience often related to knowledge workers. The intensive use of technology and difficulties in defining knowledge workers by their professions create a need for new aspects regarding KM research.

Vocational Professionals: A Missing Part

The labor force is generally categorized by profession. This categorization favors knowledge workers at the expense of other worker groups. Professions are labeled as knowledge-intensive or routine-intensive and sometimes as those in between. In practice, dividing the wide range of professions into these groups is not straightforward. First, knowledge workers form a heterogeneous group performing throughout organizations (Alvesson, 2004; Pyöriä, 2005). Second, professions change and disappear rapidly. Third, public sector workers are usually left out or treated separately when studying and defining the labor force. This is because public sector organizations are not considered firms. Hence, the traditional profession-based categorization of the labor force is problematic.

Berardi (2009) labeled knowledge workers into two categories by using the concept of mental labor. It includes cognitive labor (knowledge work) and applicative labor. According to Berardi (2009), cognitive labor is characterized by intellectual energies that are under constant creative deterritorialization. In this context, deterritorialization means decoding, blurring, and abstracting to create the best possible environment for the digitalized and abstract exchange process of information. Mental labor can also consist of a merely applicative type of labor. Castell's (2010) categorization of workers into two groups stems from the development of information technology and communication systems. Professionals with higher education are called "self-programmable labor." These workers can be described as "talents" with decision-making autonomy. They have an important position as the most valuable assets of companies. In contrast, low-skilled workers are called "generic labor." They act on instructions doing tasks that are not worth automatization. This chapter suggests that there is a substantial group of professionals not included in the present literature on labor force categorization.

A large group of skilled and experienced workers performing practical jobs is ignored although the labor market needs their competence. According to Eurostat (2010) workers performing practical tasks are a large and an increasing group within the labor force. These vocational professionals represent professions such as handicraft professionals, plumbers, electricians, firemen, chefs, mechanics, study secretaries, animal attendants in veterinary practices, and office secretaries, e.g. in universities. Obviously, many of these types of professions have changed significantly over time or vanished due to societal changes and technological development. The key point in this chapter is that vocational professionals are needed in organizations and their knowledge is worth managing. Vocational professionals cannot be described as "talents" or "generic workers." They cannot be considered cognitive workers using "intellectual energies under deterritorialization" nor do they fall into the category of purely applicative workers. Highly automatized and simplified jobs can be done without special skills, on-the-job training, or formal education. Those types of jobs can be learned in a few days, e.g., tasks in a fast food restaurant.

In contrast, vocational professionals need specific skills and experience recognized by the labor market. It is not possible to perform successfully in their vocations without professional qualifications, training, and job experience. Vocational professionals must be able to apply their theoretical and practical knowledge to changing authentic situations. They need to create new knowledge and skills according to changes in organizations, working methods, technology, customers' needs, and the society. Vocational professionals' work cannot be automatized although technology may have an important role in their job performance. Vocational professionals require KM to maintain existing skills, acquire new skills, share knowledge with others, and use knowledge creatively in organizations. The role of KM is also to encourage vocational professionals to acquire further education, gain experiences, search for profession-related knowledge from different sources, and provide feedback on the existing methods and processes.

The contemporary categorization of workers is based on the assumption that professions are knowledge-intensive or routine-intensive. This type of labeling ignores a large group of professionals doing practical tasks. These vocational professionals possess valuable knowledge suggesting that they are a relevant target group for KM actions. Vocational professionals use and create new knowledge in authentic situations. Knowledge produced by them can be used to improve the performance of the entire organization. To include vocational professionals in KM research and to define the function of KM, a new categorization of workers is needed.

Categories of the Labor Force

This chapter introduces a categorization of the labor force based on broad levels of education. In this context, education reflects competence required by the labor market. Education is chosen for the basis of categorization since it is not sensitive to constant societal changes. Education structures in different countries are relatively established in order to resist changes, e.g. in the curriculum or labor market requirements. In other words, the basic education structures are general enough to remain unchanged despite the rapidly altering environment. Education-based categorization also takes into account the entire labor force, no matter what the profession, field, or sector.

Generally, there is a decreasing number of workers with just basic or general education. They do not have formally or informally acquired qualifications recognized by employers or their qualifications are inadequate. They may have job experience, but it is not enough to make them

competent. Workers without professional qualifications perform simple tasks that may include mechanical repetition. Hence, the job can be learned without special education or skills. Typically, it is possible to perform successfully in these tasks after a few days training. The number of these types of jobs is decreasing. Automatization substitutes a part of simple tasks. Alternatively, the contents of these jobs are becoming more demanding, requiring professional qualifications. The main functions of KM in this category of workers are to gather feedback in order to detect problems and to organize tasks optimally.

This chapter calls professionally qualified non-academic workers vocational professionals. To become a vocational professional requires qualifications obtained through formal or informal education (e.g., vocational education), training, and job experience recognized by employers. These professions include a mix of theoretical and practical skills. Technology may have a significant role in these professions as a tool. Successful performance requires abilities to interact with others and to solve problems independently in varying situations. Innovativeness, creativity, and lifelong learning skills are necessary. Vocational professionals participate in many core functions of organizations, and, hence, they should be the most important target group of KM. They have a comprehensive understanding of internal and external reference groups, as well as contacts with other branches and even competitors. The strong practical aspect of the work makes vocational professionals' knowledge a valuable asset for organizations.

Theoretical and formal higher education produces highly educated professionals and experts for the labor market. In modern organizations, their tasks usually include processing digitalized information (Berardi, 2009). Highly educated professionals perform narrow tasks demanding specific knowledge. Their work has become alienated from practice and it has shifted towards an abstract and symbolic exchange of information

(Alvesson, 2001). Highly educated professionals and experts work with processes transferring information with each other. They often form teams, but their work is individual, autonomous, and invisible (Cross & Cummings, 2004; Pyöriä, 2005). In this environment, the function of KM is to coordinate the network or teams (see Table 1).

The categorization of workers according to education levels reflects the contemporary labor market. Workers with only basic or general education are a diminishing group. Their tasks are often automatized or becoming more demanding. The function of KM regarding this group of workers is mainly to coordinate tasks. Vocational professionals operate with the core processes of organizations. They have relevant and valuable knowledge about the key functions of firms. Hence, vocational professionals are considered the main target group of KM actions. Typically, highly educated professionals and experts operate as teams in digitalized networks and exchange symbolic information. The function of KM is to coordinate these teams of highly educated workers performing individual tasks.

FURTHER RESEARCH DIRECTIONS

Highly educated knowledge workers are the traditional target group of KM. Knowledge produced by them is considered vital for the survival and development of organizations. However, the relevance of their knowledge has recently been questioned. The use of technological applications in knowledge work simplifies the contents of exchange in the networks where knowledge workers operate. They handle abstract and symbolic information and perform specific and narrow tasks. In this context, knowledge acquired through practical work gains importance. Vocational professionals are performing at the heart of organizational functions. These professionals are dealing with the core processes and are able to acquire knowledge from various sources. Workers performing practical tasks are the target group for present and future KM actions.

The contemporary KM literature has difficulties in categorizing knowledge-intensive professions. Knowledge work and knowledge workers are slippery terms blurring the lines between professions. Furthermore, the contents of professions are under constant change. This chapter suggests an alternative means of education-based categorization of the labor force. Categorization by education is not sensitive to constant changes

Table 1. Labor force categorization by education

Education	Labor Market Status	Typical Tasks	KM Functions
Basic or general	Non-qualified workers	Simple, do not require professional skills (Berardi, 2009; Castells, 2010)	Feedback acquisition, coordination of tasks
Providing practical professional qualifications recognized by the labor market	Vocational Professionals	Practical, require professional skills (Albrecht, Romney, Lowry, & Moody, 2009; Davies & Ryan, 2011; Mascha, 2001; Matsuo & Kusumi, 2002; Rix & Liévre, 2008)	The main target group of KM
Higher education	Highly educated professionals or experts	Highly specified, narrow in scope, processing digitalized information (Alvesson, 2001; Berardi, 2007; Pyöriä, 2005	Coordination of the network or teams (Cross & Cummings, 2004; Demarest, 1997; Pyöriä, 2005)

in the field of professions. The categorization of the labor force presented in this chapter is general in nature. A suggestion for future research is to refine the above discussed categorization by using a formal and internationally recognized educational classification system.

CONCLUSION

The definitions of knowledge work and knowledge workers are under change. The contents of knowledge work are affected by the massive use of technological applications in organizations. The work environment based on technology requires simplified information. As a consequence, the information that knowledge workers produce and process is abstract. It is about exchanging symbols. Hence, the modern KM emphasizing highly educated knowledge workers needs to be questioned. Many employees considered to be knowledge workers do not have an opportunity to use skills obtained through higher education. Their work is narrow in range and concentrated on a specific area.

This chapter considers vocational professionals a new target group of KM research and introduces a new education-based categorization of the labor force. The chapter suggests that vocational professionals performing practical tasks are the most important subject group for KM actions. Their tasks require both practical and theoretical knowledge obtained through education and job experience. This new KM target group of vocational professionals forms the core worker group of organizations. They work with external and internal reference groups including customers and competitors. Participation in the central organizational processes provides them with valuable knowledge obtained through different sources.

Categorizing the labor force by professions is difficult. The lines between professions and tasks considered knowledge-intensive are vague and

the contents of professions are constantly changing. Furthermore, new professions emerge and some disappear. This chapter contributes to the literature by suggesting an alternative education-based categorization of the labor force. First, the labor market includes workers without professional qualifications. The numbers in this group are decreasing since firms increasingly require professionally qualified labor. Workers without professional skills are typically conducting simple tasks. Their work does not require problem solving or independent decisions. The role of KM is primarily to gather feedback in order to detect possible problems and to organize work optimally. Second, there is an increasing group of workers performing practical tasks. These vocational professionals are qualified and experienced workers. Their jobs require both theoretical and practical knowledge. Their tasks cover a substantial share of the functions of organizations. Vocational professionals acquire valuable knowledge through various sources. In sum, vocational professionals do contribute to future KM research and organizational performance. The crux of this chapter is that their knowledge is worth managing. Third, organizations employ highly educated professionals and experts. The chapter questions this group's increased emphasis in KM models. Due to technologization, highly educated professionals typically handle digitalized information in teams or networks. Hence, KM should concentrate on managing teamwork, networks, and processes.

REFERENCES

Albrecht, C. C., Romney, M., Lowry, P. B., & Moody, G. (2009). The IS core: An integration of the core IS courses. *Journal of Information Systems Education*, 20(4), 451–468.

Alvesson, M. (2001). Knowledge work: Ambiguity, image and identity. *Human Relations*, 54(7), 863–886. doi:10.1177/0018726701547004

Alvesson, M. (2004). *Knowledge work and knowledge-intensive firms*. Oxford, UK: Oxford University Press.

Alvesson, M., Kärreman, D., & Swan, J. (2002). Departures from knowledge and/or management in knowledge management. *Management Communication Quarterly, 16*(2), 282–291. doi:10.1177/089331802237242

Berardi, F. (2007). Technology and knowledge in a universe on indetermination. *SubStance, 36*(1), 57–74. doi:10.1353/sub.2007.0000

Berardi, F. (2009). *The soul at work: From alienation to autonomy*. Los Angeles, CA: Semiotext(e).

Borg, E. A. (2001). Knowledge, information and intellectual property: Implications for marketing relationships. *Technovation, 21*(8), 515–524. doi:10.1016/S0166-4972(00)00066-3

Castells, M. (2010). *The rise of the network society*. Oxford, UK: Blackwell.

Chase, R. L. (1997). The knowledge-based organization: An international survey. *Journal of Knowledge Management, 1*(1), 38–49. doi:10.1108/EUM0000000004578

Cross, R., & Cummings, J. N. (2004). Tie and network correlates of individual performance in knowledge-intensive work. *Academy of Management Journal, 47*(6), 928–937. doi:10.2307/20159632

Davenport, T. H., & Prusak, L. (1998). *Working knowledge: How organizations manage what they know*. Boston, MA: Harvard Business School Press.

Davenport, T. H., Prusak, L., & Strong, B. (2008). Business insight (A special report): Organization: Putting ideas to work: Knowledge management can make a difference – But it needs to be more pragmatic. *Wall Street Journal,* p. R11.

Davies, J., & Ryan, M. (2011). Vocational education in the 20th and 21st centuries. *Management Services, 55*(2), 31–36.

Demarest, M. (1997). Understanding knowledge management. *Long Range Planning, 30*(3), 374–384. doi:10.1016/S0024-6301(97)90250-8

Diehl, A., Grabill, J. T., & Hart-Davidson, W. (2008). Grassroots: Supporting the knowledge work of everydaylLife. *Technical Communication Quarterly, 17*(4), 413–434. doi:10.1080/10572250802324937

Drucker, P. (2000). Knowledge work. *Executive Excellence, 17*(4), 11–12.

Gherardi, S. (2009). Guest editorial: Knowing and learning in practice-based studies: An introduction. *The Learning Organization, 16*(5), 352–359. doi:10.1108/09696470910974144

Grover, V., & Davenport, T. H. (2001). General perspectives on knowledge management: Fostering a research agenda. *Journal of Management Information Systems, 18*(1), 5–21.

Heaton, L., & Taylor, J. R. (2002). Knowledge management and professional work: A communication perspective on the knowledge-based organization. *Management Communication Quarterly, 16*(2), 210–236. doi:10.1177/089331802237235

Hedlund, G. (1994). A model of knowledge management and the N-form corporation. *Strategic Management Journal, 15*, 73–90. doi:10.1002/smj.4250151006

Liu, A. (2004). *The laws of cool: Knowledge work and the culture of information*. Chicago, IL: The University of Chicago Press.

Mascha, M. F. (2001). The effect of task complexity and expert system type on the acquisition of procedural knowledge: Some new evidence. *International Journal of Accounting Information Systems, 2*(2), 103–124. doi:10.1016/S1467-0895(01)00016-1

Matsuo, M., & Kusumi, T. (2002). Salesperson's procedural knowledge, experience and performance: An empirical study in Japan. *European Journal of Marketing, 36*(7/8), 840–854. doi:10.1108/03090560210430836

McAdam, R., & McCreedy, S. (1999). A critical review of knowledge management models. *The Learning Organization, 6*(3), 91–100. doi:10.1108/09696479910270416

Powell, W. W., & Snellman, K. (2004). The knowledge economy. *Annual Review of Sociology, 30*, 199–220. doi:10.1146/annurev.soc.29.010202.100037

Pyöriä, P. (2005). The concept of knowledge work revisited. *Journal of Knowledge Management, 9*(3), 116–127. doi:10.1108/13673270510602818

Rix, G., & Lièvre, P. (2008). Towards a codification of practical knowledge. *Knowledge Management Research & Practice, 6*(3), 225–232. doi:10.1057/kmrp.2008.13

Sher, P. J., & Lee, V. C. (2004). Information technology as a facilitator for enhancing dynamic capabilities through knowledge management. *Information & Management, 41*(8), 933–945. doi:10.1016/j.im.2003.06.004

Sinha, K. K., & Van de Ven, A. H. (2005). Designing work within and between organizations. *Organization Science, 16*(4), 389–408. doi:10.1287/orsc.1050.0130

Tseng, S.-M. (2008). The effects of information technology on knowledge management systems. *Expert Systems with Applications, 35*(1-2), 150–160. doi:10.1016/j.eswa.2007.06.011

Tsoukas, H. (2002). Introduction: Knowledge-based perspectives on organizations: Situated knowledge, novelty, and communities of practice. *Management Learning, 33*(4), 419–426. doi:10.1177/1350507602334001

Wild, R., & Griggs, K. (2008). A model of information technology opportunities for facilitating the practice of knowledge management. *The Journal of Information and Knowledge Management Systems, 38*(4), 490–506.

ADDITIONAL READING

Alvesson, M. (1993). Organizations as rhetoric: Knowledge-intensive firms and the struggle with ambiguity. *Journal of Management Studies, 30*(6), 997–1015. doi:10.1111/j.1467-6486.1993.tb00476.x

Binney, D. (2001). The knowledge-management spectrum – Understanding the KM landscape. *Journal of Knowledge Management, 5*(1), 33–42. doi:10.1108/13673270110384383

Brelade, S., & Harman, C. (2007). Understanding the modern knowledge worker. *Knowledge Management Review, 10*(3), 24–27.

Butler, A., Reed, M., & Le Grice, P. (2007). Vocational training: Trust, talk and knowledge transfer in small businesses. *Journal of Small Business and Enterprise Development, 14*(2), 280–293. doi:10.1108/14626000710746709

Carlile, P. R. (2004). Transferring, translating, and transforming: An integrative framework for managing knowledge across boundaries. *Organization Science, 15*(5), 555–568. doi:10.1287/orsc.1040.0094

Cleveland, H. (1990). The age of spreading knowledge. *The Futurist, 24*(2), 35–39.

Dean, D., & Webb, C. (2011). Recovering from information overload. *The McKinsey Quarterly, 1*, 80–88.

Dobrai, K., & Farkas, F. (2009). Knowledge-intensive business services: A brief overview. *Perspectives of Innovations. Economics & Business, 3*(3), 15–17.

Donaldson, L. (2001). Reflections on knowledge and knowledge-intensive firms. *Human Relations*, *54*(7), 955–963. doi:10.1177/0018726701547008

Donnelly, R. (2006). How "free" is the free worker? An investigation into the working arrangements available to knowledge workers. *Personnel Review*, *35*(1), 78–97. doi:10.1108/00483480610636803

Duffy, J. (2000). Knowledge management: What every information professional should know. *Information Management Journal*, *34*(3), 10–16.

Lambe, P. (2011). The unacknowledged parentage of knowledge management. *Journal of Knowledge Management*, *15*(2), 175–197. doi:10.1108/13673271111119646

Lyon, A. (2005). Intellectual capital and struggles over the perceived value of members' expert knowledge in a knowledge-intensive organization. *Western Journal of Communication*, *69*(3), 251–271. doi:10.1080/10570310500202413

Malone, T. W., Laubacher, R. J., & Johns, T. (2011). The age of hyper specialization. *Harvard Business Review*, *89*(7/8), 56–65.

Martensson, M. (2000). A critical review of knowledge management as a managerial tool. *Journal of Knowledge Management*, *4*(3), 204–216. doi:10.1108/13673270010350002

Mc Campbell, A. S., Clare, L. M., & Gitters, S. H. (1999). Knowledge management: The new challenge for the 21st century. *Journal of Knowledge Management*, *3*(3), 172–179. doi:10.1108/13673279910288572

Mirghani, M., Stankosky, M., & Murray, A. (2006). Knowledge management and information technology: Can they work in perfect harmony? *Journal of Knowledge Management*, *10*(3), 103–116. doi:10.1108/13673270610670885

Nold, H. A. (2011). Making knowledge management work: Tactical to practical. *Knowledge Management Research & Practice*, *9*(1), 84–94. doi:10.1057/kmrp.2010.27

Nonaka, I., & Takeuchi, H. (1995). *The knowledge-creating company*. Oxford, UK: Oxford University Press.

Spender, J. C. (2006). Method, philosophy and empirics in KM and IC. *Journal of Intellectual Capital*, *7*(1), 12–28. doi:10.1108/14691930610639741

Stebbins, M. W., & Shani, A. B. (1995). Organization design and the knowledge worker. *Leadership and Organization Development Journal*, *16*(1), 23–30. doi:10.1108/01437739510076421

Styhre, A. (2002). The knowledge-intensive company and the economy of sharing: Rethinking utility and knowledge management. *Knowledge and Process Management*, *9*(4), 228–236. doi:10.1002/kpm.155

Wainwright, C. (2001). Knowledge management: Aspects of knowledge. *Management Services*, *45*(11), 16–19.

Weick, K. E. (1985). Cosmos vs. chaos: Sense and nonsense in electronic contexts. *Organizational Dynamics*, *14*(2), 51–64. doi:10.1016/0090-2616(85)90036-1

Winch, C. (2010). Vocational education, knowing how and intelligence concepts. *Journal of Philosophy of Education*, *44*(4), 551–567. doi:10.1111/j.1467-9752.2010.00775.x

KEY TERMS AND DEFINITIONS

Commercial Knowledge: The function of commercial knowledge is to improve the performance of organizations. It is constantly changing and partial. It is moreover social since it is produced and shared in networks consisting of human and non-human actors.

Knowledge Work: In the traditional literature, knowledge work includes expertise, autonomy, and the use of information technology. It is assumed to require intellectual abilities and decision-making. In the critical literature, knowledge work is considered narrow in scope using technological applications in producing, processing, and exchanging digitalized information in the network.

Knowledge Worker: A traditionally defined knowledge worker is a highly educated professional or expert receiving, processing, and creating new knowledge with the help of information technology. According to the emerging critical viewpoint, a knowledge worker produces, stores, and transfers simplified information in a digitalized form thus reducing work to an exchange of symbols.

Knowledge Management: With help of knowledge management organizations control, expand, and utilize knowledge in order to create economic value.

Knowledge-Intensive Organizations: Organizations where traditionally defined knowledge work and knowledge workers are in a predominant position. Knowledge management is in a central role in managing immaterial knowledge capital.

Situated Knowledge: Collective and distributed (between humans and non-humans) activities situated in time and space. Knowledge is called situated since it is located in communities of people and it travels across these communities.

Technologization: The strong presence of technology in everyday life. More widely, technologization includes the idea of utilization and productivity. Value is expressed and measured in products and tools. Simplified forms of communication are a manifestation of technologization.

Vocational Professional: A person with specialized non-academic skills, training or knowledge required by a specific trade, occupation or vocation.

Practical Knowledge: Knowledge acquired in authentic situations. It is gained through experiences but must be linked to theoretical knowledge of a specific field.

Chapter 11
The Role of Creativity, Innovation, and Invention in Knowledge Management

Sladjana Cabrilo
University Educons, Serbia

Leposava Grubic-Nesic
University of Novi Sad, Serbia

ABSTRACT

Globalization, fast-paced technological, economic, and social changes, and increased competition have affected the current business environment by changing the role of knowledge, innovation, and creativity in work, learning, and everyday life. Although Knowledge Management (KM) is usually explored separately from creativity and innovation, these concepts are closely related and in practice reinforce each other. Linking KM to innovation and creativity management in a holistic fashion has facilitated the examination of the knowledge management impact on innovation performance of organizations. In addition, this practice makes it possible to examine how creativity and invention can be used to increase the efficiency of knowledge management. This chapter focuses on the analysis of the role and importance of creativity, innovation, and invention in knowledge management. In addition, the chapter investigates the role of KM in innovation, and environmental and personal factors, which contribute to creativity, innovation, and invention in KM.

INTRODUCTION

In recent decades, corporate life has become increasingly intangible. Faced with new challenges, organizations have found themselves at crossroads. In an attempt to find new sources of wealth and long-term competitiveness, they start to turn to an inexhaustible, intangible source of wealth, such as human knowledge, innovation and creativity (Cabrilo, 2008). This hidden treasure is what really matters in a society that is in constant turmoil, especially in times of global financial cri-

DOI: 10.4018/978-1-4666-1969-2.ch011

sis (Cabrilo & Grubic-Nesic, 2010). While assets such as labor, capital, and technology continue to be important, the ability of organizations to innovate has been seen more as one of the key factors to ensure their success (Brown & Eisenhardt, 1998; Cohen & Levinthal, 1990; McGrath, 2001; Tsai, 2001; Shipton, Fay, West, Patterson, & Birdi, 2005). Through innovation, organizations are able to adapt, diversify, and reinvent themselves (Shipton, et al., 2005; Schoonhoven, Eisenhardt, & Lyman, 1990).

Innovation becomes crucial in terms of defining how a company, a city, a region, or a country evolves. However, the concept of innovation is more complex than ever before. Innovation is not something that is only embedded into products and services anymore. It is the input, the output, and the process. Innovation has become a mindset, a way to approach the world.

Knowledge, creativity, and invention are key drivers to the innovation process. Ideas present new thoughts, beliefs, or feelings that are generated as a result of some mental activity. Creativity is about combining these ideas in a unique and unexpected way. Based on these creative ideas, the process of invention creates something that is new and useful. This process is closely related to knowledge creation. Innovation is the result of combining these creative ideas, inventions and knowledge in a novel way for the full intent of creating value. This process of transforming creative ideas into vigor innovation requires just as much creativity as before.

Knowledge Management (KM) should be viewed as a holistic concept which includes a set of knowledge processes (knowledge identification, knowledge generation, knowledge codification, knowledge sharing, knowledge storing, and knowledge application) as well as the functions of supporting creativity and innovation. In KM, both innovativeness and creativity should be viewed as constant processes, as the means for optimum usage of existing knowledge and as the key drivers for generating new knowledge.

According to Nonaka and Takeuchi (1995) effectiveness of knowledge creation especially determines the level of innovation. It is impossible to innovate only by using already existing (old) knowledge and without creating new knowledge. Taking into account that learning is a production process in which knowledge is created (Weggeman, 1997), it becomes quite obvious that knowledge creation and learning are crucial for the innovation process. Analyzing the effect of organizational learning on innovation and creativity, research shows that organizational learning enhances organizations' innovativeness and capacity for adaptation (Hurley & Hult, 1988). In addition, one possibility in creating and developing knowledge is certainly through innovativeness and creativity.

Research of innovation has shown that 'domain relevant' knowledge represents one aspect of creativity (Amabile, Conti, Coon, Lazenby, & Herron, 1996) disclosing the connection between creativity and innovation. Innovation are generated and sustained through the creative efforts of individuals, groups, and organizations (West, Hirst, Richter, & Shipton, 2004). Since innovation and creativity could be viewed as individual and group phenomena, this chapter includes the research of personal and environmental factors, which contribute to individual and group creativity, innovation, as well as invention in KM.

Today, organizational innovation means creating the conditions for a continuous flow of knowledge, inventions, and creativity. Thus, the organization's ability to think and learn as well as to create, transfer, share and apply knowledge through the process of knowledge management is currently widely recognised as crucial for superior organizational performance (Senge, 1990; Drucker, 1993; Nonaka & Takeuchi, 1995; Leonard-Barton, 1995; Castells, 1996; Stewart, 1997; Weggeman, 1997; Weggeman, 2000; Kessels, 2001; Basadur & Gelade, 2006; Stam, 2007).

Creativity, invention, and innovation are connected to the process of creating and applying new knowledge. As such, they are at heart of knowledge management (Gurteen, 1998). Still, topics related to KM are usually seen as different and are separated from organizational creativity and innovation (Basadur & Gelade, 2006). Furthermore, innovation process has been mostly explored just from one perspective (deBono, 1976; Cooper, 1993). Holistic view on KM, innovation, creativity and invention as it is applied in this chapter, can contribute to the process of examining the knowledge management impact on the innovation performance of companies as well as examining how innovativeness, creativity and invention can be used in order to make KM process more effective.

BACKGROUND: WHAT ARE KNOWLEDGE, KM, CREATIVITY, INNOVATION, AND INVENTION?

Superior organizational performance is becoming increasingly dependent on knowledge, superior thinking, learning, and innovations. Therefore, terms such as knowledge management, innovation management, creativity, organizational learning, and intellectual capital are very common in the management literature. Following sections provide broad definitions and discussions of knowledge, knowledge management, creativity, invention, and innovation as the basic terms in this chapter.

The Nature of Knowledge

"Knowledge is a fluid mix of framed experience, values, contextual information, and expert insight that provides a framework for evaluating and incorporating new experiences and information. It originates and is applied in the minds of knowers" (Davenport & Prusak, 1997, p. 5). In Nonaka, Toyama, and Konno (2000) knowledge is described as dynamic, since it is created in social interactions among individuals and organisations.

Furthermore, knowledge could be defined as "information that is relevant, actionable, and based at least partially on experience" (Leonard & Sensiper, 2002, p. 485). Knowledge is linked to meaningful behavior having tacit elements born from experience. It is context specific, since it depends on a particular time and space. Knowledge can be fluid or structured, and can move from one to the other (Auernhammer, Leslie, Neumann, & Lettice, 2003). In this chapter, knowledge is considered to be a purposeful collection of information aimed to achieve its usefulness and usability in the process of value added creation. Knowledge is a deterministic and dynamic process that requires variety of perceptive, cognitive and analytical abilities, memorizing, and comprehending capacities. Knowledge is a continuous process that can be improved and developed.

Tacit and Explicit Knowledge

In today's knowledge management literature, it is common to make a distinction between tacit and explicit knowledge.

The essence of tacit knowledge is reflected in the Polanyi's (1966) statement "we know more than we can tell" (p. 4). "Tacit knowledge is highly personal and hard to formalize and, therefore, difficult to communicate to others" (Nonaka, 1991, p. 98). It encompasses personal 'know-how,' experience, skills, intuition, beliefs, ideas and values that are often taken for granted (Nonaka & Konno, 1998, p. 42). Tacit knowledge is rooted in a person's mind and memory, through experience (Cabrilo, 2008) and is represented through non-articulated knowledge (Rüdiger & Vanini, 1998, p. 469). It is bound up with the context in which it has been obtained (Stam, 2007). Knowledge is "manifested only in its application" (Grant, 1997, p. 451). Very often people express their tacit knowledge without conscious direction through instinctive reactions as 'automatic knowledge' (Spender, 1996). Due to its characteristics, tacit knowledge is very difficult to articulate and express verbally, which makes it very hard to transfer. It is acquired via personal contacts—by sharing experiences, by observation and imitation (Hall & Andriani, 2002) or via transferring tacit knowledge into explicit-codified knowledge. The use of stories and metaphors may help transference of tacit knowledge (Auernhammer, et al., 2003).

Explicit knowledge is codified knowledge, which is transmittable in formal, and systematic language (Stam, 2007). It is articulated, observable in use, simple, independent, easy teachable knowledge such as formulas, handbooks, video, and audio, etc. Explicit knowledge usually covers part of the original tacit knowledge but is not a full representation of it. Some of the reasons lie in the fact that people are unaware of the tacit dimensions of their knowledge or are unable to articulate them.

According to Leonard and Sensiper (2002), knowledge "exists on a spectrum" (p. 486). At one extreme, it is almost tacit, and at the other end of the spectrum, knowledge is almost completely explicit. Still, most knowledge exists in between the extremes.

Knowledge Productivity

The process of transforming knowledge into value is referred to as *knowledge productivity* (Stam, 2007). Explicit knowledge, tacit knowledge, information, experience, and skill are not enough to make knowledge productive. Putting knowledge into action requires a person to be competent and that means three essential elements (Gurteen, 1998). A person must have the knowledge and the skill, but most important is to have the right motivation and attitude. In other words, the mindset is important in making knowledge productive.

Holistic View on Knowledge Management

As knowledge has become the main resource in organizations, the ability to manage knowledge-based intellect represents the key managerial skill of the future (Quinn, Anderson, & Finkelstein, 1996). Although the concept of knowledge management has been intrepreted in different contexts, in this chapter, KM definitions are focused on definitions emphasizing the relations between KM, innovation, and creativity.

Stam (2007) defines KM as "deliberate initiatives that aim at stimulating the knowledge creation process, in order to enable innovation" (p. 34). Beckman (1997) views KM as the formalisation of knowledge, experience and expertise and access to them, which create new capabilities, facilitate superior performance and foster innovation. According to Drucker (1993), KM is a process of systematically creating and recreating knowledge in order to innovate, while Leonard-Barton (1995) specify it as a combination of knowledge creating activities that enable innovation. Furthermore, KM could be defined as the capability of an organization to create new knowledge, disseminate it throughout the organization, and embody it in products, services, and systems (Nonaka & Takeuchi, 1995).

Knowledge Management as a Set of Knowledge Processes

There exist numerous models and classifications of the process of knowledge management in the literature (Nonaka, 1991; Wiig, 1993; Nonaka & Takeuchi, 1995; Hedlund, 1994; Edvinsson, 1996; Snowden, 1998; Carayanis, 1999; Probst, Raub, & Romhardt, 1999; Starovic & Marr, 2003). Based on these models, KM can be defined as a set of knowledge processes that include:

- **Knowledge Identification:** The identification of what we know and what we should know including the identification of existing knowledge as well as any missing knowledge. The result should be a sufficiently accurate view of the relevant internal and external knowledge that contributes to the corporate mission.

- **Knowledge Generation:** Includes two main sub-processes, knowledge acquisition and knowledge creation, are both focused on increasing the stock of corporate knowledge (Starovic & Marr, 2003). Knowledge acquisition is a process of capturing and bringing external knowledge (knowledge from the external environment) to the company. Knowledge creation is the process of developing new knowledge within the company.

- **Knowledge Codification:** The process of knowledge formalisation into appropriate codes that involves knowledge capture, externalisation and representation.

- **Knowledge Storing:** The process of recording and maintaining knowledge within an organisation, thus making it accessible at any time.

- **Knowledge Sharing:** A process that allows knowledge to be disseminated in an organisation. Knowledge sharing can be done through formal or informal processes.

- **Knowledge application:** The process of applying knowledge within an organisation. Knowledge becomes productive only if it is transformed into value through the process of knowledge application.

These processes form the KM cycle, although they do not always occur in a linear sequence.

Knowledge Management makes Knowledge Productive

In the context of value creation, KM should be viewed as a more holistic concept, not just as a set of knowledge processes. KM needs to create knowledge and apply knowledge while making it productive (Drucker, 1993; Gurteen, 1998). According to Gurteen (1998), who has adapted an original definition given by the Gartner Group, KM is "an emerging set of organizational design and operational principles, processes, organizational structures, applications and technologies that helps knowledge workers dramatically leverage their creativity and ability to deliver business value" (p. 6). In the sense of knowledge productivity, KM's role is to fundamentally focus on 'making knowledge productive' through creativity and innovation. Thus, creativity and innovation are major ingredients of the KM process. In a holistic view, the key concerns of KM are both effective and efficient knowledge processes, as well as the functions of supporting and fostering creativity and innovation (Wickramasinghe, 2006).

Creativity: Generation of Ideas

Creativity is defined as a useful novelty that can be applied in order to add value to an organization's products and services (Oldham & Cummings, 1996). Some authors consider creativity as an internal process for generating ideas. An idea is simply 'something' that is unrealized, unproven or untested. It could be an unrealized goal, an unrealized product, an unrealized service, an unproven insight, or a new unproven concept of how something might work (Gurteen, 1998). According to Smith (1998) creativity includes the generation of ideas, alternatives, and possibilities. Meeker (1969) stated that creativity involves flexibility, individuality, and the ability to break away from conventional approaches. On the contrary, Csikszentmihalyi (1988, 1996, 1998), Amabile (1983, 1996), and Sternberg and Lubart (1991, 1995) considered creativity to be based on social interactions.

The social impact on creative behavior was originally studied by Amabile (1988). Her componential model of creativity includes cognitive, personal, motivational, and social factors, which influence all aspects of the creative process. The major contribution of the model is highlighting intrinsic motivation, domain-relevant skills and creativity-related processes as essential components to creative process.

In the contribution of Barron and Harrington (1981), creativity is the ability to produce useful ideas that concern a real value. Further, MacKinnon (1971) defined creativity as a process that involves originality, adaptation, and implementation. From a broad perspective, each individual is naturally creative, as "the need to create is a fundamental driving force in human beings" (Gurteen, 1998, p. 7). However, the creativity can be regarded as the process via which ideas are materialized (Yusuf, 2009). With respect to the result of creativity, creativity can be considered in subjective as well as in normative sense. Subjective approach to creativity reflects the notion of creative process results based on novel and original individual work. In the normative approach, the result of the creative process should be useful in a broader sense, i.e., as a new value for the society, science, art or industry.

Dynamic Nature of Creativity

Three characteristics of the creative process reveal a dynamic nature of creativity. The first refers to creativity as a thought process which is meaningful and purposeful (Csikszentmihalyi, 1988). Furthermore, a creative process typically generates something original (Amabile, 1996). Finally, the result of creative engagement has to be a value (Rank, Pace, & Frese, 2004).

Wallas's model is one of the first models of the creative process (Wallas, 1926). In this model, creative process is explained with the following stages: 1) preparation, which includes preparatory work on a problem; 2) incubation, which involves unconscious or conscious organization of gathered information; 3) illumination, where a creative idea emerges into conscious awareness; 4) verification, where the idea is consciously verified, evaluated, and then applied.

Many other models, which are developed based on the Wallas's model, contributed to the exploring of dynamic nature creativity (Osborn, 1953; Barron, 1988).

Types of Creativity

Taylor (1975) defined four possible types of creativity with the first one being expressive creativity. It is broadly defined as a spontaneous action. The second type of creativity is productive creativity, and it implies the possession of certain skills and techniques for product creation. Inventive creativity, the third type of creativity, is defined as the one driving materials and techniques behind the process. Finally, emergency creativity occurs in rare situations of emergence of original ideas, techniques, and theories.

Naturally, creativity can arise from accidental phenomena as well from processes based on experience (Boden, 1998). In such cases, the creative content is not the result of conscious intention. Since the knowledge-based creativity is vital for knowledge management, the non-conscious types of creativity are not the scope of this chapter.

Creativity and Knowledge

Weisberg (1999), and Edmonds and Candy (2002) stressed that knowledge is at heart of creativity. Specifically, the quality and the quantity of knowledge have an impact on creativity. It is worth noting that knowledge, which is the basis of change and development, should not be static. Knowledge must be considered as an inherently dynamic concept—knowledge flow, which fosters creative change and development. The flow of knowledge is prerequisite to creative performance of work.

To conclude, creativity is a process of generating ideas, which is closely related to knowledge creation. It can undoubtedly be viewed as the source of innovation (Gurteen, 1998).

Innovation: Putting Ideas into Action

Creative ideas are not sufficient for the creation of real value in business (Levitt, 1963). Someone needs to put them into action. Thus, innovation which refers to taking of new or existing ideas and turning them into action is an imperative for survival in modern business. Together with knowledge, it presents new force for gaining economic wealth in the knowledge economy (Cabrilo, 2009). Many authors have considered the ability to innovate to be equal to competitive advantage (Davenport & Prusak, 1998; Dixon, 2000; Drucker, 1993; Jacobs, 1999; Leonard-Barton, 1995; Nonaka & Takeuchi, 1995; Weggeman, 1997). Thus, knowledge management is not a goal in itself, but support of continuous innovation as a decisive factor of competitive advantage (Stam, 2007). Barnett (1953) defined innovation as "any thought, behavior or thing that is new because it is qualitatively different from existing forms" (p. 7). Innovation could be defined "as the intentional introduction and application within a role, group, or organization of ideas, processes or procedures, new to the relevant unit of adoption, designed to significantly benefit the individual, the group, organization or wider society" (West & Farr, 1990, p. 9). The World Bank (WB, 2010) refers to innovation as "technologies or practices that are new to a given society" emphasizing that "what is not disseminated and used is not an innovation" (p. 4). Linking innovation and knowledge, Cavagnoli (2011) defined innovation „as creative application

of knowledge in a new form to increase the set of techniques, products, and services commercially available in the economy (p. 111).

Types of Organizational Innovation

There are different types of organizational innovation. It may be technological innovation, which is in most literature further classified into product innovation and process innovation, and administrative innovation (Damanpour & Evan, 1984; Damanpour, Szabat, & Evan, 1989; Auernhammer, et al., 2003; Chuang, 2005). The scope of innovation can range in scope from radical/disruptive to incremental/evolutionary innovation (Trott, 1998; Christensen, 1997). Depending on the type, complexity and scope, the role of knowledge in the innovation process is crucial. For more radical innovations, it is necessary to create and apply new knowledge from very different contexts and for incremental innovations, it is more important to re-use existing knowledge in many aspects of the product's design, manufacture and delivery (Auernhammer, et al., 2003).

Open Innovation

As an answer for today's societal changes the innovation paradigm has shifted from the 'closed innovation' to the 'open innovation' model, which is based on five important elements: the establishment of ties through networking with individuals and organisations in order to exploit both, the internal knowledge and external ideas; collaboration among partners, universities, countries, users, and even competitors; 'corporate entrepreneurship,' including corporate venturing, intrapreneurship, and spin-offs, proactive management of intellectual property and internal R&D which maintains its traditional role as an important element to develop the organisation's absorptive capacity (Chesbrough, 2003).

Innovation and Knowledge

Innovation reflects a process of transforming of knowledge. This process converts new knowledge into new products and services (Audretsch, 2006). Innovation is about the creation of new knowledge or ideas and their transformation into value creating outcomes. Innovation can be better understood as a process in which the organisation creates and defines problems and then actively develops new knowledge to solve them (Nonaka, 1994, p. 14). For Hauschildt (1993, p. 18) innovation process is divided into seven subsequent steps starting with the idea and ending with the successful ongoing utilization. These steps are: idea, discovery, research, development, invention, introduction, and ongoing utilization.

In this chapter, innovation is understood as the implementation of ideas. Innovation is a process of taking of new or existing ideas and putting them into action. Since it is impossible to innovate only by application of existing knowledge, creativity in the creation of new knowledge is the driving force of innovation. Therefore, innovation management is aimed to create the conditions for a continuous flow of knowledge, creativity, and invention in order to use creative efforts to introduce new ideas, processes, products, or services.

Invention

Innovation is often confused with invention. However, the invention is only the first step in a long process of bringing a good idea to widespread and effective use (Auernhammer, et al., 2003). Some statements go in favor of the previous one, such as that "innovation refers to the commercialising of the invention" (Tidd, Bessant, & Pavitt, 1997; Ahuja & Lampert, 2001).

Invention is a creative process of creating a new (previously undiscovered) method, process, device, or material that can be used for a specific purpose. Having an idea or seeing a new possibility, connection, or relationship are the prerequisites of invention. His open and curious mind allows an inventor to see beyond what is known. Inspiration, experimentation, imagination, play, and insight (questions, doubts or hunches) are vital elements of inventive thinking which can lead to invention. Invention could be the result of conscious or unconscious actions, since a novel idea may suddenly come in a flash or in a dream.

Invention is about new processes that produce better quality or new goods or services to replace previous (old) processes. It is always connected to the break of an old familiar paradigm and replacement with the new one. Inventors experience a process of unlearning, breaking connections with past understanding and letting go of old habits and beliefs (Basadur & Gelade, 2006).

Inventing might be related to the learning in the sense of making distinction between the availability and the use of knowledge (Gordon, 1956; Gordon, 1971). If we consider learning as gaining knowledge and making new cognitive connections and inventing as using knowledge and breaking old cognitive connections, inventing and learning could be regarded as two parts of one continuous process. When we learn, we make the strange familiar and in contrast, when we invent, we make the familiar strange (Basadur & Gelade, 2006).

In the review of basic concepts in this chapter, it is worth noting that the starting point of creativity is the generation of new ideas. Invention is based on a new idea, but invention has to be introduced and successfully implemented to become innovation. Innovation is turning new or existing ideas into action and it is a far tougher proposition than creativity. Since creativity, invention, and innovation concern the process of creating and applying new knowledge, they are at heart of the KM process (Figure 1). Therefore, creativity, innovation, invention, and KM should be examined by an integrated approach as it is applied in the next section.

Figure 1. The role of knowledge, creativity, innovation, and invention in KM

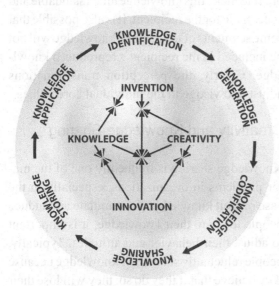

AN INTEGRATED APPROACH TO CREATIVITY, INNOVATION, INVENTION, AND KNOWLEDGE MANAGEMENT

Amabile, Schatzel, Moneta, and Kramer (2004) pointed out the difference between creativity and innovation. They defined creativity as the creation of new and useful ideas in any discipline, and innovation as the successful implementation of creative ideas. Invention refers to the idea that can be used for a special purpose. Thus, creativity and invention could be considered as the main prerequisites of innovation. In the following sections, the relationship between creativity, innovation, invention, and KM will be separately described. Since invention is a part of a long process of innovation, the role of invention in KM will be explored in the context of innovation-KM interaction.

Creativity and Knowledge Management

In majority of the KM literature, creativity has been considered as a prerequisite for the creation of

new knowledge. More generally, creativity plays an equally important role in other KM processes, such as knowledge sharing and knowledge applying. There is no consensus as to which knowledge processes are more influenced by creativity. In the following subsections, the role of creativity in some knowledge processes will be described.

Creativity and Knowledge Creation

Since the creation of new knowledge is closely related to the process of learning, exploring the role of creativity in knowledge creation has to include creativity in education. Traditional attitudes to teaching have limited and discouraged creativity, which resulted in subsequent problems in the workplace. According to Gurteen (1998), traditional methods of teaching and explanation do have a role in knowledge creation, but they are no way as effective as we might imagine. It is impossible to fully transfer knowledge from one person to another, just by turning knowledge into a string of words and trying to transplant them as the whole into the mind of someone else. The obstacles lie mainly in the practice of automatic storage of information and the usage of causal relationship between phenomena and situations. In this case, "explaining does not increase understanding, and may even lessen it" (Gurteen, 1998, p. 8).

In contrast to the previously utilized approach to learning in education, the cohesive role of creativity in knowledge creation increases understanding and contributes to the effectiveness of learning. More precisely, creative techniques for information processing enable the collection, storage, processing, and distribution of information thus facilitating the creation of knowledge that is not easily categorized and classified. Adults, like children, learn most effectively through play and through experience. Creative knowledge assimilation promotes motivation, curiosity, and commitment to learning and knowledge creation. Hence, using creative methods and techniques in knowledge creation enables the development of intrinsic motivation that is fostered by intellectual curiosity, openness to experiment, as well as by challenging individuals' abilities.

Since individual thinking process is based on perception, creativity in knowledge creation is closely related to creative perception and creative thinking. It is worthwhile to note that human perception is largely defined by personal characteristics, value frameworks and the social environment (Csikszentmihalyi, 1988). According to the personal construct psychology (Kelly, 1955), if new information is inconsistent with individual's core values, the lack of cognitive understanding has a negative impact on the knowledge extraction. In this case, the common reaction is anger or fear, which prevents the adoption of new knowledge, hinders learning and knowledge creation. These phenomena can be explained by the concepts from psychology such as the speed and quality of perceptions, called perceptual defense and perceptual accentuation. Perceptual defense is a phenomenon that manifests itself in slow processing of events or objects that are inconsistent with one's needs, values, beliefs, or attitudes. On the contrary, perceptual accentuation is reflected as easy perception and processing of pleasant events or objects. Thus, phenomena that are consistent with one's core values are perceived more quickly. Creative perception fosters creative thinking, which has a positive impact on creativity in knowledge creation.

Creativity and Knowledge Storing

Knowledge storing implies more or less permanent knowledge saving for later availability and usage (Nonaka, et al., 2000). Storage of tacit knowledge is more strongly affected by personal characteristics. Bartlett (2008) explains that during the process of storage and reproduction of the adopted tacit knowledge (i.e., knowledge storing, codification, and sharing), content is often simplified by omitting some details. Therefore, a new and simplified knowledge is created via this process;

original assimilated knowledge is rationalized in order to make this knowledge understandable and acceptable for the recipient. It is also possible that some segments of the original knowledge will not be included in the recipient's reproduced knowledge. Clearly, the perception transformations adjust knowledge to the individual core values.

Creativity and Knowledge Sharing

Knowledge sharing is frequently one of the major problems in organizations, especially in the case of tacit knowledge. To stimulate and induce people to share their knowledge, it is important to adjust their behavior and attitudes. Typically, people reluctantly share their knowledge because they believe that if they do so, they will lose their strategic advantage and competitive position within an organization.

Studies suggest that shared understanding can be beneficial to knowledge sharing (Hansen, Nohria, & Tierney, 1999). Shared understanding represents the extent to which a source's and a recipient's attitudes, work values, problem-solving approaches, and prior work experience are similar. Furthermore, shared understanding positively affects the trust between individuals, which is the main trigger of knowledge sharing. This is because without shared understanding, there is a tendency for disagreement between a source and a recipient, which might lead to poor outcomes of knowledge sharing. In fact, shared understanding removes barriers between the two parties thereby enhancing their ability to share knowledge and work together toward a common goal.

In addition, trust involves emotional and ethical categories and is mainly based on shared understanding and reciprocal expectations. Noteworthy, trust has a dual role. On one hand, it enables faster and more harmonious development of abilities that are important for knowledge sharing and learning. In addition, trust in communication is the basis for mental health, which facilitates future knowledge development. Essentially, trust is rooted in beliefs as well as in the emotional-motivational and cognitive aspects of personality.

Creativity and Knowledge Application

Knowledge application provides the greatest opportunities for creativity. In particular, recognition of the value of individual knowledge and understanding of its usability in problem-solving situations should be the focus of KM initiatives. Weick and Roberts (1993) argue that effective KM requires the adoption of a shared and correlated thinking process for the creative use of knowledge.

In knowledge management education, the development of creative thinking in knowledge sharing, knowledge assimilation and knowledge creation includes the development of creative generalization and creative differentiation (Sternberg & Lubart, 1991). Creative generalization is the ability to link unrelated facts and synthesize these facts in a new way. Creative differentiation is the opposite of creative generalization and refers to an individual's ability to notice differences in seemingly similar concepts.

Innovation and Knowledge Management

Amidon (2003) defines innovation as "knowledge in action." Thus, innovation could be regarded as the result of knowledge creation. Furthermore, innovation is "the capacity of organizations to connect internal and external knowledge through the process in which knowledge flows from the market into the company and back in the form of new products and services" (Stam, 2007, p. 37). Leonard-Barton (1995) stresses the importance of encouraging and combining knowledge creating and diffusing activities. All above disclose that KM has become an important way of approaching innovation management and change at the level of the organization.

Tacit knowledge, although being very hard to capture, is essential for both, KM and innovation

process. Tacit knowledge is used in invention and innovation through the problem solving, problem finding and framing as well as prediction and anticipation (Leonard & Sensiper, 2002). The most common is to use tacit knowledge in problem solving, because experience, which experts already have in mind helps them to recognize a pattern from their experience, to perceive and understand a problem more quickly, and to detect a solution. The first stage in innovation process is to look for and proactively sense new problems and opportunities. Creative problem framing enables the rejection of usual solution to a problem in favor of asking a wholly different question. Prediction and anticipation are inscrutable mental processes, which are very important in invention.

Innovation and Knowledge Identification

The source of creativity necessary for innovation is not only visible expertise, but also invisible experience, which needs to be identified first. Tacit knowledge enables an increased perception of ideas thus stimulating creativity and innovativeness (Shipton, et al., 2005). It is possible to activate tacit knowledge in the innovation process only if the process of knowledge identification is effective. Ability to identify relevant tacit knowledge in the organization (Seidler-de Alwis, Hartmann, & Gemünden, 2004) as well as outside the organization is important prerequisite for innovation. Trying to gain tacit knowledge in the organization, it is necessary to identify tacit knowledge capabilities of the members as well as to decide what improvements need to be done in order to meet identified knowledge gaps within the organization. These gaps could be decreased or wholly overcome through the knowledge creation—learning within the organization or knowledge acquisition—trying to gain tacit knowledge and skills through recruiting new individuals, by acquiring parts of or whole new companies, by engaging appropriate consultants or by building networks with other companies. To promote creativity, it is important that people are recruited who have the skills and knowledge required to meet identified gaps (MacDuffie, 1995; Song, Almeida, & Wu, 2003).

It is very hard to identify tacit knowledge because it is deep in the people's mind and becomes visible through its application. The main barrier to the identification of tacit knowledge is related to the fact that knowledge is increasingly viewed as a source of power. Furthermore, it is related to the willingness of individuals to publicly express their tacit knowledge and their ability to realistically perceive, evaluate, and express their own knowledge. Very often, they do not know how well they know things or they try to present themselves as good as possible (Davenport & Prusak, 1998). Identification and assessment of tacit knowledge is possible through personal contacts, face-to-face communication, social networks, know-how (Rüdiger & Vanini, 1998; Imai, 1991) and should be supported and reinforced by managerial activities and organizational culture.

Innovation and Knowledge Creation

Both, tacit and explicit knowledge are essential to the process of knowledge creation, because knowledge is created through interactions between tacit and explicit knowledge and not from either tacit or explicit knowledge alone (Nonaka, et al., 2000). The four modes of knowledge conversion are called Socialization (from tacit to tacit), Externalization (from tacit to explicit), Combination (from explicit to explicit), and Internalization (from explicit to tacit). These four stages represent the knowledge-creation spiral or the SECI-model (Nonaka & Takeuchi, 1995).

Knowledge is mostly defined as a personal ability (Kessels, 1996; Mouritsen, Bukh, Larsen, & Johansen, 2002; Sveiby, 1997; Weggeman, 1997), which means that new knowledge always begins with the individual (Nonaka, et al., 2000) or that knowledge creation is at its starting point always related to a person. It emphasizes that an organi-

zation without people cannot create knowledge (Stam, 2007). Therefore, organizational knowledge creation includes individual knowledge creation and diffusion through the organization. Making personal knowledge available to others should be the central activity of the knowledge and innovation creating company (Seidler-de Alwis, et al., 2004).

Transferring of innovation can only happen when individuals have a creative idea in the first place (West, et al., 2004). Thus, it is important for organizations to support individuals in their quest to knowledge creation. This involves making associations, considering new ideas and being open to the possibilities for growth and learning implicit in new experiences (Shipton, et al., 2005). In order to enable and facilitate knowledge creation, an organization needs to create an environment where individuals are able and motivated to experiment with new ideas without fear, to take responsibilities, and learn from mistakes. In this respect, Nonaka and Takeuchi (1995) identify five 'enabling conditions': intention, autonomy, fluctuation/creative chaos, redundancy, requisite variety. Leonard-Barton (1995) defines four 'knowledge assets' that support the growth of knowledge: the skills embodied in the people physical systems, managerial systems that enable and reward learning, underlying values like respect, tolerance and openness and unique interdependent system, which gives the organization distinctive advantage over competitors. The most effective way of creating knowledge internally is to encourage employees to be creative and keen to learn.

According to Reber (1989), it is possible to create knowledge through nonconscious process of 'implicit learning' or "independently of conscious attempts to do so" (p. 219). Rewarding can act as facilitators or barriers to individual creativity. Sometimes knowledge-based pay can promote creativity (Guthrie, 2001), but sometimes linking appraisal to remuneration tends to be unhelpful as a means of promoting better individual performance (Kessler & Purcell, 1992; Pfeffer, 1998; Wood, 1996).

Innovation and Knowledge Transfer

In the literature of knowledge management, transfer of knowledge involves passing of knowledge between cognitive systems. If knowledge transfer is to take place, interaction with others is important (Stover, 2004, p. 167). A distinction is made between intra- and interorganisational knowledge transfer (Starovic & Marr, 2003). When it takes place within an organization, it overlaps with knowledge sharing. Research on innovation suggests that new ideas and knowledge should be discussed through the organization so that they can become implemented (Damanpour, 1990). Thus, knowledge sharing is critical precondition for organizational innovation.

Innovation and Knowledge Sharing

The transfer of knowledge between individuals, knowledge sharing always assumes a collective dimension. There are many activities stimulating knowledge sharing. For example, mentoring activities enable employees to build networks across the organization, thereby facilitating knowledge transfer (Collins & Clerk, 2004; Laursen & Foss, 2003). Furthermore, career development meetings present a non-threatening environment within which employees acquire the skills necessary to work effectively with others. Effective knowledge sharing is based on the developing shared understanding between individuals and work groups, using dialogue (Shipton, et al., 2005).

Howells (1996) notes that intuition based on tacit qualities plays an important role in the innovation process. This implies that encouraging of knowledge sharing should be largely focused on sharing of tacit knowledge. There are differences in the ability to transfer knowledge directly between people, depending on the will, the communicational skills but also simply on the

language they are using (Davenport & Prusak, 1998). A certain level of personal intimacy is necessary to establish comfortable communication of tacit knowledge. Scarbrough (2003) highlighted networks of relationships, as critical resources for the combination and exchange of knowledge, required to promote innovation and create intellectual capital (Nahapiet & Ghoshal, 1998). Tacit knowledge sharing strongly depends on the distinction between face-to-face and arm's length relationships (Spring, 2003). Trust is the key driver for knowledge sharing. The closeness of the two individuals determines the degree of tacit knowledge sharing (Cavusgil, Calantone, & Zhao, 2003) and that is why sharing tacit knowledge is more successful in informal settings that in formal ones. Much tacit knowledge is generated and transferred through body language or physical demonstrations of skills (Leonard & Sensiper, 1998).

There are many barriers to knowledge sharing within the organization. One of the main obstacles is that knowledge often represents a source of power to be guarded jealously. Furthermore, if individuals who possess tacit knowledge important to the innovation are discouraged from participating in knowledge sharing process, none of benefits can be realized (Leonard & Sensiper, 2002). The willingness of individuals to share their knowledge in an organisation depends on the organisational culture (Kucza, 2001). Motivation in general, either intrinsic or extrinsic, has been shown to be a positive factor in knowledge sharing. While intrinsic motivation in an organizational setting can be influenced by appropriate personnel selection, extrinsic motivation can, on the other hand, be influenced by specific rewards for transferring knowledge. Factors such as a lack of incentives or lack of confidence are strong motivational inhibitor to knowledge sharing (King, 2006). To motivate people towards knowledge sharing, management activities should be focused on encouraging and rewarding knowledge sharing, making clear that sharing knowledge is seen as something important for the whole company.

Another problem is that knowledge is not simple as an instruction and depends on values and beliefs (Davenport & Prusak, 1998). This leads to problems when transferring knowledge. That is why the management should build a consistent vision for employee development which reinforces the value of collective endeavor and help to promote trust in the organization and its commitment to employee growth and employability (Harrison & Kessels, 2004).

Inequality in status among participants, distance, thinking and communication style preferences are also strong inhibitors to the sharing of the explicit as well as tacit dimension of knowledge (Leonard & Sensiper, 2002). Communications competence is the ability to demonstrate the appropriate communications behavior in an organizational setting. Many studies have shown that communications competence is important for resolving conflicts, having effective teams, and improving the quality of relationships; all of these outcomes are correlated with successful knowledge sharing. Among the most important communication factors influencing knowledge sharing are sender's ability to clearly put ideas into words or symbols (encoding competence) as well as recipient's ability to listen, be attentive, and respond quickly (decoding competence) (King, 2006). Many of the barriers to the sharing of tacit knowledge are the same that inhibit innovation: strong hierarchies, strong preferences for analysis over intuition, penalties for failure that discourage experimentation (Leonard & Sensiper, 2002).

In order to make knowledge sharing more efficient and effective, management of organization needs to create an atmosphere characterized by trust, safety, and openness in which organization members feel safe sharing their knowledge (Seidler-de Alwis, et al., 2004).

Innovation and Knowledge Application

"Having the necessary knowledge is important, but not knowing how to use it innovatively can render it useless" (Basadur & Gelade, 2006, p. 47). Knowledge application changes the way organizational activities are conducted. This final stage of the knowledge management cycle represents the point at which innovations are enacted. Organizational innovation will only take place where there is commitment to this stage of the KM cycle.

PERSONAL AND ENVIRONMENTAL FACTORS THAT DETERMINE CREATIVITY, INNOVATION, AND INVENTION IN KM

Depending on its holder, knowledge in an organisation can be divided on individual, group, and organisational knowledge. Contrary to individual knowledge, group knowledge is the combined knowledge of a group, being more than a sum of the knowledge of all group members. Variety of knowledge contributed by the different members results in new knowledge (Brown & Duguid, 1998). While creativity can be seen as an individual, social, and cultural phenomenon, innovation in business is usually a group process. Amidon (1997) has demonstrated the relationship between individual creativity and organizational innovation. In addition, Woodman, Sawyer, and Griffin (1993) have pointed to the relationship between individual, team, and organizational aspect of creativity. According to the previous statements, this section includes factors, which determine knowing, learning, inventing, as well as creativity and innovation by members of groups—individually and collectively.

Drivers of Individual Creativity

Numerous internal and external variables may influence creativity (Csikszentmihalyi, 1996; Grubic-Nesic, 2005). Individual creativity could be the result of personality traits, individual use of creativity and expression of creativity. In the personality domain, certain personality traits such as the intrinsic motivation, intellectual curiosity, cognitive abilities, openness to new experience, and unprejudiced thinking (Csikszentmihalyi, 1996; Gardner, 1993) are causal to individual creativity. In the same vein, behavior of creative personalities can be explained by the constant creation of new ideas, creative and flexible responses as well as by their search for a new content. Sternberg and Lubart (1991) described creative people as those who "buy low and sell high." According to this theory, creativity requires six resources: intellectual abilities, knowledge, thinking styles, personality, motivation, and life environment (Sternberg, 2006). Knowledge management must develop these personality traits, regardless of age, cultural or any other differences. As mentioned previously, trust between the sender of information and the recipients is crucial for development of these personality traits. Specifically, communication dominated by honesty, competence, persistence, and openness is the prerequisite for setting up and developing trust (Grubic-Nesic, 2005). This organizational setting is in general supposed to integrate 'open mind' participants who are willing and able to adopt new knowledge. However, in some organizations the practice of rejecting new experiences and new knowledge is common. Such a regressive organizational behavior mode only allows for new knowledge when it serves their needs and interests.

Drivers of Group Creativity, Invention, and Innovation

While individual creativity is exciting and crucial to the business, the creativity of group is even more important to the research of organizational innovation, especially if we consider complex open innovation systems, which requires cohesion of knowledge from diverse national, disciplinary, and personal-based perspectives (Leonard & Sensiper, 2002).

Social interactions have been very important for a group creativity. "When we interact with people we have an opportunity to learn, to influence, to make things happen" (Gurteen, 1998, p. 7). Therefore, it is the duty of management to support and facilitate these interactions. In a group of diverse individuals engaged in a problem solving, each individual will frame the problem and its solution by applying its own mental schema and patterns (Leonard & Sensiper, 2002; Seidler-de Alwis, et al., 2004). Intellectual diversity in a group produces energy that is possible to be converted into new ideas, inventions, and innovations (Leonard & Sensiper, 1998; Leonard-Barton, 1995). In working groups, individuals from different backgrounds (cultures, experience, cognitive styles) contribute relying on their own pools of tacit knowledge. That means that personal divergence as well as varying perspectives foster creativity of a group. A certain 'requisite variety' is desirable for innovation (Nonaka & Takeuchi, 1995), because "just hearing a very different perspective challenges the mindset of those in the majority sufficiently that they will search beyond what initially appears to be an obvious solution" (Leonard & Sensiper, 2002, p. 489). Considering that "there is clear support for a relationship between diversity and creativity" (Jackson, May, & Whitney, 1992, p. 230), it could be also concluded that intellectually heterogeneous groups are more innovative than homogeneous ones.

In addition, using ICT for inexpensive communication or virtual collaboration is vital to bring together diverse workers (Ghosh, Yates, & Orlikowski 2004). A new generation of KM technologies enables individuals in a geographically-distributed team to communicate and share knowledge. These tools contribute to their collaboration and group creativity, invention and innovation.

Facing new situations and exploring new things, people find as very challenging and intrinsically motivating. This connection between creative work and motivation is supported by motivational literature (Herzberg, Mausner, & Snyderman, 1959; White, 1959; Berlyne, 1967; Amabile, 1993; Deci & Ryan, 1985; Hackman & Oldham, 1980). As motivation is a powerful tool for building relationships within the organisation and more efficient goal achievement (Kontic & Cabrilo, 2009), creative activity stimulates team building as people help each other to solve problems. Being strongly related to the motivation and commitment of the members of the group (Basadur & Gelade, 2006), creative activity contributes to the organizational efficiency as well as effectiveness.

Creative atmosphere dominated by motivating communication encourages the development of group creativity. Motivating communication is a communication full of trust, understanding, and care about the person with whom one is communicating. It is equal and open communication with no hidden motives and intentions, focused on common goals. Unlike motivating communication, communication dominated by criticism, condemnation, ridicule, irony, sarcasm, and ignorance, has a negative impact on the development of group creativity.

If an organization wants to be innovative, to permanently innovate or invent, it should create creative thinking environment so its employees would be able to break old and out-dated paradigms and replace them with new and better ones. Thinking organizations engage the innovative abilities and creative aptitudes of all of their employees

in order to recognize the value of breaking old paradigms, replacing them with new and better ones (invent) (Basadur & Gelade, 2006). Creative culture, which is based on creativity, promotes social cohesion enabling dissemination of innovation. Thus, creative culture supports and fosters innovation.

In summary, personal factors such as intrinsic motivation, intellectual curiosity, cognitive abilities, openness to new experience and unprejudiced thinking are very beneficial to individual creativity and invention. Individual creativity, commitment, and persistence drive the innovation process. In addition, there also exist numerous environmental factors, such as motivating communication, intellectually heterogeneous team building, creative thinking environment, knowledge productive environment, creative culture, that contribute to organizational creativity and innovation as well as to effective KM process.

FUTURE RESEARCH DIRECTIONS

Many research studies have shown that it is possible to improve creativity through training (Amabile, 1983; Sternberg & Lubart, 1996) and motivation (Amabile, 1996; Amabile, et al., 2004; Zhang & Bartol, 2010). In the literature on creativity, there have been about 200 known creativity techniques usable in various aspects of work and life. Using these creative techniques in the early stage of life can improve an individual's creativity and contribute to development. To develop creativity, innovation, and invention, one requires substantial knowledge about these processes as well as individual techniques needed to develop creative and innovative approach.

Areas being identified as important for the research of KM are social networks, individual characteristics, cultural characteristics, interpersonal and team characteristics as well as motivational factors (Wang & Noe, 2010). Given all previously mentioned factors, it is difficult to determine future research directions in the field of KM. First of all, qualitative and quantitative research methodologies are complementary and both are essential to understand KM. Furthermore, for the sensible approach to KM, it is important to choose a solid theoretical framework as well as certain methodological criteria for interpretations of the results. Cultural diversity including specific cultural patterns determines the relationship to new insights. Finally, economic, social, and political factors can drive future research in a completely unexpected direction.

Although, creativity and innovation are frequently mentioned trends in business, little attention has been devoted to issues such as creativity and innovation within different cultures and cross-cultural differences in creativity and innovation (Rank, et al., 2004). Cultural values in terms of tradition, religion, and working culture, influence if and how creativity and innovation are linked and cultivated within different cultures. Therefore, a new and potentially exciting research avenue might be how to increase innovation and creativity for culturally diversified areas.

CONCLUSION

In today's knowledge-driven economy, knowledge, life-long learning, creativity, and innovation have become any company's ultimate tools in its attempts to cope with turbulence and global competition in business (Cabrilo & Grubic-Nesic, 2010).

Creativity should be viewed as the process of generating ideas and innovation as the implementation of those ideas. Invention is based on a new idea that has to be successfully implemented to become innovation. While, creativity and invention could be considered as the main prerequisites of innovation, they are not sufficient for the creation of business value. Innovation or putting new or existing ideas into action is crucial for the creation of real value in business.

Since creativity, invention and innovation concern the process of creating and applying new knowledge, they are the center of knowledge management. Therefore, KM should be viewed as a set of initiatives aimed to stimulate knowledge processes as well as to support and nurture creativity, invention and innovation. Creativity, invention, and innovation are needed at every level and every dimension within an organization (Gurteen, 1998). If KM is to have any real impact on the way we do business, then it has to be fundamentally focused on creativity, invention, and innovation, either individually or collectively.

More specifically, KM should be aimed to personal and environmental factors, which influence knowing, and learning, as well as individual and group creativity, invention and innovation. Personal and environmental factors which contribute to creativity, invention, and innovation should be stimulated by KM initiatives. We find intrinsic motivation, intellectual curiosity, openness to new experience, creative perception, creative thinking, motivating communication, intellectually heterogeneous team building, new groupware technologies, knowledge productive environment, as well as creative- promoting culture as beneficial to organizational creativity and innovation and also to effective KM process. The organizational culture is very important, because it drives people to certain attitudes, which can be, in the context of KM, either good or bad.

In addition, KM initiatives should remove all barriers to individual and group creativity, invention and innovation. We find that limiting mental models, destructive communication dominated by criticism, condemnation, ridicule, irony, and ignorance and atmosphere full of fear, punishment for failure and mistrust block individual and group creativity, invention and innovation. Therefore, these factors have a negative impact on effectiveness of KM.

Undoubtedly, we should view KM and creativity and innovation management as closely related paradigms, which jointly create reinforcing loop of value creation. Knowledge management improves innovation management, whereas it fosters individual and group creativity, invention and innovation. On the other hand, creativity and innovativeness could be regarded as the main developers of knowledge processes that improve the effectiveness of knowledge identification, knowledge generation, knowledge codification, knowledge storing, knowledge sharing, and knowledge applying. Therefore, an integrated approach to KM, innovation, creativity and invention, as applied in this chapter, should be applied in organizations. When knowledge management, creativity, invention, and innovation are embedded in systems, structures, strategy, routines, and culture and prescribed practices, they create self-reinforcing loop of value creation and guide future organizational development.

REFERENCES

Ahuja, G., & Lampert, C. (2001). Entrepreneurship in the large corporation: A longitudinal study of how established firms create breakthrough inventions. *Strategic Management Journal*, *22*, 521–543. doi:10.1002/smj.176 doi:10.1002/smj.176

Amabile, T. M. (1983). *The social psychology of creativity*. New York, NY: Springer-Verlag. doi:10.1007/978-1-4612-5533-8doi:10.1007/978-1-4612-5533-8

Amabile, T. M. (1988). A model of creativity and innovation in organizations. In B. M. Staw & L. Cummings (Eds.), *Research in Organizational Behavior* (Vol. 10). Greenwich, CT: JAI Press.

Amabile, T. M. (1993). Motivational synergy: Toward new conceptualization of intrinsic and extrinsic motivation in the workplace. *Human Resource Management Review*, *3*(3), 185–201. doi:10.1016/1053-4822(93)90012-S doi:10.1016/1053-4822(93)90012-S

Amabile, T. M. (1996). *Creativity in context*. Oxford, UK: Westview.

Amabile, T. M., Conti, R., Coon, H., Lazenby, J., & Herron, M. (1996). Assessing the work environment for creativity. *Academy of Management Journal*, *39*, 1154–1184. doi:10.2307/256995 doi:10.2307/256995

Amabile, T. M., Schatzel, E. A., Moneta, G. B., & Kramer, S. J. (2004). Leader behaviors and the work environment for creativity: Perceived leader support. *The Leadership Quarterly*, *15*(1), 5–32. doi:10.1016/j.leaqua.2003.12.003 doi:10.1016/j.leaqua.2003.12.003

Amidon, D. (1997). *Innovation strategy for the knowledge economy: The ken awakening*. Boston, MA: Butterworth-Heinemann.

Amidon, D. M. (2003). *The innovation superhighway*. Amsterdam, The Netherlands: Butterworth-Heinemann.

Audretsch, D. B. (2006). *Entrepreneurship, innovation and economic growth*. Northampton, MA: Edward Elgar Publishing Limited. doi:10.1093/acprof:oso/9780195183511.001.0001doi:10.1093/acprof:oso/9780195183511.001.0001

Auernhammer, K., Leslie, A., Neumann, M., & Lettice, F. (2003). Creation of innovation by knowledge management – A case study of a learning software organisation. In *Proceedings of WM 2003: Professionelles Wissesmanagement - Erfahrungen und Visionen*, (pp. 53-57). WM.

Barnett, H. G. (1953). *Innovation: The basis of cultural change*. New York, NY: McGraw-Hill.

Barron, F. (1988). Putting creativity to work. In R. J. Sternberg (Ed.), *The Nature of Creativity: Contemporary Psychological Perspectives*. New York, NY: Cambridge University Press.

Barron, F., & Harrington, D. (1981). Creativity, intelligence, and personality. *Annual Review of Psychology, 32*, 439–476. doi:10.1146/annurev. ps.32.020181.002255 doi:10.1146/annurev. ps.32.020181.002255

Bartlett, S. J. (2008). *The abnormal psychology of creativity and the pathology of normality.* Retrieved June 20, 2011, from http://www.mendeley. com/research/abnormal-psychology-creativity-pathology-normality/# Basadur, M., & Gelade, G. (2006). The role of knowledge management in the innovation process. *Creativity and Innovation Management, 15*(1), 45- 62.

Beckman, T. (1997). *A methodology for knowledge management.* Paper presented at the AI and Soft Computing Conference. Banff, Canada.

Berlyne, D. (1967). Arousal and reinforcement. In D. Levine (Ed.), *Nebraska Symposium on Motivation.* Lincoln, NE: University of Nebraska Press.

Boden, M. (1998). Creativity and artificial intelligence. *Artificial Intelligence, 103*(1-2), 347–356. doi:10.1016/S0004-3702(98)00055-1 doi:10.1016/S0004-3702(98)00055-1

Brown, J. S., & Duguid, P. (1998). Organizing knowledge. *California Management Review, 40*(3), 90–111.

Brown, S., & Eisenhardt, K. (1998). *Competing on the edge: Strategy as structured chaos.* Boston, MA: Harvard Business School Press.

Cabrilo, S. (2008). *Researching indicators of intellectual capital within organization.* Unpublished Doctorial Dissertation. Novi Sad, Serbia: University of Novi Sad.

Cabrilo, S. (2009). IC-based inter-industry variety in Serbia. In C. Stam & D. Andriessen (Eds.), *1st European Conference on Intellectual Capital,* (pp. 104-114). Haarlem, The Netherlands: Academic Publishing Limited.

Cabrilo, S., & Grubic-Nesic, L. (2010). A strategic model for intellectual capital reporting: Study of service industry in Serbia. In S. C. Serrano Fernandes Rodrigues (Ed.), *2nd European Conference on Intellectual Capital,* (pp. 161-170). Lisbon, Portugal: Academic Publishing Limited.

Carayanis, E. (1999). Fostering synergies between information technology and managerial and organizational cognition: The role of knowledge management. *Technovation, 19*, 219–231. doi:10.1016/S0166-4972(98)00101-1

Castells, M. (1996). *The rise of the network society: The information age: Economy, society and culture.* Oxford, UK: Blackwell.

Cavagnoli, D. (2011). A conceptual framework for innovation: An application to human resource management policies in Australia. *Innovation: Management. Policy & Practice, 13*(1), 111–125. doi:10.5172/impp.2011.13.1.111

Cavusgil, S., Calantone, R., & Zhao, Y. (2003). Tacit knowledge transfer and firm innovation capability. *Journal of Business and Industrial Marketing, 18*(1), 6–21. doi:10.1108/08858620310458615

Chesbrough, H. (2003). The new business logic of open innovation. *Strategy & Innovation, 1*(2), 11–15.

Christensen, C. (1997). *The innovators dilemma: When new technologies cause great firms to fail.* Boston, MA: Harvard Business School Press.

Chuang, L. (2005). An empirical study of the construction of measuring model for organizational innovation in Taiwanese high-tech enterprises. *The Journal of American Academy of Business, 9*(2), 299–304.

Cohen, W., & Levinthal, D. (1990). Absorptive capacity: A new perspective on learning and innovation. *Administrative Science Quarterly, 35*, 128–152. doi:10.2307/2393553

Collins, C., & Clerk, K. (2004). Strategic human resource practices, top management team social networks and firm performance: The role of human resource practices in creating organizational competitive advantage. *Academy of Management Journal, 46*, 740–751. doi:10.2307/30040665

Cooper, R. (1993). *Winning at new products: Accelerating the process from idea to launch.* Reading, MA: Perseus Books.

Csikszentmihalyi, M. (1988). Society, culture and person: A systems view of creativity. In R. J. Sternberg (Ed.), *The Nature of Creativity: Contemporary Psychological Perspectives.* New York, NY: Cambridge University Press.

Csikszentmihalyi, M. (1996). *Creativity: Flow and the psychology of discovery and invention.* New York, NY: Harper Perennial.

Csikszentmihalyi, M. (1998). *Finding flow: The psychology of engagement with everyday life.* New York, NY: Perseus Books Group.

Damanpour, F. (1990). Innovation effectiveness, adoption and organizational performance. In M. West & J. Farr (Eds.), *Innovation and Creativity at Work* (pp. 125–141). Chichester, UK: Wiley.

Damanpour, F., & Evan, W. M. (1984). Organizational innovation and performance: The problem of organizational lag. *Administrative Science Quarterly, 29*(3), 329–409. doi:10.2307/2393031

Damanpour, F., Szabat, K. A., & Evan, W. M. (1989). The relationship between types of innovation and organizational performance. *Journal of Management Studies, 26*(6), 587–601. doi:10.1111/j.1467-6486.1989.tb00746.x

Davenport, T., & Prusak, L. (1997). *Information ecology: Mastering the information and knowledge environment.* Oxford, UK: Oxford University Press.

Davenport, T., & Prusak, L. (1998). *Working knowledge: How organizations manage what they know.* Boston, MA: Harvard Business School Press.

deBono, E. (1976). *Lateral thinking for management.* New York, NY: American Management Association.

Deci, E., & Ryan, R. (1985). *Intrinsic motivation and self-determination in human behavior.* New York, NY: Plenum Press.

Dixon, N. (2000). *Common knowledge.* Boston, MA: Harvard Business School Press.

Drucker, P. (1993). *Post-capitalist society.* New York, NY: HarperCollins.

Edmonds, E., & Candy, L. (2002). Creativity, art practical and knowledge. *Communications of the ACM Special Sections on Creativity and Interface, 45*(10), 91–95.

Edvinsson, L. (1996). Developing a model for managing intellectual capital. *European Management Journal, 14*(4), 356–364. doi:10.1016/0263-2373(96)00022-9

Gardner, H. (1993). *Creating minds.* New York, NY: Basic Books.

Ghosh, T., Yates, J., & Orlikowski, W. J. (2004, October). *Using communication norms for coordination evidence from a distributed team.* Retrieved October 20, 2011, from http://seeit.mit.edu/Publications/Orlikowski_Comm_Coordination_8-05_REVISED.pdf

Gordon, W. (1956). Operational approach to creativity. *Harvard Business Review, 34*, 41–51.

Gordon, W. (1971). *The metaphorical way.* Cambridge, MA: Porpoise Books.

Grant, R. M. (1997). The knowledge-based view of the firm: Implications for management practice. *Long Range Planning, 30*(3), 450–454. doi:10.1016/S0024-6301(97)00025-3

Grubic-Nesic, L. (2005). *Razvoj ljudskih resursa.* [Development of human resources]. Novi Sad, Serbia: AB Print.

Gurteen, D. (1998). Knowledge, creativity and innovation. *Journal of Knowledge Management, 2*(1), 5–13. doi:10.1108/13673279810800744

Guthrie, J. (2001). High involvement practices, turnover and productivity. *Academy of Management Journal, 44,* 180–190. doi:10.2307/3069345

Hackman, J., & Oldham, G. (1980). *Work redesign.* Reading, MA: Addison-Wesley.

Hall, R., & Andriani, P. (2002). Managing knowledge for innovation. *Long Range Planning, 35,* 29–48. doi:10.1016/S0024-6301(02)00019-5

Hansen, M. T., Nohria, N., & Tierney, T. (1999, March-April). What's your strategy for managing knowledge? *Harvard Business Review,* 106–116.

Harrison, R., & Kessels, J. (2004). *Human resource development in a knowledge economy.* Basingstoke, UK: Palgrave Macmillan.

Hauschildt, J. (1993). *Innovationsmanagement.* München, Germany: Vahlen.

Hedlund, G. (1994, Spring). A model of knowledge management and the n-form corporation. *Strategic Management Journal,* 73–90.

Herzberg, F., Mausner, B., & Snyderman, B. (1959). *The motivation to work* (2nd ed.). New York, NY: Wiley.

Howells, J. (1996). Tacit knowledge, innovation and technology transfer. *Technology Analysis and Strategic Management, 8*(2), 91–106. doi:10.1080/09537329608524237

Hurley, R., & Hult, T. (1988). Innovation, market orientation, and organizational learning: An integration and empirical examination. *Journal of Marketing, 62,* 42–54. doi:10.2307/1251742

Imai, K. (1991). *Globalization and cross-border networks of Japanese firms.* Paper presented to Japan in a Global Economy Conference. Stockholm, Sweden.

Jackson, S. E., May, K. E., & Whitney, K. (1992). Understanding the dynamics of diversity in decision-making teams. In *Diversity in the Workplace: Human Resources Initiatives.* New York, NY: Guiford Press.

Jacobs, D. (1999). *The knowledge offensive: Smart competition in the knowledge economy.* Deventer, The Netherlands: Samson.

Kelly, G. A. (1955). *The psychology of personal constructs.* New York, NY: Norton.

Kessels, J. (1996). Knowledge productivity and the corporate curriculum. In J. Schreinemakers (Ed.), *Knowledge Management: Organization Competence and Methodology: Advances in Knowledge Management* (Vol. 1, pp. 168–174). Wurzburg, Germany: Ergon.

Kessels, J. (2001). Learning in organisations: A corporate curriculum for the knowledge economy. *Futures, 33,* 497–506. doi:10.1016/S0016-3287(00)00093-8

Kessler, I., & Purcell, J. (1992). Performance-related pay: Objectives and application. *Human Resource Management Journal, 2*(3), 16–33. doi:10.1111/j.1748-8583.1992.tb00258.x

King, W. R. (2006). Knowledge transfer. In D. G. Schwartz (Ed.), *Encyclopedia of Knowledge Management* (pp. 538–543). Hershey, PA: IGI Global. doi:10.4018/978-1-59140-573-3.ch-070doi:10.4018/978-1-59140-573-3.ch070

Kontic, L., & Cabrilo, S. (2009). A strategic model for measuring intellectual capital in Serbian industrial entreprises. *Economic Annals, 65*(183), 89–117. doi:10.2298/EKA0983089K

Kucza, T. (2001). *Knowlegde management process model*. Retrieved July 25, 2011, from http://www.vtt.fi/inf/pdf/publications/2001/P455.pdf

Laursen, K., & Foss, N. (2003). New human resource management practices, complementarities and the impact on innovation performance. *Cambridge Journal of Economics*, *27*, 243–263. doi:10.1093/cje/27.2.243

Leonard, D., & Sensiper, S. (1998). The role of tacit knowledge in group innovation. *California Management Review*, *40*(3), 112–125.

Leonard, D., & Sensiper, S. (2002). The role of tacit knowledge in group innovation. In N. Bontis & C. W. Choo (Eds.), *The Strategic Management of Intellectual Capital and Organizational Knowledge* (pp. 485–499). Oxford, UK: Oxford University Press. doi:10.1142/9789814295505_0013doi:10.1142/9789814295505_0013

Leonard-Barton, D. (1995). *Wellsprings of knowledge: Building and sustaining the sources of innovation*. Boston, MA: Harvard Business School Press.

Levitt, T. (1963, May-June). Creativity is not enough. *Harvard Business Review*, 3–10.

MacDuffie, J. (1995). Human resource bundles and manufacturing performance. *Industrial & Labor Relations Review*, *48*(2), 197–221. doi:10.2307/2524483

MacKinnon, D. (1971). Creativity and transliminal experience. *The Journal of Creative Behavior*, *5*, 227–241. doi:10.1002/j.2162-6057.1971.tb00893.x

McGrath, R. (2001). Exploratory learning, innovative capacity and managerial oversight. *Academy of Management Journal*, *44*, 118–131. doi:10.2307/3069340

Meeker, M. (1969). *The structure of intellect: Its interpretation and uses*. Columbus, OH: Charles E. Merrill Publishing Company.

Mouritsen, J., Bukh, P., Larsen, H., & Johansen, M. (2002). Developing and managing knowledge through intellectual capital statements. *Journal of Intellectual Capital*, *3*(1), 10–29. doi:10.1108/14691930210412818

Nahapiet, J., & Ghoshal, S. (1998). Social capital, intellectual capital and the organizational advantage. *Academy of Management Review*, *23*, 242–266.

Nonaka, I. (1991, November-December). The knowledge creating company. *Harvard Business Review*, 96–104.

Nonaka, I. (1994). A dynamic theory of organizational knowledge creation. *Organization Science*, *5*(1), 14–37. doi:10.1287/orsc.5.1.14

Nonaka, I., & Konno, N. (1998). The concept of "ba". *California Management Review*, *40*(3), 40–54.

Nonaka, I., & Takeuchi, H. (1995). *The knowledge creating company: How Japanese companies create the dynamics of innovation*. Oxford, UK: Oxford University Press.

Nonaka, I., Toyama, R., & Konno, N. (2000). SECI, ba and leadership: A unified model of dynamic knowledge creation. *Long Range Planning*, *33*(4), 4–34.

Oldham, G. R., & Cummings, A. (1996). Employee creativity: Personal and contextual factors at work. *Academy of Management Journal*, *39*(3), 607–634. doi:10.2307/256657

Osborn, A. (1953). *Applied imagination*. New York, NY: Charles Scribner.

Pfeffer, J. (1998). Six dangerous myths about pay. *Harvard Business Review*, *76*(3), 108–119.

Polanyi, M. (1966). *The tacit dimension*. New York, NY: Doubleday.

Probst, G., Raub, S., & Romhardt, K. (1999). *Wissen managen: Wie unternehmen ihre wertvollste ressource optimal nutzen*. Frankfurt, Germany: FAZ.

Quinn, J. B., Anderson, P., & Finkelstein, S. (1996). Managing professional intellect: Making the most of the best. *Harvard Business Review*, *74*(2), 71–80.

Rank, J., Pace, V. L., & Frese, M. (2004). Three avenues for future research on creativity, innovation, and initiative. *Applied Psychology: An International Review*, *53*, 518–528. doi:10.1111/j.1464-0597.2004.00185.x

Reber, A. (1989). Implicit learning and tacit knowledge. *Journal of Experimental Psychology*, *118*(3), 219–235.

Rüdiger, M., & Vanini, S. (1998). Das tacit knowledge phänomen und seine implikationen für das innovationsmanagement. *DBW*, *58*(4), 467–480.

Scarbrough, H. (2003). Knowledge management, HRM and the innovation process. *International Journal of Manpower*, *24*(5), 501–516. doi:10.1108/01437720310491053

Schoonhoven, C., Eisenhardt, K., & Lyman, K. (1990). Speeding products to market: Waiting time to first product introduction in new firms. *Administrative Science Quarterly*, *35*, 177–207. doi:10.2307/2393555

Seidler-de Alwis, R., Hartmann, E., & Gemünden, H. (2004). *The role of tacit knowledge in innovation management*. Competitive Paper submitted to the 20th Annual IMP Conference. Copenhagen, Denmark.

Senge, P. (1990). *The fifth discipline: The art nd practice of the learning organization*. New York, NY: Doubleday.

Shipton, H., Fay, D., West, M., Patterson, M., & Birdi, K. (2005). Managing peopple to promote innovation. *Creativity and Innovation Management*, *14*(2), 118–128. doi:10.1111/j.1467-8691.2005.00332.x

Smith, G. F. (1998). Idea-generation techniques: A formulary of active ingredients. *The Journal of Creative Behavior*, *32*(2), 107–133. doi:10.1002/j.2162-6057.1998.tb00810.x

Snowden, D. (1998). The ecology of a sustainable knowledge management program. *Knowledge Management*, *1*(6).

Song, J., Almeida, P., & Wu, G. (2003). Learning by hiring: When is mobility more likely to facilitate interfirm knowledge transfer? *Organization Science*, *49*, 351–365.

Spender, J. (1996). Competitive advantage from tacit knowledge? Unpacking the concept and its strategic implications. In B. Mosingeon & A. Edmondson (Eds.), *Organizational Learning and Competitive Advantage* (pp. 56–73). London, UK: Sage Publications. doi:10.4135/9781446250228.n4doi:10.4135/9781446250228.n4

Spring, M. (2003). Knowledge management in extended operations networks. *Journal of Knowledge Management*, *7*(4), 29–37. doi:10.1108/13673270310492921

Stam, C. (2007). *Knowledge productivity: Designing and testing a method to diagnose knowledge productivity and plan for enhancement*. Haarlem, The Netherlands: Christiaan Stam.

Starovic, D., & Marr, B. (2003). *Understanding corporate value: Managing and reporting intellectual capital*. London, UK: Chartered Institute of Management Accountants.

Sternberg, R., & Lubart, T. (1995). *Defying the crowd*. New York, NY: Free Press.

Sternberg, R., & Lubart, T. (1996). Investing in creativity. *The American Psychologist, 51*(7), 677–688. doi:10.1037/0003-066X.51.7.677

Sternberg, R. J. (2006). The nature of creativity. *Creativity Research Journal, 18*(1), 87–98. doi:10.1207/s15326934crj1801_10

Sternberg, R. J., & Lubart, T. I. (1991). An investment theory of creativity and its development. *Human Development, 34*(1), 1–31. doi:10.1159/000277029

Stewart, T. (1997). *Intellectual capital: The new wealth of organizations*. New York, NY: DoubleDay.

Stover, M. (2004). Making tacit knowledge explicit. *RSR. Reference Services Review, 32*(2), 164–173. doi:10.1108/00907320410537685

Sveiby, K. (1997). *The new organizational wealth: Managing and measuring knowledge-based assets*. San Francisco, CA: Berrett-Koehler.

Taylor, C. (1975). *Perspectives on creativity.* Chicago, IL: Aldine.

Tidd, J., Bessant, J., & Pavitt, K. (1997). *Managing Innovation: Integrating technological, market and organisational change*. Chichester, UK: John Wiley and Sons Ltd.

Trott, P. (1998). *Innovation management and new product development*. Harlow, UK: Pearson Education.

Tsai, W. (2001). Knowledge transfer in intraorganizational networks: Effects of network position and absorptive capacity on business unit innovation and performance. *Academy of Management Journal, 44*, 996–1004. doi:10.2307/3069443

Wallas, G. (1926). *The art of thought*. New York, NY: Harcourt.

Wang, S., & Noe, R. (2010). Knowledge sharing: A review and direction for future research. *Human Resource Management Review, 20*, 115–131. doi:10.1016/j.hrmr.2009.10.001

WB. (2010). *Innovation policy: A guide for developing countries*. Washington, DC: The World Bank.

Weggeman, M. (1997). *Knowledge management: Design and management of knowledge intensive organizations*. Schiedam, The Netherlands: Scriptum.

Weggeman, M. (2000). *Knowledge management in practice*. Schiedam, The Netherlands: Scriptum.

Weick, K., & Roberts, K. (1993). Collective mind in organizations: Heedful interrelating on flight decks. *Administrative Science Quarterly, 38*(3), 357–381. doi:10.2307/2393372

Weisberg, R. (1999). Creativity and knowledge: A challenge to theories. In R. Sternberg (Ed.), *Handbook of Creativity* (pp. 226–250). Cambridge, UK: Cambridge University Press.

West, M., & Farr, J. (1990). *Innovation and creativity at work: Psychologocal and organizational strategies*. Chichester, UK: John Wiley.

West, M., Hirst, G., Richter, A., & Shipton, H. (2004). Twelve steps to heaven: Successfully managing change through developing innovative teams. *European Journal of Work and Organizational Psychology, 13*, 269–299. doi:10.1080/13594320444000092

White, R. (1959). Motivation reconsidered: The concept of competence. *Psychological Review, 66*(5), 297–333. doi:10.1037/h0040934

Wickramasinghe, N. (2006). Knowledge creation. In D. G. Schwartz (Ed.), *Encyclopedia of Knowledge Management* (pp. 326–335). Hershey, PA: IGI Global. doi:10.4018/978-1-59140-573-3.ch043doi:10.4018/978-1-59140-573-3.ch043

Wiig, K. (1993). *Knowledge management foundations—Thinking about thinking - How people and organizations create, represent, and use knowledge*. Arlington, TX: Schema Press.

Wood, S. (1996). High commitment management and payment systems. *Journal of Management Studies, 33*, 53–77. doi:10.1111/j.1467-6486.1996. tb00798.x

Woodman, R., Sawyer, R., & Griffin, W. (1993). Toward a theory of organizational creativity. *Academy of Management Review, 18*(2), 293–321.

Yusuf, S. (2009). From creativity to innovation. *Technology in Society, 31*(1), 1–8. doi:10.1016/j. techsoc.2008.10.007

Zhang, X. M., & Bartol, K. M. (2010). Linking empowering leadership and employee creativity: The influence of psychological empowerment, intrinsic motivation, and creative process engagement. *Academy of Management Journal, 53*(1), 107–128. doi:10.5465/AMJ.2010.48037118

ADDITIONAL READING

Adenfelt, M., & Lagerstrom, K. (2006). Knowledge development and sharing in multinational corporations: The case of a centre of exellence and a transnational team. *International Business Review, 15*, 381–400. doi:10.1016/j.ibusrev.2006.05.002

Becerra-Fernandez, I., & Sabherwal, R. (2008). Individual, group, and organizational learning: A knowledge management perspective. In I. Becerra-Fernandez & D. Leidner (Eds.), *Knowledge Management: An Evolutionary View* (pp. 13–39). Armonk, NY: M.E. Sharpe, Inc.

Boer, N., Berends, H., & Baalen, P. (2011). Relational models for knowledge sharing behavior. *European Management Journal, 29*, 85–97. doi:10.1016/j.emj.2010.10.009

Chang, H., & Chuang, S. (2011). Social capital and individual motivations on knowledge sharing: Participant involvement as a moderator. *Information & Management, 48*, 9–18. doi:10.1016/j. im.2010.11.001

Hautala, J. (2011). International academic knowledge creation and ba: A case study from Finland. *Knowledge Management Research & Practice, 9*, 1–16. doi:10.1057/kmrp.2010.23

Jones, M., Cline, M., & Ryan, S. (2006). Exploring knowledge sharing in ERP implementation: An organizational culture framework. *Decision Support Systems, 41*, 411–434. doi:10.1016/j. dss.2004.06.017

King, W., & Marks, P. (2008). Motivating knowledge sharing though a knowledge management system. *The international Journal of Management Science, 36*, 131-146.

Koskinen, K., Pihlanto, P., & Vanharanta, H. (2003). Tacit knowledge acquisition and sharing in a project work context. *International Journal of Project Management, 21*, 281–290. doi:10.1016/ S0263-7863(02)00030-3

Leidner, D. E., & Kayworth, T. R. (2008). Knowledge management and organizational culture. In I. Becerra-Fernandez & D. Leidner (Eds.), *Knowledge Management: An Evolutionary View* (pp. 40–60). Armonk, NY: M.E. Sharpe, Inc.

Lin, W. (2008). The exploration factors of affecting knowledge sharing-The case of Taiwan's high-tech industry. *Expert Systems with Applications, 35*, 661–676. doi:10.1016/j.eswa.2007.07.038

Liu, M., & Liu, N. (2008). Sources of knowledge acquisition and patterns of knowledge-sharing behaviors: An empirical study of Taiwanese high-tech firms. *International Journal of Information Management, 28*, 423–432. doi:10.1016/j. ijinfomgt.2008.01.005

Michailova, S., & Minbaeva, D. B. (2012). Organizational values and knowledge sharing in multinational corporations: The Danisco case. *International Business Review*, *21*(1), 59–70. doi:10.1016/j.ibusrev.2010.11.006

Mitchell, W. J., Inouye, A. S., & Blumenthal, M. S. (2003). *Beyond productivity: Information, technology, innovation, and creativity*. Washington, DC: National Academies Press.

Rahimi, H., Arbabisarjou, A., Allameh, S., & Aghababaei, A. (2011). Relationship between knowledge management process and creativity among faculty members in the university. *Interdisciplinary Journal of Information. Knowledge and Management*, *6*, 1–17.

Schwartz, D. G. (2006). *Encyclopedia of knowledge management*. Hershey, PA: IGI Global.

Wang, S., & Noe, R. (2010). Knowledge sharing: A review and direction for future research. *Human Resource Management Review*, *20*, 115–131. doi:10.1016/j.hrmr.2009.10.001

Yang, J. (2007). Knowledge sharing: Investigating appropriate leadership roles and collaborative culture. *Tourism Management*, *28*, 530–543. doi:10.1016/j.tourman.2006.08.006

KEY TERMS AND DEFINITIONS

Knowledge: A deterministic and dynamic process that requires variety of perceptive, cognitive, and analytical abilities, memorizing and comprehending capacities. It includes the ability to enable action. Knowledge is linked to meaningful behavior having tacit elements born from experience.

Knowledge Management (KM): Represents deliberate initiatives aiming to stimulate knowledge processes in order to support and foster creativity, invention and innovation. As the set of knowledge processes, KM encompasses knowledge identification, knowledge generation (creation and acquisition), knowledge codification, knowledge storage, knowledge sharing, and knowledge application. These processes form the KM cycle although they do not always occur in a linear sequence.

Innovation: Successful dissemination and implementation of a new idea. It is a process of taking of new or existing ideas and putting them into action. Since it is impossible to innovate only by application of existing knowledge, creativity in knowledge processes, especially in the creation of new knowledge is the driving force of innovation.

Innovation Management: Aimed to create the conditions for a continuous flow of knowledge, creativity and invention in order to use creative efforts to introduce new ideas, processes, products or services.

Creative Knowledge Sharing: Essential for improvement of creative thinking. Creativity in knowledge sharing has a positive impact on the participants' openness to new and different ideas.

Creative Perception: Involves an individual's ability to perceive reality in different ways. It is manifested by different perceptions of the same phenomenon. Creative perception is the prerequisite of creativity.

Creative Thinking Environment: An environment in which individuals are stimulated to break old and out-dated paradigms and replace them with new and better ones. It supports creative thinking and behaviour and facilitates the knowledge management process in general, and the distinct knowledge processes in particular.

Motivating Communication: Communication full of positive emotions, trust, respect, tolerance, and openness. It contributes to group creativity.

Chapter 12
Educating and Training Organizational Knowledge Workers in Evaluating and Managing Intangible and Knowledge–Based Assets in the Knowledge Economy

Ezra Ondari-Okemwa
University of Fort Hare, South Africa

ABSTRACT

This chapter discusses the importance of training workers about the intangible assets in a knowledge economy, the nature of intangible assets, how they are different from other assets, and the concepts of a knowledge workforce in a knowledge economy. It is apparent that many organizations are engaging the services of knowledge workers, but such organizations do not provide enabling environments for these workers to be fully productive. This chapter looks at the relevance of training knowledge workers in identifying intangible assets for creating value and enhancing competitiveness and innovation in a knowledge economy. Given that it has always been difficult to gather the prerequisite information to manage such assets and create value from them, the chapter discusses the nature of intangible assets, the characteristics of a knowledge economy, and the role of knowledge workers in a knowledge economy. Training and education of knowledge workers must not be taken for granted. The chapter also discusses how training and education of knowledge workers may enhance their ability in identifying intangible assets in relation to capturing the value of such assets, the transfer of intangible assets to other owners, and the challenges of managing organizational intangible assets. In a knowledge economy, knowledge workers play a central role in managing and evaluating intangible and knowledge-based assets.

DOI: 10.4018/978-1-4666-1969-2.ch012

INTRODUCTION

With the rapid transition to the knowledge economy, workers categorized as knowledge workers are increasingly assuming crucial roles. In the knowledge economy, knowledge workers constitute an important part of a firm's intangible assets and form key sources of competitive advantages. Many are those who work as knowledge workers but have not been specifically trained as knowledge workers. The central issue is how organizations may develop appropriate training and education programmes and strategies for knowledge workers so as to attract and retain them, maximize their performance, and therefore enhance the intellectual capital of profit and nonprofit organizations in the knowledge economy. The section which follows discusses the concept of a "knowledge economy" and how such an economy differs from other economies such the industrial economy and the agricultural economy.

The Concept of a Knowledge Economy

What constitutes a "knowledge economy" and how different is it from other types of economies? The "knowledge economy" is a recent phrase in management literature that denotes the importance of knowledge management in economic growth and sustainability. To understand why knowledge management has grown in importance in recent years, it is necessary to look at the economic context within which it is developing (Morrow, 2001). The knowledge economy involves consideration of networked economy and the role of information and knowledge in economic performance. According to Morrow, networked and/or knowledge economy share common themes: (1) that developments in technology, especially information and communication technologies, are altering the economic bases of, at least developed countries; (2) that the key industries in this new economy are knowledge-intensive and heavily dependent

on knowledge workers; (3) as a consequence of globalization, competitive advantage between nations rests on the extent to which they can develop their knowledge industries and knowledge workers; and (4) that the knowledge component of all industries is increasing and value added comes from the substitution of physical resources for intangibles.

Davenport and Prusak (1998) emphasize that production of ideas and not goods is the source of economic growth. Morrow (2001) credits technology with facilitating growth in that it allows ideas in the form of techniques, research results, protocols, etc. to be globally distributed. Technology has also enabled industries to globalize and relocate to take advantage of low-cost, low-skilled labour elsewhere, while still coordinating and controlling operations from home base. Technology has further facilitated the development of a new range of industries based primarily on the production of information and knowledge.

Skyrme (1999) identifies some characteristics of a knowledge economy: every industry is becoming more knowledge intensive; industries are using knowledge to produce "smart products and services" which command premium prices; the market value of most business organizations is several times higher than the value of their physical assets as recorded in their balance sheets; and that trade in intangibles has come to mean that there is a growing range of intangibles that are traded in their own right.

Tissen, Andriessen, and Deprez (1998) identify certain signs of the presence of a knowledge economy as:

- Growth of technology-driven companies, with a major knowledge component are outgrowing almost every other company
- Many traditionally industrial companies—those designed and built to produce physical products—are being forced to knowledge products and services

- Knowledge workers are becoming the dominant factor in the Knowledge Economy, just as farmers were the dominant factor in the agricultural age, and as workers were in the industrial age
- The increase in complexity has resulted in a growing need for specialization and this trend will only increase because the knowledge sector is where the jobs are
- Employment opportunities in other sectors are decreasing in line with the increase in knowledge services
- Industrial-based economies are declining and in many countries, services are providing a significantly larger share of GNP (Tissen, Andriessen, & Deprez, 1998).

In a knowledge economy, the question should not be whether knowledge-based and intangible assets are tradable. Instead, the question should be how to identify knowledge-based and intangible assets for purposes of trade, measurement of value and management of such assets.

In the knowledge economy, many organizations are now realizing that their knowledge-based and intangible assets can generate wealth and profits. Knowledge-based and intangible assets may have been there since the beginning of human civilization, but it has always been difficult if not impossible to gather the prerequisite information to manage and value such assets. Intangible assets are those assets that are of value but cannot be physically touched such as brand, franchise, trademark, patents, copyrights, goodwill, and various types of permits. Such assets are non-monetary, created through time and/or effort, and can be identified as separate assets. Such assets can be categorized into legal and competitive intangibles. Legal intangibles are known under the generic term of 'intellectual property' and are responsible for generating legal property rights capable of defense in a court of law. Competitive intangibles may not be owned but directly impact on effectiveness, productivity, wastage,

and opportunity costs within an organization, hence, also impacting on costs, revenues, quality of customer service, satisfaction, market value and share price. In a knowledge economy, intangible assets form a significant portion of organizational assets. However, managing and valuing intangible assets may not be as straightforward as managing other organizational assets. Majority of employees in many organizations are trained in how to manage human, financial, and other tangible organizational assets but not intangible assets. This chapter therefore looks at how education and training may equip knowledge workers with a range of skills required for managing and valuing of organizational intangible assets in a knowledge economy. Training of knowledge workers is seen as a way of enabling such workers to improve an organization's performance.

Andreou, Green, and Stankosky (2007) argue that intangible assets have been identified as the most critical resource of today's business enterprise even though most business organizations are not in a position to clearly define this business driver. Very few businesses organizations, if any, have any known definition of what an intangible asset is or the best approach of valuing and/or managing intangible assets. Because of their immense importance to business organizations and their increasing importance to non-business organizations, intangibles and knowledge-based assets need to be identified for purposes of valuing and management. It is the contention of Von Krogh *et al.* (1998) that intangibles are significant factors in value creation within the business enterprise and should be managed like the traditional factors of labour, capital, and raw materials. Sullivan (1998) thinks that successful management of intangible assets within a business is likely to affect the performance and market valuation of a business enterprise. Yet, there is no evidence that intangible and knowledge-based assets are being managed like the traditional factors of labour, capital, and raw materials. Very few business and non-profit organizations have established positions specifically charged with managing intangible and knowledge-based assets. The nature of the global economy has changed so much that Teece (2000) argues that fundamental changes have been wrought in the global economy, which are continuously changing the basis of firm level competitive advantage, together with the functions of management. Because of the changes, which have been wrought on the global economy, business and non-profit organizations should look beyond managing the traditional factors of production. Hall (1992, 1993) established that many Chief Executive Officers (CEOs) believe that the three most important intangible (off-balance sheet) resources are Reputation, Employee Know-How, and Organizational Culture. In the emerging knowledge economy, both profit-making and non-profit organizations should device managerial techniques specifically meant for managing intangible and knowledge-based assets.

This chapter has the following objectives:

- Underscoring the importance of training knowledge workers in identifying intangible assets in a knowledge economy
- Examine how to determine the performance of intangible assets in a knowledge economy.

The section, which follows hereunder, discusses workers who have come to be known as "knowledge workers" in the knowledge economy.

KNOWLEDGE WORKERS

In a knowledge economy, one might want to ask the question of "who are knowledge workers and how are they different from other workers?" Because the central issue here is training, one may ask another question: "what kind of training and education do knowledge workers require so as to be productive?" In the knowledge economy,

there is a category of workers who have come to be identified as "knowledge workers." Who are the knowledge workers and what is the nature of their work? Gurteen (2006) defines knowledge workers thus:

Knowledge workers are those people who have taken responsibility for their work lives. They continually strive to understand the world about them and modify their work practices and behaviours to better meet their personal and organisational objectives. No one tells them what to do. They do not take 'no' for an answer. They are self-motivated.

Gurteen (2006) outlines the characteristics of knowledge workers as people who take responsibility for their work; workers, whom cannot be coerced; they cannot be bribed, manipulated, or rewarded; no amount of money or fancy technology may 'incentivize' knowledge workers to do a better job; knowledge workers see the benefits of working differently for themselves; and they are not 'wage slaves'—they take responsibility for their work and drive improvement.

Kumar (2004) defines a knowledge worker:

A knowledge worker is the one who creates new ideas, or is engaged in communicating or disseminating knowledge or uses knowledge as a resource. These individuals create new ideas and are involved in research and development (popularly known as R&D). They are actively associated with innovations and knowledge advancements. Those who disseminate knowledge are teachers, trainers and consultants. The other categories of workers using knowledge as a resource of value creation are IT professionals who create software programs. Thus, the common thread running through all these individuals is that all of them deal with data (information) and ideas. This group of knowledge workers is ever increasing, both in numerical strength and job varieties (Kumar, 2004, p. 18).

In a knowledge economy, more and more work is knowledge-based (Drucker, 1993). Drucker argues that even manufacturing jobs in a knowledge economy require professional expertise and mastery of a large body of knowledge. Most workers in the knowledge economy in effect are knowledge workers. This same trend towards more knowledge workers is present in service industries, not-for-profits organizations and in government. Drucker suggests that one-third of all jobs in a knowledge economy are filled by the highly productive group he calls knowledge workers.

Knowledge work involves information gathering, imagination, experiment, discovery, and integration of new knowledge with larger systems (Myers, 1996). Given this nature of knowledge work, Myers argues that bosses cannot order about knowledge workers like the ditch diggers or assembly-line bolt turners of yore. Myers further contends that if knowledge workers are any good at all, they soon learn more about what they are doing on a specific project than their bosses can. Knowledge work inherently has a large component of self-direction and team and may be hampered by remote control from distant bosses. As we move further into the knowledge economy and beyond bureaucracy, ways should be found to organize in such a way that all work is knowledge-based, bringing everyone's native intelligence and collaborative abilities to bear on constantly changing ways of achieving shared goals.

In order to be effective in identifying and managing knowledge-based and intangible assets in a knowledge economy, knowledge workers need to have an understanding of the nature of knowledge-based and intangible assets. The following section discusses the nature of knowledge-based and intangible assets in the knowledge economy.

THE NATURE OF KNOWLEDGE-BASED AND INTANGIBLE ASSETS

Knowledge workers need to have an understanding of the nature of knowledge-based and intangible assets and how the performance of such assets is assessed. It is not unusual to evaluate an organization's performance and success by considering only its tangible financial assets such as market value and share and net book value. There is however another very important "hidden" component known as the intangible value that does not appear on many organizations' balance sheets. The Intangible Value of an organization is the difference between its market value (share price multiplied by the number of shares issued) and its Net Book Value (recorded value of all tangible assets). The intangible value is rarely lower than 50% of the market value and in larger quoted companies, it is frequently much higher. Microsoft's intangible value is said to be well over of 85% of its market value while Nokia's intangible value is in excess of 90% of its market value.

Given that majority of companies only manage what is measureable—that is the tangible values, it is patently clear that not identifying, understanding, and managing intangible values constitutes a major corporate "blind spot" that may have far reaching economic implications. With companies such as Ford whose intangible assets are in the region of 35 billion US dollars, even a 1% loss through poor intangible value management constitutes a significant loss for shareholders. On the other hand, a 1% gain through efficient intangible value management represents substantial shareholder profits.

A growing body of research is providing conclusive evidence that an intangible value management programme is the most important and significant enterprise-wide intervention any organization can undertake. In a knowledge economy, a company's ability to flourish depends on its capacity to create, develop, and integrate the full spectrum of its intangibles. When intangibles are not properly identified, accounted for and managed, they get diluted and dissipated within the system in much the same way that untrained eyes overlook diamonds in the rough.

The United Kingdom's Department of Trade and Industry (DTI) (2001) published a document titled "Creating Value from your Intangible Assets," which identified seven key intangible assets as:

- **Relationships:** A company may only hope to achieve its full potential by developing an effective strategy for managing and maintaining excellent relationships with both its external and internal customers.
- **Knowledge:** It is essential for an organization to continuously expand its knowledge base and also make sure that this knowledge is shared and used effectively throughout the organization. Explicit knowledge can be written down and easily replicated and copied. Tacit knowledge on the other hand is held in the minds and hearts of individuals and is shared through stories, dialogues, and gatherings.
- **Leadership and Communication:** Clear goals and strategies must be embedded throughout the organization and this is only possible through strong and visionary leadership and effective and authentic communication. Good leadership involves responding to change by encouraging new innovative thinking that seeks a sustainable future rather than seeking to sustain the past.
- **Culture and Values:** These contribute to the quality of the workplace environment, the care for each other, and the tangible assets, the happiness, safety, openness, cooperation, teamwork, empathy, and other important human dynamics. These contribute to ensuring the continual health and maintenance of these values and also recognizing that different groups have different cultures that need to be integrated and managed, is essential for optimal functioning.
- **Reputation and Trust:** while these may be influenced by tangible assets, location of property or intellectual property, in the long run, things such as empathy with needs, reliability, responsiveness, friendliness and quality sustain image, brand, trust and reputation. Issues, which could damage these key intangible assets, need to be continually monitored and steps taken to reduce the risks as far as possible.
- **Skills and Competencies:** It is not sufficient to only know about things, to possess the tangible facilities or to own the intellectual property. What is needed is the talent to make use of resources to create value for the organization. Core competencies are identified as the ability to seize opportunities at the right time and to be innovative in order to create value for all concerned. The importance of creating the space and opportunity for everyone to continuously learn both individually and collectively cannot be overemphasized.
- **Processes and Systems:** It is important to consider in a balanced fashion not only how to do things but also to consider the implications of the way in which things are done. Investing in systems is primarily about improving efficiency, but simply putting a system into place will not fix a broken process. Processes must be sorted out first and then systems introduced to automate them.

The reporting of intangible value in UK companies has been strongly recommended for implementation. The primary purpose of the Operating and Financial Review (OFR) would be to provide greater transparency and to improve the quality, usefulness, and relevance of information that is provided by quoted companies. This would enable shareholders to exercise effective and responsible control.

The seven areas outlined above comprise the intangible raw materials that talented people use to collaborate with each other in order to achieve goals, solve problems, seize opportunities, and unlock their full potential. Since all organizations have a diverse mix of assets, both tangible and intangible, there is no simple formula that will fit all circumstances. What is clear however is that these seven areas require investment, maintenance, and management in a strategic and forward-looking way in order to yield new areas of business ventures and profit.

In the opinion of Andreou, Green, and Stankosky (2007), intangible assets have been identified as the most critical resource of today's business enterprise even though most business organizations are not in a position to clearly define this business driver. The management of intangible assets can be tricky because as yet, there is not a universally accepted method of measuring their value. Flignor and Orozco (2012) cite Sir William Thompson, Lord Kelvin (1824-1907) as saying, "When you measure what you are speaking about and express it in numbers, you know something about it, but when you cannot (or do not) measure it, when you cannot (or do not) express it in numbers, then your knowledge is of a meager and unsatisfactory kind." Intangible assets are said to refer to knowledge and skills (people's know-how) largely stored in the mind of men (Nelson & Winter, 1982; Itami, 1984) which cannot be easily codified or even transferred to other agents. This is because such assets are considered to have an important tacit component (Polanyi, 1958; Lazaric & Marengo, 2000).

In addition to the above characteristics of intangible assets, Diefenbach (2006) identifies a rather unique characteristic of intangible resources—the stock of intangible resources can increase while being used. For example, to use knowledge in a conversation and further it as information to another person leads often to the result

that the amount (and/or the quality) of knowledge has increased—probably for both parties. This characteristic—a (possible) increase while being used—might be seen as "the" decisive criterion of demarcation against tangible assets. Taking the general idea and all three criteria together, Diefenbach defines intangible resources as:

An intangible resource is everything of immaterial existence, which is used or potentially usable for whatever purpose, which is renewable after use, and which not only decreases, but can remain or increase in quantity and/or quality while being used. (Diefenbach, 2006, p. 409)

A Swedish financial services company by the name of Skandia AFS is reputed to be one of the first to report "intangibles" as business assets. In 1995, a supplement to the company's annual report used for the first time the word "IC," instead of the accounting term "intangible assets" (Edvinsson & Malone, 1997). The Skandia Value Scheme which is shown in Figure 1 was developed by Edvinsson in 1993. It interprets the market value of a firm as comprising the financial capital (inclusive of all tangible assets) and the IC (non-financial value). It further divides IC into Structural Capital (SC) and Human Capital (HC). SC includes customer and organizational capital that relates to the external and the internal focus of SC. CC represents the external focus of the company and is a valuation of the customer relationships. Organizational capital consists of innovation and process capital. Process capital represents the know-how (for example, manuals and best practices) in the company. Innovation capital is that which creates success in the future and includes intellectual assets and intellectual property, both of which are intangible.

Another approach towards classifying organizational resources is the one adopted by Haanes and Lowendahl (1997). This approach classifies an organization's resources into tangible and intangible resources as shown in Figure 2. Intan-

Figure 1. The Skandia value scheme

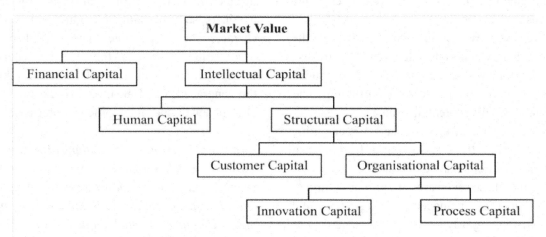

Source: Edvinsson and Malone (1997, p. 52)

gible resources are the Intellectual Capital (IC) of an organization, which are further categorized into competence and relational resources. Competence is viewed as the ability to perform a given task. Competence exists at two levels – individual (knowledge, skills, aptitude, or capa-

bilities) and organizational (information-based elements like databases, technology, and procedures). Relational resource refers to the reputation of the company, client loyalty and the relationships it has with customers. Lowendahl (1997) further divides the competence and relational categories

Figure 2. Haanes and Lowendahl model of organizational resources

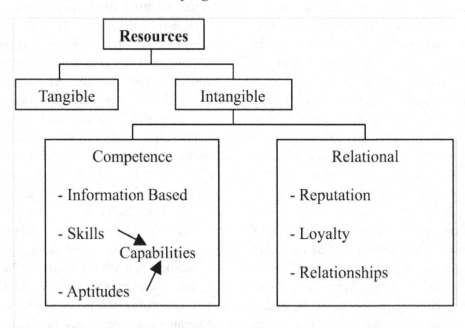

Source: Haanes and Lowendahl (1997)

into two subgroups, Individual and Collective, depending on whether the resource is employee or organizationally focused as shown in Figure 3. This added division distinguishes between IC that is people-dependent and IC that is organizational-dependent.

In categorizing organizational resources, Stewart (1997) uses a different conceptual scheme and divides Intellectual Capital (IC) into three basic forms: Human Capital (HC), Structural Capital (SC), and Customer Capital (CC). Human capital is the accumulated capabilities of individuals charged with providing customer solutions. Structural capital refers to the capabilities of the organization to meet market requirements. Unlike human capital, structural capital can be formally captured and embedded. Customer capital points to the extent and intensity of the organization's relationships with customers. The three types are interrelated—each one positively or negatively affecting the other. Figure 3 shows the components of intellectual capital espoused by Stewart.

Rodgers (2003) has divided knowledge-based assets into three categories:

1. **Human:** Attitudes, perceptions, and abilities of employees; and their motivation, commitment and adaptability to the organization. This is the knowledge that each individual has and is capable of generating. Human capital is essential in that it is the source of innovation and renewal, whether from

brainstorming activities or a list of quality suppliers. Areas that are key to managing human capital include:

a. Building an inventory of employee competencies
b. Developing a system to transfer the needed knowledge, skill, or intellectual addition when required
c. Acquiring an evaluation and reward system anchored to the acquisition and application of competency that aligns with the organization's objectives

2. **Organizational:** Intellectual properties such as brands, copyrights, patents, and trademarks; and infrastructures including culture, and process capability. Organizational (structural) capital also includes knowledge that has been captured/institutionalized within the structure, processes, and culture of an organization. Sharing and transporting knowledge needs structural intellectual assets such as distribution channels, communication systems, laboratories, competitive and market channels, which turn individual know-how into the property of the organization.

3. **Relational:** Knowledge of and acquaintance with communities, competitors, customers, governments, and suppliers in which the organization operates. It also provides the perception of value obtained by a customer from conducting business with a supplier of goods and/or services. Reputation capi-

Figure 3. Elements of intellectual capital

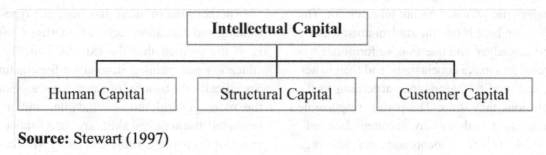

Source: Stewart (1997)

tal can be considered as part of relational knowledge-based assets. Reputation capital is dependent on the measures of the societal value that the organization puts back into the economy; partnering and joint venturing; the license to operate in society; reputation among customers; and shareholder value as influenced by an organization's ethics.

It is suggested that education and training for knowledge workers on identifying and managing intangible assets in a knowledge economy may help to capture the value of such assets. The following section discusses the differences between education and training as well as the specific areas in which knowledge workers should be educated and trained in.

TRAINING VS. EDUCATION

Training and education are terms, which are frequently used interchangeably even though they do not necessarily mean the same thing. Some aspects of training and educating may be similar, but the two are not quite the same. According to Carney (2003), training and education are not one and the same thing. Training seeks to impart a set of established facts and skills and to obtain a uniform predictable behavior from the trainees without the necessity of their understanding why they should act in a prescribed manner. Carney further argues that to a great extent, such learning is primarily passive and incorporates conditioned reflex action within a time constraint. Education, according to Carney, seeks to have the student learn skills and to understand why actions are taken or not. The implication here is that the student must learn to observe, analyze and question, to formulate hypotheses and make conclusions, and then to act, live, and modify their actions according to the conclusions they draw. The person responsible for educating students may accommodate individual talents in the students and even encourage

competition between them. This kind of learning is an active process. However, all education must include training especially in the acquisition of factual information. Training is built around rote memory, repetition, and conditioning reflexes ala Skinner. Education is built on the organization of knowledge, mastery of the detail and active analysis ala Socrates.

EFFECTS OF EDUCATION AND TRAINING

Can training and education have any effect on knowledge workers? According to the European Commission (2005), the importance of education and training in a lifelong learning perspective for the knowledge-based society and the achievement of the Lisbon goals increase the overall need for investment in human capital. Investing in human resources is indeed essential to increase employability, economic prosperity, and social welfare

Some studies have been carried out in a bid to explicitly measure the effects of education and training on an organization's productivity and have found consistent positive effects. A study conducted by Dearden *et al*. (2004) came to the conclusion that training has a significant effect on industrial productivity in a panel of British companies. Their estimations are that a five percent increase in training is associated with a four percentage point increase in productivity and a 1.6 percent increase in wages. This implies that research focusing exclusively on individual wages has underestimated the effect of training to a significant extent.

Another area of study has been the type of training and education received. Martins (2004) is of the opinion that the external benefits of education and training depend on their nature. Specifically, the benefits of education are greater, the more general, non-excludable, and non-reversible the acquired skills are. In a study of a panel of Portuguese firms and using Mincerian equations, Martins estimates firms' average real earnings returns of schooling at 14-23%, which are considerably larger than normal private returns estimates. More importantly, these returns are also considerably higher than social returns calculated in the conventional way. Martins also estimates Mincerian wage regressions and finds education increases wages at an average of 2-3% for less educated workers, confirming the existence of externalities at firm level.

Whereas education and training result in benefits to organizations, since the original research by Becker (1975), it has been argued that firms might be deterred from investing in the training of workers because of fear of them being poached by other companies. An organization may take advantage of gains in human capital generated by other organizations' investments without paying for its acquisition. In this context, an organization may only engage in training programmes in non-competitive labour markets where there is a low risk of workers drainage. In competitive labour markets with transferable and non-excludable skills, employers may elect to train fewer workers because of the projected risk of losing trained employees. Thus, public subsidies for worker training may be warranted because without government intervention the level of training would be below the social optimum. Despite these recent developments in the literature, the benefits of training and education to organizations are still relatively little understood. Although the weight of empirical evidence may suggest that education and training may result in higher wages for workers and higher productivity for organizations, further research is needed to establish the precise mechanism behind those effects and particularly on knowledge workers. Knowledge workers are identified by the kind of tasks they perform, but many organizations have not as yet specifically identified knowledge workers *per se*. However, productivity increases from education and training are implicitly recognized by organizations, which in many cases customarily pay for the training of their employees. It may hence be said that training of knowledge workers may increase the productivity of the organizations they work for. This chapter proposes specific areas in which organizations may need to train their knowledge workers. It may not be possible for an organization to train its knowledge workers in every area that is suggested herein but organizations do not lose anything by being aware of the suggested areas.

EDUCATION AND TRAINING ON IDENTIFYING POSSIBLE KNOWLEDGE-BASED ASSETS VALUATION METHODS

How to assess and measure the value of knowledge-based and intangible assets are issues debated in the available literature on knowledge-based and intangible assets management and it does not seem that methods and standards of assessing, measuring and valuing such assets have been agreed on. Measuring and valuing of knowledge-based and intangible assets management successes or failures are still challenges that organizational managers have to contend with. It has generally not been easy to assess, measure, and/or value knowledge-based and intangible assets. One unique characteristic of the knowledge-based and intangible assets is that they are governed by increasing returns, as opposed to the decreasing returns which are known to characterize the traditional resources of land, labour, and capital (Arthur, 1996).

Many organizations have no or little understanding of the value they derive from the investments they make in the management of knowledge-based and intangible assets (Ahmed, Lim, & Zairi, 1999). The reason for failing to derive any value from knowledge-based and intangible assets management investment is because many organizations fail to put in place tracking systems to measure progress in knowledge-based and intangible assets management, hence enforcing the case for measurement. According to Ahmed,

Lim, and Zairi (1999), the importance of measuring knowledge-based and intangible assets are derived from the following:

- One cannot manage what one cannot measure.
- It is important for organizations to determine what to pay attention to and improve.
- To provide a scorecard for people to monitor their own performance levels.
- To give an indication of the cost of poor implementation.
- To give a standard for making comparisons.
- To help efforts comply with organizational objectives.

Knowledge workers and managers need to understand how to evaluate intangible assets or knowledge-based assets so that they are in a position of communicating value to stakeholders (Edvinsson, 2000; Rodgers, 2003). The understanding may only be gained through education and training. Knowledge-based assets may be looked at as strategic resources, but the traditional accounting systems may still be having problems in determining the exact book value of such assets. Blair and Wallman (2001) suggest that knowledge-based and intangible assets may be defined as non-physical features that contribute to, or are used in, producing products, or rendering services, that are expected to generate future productive benefits for individuals or companies that control the use of those features.

It is important to identify knowledge-based and intangible assets, as they are invisible and intangible. Because of their nature, knowledge-based and intangible assets are not captured very well by any of the traditional measures, accounting or otherwise, that corporations master in their everyday operations (Bontis, et al., 1999; Hauser & Katz, 1998). Because of the nature of knowledge-based and intangible assets, Bontis *et al.* think that managers may run the risk of 'forgetting' that the knowledge-based and intangible assets are there.

Managers may also underestimate the value and contribution of knowledge-based and intangible assets of an organization. Decisions may thus be made which in the long-term might prove harmful and costly precisely because of the damage the 'intangible asset stock' of the organization may cause. Wrong decisions may be made if decision makers of an organization ignore or do not make use of the knowledge-based and intangible assets available within the organization.

It is one thing to invest in intangible assets and it is another thing understanding and accounting adequately for investments in intangibles. Not understanding and consequently not accounting properly for investments in intangibles can have negative consequences. Blair and Wallman (2001) believe that failure to account adequately for investments in intangibles results in understatement of GDP, of corporate profits, and of personal savings because of accounting systems, which treat investments in intangibles as expenses, therefore overstating the cost of producing current output. Blair and Wallman further argue that failure to understand the role of intangible assets in the aggregate economy will repeatedly lead to misdiagnoses of economic problems and inappropriate policy responses.

Some of the methods which have been suggested for evaluating and measuring intangible and knowledge-based assets and which knowledge workers may need to be trained in include:

- Human Resources Accounting (HRA)
- Economic Value Added (EVA)
- Balanced Scorecard
- Intellectual Capital
- Valmatrix.

The Human Resource Accounting (HRA) system takes into account the fact that human capital represents the human factor in the organization; the combined intelligence, skills and expertise that gives the organization its distinctive character. Sackman *et al.* (1989) state that the objective of

HRA is to quantify the economic value of people to the organization in order to provide input for managerial and financial decisions. As far as they go, human resource accounting models attempt to calculate the contribution that human assets make to firms by capitalizing salary expenditure.

Bontis *et al.* (1999) identify three basic uses to which HRA information may be put as part of the official audited reporting of results to external users of the organizations financial data (e.g. creditors, investors, government, regulatory bodies); internal feedback to organization members on the accomplishment of strategic goals; and as a starting point to develop future plans and strategy by recognizing the core competencies inherent in unique intellectual capital resident in the organization.

As a method of assessing, measuring, and evaluating intangible assets, the human resource accounting has some weaknesses including the fact that too many assumptions must be made when using HRA models for assessing, measuring, and evaluating knowledge-based assets. All the HRA models suffer from subjectivity, uncertainty, and lack of reliability in that their measures cannot be audited with any assurance; and it may not be morally acceptable to treat human beings as assets.

Economic Value Added (EVA) is another possible assessment, measurement and valuation method of knowledge-based assets that Bontis *et al.* (1999) identify. EVA is looked upon as a comprehensive financial management measurement system that can be used to tie together capital budgeting, financial planning, goal setting, performance measurement, shareholder communication, and incentive compensation. The objective of EVA is to develop a performance measure that properly accounts for all ways in which corporate value could be added or lost. EVA is purported by its proponents to be the only measure of performance that properly accounts for all the complex trade-offs involved in creating value. Economic value added may not explicitly relate to the management of knowledge-based assets,

but it may be implicitly argued that the effective management of knowledge-based assets may increase economic added value.

Economic value added as a technique of measuring, assessing, and evaluating knowledge-based and intangible assets has some weaknesses. Given the ephemeral nature of knowledge-based and intangible assets, EVA may not be effectively used to estimate the value of a training programme or evaluate the value of a best practice database.

Economic added value is subject to several areas of performance adjustments that are supposed to address shortcomings in conventional accounting practices, and thus solve problems such as the accounting of intangibles and long-term investments with a high degree of uncertainty. Among the problematic areas, Bontis *et al.* (1999) identify depreciation, capitalization, and amortization of research and development, market building, outlays, restructuring charges, acquisition premiums, and other 'strategic' investments with deferred pay off patterns.

Dodd and Chen (1997) report that in their study on EVA, they found out that it may be a useful measure of corporate performance. However, they do not find EVA to be as perfect as its advocates claim, nor do they find it to be the only performance measure that may show how to achieve a superior stock return. Dodd and Chen do not necessarily emphasize the use of EVA as a measurement technique for knowledge-based assets of an organization.

Roos and Roos (1997) identify the Balanced Scorecard as another technique of measuring the value of knowledge-based assets of an organization. The Balanced Scorecard is suggested as a measure for non-financial measures such as cycle times, quality rates, customer satisfaction and market shares. According to Roos and Roos, the issues that are involved in the Balanced Scorecard include treating intellectual capital as the sum of the organization's hidden assets, which are the most important source of competitive advantage, and visualizing intellectual capital systematically.

The Balanced Scorecard organizes its measurement system in four perspectives, namely, financial perspective, customer perspective, internal business perspective, and the learning and growth perspective. The financial perspective includes traditional accounting measures. Customer perspective focuses on identification of target groups, customer satisfaction, and customer retention. The internal business process draws heavily from the concept of the value chain. The learning and growth perspective includes all measures relating to employees and systems the organization has in place to facilitate learning and knowledge diffusion.

Intellectual capital has also been identified as a technique of assessing and measuring knowledge-based assets by Bontis *et al.* (1999). They look at intellectual capital as the collection of intangible resources and their flows. Intellectual capital is something peculiar to every organization. What may qualify as intellectual capital for one organization may not necessarily qualify as intellectual capital for another organization. For that, intellectual capital is context specific. Pearlson and Saunders (2004) report that Skandia; a Swedish insurance company divides intellectual capital into two major categories: (1) human capital, which exists in the minds of individuals: their knowledge, skills, experience, creativity and innovation; (2) structural capital, which includes both (a) organizational capital, the infrastructure which supports human capital (information systems, internal processes, proprietary software, and documentation) and (b) customer capital, the relationships, satisfaction, longevity, price sensitivity, and financial well-being of long-term customers. Skandia uses these categories to develop a set of measures for progress in managing knowledge.

It is hard to put a value on intellectual assets because they take a less defined form (Stewart, 1997) than other assets. Stewart however suggests three ways of measuring the value of intellectual capital although he says they are not the best. One

way Stewart gives of valuing intellectual capital is by cost. He calls it a "lousy" way of valuing intellectual capital but he says it can be used. The cost of creating intellectual capital is not necessarily related to the value of what is created, Stewart argues. He also says that intellectual capital may be valued by rating the relative strength of an organization's assets versus comparables. He is not very specific on the comparables, even so. There could be very few comparables that one may compare with intellectual capital.

Stewart (1997) suggests "Valmatrix" as another way of measuring the value of intellectual capital. It lists twenty factors such as pretax margins, breadth of product line, potential for line extensions, barriers to entry, and licensing potential. For each factor, the asset can be scored from 0 to 5 based on how it is assessed. The best possible score is 100, which may be earned by a rare intangible asset that could be top-of-the-line for all twenty factors. The score can be plugged into an established method of evaluating intangibles (such as royalty rates, asset sales, or even costs).

Most organizations carry out detailed financial measurement and reporting, but few do the same for their intellectual and knowledge-based assets that are much more valuable (Skyrme, 1999). Skyrme further contends that this has led in part to the introduction of non-financial performance measurement systems to guide day-to-day management actions. Skyrme gives examples as the Balanced Business Scorecard and the European Foundation for Quality Management Excellence Model. He, however, thinks that these systems do not explicitly capture knowledge measures nor do they help managers identify the underlying cause of different outcomes. In the economies where knowledge and information are not highly valued, top corporate managers are likely to question how one may justify investing in an intangible assets which cannot be measured by conventional methods and standards.

EDUCATION AND TRAINING IN INTANGIBLE ASSETS AND THE PROPERTY RIGHTS

One important characteristic of an asset or a resource is that it should be owned by a person or a community or an organization. In the property rights view, a firm is considered to be a bundle of rights to control the resources it owns. Farok (2001) cites Williamson (1991) as contending that a central position of this view is that "economic performance is largely determined by the way in which property rights are defined." A resource or an asset has several other attributes that, under appropriate circumstances, may enable the use of that resource to generate rents or wealth for its owner. Examples of the attributes of a resource or asset include the resource being unique or ubiquitous, attributes, which enable synergistic uses of the resource in combination with other complementary assets. Intangible assets have the attributes of being unique; they can be used in combination with other complementary resources to generate wealth and they are usually owned by a particular individual, a community or by an organization. The control over these attributes (i.e. the right to use the resources, the right to appropriate the returns from the resources, and the right to transfer the location) are called property rights (Furubotn & Pejovich, 1974).

Property rights over an asset, whether intangible or physical can be considered the source of wealth associated with the asset in that they provide the necessary conditions for value-creating decisions to be made concerning the asset. The ability of an organization or firm to make such decisions essentially depend on various rights identified and highlighted by the property rights approach. According to Farok (2001), such property rights include the right to exclude others from use of the asset; the right to combine the assets with other types of assets; the right to modify the assets; and the right to transfer the asset. It is true that none of these rights may individually be sufficient to create value. However, exercising various rights in combination may lead to creation of value.

EDUCATION AND TRAINING IN THE RIGHT TO COMBINE AND/OR MODIFY

The mere possession of an asset is no guarantee that it will generate wealth. However, the appropriate use of the asset under conditions of environmental uncertainty, that generate rents (Ramanathan, Seth, & Thomas, 2001). Putting an asset to appropriate use so as to generate wealth involves invoking the right to use the asset, combine it with other resources, and/or to modify the resources. Ramanathan, Seth, and Thomas argue that the uncertainty associated with the outcomes of these decisions results in the possibility of entrepreneurial rents, which may be realized by risk taking and entrepreneurial insight in an uncertain and complex environment. However, once the rent-generating potential of the resource has been identified with relative certainty, other rent-seekers or investors may attempt to acquire these resources or substitutes and to imitate the rent-generating process. So as to sustain the entrepreneurial rents from an asset or a resource, owners of rent-yielding resources or assets may need to protect against the erosion of rents. The right to exclude others from unauthorized use of a resource may be invoked to provide such protection. Intangible assets, which are not well identified and protected, may be subjected to duplication and may be accessed by unauthorized rent seekers. This may lead to the reduction of the rents or wealth generated by such assets.

EDUCATION AND TRAINING IN CHANGE OF LOCATION OF KNOWLEDGE-BASED AND INTANGIBLE ASSETS

The issue of location of intangible assets may cause confusion as such assets are not material objects which may occupy a physical location. However, intangible assets exist in various media where they are generated, stored, used, or developed (Diefenbach, 2006). Location of intangible assets is important possibly because ownership, access to, and transfer of things, i.e. trade of commodities, are some of the most basic and important aspects of economics and business. The media in which knowledge-based and intangible assets exist can be located for purposes of transfer of ownership, change of location and access to such assets. An asset that is not accessible may not be identified and may not be valued for purposes of determining its market value. Diefenbach (2006) suggests that one aspect of identifying knowledge-based and intangible assets is to look at what kind of media they are in. Diefenbach however concedes that it is quite difficult to identify where some knowledge-based and intangible assets are located. Knowledge-based and intangible assets like skills, social capital, organizational culture, and technology may be difficult to locate.

However, Diefenbach (2006) looks at location as a leading principle of identifying and differentiating knowledge-based and intangible assets. He contends that some intangible assets can be in "our heads" or belong to us as individuals; such may include tacit knowledge based on, and comprising, qualifications, experiences, skills, and abilities of an individual; individual feelings and values, hopes and objectives; personal health, wellbeing and manpower; individual competence of assessing, deciding, acting, and behaving; personality; and formal qualifications and degrees (legally protected).

Intangible Business (2008) suggests that the common approaches for valuing intangible assets, including customer-related intangibles, are:

- **Cost Approach:** How much did it cost to create the asset or how much would it cost to replace it?
- **Market Approach:** The amount paid for the asset or similar assets on the open market.
- **Income Approach:** The present value of future cash flows, that is, how much income the asset will generate throughout its useful life, accounting for the time value of money and associated risks.

EDUCATION AND TRAINING IN APPROPRIATION OF RETURNS FROM KNOWLEDGE-BASED AND INTANGIBLE ASSETS

Assets, whether tangible or intangible, are supposed to generate some form of income or wealth for the owner/s. It is important to identify knowledge-based and intangible assets for the purposes of appropriating returns or rent for that matter. Income approaches are based around the concept that an asset is worth is equal to the present value of the future returns the asset is expected to generate. This involves forecasting the entity or asset's ability to generate cash and adjusting the future income streams to today's value by discounting for risk.

Forbes (2008) suggests a number of income-based methods as being ideal for appropriation of returns from knowledge-based and intangible assets. The methods include royalty relief, intangible asset contribution, and multiple-period excess earnings.

- **Royalty Relief:** This is an estimate of the present value of the royalties less tax and associated costs that the business would have to pay if it did not own the asset in question. This approach is commonly used for brands and patents because there is an active licensing market that makes it relatively straightforward to find comparable licensing transactions to estimate an appropriate valuation royalty rate. This approach is not very helpful when valuing a customer relationship as it is not an asset that is typically licensed, and hence there is no universe of comparable transactions.

- **Intangible Asset Contribution:** This is where recognition is given to the contribution of intangible assets to the business earnings. These are then discounted back to give a present value. The weakness of this approach is in determining the appropriate intangible asset contribution –as internal and external benchmarks are difficult to assess and obtain while econometric analysis or trade-off research needed to obtain a reasonable level of accuracy would be expensive and still not be particularly robust. Using this approach, the intangible assets of a loss-making business would be worth nothing, which, in the case of a business whose manufacturing base is expensive or inefficient, may be very far from the truth such that only the intangible assets have a disposal value in the event the business may go bust.

- **Multiple-Period Excess Earnings:** The value of expected economic benefits that exceed an appropriate rate of return on the value of a selected asset base being used to generate anticipated economic benefits. Basically, subtract the present value of cost-based returns for each operating func-

tion and any separately identifiable intangibles from the entity's business value. This is a commonly used approach for valuing customer-related intangibles.

Table 1 presents a simplistic example of the multiple excess earnings approach. First, the business value is calculated. Future returns on the costs of key functions are discounted to a present value; a more detailed analysis would include the present value of returns of a larger number of discrete functions such as IT, HR, and R&D. By calculating brand value using the royalty relief approach, there is no need to determine the present value of functional returns on marketing expenditure. Subtracting the value of all identified intangibles and the present value of functional returns from the business value leaves a residual amount of excess returns. Assuming a value has been allocated to all operating functions and intangible assets, the value of the excess returns is equivalent to the value of the customer relationship.

This approach and rational is similar to the concept of the value chain framework where the value of the whole chain is greater than the sum of its parts. In this way, the value of the customer relationship can be considered as the additional value created from assets employed in combination over and above normal functional returns.

The major weakness of the multiple excess earnings approach is that it is rather complicated to carry out. Furthermore, correctly identifying all the value drivers (operating functions and intangible assets employed) and calculating their respective functional returns and present values is open to distortion and inaccuracy due to the sensitivity of the valuation to key assumptions and source data. In the case of an acquisition, the excess returns will also include the value of any synergies resulting from the business combination.

Table 1. Multiple-period excess earnings example

Business Value			109.0
	Rate of Return	**Present Value of Functional Returns**	
Manufacturing	8%	45.6	
Distribution	11%	5.5	
Administration	13%	8.7	
			59.9
	Royalty Rate	**Present Value of Royalty Income**	
Brand Value	5%	41.9	
			41.9
Excess Returns			7.2

Source: Forbes (2008, p. 5)

METHODS OF EDUCATING AND TRAINING KNOWLEDGE WORKERS

All the suggested areas of training and education are important for knowledge workers in a knowledge economy. Organizations may not find it easy to train in all the areas at the same time. Methods of training may include on-the-job training and long-term training for younger knowledge workers. Younger knowledge workers may be sponsored to go for long-term training while older knowledge workers may be trained on-the-job.

CONCLUSION

Many organizational employees currently working as knowledge workers are not specifically trained as knowledge workers. In a knowledge economy, organizations are discovering that they are increasingly infesting in intangible and knowledge-based assets and hiring employees who work as knowledge workers. Relationships with stakeholders and creativity of employees are good examples of intangible assets of an organization. Intangible assets are considered critical for most organizations, especially those operating in knowledge intensive industries. Training of knowledge workers results in increasing their competencies,

which in turn may help to improve productivity and profitability for profit-making organizations and improvement of service delivery for non-profit organizations.

The discussion in this chapter suggests that in a knowledge economy, intangible assets are important in generating wealth and contributing to GDPs of countries around the world. Valuing knowledge-based and intangible assets is clearly not a straightforward exercise. Knowledge workers and managers need to be educated and trained in every aspect of managing and valuing knowledge-based and intangible assets. Each valuation method prescribed by accountants is subject to strengths, weaknesses, and complexities and yet none - is able to provide a universally indisputable, accurate, and reliable value. Although these values are not as robust as we would hope, it is certainly better to attempt to attribute value to intangible assets than to classify everything as either goodwill or organizational culture.

Many appraisers specializing in intangible assets would typically consider all the available valuation approaches but in most instances rely on an income-based approach as a primary method and use market-based approaches for supporting evidence. Multiples of revenues, profits and assets, and other such rules of thumb are sufficient for benchmarking and as a sense check but are by no means robust enough to be relied upon in their own right. In this way, valuing intangible assets is more of an art than a science; applying several supporting methodologies and a modicum of common sense provides sufficient confidence in a valuation result. Valuation practitioners and investors in intangible assets should devise ways of identifying and appreciating intangible assets. Many organizations do not as yet have ways of identifying the value of their intangible assets, which makes it hard for valuation and tax assessment.

Further research should be conducted on the best methods of valuing and managing intangible and knowledge-based assets, how best knowledge workers may be trained in evaluating and managing such assets and the most important areas in which knowledge managers should be trained.

REFERENCES

Ahmed, P. K., Lim, K. K., & Zairi, M. (1999). Measurement practice for knowledge management. *Journal of Workplace Learning: Employee Counseling Today, 11*, 304–311.

Andreou, A. N., Green, A., & Stankosky, M. (2007). A framework of intangible valuation areas and antecedents. *Journal of Intellectual Capital, 8*, 52–75. doi:10.1108/14691930710715060

Arthur, W. B. (1996). Increasing returns and the new world of business. *Harvard Business Review, 74*(4), 100–109.

Becker, G. S. (1975). *Human capital: A theoretical and empirical analysis, with special reference to education*. Chicago, IL: University of Chicago Press.

Blair, M. M. (2005). Closing the theory gap: How the economic theory of property rights can help bring "stakeholders" back into theories of the firm. *Journal of Management and Government, 9*, 33–39. Retrieved from http://www.springerlink.com/content/p744646n5qw22h66/ doi:10.1007/s10997-005-1566-y

Blair, M. M., & Wallman, S. M. (2001). *Unseen wealth: Report of the Brookings task force on intangibles*. Washington, DC: Brookings Institution Press.

Bontis, N. (1999). The knowledge toolbox: A review of the tools available to measure and manage intangible resources. *European Management Journal, 17*, 391–402. doi:10.1016/S0263-2373(99)00019-5

Carney, A. (2003). *Factors in instructional design: Training versus education*. Retrieved from http://www.uic.edu/depts/accc/itl/conf2003/usetech2enhance/carney2.pdf

Davenport, T., & Prusak, L. (1998). *Working knowledge: How organizations manage what they know*. Boston, MA: Harvard Business School Press.

Dearden, L., McGranahan, L., & Sianesi, B. (2004). The role of credit constraints in educational choices: Evidence from NCDS and BCS70. *Centre for the Economics of Education*. Retrieved from http://cee.lse.ac.uk/ceedps//ceedp48.pdf

Diefenbach, T. (2006). Intangible resources: A categorical system of knowledge and other intangible assets. *Journal of Intellectual Capital, 7*, 406–420. Retrieved from http://www.emeraldinsight.com/Insight/ViewContentServlet?Filename=/published/emeraldfulltextarticle/pdf/2500070308.pdf doi:10.1108/14691930610681483

Dodd, J. L., & Chen, S. (1997). Economic value added (EVA super TM): An empirical examination of a new corporate performance measure. *Journal of Managerial Issues*, *9*, 318–333.

Drucker, P. (1993). *Post-capitalist society*. Oxford, UK: Butterworth Heinemann.

DTI. (2001). *Creating value from your intangible assets*. Retrieved from http://www.exinfm.com/pdffiles/intangible_assets.pdf

Edvinsson, L. (2000). Some perspectives on intangibles and intellectual capital. *Journal of Intellectual Capital*, *1*, 12–16. doi:10.1108/14691930010371618

Edvinsson, L., & Malone, M. (1997). *Intellectual capital: Realizing your company's true value by finding its hidden brainpower*. New York, NY: Harper Collins.

European Commission. (2005). *A study on returns of various types of investment in education and training*. Retrieved from http://www.londecon.co.uk/le/publications/pdf/invest05_en.pdf

Farok, J. (Ed.). (2001). *Valuation of intangible assets in global operations*. Westport, CT: Quorum Books.

Flignor, P., & Orozco, D. (2012). *Intangible assets and intellectual property valuation: A multidisciplinary perspective*. Retrieved from http://www.wipo.int/sme/en/documents/ip_valuation.htm#legal

Forbes, T. (2008). Valuing customers. *Database Marketing and Customer Strategy Management*. Retrieved from http://www.intangiblebusiness.us/store/data/files/389-Valuing_Customers_Thayne_Forbes_Database_of_Customer_Marketing_January_2008.pdf

Furubotn, E. G., & Pejovich, S. (1974). Introduction: The new property rights literature. In Furubtn, E. G., & Pejovich, S. (Eds.), *The Economics of Property Rights*. Cambridge, MA: Ballinger Publishing Company.

Gurteen, D. (2006). *The gurteen perspective*. Retrieved from http://www.ikmagazine.com/display.asp?articleid=AE03F1CA-F94B-4BD5-9BE9-0CB68079CB6F

Hall, R. (1992). The strategic analysis of intangible resources. *Strategic Management Journal*, *13*, 135–144. doi:10.1002/smj.4250130205

Hall, R. (1993). A framework for linking intangible resources and capabilities to sustainable competitive advantage. *Strategic Management Journal*, *14*, 607–618. doi:10.1002/smj.4250140804

Hauser, J. R., & Katz, G. M. (1998). Metrics: You are what you measure. *European Management Journal*, *16*, 517–528. doi:10.1016/S0263-2373(98)00029-2

Investopedia. (2009). *Intangible asset*. Retrieved from http://investopedia.com/terms/i/intangible-asset.asp

Itami, H. (1984). Invisible resources and their accumulation for corporate growth. *Hitotsubahi Journal of Commerce & Management*, *19*, 20–39.

Kumar, J. (2004). *Transition from production-based to knowledge-based economy: An overview*. Retrieved from http://www.apo-tokyo.org/00e-books/IS-02_TrainingKnowledgeWorkers.htm

Lazaric, N., & Marengo, L. (2000). Towards a characterization of assets and knowledge created in technological agreements: Some evidence from the automobile robotics sector. *Industrial and Corporate Change*, *9*, 53–86. doi:10.1093/icc/9.1.53

Lowendahl, B. (1997). *Strategic management of professional service firms*. Copenhagen, Denmark: Handelshojskolens Forlag.

Martins, P. S. (2004). *Firm-level social returns to education*. IZA Discussion Paper, 1382. Retrieved from http://www.econstor.eu/bitstream/10419/20678/1/dp1382.pdf

Morrow, N. M. (2001). Knowledge management: An introduction. In M. E. Williams (Ed.), *Annual Review of Information Science and Technology (ARIST), 35,* 381-422.

Myers, S. P. (1996). *Knowledge management and organizational design.* Boston, MA: Butterworth-Heinemann.

Nelson, R., & Winter, S. (1982). *An evolutionary theory of economic change.* Boston, MA: Harvard University Press.

Pearlson, K. E., & Saunders, C. S. (2004). *Managing and using information systems: A strategic approach.* New York, NY: John Wiley and Sons.

Polanyi, M. (1958). *Personal knowledge: Towards a post-critical philosophy.* New York, NY: Routledge.

Ramanathan, K., Seth, A., & Thomas, H. (2001). The value of new knowledge-based intangible assets: An examination of in the global pharmaceutical industry. In Forak, J. (Ed.), *Valuation of Intangible Assets in Global Operations.* Westport, CT: Quorum Books.

Rodgers, W. (2003). Measurement and reporting of knowledge-based assets. *Journal of Intellectual Capital, 4,* 181–190. doi:10.1108/14691930310472802

Roos, G., & Roos, J. (1997). Measuring your company's intellectual performance. *Long Range Planning, 30,* 413–426. doi:10.1016/S0024-6301(97)90260-0

Sackman, S. A., Flamholtz, E. G., & Bullen, M. L. (1989). Human resource accounting: A state of the art review. *Journal of Accounting Literature, 8,* 235–264.

Stewart, T. A. (1997). *Intellectual capital: The wealth of new organizations.* London, UK: Nicholas Brealey Publishing.

Sullivan, P. H. (1998). *Profiting from intellectual capital: Extracting value from innovation.* New York, NY: Wiley.

Teece, D. J. (2000). *Managing intellectual capital.* Oxford, UK: Oxford University Press.

Thomas, H. (Ed.). (1997). *The unit of activity: Towards an alternative to the theories of the firm, strategy, structure and style.* Copenhagen, Denmark: Wiley.

Tissen, R., Andriessen, D., & Deprezz, F. L. (1998). *Value-based knowledge management.* Amsterdam, The Netherlands: Addison Wesley Longman.

Von Krogh, G., Roos, J., & Klein, D. (Eds.). (1998). *Knowing firms: Understanding, managing, and measuring knowledge.* London, UK: Sage Publications.

Chapter 13

The Influence of the Application of Business Continuity Management, Knowledge Management, and Knowledge Continuity Management on the Innovation in Organizations

Hana Urbancová
Czech University of Life Sciences, Czech Republic

Martina Königová
Czech University of Life Sciences, Czech Republic

ABSTRACT

The aim of organizations is efficient management leading to a competitive advantage. In the current knowledge economy, employees, their knowledge, and potential are considered to be an organization's main competitive advantage and the most important asset towards determining performance and success. By introducing modern areas of management, organizations can quickly identify and utilize knowledge, which enables an early application of knowledge in innovations and key processes. Thus, putting them ahead of their competitors and gaining a competitive advantage in the market. This chapter focuses on the impact of applying Business Continuity Management, Knowledge Management, and Knowledge Continuity Management on innovations in organizations and their productivity.

DOI: 10.4018/978-1-4666-1969-2.ch013

INTRODUCTION

In the present situation characterised by dynamic changes, organizations concentrate their effort on efficient management aimed at gaining a competitive advantage. In the course of their activities, organizations are threatened by both the external and internal environment. This is why organizations pay more and more attention to the so-called Business Continuity Management whose task is to help anticipate potential threats and their consequences, which might have a negative impact on organizations' key processes as well as organizations as a whole. In order for an organization to be successful in the market and improve its performance, it is necessary to monitor all changes and ensure not only the continuity of processes, but also of knowledge as, in compliance with the resource approach, this contributes to achieving a competitive advantage.

The dynamic changes directly or indirectly impact all organizations including higher education institutions. Those changes are connected with both information and communication technologies, and with the age and national structure of students at the universities and involve requirements on international cooperation in the research and development. It is important that the pedagogues have interdisciplinary education. The BCM, KM, and KCM significantly participate in such interdisciplinarity, and the pedagogues ability to adapt to changes in global environment.

Organizations wish to have efficient management in place. In order to achieve their goals, organizations have to ensure the proper and efficient functioning of individual innovation-based processes in which organization employees, who are the holders of knowledge, take part. If employees change their positions, they take the knowledge with them, and this may affect the quality of such processes. The problem of not ensuring the transfer of knowledge results in time and material losses in the quality of process management.

Based on the analysis of primary and secondary data, this chapter will attempt to identify the following:

- The importance of knowledge in the process of innovations and modern areas of management that also employ knowledge.
- The impact of the implementation of these areas on innovative development that determines an organization's performance.

The primary sources have been obtained through a survey. The data for the evaluation of benefits has been gathered through a quantitative survey (i.e. a questionnaire survey), in which 167 higher and middle management managers from 580 various organizations took part; the branch in which the organizations operate has not been taken into account in 2010. The questionnaire was distributed to 814 respondents. The overall questionnaire return was 20.52%, i.e. 167 respondents took part. 55.1% hold a senior management position, 68.9% have university education, 45.5% are in the age group 46-62 years, 70.1% are employees of Czech organizations, 51.5% work in tertiary sector, and 38.9% work in the primary sector. 76.6% of respondents were male. The data have been processed by means of absolute and relative frequencies using the LimeSurvey application and the Excel 2007 programme.

The secondary sources include research works targeted at Business Continuity Management (hereafter BCM), Knowledge Management (hereafter KM), Knowledge Continuity Management (hereafter KCM), and innovations. Data obtained has been processed by methods of induction, deduction, analysis, and synthesis of knowledge and through the review of outcomes of the survey carried out among middle- and higher-level managers in organizations in the Czech Republic. On the basis of the survey, we have identified areas in which the application of BCM, KM, and KCM turned beneficial.

THEORETICAL BACKGROUND OF THE CHAPTER

Business Continuity Management

Currently, Business Continuity Management is considered a managerial discipline that focuses on the identification of potential impacts arising from negative circumstances that can threaten organizations. BCM therefore creates a framework to ensure a certain level of resistance and ability to respond to unexpected events and thus to protect not only the key organization's processes, but also its interests, for instance the market value of shares. The main areas of BCM implementation include: employee safety, internal communication in organizations, restoration of critical business processes and functions, efficient risk management and knowledge continuity. BCM may be implemented by all organizations regardless of their size or purpose of business (Ercan, 2010; Herbane, 2010). What is important is the support of the top management and anchoring BCM into the organizational culture in order to make all employees understand its role. BCM can be expressed by the so-called BCM lifecycle in which BCM is viewed as a continuous process (Figure 1).

According to Wong (2009), the basic roles of BCM in strategic management deal with four basic factors, which are as follows: long-term character, achievement of a competitive advantage, adequate means to achieve an organization's goals and organizational decisions. Strategic management is associated with a longer time horizon when goals and plans are set and directed, using organizational means, at the achievement of these long-term goals. It is therefore possible to say that BCM could be considered one of the organization's crucial strategic goals that contribute to the competitiveness of this organization. Recently achieving a competitive advantage has meant being ahead of competitors, being in the lead, and doing something that is difficult to copy. It is possible, for example, to place a strategy above the frame of accepted experience while paying more attention to knowledge strategies and innovation. These innovative approaches can, according to Wong (2009), be transformed into strategies ensuring business continuity and plans that maintain and protect organizations' critical

Figure 1. Business continuity management lifecycle diagram (BS 25999-1:2006)

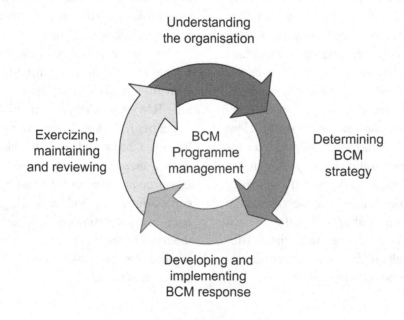

activities. Organizations that have incorporated BCM in their strategic management could achieve the so-called distinctive character, i.e. better performance compared to their competitors (Wong, 2009). In conclusion, it can be summarized that BCM is based on three essential aspects—technologies, people, and processes.

Knowledge Management and Intellectual Capital

Knowledge Management, like BCM, is another important area that an organization must focus on. According to Young (2003), knowledge management is the discipline of enabling individuals, teams, and entire organizations to collectively and systematically capture, store, create, share, and apply knowledge to better achieve their objectives. Dalkir (2005) adds that knowledge management is the deliberate and systematic coordination of an organization's people, technology, processes, and organization structure in order to add value through reuse and innovation. This coordination is achieved through creating, sharing, and applying knowledge, as well as through feeding the valuable lessons learned and best practices into corporate memory in order to foster continued organization learning. The definition of KM is still quite broad, but generally, it is viewed as a process of systematic and active management and shaping of organizations' knowledge, which concentrates both on the state as well as the movement of knowledge (Truneček, 2004). The objective of KM in organizations is to focus employees' knowledge on goal achieving (Altmeyer & Georg, 2002). Davenport and Prusak (1998) define KM as a systematic process of searching for, selecting, organizing, distilling, and presenting information in a way that improves an employee's understanding of the specific area of interest (Seeley-Brown & Duquid, 2000).

Wilson (1998) specifies the above definition by adding that it encompasses the formulation of a strategy to develop and apply knowledge that

contributes to the improvement of processes and the ability to respond. Collison and Parcel (2005) speak about an interconnected spectrum of KM activities, one end of which is characterised by "knowledge retaining" and the other by "communication" of people. The relationship between knowledge recording and communication may then be perceived as a relationship between what other people know and what is known. From the point of view of an organization's management, this means in particular managing and supporting knowledge of employees who by its application create new ideas that represent a competitive advantage, and as Drucker (1998) adds, the only competitive advantage of the organization. The above-mentioned definitions are supported by Jirásek (2004) who accents yet another benefit of KM, which lies in that organizations not only receive, but also generate knowledge and thus reproduce and broaden their productive potential and invest in themselves.

With respect to the above, the basic elements of successful KM can be summarized as follows:

- Reliable common technological infrastructure that permits knowledge sharing,
- Alliance of people who possess knowledge and are willing to share it, ask questions and listen to others,
- Organizational culture and organizational structure encouraging knowledge sharing,
- Proven processes to facilitate knowledge sharing, review, and extraction.

According to Anatan (2007), knowledge management is the foundation of organizational learning. Through the process of learning, knowledge ultimately provides the creative potential of innovation through which organizations will find the ways to improve the innovative performance. As new outputs, innovations may come from new knowledge as well as from the combination of existing knowledge to create architectural innovations, using combinative capabilities. Radical and incremental innovations refer to high and low degrees of new knowledge, involving high and low degrees of organizational transformation.

The Knowledge management works with intangible assets. Thomas Stewart, a pioneer in the study of such intangible assets, is credited with having coined the term "Intellectual Capital" to refer to these assets. After more than a decade of studies by various other scholars in this area, there is general agreement that Intellectual Capital itself is composed of three distinct types of capital—Human Capital, Structural Capital, and Relational Capital.

Human Capital is the availability of skills, talent, and know-how of employees that is required to perform the everyday tasks that are required by the organizational strategy (Talukdar, 2008). According to this, the enhancement of Intellectual Capital can be expected as a result by stimulating the Knowledge management.

Knowledge Continuity Management

Knowledge continuity management is a branch of knowledge management (see Figure 2). While knowledge management focuses on the capturing and sharing of know-how important for colleagues who have similar tasks in the organization, knowledge continuity management is targeted at the transfer of critical knowledge (minimum knowledge base, knowledge decrease below this level leads to the knowledge discontinuity) from departing employees to their successors (Beazley, et al., 2002; Beazley, 2003).

If the leaving of an employee does not lead to changes in the original knowledge base, the successor has taken over all critical knowledge of the leaving employee. In other words, the aim of knowledge continuity is to maintain the original knowledge base of the leaving employee.

As a result, newcomers who replace leaving employees spend more time to start working as important findings and information of their predecessors is lost. The problem of unsecured

Figure 2. Management of knowledge base continuity (own elaborate)

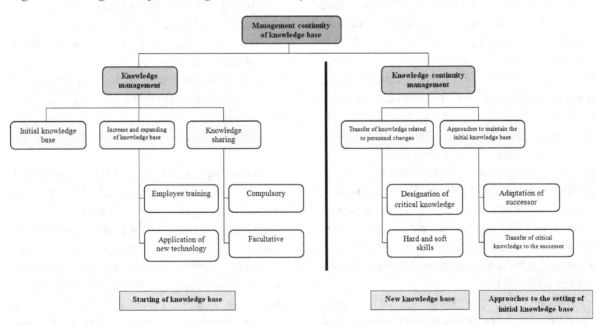

transfer leads to time and material losses in the quality of process management. This paralyses organizations' abilities to act flexibly and keep track (Stam, 2009).

The above implies that managers have to pay attention to knowledge continuity and make this activity part of managerial roles in order to achieve an optimal level of business continuity, as without knowledge employees holding knowledge critical for the organization it is impossible to ensure business continuity.

In other words, it can be said that knowledge management serves to develop the current potential of an organization's knowledge employees and by then applying knowledge continuity management, the preservation of this potential by the organization can be ensured despite personnel changes that involve the leaving of key knowledge employees. The efficient utilization of knowledge management in combination with BCM and knowledge continuity management leads to the improvement of productivity of organizations and the enhancement of their competitiveness in the market.

Innovation

Kiernan (1995) states that in the past there was no need for continuous innovation. The pace of competition used to be quite slow and innovations once in several years were sufficient. However, for a number of sectors this is no longer true in the present conditions. Today's super-competition leaves no space for rest, requiring organizations to innovate on an ongoing basis. It is a competitive necessity.

The term of innovation originates from a Latin expression "innovare" (renovate). In the most general sense of the word, innovation means a change (Drucker, 1993). Innovations are a series of scientific, technical, organizational, financial, business, and other activities, the goal of which are to produce a new or significantly improved product (goods, technology, or service) efficiently

launched in the market (Švejda, et al., 2007). Innovation also means re-launching and broadening of a range of products, services, and related markets, developing new production, supply, and distribution methods, introducing changes in management, organization of work, working conditions, and labour qualification. Innovation is aimed at increasing the market value of the final product. It can be understood as an ongoing process of searching for resources and new results (Mlčoch, 2002). Innovation means a change in the resource profitability, a change of values and consumer satisfaction brought about by such resources (Drucker, 1993; Švejda, et al., 2007).

Schumpeter (1961) saw innovations as the basis for dynamic development. He defined them as follows:

- Launch of production of a new type of product or of an existing product with new features.
- Introduction of a new manufacturing process (procedure) in production or a new kind of sale or acquisition.
- Opening of a new market.
- Use of new sources of raw materials or new semi-finished products.
- Introduction of a new production system (a new form of organization of work) or of a new production or business group.

The basis for innovation production, however, lies in the generation of knowledge (Košturiak & Chaľ, 2008). Thanks to knowledge, employees come up with new, often better, solutions (Tsoukas, 2009; Tsoukas & Mylonopoulos, 2004). Based on the summary of previous chapter, it is possible to state that knowledge continuity ensuring has a significant meaning for and impact on the quality of processes, innovation and the quality of operational, tactical and strategic decision-making based on timely, precise and complex knowledge of the matter in question. The importance of knowledge continuity ensuring also follows from the fact that a leaving employee from an organisation where knowledge continuity is not ensured will carry away with him not only the know-how, but also relationships s/he has established with his/her collaborators in the organization. Where knowledge continuity is ensured, if an employee with critical knowledge decides to leave, the organization will not lose the knowledge since it has been transferred to a different employee. In addition, the quality of company processes will be preserved. Systematic knowledge continuity ensuring is therefore aimed at the continuity of an organization's development and decision-making. Thanks to new findings, innovations enhance or redesign an already existing process or add a missing element (Seeley-Brown & Solomon-Gray, 1995).

Innovations arising from new knowledge are, in fact, authentic "real" innovations as primarily defined by Schumpeter (1961). Bartes (in Drucker, 1985) says that time periods for invention implementation continue to shorten. The shortening of implementation periods is closely connected with the strengthening of the scientific and technical potential of the given country. According to Europe Priorities (2011), this could be endorsed by the European Union's goals in the area of intelligent development, which are as follows:

- To invest 3% of the European Union's GDP in research and development (by combining private and public funds) and to improve overall general conditions for research, development and innovation.
- To increase, by 2020, the employment rate of men and women in the 20 to 64 age group to 75% by encouraging higher employment of women, young people, older people, people with low qualifications and legal immigrants.
- To increase the level of erudition, in particular by means of the following measures:
  - To decrease the level of early termination of school attendance to less than 10%,
  - To increase the number of university graduates (or graduates at a comparable level of education) in the age group of 30 to 34 to at least 40%.

It is necessary to realize that measuring innovations (innovative ability and performance) is strongly influenced by employee training. Their education is an essential indicator as human resources and innovations are very closely linked areas. Ultimately, proposals for innovation are always formulated by man. This indicator may be expressed by the percentage of expenditures incurred from the wage fund in respect to employees' education and by the percentage of employees trained in the area of innovations (evaluation of innovative proposals, innovation prospecting, etc.). Simultaneously, it is important to measure the capital invested in know-how acquisition. Investments in know-how acquisition are a typical indicator of the innovative ability. The precondition is that an organization acquires such know-how for the purpose of its commercial use, i.e. that it will use the purchased (or otherwise acquired) knowledge (licenses, patents, utility models) to produce its products or provide services. This category can also cover software purchases permitting better or more efficient management and transfer of information within the organization.

Based on the above-mentioned definitions, common features can be identified and innovations defined as follows:

- Innovation is a targeted and desired change in the current state.
- The change has to have a practical use and has to be new at least for the given organization.
- The subject of the change is products, services, production and organizational procedures or processes.
- The outcome of the changes implemented is a technical, economic, or general social benefit.

- Innovation is based on knowledge, the holders of which are people.

Processes

Innovative development which falls within the category of aggressive strategies can be, according to Pitra (1997), defined as measures in the internal environment of an organization that result in the improvement of the quality of products and services offered. However, it is necessary to add that innovative development in innovative processes is very costly and for a longer period of time consumes a major part of the funds that the given organization has available. The organization has to re-earn the effort and means employed; otherwise it has no chance of surviving in the strongly competitive environment (Drucker, 1993).

The innovative process in an organization consists of a broad variety of activities covering the entire process, from the very first idea to its implementation. A simple representation of the innovative process is shown in the following scheme: invent, design, produce, and sell (see Figure 3).

An innovative process can be determined in two ways. The first is the identification of innovative processes with activities. Innovative processes are targeted at turning innovative inputs into outputs, or at transforming inventions into innovations. The innovative process is therefore a set of steps and activities focusing on the transformation of an innovative ability into innovative performance (Drucker, 1993). For a detailed description of the innovative process see Figure 4.

The second (more general) approach to the innovative process covers all activities associated with innovations, starting from the idea to its launch in the market. In this case, innovations are considered the innovative process as such. The innovative process thus also includes research and development, industrial and legal protection, introduction into production and final use. However, it would be impossible to carry out all activities if there were a lack of experienced and enthusiastic people in organizations. Therefore, it is important to continuously improve educational programmes and training centres and en-

Figure 3. Innovation process (own elaborate)

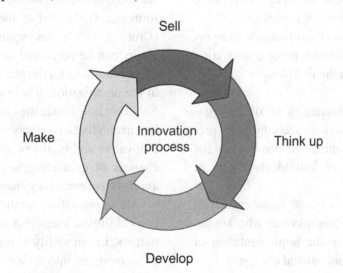

261

Figure 4. Detailed innovation process (own elaborate)

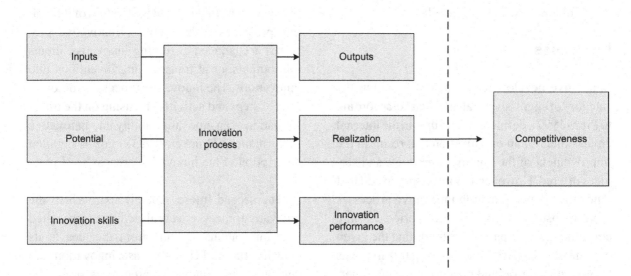

courage creativity to intensify efforts in the area of improvement proposals.

Process innovations mean introducing something new and have to be supervised by the representatives of an organization's top management (Pitra, 1997). The human factor, i.e. abilities, knowledge and skills of employees, is essential for the innovation of individual processes in organizations. According to Pitra (1997), the human factor is the main prerequisite for the innovation of relationships between individual innovative projects and their supporting processes.

Pitra (1997) also says that in relation to an organization's human resources, process innovation is also connected with the following:

*   Education and training of all of the organization's employees according to pre-designed programmes responsive to the different needs of individual groups of employees.
*   Efficient stimulation and remuneration of the organization's employees who are actively involved in the implementation of the required organizational change.

Mutual Relations and the Impact of Applying These Areas on Innovations and Subsequently on Organization Performance

Innovative ability and performance are terms that are frequently interchanged and often "blend." In terms of innovative process which is understood as the transformation of inputs into outputs, both terms represent poles, with innovative ability standing at the beginning and innovative performance at the end of the innovative process (Drucker, 1993). An organization's innovative ability can be perceived as its potential, a basis of preconditions for the generation of innovations in the organization. These preconditions can be found not only inside the organization, but also in its surroundings. By improving the organization's innovative ability, the organization increases its chances of generating innovations. Innovative ability is represented by innovation process inputs.

An organization's innovative performance is an ability to transform innovative inputs into outputs, i.e. an ability to transform the potential of innovations into their realization. Innovative performance is manifested by the company's success in introducing innovations in the market.

Competitiveness may be defined as an ability of the company to fight its competitors in placing its products or services on the market under the precondition of an efficient use of production factors employed in the course of product manufacturing or service provision (Drucker, 1993).

Organizations that wish to survive in the competitive global market environment and attempt to strengthen their position in the market may not ignore product, service and process improvement (Tureková & Mičieta, 2003). According to Stachová and Stacho (2010), innovation can be defined as a practical implementation of new ideas with the aim of improving the current state. The generation, development, and realization of innovations are part of the innovative process, which also includes the implementation of an innovative idea, i.e. of the very change from the original to a new condition. In order for the change to be positive, all factors, not only of material and financial nature, but in particular the human factor need to be preset pro-innovatively (Tureková & Mičieta, 2003). The fact that the process of introducing innovations requires that focus be placed on employees stimulates organizations to build the environment of an innovative organization (Stachová & Stacho, 2010). According to Stachová and Stacho (2010), Kiernan (1995), and Douglas and Seely-Brown (2011), the factors that influence innovative organizations include the following: involvement of management in innovations, creative leaders (innovators), innovative organizational culture, focus on customers, open efficient communication, learning organization, flexible organizational structure, intense engagement in innovations, talent management, and team co-operation. It is possible to say that the higher is the level of the innovative organization factors in the company, the higher the number of qualified and talented employees (potential employees) willing to work for it. These employees will represent a competitive advantage for the company.

Figure 5 shows space for the application of product and service innovations.

RESULTS

Organizational measures directed at the application of research and development knowledge that contributes to the success of an innovation are theoretically grounded on three basic principles (Pitra, 1997). These measures, however, need to be respected by organizations, as they may, in the final effect, contribute to a higher efficiency of individual processes and help gain a competitive advantage (see Figure 6). The figure provided shows both the theoretical principals as well as practical recommendations for organizations.

Figure 6 clearly shows that the measures regard the following:

- **Knowledge Application:** The success of an organization's innovative efforts is determined by the ability of its employees to acquire and generate the necessary knowledge, but also to distribute it for the general benefit of the organization.
- **Creative Skills:** People's creative skills are the decisive indicator of performance efficiency. In order to develop and exploit these creative activities, it is necessary to develop favourable conditions[1].
- **Activity Synergy:** Concentrating attention on the openness of relations between knowledge resources and consumers. In other words, it refers to an efficient transfer of all organizational resources and knowledge throughout the whole innovation process. Competitive advantage durability can derive from the fact that innovations based on new knowledge extend current knowledge in a unique way and thus provide an opportunity for achieving a synergic effect. The efficient management, strengthening, sharing and preserving of employ-

Figure 5. Space for use the innovation of products and services

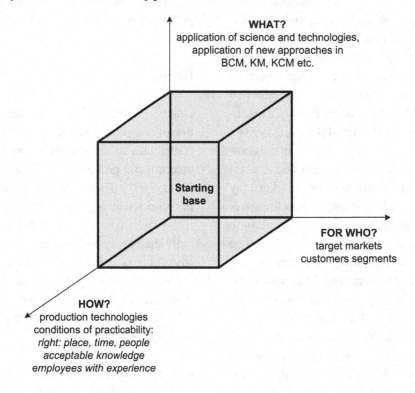

Figure 6. Organizational arrangements (own elaborate)

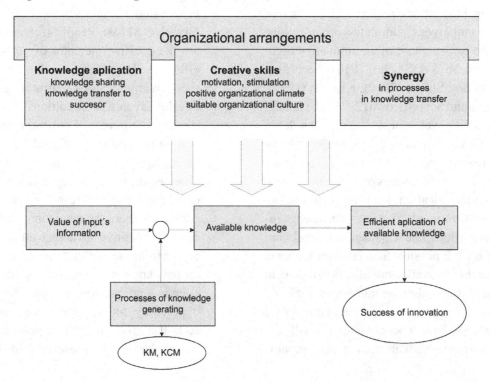

ees' knowledge are likely to broaden the knowledge of individuals as well as the so-called organizational knowledge. On the global scale, the introduction of knowledge processes enhances the performance of the entire organization. There are also long-term advantages as there are activities in which the transfer of knowledge, experience, and skills takes a longer period of time. This, however, requires respecting individual functional strategies that determine the implementation of the overall innovative strategy of the given organization, i.e. accomplishing the synergic effect from the combination of individual strategies (Figure 7). By linking and interconnecting individual strategies, organizations can reach better results than by gradual implementation of individual strategies.

One of the factors that support an organization's innovative activities is a functioning knowledge market within the organization, i.e. the sharing and transfer of knowledge between current

employees as well as between generations of employees. The introduction of KM and KCM produces benefits that can be divided into two groups. One of them includes benefits associated with the implementation of knowledge processes and the other comprises benefits directly connected with the basic business goals of the organization that have an impact on the following:

- Company processes
- Innovation
- Customers
- Employees and their knowledge
- Financial results

Based on the surveys carried out it can be stated that in the area of innovations major benefits include the application of new technologies, launch of new products and services, introduction of new business segments and improvements in research and development and generally in all knowledge-based processes. While practice offers a number of examples of benefits arising from the implementation of knowledge management strategies

Figure 7. Support of strategy

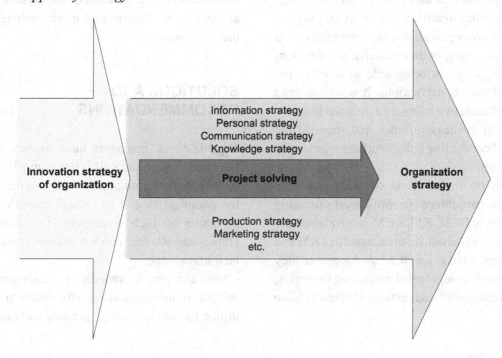

in organizations (Jones, 2003), technical literature provides only limited background information concerning the methods of their measurement. In his survey, Jones (2003) tried to demonstrate the benefits of knowledge management by measuring its impacts through the Balanced Scorecard conception. This conception helps organizations link strategic goals with operational activities and allows for their measurement (by EVA, Intellectual Capital). Since its first publication by Norton and Kaplan in the early 1990s, many organizations have applied it to measure four key aspects of their organization's performance: Financial, Customer, Internal Business Process, Learning and Growth. Simultaneously, it matches an organization's vision and strategy and monitors the performance of the organization from five perspectives that were examined in the surveys carried out. Organizations should realise that this system of measuring of their performance is targeted at developing their future growth opportunities and should place emphasis on balancing all five perspectives. This means that for an organization to be successful in the long term, it has to focus not only on generating the biggest possible profit today, but also on satisfying future customers, an efficient arrangement of internal production and management processes and improving qualifications of its employees. In fact, many organizations are losing important opportunities to spur their research and development results by not being able to quantify the results of such collaborations. It was confirmed that a collaborative balanced scorecard is a very useful tool to measure, track and improve the impact of conducting collaborative projects with universities.

Based on the analysis of secondary data sources, in particular of scientific works focusing on the area of BCM, KM, KCM, innovations, and the survey carried out, it can be stated that KM and KCM form a basis for BCM, and together they support the development of innovative strategies, lead to a competitive advantage, efficiency, more

efficient identification of potential threats, and better decision-making with lower risks.

It is clear from the above that an efficient transfer of knowledge produces benefits and contributes to the improvement of processes and higher competitiveness of the given organization. If an organization decides to focus on ensuring BCM, KM, and KCM, i.e. if it is able to anticipate potential threats and their impacts on the organization, realise that the knowledge of its employees is the greatest asset and efficiently support knowledge sharing and transfer between current employees as well as generations of employees, benefits are likely to occur not only in the area of knowledge utilization and team co-operation, but consequently also in the improvement of performance of the entire organization, cost decreasing and increasing of productivity, including economic and non-economic aspects.

In conclusion, it can be said that organizations are aware of the fact that an efficient transfer of knowledge generates benefits and helps increase competitiveness of the given organization. This is also confirmed by North and Hornung (2003) who also point out that benefits arising from knowledge management and knowledge continuity management are dependent on the organization's acceptance and application of and adherence to the conception.

SOLUTIONS AND RECOMMENDATIONS

Organizations' managers have already started to realise that in the still faster competitive environment they cannot rely solely on the size of the organization and its capital strength, but in particular on their employees, i.e. knowledge employees, who are carriers of both explicit and tacit knowledge.

By applying knowledge management, successful organizations acquire the ability to readily utilize knowledge, which permits them an early application of knowledge in key production processes and thus keeping ahead of their competitors and gaining a competitive advantage in the market. Knowledge management thus becomes the basic prerequisite for innovation management implemented through knowledge employees who are, thanks to their creativity, involved in innovations.

Should these employees change their position, they take their knowledge with them and this may threaten the quality of processes. Therefore, it is important to ensure knowledge continuity management, which is a branch of knowledge management. Without the right process aimed at preserving this knowledge and its transfer to successors, organizations would lose this knowledge and its efficiency would be threatened. The problem of not ensuring knowledge transfer results in time and material losses in the quality of process management.

The enhancement of quality of processes by means of ensuring knowledge continuity can be achieved by organizations in the following ways:

- By identifying key employees with critical knowledge pursuant to decision-making situations (transfer of structured knowledge followed by the transfer of critical knowledge, which will project in the quality of decision-making).
- By a suitable personnel policy; it is in particular important to make sure that employees who are carriers of critical knowledge do not leave before they transfer the critical knowledge to a suitable successor (at the time when the employee leaves, the organization should already have a successor who has the same critical knowledge necessary for his work as his predecessor).
- By continuous transfer of knowledge that must be ensured during the professional history of employees and not only at the time when they are about to leave the organization.

- By developing a high-quality organizational culture in terms of natural knowledge sharing and transfer and idea brainstorming => the necessity of anchoring the area of knowledge continuity ensuring in the organizational culture of codes of conduct that have to be binding on an organization's employee and into the system of shared values (integration values) that maintain, strengthen, and improve the compactness of the organization and its processes (ensure integrity), improve process efficiency as they shorten links (distances) between individual elements.
- By creating systems of gradual enhancement of quality of processes.
- By deliberate establishment of a suitable organizational climate.
- By setting a suitable organizational structure encouraging communication among employees; the personality of the manager responsible at the given level for adequate adherence to efficient measures of knowledge continuity ensuring.

In case the conditions leading to knowledge continuity ensuring are not met, it will lead to the raising of barriers to knowledge sharing and transfer and the key processes in organizations will not work appropriately.

According to Bersin and Associates research study (O'Leonard, 2009), succession planning is critical to the long-term health of any organization. Only 26 percent of organizations say they have successors identified for the majority their executive positions. It is troubling, given the number of impending retirements within most organizations. These organizations will likely find themselves responding reactively to changes in leadership, relying on the external market for succession candidates – or on ill-prepared internal candidates. In addition, a formalized succession management process helps an organization retain its best people. Organizations with such a process have 50 percent lower turnover among high performers, who are more likely to be committed to a career with an organization if they are being groomed for a future position.

The main recommendations for organizations are thus to support innovations, and develop strategies and mechanisms, encouraging innovations in all processes and to make continuous attempts to surpass themselves. Innovations are part of all business segments, however, it is necessary to realise that it is manageable to accomplish excellent results once, but it is much harder to excel repeatedly and in the long term. Simultaneously, what distinguishes truly excellent innovators from competitors is their ability to develop such mechanisms that will continuously support innovations. Successful innovation also encompasses monitoring of key indicators, i.e. the growth rate of innovations, intensity of information and communication technology application, investments in education, ensuring knowledge continuity and business continuity.

FUTURE RESEARCH DIRECTIONS

It is important for organizations to increasingly realise and place more emphasis on their employees' knowledge in order to prevent loss of such knowledge and ensure its preservation for the organization and for the purposes of employees' successors, should an employee who is the holder of critical knowledge decide to leave the organization. Simultaneously, it is necessary for organizations to shorten and speed up the innovative process. Knowledge-based innovations represent a source of relatively durable competitive advantage. It is also true that the more knowledge an organization has, the more it is able to learn. Furthermore, it is necessary to focus on the development of competencies in knowledge-oriented organizations and on the examination of organizational culture that would encourage the ensuring of BCM, KM, and KCM in organizations. The introduction of these

modern areas of management together with a suitably pre-set organizational culture will contribute to the increase of the innovative potential of the given organization.

CONCLUSION

BCM, KM and KCM ensuring has a substantial significance for and impact on the quality of processes, the quality of innovations and the quality of operational, tactical, and strategic decision-making based on timely, precise, and complex understanding of the situation. To achieve a better quality of processes, faster and correct innovations, and thus increase efficiency leading to a competitive advantage, it is necessary for organizations to ensure BCM, KM and KCM. The reasons are as follows:

- Each employee in an organization takes part in its processes and needs knowledge for his/her activities, thus innovations are also based on knowledge.
- By ensuring KM and KCM, it is possible to eliminate the negative consequences of knowledge loss (due to personnel changes) and to maintain the quality of processes and knowledge necessary for further innovations.
- They improve and speed up the process of initial training of new employees, facilitate adaptation to changing internal and external conditions and thus increase the flexibility of decision-making in the field of innovations.

Organizations that have made a decision to apply BCM, KM, and KCM may expect benefits not only in the area of knowledge utilization, innovations, and innovative potential, but subsequently also in the increasing of efficiency of the entire organization. The goal of the future success of organizations in the strongly competitive environment is to develop knowledge- and innovation-based economy as knowledge, research, development and innovations are the pillars of competitiveness.

ACKNOWLEDGMENT

This chapter is a follow-up to the research project of University - wide internal grant agency (CIGA), registration number 20121001 - Business continuity management contributing to higher performance in organizations and is associated with the running research project of the grant Project of the Grant Agency of the Czech Republic GP402/09/P616 - Use of Competencies in Knowledge-Based Organization. Contact address - Czech University of Life Sciences Prague, Faculty of Economics and Management, Department of Management.

REFERENCES

Altmeyer, D., & Georg, S. (2002). *Die bedeutung von wissensmanagement für unternehmen.* Aachen, Germany: Shaker Verlag.

Anatan, L. (2007). Innovation as core competencies: The role of knowledge and organizational learning in knowledge-based competition era. *Jurnal Manajemen, 9*(2), 87–99.

Beazley, H. (2003*). Knowledge continuity: The new competitive advantage.* Retrieved April 13, 2010, from http://www.asaecenter.org/PublicationsResources/EUArticle.cfm?ItemNumber=11836

Beazley, H., Boenisch, J., & Harden, D. (2002). *Continuity management: Preserving corporate knowledge and productivity when employees leave.* New York, NY: Wiley.

Collison, C., & Parcel, G. (2005). *Knowledge management.* Brno, Czech Republic: Computer Press.

Dalkir, K. (2005). *Knowledge management in theory and practice.* Burlington, VT: Elsevier.

Davenport, T., & Prusak, L. (1998). *Working knowledge.* Boston, MA: Harvard Business School Press.

Douglas, T., & Seely-Brown, J. (2011). *A new culture of learning: Cultivating the imagination for a world of constant change.* New York, NY: CreateSpace.

Drucker, P. (1985). Creating strategies of innovation. *Strategy and Leadership, 13*(6), 8–45. doi:10.1108/eb054121

Drucker, P. (1993). *Innovation and entrepreneurship.* Prague, Czech Republic: Management Press.

Drucker, P. (1998). Management's new paradigms. *Forbes, 162*(7), 152–177.

Ercan, T. (2010). Towards virtualization: A competitive business continuity. *African Journal of Business Management, 4*(10), 2164–2173.

Europe. (2012). *Smart growth.* Retrieved April 15, 2011, from http://ec.europa.eu/europe2020/priorities/smart-growth/index_en.htm

Herbane, B. (2010). The evolution of business kontinuity management: A historical review of practices nad drives. *Business History, 52*(6), 978–1002. doi:10.1080/00076791.2010.511185

Jirásek, J. A. (2004). *Duel of the brains.* Prague, Czech Republic: Alfa Publishing.

Jones, R. (2003). Measuring the benefits of knowledge management at the financial services authority: A case study. *Journal of Information Science, 29*(6), 475–487. doi:10.1177/0165551503296005

Kiernan, M. J. (1995). *Get innovative or get dead! Building competitive companies for the 21st century.* Vancouver, Canada: Douglas & McIntyre.

Košturiak, J., & Chaľ, J. (2008). *Innovation your competitive advantage!* Brno, Czech Republic: Computer Press.

Mlčoch, J. (2002). *Innovation and organizational productivity*. Prague, Czech Republic: Linde.

North, K., & Hornung, T. (2003). The benefits of knowledge management - Results of the German award "knowledge manager 2002". *Journal of Universal Computer Science, 9*(6), 463–471.

O'Leonard, K. (2009). *Bersin & associates 2009 talent management factbook: Executive summary*. Retrieved April 20, 2011, from http://www.bersin.com/uploadedFiles/052909_ES_TM-Factbook2009_KOL_Final.pdf

Pitra, Z. (1997). *The role of innovations in business strategy*. Prague, Czech Republic: Grada Publishing.

Schumpeter, J. A. (1961). *Theory of economic development*. Oxford, UK: Oxford University Press.

Seeley-Brown, J., & Duquid, P. (2000). *The social life of information*. Boston, MA: Harvard Business Press.

Seeley-Brown, J., & Solomon-Gray, E. (1995). *The people are the company*. Retrieved from http://www.fastcompany.com

Stachová, K., & Stacho, Z. (2010). Organisations operating in Slovakia are aware of the need to focus on "innovative organisation", but they have problems to practically adopt it. In *TOIOTARITY: Knowledge Using is Service Management* (pp. 65–76). Warszawa, Poland: Publisher Institute Wydawniczy PTM.

Stam, C. (2009). *Knowledge and the ageing employee: A research agenda*. Haarlem, The Netherlands: Holland University of Applied Sciences.

Švejda, P. (2007). *Business innovation*. Prague, Czech Republic: Association of Business Innovation.

Talukdar, A. (2008). *What is intellectual capital: And why it should be measured*. Founder, Czech Republic: Attainix Consulting.

Tsoukas, H. (2009). A dialogical approach to the creation of new knowledge in organizations. *Organization Science, 20*(6), 941–957. doi:10.1287/orsc.1090.0435

Tsoukas, H., & Mylonopoulos, N. (2004). *Organizations as knowledge systems: Knowledge, learning and dynamic capabilities*. London, UK: Palgrave Macmillan.

Tureková, H., & Mičieta, B. (2003). *Innovative management*. Žilina, Slovakia: EDIS.

Wilson, O. (1998). Knowledge management: Putting a good idea to work. *Managing Information, 5*(2), 31–33.

Wong, N. W. (2009). Paper. *Journal of Business Continuity & Emergency Planning, 4*(1), 62–68.

Young, R. (2005). Knowledge management - Back to basic principles. *Knowledge-management-online.com*. Retrieved April 5, 2010, from http://www.knowledge-management-online.com/knowledge-management-back-to-basic-principles.html

ADDITIONAL READING

Argote, L., & Ingram, P. (2002). Knowledge transfer: A basis for competitive advantage in firms. *Organizational Behavior and Human Decision Processes, 82*, 150–169. doi:10.1006/obhd.2000.2893

Beijerse, R. P. (2002). Knowledge management in small and medium-sized companies: Knowledge management for entrepreneurs. *Journal of Knowledge Management, 4*(2), 162–179. doi:10.1108/13673270010372297

British Standards Institution. (2010). *BS 25999 business continuity*. Retrieved July 20, 2011, from http://www.bsigroup.com/en/Assessment-and-certification-services/management-systems/Standards-and-Schemes/BS-25999/

Brockmann, E., & Simmonds, P. G. (1997). Strategic decision making: The influence of CEO experience and use of tacit knowledge. *Journal of Managerial Issues, 9*(4), 454–467.

Chen, S. (2011). Empirical research on knowledge integration improving innovation ability of IT enterprise- Based on structural equation model. *Information-An International Interdisciplinary Journal, 14*(3), 753–758.

Crevani, L., Palm, K., & Schilling, A. (2011). Innovation management in service firms: A research agenda. *Service Business, 5*(2), 177–193. doi:10.1007/s11628-011-0109-7

Dalkir, K. (2005). *Knowledge management in theory and practice*. Burlington, VT: Elsevier.

Davenport, T., & Prusak, L. (1998). *Working knowledge*. Boston, MA: Harvard Business School Press.

Forsman, H. (2011). Innovation capacity and innovation development in small enterprises: A comparison between the manufacturing and service sectors. *Research Policy, 40*(5), 739–750. doi:10.1016/j.respol.2011.02.003

Goldratt, E. M. (2009). *Isn't it obvious?* Great Barrington, MA: North River Press.

Haldin-Herrgard, T. (2000). Difficulties in diffusion of tacit knowledge in organizations. *Journal of Intellectual Capital, 1*(4), 357–365. doi:10.1108/14691930010359252

Harsh, O. K. (2009). Three dimensional KM and explicit knowledge reuse. *Journal of Knowledge Management Practice, 10*(2), 1–10.

Herbane, B. (2010). The evolution of business continuity management: A historical review of practices and drivers. *Business History, 52*(6), 978–1002. doi:10.1080/00076791.2010.511185

Hibbard, J. (1997). Knowledge management – Knowing what we know. *Information Week, 653*, 46–64.

Johannessen, J., & Olsen, B. (2003). Knowledge management and sustainable competitive advantages: The impact of dynamic contextual training. *International Journal of Information Management, 23*(4), 277–289. doi:10.1016/S0268-4012(03)00050-1

Kachaňáková, A., & Stachová, K. (2011). The level of education and development of employees in organisations operating in Slovakia. *Scientia Agriculturae Bohemica, 42*(2), 87–92.

Massingham, P. (2010). Knowledge risk management: A framework. *Journal of Knowledge Management, 14*(3), 464–485. doi:10.1108/13673271011050166

Münstermnn, B., Eckhardt, A., & Weitzel, T. (2010). The performance impact of business process standardization: An empiric evaluation of the recruitment process. *Business Process Management Journal, 16*(1).

Ordaz, C. C. (2006). The influence of human resource management on knowledge sharing and innovation in Spain: The mediating role of affective commitment. *International Journal of Human Resource Management, 22*(7), 1442–1463. doi:10.1080/09585192.2011.561960

Palacios-Marques, D., Gil-Pechuan, I., & Lim, S. (2011). Improving human capital through knowledge management practices in knowledge-intensive business services. *Service Business, 5*(2), 99–112. doi:10.1007/s11628-011-0104-z

Smith, M., & Sherwood, J. (1995). Business continuity planning. *Computers & Security, 14*, 14–23. doi:10.1016/0167-4048(95)96991-B

Sternberg, R. J., & Wagner, R. K. (1992). Tacit knowledge: An unspoken key to managerial success. *Creativity and Innovation Management, 1*(1), 5–13. doi:10.1111/j.1467-8691.1992. tb00016.x

Swap, W. (2001). Using mentoring and storytelling to transfer knowledge in the workplace. *Journal of Management Information Systems, 18*(1), 95–114.

Swart, J. (2006). Intellectual capital: Disentangling an enigmatic concept. *Journal of Intellectual Capital, 2*(7), 136–159. doi:10.1108/14691930610661827

Swart, J. (2011). Thatś why it matters: How knowing creates value. *Management Learning, 42*(3), 319–332. doi:10.1177/1350507610391591

Truneček, J. (2004). *Knowledge management.* Prague, Czech Republic: C. H. Beck.

Urbancová, H. (2011). *Knowledge and experience continuity in organizations.* Unpublished Doctoral Dissertation. Prague, Czech Republic: Czech University of Life Sciences Prague.

Urbancová, H., & Königová, M. (2010a). Control and its role in the process of ensuring knowledge continuity. *Journal of Modern Accounting and Auditing, 6*(7), 38–45.

Urbancová, H., & Königová, M. (2010b). Role of knowledge continuity, experience and competencies in process of delegation. *Scientia Agriculturae Bohemica, 41*(2), 115–120.

Urbancová, H., & Königová, M. (2011). New management disciplines in the area of business continuity. *Scientia Agriculturae Bohemica, 42*(1), 37–43.

KEY TERMS AND DEFINITIONS

Business Continuity Management: A managerial discipline that focuses on the identification of potential impacts arising from negative circumstances that can threaten organizations (Wong, 2009).

Competitive Advantage: Long-term ability of organizations to generate more value for customers than competition (Mlčoch, 2002).

Innovation: A series of scientific, technical, organizational, financial, business and other activities, the goal of which is to produce a new or significantly improved product (goods, technology or service) efficiently launched in the market (Švejda, 2007).

Knowledge Continuity Management: Is targeted at the transfer of critical knowledge (Beazley, et al., 2002).

Knowledge Management: The discipline of enabling individuals, teams, and entire organizations to collectively and systematically capture, store, create, share, and apply knowledge, to better achieve their objectives (Young, 2003).

Performance: The ability to transform inputs into outputs (Pitra, 1997).

Processes: Includes various activities which transform inputs to outputs and from them creates products and services (Mlčoch, 2002).

ENDNOTE

[1] The outcomes of the survey carried out in the Czech Republic reveal the extent to which the decisive internal factors influence knowledge continuity, ensuring that it contributes to the improvement of the efficiency of individual processes. With respect to knowledge continuity ensuring, it has been found that organizational climate is the strongest factor in all organizations examined. Other important factors include stimulation and organizational culture. Or-

ganizational structure is the least important factor. At an individual level, motivation is the most significant factor, followed by the will to share knowledge and trust. It can be concluded that large organizations are more strongly influenced by factors at the organizational level while factors at an individual level play a more important role in small organizations. Knowledge continuity ensuring determines individual process in organizations. This means that knowledge continuity is one of the strengthening factors of an organization's performance.

Chapter 14
Slow Knowledge:
The Case for Savouring Learning and Innovation

John Tull
Inclusive Capital, Australia

ABSTRACT

Breathless announcements of the latest information access devices occupy whole sections of our daily news, itself increasingly accessed online and on-the-go. This reinforces to the manager or educator the conventional wisdom that strategies for developing organisational capabilities inherently involve ever-quicker access and sharing of information—a belief reflected widely in organisational learning and strategy literatures. However, Knowledge Management's role in translating learning into performance-enhancing capabilities remains opaque; "macro" evaluations are too abstract, leading to recent calls for empirical or "micro" studies. Furthermore, while rare breakthroughs attract headlines and research, customers and clients are mostly won or lost in the more mundane interactions of daily work. The evolution of organisational capabilities and how they rely on the medium of knowledge practices can be unpacked using the construct of an organisation's "absorptive capacity," a construct essentially unknown to KM. That construct can be improved by incorporating "tempo" as a crucial design and governance element. Analysing KM practices as supporting absorptive capacity is a new idea that provides both the manager and the educator with implementable recommendations. A detailed case study identifies the four key factors of capability development via KM, highlighting that "slow knowledge"—gearing knowledge processes to the appropriate absorptive capacity framework—can yield more effective organisational outcomes.

1. INTRODUCTION

Even a cursory online browse of the writings of a Sun Tse or Caesar is enough to demonstrate that knowledge has always been vitally important for the effective exercise of organizational capabili-ties; yet it is only very recently that reseachers have turned to the formal study of knowledge within institutional capabilities. Development of the 'knowledge based view of the firm' (Grant, 1996) for the first time added intangibles as an identifiable and valuable resource (Barney, 1991) of the organization. This prompted managerial at-

DOI: 10.4018/978-1-4666-1969-2.ch014

tention to swing to the issue of how best to manage that resource. Knowledge Management (KM), which began as an initially *'Utopian'* response (Wilson, 2005) arguably producing more disappointment than success, has since evolved into a more nuanced, albeit fragmented, set of practices that provoke ongoing debate about the relationship between KM and value creation (Easterby-Smith & Lyles, 2003). We need not look far to see evidence that the KM discourse has enduring appeal however; Long Range Planning, a leading business practitioner-oriented academic journal, states that four of its five all-time most highly cited papers feature 'Knowledge Management' in their titles—and the fifth addresses 'Intellectual Capital.'

This discovery of knowledge as a manageable resource is important in a landscape increasingly analysed as 'dynamic' (Eisenhardt & Martin, 2000; Teece, Pisano, & Shuen, 1997), where the degree of 'evolutionary fitness' of a resource (Helfat & Peteraf, 2003) is crucial to sustainable competitive advantage. And yet simply possessing the resource of knowledge doesn't create that advantage; we need to transform and apply it in some value-creating way (Spender, 1996). New technologies present us with many different ways to try to perform that value-adding; we experience this in the plethora of new ways in which we use knowledge to work, communicate and collaborate. Data-rich mobile technologies even untether the place and time of those activities:

If the iPhone 4, Google's Android applications, and Tablet PCs are weak signals, we are stepping into a very different world at an increasing pace. (Despres, 2011, p. 25)

1.1. Two Challenges in Managing Knowledge

Administrators and educators face at least two pressing challenges in assessing what is KM's role in this environment. The first challenge is to reconcile the sheer open-ended technological possibilities that drive the evolution of modern KM with the unforgiving managerial imperative to improve organisational performance (Marqués & Simón, 2006). The second challenge is for research staff and marketers to reconcile their legendary differences by finding ways to create knowledge that is both new and valuable, a conciliation that some authors argue begins with our acknowledging that learning processes are valuable only to the extent that they are closely aligned to strategy (Vera & Crossan, 2003).

The first challenge arises from the way that KM and Information Technology (IT) have co-evolved. The key issues with 'first generation' understanding and implementation of KM technologies, processes, and artifacts are well-rehearsed (see for example Brown & Duguid, 1991; McElroy, 2000; Senge, 1994). In those early accounts, technological possibilities were often mistaken as representing what actually creates sustainable value. That technology-focused KM paradigm tended to 'ignore the social architecture of knowledge exchange within organizations' (Easterby-Smith & Lyles, 2003). Managers and educators largely identified KM as the application of efficient knowledge accumulation, aggregation, and manipulation functionalities to business operations; KM became largely 'inventory control' of data. This is a potentially dangerous metaphor; for example, while knowledge creation exhibits a pronounced path dependency, meaning that all our learning draws initially on our organisation's prior stock of knowledge (see, for example, Grant, 1996; Ahuja & Katila, 2001), the needed information 'stock' transformations may therefore be misconstrued as essentially an IT problem. This ignores important issues, such as how innovation is possible and where new knowledge gets created (McElroy, 2000), along with the prior question of who is it that decides what is worth acquiring anyway (Antona Copoulou & Easterby-Smith, 2005).

By contrast, 'second generation' KM, emphasizing self-organising knowledge creation, fluid knowledge transfers, and their relationship to action (Tuomi, 2002) seems more grounded in human interaction. This central idea closely links organisational learning to strategic management priorities: knowledge becomes most valuable to the organisation precisely by existing as a dynamic 'flow' that can be managed, rather than as any stock of artifacts *per-se* (Nonaka, et al., 2008). But the desired link to improved performance outcomes remains problematic; the second challenge noted above, of aligning knowledge creation with value-addition performance, remains unanswered. If Despres is right in claiming that 'most actors agree that for five years or more KM has been on the downswing of the management fashion wave' (Despres, 2011, p. ix), then practitioners need to heed his call for KM's rehabilitation via 'less euphoria, more deliberation, results-oriented [analyses with] more depth…fewer gurus, better methodologies' (p. x).

If we instead characterise KM as the goal-seeking practice of knowledge—or rather, of 'knowing' (Eisenhardt & Santos, 2002)—we may discover the needed connection between the research agendas for organisational learning and strategic management. In this vein, we could redefine second generation KM practices as the 'implementation strategy' for adaptive learning and knowledge creation (McElroy, 2000, p. 201), addressing the second KM challenge noted above. Viewing KM as practices that enable goal-directed learning to support performance imperatives reflects the realisation that 'in a continuous movement…subjective experience grows into knowledge through action and practice' (Nonaka, et al., 2008, p. 33). Viewed as dynamic practice

rather than as the sum of knowledge resources, KM can thereby provide managerial tools for promoting the right conditions for knowledge creation and application that will produce desired business results.

While the idea of KM as dynamic practice looks promising, the devil is, as always, in the detail of identifying what those 'right conditions' are and how they may be implemented. Our core issue here is how knowledge is generated and then applied to create organizational capabilities. We typically experience the flow of knowledge acquisition as an individual phenomenon, a personal learning. However, if Daneels (2003) is correct in arguing that experiential (self) learning is limiting, it is difficult to link learning to organisational performance. On the other hand, at an aggregated level, if the interpretive flexibility of people in bureaucratic organisations is low (Orlikowski, 1992), collective learning may occur within a systemic and entrenched 'learning myopia' (Levinthal & March, 1993) that equally reduces the organisation's strategic capabilities. This set of practice issues about aligning learning to developing and applying outcome-producing capabilities is important; practitioners recognise that organisational competitiveness is ultimately at stake (see, for example, Leinwand & Mainardi, 2011, for a recent discussion). Constant renewal of capabilities comes at a cost, however—the 'dynamic capability' of learning is expensive to maintain (Zollo & Winter, 2002).

1.2. Objectives of this Chapter

This chapter takes as its point of departure Easterby-Smith & Prieto's (2008) concluding remarks to their analysis linking dynamic capabilities and knowledge management:

[T]here is a need to understand the critical importance of learning processes, both because they underpin resource and operational renewal processes and because they mediate between

environmental dynamism and the appropriate configuration of organizational capabilities. (p. 246)

The following discussion makes the empirically grounded case that, by attending to the 'micro' details of how KM practices and resources can be incorporated in organisational capability development, we gain new insights into how learning sometimes transmutes into effective change. In contrast to the 'speed' ethos of IT-based paradigms, the guiding metaphor here instead borrows from the 'slow food' phenomenon, as stated at their eponymous website:

slow [knowledge] unites the pleasure of [learning] with responsibility, sustainability, and harmony with the context.

By exploring how the pace and manner in which learning is accomplished shapes the development of needed capabilities, we can more clearly link organisational knowledge creation and absorption to performance outcomes. The proposed approach provides the first direct integration of KM with the influential 'Absorptive Capacity' (ACAP) construct from the strategy literature. In so doing, it also provides the first explicit extension of KM to organisational capability development theory, by identifying the need to add a temporal dimension to ACAP to better articulate absorbed practice. The next section will overview the ACAP construct and its uses, in order to derive an initial framework for assessing KM within the context of organisational capability development through a detailed case study.

2. ABSORPTIVE CAPACITY

In an environment of constant change, it is important to better understand the applied practices, resources, and structures required to create and support organisational performance. Dynamic Capabilities theorising in the strategic manage-

ment literature grapples with the issue of how performance improvement can be managed in such environments (Zollo & Winter, 2002); one of its most widely used constructs is that of Absorptive Capacity. The ACAP construct seems sufficiently flexible *prima-facie* to be applied to KM; it has previously provided a framework for identifying and analysing factors such as diversity and feedback (Cohen & Levinthal, 1990), social context (Zahra & George, 2002), and political power (Todorova & Durisin, 2007) in knowledge creation processes. It has also been used to assess the effects of learning on the competitive environment (Van den Bosch, et al., 1999).

What then is ACAP and what does it offer us? Cohen and Levinthal provide the seminal definition of ACAP as the organisation's 'ability to identify, assimilate, and exploit knowledge to commercial ends' (1990, p. 128). They argue that development of knowledge is cumulative and path dependent, originating primarily from external sources. Thus, ACAP begets further ACAP, through an incremental process in which prior knowledge is applied to the creation of new knowledge when triggered by some event, thereby increasing the organisation's knowledge stock (and capacity for absorption) for the following cycle. Originally developed within the context of technology R&D, the ACAP concept has been broadened to address organizational learning in fields ranging from general innovation (for example, Van den Bosch, et al., 1999) and strategic alliances (Lane & Lubatkin, 1998) to strategic change (Kogut & Zander, 1992).

Zahra and George (2002) provide a more practical redefinition of ACAP as 'a set of organizational routines and processes by which firms acquire, assimilate, transform, and exploit knowledge to produce a dynamic organizational capability' (p. 186). ACAP thereby becomes a broadly sequenced process of four stages spanning the spectrum from 'potential' to 'realized' capability (see Table 1). Thus, ACAP is a complete process that we might interpret as capable of explicitly relating strategic

Table 1. ACAP framework

Acquisition	the firm's ability to identify and acquire (primarily) externally-sourced knowledge	**Potential ACAP:** Related to strategic flexibility and a firm's capacity to adapt, learn and evolve; insufficient by itself to produce innovation
Assimilation	analysing, processing, interpreting, and understanding this knowledge	
Transformation	processes for the development of new routines that combine existing knowledge with newly acquired and assimilated knowledge	**Realized ACAP:** Processes to leverage absorbed knowledge; show an explicit link to organisational performance
Exploitation	processes for refining, leveraging, or extending existing competencies, or to creating new ones	

(Source: author's summary, after Zahra & George, 2002)

management (the creation of competitive advantage) with organisational learning (innovation processes) and knowledge management (creation and adoption of knowledge). The following three paragraphs briefly describe these linkages.

ACAP has one primary role on this account: it is embedded within organisational processes and routines to produce adaptive capabilities that improve performance. ACAP is therefore positively associated with organisational change and innovation (Szulanski, 1996), a key theme in Strategic Management literature of dynamic capabilities (Teece, et al., 1997). In fact, Zahra and George (2002) explicitly identify ACAP as the learning mechanism in strategic adaptation: 'We recognize ACAP as a dynamic capability that influences the nature and sustainability of a firm's competitive advantage' (p. 185), with learning leading to both innovation and 'the creation of other organizational competencies' (p. 186).

To remain innovative and competent, an organisation must develop a full understanding of the processes that transform its knowledge into capabilities and how these capabilities can meet environmental demands (Van den Bosch, et al., 1999; Lane & Lubatkin, 1998). Zahra and George (2002) conceptualise ACAP as being ultimately the capability to create new outputs such as goods, services and new ventures through learning-directed behavioural change. This links ACAP to the Organisational Learning literature

and the latter's distinction between learning as 'exploration' versus 'exploitation' (March, 1991).

By contrast, we find only implicit recognition of a relationship between ACAP and KM in the current literature. An extensive database search in July 2011 identified only a handful of mentions—ranging from a working paper focusing on KM systems as antecedents to ACAP (Moos, et al., 2010); to an SME study citing a relationship (Gray, 2006). This is a significant omission, given the prominence of the requirement for knowledge resource management highlighted by Lane et al. (2006) in probably the widest-ranging literature review of the ACAP construct. That analysis of 289 papers concluded ACAP 'depends on the organization's ability to share knowledge and communicate internally,' with a 'critical' dependency being 'the relevant prior knowledge that is the basis of absorptive capacity also includes awareness of what knowledge the organization already possesses, as well as where and how it is used' (p. 838). These statements imply that the ACAP involved in enabling new capabilities is at least in part the outcome of that organisation's KM capability.

For the purposes of addressing this gap, we can adopt the broad Zahra and George (2002) structure of four major knowledge processes comprising ACAP (Table 1), noting the mediation of contingent conditions including 'social integration mechanisms' in generating actual performance outcomes. Such mechanisms are important for explicating shared practice rather than solitary learning (see Section 1.1), consistent with the view that 'learning as increasing participation in communities of practice concerns the whole person acting in the world' (Lave & Wenger, 1991; see also Brown & Duguid, 1991).

Thus, the central research question for this discussion is: *How can KM be enacted in ways that enhance the organisation's absorptive capacity for new capability development?* Consistent with the earlier emphasis on practice-oriented 'micro' approaches, this chapter addresses the research question through an empirical study of a major capability development initiative executed as an integrated KM project and associated consulting skills development program.

3. CASE STUDY: KM AS CAPABILITY DEVELOPMENT ENABLER

The following case study presents a 'comparative case analysis' of two attempts by a single multinational organisation to effect its strategy of implementing and exploiting an organisation-wide capability development that in large part depended upon the KM practices that enable effective learning and adoption (ACAP).

Case studies are a preferred vehicle for exploring emergent issues, capturing the richness of micro detail (Salvato, 2003) while retaining theoretical relevance by linking back to the literature (Eisenhardt, 1989; Yin, 2003). The last requirement is particularly important for 'micro' practice studies, to avoid remaining at the level of rich idiosyncratic detail. Johnson et al. (2003) recommend that such studies 'span levels' and involve 'a close engagement with practice' in order to improve theoretical integration. A single in-depth case study is consistent with those authors' call for 'an activity-based view of strategy that focuses on the detailed processes and prac-

tices which constitute the day-to-day activities of organizational life and which relate to strategic outcomes' (p. 6).

Echoing these sentiments, Cook and Brown (1999) identify the value of empirical studies of specifically KM practices and their role in supporting innovation capability:

There is a need for more case studies of knowledge creating organizations, knowledge work, and knowledge management... Equally important are the ways organizations can dynamically afford, within the situated practices of ordinary daily work, the productive inquiry essential to ongoing innovation. (p. 398)

To enhance the quality of the research design, multiple people were engaged within each unit, along with multiple sources of information—interviews, survey instruments, extended observation, and document reviews (Yin, 2003). To improve theoretical validation, the emerging framework was continuously compared to the initial inductively derived framework, as a form of hypothesis testing. Treating the two studied projects as 'strategic episodes' (Hendry & Seidl, 2003), and the country-level finding as 'cases' within either episode (Yin, 2003), allows for cross-case comparison of what were similar initiatives governed by a common strategy but separated by five years. The 'strategic episodes' chosen are quite familiar to organisations attempting to compete on the basis of better knowledge capabilities; for Johnson et al. (2003) this is important, as choice of readily recognisable situations helps to strengthen and broaden analytical generalisations (p. 17). The capability development framework was subjected to iterative 'interrogation' through open debate with a number of interview participants as the data collection proceeded over 18 months, a useful filter for arriving at more robust explanatory factors (Yin, 2003).

3.1. The McKinsey of Development

By the start of the twenty-first century, the hundred billion dollar International Aid sector was transforming rapidly as Western donors sought models that delivered clearer results. Attention had swung increasingly to economic development and development of the small and medium enterprise sector, supported by popularisation of 'bottom of the pyramid' commercial approaches by Prahalad (2004) and Yunus (2003), and by the entry of new foundations established by Internet-era billionaires.

TechnoServe, a 32-year-old not-for-profit organisation with 300 employees and an annual donor budget of $15 million in 2000, had enjoyed a clear decades-long differentiation from its singular focus on business consulting, extending private sector ethos and skills to farmers and entrepreneurs based on rigorous value chain analysis. Attracted by the newly galvanised market for commercially oriented development, however, larger and broader-based competitors vigorously upgraded their capabilities. By 2005, the top five private competitors had annual 'revenues' (grants and income) totaling $1,042 million, with the top two contractors winning an average of $452 million in annual contract awards between 2000-2005 from the United States government agency USAID alone (according to the 'Fedspending' database).

In 2002, TechnoServe launched an internal strategic capabilities program centred on improving business consulting skills that would enable this mid-ranking player to outpace the broader market by seizing several 'whole of sector' projects in areas like specialty coffee and region-wide cashew growing. Most major direct competitors were also styling themselves as 'consultants' however—for example DAI declared its 'global project management and consulting' capabilities, while Chemonics reinforced its positioning as 'a global consulting firm' by establishing a Knowledge and Innovation Department in 2006. These investments indicated growing 'knowledge inten-

sity' in the sector, creating new sources of both uncertainty and potential competitive advantage for firms (Autio, et al., 2000).

TechnoServe management concluded that their top priority was to develop the capabilities needed for deep value-added services; they hypothesised this required an organisation-wide learning program centered on consulting skills. That strategic program would support the written corporate policy of 'enabling rather than doing,' through disciplined practices that 'support market structures…that become self-sustaining, allowing us to move on to the next area in need.' In 2003, a consulting skills program comprising a five day residential 'mini-MBA' format was launched, a program in which the majority of Business Advisor (BA), Program Manager (PM) and Country Director (CD) staff would participate. Management hoped that such capabilities would allow TechnoServe to become what the then-CEO recalled in an interview with the author (July 2011) as 'the McKinsey of Development.'

By early 2005 however, the leadership concluded that quality of execution was being impeded by widely disparate skill-sets, work practices, and strategic awareness. A strategic review recommended more integrated capability development, with KM being the critical but most challenging component; 'TechnoServe does not have functional leadership in KM—a key focus of our larger competitors.' Their recommendations included (1) 'to make quality of execution a key part of TechnoServe's mind-set/culture'; and (2) 'to integrate knowledge management, program evaluation and product R&D to ensure learning gets captured and leveraged.'

3.2. Strategic Episode 1: Resource-Oriented KM Implementation

Management's response to the above was to expand the consulting skills program and initiate plans for universal access to tools, case studies, and sharing facilities. The latter elements involved the organisation's first-ever implementation of an enterprise-level KM strategy, one designed to provide internal capability development at two levels:

- A tier-one enterprise knowledge management platform (using SharePoint)
- 'Best practice' tools aligned to Communities of Practice.

The resulting implementation in 2005 reflected a classic 'first generation' KM launch (McElroy, 2000; Tuomi, 2002). A large volume of documents was lodged, ranging from market analyses, sector studies and proposals, to business plans, analytical models, and donor reports. The launch was supported in multiple ways: computers and cell phones for all staff, internal newsletters, promotional competitions, a Web-based instructional tutorial program, and management messaging. By 2006 and 2007, some successes were noted—cases of effective replication, complementary local websites and process developments in major field programs. However, internal reviews highlighted that the KM system, toolkits, and consulting training had not become integral to the work of most staff; the consulting training had remained an 'island' of activity and was finally discontinued globally in 2007.

A limited field study of TechnoServe's KM status, conducted in early 2009 by three external consultants, provided various qualitative inputs regarding the likely causes and implications for practice. They found that 'the state of knowledge management is relatively primitive,' noting the lack of 'systematic efforts to capture, analyze (and to some extent even recognize) lessons learned and best practices.' The strategic significance of 'potential' versus 'realised' (Zahra & George, 2002) was everywhere evident: 'most importantly, TNS…sits on top of a mine of stories and lessons about technique and about basic principles. That mine is unopened and untapped.' The KM

resource and related practices had instead 'fallen into disuse.'

An analysis of the KM library in 2011 by this author highlights the extent of that rapid decline, taken to reflect lack of staff demand or 'knowledge pull.' Document lodgment had declined steeply after 2006 (Figure 1), with usage tapering off to negligible levels, in sharp contrast with the doubling of staff numbers over the duration as several complex, knowledge-intensive projects were won.

By 2009 the country and regional management reflected on what they acknowledged was a failed capability development program. In a survey of senior leaders that year, 60% rated TechnoServe's KM as 'falling short,' second only to the 70% dissatisfaction with the related issue of staff training. Poor basic disciplines in file management made any use of the KM system a hit-and-miss investment of time over slow Internet connections, curtailing field staff usage. Skills development was thus impaired by these higher 'search costs' (Nelson & Winter, 1982) which those scholars show significantly influences the development of organisational routines which constitute capabilities (Zollo & Winter, 2002). This author's study found that use of the KM system, by managers or professionals, was very largely confined to Headquarters staff; the KM system had become an unstructured repository.

Thus a carefully planned and ostensibly integrated strategic capability program, one based on claimed KM best practice and sponsored strongly at CEO level, had nevertheless failed. Potential causal factors are noted above but do not provide a coherent description. The ACAP four-element model provides us with a more structured diagnosis:

- **Acquisition/Creation:** The consultancy training was not integrated into the design of new programs and related investment; 'There were no tools I could find to help me create or adapt new learnings, and no

281

Figure 1. Document deposits to KM system 2004-2010 (source: the author)

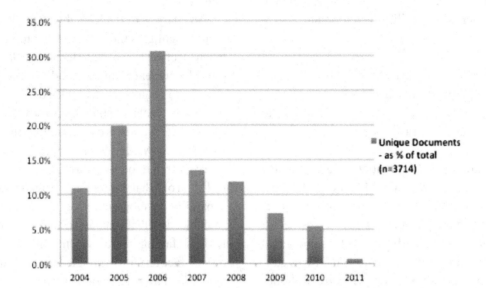

reliable way to share anything if I did' (PM, Africa).

- **Assimilation:** Realignment of workflow and prioritisation of learning was inconsistent at best, with short term task focus dominating; 'The main reason for limited participation? Everyone is completely swamped!' (BA, South America).

- **Transformation:** KM processes and IT resources were inadequate for collaboration; 'The Senior BA's have all the documents on their laptops; the office server crashes' (CD, Central America).

- **Exploitation:** Most staff discovered little practical application to the job, due to poor integration of processes; 'I don't think the majority of the field BAs will use SharePoint unless the Director specifically assigns them a task' (Snr. BA, Africa).

ACAP provides a useful diagnostic analysis of a flawed process design and practice that combined to frustrate the creation, adoption and application of new or adapted, valuable knowledge. It highlights the interdependencies between successive steps and the ways they created the lived experience of participants increasingly frustrated by obstacles to improving their operational capabilities.

However, these categories lack sufficient granularity to help us identify just what, at a day-to-day practice level, constitutes effective absorption of knowledge. For example: 'acquisition' is expensive and the interpretation of outputs is often contested, especially at the early stages—therefore what should the organisation do? Simply improving scanning and filtering subprocesses may provide a 'technician's' solution for matching the right content, intentions and rigour in implementation. That, however, may lead us to ignore the more fundamental issue that undermines much well-executed Development Aid: why is it that sound expert advice is often ignored by the poor? Both KM and ACAP lack a reflective process that (re)assesses whether the right knowledge is being sought and adopted, at the risk of simply maintaining the organisation's 'dominant logic' (Prahalad & Bettis, 1986). Thus, we can now recast the research question in Section 2 in more concrete terms: *Can we develop an ACAP-based framework that better integrates KM practice to capability development through a dynamically adjusted orientation towards the goals of practice rather than just their particulars?* This question motivated the study summarised below.

3.3. Method for the Participative Study

The attempt to address the research question given above was conducted as a participant-observer study from September 2009 to March 2011 in two phases:

1. An inductive process of accumulating data, primarily by interview and observation of a sample of the advisory staff working with clients. Reflections on the findings were used to create a working hypothesis for capability development and its KM support;

2. A subsequent deductive testing process, using that working hypothesis to structure a larger program of interviews and direct observation, supported by a survey instrument; interview participants were invited to engage with the hypothesis and help co-create it.

The data collection process is summarised in Table 2.

3.3.1. Initial "Inductive" Phase

Based on the initial data collection and discussions with management, the author developed a framework based on four factors that seemed to determine the learning practices that promote capability development within consulting practice. These were: (1) investment in KM facilities and specific tools content; (2) training processes to acquire use of those assets; (3) the experience of applying that training in practice; and (4) management's role in providing the internal environment, incentives, and infrastructure that shape and monitor these processes. This is represented in Figure 2, a simple schematic used to engage with selected participants in the later 'deductive' phase.

3.3.2. In-Depth "Deductive" Phase

In addition to the 91 interviews in this phase, an 86% response to a follow-up survey of all interviewed staff provided additional insights about the context and the relative importance of 20 elements that affect performance at both individual and team levels. The main areas of focus were Tools and KM facilities; Training and Development processes; Learning application experience; and related Management processes.

Table 2. Data collection and framework development approach

	Inductive Framework	- Deductive Framework and Test
Method	Interviews, observation, document reviews; develop a working hypothesis	Interviews, observation, 'co-production' of the framework conceptually, then realised through joint design of the consulting workshop and KM facilities with selected participants; tested in a major pilot 2011.
Dimensions	7 interviews (90 minutes average); 2 months in-field observation in 2 countries	91 interviews (averaging 75 minutes) including 6 with executive/non-executive board members. 11 observation periods (training events); 16 months of in-field and HQ full time observation/participation; extensive formal and informal management meetings.
Theoretical Sampling: Engage voluntary participants with a range of job levels and types, years of experience in the organisation, and (undisclosed) individual performance ratings.		

(Source: the author)

Figure 2. Capability development: initial view (source: the author)

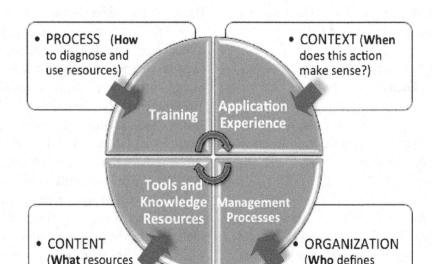

In both the interviews and surveys, one strikingly strong observation was the pervasive 'mission zeal,' an intellectual and emotional alignment expressed by 88% of respondents centred on a corporate culture of providing business-oriented self-help opportunities to the disadvantaged. The majority of respondents also reflected a high sense of internal cooperation during in-person encounters, but with considerable uncertainty over whether this could be maintained amidst rapid growth.

The strongest notes of concern arose in regards to the operational isolation of teams and even country units, expressed in a sense of lost opportunities for sharing and adapting knowledge. This had been a persistent issue: 'in 2005, it was hard to see any common thread except for mission' (Corporate Executive). In the interviews, 71% of interviewees reported significant concerns about inadequate individual and group capability development, and 82% experienced no effective role for formal KM in their jobs.

Applying the practice-oriented framework in Figure 2:

- The majority of interviewees saw only limited relevance, access, and potential use of tools and KM resources: 'the problem is, we are hard science people—but it is 'soft' issues that take up all our time" (Snr. BA, South America)
- The consulting training process was conceptually elegant but unwieldy: 'too much content, not enough absorption or application' (Regional Executive); 'we need to learn to listen instead of tell; you can't change behaviour by telling' (CD, Africa);
- As a result, fewer than 15% of respondents could tell a story about productive practice experience or application of that training and associated KM assets: 'good information, but it wasn't skill-building; I didn't know what to do with it next Monday' (BA, Africa);

• Management processes only partly supported KM integration into the work: 'we were given no incentive or time to change what we were doing, to invest time in disseminating information' (PM, Africa).

Thus, in this context an ACAP process of 'acquisition,' interpreted as the efficient creation of constant streams of new tools or techniques, would likely become seriously counter-productive. Pointing a 'fire hose' of information towards a context of bad roads, slow Internet, glacial trust-building customs, and the like, can result in severe mismatch of resources to needs; that creates confusion and frustration and likely obscures identification of more effective resources (or people). This concern applies to each of the ACAP components.

These insights provided a set of design principles for a second strategic initiative to develop consulting capabilities and supporting KM practices, as described in Section 3.4.

3.4. Strategic Episode 2: Practice-Oriented KM Implementation

By 2010, management had embraced the strategic importance of embarking on a 'second generation' KM initiative emphasizing collaborative discovery, sharing and self-organisation rather than compliance. This matched the historically decentralised corporate style of the organisation. An extensive search for a KM technical solution therefore prioritized collaborative functionality and intuitive user interfaces. The research findings above centre-staged actual needs, the importance of the organisation's ability to assimilate and deploy, and realistic implications for management systems and practices. The KM re-launch was positioned in the 2010 corporate strategy update document to 'result in a revitalized culture and organization for TechnoServe.'

3.4.1. Joint Theory Building Approach

Many participants in the study cited some version of the 'fire hose' issue noted above as a major concern. A typical account by a participant in the original consulting training was that it was a heady week of 'downloads and drills,' a 'boot-camp' with 'no time for absorbing, trying it out, making sure I understood before we were on to the next topic' (Snr. BA, Africa). An important initial design reorientation was to translate the ACAP process principles into a more practice-oriented design. This entailed envisaging the process from the 'lived reality' of the business advisor staff, most of whom operate out of four-wheel drive vehicles far from home base, working with client groups immersed in traditional customs and folk knowledge bases far from the university classroom. Effective 'knowing' practices require not 'acquisition' or 'transformation' in the abstract, but instead demands practice skills and tools such as those that enable better situational awareness ('who gains here; who loses?'), commercial instincts ('is this business or a disguised social program?'), and an overarching reflexive awareness ('am I getting this right? how can I find out?').

The research findings, collected and analysed iteratively with feedback from a sample of participants, led to refinement of the capability development framework, along with an important reorientation essentially from noun to verb: a new focus on the activity areas that interact to develop capabilities as practices, rather than their artifacts. This revised framework is active and purposive, providing impetus for the framework to be continuously reflexively monitored by all participants and modified adaptively—a concept informed by Giddens' Structuration Theory (1994; see Tull & Dumay, 2007, for an example within the context of strategic change management).

The one constant principle would be that of 'tempo,' the perhaps largely tacit regulation and alignment of the time-based enactments involved in the acquisition and absorption of innovation and application. Tempo is especially important in the context of work that requires complex performances by individual and teams over durations of months and years. In collaborative discussion, we jointly hypothesized that recognising 'tempo' explicitly in the framework would provide all the involved agents (managers, professionals, and other actors) with a monitoring guidance that helps them avoid the performance implications of inadvertent under- or over-emphasis in any quadrant.

Upon reflection subsequent to this framework development, we decided we could view these elements as mapping broadly to the ACAP categories, with tempo directed by the organisational purpose of realising value, generating a recursive feedback loop in those learning interactions. The resulting reconceptualisation of the framework is illustrated in Figure 3.

This practice-based model hypothesis that the development of business capabilities occurs at two levels:

- The 'above-the-line' level of the agent— whether individual or their Community of Practice (CoP); the development learning and experience made available to become 'internalised' as part of their professional repertoire of capabilities;
- The 'below-the-line' level of the organisation, its resources and capacity; these become 'institutionalised' as a shared epistemic resource and set of norms.

Interviewees strongly engaged with this framework, finding it spoke directly to the specific investments needed to improve their practice of consulting with an intuitive accessibility that encouraged any of them to monitor the 'fitness' of those settings. This established a framework for the design of a specific program that could serve as a test of the underlying hypothesis. That collaborative design process and test process is described in the following section.

Figure 3. Practice-oriented capability development framework (source: the author)

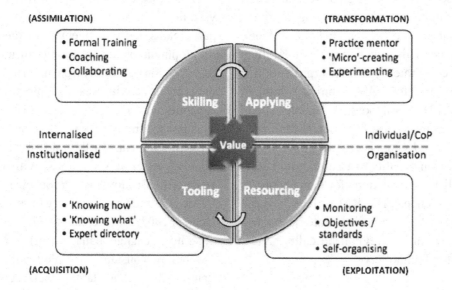

3.5. Designing an Integrated Capability Development

Staff at all levels had identified the consulting training that had fallen into disuse as the candidate for redevelopment—it arose as the most frequently cited need in the interviews, with client engagement, stakeholder motivation, change management, and relevant quantitative skills singled out as the four priority skill areas needed. Many recognised that within TechnoServe, best practice existed largely as tacit knowledge: the corporate strategy update summed it up as 'quality is driven by individual staff skills instead of global corporate intellectual capital.'

The design principles needed to recognise several persistent impediments:

- An only partially-completed 'transition from the organizational competence being technical to business' (2005 internal strategy document).
- Infrequent formal training opportunities due to widely dispersed work locations
- An embedded 'apprenticeship' model that reinforced siloed thinking.

The design aimed to integrate KM functionality and processes with a suite of self-learning tools and opportunities for collaboration, to create a more effective consultancy practice at individual and at group level. Performance-enhancing capabilities would be underpinned by the deployment of KM practices supportive of ACAP processes.

Shifting to the practice performative, knowing emerged spontaneously in multiple discussions as the explicit and overarching priority for most respondents: 'KM has to be about more than a library. We need to analyse what we do and how we do it, for best practices' (CD, Africa); 'it's when we are 'in the moment' that we need to be able to apply our collective wisdom to ask: 'what's going on here? How should we work with these smart but vulnerable people?" (Snr. BA, Africa).

Adopting the framework in Figure 3 provided the 'core micro-strategies engineering' design approach (Salvato, 2003) that enabled the capability development team to converge on four design priorities for creating an effective knowledge-building cycle for the change management consulting practice. Described in the performative style, they were:

- **Tooling:** Intuitive, adaptable tools that could be internalised by clients themselves, motivating self-directed change and enabling creation on a 'just-in-time' basis.
- **Skilling:** Listening and related motivation-building skills to 'ignite passion' in clients; discovery through reflection ('what is the current reality for them; what will be different?'), rather than lecture; techniques to adapt any learnings.
- **Applying:** Maintaining a collaboration community via two types of investment—technical (self-authoring Web tools, intuitive access interface); and operational (management practices supporting reflective awareness and experimental 'space').
- **Resourcing:** Investing in managerial systems support for engaging colleagues, managers, partners, and others, ultimately including a realignment of incentives.

The first opportunity for translating these principles into practical action was the 'strategic episode' of launching the second attempt at an integrated consulting capability development program. Beta-testing in Chile was followed by a full pilot program in Africa in January 2011. The strategic episode is summarised in Figure 4, with an annotation shown for each of the four framework steps as discussed above.

3.5.1. Pilot Outcomes and Interpretation

Based on program feedback surveys, management reviews, and subsequent interactions with participants, the pilot was largely successful. Sixty-seven percent of the 21 participants drawn from six African countries completed the 'pre-work' reflection exercises via the dedicated KM Web page to post their observations on assigned reading and summaries of reflective discussions with their manager. During the workshop, 100% of participants made a two to five minute personal video testimony posted to the KM website. In the seven months following return to the workplace, over 75% of participants have documented how they had applied the learning and tools developed in that workshop, via the KM platform. Similar results have been reported with subsequent delivery of the workshop elsewhere.

The majority of these responses demonstrated practical applications that created incremental new knowledge, such as the BA who adapted the 'Behaviour-Impact-Consequence' module to help resolve deep conflict within a client organisation. In several cases, full documentation and advice was shared, converting the KM website into an ongoing CoP facility for new knowledge assimilation:

We stopped trying to provide financial and logical arguments and instead sat down and learned to see things through their eyes, applying our empathy training.... It turned out their biggest worry was drinking water, not crop yields. So now we're addressing water first. (Snr. BA, Africa)

A detailed debrief enabled feedback and reflection to be incorporated into planning for the full implementation of this strategic change initiative, applying the new framework. The integrated program of capability development and KM support is now proceeding to global rollout (see Table 3).

Figure 4. Recursive integration of KM into capability development (source: the author)

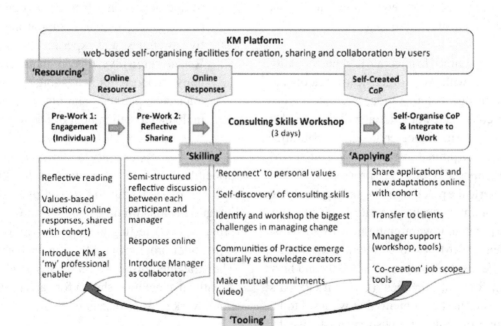

Table 3. Implementation of the framework 2011-2012

	Capability Development	KM Practices
Tooling	Global rollout of workshop in 2011-2012; extend design to other skill areas	Enroll and enable 100% of staff to create, adapt and share knowledge assets
Skilling	Incorporate KM-based consulting practices into work program design	'Knowledge Champions' in all 30 organisational units
Applying	Initiate Communities of Practice for all key business areas	Self-authoring tools and collaboration are available to 100% of staff
Resourcing	Complementary managerial coaching skills	Modify incentives to promote knowledge creation and sharing

(Source: the author)

Participants and facilitators experienced the framework's diagnostic utility directly in its directing our attention to interdependencies and the role of appropriate 'tempo' in the introduction of new information and facilities. It also highlighted some weaknesses identified during the initial implementation: in a few cases, a deep task-orientation within management ranks impeded allowing enough time for assimilation and co-creation by staff; whereas corporate executive enthusiasm to accelerate the rollout is constrained by ongoing dependence on donor funding.

These issues suggest the need to further improve the framework in Figure 3 by developing a higher-order reflective process that constantly monitors not only activity but also its 'fitness' to the purpose and value of the work. Developing this higher-order capability, with appropriate resource-switching capacity, itself requires some reconfiguration of internal tooling, skilling, applying, and resourcing capabilities, in an iterative process subject to monitoring and critique by fellow practitioners.

4. DISCUSSION AND FUTURE RESEARCH

Through this in-depth case analysis of successive capability development attempts within a global services organisation, we have examined the familiar 'strategic episode' of launching KM-supported capability development. The extended, participative, multi-method, practice-based study reflects a research design that meets key criteria for robust framework development.

The second attempt at an integrated capability development initiative was clearly an improvement, in significant part due to a design philosophy that emphasised reflection, experimentation, spontaneous CoP formation (Wenger, 1998), and self-directed 'trying on for size' rather than didactic delivery. These differences are well captured in Brown and Duguid's commendation of Lave's distinction between technologies designed for teaching and technologies intended for learning (1992, sec. 2.1). In this current study, we can identify three specific differences that each contributed to the successful application of the ACAP-based framework. These additional elements emerged from the case analysis; they are identified in the following paragraphs as the issues of: absorbed practice, tempo and the implication for aligning KM to practice capabilities.

4.1. Absorbed Practice

The design approach outlined in the second case study embraces 'less is more'—fewer, but better, tools, with considerably more time for each participant to think, commit to engaging, try out the practice skill, critique it, form co-creation alliances, and then modify and finally own the material. That design drew on ACAP process research to articulate the new orientation, materialising a 'slow knowledge' approach that is suitable for the context. That articulation was largely implemented through the new KM platform, but the emphasis remained on absorbed practice rather than resources. The KM practice was in turn designed to support the absorptive capacity of the organisation as a system of interactions rather than as a suite of resources. This recognised that performance in this context involves people engaged in complex issues where the quick answer may ultimately prove to be the wrong answer.

Echoing Orr's lone plea for the value of knowledge 'slowness'—the seeking of wisdom through our use of information (Orr, 1996)—this chapter raises a similarly aesthetic appeal to provide facilities that support our tacit grasp of what constitutes meaningful engagement. Peter Drucker summed up the ultimate role of human agency perhaps the most concisely, stating that 'Knowledge [exists]… only between two ears' (Kontzer, 2001). Thus, ACAP systems and processes must be geared to the human absorptive scale, a consideration that led to introducing the concept of 'tempo.'

4.2. Tempo

Tempo is a defining difference in the case 'episodes,' in respect of the design and the governance of activity within either case. By contrast, with the design approach in Figure 4, the earlier project had emphasised 'hard' knowledge and skills, delivered fast, uniformly consumed, and applied. This was expressed materially in the weighting given to driving 'hard' KM activities: fill the database with documents; deploy servers, laptops, and data analysis tools; drill the classroom participants with crash courses in advanced finance, marketing, and negotiation (see Table 4). That tempo proved to be poorly aligned to practice needs: focusing on the volume of supply of artifacts and technology—documents, training materials, templates—largely denied investment of money or time to foster less definable outputs. However, it was these latter outputs, such as appreciative inquiry skills and co-creation management systems, which were most required to begin addressing the types of socio-political challenges that have the greatest impact on performance. That 'first generation' approach

Table 4. Between-case comparison of capability and KM priorities

ACAP factors in Capability Development	Episode 1: 1st generation program		Episode 2: 2nd generation program	
	Capability Tempo (High/Medium/Low)	**KM Focus**	**Capability Tempo (High/Medium/Low)**	**KM Focus**
Acquire/Create	Best practice tools, techniques **(H)**	Big repository, DB access, content 'dump'	Best practices for inspiring change **(M)**	Create/adapt processes, tools; semantic tagging
Assimilate	Select tools, learn, apply proficientl **(H)**	Database search, personal contacts, email	Right questions guide selection **(M)**	Intuitive Web search, chat, 'go-to' experts
Transform	Edit and deposit new version in DB **(L)**	Self author offline; email/call for peer support	Engage peers and the client in co-creation **(H)**	Self-author online; peer collaboration
Exploit	Diagnose, analyse, and deliver business solutions **(M)**	Repository of final documents; but no manager tools	Enable clients to develop self-help capabilities **(H)**	CoP mentoring, multi-media tools
+ Social factor	Organisation and mobilisation skills **(L)**	Minimal use	Motivation, 'EQ' skills **(H)**	CoP mentoring Management engagement
+ Power factor	Negotiation skills Stakeholder plans **(M)**	Centralised DB Decentralised knowledge owners	Stakeholder mapping and motivating skills **(H)**	Self-creation tools; CoP mentoring Centralised DB

(Source: the author)

'provided little management infrastructure, and frankly, little incentive' (CD, Africa) to embed these skills in the routines, work cycles and time investment for knowledge renewal that comprise genuine capability.

The two cases reflect a distinct difference in where the 'High' priority assignment of activity and attention was placed, resulting in clearly different resourcing decisions and very different outcomes (Table 4). The tempo concept provides a promising extension to ACAP because it actually has two important aspects, as already commonly recognised in the context of music. Time is the obvious facet; by itself, it just highlights coordination or synchronisation, the concern of the technician. ACAP discourse focuses on such technical-level considerations. But music practitioners also recognise a second aspect of tempo— 'mood' or 'style,' the performative and interpretative facet that can only find expression through skillful human agency. Within the context of applying ACAP to support capability development, the case study revealed this second aspect of tempo as being important to the performance of organisational learning that genuinely supports the creation and maintenance of value. That value creation must be enacted by practitioners, leading to the third issue of how KM aligns to this performative challenge.

4.3. KM Alignment to Practice

Table 4 illustrates the range of support that KM can provide to a capability development initiative designed for effective absorption. But even in restraining our immersion in the technological possibilities of KM to those 'collaborative,' 'social,' and 'open access' functionalities that seem most productive, the sheer ubiquity of technology reminds us of Orlikowski's (2007) warning that technologies and knowledge artifacts work through us equally as much as we work through them. On her account, this creates an 'entangle-ment' of materiality (p. 1435) that may invisibly shape our behaviours in practice.

We can see evidence of this effect in the case study description of the first strategic episode. By loading up databases and issuing laptops, TechnoServe enacted the tangible symbols of becoming a more capable 'knowledge based organisation.' This program ran aground however, largely due to the lack of any mechanism for managing 'tempo,' the governance system that balances activities ostensibly relating to capability development with the performative needs and contextual conditions of actual practice. That omission confused and ultimately frustrated many of the practitioners; yet the very materiality of the KM investment and related training activities had concealed much of this dysfunction until its contribution to disappointing performance improvement was irrefutable.

5. CONCLUSION

This chapter directly connects the rich ACAP literature and diverse KM literature for the first time, doing so specifically in terms of offering a micro-level framework for translating KM practice into support for ACAP required in effective capability development. This latter step links KM to the organisation capability literature, a linkage also greatly under-researched to date.

ACAP is value creating for the organisation to the extent that it supports the development of organisational capabilities that create competitive sustainability or advantage. This discussion shows that the ACAP construct provides a useful framework at a process level for relating learning and innovation to absorbed practice. As an integrated time-bounded set of processes under the direction of practice-building imperatives, ACAP enables the four 'micro-strategies' that constitute capability development (tooling, skilling, applying, and resourcing). This conceptualisation both directs

ACAP to value-creating priorities, and locates the decisions that practice participants must make every day (where to invest effort; what to buy versus build), within a governing time-based framework. Resources such as the enabling KM facilities and processes can then be marshaled coherently, thereby improving the ACAP of the organisation for continuous practice improvement.

This new framework emerges from two novel extensions to ACAP theorising, namely tempo and practice. These extensions provide a concrete way to apply ACAP to the question of how KM contributes to the realisation of new capabilities within an organisation's specific context in performance-enhancing ways.

The first extension is tempo, which is rarely evaluated in this context (for the one known exception, see Holtham, et al., 2002). The case study shows that tempo emerged as being a substantive factor in the design, construction, and maintenance of effective capabilities. This is a departure from Zahra and George (2002), who highlight 'intensity and speed' of knowledge acquisition as apparently unproblematic key success factors for firm performance (p. 189), without discussing the likely tradeoff with 'quality,' their third listed success factor. Here instead we incorporate tempo as an important new regulating factor in the effectiveness of knowledge absorption within capabilities development.

The second extension lies in developing ACAP discourse towards a practice focus. The extended longitudinal case study allowed us to reinterpret ACAP functionality as constituting dynamic interactions between systems, artifacts, interactions, and actors, thereby providing a clearer linkage to capability-based performance governed by a sense of appropriate tempo. It thereby explicated KM as the set of practices that apply sets of technologies and content to support (or subvert) that tempo. This explication was presented at a 'micro' level, so that we could avoid the 'cul-de-sac of high abstraction' (by providing instead) 'more direct confrontation with the complexities of managerial

and organizational action' (Johnson, et al., 2003, p. 6). The proposed new framework therefore extends beyond the valuable ACAP process descriptions to a more concrete and granular framework for the practice of situated 'slow knowledge.' Thus recast in practice rather than resource terms, KM is more readily integrated with each of the four ACAP processes that create and sustain capability renewal and growth.

The proposed framework is emergent. As a case-based analysis of a pair of strategic episodes within a single organisation, the study was designed to attempt to counteract the attendant risks of idiosyncrasy and bias. Key elements of that design were the longitudinal scale, duration, data diversity, iterative participant critique of the emerging capability development framework and the pilot test, in order to improve the validity of the framework development process.

'Slow knowledge' represents richly experienced, human-centric, context-aware knowledge creation, and application that practitioners 'savour' in order to apprehend its application towards practice-oriented goals. Future research may further incorporate 'slow knowledge' into development of the capability development framework outlined here by, for example, examining how KM can be managed to support the absorptive tempo appropriate to actual practice needs. Developing KM practices to support human-scaled tempo 'brings the whole person back in' to the organisational encounter with a changing environment, enabling the menu of knowledge *techne* to better support the capabilities that contribute to achieving performance goals.

ACKNOWLEDGMENT

The author wishes to thank TechnoServe for its generous access to case study sources, and in particular acknowledges the extensive support of Dr. Simon Winter, SVP, TechnoServe.

REFERENCES

Ahuja, G., & Katila, R. (2001). Technological acquisitions and the innovation performance of acquiring firms: A longitudinal study. *Strategic Management Journal, 22,* 197–220. doi:10.1002/smj.157

Antonacopoulou, E., & Easterby-Smith, M. (2005). *Dynamic capabilities and organizational learning: Advanced institute of* management research paper no. 014. Retrieved 14/08/2010 from http://papers.ssrn.com/sol3/papers.cfm?abstract_id=1306958

Autio, E., Sapienza, H. J., & Almeida, J. G. (2000). Effects of age at entry, knowledge intensity, and imitability on international growth. *Organization Science, 43*(5), 909–924.

Barkema, H. G., & Vermeulen, F. (1998). International expansion through start-up or acquisition: A learning perspective. *Academy of Management Journal, 41*(1), 7–26. doi:10.2307/256894

Barney, J. B. (1991). Firm resources and sustained competitive advantage. *Journal of Management, 17*(1), 99–120. doi:10.1177/014920639101700108

Bettis, R. A., & Prahalad, C. K. (1995). The dominant logic: Retrospective and extension. *Strategic Management Journal, 16*(1), 5–14. doi:10.1002/smj.4250160104

Brown, J. S., & Duguid, P. (1991). Organizational learning and communities-of-practice: Toward a unified view of working, learning and innovation. *Organization Science, 2*(1), 40–57. doi:10.1287/orsc.2.1.40

Brown, J. S., & Duguid, P. (1992). *Stolen knowledge*. Retrieved 10/08/2011 from http://www2.parc.com/ops/members/brown/papers/stolen-know.html

Cohen, W. M., & Levinthal, D. A. (1990). Absorptive capacity : A new perspective on learning and innovation. *Administrative Science Quarterly, 35*(1), 128–152. doi:10.2307/2393553

Cook, S. D. N., & Brown, J. S. (1999). Bridging epistemologies: The generative dance between organizational knowledge and organizational knowing. *Organization Science, 10*(4), 381–400. doi:10.1287/orsc.10.4.381

Daneels, E. (2003). Tight-loose coupling with customers: The enactment of a customer orientation. *Strategic Management Journal, 24*(6), 559–576. doi:10.1002/smj.319

Despres, C. (2011). *Leading issues in knowledge management research*. Reading, UK: Academic Publishing International.

Easterby-Smith, M., & Lyles, M. A. (2003). Introduction: Watersheds of organizational learning and knowledge management. In Easterby-Smith, M., & Lyles, M. A. (Eds.), *The Blackwell Handbook of Organizational Learning and Knowledge* (pp. 1–15). Oxford, UK: Blackwell Publishers.

Easterby-Smith, M., & Prieto, I. M. (2008). Dynamic capabilities and knowledge management: an integrative role for learning? *British Journal of Management, 19*(3), 235–249. doi:10.1111/j.1467-8551.2007.00543.x

Eisenhardt, K. M. (1989). Building theories from case study research. *Strategic Management Journal, 14*(4), 532–549.

Eisenhardt, K. M., & Martin, J. (2000). Dynamic capabilities: What are they? *Strategic Management Journal, 21*(10-11), 1105–1121. doi:10.1002/1097-0266(200010/11)21:10/11<1105::AID-SMJ133>3.0.CO;2-E

Eisenhardt, K. M., & Santos, F. M. (2002). Knowledge-based view : A new theory of strategy? In Pettigrew, A., Thomas, H., & Whittington, R. (Eds.), *Handbook of Strategy and Management.* Thousand Oaks, CA: Sage Publications Inc. doi:10.4135/9781848608313.n7

Giddens, A. (1984). *The constitution of society-Outlines of the theory of structure.* Cambridge, UK: Polity Press.

Grant, R. M. (1996). Toward a knowledge-based theory of the firm. *Strategic Management Journal, 17,* 109–117.

Gray, C. (2006). Absorptive capacity, knowledge management and innovation in entrepreneurial small firms. *International Journal of Entrepreneurial Behaviour & Research, 12*(6), 345–360. doi:10.1108/13552550610710144

Helfat, C. E., & Peteraf, M. A. (2003). The dynamic resource-based view: Capability lifecycles. *Strategic Management Journal, 24*(10), 997–1010. doi:10.1002/smj.332

Hendry, J., & Seidl, D. (2003). The structure and significance of strategic episodes: Social systems theory and the routine practices of strategic change. *Journal of Management Studies, 40*(1), 175–196. doi:10.1111/1467-6486.00008

Holtham, C., Ward, V., & Bohn, M. (2002). *Slow knowledge: The importance of in team debriefing and in individual learning.* Unpublished. Retrieved 18/7/2011 from http://www2.warwick.ac.uk/fac/soc/wbs/conf/olkc/archive/oklc3/papers/id246.pdf

Johnson, G., Melin, L., & Whittington, R. (2003). Guest editors' introduction micro strategy and strategizing : Towards an activity-based view. *Journal of Management Studies, 40,* 3–22. doi:10.1111/1467-6486.t01-2-00002

Kogut, B., & Zander, U. (1992). Knowledge of the firm, combinative capabilities, and the replication of technology. *Organization Science, 3*(3), 383–397. doi:10.1287/orsc.3.3.383

Kontzer, T. (2001). Management legend: Trust never goes out of style. *Information Week.* Retrieved 05/07/2011 from http://www.informationweek.com/news/6507112

Lane, P. J., Koka, B. R., & Pathak, S. (2006). The reification of absorptive capacity: A critical review and rejuvenation of the construct. *Academy of Management Review, 31*(4), 833–863. doi:10.5465/AMR.2006.22527456

Lane, P. J., & Lubatkin, M. (1998). Relative absorptive capacity and interorganizational learning. *Strategic Management Journal, 19,* 461–478. doi:10.1002/(SICI)1097-0266(199805)19:5<461::AID-SMJ953>3.0.CO;2-L

Lave, J., & Wenger, E. (1991). *Situated learning: Legitimate peripheral participation.* Cambridge, UK: Cambridge University Press.

Leinwand, P., & Mainardi, C. (2011). *the essential advantage: how to win with a capabilities-driven strategy.* Cambridge, MA: Harvard Business Review Press.

Levinthal, D. A., & March, J. G. (1993). The myopia of learning. *Strategic Management Journal, 14*(8), 95–112. doi:10.1002/smj.4250141009

Lubatkin, M., Florin, J., & Lane, P. (2001). Learning together and apart: A model of reciprocal interfirm learning. *Human Relations, 54*(10), 1353–1382.

March, J. G. (1991). Exploration and exploitation in organizational learning. *Organization Science, 2*(1), 71–87. doi:10.1287/orsc.2.1.71

Marqués, D. P., & Simón, F. J. G. (2006). The effect of knowledge management practices on firm performance. *Journal of Knowledge Management, 10*(3), 143–156. doi:10.1108/13673270610670911

McElroy, M. W. (2000). Integrating complexity theory, knowledge management and organizational learning. *Journal of Knowledge Management, 4*(3), 195–203. doi:10.1108/13673270010377652

Moos, B., Beimborn, D., Wagner, H.-T., & Weitzel, T. (2010). *Knowledge management systems, absorptive capacity, and innovation success.* Unpublished. Retrieved 06/08/2011 from http://is2.lse.ac.uk/asp/aspecis/20110149.pdf

Nelson, R. R., & Winter, S. G. (1982). *An evolutionary theory of economic change.* Cambridge, MA: Harvard University Press.

Nonaka, I., Toyama, R., & Hirata, T. (2008). *Managing flow: A process theory of the knowledge-based firm.* Hampshire, UK: Palgrave Macmillan Ltd.

Orlikowski, W. J. (1992). The duality of technology: Rethinking the concept of technology in organizations. *Organization Science, 3*(3), 398–427. doi:10.1287/orsc.3.3.398

Orlikowski, W. J. (2007). Sociomaterial practices: Exploring technology at work. *Organization Studies, 28*(9), 1435–1448. doi:10.1177/0170840607081138

Orr, D. W. (1996). Slow knowledge. *Conservation Biology, 10*(3), 699–702. doi:10.1046/j.1523-1739.1996.10030699.x

Prahalad, C. K., & Bettis, R. A. (1986). The dominant logic: A new linkage between diversity and performance. *Strategic Management Journal, 7*(6), 485–501. doi:10.1002/smj.4250070602

Salvato, C. (2003). The role of micro-strategies in the engineering of firm evolution. *Journal of Management Studies, 40*(1), 83–108. doi:10.1111/1467-6486.t01-2-00005

Senge, P. M. (1994). *The fifth discipline: The art and practice of the learning organization.* Boston, MA: Doubleday Business.

Spender, J.-C. (1996). Making knowledge as the basis of a dynamic theory of the firm. *Strategic Management Journal, 17*, 45–62.

Szulanski, G. (1996). Exploring internal stickiness: Impediments to the transfer of best practices within the firm. *Strategic Management Journal, 22*, 27–44.

Teece, D. J. (2007). Explicating dynamic capabilities: The nature and microfoundations of (sustainable) enterprise performance. *Strategic Management Journal, 28*, 1319–1350. doi:10.1002/smj.640

Teece, D. J., Pisano, G., & Shuen, A. (1997). Dynamic capabilities and strategic management. *Strategic Management Journal, 18*(7), 509–533. doi:10.1002/(SICI)1097-0266(199708)18:7<509::AID-SMJ882>3.0.CO;2-Z

Todorova, G., & Durisin, B. (2007, September). The concept and the reconceptualization of absorptive capacity: Recognizing the value. *Academy of Management Review.*

Tull, J., & Dumay, J. (2007). Does IC management 'make a difference'? A critical case study application of structuration theory. *Electronic Journal of Knowledge Management, 5*(4), 515–526.

Tuomi, I. (2002). The future of knowledge management. *Lifelong Learning in Europe, 7*(2), 69–79.

Van den Bosch, F. A., Volberda, H. W., & de Boer, M. (1999). Coevolution of firm absorptive capacity and knowledge environment : Organizational forms and combinative capabilities. *Organization Science, 10*(5), 551–568. doi:10.1287/orsc.10.5.551

Vera, D., & Crossan, M. (2003). Organizational learning and knowledge management: Toward an integrative framework. In Easterby-Smith, M., & Lyles, M. A. (Eds.), *The Blackwell Handbook of Organizational Learning and Knowledge* (pp. 122–142). Oxford, UK: Blackwell Publishers.

von Hippel, E. (1986). Lead users: A source of novel product concepts. *Management Science*, *32*(7), 791–805. doi:10.1287/mnsc.32.7.791

Wenger, E. (1998). *Communities of practice: Learning, meaning and identity*. Cambridge, UK: Cambridge University Press.

Wilson, T. D. (2005). The nonsense of knowledge management revisited. In Maceviciute, E., & Wilson, T. D. (Eds.), *Introducing Information Management: An Information Research Reader* (pp. 151–164). London, UK: Facet Publishing.

Yin, R. K. (2003). *Case study research: Design and methods* (3rd ed.). Thousand Oaks, CA: Sage Publications.

Zahra, S. A., & George, G. (2002). Absorptive capacity: A review, reconceptualization, and extension. *Academy of Management Review*, *27*(2), 185–203.

Zollo, M., & Winter, S. G. (2002). Deliberate learning and the evolution of dynamic capabilities. *Organization Science*, *13*(3), 339–351. doi:10.1287/orsc.13.3.339.2780

ADDITIONAL READING

Akscyn, R. M., McCracken, D. L., & Yoder, E. A. (1988). KMS: A distributed hypermedia system for managing knowledge in organizations. *Communications of the ACM*, *31*(7), 820–835. doi:10.1145/48511.48513

Argyris, C., & Schön, D. (1978). *Organizational learning*. Reading, MA: Addison-Wesley.

Barney, J. B. (1997). *Gaining and sustaining competitive advantage*. Reading, MA: Addison-Wesley Publishing.

Bougon, M. G., Weick, K. E., & Binkhorst, D. (1977). Cognition in organizations: An analysis of the Utrecht Jazz Orchestra. *Administrative Science Quarterly*, *22*, 606–639. doi:10.2307/2392403

Brown, J. S., & Duguid, P. (2000). Balancing act: How to capture knowledge without killing it. *Harvard Business Review*, *78*(3), 73–80.

D'Aveni, R. A. (2010). *Beating the commodity trap*. Boston, MA: Harvard Business School Press.

Davenport, E. (2002). Mundane knowledge management and microlevel organizational learning: An ethological approach. *Journal of the American Society for Information Science and Technology*, *53*(12), 1038–1046. doi:10.1002/asi.10110

Hailey, J., & James, R. (2002). Learning leaders: The key to learning organisations. *Development in Practice*, *12*(3/4), 398–408. doi:10.1080/0961450220149753

Helfat, C. E. (1997). Know-how and asset complementarity and dynamic capability accumulation: The case of R&D. *Strategic Management Journal*, *18*(5), 339–360. doi:10.1002/(SICI)1097-0266(199705)18:5<339::AID-SMJ883>3.0.CO;2-7

Huff, A. S. (1982). Industry influences on strategy reformulation. *Strategic Management Journal*, *3*(2), 119–131. doi:10.1002/smj.4250030204

Jarzabkowski, P., & Spee, P. A. (2009). Strategy-as-practice: A review and future directions for the field. *International Journal of Management Reviews*, *11*(1), 69–95. doi:10.1111/j.1468-2370.2008.00250.x

Nutley, S., Walter, I., & Davies, H. (2002). *From knowing to doing: A framework for understanding the evidence-into-practice agenda*. Discussion Paper 1. St Andrews, UK: University of St Andrews. Retrieved 16/02/2010 from http://www.stand.ac.uk/~cppm/ under RURU

O'Malley, D., & O'Donoghue, G. (2001). *NGOs and the learning organisation*. London, UK: British Overseas NGOs for Development. Retrieved 10/09/2009 from www.bond.org.uk/lte/lngo.htm

Pasteur, K., & Villiers, P. S. (2003). Minding the gap through organisational learning. In Groves, L., & Hinton, R. (Eds.), *Inclusive Aid: Changing Power and Relationships in International Development*. London, UK: Earthscan.

Prahalad, C. K., & Hamel, G. (1990, May-June). The core competence of the corporation. *Harvard Business Review, 68*, 79–91.

Regner, P. (2008). Strategy-as-practice and dynamic capabilities: Steps towards a dynamic view of strategy. *Human Relations, 61*(4), 565–588. doi:10.1177/0018726708091020

Suchman, L. (2000). Making a case: 'Knowledge' and 'routine' work in document production. In Luff, P., Hindmarsh, J., & Heath, C. (Eds.), *Workplace Studies: Recovering Work Practice and Informing System Design* (pp. 29–45). Cambridge, UK: Cambridge University Press. doi:10.1017/CBO9780511628122.003

Weick, K. (1995). *Sensemaking in organizations*. Thousand Oaks, CA: Sage Publications.

KEY TERMS AND DEFINITIONS

Absorptive Capacity: The set of organisational practices for acquiring or creating, assimilating, transforming and applying knowledge to create the dynamic capabilities needed to achieve organisational priorities.

Dynamic Capabilities: An organisation's routine (repeatable) ability to build, integrate and transform internal and external competences in response to rapidly changing environments.

Knowledge Management: The broad suite of strategies and practices used by actors within a network to identify, create, represent, distribute, and make accessible insights and learnings for organisational purposes.

Tempo: The speed or pace of an activity that, within the context of complex and sustained inter-personal performance, invokes a purposive regulation of activities to synthesise individual elements into a coherent, value-directed whole.

Practice: The everyday activities of working life relating to organisational outcomes centred on the performances of the social agent within 'given' social structures and symbolic orders.

Chapter 15
The Role of a Knowledge-Centric Capability in Innovation:
A Case Study

Marié Cruywagen
University of Stellenbosch Business School, South Africa

Juani Swart
University of Bath, UK

Wim Gevers
University of Stellenbosch Business School, South Africa

ABSTRACT

The ability to provide an organisational context for the creation, sharing, and integration of knowledge, called the knowledge-centric capability, is a key strategic resource of an organisation and an enabler of innovation. This view is informed by dynamic capabilities, which focus on the ability of an organisation to modify and renew its resource base by creating, integrating, recombining, and releasing its resources in order to adapt to current changes or to affect change in its environment. A knowledge-centric capability comprises three core elements that enable innovation. Organisational intent is the resolve of an organisation to provide the context in which knowledge can serve as a strategic resource in the organisation. Knowledge orientation is the way in which an organisation orientates itself towards its knowledge environment in terms of knowledge types and the role of knowledge in the organisation. Enactment includes elements of knowledge coordination, creation, use, and integration. The authors review how the extent to which the three core elements that are present in an organisation could give an indication of the organisation's ability to innovate by comparing these insights with the practices of Fundamo, one of the world's leading specialist mobile financial services companies.

DOI: 10.4018/978-1-4666-1969-2.ch015

INTRODUCTION

The requirement for long-term competitiveness is central to an organisation's strategy and management. An organisation is unavoidably connected to the conditions of its environment and to sustain a competitive advantage. It needs to be able to sense changes in both its internal and external environments and adapt in an appropriate manner. This alignment with the environment implies an organisation must be able to learn, unlearn, or relearn based on its past behaviours (Cyert & March, 1963; Fiol & Lyles, 1985; Levitt & March, 1988; Miller & Friesen, 1980). Applying this view to knowledge management, a knowledge-centric perspective thus needs to address the issue of how organisations employ knowledge to create, maintain, and renew their competitive advantage in a dynamic environment.

The objective of this chapter is to illustrate that the capacity to provide an organisational context for the creation, sharing, and integration of knowledge, called the knowledge-centric capability (Cruywagen, 2010), is a key strategic resource of an organisation and an enabler of innovation.

To achieve this objective, we will explore in what manner a knowledge-centric capability enables an organisation to develop its capacity for innovation, and identify the configuration of capabilities which comprise the knowledge-centric capability of Fundamo, a global specialist mobile financial services provider, in order to garner some lessons for both theory and practice.

The chapter is structured as follows. Following this introduction, we will review the extant literature on the dynamic capability view as an extension of the resource-based view. The third section provides a brief overview of the knowledge-centric capability framework, as introduced by Cruywagen (2010). The following section presents the Fundamo case study and outlines the company's knowledge-centric capability as an enabler of innovation. The final two sections present some directions for future research and the conclusions.

BACKGROUND

This section reviews the literature concerned with the dynamic capability view which formed the foundation for the knowledge-centric capability framework (Cruywagen, 2010).

Dynamic Capabilities

The dynamic capability approach is partly based on the work of Schumpeter (1934), Penrose (1959), and Nelson and Winter (1982), and is focused on the ability of an organisation to modify an renew its resource base by creating, integrating, recombining, and releasing its resources in order to adapt to current changes or to effect change in its environment (Eisenhardt & Martin, 2000). From a dynamic knowledge-centric perspective, this means focusing on the ability of an organisation to modify and renew its knowledge base by creating, integrating, recombining, and releasing its knowledge resources in order to effect change or to adapt to change in its environment. The evolutionary view of competitive advantage is discussed under various names in the literature, for example core competencies (Prahalad & Hamel, 1990), capacity for regeneration (Ambrosini, Bowman, & Collier, 2009; Hogarth, Michaud, Doz, & Van der Heyden, 1991), and dynamic capabilities (Teece, 2007; Teece & Pisano, 1994; Teece, Pisano, & Shuen, 1997). From these perspectives, a sustainable competitive advantage is dependent not only on the ownership of distinctive resources, but also distinctive and dynamic capabilities.

The concept of dynamic capabilities was originally defined as "the firm's ability to integrate, build, and reconfigure internal and external competencies to address rapidly changing environments" (Teece, et al., 1997, p. 516). In this definition, competencies included managerial and organisational processes, in turn comprising coordination or integration, learning and reconfiguration (Teece, et al., 1997).

The competence of an organisation has been shown to be embedded in its distinct ways of coordinating and integrating activities (Faraj & Sproull, 2000; Garvin, 1998; Iansiti & Clark, 1994). The role of the organisation is therefore to provide an environment that integrates individual effort, activities, learning processes and strategies in a coherent manner (Foss & Christensen, 2001). Additionally, organisational processes display varying degrees of coherence and Teece *et al.* (1997) explain that recognising congruence and complementarities among processes, and between processes and incentives is key to understanding the capabilities of an organisation. Corporate coherence then is the ability of an organisation to generate and exploit synergies of various types (Foss & Christensen, 2001; Teece, Rumelt, Dosi, & Winter, 1994).

Also important in Teece *et al.* (1997) and other (Eisenhardt & Martin, 2000; Zollo & Winter, 2002) conceptions of dynamic capabilities, is the notion that dynamic capabilities emerge from organisational learning. To a large extent the various authors draw on Levitt and March's (1988) discussion of organisational learning as routine-based, history-dependent, and target-oriented. Learning is seen as a social and collective process that occurs both through imitation or emulation, and through developing collective understandings or interpretations of history and complex problems (Levitt & March, 1988; Teece, et al., 1997). The resulting organisational knowledge is then absorbed into routines, that becomes the collective organisational memory and guides future behaviour (Levitt & March, 1988).

Another important aspect of organisational learning in the context of dynamic capabilities is its role in solving the evolutionary economic problem of creating variety. This is accomplished through the reconfiguration of organisational resources in order to accomplish the required internal and external transformation to align with changes in the environment (Teece, et al., 1997). A simulation study by Marengo (1994) has demonstrated how new organisational knowledge emerges from the interaction of coordinated learning processes

within organisations. The study also highlighted an apparent tension between the necessity to keep the organisation together and to allow for diversity of experimentation. This observation concurs with March's (1991) observation of a trade-off between the exploitation of old certainties and the exploration of new possibilities, with an emphasis on improved competence in the exploitation of existing knowledge rendering the exploration of new knowledge less attractive, and the exploration of new knowledge reducing the speed at which existing skills are improved. "Maintaining an appropriate balance between exploration and exploitation is a primary factor in system survival and prosperity" (March, 1991, p. 71).

Organisational learning is also cumulative and path-dependent, which means that new capabilities can only be developed on existing capabilities (Dierickx & Cool, 1989). The notion of path dependency recognises that an organisation's current position and path ahead are shaped and constrained by previous activities and learning (Teece, et al., 1997). It is, however, not only learning processes and the coherence of processes that determine an organisation's position, but also its specific resources, as argued in the resource-based view.

Furthermore, dynamic capabilities and competences can only provide a competitive advantage if the routines, skills and resources they are based on are distinctive, meaning they should be difficult to imitate (Dierickx & Cool, 1989; Teece, et al., 1997). Factors like the tacit nature of knowledge, unobservable processes, or intellectual property protection could act as barriers to the imitation of competences (Teece, et al., 1997).

Dynamic capabilities can exist at different levels in relation to managerial perceptions of the environment, namely incremental, renewing and regenerative dynamic capabilities (Ambrosini, et al., 2009). Where incremental dynamic capabilities are concerned with continuing improving an organisation's resource base, renewing dynamic capabilities is concerned with refreshing, adapting, and augmenting the resource base. Regenerative dynamic capabilities change the manner by which an organisation changes its resources base, therefore impacting on an organisation's current collection of dynamic capabilities (Ambrosini, et al., 2009).

Eisenhardt and Martin (2000, p. 1117) argue that long-term competitive advantage lies in the resource configurations that managers build using dynamic capabilities, and not in the capabilities themselves. This is particularly true in high-velocity markets where dynamic capabilities are characterised as simple not complicated, experiential not analytic, and iterative not linear processes (Eisenhardt & Martin, 2000).

From a dynamic knowledge-based perspective then, a sustainable competitive advantage cannot solely be achieved through the ownership of distinctive knowledge or the ownership of dynamic capabilities. Additional to a unique knowledge base, distinctive and dynamic capabilities are required to provide an organisational context for creating, transferring and integrating such knowledge as unique configurations of knowledge. Cruywagen (2010) refers to this as an organisation's knowledge-centric capability. Scholars have quite extensively elaborated on the initial idea of dynamic capabilities, diffusing rather than consolidating the meaning of dynamic capabilities as a concept. In an attempt to provide a more precise definition of dynamic capabilities that can serve as a basis for future work, Helfat *et al.* (2007) define a dynamic capability as "the capacity of an organisation to purposefully create, extend, or modify its resource base." This definition has been adopted by Cruywagen (2010) to form the basis of the conception of the knowledge-centric capability, which is briefly discussed in the following section.

Overview of the Knowledge-Centric Capability Framework

The concept of a knowledge-centric capability (Cruywagen, 2010) is built on the foundations of the dynamic capability view which developed in response to the inadequacies of the resource-based view, and builds on it by conceptualising the resource-based approach in a dynamic context. A brief overview of the knowledge-centric capability framework is included here to set the context for the remainder of the chapter, yet we refer the reader to Cruywagen (2010) for a full discussion on the knowledge-centric capability framework and an in-depth explanation of how the sub-dimensions were derived from an extensive review of the literature.

The key concepts in Helfat *et al.'s* (2007) definition of dynamic capabilities were used as foundation for the conception of the term "knowledge-centric capability" (Cruywagen, 2010), which refers to an organisation's ability to provide an organisational context for creating, transferring and integrating knowledge. The dimensions of a knowledge-centric capability are presented in Figure 1.

The term "purposefully" refers to some degree of intent as opposed to routine organisational activities. Cruywagen (2010) refers to this as organisational intent, which is represented by the sub-dimensions of KM strategy, KM benefits, KM structure, KM technology, KM budget, Human Resource Management practices, and learning culture. In the concept of knowledge-centric capability, "resource base" refers to the knowledge base of the organisation. An organisation's orientation towards its knowledge resources will therefore have a significant impact on its capability to leverage those resources. From a knowledge-centric capability perspective this is referred to as an organisation's knowledge orientation (Cruywagen, 2010) which is represented by the role of knowledge, type of knowledge, sources of knowledge, and origin of knowledge as sub-dimensions. The phrase "create, extend, or modify" refers to actions undertaken by an organisation to modify its resource base into unique configurations, which in the conception of a knowledge-centric capability is referred to as "enactment" (Cruywagen,

Figure 1. Dimensions of a knowledge-centric capability (Cruywagen (2010)

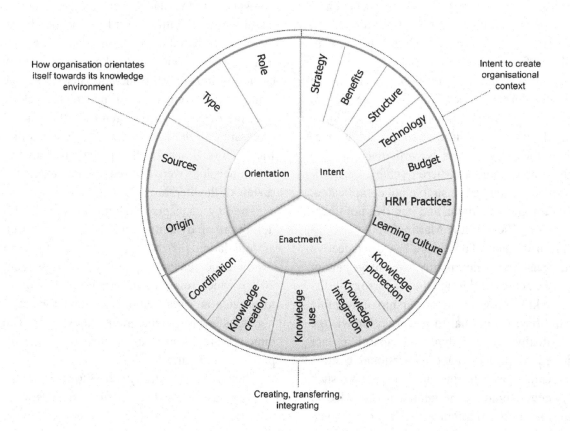

2010). Enactment is represented by coordination, knowledge creation, knowledge use, knowledge integration, and knowledge protection as sub-dimensions. Also of great importance is the notion that "capacity" refers to the potential to perform a task adequately—it does not necessarily refer to superior performance. "Capacity" also implies that the dynamic capability can reliably be replicated and that it is not merely a once-off activity or luck (Helfat, et al., 2007). In terms of the concept of a knowledge-centric capability, the term "capability" thus refers to the ability to adequately provide an organisational context for creating, transferring, and integrating knowledge.

The next section will explore how a knowledge-centric capability enables an organisation to enhance its innovation capabilities.

A KNOWLEDGE-CENTRIC CAPABILITY AS AN ENABLER OF INNOVATION

Fundamo Case Study

Fundamo, a South Africa-based company, is the world's largest global specialist provider of mobile financial services solutions. The company provides mobile banking and payment solutions, which can be deployed by either mobile operators or banks. Fundamo's comprehensive enterprise mobile financial services platform comprises the Mobile Wallet, Mobile Banking, Mobile Remittance, Mobile Commerce and Mobile Debit Card modules.

Founded in 2000, the company has been a visionary in predicting the trend towards providing financial services through mobile phones, and the impact this will have on the financial services industry in both the developed and developing markets. Gartner (2009) predicts that mobile money transfer, SMS payment, and mobile banking, domains in which Fundamo operates, is expected to achieve mainstream adoption within two to five years, with a moderate to high transformational impact on the industry. This gives an indication that Fundamo is a step ahead of the expected changes in their industry.

The mobile phone industry has experienced rapid growth since its inception, increasing from just over 11 million mobile phone subscribers in 1990 to an estimated 4.6 billion in 2009. The growth is not limited to the developed world, as the growth is impressive in developing economies as well. The prevalence of mobile devices in developing countries presents an opportunity to provide access to financial services not only to the banked, but also to the under-banked section of a population. It is estimated that 200 million international migrant workers were responsible for remittance flows of US$351 billion to developing countries in 2011 alone, representing an 8% increase from 2010 (Ratha, 2011). Mobile financial services make remittances more affordable by removing the need for physical points of presence and by providing a real-time and secure method of transacting, removing some dependency on cash (Fundamo, 2011).

Fundamo has more than 150 employees and is currently operational in more than 40 countries, including 27 countries in Africa, Asia, and the Middle East. Their solutions are tailored to emerging economies, more specifically to be utilised for customers who do not have access to financial services or bank accounts.

Fundamo deployed its first commercial customer, CelTel in Zambia, in 2003. In 2004, Fundamo was awarded the contract for the MTN/ Standard Bank Joint Venture in mobile banking.

In 2007, HBD Venture Capital, a South African company, invested ZAR36 million (US$5.1 million) in Fundamo and the following year Fundamo signed a partnership agreement with Accenture for the provision of mobile wallets worldwide. In 2009, Fundamo was awarded a ZAR100 million (US$ 9.7 million) contract, which would expand MTN's MobileMoney from South Africa to 20 additional African countries, making it the largest global rollout of mobile banking. By 2009, Fundamo had 40 deployments in more than 30 countries, including 27 countries in Africa and the Middle East and another 10 globally. In 2010, Yellow Pepper partnered with Fundamo to launch mobile banking and money transfer services in Latin America, and MTN Uganda's MobileMoney service, which is powered by Fundamo, reached 890,000 users in just over 12 months. The same year Fundamo also partnered with Vodafone Qatar's money transfer service—the world's first international mobile remittance service. Fundamo also partnered with AndaraLink in Indonesia providing the world's first network of microfinance institutions connected via mobile technology. In 2011, Visa acquired Fundamo for US$110 million. By September 2011, Fundamo has rolled out to 34 developing countries up from 27 in June 2011. Being a private company, Fundamo does not disclose growth figures or transaction volumes; however, Fundamo succeeds in maintaining 30% to 50% market share in the countries where it operates. The company is considered the market leader not only in Africa, but globally, with their technology being used more widely than any other supplier in the mobile financial services domain.

The company started out with four employees, and was committed to providing the best in class technology from its inception, with a strong emphasis on research and development. Fundamo prides itself on its specialised knowledge and expertise in the field of providing financial services to the poor, viewing it as a key differentiator. Fundamo is also performing well financially, boasting a 50% growth in earnings year-on-year

(Armitage, 2010), and recognises that such phenomenal growth could pose enormous challenges to the company in the future.

Although Fundamo does not have a formal knowledge management strategy, the increasing importance of formalising knowledge management is understood. Knowledge, experience, and expertise are viewed as the core of its competitive advantage. While the company was still small, it was relatively easy to share knowledge without a formal strategy in place. The rapid growth of the company is, however, making it increasingly difficult to keep track of "who knows what," which highlights the need for a more formal approach to knowledge management.

Fundamo has a well-established learning culture with a number of activities to reinforce it. A good example is called pair-programming, where an experienced developer is paired with a lesser experienced developer to share knowledge and to prevent the emergence of isolated pockets of expertise in the software platform.

Other activities that reinforce the learning culture include specially arranged talks by industry experts, and so-called brown-bag sessions, where any employee can arrange a lunchtime session with colleagues to discuss new ideas and developments. Also considered important is Fundamo's interaction with a number of large companies, for example Accenture and S1 Corporation. Fundamo also has a culture that celebrates new thoughts, while the impressive open-plan arrangement of the office facilitates knowledge sharing.

Fundamo does not have formal knowledge management technology in place. Most business units only store information in file structures on the network drive. Although everyone in the company has access to it, the information is not stored in a standard manner across business units. This complicates the processes of retrieving and sharing digitised information in the company. The company was in the process of deploying a wiki, which would serve as an informal knowledge base where employees could share their thoughts and ideas.

The majority of Fundamo's clients operate in developing countries in Africa and the Middle East, where Internet infrastructure is often wanting. This means employees working at the client's site need to document all relevant information on their laptops and synchronise the documents back to the file structure when they have access to the Internet, or when they are back in South Africa. Moreover, employees operate in a high-pressure environment, which means they often do not get the time to synchronise their information back to the file structure in a timely manner.

The nature of Fundamo's operational environment and the conditions under which it operates highlights the challenge the company faces in using technology to capture and share knowledge and emphasize the importance of personal interaction in sharing and integrating knowledge.

Fundamo uses information from its research team and sales team to inform its product strategy and company strategy and to decide which features need to be built into a product. A formal process is used collate different knowledge sources, to prioritise features and to decide which features will be included in a product. The product development specifications are also well documented and structured. Fundamo believes their approach to product development enables them to stay ahead of their competitors.

Fundamo has also gone through an exercise to reduce the amount of information that needs to be documented so that only what is absolutely necessary is captured. The result is more effective product documentation and of course higher productivity because of the reduction in time spent producing the documents.

Product development and improvement is an iterative process. Features included in a product are refined over time through an improvement cycle. This approach inevitably also leads to other new features being included. Because Fundamo develops leading edge technology, the solutions are not always known beforehand. They therefore follow a process of continuous refinement and improvement.

Over time, Fundamo has also improved their abilities in project estimation and quality assurance. By building on experiences from previous projects, these processes have almost been perfected. These capabilities enable Fundamo to deliver a timeous product of the highest standard, which results in satisfied clients.

Fundamo has also mastered the skill of integrating new insights gained from the training of clients into the company's stock of knowledge and expertise. Through the training they offer to clients, Fundamo experiences the reality of what people or the market wants. These insights are documented in the evening after the training and incorporated into the following day's training by looking at new case studies. These insights are also presented and shared with relevant colleagues.

One of Fundamo's biggest challenges is the fact that every client environment demands a new approach to providing a solution. This challenge is addressed through Fundamo's deployment methodology, which captures the experience of more than nine years of mobile banking and payment production deployments and makes it available to each new project.

Fundamo is driven by its ability to innovate. The company invests around 35% of annual revenues in research and development to ensure it maintains its leadership position. Its innovative ability is evident in the numerous local and international nominations and awards it has received for its mobile payment platform. In 2006, Fundamo was awarded the Frost and Sullivan technology leadership award.

Its products have extended the prospect of mobile banking to a larger number of South Africans and are enabling African countries to be amongst the most innovative when it comes to mobile banking. This has great applicability in the global markets

where the company is headed next (McDonald, 2006).

In 2009, Fundamo was nominated for the World Communication Awards and in 2011 in was shortlisted in the "Mobile Money for the Unbanked Award" in the Global Mobile Awards.

Fundamo currently has more than 30 registered patents and considers their formal process to harvest and manage patents as an important contributor to building and protecting their ability to remain competitive.

In June 2011, Visa acquired Fundamo for US$110 million in a bid to lead the mobile payment race. This important milestone in Fundamo's relatively short history clearly underlines the company's leadership in the mobile financial services industry.

A qualitative research approach underpinned the empirical work undertaken at Fundamo (also see Cruywagen, 2010). The aim was to gain a detailed understanding of the activities at Fundamo, which supports innovation and the perceived value derived from them. A comprehensive case study process were employed which included a number of design tests to ensure a valid and rigorous case study, as recommended by Gibbert, Ruigrok, and Wicki (2008) and Yin (2003). The data were collected through semi-structured interviews with the Chief Software Architect and the CEO, as well as focus group sessions with a number of employees. The interviews and focus group sessions were conducted at Fundamo's head office in Cape Town. Secondary data were obtained from company information available in the public domain. Recordings of the interview and focus group sessions were transcribed and subsequently coded. Two coding cycles (Saldaña, 2009) were used to transition from data collection to the more extensive data analysis. A process of explanation building was used to identify the interrelationships that emerged between the various themes, ensuring the internal validity of the case study.

Inside Fundamo's Knowledge-Centric Capability

From the review of dynamic capability literature and the presentation of the Fundamo case study, it is apparent that a knowledge-centric capability is not a separately identifiable construct, but rather that it is composed of a number of reinforcing practices and processes within an organisation. This section therefore turns to identifying the elements that comprise Fundamo's knowledge-centric capability with a view on how it enables the company to innovate.

Organisational Intent

"To be capable of something is to have a generally reliable capacity to bring that thing about as result of an intended action" (Dosi, Nelson, & Winter, 2000, p. 2). The intent should therefore also be reflected in the activities of the organisation, which are aimed at facilitating the desired outcome. With a knowledge-centric capability, this is reflected in the intent to provide an environment that is conducive to the creation, transfer, and integration of knowledge as a strategic resource.

R&D Budget

Organisations that conduct their own research and development are better able to use externally available information (Cohen & Levinthal, 1990). Fundamo's investment of 35% of annual revenue in research and development, not only affords the opportunity to create new knowledge, but also contributes to their absorptive capacity, i.e. its ability to recognise the value of new information, assimilate it and apply it to commercial ends, as argued by Cohen and Levinthal (1990).

Learning Culture

Fundamo's intent to create such an environment conducive to the creation, transfer, and integration of knowledge is particularly evident through its well-established learning culture. As the Chief Software Architect explains:

In the development area we practise what they call pair-programming. It is formalised. So the idea is to pair an experienced person with a lesser experienced person in order to share knowledge and to prevent that you get stuck with specialists in certain areas of the software. This enables us to transfer knowledge across all the different aspects of the software. (Cruywagen, 2010)

Learning activities such as pair-programming, the brown-bag sessions, and working closely with external experts afford Fundamo the opportunity to create variety in their internal environment which ultimately leads to the emergence of novelty and the creation of new knowledge and innovation (Foss & Christensen, 2001).

Knowledge Orientation

The way in which an organisation orientates itself towards its knowledge environment will have a profound impact on the way in which knowledge is used as a resource for creating a competitive advantage.

Types of Knowledge

Sustained competitive advantage is dependent on an organisation's capacity to innovate, which in turn depends upon the individual and collective expertise of individuals (Leonard & Sensiper, 2002). This expertise or knowledge can either be explicit or tacit in nature. Tacit knowledge is a source of competitive advantage because it is hard to replicate by its competitors (Leonard & Sensiper, 2002; Teece, et al., 1997). Explicit knowledge, on the other hand, is accessible to people other than the individuals or groups originating it and therefore easier to imitate or even substitute (Teece, et al., 1997). The perceived importance of these forms of knowledge in an organisation can therefore give an indication of the organisation's capacity to innovate and to create a sustainable competitive advantage.

Inadvertently, Fundamo's approach to knowledge management includes both codification and personal interaction activities. As part of the codification approach, electronic file structures are used to store and share important documentation, while the wiki will be used as an informal platform for sharing knowledge. Product specifications are also well structured and documented. The strength of Fundamo's knowledge activities, however, lies in the transfer and integration of tacit knowledge through activities such as pair-programming, project estimation, quality assurance and the product development and improvement process, which suggests a strong capacity for innovation and creating a sustainable competitive advantage.

Sources of Knowledge

Another of Fundamo's strengths is their ability to scan the environment and to identify and develop sources of ideas and innovation. This concurs with earlier findings (Desouza & Awazu, 2006; Robinson, 1982) that SMEs are particularly skilled at exploiting external sources of knowledge. External sources of knowledge enable an organisation to develop a broader knowledge base, which in turn enables greater strategic flexibility and fuels the innovation process (Bierly & Daly, 2002; Cohen & Levinthal, 1990; Grant, 1996; Hargadon, 1998). Two important sources of knowledge for Fundamo are clients and technology partners. The CEO explains:

Our exposure to different companies and their view of things… it's almost like we see things

that we like or that's applicable to us. I think that is a big stimulation for how we do things. (Cruywagen, 2010)

She's now busy training in Bahrain, and she experiences the reality of what the people want, or the market or whatever, and then she documents it in the evening. She gets new insights, she documents it, and she shares it with us. (Cruywagen, 2010)

The importance of these external knowledge sources in Fundamo's success serves as an indicator of Fundamo's capacity to scan their external environment and to explore external knowledge sources for potential innovation opportunities.

Enactment

The essence of organisational capabilities resides in organisational processes, which from a dynamic capabilities perspective include elements of coordination, integration, reconfiguration and learning. The extent to which such processes are deployed in an organisation could therefore give an indication of the organisation's capacity to become knowledge-centric.

Knowledge Creation

Knowledge creation activities are aimed at introducing variety in an organisation, thereby stimulating the generation of new ideas that may eventually result in innovation. These processes coincide with knowledge exploration activities (March, 1991), or what Foss and Christensen (2001) refer to as Knowledge Problem 2, which in essence is the creation of new knowledge in order to render a competitive advantage sustainable. Stimuli of exploration activities could include knowledge of customers, suppliers, business partners, industry developments, or competitors. Fundamo is quite proficient at creating new knowledge based on customer interaction, as was pointed out earlier. This ability, along with the value Fundamo derives from interacting with technology partners enhances the company's ability to innovate.

Knowledge Use

Knowledge use activities are aimed at knowledge exploitation, in other words leveraging existing knowledge in new contexts. Exploitation activities are aimed at increasing efficiency and ensuring current viability (Easterby-Smith & Prieto, 2008; Levinthal & March, 1993; March, 1991). Knowledge exploitation typically emerges in activities aimed at improving products, services, or efficiency. Examples of knowledge use activities in Fundamo include the iterative product development process, as well as the project estimation process. Both these processes increase Fundamo's efficiency and viability in the long-term. The following statement by an employee illustrates how Fundamo's environment forces them to use their existing knowledge to find solutions to new problems, thereby also creating new knowledge:

I think the kind of environment we move in forces us to learn all the way, otherwise it would be easy. You cannot have five developers, copy and paste, and just change the labels and stuff. Every new client we have to go back to have a session thinking about how we are going to do that. I think it forces us to learn all the way. (Cruywagen, 2010)

Knowledge Integration

Knowledge integration activities are deployed to solve what Foss and Christensen (2001) refer to as Knowledge Problem 1, namely the integration of dispersed knowledge. An organisation's capacity to absorb and share external knowledge does not only depend on its interface with the external environment, but also on the transfer of that knowledge across the organisation (Cohen & Levinthal, 1990). Knowledge can be shared and integrated through social interaction, for example

communities of practice or storytelling, or by means of codification of knowledge, for example electronic documents (Haas & Hansen, 2007). The integration of knowledge results in an organisation's collective memory, often with frequently used concepts, methodologies, and commonly used terminology as foundation. Knowledge integration plays an important role in Fundamo's product development process. Knowledge from various sources, e.g. the research team, sales team, customer training, and technology partners, are integrated and prioritised in order to decide which features will be included in a product. Fundamo's deployment methodology represents the experience of more than nine years of production deployment and forms the foundation of the company's collective memory.

Knowledge Protection

For knowledge to be a source of competitive advantage, it has to be rare and inimitable. Codified knowledge can be protected to some extent by general patents, copyright and trade secrets (Liebeskind, 1996). Fundamo values the protection of organisational knowledge and has an active patent management and harvesting process with approximately 30 registered patents. Through these processes, Fundamo hopes to be able to sustain their competitive advantage though innovation.

Evolving the Knowledge-Centric Capability

The discussion has shown that Fundamo's knowledge-centric capability, presented in Figure 2, plays an important role in the company's ability to innovate.

However, the rapid growth of the company poses new challenges and their knowledge-centric capability will have to be developed further by addressing key areas, such as developing a KM strategy, identifying KM benefits, putting a KM structure in place, aligning KM technology with

Figure 2. Fundamo's knowledge-centric capability

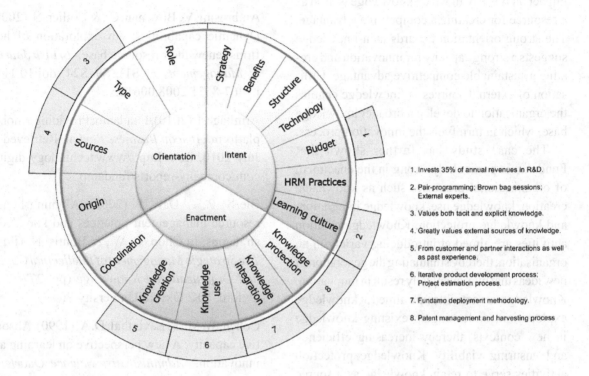

1. Invests 35% of annual revenues in R&D.

2. Pair-programming; Brown bag sessions; External experts.

3. Values both tacit and explicit knowledge.

4. Greatly values external sources of knowledge.

5. From customer and partner interactions as well as past experience.

6. Iterative product development process; Project estimation process.

7. Fundamo deployment methodology.

8. Patent management and harvesting process

the strategy, implementing knowledge-sharing incentives, aligning the KM strategy with the role of knowledge in the organisation, better understanding the origin and flow of knowledge in the organisation, and implementing effective coordination on a personal and group level to ensure the innovation capability remains viable in the long-term.

FUTURE RESEARCH DIRECTIONS

This chapter serves as an introduction to the view that a knowledge-centric capability acts as an enabler of innovation. Additional research into the composition of the knowledge-centric capabilities of companies renowned for their abilities to innovate could provide useful insight into the relative importance of elements such organisational intent, knowledge orientation, and enactment in an innovation capability.

CONCLUSION

A knowledge-centric capability is built on the foundation of dynamic capabilities and provides organisations with the context and processes, and therefore, the capacity to innovate. A knowledge-centric capability comprises three core elements, namely organisational intent, knowledge orientation, and enactment. The Fundamo case study identified a strong learning culture as an important indicator of organisational intent. The culture in an organisation is considered central to its ability to learn and to use knowledge as a source of competitive advantage. Learning processes also contribute to the development of dynamic capabilities. The prevalence of activities aimed at creating a learning culture is therefore considered an indicator of an organisation's intent to create, share, and use knowledge as a strategic resource.

The case study also showed that the way in which an organisation orientates itself towards its knowledge environment will have a profound impact on the way in which knowledge is used as a resource for creating a competitive advantage. The strong orientation towards tacit knowledge suggests a strong capacity for innovation and creating a sustainable competitive advantage. Utilisation of external sources of knowledge enables the organisation to develop a broader knowledge base, which in turn fuels the innovation process.

The case study has further shown that Fundamo is particularly strong in the enactment of organisational processes such as knowledge creation, knowledge use, knowledge integration, and knowledge protection. Knowledge creation activities are aimed at introducing variety in an organisation, thereby stimulating the generation of new ideas that may eventually result in innovation. Knowledge use activities are aimed at knowledge exploitation, or leveraging existing knowledge in new contexts, thereby increasing efficiency and ensuring viability. Knowledge protection activities serve to retain knowledge as a source of competitive advantage by keeping it rare and inimitable. In particular, codified knowledge can be protected to some extent by general patents, copyright, and trade secrets.

It is recognised that different organisations' knowledge-centric capabilities could be configured in different ways. The elements discussed in this chapter, however, were identified as the essential elements of Fundamo's knowledge-centric capability that contributes to the company's ability to innovate. This configuration of a knowledge-centric capability thus provides a point of departure for further exploring the relationship between knowledge-centric capabilities and innovation.

REFERENCES

Ambrosini, V., Bowman, C., & Collier, N. (2009). Dynamic capabilities: An exploration of how firms renew their resource base. *British Journal of Management*, *20*(S1), S9–S24. doi:10.1111/j.1467-8551.2008.00610.x

Armitage, I. (2010). Fundamo: Providing a mobile platform. *African Business Review*. Retrieved 10 July 2010, from http://www.technology-digital.com/company-reports/fundamo

Bierly, P., & Daly, P. (2002). Aligning human resource management practices and knowledge strategies. In Choo, C. W., & Bontis, N. (Eds.), *The Strategic Management of Intellectual Capital and Organizational Knowledge* (pp. 277–295). Oxford, UK: Oxford University Press.

Cohen, W. M., & Levinthal, D. A. (1990). Absorptive capacity: A new perspective on learning and innovation. *Administrative Science Quarterly*, *35*, 128–152. doi:10.2307/2393553

Cruywagen, M. (2010). *Knowledge-centric capabilities: A configurational approach*. Unpublished Doctotal Dissertation. Stellenbosch, South Africa: University of Stellenbosch.

Cyert, R. M., & March, J. G. (1963). *Behavioral theory of the firm*. Malden, MA: Blackwell Publishers.

Desouza, K. C., & Awazu, Y. (2006). Knowledge management at SMEs: 5 peculiarities. *Journal of Knowledge Management*, *10*(1), 32–43. doi:10.1108/13673270610650085

Dierickx, I., & Cool, K. (1989). Asset stock accumulation and sustainability of competitive advantage. *Management Science*, *35*(12), 1504–1511. doi:10.1287/mnsc.35.12.1504

Dosi, G., Nelson, R. R., & Winter, S. G. (2000). Introduction: The nature and dynamics of organizational capabilities. In Dosi, G., Nelson, R. R., & Winter, S. G. (Eds.), *The Nature and Dynamics of Organizational Capabilities*. Oxford, UK: Oxford University Press. doi:10.1093/0199248540.003.0001

Easterby-Smith, M., & Prieto, I. M. (2008). Dynamic capabilities and knowledge management: An integrative role for learning. *British Journal of Management, 19*, 235–249. doi:10.1111/j.1467-8551.2007.00543.x

Eisenhardt, K. M., & Martin, J. A. (2000). Dynamic capabilities: What are they? *Strategic Management Journal, 21*, 1105–1121. doi:10.1002/1097-0266(200010/11)21:10/11<1105::AID-SMJ133>3.0.CO;2-E

Faraj, S., & Sproull, L. (2000). Coordinating expertise in software development teams. *Management Science, 46*(12), 1554–1568. doi:10.1287/mnsc.46.12.1554.12072

Fiol, C. M., & Lyles, M. A. (1985). Organizational learning. *Academy of Management Review, 10*(4), 803–813.

Foss, N. J., & Christensen, J. F. (2001). A market-process approach to corporate coherence. *Managerial and Decision Economics, 22*, 213–226. doi:10.1002/mde.1012

Fundamo. (2011). *Fundamo enterprise platform*. Retrieved 23 June, 2011, from http://www.fundamo.com

Gartner. (2009). *Hype cycle for consumer mobile applications, 2009*. Washington, DC: Gartner.

Garvin, D. A. (1998). The processes of organization and management. *Sloan Management Review, 39*(4), 33–50.

Gibbert, M., Ruigrok, W., & Wicki, B. (2008). What passes as a rigorous case study? *Strategic Management Journal, 29*(13), 1465–1474. doi:10.1002/smj.722

Grant, R. M. (1996). Prospering in dynamically-cometitive environments: Organizational capability as knowledge integration. *Organization Science, 7*(4), 375–387. doi:10.1287/orsc.7.4.375

Haas, M. R., & Hansen, M. T. (2007). Different knowledge, different benefits: Towards a productivity perspective on knowledge sharing in organizations. *Strategic Management Journal, 28*, 1133–1153. doi:10.1002/smj.631

Hargadon, A. B. (1998). Firms as knowledge brokers: Lessons in pursuing continuous innovation. *California Management Review, 40*, 209–227.

Helfat, C. E., Finkelstein, S., Mitchell, W., Peteraf, M. A., Singh, H., & Teece, D. J. (2007). *Dynamic capabilities: Understanding strategic change in organisations*. Oxford, UK: Blackwell Publishing.

Hogarth, R. M., Michaud, C., Doz, Y., & Van der Heyden, L. (1991). *Longevity of business firms: A four-stage framework for analysis*. Unpublished Manuscript.

Iansiti, M., & Clark, K. B. (1994). Integration and dynamic capability: Evidence from product development in automobiles and mainframe computers. *Industrial and Corporate Change, 3*(3), 557–605. doi:10.1093/icc/3.3.557

Leonard, D., & Sensiper, S. (2002). The role of tacit knowledge in group innovation. In Choo, C. W., & Bontis, N. (Eds.), *The Strategic Management of Intellectual Capital and Organizational Knowledge* (pp. 485–499). Oxford, UK: Oxford University Press. doi:10.1142/9789814295505_0013

Levinthal, D. A., & March, J. G. (1993). The myopia of learning. *Strategic Management Journal, 14*, 95–112. doi:10.1002/smj.4250141009

Levitt, B., & March, J. G. (1988). Organizational learning. *Annual Review of Sociology, 14,* 319–340. doi:10.1146/annurev.so.14.080188.001535

Liebeskind, J. P. (1996). Knowledge, strategy, and the theory of the firm. *Strategic Management Journal, 17,* 93–107.

March, J. G. (1991). Exploration and exploitation in organizational learning. *Organization Science, 2*(1), 71–87. doi:10.1287/orsc.2.1.71

Marengo, L. (1994). *Structure, competence and learning in an adaptive model of the firm. Papers in Economics and Evolution no. 9203.* Freiburg, Germany: European Study Group for Evolutionary Economics.

McDonald, L. (2006). *Fundamo awarded technology leadership award.* Retrieved 15 July, 2010, from http://www.cbr.co.za/news.aspx?pklnewsid=22202

Miller, D., & Friesen, P. H. (1980). Momentum and revolution in organizational adaptation. *Academy of Management Journal, 23,* 591–614. doi:10.2307/255551

Nelson, R. R., & Winter, S. G. (1982). *An evolutionary theory of economic change.* Cambridge, MA: Belknap Press.

Penrose, E. T. (1959). *The theory of the growth of the firm.* New York, NY: John Wiley.

Prahalad, C. K., & Hamel, G. (1990, May-June). The core competence of the corporation. *Harvard Business Review,* 79–91.

Ratha, D. (2011). Worldwide remittance flows updated to $483 billion for 2011. *People Move (World Bank).* Retrieved 7 December, 2011, from http://blogs.worldbank.org/peoplemove/worldwide-remittance-flows-updated-to-483-billion-for-2011

Robinson, R. B. (1982). The importance of "outsiders" in small firm strategic planning. *Academy of Management Journal, 25*(1), 80–93. doi:10.2307/256025

Saldaña, J. (2009). *The coding manual for qualitative researchers.* Thousand Oaks, CA: Sage Publications.

Schumpeter, J. A. (1934). *The theory of economic development: An inquiry into profits, capital, credit, interest, and the business cycle* (Opie, R., Trans.). Cambridge, MA: Harvard University Press.

Teece, D. J. (2007). Explicating dynamic capabilities: The nature and misfoundations of (sustainable) enterprise performance. *Strategic Management Journal, 28,* 1319–1350. doi:10.1002/smj.640

Teece, D. J., & Pisano, G. (1994). The dynamic capabilities of firms: An introduction. *Industrial and Corporate Change, 3*(3), 537–556. doi:10.1093/icc/3.3.537-a

Teece, D. J., Pisano, G., & Shuen, A. (1997). Dynamic capabilities and strategic management. *Strategic Management Journal, 18*(7), 509–533. doi:10.1002/(SICI)1097-0266(199708)18:7<509::AID-SMJ882>3.0.CO;2-Z

Teece, D. J., Rumelt, R., Dosi, G., & Winter, S. (1994). Understanding corporate coherence: Theory and evidence. *Journal of Economic Behavior & Organization, 23*(1), 1–30. doi:10.1016/0167-2681(94)90094-9

Yin, R. K. (2003). *Case study research design and methods* (3rd ed.). Thousand Oaks, CA: Sage Publishing.

Zollo, M., & Winter, S. G. (2002). Deliberate learning and the evolution of dynamic capabilities. *Organization Science, 13*(3), 339–351. doi:10.1287/orsc.13.3.339.2780

ADDITIONAL READING

Argote, L., McEvily, B., & Reagans, R. (2003). Managing knowledge in organizations: An integrative framework and review of emerging themes. *Management Science, 49*(4), 571–582. doi:10.1287/mnsc.49.4.571.14424

Brown, J. S., & Duguid, P. (1998). Organizing knowledge. *California Management Review, 40*(3), 90–111.

Choo, C. W., & Bontis, N. (Eds.). (2002). *The strategic management of intellectual capital and organizational knowledge.* Oxford, UK: Oxford University Press.

Davenport, T. H., De Long, D. W., & Beers, M. C. (1998). Successful knowledge management projects. *MIT Sloan Management Review, 39*(2), 43–57.

Easterby-Smith, M., & Lyles, M. A. (Eds.). (2003). *The Blackwell handbook of organizational learning and knowledge management.* Oxford, UK: Blackwell Publishing.

Easterby-Smith, M., Lyles, M. A., & Peteraf, M. A. (2009). Dynamic capabilities: Current debates and future directions. *British Journal of Management, 20*(s1), S1–S8. doi:10.1111/j.1467-8551.2008.00609.x

Grover, V., & Davenport, T. H. (2001). General perspectives on knowledge management: Fostering a research agenda. *Journal of Management Information Systems, 18*(1), 5–21.

Helfat, C. E., Finkelstein, S., Mitchell, W., Peteraf, M. A., Singh, H., & Teece, D. J. (2007). *Dynamic capabilities: Understanding strategic change in organisations.* Oxford, UK: Blackwell Publishing.

Katz, D., & Kahn, R. L. (1966). *The social psychology of organizations.* Hoboken, NJ: John Wiley & Sons.

Kogut, B., & Zander, U. (1992). Knowledge of the firm, combinative capabilities, and the replication of technology. *Organization Science, 3*(3), 383–397. doi:10.1287/orsc.3.3.383

Leonard-Barton, D. (1995). *Wellsprings of knowledge: Building and sustaining sources of innovation.* Boston, MA: Harvard Business School Press.

Liao, J., Kickul, J. R., & Ma, H. (2009). Organizational dynamic capability and innovation: An empirical examination of internet firms. *Journal of Small Business Management, 47*(3), 263–286. doi:10.1111/j.1540-627X.2009.00271.x

Nelson, R. R. (1991). Why do firms differ, and how does it matter? *Strategic Management Journal, 12*, 61–74. doi:10.1002/smj.4250121006

Nonaka, I., Kohlbacher, F., Hirata, T., & Toyama, R. (2008). *Managing flow: A process theory of the knowledge-based firm.* New York, NY: Palgrave Macmillan.

O'Dell, C. S., Grayson, C. J., & Essaides, N. (1998). *If only we knew what we know: The transfer of internal knowledge and best practice.* New York, NY: Free Press.

Peteraf, M. A. (1993). The cornerstones of competitive advantage. *Strategic Management Journal, 14*(3), 179–191. doi:10.1002/smj.4250140303

Polanyi, M. (1966). *The tacit dimension.* Garden City, NY: Doubleday.

Tsoukas, H. (2003). Do we really understand tacit knowledge? In Easterby-Smith, M., & Lyles, M. A. (Eds.), *The Blackwell Handbook of Organizational Learning and Knowledge Management* (pp. 410–427). Oxford, UK: Blackwell Publishing.

Tsoukas, H., & Vladimirou, E. (2001). What is organizational knowledge? *Journal of Management Studies, 38*(7), 973–993. doi:10.1111/1467-6486.00268

Von Krogh, G., & Grand, S. (2002). From economic theory toward a knowledge-based theory of the firm. In Choo, C. W., & Bontis, N. (Eds.), *The Strategic Management of Intellectual Capital and Organizational Knowledge* (pp. 163–184). Oxford, UK: Oxford University Press.

Zack, M. H. (1999). Managing codified knowledge. *Sloan Management Review, 40*(4), 45–58.

KEY TERMS AND DEFINITIONS

Absorptive Capacity: Ability of an organisation to recognise the value of new, external information, assimilate it, and apply it to commercial ends.

Dynamic Capabilities: Capacity to intentionally create, extend or modify the resource base of an organisation.

Knowledge-Centric Capability: Capacity to provide the organisational context for creating, transferring and integrating knowledge into new configurations.

Organisational Learning: Continuous process that enhances the collective ability of an organisation to make sense of and adapt to changes in both internal and external environments.

Explicit Knowledge: Knowledge that can be communicated explicitly or codified.

Tacit Knowledge: Knowledge that can only be transferred through observation or engagement in the activity; cannot be codified or communicated explicitly; skills; know-how.

Knowledge Exploitation: Leveraging existing knowledge in new contexts.

Knowledge Exploration: Creation of new knowledge, typically from sources external to the organisation.

Section 3
Knowledge Management, Innovation, and Technology

Chapter 16
Technology and Tools Supporting CoPs

Sheryl Buckley
University of South Africa, South Africa

Paul Giannakopoulos
University of Johannesburg, South Africa

ABSTRACT

The role of technology in organisations over the past two decades, whether centred on business or education, has varied from performing simple day-to-day tasks to performing highly sophisticated problem-solving tasks. Many organisations have either adjusted their daily routines to accommodate new technology or developed technologies to satisfy their needs. At the same time, the credo "knowledge is power" was changing to one of "knowledge sharing is power." Once this change was recognized, Communities of Practice (CoPs), a special type of community of practitioners sharing knowledge voluntarily, began to play a very important role in Knowledge Management (KM). Such communities relied heavily on technology in order to prosper. One of the greatest advantages of these communities is the sharing of tacit knowledge, in a disciplinary as well as interdisciplinary environment, which is an "ingredient" of innovation and competitive advantage. This chapter will review the ongoing evolution of the tools, types of technology, and innovations that can be used by both online and offline CoPs. It will further address the matter of which technological innovations and tools academics can use to support CoPs and the design of technology used for this purpose.

INTRODUCTION

It is common knowledge nowadays that communication technologies are changing faster than the speed at which people, in general, are mastering them. However, there are many specific technologies that see changes not in their underlying concepts, but in the extra utilities that are added—some of which are used and others not. Examples of such technologies would be cell phones and word processors. Improvements in communication and transportation technology

DOI: 10.4018/978-1-4666-1969-2.ch016

over recent centuries have resulted in shifts in community ties, which have moved from being primarily people-to-people, geographically bound, to being people-to-people irrespective of local geography (Jones & Grandhi, 2005, p. 216). Considerable effort has gone into freeing interpersonal interactions from geographic constraints and enabling communication anywhere, any time. Until recently, state Jones and Grandhi (2005), our ability to use technology to seamlessly locate individuals and provide them with geographical, contextualized, personal information management tools was quite limited. However, this situation is now changing with the widespread adoption of wireless technologies such as the Global Positioning System (GPS), 802.11, Bluetooth, Radio Frequency Identification (RFID), and other geographical routing technologies. Using such technologies, Computer-Mediated Communication (CMC), and location data, such as the geographical location a user is communicating from or to, can be combined to provide appropriate geographic context to interactions. As a result, face-to-face communication can be replaced or complemented by these technologies. Thus, online communities other than face-to-face have begun to emerge—such as CoPs or COP/face-to-face hybrids. For the rest of this chapter, the terms 'online communities' and 'CoPs' will be used interchangeably.

Jones and Grandhi (2005, p. 220) state that online communities can be networked communities, whose interactions are mediated primarily through the Internet, and with non-geographic affinities leading to shared social ties. These online communities are often built through online community spaces such as e-mail lists, newsgroups, Internet Relay Chat (IRC) channels and others, which enable a wide range of individuals to attend and contribute to a shared set of computer-mediated interpersonal interactions. They can, therefore, be considered relatively transparent and open. These spaces support online communities by providing a space in which ties can be formed between people through public shared interactions. Such spaces are different from personal spaces, such as e-mail inboxes, where interactions are not publicly shared between members of the online community.

Sharing of knowledge, especially tacit knowledge, has been accepted as the way forward for innovation and competitive advantage (Wenger, 2001). Because the aim of KM is the creation, sharing, and flow or transfer of knowledge in an organisation, a CoP can be one of the most informal ways to achieve this aim. In fact, CoPs can be seen as a way to eliminate the limitations of a purely technology-based KM. This chapter aims at discussing, in depth, communication tools that can be used by CoPs (face-to-face, or virtual, or both).

BACKGROUND

For a community to be called a CoP it has to satisfy a number of criteria as described by the orginators of CoPs, Wenger and Lave (1991) and McDermott (2000). Akoumianakis (2009) adds that a CoP is conceived as being virtual, and formed and maintained using a variety of tools such as listservs, e-mails, blogs, and wikis and sees a CoP as "an organisation within an organisation." The most important criterion of a CoP is "sharing knowledge in a voluntary manner." Online communities are just one of many types of communities: They have a purpose, are supported by technology, and are guided by norms and policies (Preece, 2000). The term 'online community' broadly refers to all communities that exist predominantly online, but we acknowledge that online communities vary depending on:

- Whether they have a physical as well as a virtual (i.e., networked, physi-virtual) presence (Lazar, Tsao, & Preece, 1999).
- Purpose (e.g., health support, education, business, neighborhood activities).

- The software environment supporting them (e.g., listserver, bulletin board, chat, instant messaging, or, more often these days, some combination of these).
- Size (small communities of fifty people are different from those of 5000 or 50000).
- The duration of their existence.
- The stage in their life cycle.
- The culture of their members (e.g., international, national, local, and influences that may be related to politics, religion, gender, professional norms).
- Their governance structure (e.g., the kind of governance structure that develops and the types of norms and rules associated with it).

Basdekis, Klironomos, Antona, and Stephanidis (2006) indicate that, during recent years, important changes have been experienced in the ways people use and interact with the Internet and Information and Communication Technologies (ICT) in general, as well as in the ways people communicate and interact with each other through the use of such technologies. Access to information is a basic right and the increasing amount of publicly available information is even more important for people with disabilities and other groups at risk of exclusion.

Lewis and Allan (2005, pp. 36-37) state that there are two main types of virtual communication tools and that these enable different types of contacts between community members and facilitators:

- **Asynchronous Tools:** Enable people to communicate at a time that suits them. Individuals post a message that is held by the system. This message can be read and responded to as and when the recipient comes online. Asynchronous communications take place over time rather than at the same time, e.g. e-mail, bulletin boards, and mailing lists.

- **Synchronous Tools:** Enable people to communicate when they log onto the same system at the same time, that is, they are immediate and live communications. Unlike face-to-face communications, a transcript or record of the communication process is provided by many synchronous tools, e.g. conference or chat rooms, instant messaging, Internet telephony, and video conferencing.

Table 1 briefly describes these tools and gives examples of their application for virtual learning communities.

For Long and Schweitzer (2004), synchronous discussions, community news, community resources, document exchange, quiz or survey, picture exchange, personal identity, and search are key CoP features. Asynchronous discussion means that users are not communicating in 'real time.' They are merely posting and responding when they are at the community site. Synchronous discussion is anything that allows the community user to carry on a live conversation.

Wenger (2001) identifies the most common online facilities that CoPs can use:

- A home page to assert their existence and describe their domain and activities.
- A conversation space for online discussions of a variety of topics.
- A facility for floating questions to the community or a subset of the community.
- A directory of membership with some information about members' areas of expertise in the domain, electronic collaboration, discussion, or meeting.
- A document repository for their knowledge base.
- A search engine that enables them to retrieve things they need from their knowledge base.
- Community management tools, mostly for the coordinator but sometimes also for the

Table 1. Characteristics of virtual communication tools (Lewis & Allan, 2005, p. 37)

	Type of Communication	Asynchronous/ Synchronous	Virtual Learning Community Applications
E-mail	1 to 1, 1 to many	Asynchronous	Exchange information Provide detailed instruction Discussion Collaborative or project work Knowledge construction Training delivery Follow-up coaching or mentoring sessions Networking
Mailing lists	1 to many	Asynchronous	Exchange information Provide detailed instruction Discussion Collaborative or project work Knowledge construction Network
Bulletin boards	1 to many	Asynchronous	Exchange information Provide detailed instruction Discussion Collaborative or project work Knowledge construction Follow-up coaching or mentoring sessions
Polling	1 to many	Asynchronous	Collect information Decision making
Instant messaging	1 to 1, 1 to many	Synchronous	Exchange information Provide detailed instruction Discussion Knowledge construction
Chat or conferencing	1 to 1, 1 to many	Synchronous	Exchange information Provide detailed instruction Discussion Collaborative or project work Knowledge construction Follow-up coaching or mentoring sessions
Internet telephony	1 to 1, 1 to a few	Synchronous	Exchange information Provide detailed instruction Discussion Knowledge construction Training events, meetings
Video conferencing	1 to 1, 1 to a few	Synchronous	Exchange information Provide detailed instruction Discussion Knowledge construction Training events, meetings

community at large, including the ability to know who is participating actively, which documents are downloaded, how much traffic there is, which documents need updating, etc.

- The ability to spawn subcommunities, subgroups, and project teams.

Furthermore, a technological platform for CoPs should ideally be (Wenger, 2001):

- Easy to learn and use because CoPs are usually not people's main jobs.
- Easily integrated with the other software that members of the community are using

for their regular work so that participation in the community requires as few extra steps as possible.

• Not too expensive. If it requires a lot of investment up front, potentially useful communities will not be able to take advantage of the platform.

For Arguello, Butler, Joyce, Kraut, Ling, and Wang (2006), since the 1970s, when the first Usenet news-sharing programs were created, online communities have co-evolved with computer networking. Three decades later, people share information, jokes, discussions, data, and social support in thousands of online communities across a variety of contribution lists, and the Usenet is still one of these. People benefit from the presence and activity of others in online communities—from the information and support they provide and the conversations in which they participate. Online communities are particularly well suited to adapting general information for individuals' specific needs. In order to succeed, online communities, like smaller groups, need to meet the needs of individual members and maintain themselves over time. The first need to be met is the community's willingness to respond to a member's message, because the responses provide the content through which participants gain benefit from others in the group.

The second is members' commitment to the community, which reflects their satisfaction with their experience. To survive and thrive, online communities must provide the benefits and experiences that members seek. In online groups, conversation is the basic mechanism by which participants derive benefit. Whether they are explicitly soliciting information or assistance or implicitly seeking to direct the group's attention to topics in which they are interested, individuals who attempt to start conversations are trying to increase the likelihood that the group will provide benefits they value. The community's response, if any, is what satisfies the poster's needs. Thus, community responsiveness to attempts to initiate conversations is an essential element of community success.

The viability of a community also depends on the willingness of individuals to stick with the group over time. A self-interest model of group commitment holds that people remain committed to a group only as long as the group meets their various social, instrumental, and emotional needs better than alternative uses of their time. In discussion-based communities, getting talked to is a basic mechanism for obtaining a benefit. If others fail to respond, the silence calls into question one's reason for commitment. This hypothesis is consistent with research showing that individuals who post for the first time to an online group are more likely to return when others respond to them. Other research has found that receiving a response increases the speed of posting a second time, although not the probability of posting again.

Online communities consist of people and the content they exchange. While there are cases of extremely long-lived discussions involving hundreds of people, most online conversations are smaller, shorter and more focused, with a clear initiating message, a small number of participants, a limited duration, and a relatively circumscribed topic. It is through these online conversations, typically presented in threaded form, that many individuals experience an online community. To increase the benefit that people receive from online communities, and ultimately the viability of the community itself, it is important to understand the factors that influence the interaction through which people experience the community. Unlike most user interfaces through which users engage with computers, discussion does not follow a designed formula. What is said (topic), how it is said (style and structure), who says it (author characteristics), and where it is said (group characteristics) all interact to shape the way in which an individual's interaction with a community plays out.

Infrastructures designed to support the formation of viable communities that are usable by a wide audience must help individuals engage with communities in a way that is likely to prompt beneficial responses and build commitment. The context matters. Different groups have evolved different interaction patterns, including the likelihood of response to individual messages. Efforts to develop technology to support the formation of viable and effective online communities can do more than simply provide access to an infrastructure that allows for sharing and structuring ongoing group discussion. Tools can be developed to help members use appropriate rhetorical strategies, at the right time, and in the right place to effectively benefit from and contribute to online communities—and in doing so, to improve both the experience for the individual and the success of the community as a whole.

Beenen, Ling, Wang, Chang, Resnick, and Kraut (2004) argue that, despite the vibrancy of online communities, large numbers of them fail. For example, Butler found that 50% of social, hobby, and work mailing lists had no traffic over a four-month period. Under-contribution is a problem even in communities that do survive. In a majority of active mailing lists, fewer than 50% of subscribers posted even a single message in a four-month period. Similarly, on the popular peer-to-peer music sharing service, Gnutella, two-thirds of users share no music files and ten percent provide 87% of all the music. In open source development communities, four percent of members account for 50 percent of answers on a user-to-user help site, and four percent of developers contribute 88% of new code and 66% of code fixes. Although not everyone needs to contribute for a group to be successful, groups with a large proportion of non-contributors have difficulty providing needed services to members.

A number of changes in the technological environment are slowly providing large numbers of people with one or more devices that enable mobile, location aware, hi-speed, and multimedia communication. There is a general movement to provide Wi-Fi (wireless technology owned by the Wi-Fi Alliance) coverage by universities, public network activists, cities, rural communities and businesses (Jones & Grandhi, 2005, p. 221). Many new top-end laptops and Personal Digital Assistants (PDAs) now have in-built Wi-Fi. Wi-Fi is fast enough to enable high-speed delivery of rich multimedia and many operators are offering mobile phones capable of playing, recording, and delivering multimedia. Further, PDA phones are coming to market with both broadband capabilities and Wi-Fi connectivity.

In addition to wireless personal communication infrastructure, and devices becoming more sophisticated, 'things' are getting smarter with the advent of technologies such as RFID. RFID potentially enables communication to be placed within a very rich geographic-digital context. The trend appears to be towards numerous real-world environments in which everything is digitally labeled, everything is connected and everyone can communicate from anywhere (Jones & Grandhi, 2005, p. 224).

TOOLS SUPPORTING COPS

The survival and flourishing of established and future CoPs depends, among other factors, on communication. In the absence of face-to-face communication, members of CoPs must be aware of alternative ways of communicating. This implies that they must be aware of all possible communication tools, which will enhance their cause. What they should be careful of is choosing the appropriate tools that suit their needs. With the use of technology comes also the 'abuse'—thus the use of technology can also be counterproductive (e.g. spending too much time using Facebook for private purposes). A number of well-known tools, as well as less well-known tools, that CoP members can use, will be discussed in detail in the next few sections. Akoumianakis (2009) discusses some of the criticisms of CoPs and the tools used. He cites Wenger et al. (2002) where even the originator of CoPs admits that the strongest points of a CoP can become the weakest link because trust, domain, and established practices can hold it hostage. The author further mentions Roberts (2006) and Franke and Piller (2004) who found that some toolkits can be abused, or render themselves useless, because the users themselves have not made any input into their design.

Facebook

Facebook and MySpace are examples of Web 2.0 Social Networking Sites (SNS) which have enormous potential in the field of education, despite the fact that they were not designed as an environment for constructing and managing learning experiences (Llorens & Capdeferro, 2011, p. 199). YouTube and Flickr allow individuals to present themselves, articulate their social networks and establish or maintain connections with others (McCarthy, 2009, p. 39). Facebook is currently the most popular SNS on the Internet, but it has not been used in tertiary education beyond basic marketing strategies such as universities presenting themselves to prospective students (McCarthy, 2009, p. 39). It operates as an open platform, unlike other systems organised around courses or formally structured content. While Facebook is not a learning environment, it can serve as a very valuable support for the new social orientations now prevailing in approaches to educational processes. For Llorens and Capdeferro (2011, p. 199) learning communities represent a fusion between the individual realm and the shared realm. In this context, Facebook provides educators with a good opportunity to generate knowledge and inter-group cohesion. Research carried out by the University of California in Los Angeles found that over 94% of first-year students spent at least some time on social networking sites in a typical week (Panckhurst, 2008).

Facebook constructs sociality by means of a strategy that connects users not only with each other, but also with numerous circles of sub-networks, events, and groups. It assumes that the production of creative experiences is a social event, which is based on pooling resources and content contributed by people and processed using shared-use tools (Llorens & Capdeferro, 2011, p. 199).

Twitter

Twitter is primarily a communication tool and has often been described as filling the gap between e-mail and Instant Messaging (IM). It is a form of microblogging that was launched in July 2006. It has grown very quickly and, within eight months of its launch, attracted 94 000 users; it now has over a million users, more than 200 000 of them active weekly (Arrington & Schonfeld, 2008). Twitter allows users to post their latest 140-character-or-less updates through one of three methods: Web form, text message, or instant message. It is also a means of communication with the ability to form distributed communities. The number of educators microblogging has recently escalated and is "becoming serious in informal learning" (Costa, Benham, Reinhardt, & Sillaots, 2008). The reasons that many educators are part of this are the ease with which knowledge can be shared and developed, and the way in which meanings attributed to situations and experiences common to educators in developed English speaking countries can be negotiated. Educators who have joined Twitter have done so because it is easy, and because people they already know and trust have joined it.

Blogs

The current largest fad on the Web is weblogs or blogs. While often regarded as a platform for people to share their personal stories, a blog can also be used to tell the story of an organisation (CommunIT, 2012). Austin Free-Net (2012) explains that blogs are Web pages that are updated frequently with new content. Bloggers (people who blog) typically offer their readers' links to interesting information along with the blogger's own commentary. Blogs have also become popular among diary and journal keepers. They are an efficient and exciting way to keep people abreast of each other's worlds and the world we all live in. It is estimated that there are over one million bloggers around the world—from the US to Brazil to Iran. Many authors and journalists also blog as a way of freeing their work from editors. The 2004 US presidential candidates used blogs on their campaign sites.

A blog is a simple content management system that allows individuals to post to a website in a fashion organised by date. This is the simplest form of an asynchronous discussion forum. It is a discussion that only one person can post to. While this makes it not really a discussion, the argument is simply intended to emphasise how close a blog is to a simple discussion posting. The interesting part about blogs is how they organise themselves, and how most of them provide some mechanism for users to post comments about the blog. The blogging community is the beginning of a semantic organisation (Daconta, Obrst, & Smith, 2003). It can be said that a potential emerging trend in CoPs will be that each member will keep a personal blog that other community members can read. In this way, a stronger common ground will be established, ultimately leading to greater interaction in the community.

Paquet (2002) refers to blogs as weblogs. This term, which was coined by Jorn Barger in 1997, refers to a website that is a log of the Web, indicating a record that points to material available on the World Wide Web. A weblog editor is often called a weblogger. The first weblog was Tim Berners-Lee's 'What's New?' page at http://info.cern.ch/, which pointed to new websites as they came online. The second weblog was Marc Andreessen's 'What's New?' page at the National Center for Supercomputing Applications, which performed a similar function until mid-1996.

Several new weblogs appeared with the explosion of the Web in 1996/1997. Early weblogs included Dave Winer's 'Scripting News,' Jorn Barger's 'Robot Wisdom,' and Cameron Barrett's 'CamWorld.' The content of early weblogs was most often a mix of links and commentary that was tailor-made to their editor's taste. Over time, these weblogs built sizable followings because they provided a unique selection of fresh content that appealed to a segment of the online population and because of their personal flavour.

Blogs are good for (Paquet, 2002):

- Sharing/distributing information of all kinds
- Producing a user's own 'information' and self-expression
- Documenting the experiences that users and their colleagues are having and or work that they are doing.

CommunIT (2012) states that blogging tools are designed to be easy to use. To this end, they can help a person create posts, display posts to visitors, moderate, publish RSS (Really Simple Syndication) feeds, configure the appearance and layout, find support, host a blog, and get statistics on a blog. There are different kinds of blogs, and some are easier to manage than others. A blog can be run off a person's own server or through a service. The latter option is far easier for beginner bloggers. A blogging client allows text to be typed in, formatted, and published to the Web with just a few mouse clicks. Examples of blog services are blogger.com, blog-city.com, angelfire.com, easyjournal.com, and blurty.com. Blogs are about text, links, and images.

White (2006) explains that blog communities show up in three main patterns (see Figure 1) with a wide variety of hybrid forms emerging between the three: The single blog/blogger-centric community, the central connecting topic community, and the boundaried community.

Figure 1. Blog-based communities (White, 2006)

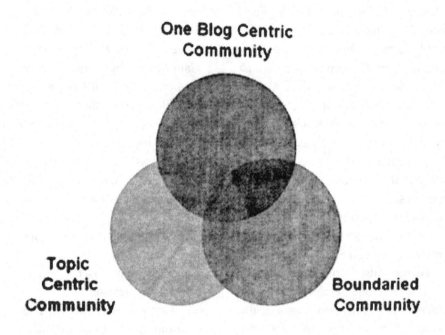

Furthermore, by looking at the patterns we can start thinking about strategic approaches to blogs as a medium for community development. They can be considered in terms of their (White, 2006):

- **Technology/Design:** The impact of how the blogging tools are deployed and their impact on the community.
- **Social Architecture:** Locus of control and power, identity, and interaction processes.
- The role of content or subject matter.
- Other issues, such as scalability and life cycle.

On the other hand, in the single blog/blogger-centric community (see Figure 2), the first and most visible model is the hub-and-spoke model of 'one blog/blogger.'

Instead of a hub and spoke, the central connecting topic-centric blog community (see Figure 3) is a network formation. This form is a community that arises between blogs linked by a common passion or topic. The boundary of the network is a combination of subject matter (domain) and membership (community). Beyond the visible membership of linked blogs is the wider and mostly invisible network of readers.

This form is exemplified by groups such as food bloggers, mummy bloggers, travel bloggers, and political bloggers with a particular party or issue identification. They may be far less interested in positioning themselves than they are in the topic they blog about. As these grow, they are more network-like than community-like. Communities form within the network as people find more specific niches and interests.

Boundaried communities (see Figure 4) are collections of blogs and blog readers hosted on a single site or platform.

Typically, according to White (2006), members register and 'join' the community and are offered the chance to create a blog. This boundary makes them the closest form to traditional forum-based communities. Examples include the huge teen-oriented site MySpace.com, as well as Yahoo 360, March of Dimes, and Share Your Story, as well

Figure 2. Single blog/blogger-centric community (White, 2006)

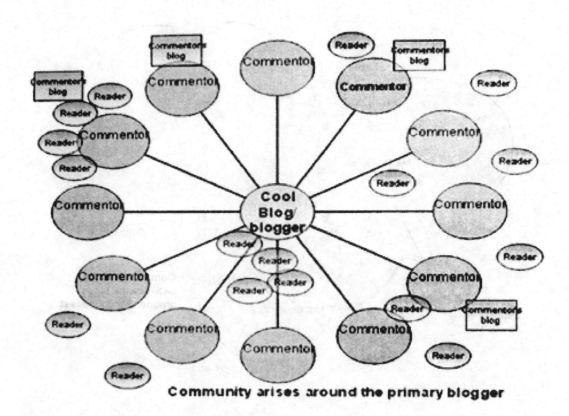

Community arises around the primary blogger

as Australian free educational blogging sites such as Edublogs, ESLblogs, Uniblogs, and Learnerblogs.

Often these communities have other tools built in, such as discussion boards, social networking features, wikis, and instant messaging. The blogs are part of the overall ecosystem. There is less emphasis on RSS and cross-linking because those features are built into the technology in other ways. Because they are within a defined boundary, bloggers can see and easily access other blogs. They can, if they wish, link. Linking takes place mostly within this closed system and bloggers seem to link less often outside of the community. This leads to denser and faster possible internal connections and, possibly, to community building.

Weblogs, says Paquet (2002), serve a number of important functions, such as selection of materials,

personal knowledge management, conversation, social networking, and information routing.

E-Mail

E-mail is a technology based on the Internet, providing for the sending and receiving of text-based messages as personal communications. A mailing list offers a facility for asynchronous e-mail communications between members of a group connected by virtue of a common interest or affiliation, providing a means for public dialogue. The World Wide Web is a set of electronic protocols to access and publish information—in the form of hypermedia as well as text documents (Wild, 1999).

From a person's desktop, e-mail provides a quick, reliable, and cost-effective link to the

Figure 3. Topic-centric community (White, 2006)

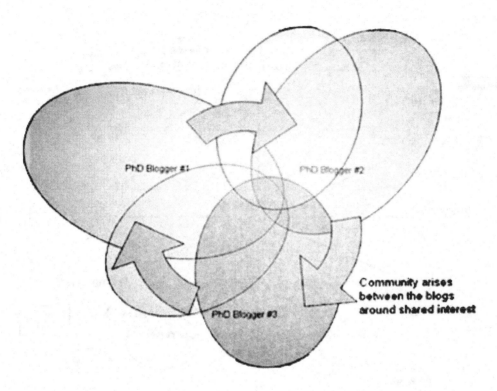

Figure 4. Boundaried communities (White, 2006)

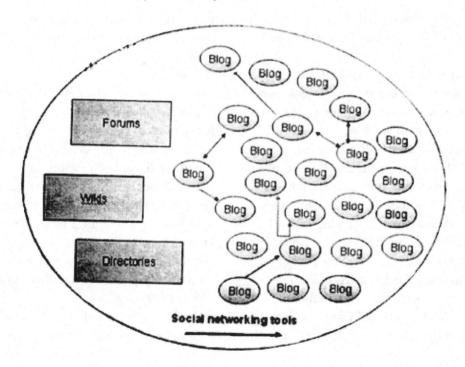

world at large and consequently, e-mail lists have evolved as a powerful tool for collaboration in Africa, Asia, and Latin America. However, for the inexperienced user, participating in such a list can be a frustrating and sometimes intimidating experience (James & Rykert, 1998, p. 68).

For Tyler, Wilkinson, and Huberman (2012), e-mail has become the predominant means of communication in the information society. It pervades business, social and technical exchanges and, as such, it is a highly relevant area for research on communities and social networks. E-mail has been established as an indicator of collaboration and knowledge exchange (Wellman, 2002; Whittaker & Sidner, 1996). E-mail is also a tantalising medium for research because it provides plentiful data on personal communication in an electronic form. This volume of data enables the discovery of shared interests and relationships where none were previously known (Schwartz & Woods, 1993). Given its ubiquity, it is a promising resource for tapping into the dynamics of information within organisations, and for extracting the hidden patterns of collaboration and leadership that are at the heart of CoPs.

Preece, Maloney-Krichmar, and Abras (2003) indicate that e-mail, the first and still the most frequently used communication tool on the Internet (Project, 2002), was developed by ARPAnet in 1972. Early systems were point to point—one person could send a note to just one other person. Listservers, which allow one to do many postings, were not invented until 1975. The basic form of this technology has not changed much since that time, although e-mail readers have improved greatly. Listservers are used in two ways: trickle through and digests. Trickle-through systems distribute each message as it is received. Digests comprise a list of messages presented one after the other, usually in chronological order of receipt. In the mid to late 1980s, systems with improved graphical user interfaces started to appear.

Kollock and Smith (1999) indicate that, in an e-mail discussion list, a message sent to a group address is then copied and sent to all the e-mail addresses on a list. When people direct a series of messages and responses to the list, a group discussion can develop. As of 1997, there are tens of millions of e-mail users and thousands of public mailing lists, as well as hundreds of thousands of less formal discussion lists, in existence. These lists are maintained for the discussion and distribution of information on thousands of topics. This may be the most common form of group interaction on the Internet, and some lists contain thousands or tens of thousands of members.

E-mail discussion lists have some important qualities that distinguish them from other Internet communication tools. E-mail lists are typically owned by a single individual or small group. Since all messages sent to the list must pass through a single point, e-mail lists offer their owners significant control over who can contribute to their group. List owners can personally review all requests to be added to a list, can forbid anyone from contributing to the list if they are not on the list themselves, and even censor specific messages that they do not want broadcast to the list as a whole. Because active review requires significant time and effort, most e-mail lists are run as open spaces, allowing anyone to join the list and anyone to contribute to it. Even open lists can be selectively closed or controlled by their owners when faced with disruption (Kollock & Smith, 1999).

E-mail discussion lists are asynchronous media. Interaction is structured into turns, but a reply may occur minutes or months after the prior turn. There are a number of benefits to asynchronous interaction. A group can interact without everyone gathering at a particular time. As a result, people on very different schedules or in distant time zones can still exchange messages and sustain discussions (Kollock & Smith, 1999).

Wikis

APC (2005) describes a wiki as an online database-driven website for simple, quick, and versatile online publishing. The graphic layout of published content is a lot simpler than can be achieved with most 'real' content management systems. It is easy to use and extremely flexible in terms of structuring content and, as opposed to a Content Management System (CMS), does not need strong administrative or Web design skills.

The first wiki was created in 1994 as an open source solution to collaboratively develop software patterns on the Web (Lachkovics, Metz, Goldberg, Alluri, & Quek, 2006). Since then, they have been adopted for many other uses and their popularity continues to grow. Possibly the most successful wiki is Wikipedia, a free encyclopedia composed entirely of volunteer contributions. It has produced over 160000 articles in less than three years.

Wiki is short for 'wikiwikiWeb,' first coined by Ward Cunningham in 1995. 'Wiki' means 'quick' in Hawaiian (LeFever, 2006). Wikis are different from normal websites in that normal websites are usually developed offline and then presented to users as a finished product. By comparison, wikis are first presented to users as a blank slate—an empty page. A new wiki is an empty wiki with no pages and no links. Instead of a team of designers developing a website in private, a wiki is developed in public by the users of the wiki over the life of the wiki. The users are responsible for the direction and content of the wiki website over time. Everyone who uses the wiki has the opportunity to contribute to it and/or edit in the way that he or she sees fit. This allows a wiki to change constantly and morph to represent the needs of the users over time. Wikis grow to represent the community of users. All wiki pages are equipped with a publicly available link that usually says 'Edit this page' or 'Edit text.' Whenever a user wants to update or change a page, he or she clicks the 'Edit this page' link, makes the desired changes using plain text

and then clicks 'Save' to finalise the change. It is this editing ability that makes a wiki so efficient in collecting information—users need only to edit a page to update the website—no programming skill is required (LeFever, 2006).

LeFever (2006) reports that wikis are not appropriate for:

- **Threaded Discussions:** Without attribution or chronology, discussions do not work.
- **Weblogging:** There is no attribution or chronology.
- **Instant Messaging/Presence:** There is no way to know when someone else is 'on' the wiki or to contact them directly via the wiki.

Wikis are best used for a purpose—to serve a need. They are tools and their value is related to how they are used. Wikis are not predefined by any structure or requirements.

APC (2005) explains that wikis are useful when working on a single document or a relatively self-contained topic, section or page. They might also be useful in the idea stage of jotting down and adding information. Wikis are not ideal if there is a need to see who has made what changes where, or to comment directly on text. Each page shows who saved the last changes, but who wrote which parts of the text cannot be tracked.

Creating a wiki using a third-party wiki-hosting service is a sensible choice for many non-profit organisations because this option requires minimal setup and no advanced technical knowledge. In addition, some organisations are likely to treat their first wiki as a sort of experiment, evaluating its effectiveness as a communication tool and noting whether users adopt it. Some examples of hosted and free wiki services are BluWiki, EditMe, EditThis.info, JotSpot, PB Wiki, StikiPad, Wikia, and Wikispaces (Satterfield, 2006).

Satterfield (2006) divides wikis into three basic categories: public, protected, and private. A public wiki has an active and engaged community of users and can come to be a valuable vault of shared knowledge that evolves and expands over time. Public wikis such as Wikipedia allow anyone on the Internet to view, create, and edit pages. Although some public wikis require an account to be created before content can be altered, others let anonymous users add or change pages.

Protected wikis, on the other hand, are visible to the general public but can only be changed by authorised users. Most wikis have a designated administrator (or wikimaster) who grants users the permissions required to edit, add, or delete information. The wikimaster also makes general rules and enforces standards of conduct to help maintain the integrity of the content.

Private wikis are most often used for internal communications within a company or organisation; only those who are authorised by the administrator can edit, or even view, the wiki (Satterfield, 2006).

Polling Software and Instant Messaging

Polling software enables a community facilitator to collect information from the whole group. It is particularly useful for identifying the optimum time(s) for online conferences (Lewis & Allan, 2005, p. 40).

Instant messaging enables a user to send and display a message on someone else's screen in a matter of seconds. Instant message systems often have friend or buddy lists that enable individuals to track when one of the people on their list comes online so that they know the instant they can start sending messages to him or her. This facility may be used by a virtual learning community (Lewis & Allan, 2005, p. 40).

Chat systems, instant messaging and texting systems are synchronous, which means that correspondents must be co-present online. Conversations are rapid and each individual comment is short. In busy systems, messages scroll off the screen as they are replaced by more recent ones. Internet Relay Chat (IRC) was developed in 1988 by Jarkko Okarinen. Instant messaging was made famous by ICQ and AOL Instant Messenger has appeared in the last five years. Texting, a related technology, occurs across phone lines. Texting is popular in some parts of the world, particularly Europe, parts of Africa, and the Middle East (Preece, Maloney-Krichmar, & Abras, 2003).

WorldsAway was an online graphical 'virtual chat' environment in which users designed their own two dimensionally represented avatars. It was the first visual virtual world. In 1996 it was one of the top 20 most popular forums on CompuServe (Basdekis, Klironomos, Antona, & Stephanidis, 2006).

Kollock and Smith (1999) indicate that text chat differs from e-mail lists and BBSs in that it supports synchronous communication—a number of people can chat in real time by sending lines of text to one another. Chat is one of the most popular forms of interaction on the Internet, and accounts for a sizeable proportion of the revenue of the commercial online providers such as America Online. Text chat is often organised around the idea of channels on a text-based 'CB-radio' system. Most chat systems support a great number of 'channels' dedicated to a vast array of subjects and interests.

Text chat also uses a centralised server that grants the server owner a great deal of power over access to the system and to individual channels. In commercial chat services, chat channels are frequently policed by the provider's staff or by appointed volunteers. In the largest non-commercial system—IRC (Internet Relay Chat)—each channel has an owner who can eject people from the channel, control who enters the channel, and decide how many people can enter.

Internet Telephony and Video Conferencing

Synchronous communications now include internet telephony, which is the ability to make phone calls via the Internet. Internet telephony enables individuals to make long-distance phone calls through the computer and the Internet without paying expensive long-distance phone charges. However, it requires up-to-date computers with access to a fast modem and a large amount of RAM, otherwise the sound quality may be poor (Lewis & Allan, 2005, p. 41).

Video conferencing has been available for years but previously required specialist and very expensive equipment installed in specialised rooms. The use of desktop video conferencing is becoming more common and offers a way in which members of the virtual learning community can 'come together' relatively easily (Lewis & Allan, 2005, p. 41).

Group Communication Software and Collaboration

Many organisations are using commercial communications software packages that offer a mix of e-mail, messaging, bulletin board and conference room facilities. One advantage of this approach is that it means that employers are familiar with these electronic tools and use them as an everyday part of their work (Lewis & Allan, 2005, p. 42).

For Tyler, Wilkinson, and Huberman (2012), CoPs are the informal networks of collaboration that naturally grow and coalesce within organisations. Any institution that provides opportunities for communication among its members is eventually threaded by communities of people who have similar goals and a shared understanding of their activities. These communities have been the subject of much research as a way to uncover the structure and communication patterns within an organisation—the reality of how people find information and execute their tasks.

Bulletin Boards

Bulletin boards are designed based on the metaphor of a physical bulletin board. People post messages to the board and these are displayed in various ways. The messages are usually threaded, meaning that messages on the same topic are associated with each other. The first message forms the beginning of the thread and responses are stacked beneath it. Over the years systems have appeared that offer many fine enhancements: search engines enable users to search according to topic, username, date; emoticons; private conversation spaces; links to e-mail, user profiles and Web pages; as well as graphical two dimensional pictures and avatars (Preece, Maloney-Krichmar, & Abras, 2003).

For Kollock and Smith (1999), BBSs (Bulletin Board Systems—also known as conferencing systems) are another form of asynchronous communication that refines e-mail discussion lists in a number of ways. Most BBSs allow participants to create topical groups in which a series of messages, similar to e-mail messages, can be strung together one after another. There are a number of conferencing systems. Well-known ones include the Usenet, the WELL (picospan), ECHO (caucus), and the bulletin board discussion groups run on commercial online services such as America Online and the Microsoft Network. Each sustains a wide collection of topics of discussion and an ongoing give-and-take between participants. BBSs differ from e-mail discussion lists in another way. E-mail is a 'push' media—messages are sent to people without them necessarily doing anything. In contrast, conferencing systems are 'pull' media; people must select the groups and messages they want to read and actively request them.

Kollock and Smith (1999) state that Usenet is the largest conferencing system and has a unique form of social organisation. Usenet is composed of a distributed database of messages that is passed through an informal global network of systems that agree to a standard message format. More than tens of thousands of 'newsgroups' are carried over the Usenet, each containing from a few dozen to tens of thousands of messages. On an average day, tens of thousands of different people contribute hundreds of thousands of messages to the Usenet. A new site 'joins' Usenet simply by finding any existing site that is willing to pass along a copy of the daily 'feed' (the collection of messages it receives). As a result, Usenet has no central authority, no single source of power that can enforce boundaries and police behaviour. No one owns most Usenet newsgroups; most news-groups are anarchic in the technical sense of the term—they have no central authority though they do have an order and structure. Almost anyone can read the contents of a Usenet newsgroup, create entirely new newsgroups, or contribute to one. This makes Usenet a more interesting and chal-lenging social space than systems that are ruled by central authorities.

MUDs

MUDs (Multiple User Domains/Dungeons) at-tempt to model physical places as well as face-to-face interaction (Kollock & Smith, 1999). MUDs are text-based virtual realities that maintain a sense of space by linking different 'rooms' together. MUDs grew out of the interest in adventure-style games that presented a textual description of dif-ferent rooms and the objects in them and allowed the player to move from room to room, take and drop objects, and do things such as fight dragons and solve puzzles. With the growing availability of networked computers on university campuses in the late 1970s, MUDs were developed to allow people to play adventure games with other people instead of against computers.

Over the past fifteen years, MUDs have become increasing sophisticated and complex. Modern social MUDs allow users to build new spaces, create objects, and to use powerful programming languages to automate their behaviour. While many MUDs continue to focus on combat role-playing, many social MUDs have become a means

for widely dispersed groups to maintain personal contact. MUDs incorporate a range of other modes of communication, such as e-mail and discussion groups, to link users with other users. However, like text chat, their key quality is that they support synchronous communication—people interact with each other in real time. MUDs allow a number of people in the same 'room' to meet and talk by sending lines of text to one another. MUDs often support simulations of the multi-channel quality and nuances of face-to-face interaction by framing the lines of text users send to one another as 'say,' 'think,' or 'emote' messages. This allows users to provide meta-commentary on their turns of talk and to create 'gestures' or make parenthetical comments (Kollock & Smith, 1999).

Like e-mail lists, MUDs are typically owned by the individuals or groups that provide the hardware and software and the technical skill needed to maintain the system. Because these skills and re-sources have until very recently been rare, owners of MUD servers have had nearly complete control over the system. MUD owners are often referred to as 'Gods.' Gods can delegate their power in whole or in part to selected participants, who commonly take on the status of 'wizards.' Other users can be granted more access to the computer's memory and network capacity, allowing them to build larger and more elaborate virtual spaces and objects. Users can be granted or denied the right to enter the MUD, be given the power to build new objects or enter specific rooms, and can have limited abilities to communicate with other users. MUDs may contain sophisticated forms of social stratification and elaborate hierarchies.

MP3 and the Mobile Community

MP3, another technology innovation, also has an impact on the concept of community. It provides an interesting example of how a community can form around a particular technology designed to facilitate the distribution, sharing and stealing of music (Preece, Maloney-Krichmar, & Abras, 2003).

According to Varey (2005, p. 142), the widespread adoption of mobile telephones and other Information and Communication Technology (ICT) may indicate that we are creating an interaction society.

People are interdependent on one another and thus attempt, abort, avoid and accomplish the exchange of things. This requires agreement on who does, and should exchange, what with whom, for what reason and on what terms. The necessary interaction as individuals and as a group member is through shared meanings and learned values and through social role enactment. Within interaction, people offer (or do not offer) things to one another and demand, accept or reject things from one another (Varey, 2005, p. 148).

ABI Research (2007) found that mobile social communities currently number nearly 50 million members worldwide, a number that is expected to reach 174 million in 2011. Furthermore, they claim that "[t]he rapid rise of online social communities—gathering places such as MySpace and Facebook—has done more than bring the 'pen pal' concept into the 21st century. It has created a new paradigm for personal networking. In a logical progression, many social communities are now based on the mobile phone and other portable wireless devices instead of the PC. Such mobile social communities extend the reach of electronic social interaction to millions of people who don't have regular or easy access to computers."

Axup (2012) defines a mobile community as a network of interpersonal ties that provides sociability, support, information, a sense of belonging and social identity, and that always connects its members regardless of where they are. Furthermore, users of mobile devices often end up developing intimate connections to them. This is probably because the devices are with them all the time, increase safety and perform both social and private functions. Consequently, they often become embedded as part of the user's identity.

The question arises: what happens when this is applied to existing online communities?

Howard Rheingold is the world's foremost authority on virtual communities. He served as an online host for The Well from 1985, and sat on The Well's Board of Directors. In 1994, he was the founding Executive Editor of HotWired, the first commercial webzine with a virtual community known as Threads. Rheingold is already seeing the movement of virtual communities off the desktop and out of classical cyberspace. Billions of SMSs are transmitted every day (Rheingold, 2003). The current state of mobile communities is somewhat parallel to the early days of the Bulletin Board System (BBS). People are connecting one to one via their mobile devices to exchange information. It will not take long for this style of communication to become more centralised. The emergence of mobile communities will mean that participants in online communities will remain in continuous contact over multiple platforms on desktops and mobile devices. This continuous contact will perhaps be a truer form of what is meant by a community.

People become intimately attached to groups of people. They share private information, meet people more often, and grow to trust social networks. Consequently, new opportunities for collective action develop. Communities of people could, in some cases, establish powerful group identities, find new ways to coordinate and orchestrate policies, and eventually gain power to influence governments and politics. On the other hand, these communities are more personal than ever. They know a lot about a person and have an almost super-human ability to connect one person with other people and find the resources he or she needs. All of this theorising is dependent on having tools, which enable and possibly encourage people in this direction. Communities do not just happen, they must be built. Technology greatly influences how people act, simply because it makes so many things possible (Axup, 2012). A few examples are listed below:

- Instant messaging on Danger's Hiptop enables mobile users to chat with groups while on the move.
- Networks of friends send SMSs to members of their friend groups to coordinate activities.
- Families use mobile phones to keep in touch with loved ones as they travel or commute.
- Moblogging allows people to post pictures (or other media) to a community website from anywhere, and a few sites now allow readers to respond using similar media via their mobile devices.

Discussion and Mailing List

There are thousands of discussion lists available on the Internet and each is devoted to a particular topic and is aimed at a specific audience. They provide a quick and easy method of communication and often have very speedy response time. They are a good method of keeping up to date and also tapping into practical experience and expertise. The vast majority of discussion lists are open to anyone who wants to subscribe and such lists may have a membership of thousands—that is, they are used by communities of interest rather than virtual learning communities or CoPs (Lewis & Allan, 2005, p. 39).

A mailing list allows a group of people to work together online and to discuss, share and produce information. On a more technical level, a mailing list is an automatic message-sending program that stores a list of e-mail addresses of a group of people who are members of or subscribers to that mailing list. This list (with addresses) is based at a host computer connected to the Internet. The mailing list distributes each message sent to it to all members of the mailing list. The mailing list software offers several functions to manage the mailing list. According to IDRC (2012), a mailing list allows any number of people with e-mail addresses to communicate amongst one another

on issues of common interest. Participants 'subscribe' to the list. If they decide they no longer want to receive messages from the list, they can 'unsubscribe.' Each discussion has its own e-mail address (e.g. ashbev@gmail.com). Each time a message is posted to the list address, everyone subscribed to the mailing list receives it.

Sharp (1997) asserts that one or more local CoPs can act to create critical mass for a mailing list community of discourse by acting as facilitators, helping to ensure that answers are given and phone calls are made to participants requesting help, to mention just a few functions. These local CoPs will reinforce and encourage other local members to participate in and support a mailing list. After reaching a critical mass, other conditions being equal, the original facilitating group will become less critical.

Several studies have found that people communicating by BBS, mailing lists and moving to e-mail will then seek to meet face to face. CMC, while supporting communications, cannot build a community. Trust, cooperation, friendship, and community are based on contacts in the sensory world. People communicate through networks but do not live in them. The more face-to-face opportunities there are, and the more time to develop judgments of competency and trust in fellow practitioners there is, the more likely it is that mailing lists will to be used for a full array of services such as asking for help (Sharp, 1997).

A mailing list can act as a human knowledge filter, for its members are often experts on differing subjects have worked on different projects, and can be approached by others in the community of discourse to quickly supply answers.

A successful mailing list will take on many attributes of a community. Interaction in virtual spaces can come to share many of the characteristics of 'real' interaction—people discuss, argue, fight, reconcile, amuse, and offend just as much as, and perhaps more than, in a real-world community. In mailing lists, examples can be seen of attempts to control behaviour by correction, by suggestion, by appealing to the rules of the group, by attempting to keep posters on topic, and so on.

Another type of mailing list is a listserv. List-servs, or electronic discussion groups, are dynamic electronic Schelling points. In *The Strategy of Conflict* (1960), Schelling developed the idea of natural and constructed points that focus interactions, places that facilitate connections with people interested in participating in a common line of action. The clock at Grand Central Station is an example, as are singles bars and marketplaces. Each is a space designated as a point of congregation for people of like interests (Sharp, 1997).

Sharp (1997) argues that, because of the public and shared communication of written messages on a listserv, others can quickly and easily comment on and add to any given answer. Many users turn to listservs as a convenient way to find information quickly. The mailing list acts as an organic information filter (Sharp, 1997). Even without face-to-face contact, regular readers of a listserv will come to judge the competence of frequent contributors by the perceived reasonableness of their answers and by certification, both in online replies and from comments from their local CoP, that a particular contributor is competent or not so competent.

Networks enhance the flexibility of Schelling points by radically altering the economies of their production and use. Members of these virtual social networks frequently identify their groups (and groups of groups) as virtual communities.

TECHNOLOGY DESIGN FOR COPS

Irrespective of the environment, providing technology for communities is not very different from providing technology for other purposes. Wenger et al. (2005) maintain that great care should be taken in the design process of technological tools. The authors suggest that such tools should be easy to use, designed for learning, within the reach of the CoP members and capable of evolution.

Design for Ease of Use and Learning

Because communities are rarely their members' highest priority, the general principle of simplicity is doubly important. A team that will spend extensive time working together may be ready to invest in learning a complex system, but community members rarely have such luxury. Difficulties in learning to use the technology will quickly discourage participation. A community-centric approach to implementation of new technologies implies that the technology steward looks for existing tools in the environment available for community adoption—as is, or with minor modifications. Adoption of familiar tools is faster and less painful than of tools that seem too new or too different. At the same time, sustained interaction with other community members can lead to high levels of sophistication, so community members can come to tolerate and exploit a great deal of complexity. Learning in, around and about technology for CoPs happens not only at individual level, but also at the level of the group (Wenger, et al., 2005).

Design for Evolution

It is always a good idea to design technology that can evolve, but with communities, the need to design for evolution is paramount. The community's needs at the beginning of its life will evolve over time—a challenge for technology providers. Unlike the trajectory of a team, which can often be fairly well planned from the start, the life of a community is a voyage of discovery. Communities change. They often start rather tentatively, with only an initial sense of why they should come together. They reinvent themselves continuously. Their understanding of their domain expands. New members join. Their practice evolves. The technologies need to support the intertwined evolution of domain, community, and practice without overbuilding. Leading with too much, or overdesigned, technology will burden community members if the environment gets too difficult to use, or introduces too much change. The community leaders represent the community in facing these challenges (Wenger, et al., 2005).

Design for "Closeness at Hand"

Community members often do not work together on a day-to-day basis, but what they interact about is often related to their main occupations. Solutions that are 'one click away' from the tools that members use day-to-day are preferable to those that seem farther away from their working environment and that require effort to switch context. Providing close-at-hand access to a CoP can be complicated by the fact that members may want to participate from home, from the office, or while they are on the road. This is one reason e-mail is still a very successful community tool in spite of all the recent developments: it integrates community interactions in the tool where people spend a large portion of their working and social lives (Wenger, et al., 2005).

Design from a User's Perspective

Like most users of technology, communities come together for a purpose, which is rarely a fascination with technology for its own sake. As in any technology design, the user perspective has to be the focus. However, because community technology is designed for communities but experienced by individuals, the process has to balance community and individual perspectives. Individual participation is shaped by many forces, including different needs and preferences, personal learning goals in the community context, as well as familiarity with the technology (Wenger, et al., 2005).

TECHNOLOGY FOR SUCCESSFUL CoPs

There are fundamental elements in a CoP according to which technology can have either a positive or negative effect (Wenger, 2001).

- **Time and Space**
  - **Presence and Visibility:** A community needs to have a presence in the lives of its members and make themselves visible to each other.
  - **Rhythm:** Communities live in time and they have rhythms of events and rituals that reaffirm their bonds and value.
- **Participation**
  - **Variety of Interactions:** Members of a CoP need to interact in order to build their shared practice.
  - **Efficiency of Involvement:** CoPs compete with other priorities in the lives of their members. Participation must be easy.
- **Value Creation**
  - **Short-Term Value:** CoPs thrive on the value they deliver to their members and to their organisational context. Each interaction needs to create some value.
  - **Long-Term Value:** Because members identify with the domain of the community, they have a long-term commitment to its development.
- **Connections**
  - **Connection to the World:** A CoP can create value by providing a connection to a broader field or community that its members care to keep abreast of.
- **Identity**
  - **Personal Identity:** Belonging to a CoP is part of one's identity as a competent practitioner.

- ○ **Communal Identity:** Successful communities have a strong identity that members inherit in their own lives.
- **Community Membership**
  - ○ **Belonging and Relationships:** the value of belonging is not merely instrumental, but personal as well: interacting with colleagues, developing friendships, building trust.
  - ○ **Complex Boundaries:** CoPs have multiple levels and types of participation. It is important for people on the periphery to be able to participate in some way. And inside communities too, people form sub-communities around areas of interest.
- **Community Development**
  - ○ **Evolution:** Maturation and integration—CoPs evolve as they go through stages of development and find new connections to the world.
  - ○ **Active Community-Building:** Successful CoPs usually have a person or core group that takes some active responsibility for moving the community along.

Wikibooks (2008) states that, in order for an online CoP to be successful, the technology supporting it needs to meet the needs of the community (and support its identity) as well as the needs of the individual (and support his or her identity). Wenger (2001) outlines that a technology steward is a good prerequisite for a successful online CoP. The technology steward role requires understanding of the relevant technologies for communities, the inventiveness of the technology for serving the community perspective, and supporting the way the community uses technology and ideas about the technology, which come from inside the community. Once the technology to support the CoP is in place, Wenger states that ongoing monitoring by the technology steward is essential to ensure ease of use and learning, to search for possible opportunities for evolution of the technology, and to ensure ease of use for participants from the user's perspective.

Examples of technologies, both synchronous and asynchronous, that have been developed for online communities include Communispace (http://www.communispace.com/), CommunityZero (http://www.ramius.net/products/communityzero/index.cfm), iCohere (http://www.icohere.com/), and Web Crossing (http://www.webcrossing.com/Home/).

Other technologies which have been adapted for CoPs and not specifically designed for them include eRoom, Groove, Quickplace, Blackboard, Moodle, WebCity, Livelink, Meetme, Mindshare, SharePoint, or WebSphere, PhP Nuke, Plone, Vignette, WebEx, PlaceWare, HorizonLive, and NetMeeting, as well as MSN Messenger, Usenet, and Yahoo Groups.

INVESTMENT STRATEGIES AND CHALLENGES FOR TECHNOLOGY

Wenger (2001) identified four strategies in increasing order of complexity and investment.

Just Use What You Have

CoPs functioned in organisations long before technologists and managers tried to provide specific facilities for them. The basic communication technologies that most organisations already have can be enough for some communities. E-mail systems usually have facilities for creating simple distribution lists. Most organisations have some kind of file repository system. Teleconferencing facilities are almost ubiquitous. This simple approach may not be very exciting for the technology savvy, but it is a way to get going until more specific needs are established.

Start with a Simple Facility

Using this approach, a platform is built by providing a useful but limited facility in one product category to jumpstart the process:

- The product categories that best fit the main activities of the communities are determined.
- A base system, depending on the primary needs of the communities, is provided.
- In due time, an expanded platform is built by adapting the base and adding components.

Deploy a Community-Oriented System

A number of community-oriented companies, such as Communispace, RealCommunities, and ArsDigita, aspire to become integrators of facilities and applications that expand the basic community framework they offer. They do this through partnerships and by building compatibility and modularity into their systems.

Build on an Enterprise Collaboration System

If price were no object, a knowledge worker's desktop, such as Intraspect, LiveLink, or Engenia Unity would be attractive because many of the more complex facilities are in place. These systems often do not have the kind of specialised communal space that community-oriented systems can create. As a result, they are not as good at giving a community a sense of identity and distinct style. However, given the complex facilities they provide, it is usually relatively easy to add on community spaces with a distinct identity. Further, no matter the approach adopted, the following issues need to be considered.

1. **What types of communities are you trying to support?** It is crucial to understand the kind of communities you want to support, the kinds of activities they engage in, and the relationships they develop.
    a. How well defined is the domain of knowledge?
    b. How tightly knit is the community?
    c. Are they likely to know each other? To have established reputations?
    d. What is the main goal of the community?
    e. How much common knowledge are they building?
    f. How much work are they doing together?
    g. Are interactions mainly discussions, such as expressing opinions?
    h. How important are documents, tools, and other artifacts?

    These questions will help you form an understanding of the product categories best suited for these communities, and of the best entry point into the development of a technology platform for CoPs. For instance, if the communities mostly want to have good conversations online and share a few documents, fairly cheap solutions can be developed easily and made available for wide use at low cost.

2. **What are you trying to accomplish with technology?** You need to decide which community success factors you are trying to prop up and then evaluate your technology choices accordingly.
    a. What aspects of community life does technology need to enhance?
    b. What is the practice of the community and how can technology support it?
    c. Does the design of the system address the necessary success factors appropriately?

d. How well do the pieces together?

e. How easy is it to integrate potential new pieces?

3. **Do you want technology to modify behavior?** You also need to decide what the system says about the place and role of communities in the organisation. An aspect of this question is how much behavior modification you want to promote. All technologies, to some extent, influence behavior by placing emphasis on or facilitating certain processes, but some companies also take intentional steps to make their technologies reflect some principles or processes and influence behaviour accordingly.

Some systems are designed as general utilities and some are designed to encourage certain behaviors. Some are meant to blend seamlessly into the way people behave already, for instance by using e-mail a great deal. Others are meant to encourage specific behaviors, such as logging on to a distinct community space or reflecting on a model of how a community behaves.

a. How well is the system integrated into how people work?

b. What model of collaboration does a system reflect?

c. How much work will the behavioral modification require?

d. Is it worth the trouble?

e. How well are the community-oriented facilities integrated with existing systems that provide some of the needed functionality (e.g., databases, document management, enterprise systems, and portals)?

4. **What are the requirements of the technology?**

a. **Support:** You need to consider the requirement for local support. For instance, some systems require a thick-client component on local machines, which must be installed by an IT department, while browser-based or thin-client applications, which are increasingly common, do not require local technical support.

b. **Programming:** You need to consider the requirement for programming skills. For instance, ACT is free, but unless you hire the services of ArsDigita, using the system requires a group of skilled programmers who are interested in joining the ArsDigita community.

c. **Systems Requirements:** These issues are important in the selection of particular products, though the trend towards ASP and the increasing use of open standards like Java and XML may decrease the prominence of these types of question.

However, there is no step-by-step recipe that can be followed that will guarantee a specific outcome. Building community is an activity fundamentally different from writing computer code. The tendency of those involved in building graphical virtual worlds is to create visually compelling worlds that look good, but do a poor job of fostering social interaction. Many of these systems have more in common with lonely museums than with the vibrant communities they set out to create.

As Kollock and Smith (1996, p. 109) state: 'At the root of the problem of cooperation is the fact that there is often a tension between individual and collective rationality. This is to say that, in many situations, behavior that is reasonable and justifiable for the individual leads to a poorer outcome for all. Such situations are termed social dilemmas and underlie many of the most serious social problems we face.'

For Bilodeau (2003) the technology used to support CoPs can be expected to have a strong bias towards explicit knowledge. This introduces a risk that only the explicit knowledge of the community will be made available to its members, leaving out the tacit portions. This incomplete rendering of the community may make it difficult for people to engage in authentic practice through the technology alone. To address this, designers must consider the technology within the context of the practice, mindful of how it will be used by students to gain an understanding of the material (i.e. the practice) through social interactions centered around reified artifacts, explicit knowledge that has been encoded as text, multimedia, or even software (i.e. simulations) (Haneda, 1997).

The main emphasis of technology should be to enable community participants to share experience (Finerty, 1997). Computers can help students locate community resources (people, information, etc.) based on their needs (Hay, 1993). In addition, computers can be used to create connections between people in a community and across community boundaries. For example, IT makes it easier to allow practitioners to interact with students in the classroom (Hung & Nichani, 2002). These are connections that traditionally, for a variety of reasons, may have been difficult or not even possible. Bilodeau (2003) claims that advancements in technology can have an impact on three broad arenas of Higher Education (HE):

- The nature of knowledge
- The process of teaching and learning, and
- The social organisation of teaching and learning in HE

At the most basic level, technology has affected the nature of knowledge itself. It shapes what counts as knowledge, how knowledge is produced, how people are involved in the production of knowledge, and how academic knowledge is valued. There is a burgeoning assumption that legitimate knowledge must be capable of being computerised. Knowledge is increasingly created, processed, manipulated, and stored using technology. In addition, the way in which knowledge is produced in academic settings has been greatly expanded; new ways to conduct research are only now possible because of technological advances. Finally, technology is a critical building block and should be viewed as a support to the social aspects of sharing knowledge. To be effective (Worldbank.org, 2012), technology should be adapted and customised to the needs of the community. The 'best' technology involves tools that help community members find, disseminate and apply knowledge, and that enhances communication among them.

Solutions and Recommendations

KM aims at creation, sharing, and preserving knowledge, but such activities do not take place in a vacuum. They are driven by the human beings who form the human and the intellectual capital—as well as the backbone—of a modern organisation. However, for them to utilise their explicit and tacit knowledge, the organisation has to create an atmosphere conducive to such activities and be given the tools to perform not only their duties, but in a voluntary manner share their tacit knowledge. Nowadays, it has been accepted that CoPs are ideal for the achievement of the KM aims.

Although the original idea of a CoP was one of voluntary participation with management playing the role of an observer, research has shown that an active, non–interfering/non-controlling approach by management could achieve better results. For example, at the University of Johannesburg (UJ) a survey showed that a very small percentage of academics were aware of CoPs (Buckley, 2009). How can one create a CoP, or participate in one, if one is not aware of them? Toshiba was one of the first organisations to have its management introduce CoPs and, within a year, more than 90% of the employees belonged to one or more

CoPs. This is what UJ is also doing. The question of using incentives to encourage participation in CoPs is supported by Buckley (2009) who claims that such incentives could eliminate a number of inhibitors for such participation.

In a university setup, it is assumed that all academics are aware of the existing technologies. At UJ, it was established that almost all academics used e-mail and part of the Intranet and Internet, but this was as far as it went. Attempts were made by the IT department and the Research and Innovation division to improve the situation. Schienstock (2011, p. 67) has also seen the important role of CoPs in innovation and argues that technological innovations are embedded in social activities which take place in specific socio-cultural settings. Furthermore, a major assumption of the community concept is that one cannot separate learning and techno-organisational innovations from work. Instead, learning occurs and innovations are developed mainly through conversations and interactions between people within the work process (Schienstock, 2011, p. 67).

As online/offline CoPs depend more and more on technology, one of the most important factors identified in the literature (Buckley, 2009), as well as at UJ, is the perceived risk that one will lose the uniqueness of one's own knowledge. However, this perception is in line with the idea that 'knowledge is power' (an industrial era approach to knowledge) rather than 'knowledge sharing is power' (a knowledge era approach). This perception is directly related to trust. The building of trust among members who aim at sharing their knowledge is therefore a precondition. This is, of course, true for any CoP (virtual or otherwise).

Management support (of any form), along with the enlightenment of academics, could be among the most important factors contributing to the establishment and flourishing of CoPs in any organisation.

FUTURE RESEARCH DIRECTIONS

Online communication opens up vast opportunities for human interaction and association across time and space. Technology is still changing at a pace faster than the speed at which users of technology become accustomed to new technology. Thus, if technology is to be used as a main tool for communication in a CoP then a modification of the original concept is necessary. Research into the role of management in CoPs will have to become research into the originating and supporting of CoPs. Voluntary participation of members must be maintained and pilot projects should be established to determine such roles.

From the conception of CoPs by Lave and Wenger in 1991, research on the value of CoPs in organisations has shed light on one of the most important functions of a CoP—the sharing of knowledge, especially the tacit knowledge. Since then, tacit knowledge has been recognised as an important aspect of competitive advantage. Creation of new knowledge and innovation are also interlinked with knowledge sharing. However, the effects of knowledge sharing on the creation of new knowledge and innovation have not been yet established. It can be hypothesised that, by sharing knowledge with another person, that knowledge can become an activator of thinking processes which otherwise would have remained dormant.

Another important issue that needs to be studied in depth is research on formal creators of new knowledge, namely institutions of higher learning. For centuries, universities and colleges have been the curators of knowledge, the creators of new knowledge and the ones entrusted with the dissemination of knowledge for continuity to prevail. Academics find themselves in a precarious situation: they are considered to be the experts of knowledge in the various fields and they train novices. On the other hand, through research, they have to create new knowledge. Forming CoPs then could, then, be problematic. It will be of great interest to the knowledge society to investigate the barriers to the establishment of CoPs as well as the factors that promote the establishment of CoPs—or why academics share, or do not share, their tacit knowledge with other academics.

Finally, adding a pragmatic dimension to situated learning—which gives rise to a psycho-pragmatic approach to learning and knowledge creation and acquisition—opens a new field of research. Concentrating on the utility of knowledge to be acquired, it gives the choice to the individual to decide whether it is worthwhile acquiring such knowledge. In a knowledge society, there is no room for "inert" knowledge.

CONCLUSION

This chapter has illustrated that technology can play a very important role in improving communication between members of a CoP, unconstrained by space or time. Awareness of the various communication tools, and the proper use of them, increases the chances that a CoP will flourish. Be it via wireless or landline connectivity between members of CoP (any means other than face to face), its members can communicate their ideas effectively. It must be borne in mind that technology cannot give rise to a CoP; it can only complement it and enhance communication. The nature of CoPs will dictate the tools to be used and, for this reason, knowledge of the function of each tool is necessary.

The foundation of the community's architecture is the technology infrastructure that supports collaboration and learning. Current demands on most organisations mean that a community's collaborative space must be accessed via multiple channels. The virtual space needs to be complemented by opportunities to meet face to face, on the telephone and by e-mail. To support the many different kinds of conversations that will take place, the organisation needs to provide the community with a variety of tools and approaches to maximise the opportunity for knowledge creation, access and exchange. The tools used to support the community should be fairly standard across the organisation. The object is to have people become familiar with a tool so that, when they encounter it again, they know how to use it. Creating a level of computer literacy within the community helps create greater readiness across the organisation for the adoption of new technology. The key challenge for technology that supports communities is incorporating the social aspects of community at the lowest possible bandwidth.

Perhaps answering Wenger's (2001) four fundamental questions is a good way of establishing the role that technology will play in a CoP. The situation (e.g. availability of tools or availability of funds to purchase tools, as well as the way members operate) will dictate how the tools will contribute to enhancing the cause of the particular CoP.

Finally, when a new communication tool is designed, this should satisfy the needs of the user and not vice versa (i.e. the user should not have to adapt to technology). The new tool should be easy to use, designed for learning, within reach of the CoP members and capable of evolution.

REFERENCES

APC.org. (2005). *Internet & ICTs for social justice and development news*. Retrieved from http://www.apc.org/english/news/index.shtml?x=5038198

Arguello, J., Butler, B., Joyce, E., Kraut, R., Ling, K. S., & Wang, X. (2006). Talk to me: Foundations for successful individual-Group interactions in online communities. In *Proceedings of CHI 2006*. ACM Press.

Arrington, M., & Schonfeld, E. (2008). *The real twitter usage numbers*. Retrieved from http://www.techcrunch.com/2008/04/29/end-of-speculation-the-reral-twitter-usage-numbers/

Austin Free-Net. (2012). *Blogging!* Retrieved from http://www.austinfree.net/curricula/blogging_curriculum.html

Axup, J. (2012). *Mobile community design*. Retrieved from http://www.mobilecommunitydesign.com/pages/faq.html

Basdekis, I., Klironomos, I., Antona, M., & Stephanidis, C. (2006). *Online communities for all: The role of design for all in the formation and support of inclusive online communities*. Paper presented at the International Design for All Conference 2006. Rovaniemi, Finland.

Beenen, G., Ling, K., Wang, X., Chang, K., Resnick, P., & Kraut, R. E. (2004). *Using social psychology to motivate contributions to online communities*. Retrieved from http://www.si.umich.edu/~presnick/papers/cscw04preprint.pdf

Bilodeau, E. (2003). *Using communities of practice to enhance student learning: Examples and issues*. Retrieved from http://www.coolweblog.com/bilodeau/docs/2003-10-01-cop-enhancing-student-learning.pdf

Buckley, S. B. (2009). *Knowledge sharing through communities of practice at institutions of higher education*. Johannesburg, South Africa: University of Johannesburg.

Commun, I. T. (2006). *Getting started with blogging software*. Retrieved from http://www.communit.info/index.php?option=com_content&task=view&id=779&Itemid=60

Costa, C., Benham, G., Reinhardt, W., & Sillaots, M. (2008). *Microblogging in technology enhanced learning: A use-case inspection of PPE summer school 2008*. Retrieved from ftp.informatik.rwth-aachen.de/Publications/CEUR-WS/Vol-382/paper3.pdf

Daconta, M., Obrst, L., & Smith, K. (2003). *The semantic web*. New York, NY: Wiley Publishing.

Finerty, T. (1997). Integrating learning and knowledge infrastructure. *Journal of Knowledge Management*, *1*(2), 98–104. doi:10.1108/EUM0000000004584

Haneda, M. (1997). Second language learning in a 'community of practice': A case study of adult Japanese learners. *Canadian Modern Language Review*, *54*(1), 11–27. doi:10.3138/cmlr.54.1.11

Hay, K. E. (1993). Legitimate peripheral participation, instructionism, and constructivism: Whose situation is it anyway? *Educational Technology*, *33*(3), 33–38.

Hung, D., & Nichani, M. (2002). Bringing communities of practice into schools: Implications for instructional technologies from Vygotskian perspectives. *International Journal of Instructional Media*, *29*(2), 171–184.

IDRC. (2012a). *Part 1: Getting set up*. Retrieved from http://www.idrc.ca/en/ev-31833-201-1-DO_TOPIC.html

IDRC. (2012b). *Part 2: Working together*. Retrieved from http://www.idrc.ca/en/ev-31838-201-1-DO_TOPIC.html

IDRC. (2012c). *Part 3: Resources*. Retrieved from http://www.idrc.ca/en/ev-31839-201-1-DO_TOPIC.html

James, M., & Rykert, L. (1998). *From workplace to workspace: Using Email lists to work together*. IDRC Publications.

Jones, Q., & Grandhi, S. A. (2005). *Supporting proximate communities with P3-systems: Technology for connecting people-to-people-to-geographical-places*. In M. Wilber (Ed.), *The Interaction Society: Practice, Theories and Supportive Technologies*, (pp. 215-224). Hershey, PA: IGI Global.

Kollock, P., & Smith, M. (1999). *Communities in cyberspace*. London, UK: Routledge.

Lachkovics, A., Metz, T., Goldberg, E., Alluri, K., & Quek, P. (2006). *Innovative use of internet-based collaboration tools and methods in an institutional context*. Retrieved from http://www.col.org/pcf3/Papers/PDFs/Lachkovics_etal_Alluri.pdf

Lave, J., & Wenger, E. (1991). *Situated learning: Legitimate peripheral participation*. New York, NY: Cambridge University Press.

Lazar, J. R., Tsao, R., & Preece, J. (1999). One foot in cyberspace and the other on the ground: A case study of analysis and design issues in a hybrid virtual and physical community. *WebNet Journal: Internet Technologies. Applications and Issues, 1*(3), 49–57.

LeFever, L. (2006). *Wikis described in plain English*. Retrieved from http://www.commoncraft.com/archives/000644.html

Lewis, D., & Allan, B. (2005). *Virtual learning communities: A guide for practitioners*. London, UK: Open University Press.

Llorens, F., & Capdeferro, N. (2011). Facebook's potential for collaborative e-learning. *Revista de Universidad y Sociedad del Conocimiento, 8*(2), 197–210.

Long, L. N., & Schweitzer, S. J. (2004). *Information and knowledge transfer through archival journals and on-line communities*. Retrieved from http://www.personal.psu.edu/lnl/papers/aiaa2004_1264.pdf

McCarthy, J. (2009). Utilising Facebook: Immersing generation-Y students into first year university. *Ergo, 1*(2), 39–49.

McDermott, R. (2000). *Learning across teams: The role of communities of practice in team organisations*. Retrieved from http://home.att.net/~discon/KM/Learning.pdf

Panckhurst, R. (2008). *Communities of practice: Using the open web as a collaborative learning platform*. Retrieved from http://halshs.archives-ouvertes.fr/hal-00291874/

Paquet, S. (2002). *Personal knowledge publishing and its uses in research*. Retrieved from http://weblogs.com/0110772/stories/2002/10/03/

Preece, J. (2000). *Online communities: Designing usability, supporting sociability*. New York, NY: John Wiley & Sons, Inc.

Preece, J., Maloney-Krichmar, D., & Abras, C. (2003). History and emergence of online communities. In Wellman, B. (Ed.), *Encyclopedia of Community*. Thousand Oaks, CA: Sage.

Research, A. B. I. (2007). *Social communities go mobile: 174 million members forecasted by 2011*. Retrieved from http://www.abiresearch.com/abiprdisplay.jsp?pressid=780

Rheingold, H. (2003). Mobile virtual communities. *The Feature*. Retrieved from http://www.thefeaturearchives.com/topic/Culture/Mobile_Virtual_Communities.html

Satterfield, B. (2006). *Exploring the world of wikis: Collaborative Web sites organize information, encourage participation*. Retrieved from http://www.techsoup.org/learningcenter/webbuilding/

Schienstock, G. (2011). Path dependency and path creation: Continuity vs. fundamental change in national economies. *Journal of Future Studies, 12*(4), 63–67.

Schwartz, M. F., & Woods, D. C. M. (1993). Discovering shared interests among people using graph analysis. *Communications of the ACM, 36*(8), 78–89. doi:10.1145/163381.163402

Sharp, J. (1997). *Key hypotheses in supporting communities of practice*. Retrieved from http://www.tfriend.com/hypothesis.html

Tyler, J. R., Wilkinson, D. M., & Huberman. (2012). *Email as spectroscopy: Automated discovery of community structure within organisations*. Retrieved from http://www.hpl.hp.com/research/idl/papers/email/email.pdf

Varey, R. J. (2005). Informational and communicational explanations of corporations as interaction systems. In Wiberg, M. (Ed.), *The Interaction Society: Practice, Theories and Supportive Technologies*. Hershey, PA: IGI Global. doi:10.4018/978-1-59140-530-6.ch006

Wellman, B. (2002). Designing the Internet for a networked society: Little boxes, globalisation and networked individualism. *Communications of the ACM, 45*(5), 91–96. doi:10.1145/506218.506221

Wenger, E. (2001). *Supporting communities of practice: A survey of community-oriented technologies*. Retrieved from http://www.ewenger.com/theory/communities_of_practice_intro.htm

Wenger, E., White, N., Smith, J. D., & Rowe, K. (2005). *Technology for communities*. Retrieved from http://www.technologyforcommunities.com

White, N. (2006). *Blogs and community – Launching a new paradigm for online community?* Retrieved from http://kt.flexiblelearning.net.au

Whittaker, S., & Sidner, C. (1996). Email overload: Exploring personal information management of email. In *Proceedings of CHI 1996*, (pp. 276-283). ACM Press.

Wikibooks. (2008). *Online learning communities and communities of practice*. Retrieved from http://en.wikibooks.org/wiki/Online_Learning_Communities_and_Communities_of_Practice

Wild, M. (1999). The anatomy of practice in the use of mailing lists: A case study. *Australian Journal of Educational Technology, 15*(2), 117–135.

Worldbank.org. (2012). *Communities of practice, questions and answers*. Retrieved from http://siteresources.worldbank.org/WBI/Resources/CoP_QA.pdf

ADDITIONAL READING

APQC. (2001). *Building and sustaining communities of practice*. Retrieved from http://www.researchandmarkets.com/reports/40877

Baumard, P. (1999). *Tacit knowledge in organizations*. Thousand Oaks, CA: Sage.

Chetley, A., & Vincent, R. (2003). *Learning to share learning: An exploration of methods to improve and share learning*. Retrieved from www.healthcomms.org

De Laat, M. F., & Simons, P. R. J. (2002). Collective learning: Theoretical perspectives and ways to support networked learning. *European Journal of Vocational Training, 27*, 13–24.

Denning, S. (2004). *Communities for knowledge management*. Retrieved from http://www.steve-denning.com/communities_knowledge_management.html

Dixon, N. (2000). *Common knowledge: How companies thrive by sharing what they know*. Boston, MA: Harvard Business School Press.

Huber, G. (1991). Organizational learning: The contributing processes and the literature. *Organization Science, 2*(1), 88–115. doi:10.1287/orsc.2.1.88

Johnson, H. (2007). Communities of practice and international development. *Progress in Development Studies, 7*(4), 277–290. doi:10.1177/146499340700700401

Juriado, R., & Gustafsson, N. (2007). Emergent communities of practice in temporary inter-organisational partnerships. *The International Journal of Knowledge and Organisational Learning Management, 14*(1), 50–61.

Keka¨le, T., & Viitala, R. (2003). Do networks learn? *Journal of Workplace Learning, 15*(6), 245–247. doi:10.1108/13665620310488539

King, P. M., & Baxter-Magolda, M. B. (1996). A developmental perspective on learning. *Journal of College Student Development, 37*(2), 163–173.

Locke, K. (2001). *Grounded theory in management research.* Thousand Oaks, CA: Sage.

Malone, S. A. (2003). *Learning about learning: An A-Z training and development tools and techniques.* Trowbridge, UK: The Cromwell Press.

McDermott, R. (1999). Nurturing three dimensional communities of practice: How to get the most out of human networks. *Knowledge Management Review.* Retrieved from http://www.co-i-l.com/coil/knowledge-garden/cop/dimensional.shtml

Nath, V. (2000). *Heralding ICT enabled knowledge societies, way forward for the developing countries.* Retrieved from http://www.cddc.vt.edu/knownet/articles/heralding.htm

Nonaka, I. (1994). The knowledge-creating company. *Harvard Business Review, 69*(6), 96–104.

Nonaka, I., & Takeuchi, H. (1995). *The knowledge-creating company: How Japanese companies create the dynsmics of innovation.* Oxford, UK: Oxford University Press.

Polanyi, M. (1958). *Personal knowledge: Towards a post-critical philosophy.* Chicago, IL: University of Chicago Press.

Polanyi, M. (1961). Knowing and being. *Mind, 70*(280), 458–470. doi:10.1093/mind/LXX.280.458

Polanyi, M. (1966). *The tacit dimension.* New York, NY: Anchor Day Books.

Renzl, B. (2007). Language as a vehicle of knowing: The role of language and meaning constructing knowledge. *Knowledge Management Research and Practice, 5,* 44–53. doi:10.1057/palgrave.kmrp.8500126

Roberts, J. (2000). From know-how to show-how: The role of information and communications technology in the transfer of knowledge. *Technology Analysis and Strategic Management, 12*(4), 429–443. doi:10.1080/713698499

Sandelands, E. (1999). Learning organizations: A review of the literature relating to strategies, building blocks and barriers. *Management Literature in Review, 1.* Retrieved from http://www.helpdesk.net.au/training/organisational/Learning%20organizations%20a%20review.htm

Senge, P. (1993). *The fifth discipline: The art and practice of a learning organisation.* London, UK: Century Business.

Strauss, A. L., & Corbin, J. (1990). *Basics of qualitative research: Grounded theory procedures and techniques.* Newbury Park, CA: Sage.

Sun, R. (2002). *Duality of the mind.* Englewood Hills, NJ: Lawrence Erlbaum Associates.

Tjepkema, S., ter Horst, H., & Mulder, M. (2002). Learning organisations and HRD. In Tjepkema, S. (Ed.), *HRD and Learning Organisations in Europe.* London, UK: Routledge.

Tsoukas, H. (2003). Paper. *Organization Studies, 24*(9).

Van Maanen, J. (1988). *Qualitative methodology.* Beverley Hills, CA: Sage.

Varela, F. J., & Maturana, H. R. (1992). *The tree of knowledge.* Boston, MA: Shambhala.

Vestal, W. (2006). *Sustaining communities of practice*. Retrieved from http://www.kmworld.com/Articles/ReadArticle.aspx?-ArticleID=15159&PageNum=4

Wenger, E. (1996). *Communities of practice: The social fabric of a learning organisation*. Retrieved from http://www.ewenger.com/pub/pubhealthcareforum.htm

Wenger, E. (1998). *Communities of practice: Learning, meaning and identity*. Cambridge, UK: Cambridge University Press.

Wenger, E., McDermott, R., & Snyder, W. M. (2002). *Cultivating communities of practice: A guide to managing knowledge*. Washington, DC: Library of Congress Cataloging-in-Publication Data.

KEY TERMS AND DEFINITIONS

Knowledge: Knowledge is a fluid mix of framed experience, values, contextual information, expert insight, and grounded intuition that provides an environment and framework for evaluating and encompassing new experiences and information. It originates and is applied in the minds of the knower. In organisations it often becomes embedded, not only in documents or repositories, but also in organisational routines, processes, practices and norms.

Blog (from Weblog): A website containing entries about a topic. Entries are dated and pre-sented in reverse chronological order, that is, most recent first. Blogs can be written by individuals or groups of contributors. Blog posts may contain commentary and links to other websites and a search facility may be included.

Blog Communities: Blog communities show up in three different patterns. By looking at the patterns, we can start thinking about the strategies necessary to use blogs as a medium in community development.

Communities of Practice: Groups of people who share information, insight, experience, and tools around an area of common interest.

Knowledge Management (KM): A sharing of knowledge among communities leading to innovation and competitive advantage. CoPs are said to be key to achieving KM. Technology is the building block for knowledge management.

Website: A collection of interconnected webpages, usually located on the same server. A website may be built and maintained as a collection of information by a person, group, or organisation and is usually navigated from a nominated home page.

Wiki (from WikiWikiWeb): An online, database-driven website for simple, quick, versatile online publishing.

Communication Tools: These facilitate interaction between communities and facilitators. They include synchronous tools and asynchronous tools. Synchronous tools involve communication at the same time, whereas asynchronous tools relate to communication over time.

Chapter 17
Challenges and Opportunities for Innovation in Teaching and Learning in an Interdisciplinary Environment

Alina Mihaela Dima
Bucharest Academy of Economic Studies, Romania

ABSTRACT

Keeping up-to-date with ever-changing technologies and striving to find innovative ways to integrate them into a classroom setting are constant challenges to all educators. Clearly, technology is associated with changes in practice, but the nature of this association is complex and contested. Innovation in education has always been related to technological developments, but it can also be achieved by introducing changes to teaching practices, curricula, and learning activities, all of which can be regarded as activities included in the knowledge management and transfer paradigm.

INTRODUCTION

Innovation is a very powerful concept with a large spectrum of meanings and fields of applications (Bratianu & Vasilache, 2009). However, its Latin root *nova* is very clear, designating something new, and *innovare* means to make something new (Tidd, Bessant, & Pavitt, 2001). The concept of innovation refers to a new idea, which can be obtained by using old ideas, by presenting an idea that challenges the established order, or by doing

or seeing things in a new way. The stress should always be put on the idea being innovative for the ones involved in the process, not in an abstract, general way (Van de Ven, 1986; OECD, 2005). According to the OECD (2005, p. 46) innovation is an umbrella term that unites the "implementation of a new or significantly improved product (good or service), or process, a new marketing method, or a new organizational method in business practices, workplace organization or external relations." For the study of innovation in education, we need to

DOI: 10.4018/978-1-4666-1969-2.ch017

focus on two main aspects of this concept: on the process innovation and on innovation as a process. The first term is defined as "a new or significantly improved production or delivery method" (OECD, 2005, p. 55). This includes significant changes in techniques, equipment, and/or software. In education, this can for example be a new or significantly improved pedagogy" (OECD, 2005). The process of innovation is defined by Van de Ven (1986) as the development and implementation of new ideas by people who over time engage in transactions with others within an institutional context.

Innovation in education has always been related to innovations in technologies, but, as we will argue in the following sections, innovation does not have to depend on new devices or software solutions; it can also be achieved by introducing changes to teaching practices, curricula and learning activities, all of which can be regarded as activities included in the knowledge management and transfer paradigm (Laine, et al., 2008). Educational and research institutions, especially universities, create an important amount of knowledge which becomes valuable only if it is used to increase the common welfare of citizens by being transferred to the stakeholders. This is done through knowledge transfer, a process by which one individual or organization transmits its experience to another and systematically organized information and skills are exchanged between entities (Argote & Ingram, 2000; Duan, et al., 2010; Hubig & Jonen, 2006).

The take we have on innovation is based on the opinions of those authors who regard technology as a catalyst, not an initiator, of innovation in education, authors who argue that other major societal forces are the true reasons behind the inclination toward change and that technology is just another solution (McCreadie, et al., 2009; Taylor, 1999; cited in Price, et al., 2005). However, before arguing in favor of more proactive means of innovating, we need to address the issue of the relationship between change in education and technology within the interdisciplinary environment.

Interdisciplinary studies have grown in popularity over the last decades and they are regarded by Boix-Mansilla (2010) as a solution to changes in global labor markets that require individuals who are able to frame and address new problems, employ expert thinking in a flexible manner, and communicate effectively with people who hold different perspectives on the problems at hand. Moreover, many of the problems faced by our society today, such as climate change and global migration, lie at the intersection of many different disciplines, and their analysis and solution demand a general view of the world which can be acquired only by transgressing the boundaries of the traditional notion of discipline and by recognizing the subtleties of the nature of academic disciplines which cannot be viewed as discrete and autonomous as before anymore.

Thus, we can conclude that interdisciplinarity can be regarded as a solution to the complex problems encountered in today's world and that it lacks some of the challenges posed by using only technology as a means to solve these issues. With an interdisciplinary approach, the focus is never on "what," but always on "how," on "why," and the end result is always in sight from the beginning of the process. Irrespective of the definition we give to interdisciplinarity, the value of the interdisciplinary approach with regard to innovation lies in the emphasis put on using the inherent strengths of the agents involved in the educational process, and not on external devices, while not contesting their usefulness. Thus, in its study we can get a complete view of what is happening in the teaching and learning practices today. Teaching and learning are tightly connected with knowledge. Knowledge is gained either by experience, learning, and perception, or through association and reasoning. The term knowledge is also used to mean the confident understanding of a subject, potentially with the ability to use it for a specific purpose. Knowledge Management programs are typically tied to organizational objectives and are intended to lead to the achievement of specific outcomes, such as shared intelligence, improved performance, competitive advantage, or higher levels of innovation.

Conclusions of this chapter underline that the process of knowledge management becomes the essential point of innovation process in education where the educators should play the most important role and facilitate the creation, transfer and sharing of knowledge.

INNOVATION IN TEACHING AND LEARNING

Challenges of Technology-Based Innovation in Education

Despite limited or no reward for quality teaching, instructors still pursue various teaching techniques and experimentations to improve teaching effectiveness. Quality of education is intimately related to technology in terms of delivery, research, practice, and policy (Fadaei, 2010).

The pattern of growth in the use of technology in higher education can be seen through:

- Increasing computing resources, including Web-based technologies, encouraging supplemental instructional activities; a growth of academic resources online; and administrative services provided through networked resources
- Organizational changes in policies and approaches
- An increasing emphasis on quality of teaching and the importance of staff development
- Changes in social practice, e.g. a growth in demand for lifelong learning opportunities, which consequently affect the need to adapt technology into instructional delivery; and an increase in average age of students (Price, et al., 2005).

The most recent innovation in technology is the intelligent software agents, called avatars or virtual characters, which are now becoming part of simulation games. Many business schools have adopted business simulations to overcome some of the deficiencies in the traditional business curriculum. Simulations are useful because many of the competencies of successful managers can only be learned through practice. Simulation has been defined as any artificial or synthetic environment that is created to manage an individual's (or team's) experiences with reality (Bell, Kanar, & Kozlowski, 2008). Simulations can encompass a wide range of activities, from role-playing simulations to computer-based simulations (Salas, Wildman, & Piccolo, 2009).

Salas, Wildman, and Piccolo (2009) point out that leadership skills, strategic decision-making, and effective communication are all behavioral skills that cannot be truly developed simply through knowledge-based training methods. Successful business schools are therefore looking for creative pedagogy that involves students in active rather than passive learning (Albrecht, 2000).

In the top management games, students are responsible for running an entire business rather than on a specific function or area of the company. The majority of the business simulations involve running a whole business such as RealGame, which is based on the operations of a manufacturing company (Lainema & Lainema, 2008). Many companies such as Innovative learning Systems, Oak Tree Simulations, and CapSim offer Internet based whole business simulations.

Simulations and virtual worlds are useful in education for two main reasons. First students are accustomed to communicating and playing games on the Internet and the simulations have been shown to increase student engagement (Faria, et al., 2004). The second reason is related to the way we learn, in that gaming draws on whole brain activity and taps into the powerful nature of learning from doing (De Freitas, 2009). Coventry University's Serious Games Institute has produced a report that provides an overview of the available virtual worlds and categorizes them to help practitioners identify the worlds that are most relevant for the learning context (Gurley, Wilson, & Jackson, 2010). As presented in Table 1 across all virtual worlds categories there can be identified several ways in which these virtual environments can influence and contribute to the learning process. The main aspects sought after include the levels of variables such as learner control, collaboration, persistence, requirement for 3D interactions and experiences, immersion and interactivity, and inclusion of sharable and user generated digital content, which characterize a particular virtual world (De Freitas, 2008).

De Freitas (2008) identifies as the most relevant virtual worlds, in terms of potential contribution to education and training, the social, training and corporate ones. Although multiplayer role-play games may bring significant results on the long run, further research is needed to confirm it. Mir-ror worlds may too play an important part in education and training in the future.

Apart a wide range of application like mentoring, exploratory trails and quests, role plays and rehearsals of skills, these worlds bring a tremendous contribution through their facilitating of cross-disciplinary collaborative research and learning opportunities. Moreover, virtual worlds have also influenced the learning style though the emergence of learning communities, thus bringing forth potential pedagogical implications (de Freitas, 2008). The literature reports many efforts to integrate industry-leading technologies into classrooms (Alford, et al., 2004; Courte & Bishop-Clark, 2005; Jarzabek & Pettersson, 2006; Kourik & Wang, 2009; Suchan, et al., 2006; Swain, 2009). A very reliable infrastructure supporting business-critical applications is important in industry. Students with exposure to such industrial-strength software will expand their job and career opportunities worldwide (Cameron, 2008). One example of a program designed to assist colleges

Table 1. Categories of virtual worlds

Category of Virtual World	Examples	Value for Learning and Education
Role Play Worlds	World of Warcraft, Everquest, Guild Wars	Display significant potential for indirect learning, contributing to the development of team-working skills, leadership skills and communication skills. Possible applications may include role-play designed to enhance professional development.
Social Worlds	Second Life, CyWorld, ActiveWorlds For children Habbo Hotel, Club Penguin	Have as main focus activities that involve socializing, community building and communications between friends and colleagues. Besides these, children use them also for sharing content. They come in different dimensions and some may include real-life advertising content. Because of their nature, they rank very high in terms of immersion and interactivity.
Working Worlds	Project Wonderland, IBM's Metaverse	Dedicated to corporate communications and business support facilities. Use 3D rich environments to connect staff located all over the world, facilitating collaboration and reducing cost.
Training Worlds	America's Army, platforms such as the OLIVE platform	Designed especially for offering the training needed in professions involving high risk, life threatening or hard to perform situations. They have great applicability in military training and medical education and training.
Mirror Worlds	Google Earth, Planet Earth, Unype	Created as a 3D visual representation of the real world, mirror worlds broadened their scope of use due to their interoperability with other applications. They may play an important part in the field trips area and multimedia production.

Source: Adapted from de Freitas (2008)

and universities in the education of students in leading technologies and concepts is the IBM Academic Initiative and its Hub-Connection Center (HUB). The program provides members with access to IBM software, hardware, faculty education, courseware, and many other valuable resources. Faculty can teach fundamentals using the leading software systems and incorporate real world examples through lab exercises and practical applications.

Wang et al. (2010) explain the benefits of this technology applied at Webster University. The program includes a worldwide community of participating schools and universities, IBM technical experts, customers and business partners. This community encourages technology content to be relevant to the real world. The HUB connects educators and students with IBM's clients and business partners and assists in establishing relationships with the business community. For example, a recent roundtable at Webster University included faculty members from local universities and colleges, vendor representatives, and professionals from local IT companies. Participants discussed next generation IT technologies, potential curriculum enhancements, customer needs and future job opportunities (Wang, et al., 2010).

Technology dependency is also an issue in online courses. The basic concept of on-line education is founded on the idea of offering immediate access to information gathered from a wide spectrum of sources through the use of technology. Programs include video, audio, sophisticated imaging, Internet, e-mail, document share capabilities, and chat rooms. This new mode of education, sometimes called webucation, can link hundreds of students, classrooms, and instructors in minutes.

Online education is growing rapidly as more and more students are finding such a learning method to be more conducive to their lifestyle. The development and growth of the Internet and World Wide Web have led to global information dissemination and provided radical changes to global communication and interaction. Demand for teaching via the Internet has therefore increased, promoting further development of online and distance learning. Thus, primary changes in higher education of late can be seen through: (a) an increase in computing resources in campuses worldwide, and (b) the increased use of Web-based technologies to supplement instructional activities.

The impact of such technology developments can be seen to cut across different levels of institutional structure, for example, organizational changes in policies and institutional approaches toward the use of technology for teaching and learning; an increase of emphasis and volume in staff development modules in campuses worldwide to support academics' use of technology in their teaching; and an increase in emphasis on quality of teaching, as instructional activities become more transparent online.

Despite the benefits of technology in teaching and learning, a lot of papers reveal the shortcomings or partial impact on their developments. Although developing behavioral skills has been a desired outcome of instructors these skills are typically not directly learned from a computer simulation or the use of technology in class. Recent reviews of the research on business simulations (Faria, et al., 2009; Anderson & Lawton, 2009) have documented that building teamwork skills and improving students' ability to work with peers are common objectives of instructors who use simulations. These reviews point out that the behavioral outcomes are learned because students are often asked to work in teams. For example, Svoboda and Whalen (2005) used a business simulation to teach sustainability, noting that it allowed students to utilize cross-group collaboration as well as providing a consequence-free environment allowing students to try new behaviors and techniques and receive immediate feedback.

Direct communication, face-to-face interaction, immediate feedback, which builds the relationship between student and teacher, are considered essential tools in education even in the modern era. Teacher-student relationships were developed through interaction, feedback, and assistance (Kember, Leung, & Ma, 2007). The main motivational tool available in traditional forms of education is the daily interaction between student and instructor. This relationship is the driving force that challenges the student to excel, and helps the instructor foresee a potential problem in the process. The exchange of information is direct, providing the student an immediate opportunity to question concepts and intent. Working together in a one-to-one setting helps to fortify a strong teacher/student relationship.

The communication challenge is not new to educators and continues to be present in all forms of distance education. However, to the on-line student, who is sitting at home, logged onto a program site, this problem is intensified. Feedback on questions is not immediate, there are no phone calls with an encouraging voice to sooth the worries, and neither the student nor the teacher has a visual representation to place with a name. It is a lonely existence and a partnership forged primarily with a piece of computer hardware and not a real campus.

Campus life means living within a community that is totally focused on learning. Every breath inhaled has as purpose to expand the lungs of creativity and develop the mind of the student. For the online student, however, there is no campus life to experience or fond memories to share with new incoming freshman; any encouraging words about schedules, classes or teachers, can be posted on a Web-based bulletin board, but that lacks the touch, feel, and taste of real sharing.

Technology has not only become part of the classroom, but it has also extended it beyond the confines of its physical boundaries through audio-conferences, video-conferences, e-mail, instant messaging, and many more. Most of the technologies enumerated above are used in combination with face-to-face interaction, in order to improve the teaching and learning outcomes.

As a result, with the introduction of technology in the educational process, new concepts of university teaching, such as "distributed learning," "flexible learning," "distance learning," and "webucation," have become important in today's educational landscape, emphasizing the many advantages of using technology: the access to high-quality teaching and learning at any time and place, information available on demand, the efficiency of multimedia materials in helping students learn, and the increase in interaction with teachers through on-line communication (Bates, 2000). However, many universities have not integrated properly technology into their educational practices due to lack of experience with the new technology, the rapid change in this environment, the emphasis on "what" instead of "how" (focus on the technology rather than the meaningfulness of its applications) and many more (Price, et al., 2005).

Due to the aforementioned challenges, the relationship between education innovation and technology remains a controversial subject. It has been regarded by some authors as benefic, the former having the potential to transform educational practice or to create more flexible opportunities for learning (Price, et al., 2005).

Many commentators have argued that technology has the potential to transform educational practice, typically as an element of wider organizational transformation such as the development of mega-universities (Daniel, 1998) or as a consequence of competition in international educational markets (Hannah, 1998). Others have taken a less deterministic position, but see a link between technology and changing educational practices such as the creation of more flexible opportunities for learning (e.g. de Boer & Collis, 2005). Clearly, technology is associated with changes in practice but the nature of this association is complex and contested.

However, there are others for whom this relationship's potential still remains to be proved, or who believe, as Taylor (1999; as cited in Price, et al., 2005) does, that technology plays a part in the ongoing process of academic re-invention, but it does not cause change all by itself. After reviewing the scientific literature related to the introduction of technology as a means to innovate, we can argue that, preponderantly, what changes is the form of the delivery of the academic material, not the content itself. Although changing the form eventually leads to changes in content, in order to hasten the pace of educational innovation, we need to look at proactive means of initiating change, at ideas that shape educational practices, not at the means used to achieve those ideas. Consequently, the next section analyzes the innovation in teaching and learning practices that do not necessarily depend on technology, but on changing the perceptions of the actors involved in these processes.

Challenges of Non-Technology-Based Innovation in Education

Introducing technology into the classroom does increase the degree of student engagement, but this might be due to their novelty rather than other inherent characteristics. Stupans et al. (2010) consider that any activity that takes students into different learning experiences contexts will improve outcomes. Being able to visualize abstract concepts, interacting and collaborating with peers, facilitates learning, but, the authors do agree that placing the teaching material in the form of a game can distract students attention, the medium risking to become more important than the message being presented (Allery, 2004; as cited in Stupans, et al., 2010).

Smith and O'Neil (2003) consider that he educational methods could be viewed also from the framework of action learning, characterized by a commitment to capture, and build on what is rather than operate in a pure, detached, analytical, and rational world of what should be. By focusing on this approach, we put an emphasis on

introducing into the classroom not only something fun and novel, but also something taken from the daily life, which can be accomplished by using case-studies (Williams, 2005), high-fidelity simulations (Marlow, et al., 2008), inviting guest lecturers who can share valuable insights from industry (Van Hoek, et al., 2011), and embedding research activities (Webster & Kenney, 2011). However, educational activities might not only concern what happens in the classroom, and should be viewed from a broader perspective as classroom activities that can be supported by activities carried out by students inside external organizations, in the form of internships which provide valuable skills and training to a group of students in bridging academic research to real world solutions (Hynie, et al., 2011).

As a means of increasing motivation and student participation, Lee and Horsfall (2010) discuss the use of accelerated learning, defined as a course delivered in a shorter length of time than normal. In their study, they show that students experience significant benefits due to the shortened timeframes (increased sense of community, responsibility to their peers, frequency of feedback, and immersion into a single topic), but, on the other hand, the authors point that the success of accelerated learning practices depends on active learning techniques, adapting course content and assessment, and providing sufficient feedback.

Moreover, the curriculum change can also regard the shift towards learning types, "with the goal of producing graduates who have the ability to complete the transition from novice to expert after graduation and continue to deepen their expertise throughout their careers" (Harris & Cullen, 2008, p. 51). They propose a curriculum review based on the three learning types identified by Miller and Seller (1990) as cited in Harris and Cullen (2008): transmissive, transactional, and transformative, with a gradual pass from the first types to the later one, which sees learners as individuals in control of their own learning and view learning as a holistic process, promoting the social function of learning. However, this approach specifically addresses the needs of the university and the organizations in which the learners will work, and does not focus on the specificity of the learners needs. Kirkgoz (2009) describes a different approach to curriculum renewal, one that starts with a multi-dimensional needs analysis of the students and then builds a new curriculum based on these findings. The author stresses that curriculum innovation should be introduced gradually and that it should involve all participants for the development of consensus, commitment, and motivation.

Innovation can come not only as new educational practices, but also as new subjects introduced in the curricula. Most of these new courses are based on the interdisciplinary approach, which puts an emphasis on "overlapping" skills. At the moment there are countless definitions of the concept of interdisciplinarity, and there is also a lot of confusion in regards to the delimitation of this concept from related ones such as transdiciplinarity, multidisciplinarity, and pluridisciplinarity (Davies & Devlin, 2007; Shailer, 2005). What seems to create most of the misunderstanding is the actual meaning of the prefix "inter," which, as Repko (2008, p. 6) notes, for some implies "the contested space between disciplines," "the action taken on these insights, called integration," or "something altogether new that results from integration and is additive to knowledge."

As interdisciplinarians break new grounds and are usually regarded as pioneers of new insights, Welch (2007, pp. 146-147) believes that intuition should play a more important role in interdisciplinary teaching and learning as well: "its inclusion in interdisciplinary instruction is crucial to preparing our students for the practical necessities of complex problem solving in the 'real world.'" In order to incorporate intuition into interdisciplinary teaching, an emphasis on creativity and a tolerance for uncertainty is needed (Ruth-Sahd, 2003; as cited in Welch, 2007). This can be accomplished by forcing students to make

decisions in a short period of time and with insufficient data (Birgerstam, 2002; as cited in Welch, 2007), by "presenting material in such a way as to trigger thought in multiple, simultaneous matrices, to provide a supportive environment which encourages and rewards divergent thinking" (Sill, 1996; as cited in Welch, 2007, p. 148) or by making use of paradoxes.

If we accept that interdisciplinarity mainly implies the combining of two or more disciplines into one cohesive whole, we have to also accept that we will encounter different issues related to the use of different cognitive maps or paradigms. As insurmountable as they may seem, the epistemological problems can be tackled and are dealt with in practice, constituting a fertile ground for innovation in education. Interdisciplinary studies can be regarded as creative processes and thus we can apply creative thinking tools in order to promote integration and to foster innovation (Spooner, 2004). For example, learning to apprehend certain aspects of reality through developing a wider range of different perspectives leads to an enhanced ability for complex understanding. This can be translated into the teaching practice as processes which enable students to surmount their perceptual habits of counting on just a few of their senses and, instead, start considering using all of them (Spooner, 2004). Perfectly coupled with observing, imaging and abstracting stress, is the importance of being able to see only with the mind's eye parts of complex wholes or to explore hidden connections. By abstracting, we cannot only recognize the underlying patters and observe discrepancies, but also form new patterns. There are numerous other creative processes that may help the interdisciplinary teachers and learners and, as Spooner (2004, p. 23) nicely puts it, "future research will need to examine more precisely how each of the creative thinking skills or tools factor into the interdisciplinary process and play a role in the development of knowledge integration and synthesis."

INNOVATION IN EDUCATION: THE KNOWLEDGE MANAGEMENT PERSPECTIVE

The higher education landscape is undergoing significant change as new educational technologies, a new generation of students, innovative competitors and the shortage of public funding create what Kirp (2003) has labeled "academic capitalism." Equally, the format and delivery of lectures is evolving with the traditional university model being radically altered. Demands from industry, financial pressures and increased competition in the education marketplace are leading to the emergence of practice-based learning (Brennan, 2005), competence-based skills or generic capabilities necessary for lifelong learning (Kember, Leung, & Ma, 2007). However, in a nascent stage in the field of management education, this movement exemplifies successful examples of management education programs, programs directed toward business development and knowledge creation with the beginnings of research rooted in practice (Nixon, et al., 2006).

Research on knowledge and knowledge management spans the disciplines of economics, information systems, organizational behavior and theory, psychology, strategic management, and sociology. This diversity has contributed to the rapid advance of research in specialized areas of inquiry that investigate different aspects of organizational learning and knowledge management (Evangelista, Esposito, Lauro, & Raffa, 2010).

Knowledge is a fluid mix of framed experience, values, contextual information, and expert insight that provides a framework for evaluating and incorporating new experiences and information (Davenport & Prusak, 1998). Murthy (2007) states that knowledge is gained either by experience, learning, and perception or by association and reasoning. The term knowledge is also used to mean the confident understanding of a subject, potentially with the ability to use it for a specific purpose.

Knowledge is increasingly being embedded into the systems that are supporting, if not driving industry, while the need is to sharpen the methods of "Thinking," so that the embedded knowledge can be effectively and quickly harnessed for carrying out tasks. The needs of training are therefore, not so much for repetitively physical activity or 'hands-on' experience, which in any case cannot be simulated in the University outside industry, but for training the mind so as to develop training 'skills' in thinking and acting. The required skill set is the following:

- Basic knowledge of the relevant area, including allied subjects.
- The ability to quickly gather and internalize knowledge.
- The ability to perceive and understand situations that need a knowledgeable response.
- The ability to evolve appropriate and effective responses to deal with such situations.

Knowledge Management refers to a range of practices used by organizations to identify, create, represent, and distribute knowledge for reuse, awareness, and learning across the organizations. In a broad sense, Quintas et al. (1997) define knowledge management as the process of continually managing knowledge of all kinds to meet existing and emerging needs, to identify and exploit existing and acquired knowledge assets and to develop new opportunities. Palmer and Marra (2004) focused their attention on differences in epistemological conceptions of students from different disciplinary fields. Their results further confirm that activities suggested during the course, teachers' teaching strategies, and student diversity, influence the changing of one's conception of teaching, creating new conceptions regarding the meaning of learning.

We could summarize that the basic dimensions of the knowledge management process in universities are the following:

- To create courses those are 'market-oriented,' focused on the required competencies of the labor market
- To transform teaching methods that enable 'new' skill development and personal long term development
- To produce not a mass scale of graduates, but a selective mass that possess such qualifications that have been shaped by modern methods so as to absorb and internalize such 'new' skills.

This perspective implies the shift from traditional way of teaching as the transmission of knowledge to the modern perspective of teaching as the facilitation of learning has implications for the role of the teacher. While lecturing may remain important, it loses ground relative to the design of learning tasks and learning environments as a focus of the teacher's concern. Teachers spend proportionately more time designing useful learning tasks and identifying and improving access to good learning resources. This shift is related to changes in technology in complex ways and the new role signifies a shift in the locus of control over student learning (Crook, 2002).

Additionally, we could say that facilitation of learning in the context of Knowledge-Based Management is basically a process of creation, generation and transfer of knowledge. The shift from teaching as simple transmission of information to teaching as transfer of knowledge become the challenge and opportunity for innovation in teaching and learning in an interdisciplinary environment. By definition, institutions of higher learning are knowledge-creating organizations.

The development of Knowledge-Based Learning Management systems is a key component to enabling active, continuous (Raisinghani, 2001) long life learning and to facilitate instruction (Suter, 2001). Knowledge Management systems are a particularly helpful tool to assist in the conversion of tacit to explicit knowledge. An organization adopting such a system will be more aware of how

it can enable the extrinsic and intrinsic motivations of its stakeholders, as well as foster better communication, and thus, through the facilitation of the tacit knowledge conversion process, create a more favorable environment for creativity and innovation to boost (Byosiere & Luethge, 2008). Moreover, when faced with a multitude of situations involving teamwork, designing new ideas or projects, feedback, fast decisions or simply uncertainty, the stakeholders will mostly rely on their previous experiences, perceptions, intuition and creativity. This will enable an externalization of all these tacit knowledge elements and their transformation into explicit knowledge, as best practices, models, analogies, comments and other learning outcomes or activities are being coded and shared (Liyanage, et al., 2009; Seidler-de Alwis & Hartmann, 2008). In this later stage, we can see the importance that the values and the knowledge management approaches adopted by the organization have to the success of the externalization process and to that of internalization as well (Seidler-de Alwis & Hartmann, 2008) (see Table 2).

Polanyi (1962) identifies three main dimensions of tacit knowledge: the personal, the social and the context specific one, that are behind the mechanism of knowledge transfer. He argues that while the context determines the nature of the experiences and the person's perception upon them, the social factor influences the behavior, in general, and more specifically the skills and abilities a person possesses through the transfer of tacit knowledge. However, not all the tacit knowledge can be transferred, as the dissimilarity of elements such as the common background, basic knowledge and personal values between the people involved in the process creates a personal filter (McNichols, 2010). Finally, the tacit knowledge a person possesses is personal, all their abilities, skills and insights being closely related to their experiences and background (Polanyi, 1962; Joia & Lemos, 2010). The study of such limitations and many more, along with the very

Table 2. Old vs. new approach of knowledge management in teaching

Teaching as transmission of information	Teaching as passing information and making it easier for students to understand	Traditional techniques with emphasis on syllabus coverage or meeting exam requirements	Transfer of information and data	Short term individual development	Single discipline focus
Teaching as creation, generation and transfer of knowledge	Innovative teaching strategies to facilitate learning	Complex technology based techniques and non-technology based techniques to stimulate active, continuous learning, long-life learning	Conversion of tacit to explicit knowledge, tacit to tacit, explicit to explicit and explicit to tacit	Long term personal development	Interdisciplinary learning environment

reason of existence of knowledge management is called epistemology—the philosophy of science—but epistemology plays an important part in bringing forth the interdependence between other fields of study and knowledge management as well as across industries and different sciences, through the attempt of understanding the complex nature of reality (Williams, 2008). Within the knowledge management context, the epistemologies that have been developed may serve as a check for any organization willing to understand in-depth and constantly evaluate the direction towards which is heading in order to improve performance and achieve its goals. Because there is a high temptation to focus on the quantitative side due to the simplified version of the objectives' complex nature it can offer, many organizations find themselves in the numbers race, striving to attain or even surpass certain goals defined in such terms, while losing sight of the real purpose at a rather holistic perspective (Cook & Brown, 1999).

Epistemologies also go beyond this, trying to understand the challenges the world today places for the knowledge management systems. The promise of a knowledge driven society sets forth the temptation to believe that greater knowledge will provide for societal regulation. However, the type of knowledge perceived as appropriate for this is represented only by knowledge as "information (to be precise, as objectified, abstract, decontextualized representations)." Even though

transparency seems to be one of the characteristics of this high-volume, high-connectivity, high-interaction and high-accessibility society, doubt, disorientation and uncertainty come as great forces that hinder the knowledge transfer process (Tsoukas, 2005).

Economic progress then becomes dependent upon progressing towards a knowledge-based society, which requires a workforce with the types of capabilities needed for lifelong learning. To move in this direction there has been a major expansion in the numbers entering higher education and universities have been exhorted to produce graduates with lifelong learning capabilities (Candy & Crebert, 1991; Leckey & McGuigan, 1997; Longworth & Davies, 1996; Tait & Godfrey, 1999). While the literature on factors affecting the development of generic capabilities is limited, there has been a considerable volume of research on classroom-related learning environments and their effect on student learning outcomes. The following elements are designated to describe the teaching and learning environment (Kember & Leung, 2005b): active learning, teaching for understanding, assessment, coherence of curriculum, teacher-student interaction, feedback to assist learning, assistance from teaching staff, relationship with other students, cooperative learning. We could add to this list the transfer of knowledge. While the role of technology is not clearly stated in defining the teaching and learning environment, the role of teacher is emphasized as a facilitator of learning.

Facilitation of learning stimulates integration of learning management systems into larger life-time personal knowledge management systems and collaborative systems for cross-disciplinary work within the institution. Knowledge based learning management systems are an essential component of higher education in the future (Francisco, 2006). However, research demonstrates that knowledge management in the academic world requires integrating and balancing leadership, organization, education and technologies used in the interdisciplinary learning environment of that specific institution (Irlbeck, 2002).

CONCLUSION

There are many reasons why the relationship between education and technology has remained obscure. In evaluating the impact of technology-stimulated changes in education, we are facing various major challenges. One main reason could be that practice in Higher Education has always been fluid and complex (many things changed from one moment to another and instructors generally had considerable freedom in how they organized their teaching); on the other hand, institutes for Higher Education are complex organizations with many actors and factors that (can) all affect each other.

Henkel (2000), for example, discusses the way that academics' identities are shaped by the communities they participate in (such as the institution and the discipline), the values they hold, and the practices they engage in as professionals. These identities, have had to change in the wake of successive policies that have re-shaped Higher Education, such as massification, the changing relationship between institution and state (especially in terms of the way funding is allocated), the rise of managerialism and instrumentalism, and the subsequent re-positioning of Higher Education as

a competitive market. Social technologies such as quality assurance and accountability systems have further influenced notions of academic work and identity. Within all of this, there have been particular changes to academics' identities as teachers. The increasing number of students has led to a change in terms of teaching relationships, which are sustainable, based on the transfer of knowledge that should be embedded in the valuable skills required by the complex market, which is permanently under change and is highly influenced by uncertainty. Thus, in the academic environment, knowledge management is a management of change, innovation, uncertainty, and complexity. Additionally, many students entering Higher Education now have markedly different views on what universities are for, from those who teach them.

In this context, the challenge for the university system is to re-vamp its system of education. This raises the question of what is seen as the traditional system of knowledge and teaching in the university and what should be the nature of innovation in knowledge management within universities so as to provide a sustainable learning environment.

ACKNOWLEDGMENT

This work was supported by CNCSIS-UEFISCSU, project PN II-RU-TE_351/2010.

REFERENCES

Albrecht, W. (2002, March-April). Accounting education on the edge. *BizEd*, 41-45.

Alford, K. L., Carter, C. A., Ragsdale, D. J., Ressler, E. K., & Reynolds, C. W. (2004). Specification and managed development of information technology curricula. In *Proceedings of the 5th Conference on Information Technology Education*, (pp. 261-266). IEEE.

Anderson, P. H., & Lawton, L. (2009). Business simulations and cognitive learning. *Simulation & Gaming, 40*, 193–216. doi:10.1177/1046878108321624

Argote, L., & Ingram, P. (2000). Knowledge transfer: A basis for competitive advantage in firms. *Organizational Behavior and Human Decision Processes, 82*(1), 150–169. doi:10.1006/obhd.2000.2893

Bates, T. (2000). *Managing technological change: Strategies for college and university leaders.* San Francisco, CA: Jossey-Bass.

Bell, B. S., Kanar, A. M., & Kozlowski, S. W. (2008). Current issues and future directions in simulation-based training in North America. *International Journal of Human Resource Management, 19*, 1416–1434. doi:10.1080/09585190802200173

Boix-Mansilla, V. (2010). *MYP guide to interdisciplinary teaching and learning.* Wales, UK: International Baccalaureate.

Bratianu, C., & Vasilache, S. (2009). Implementing innovation and knowledge management in the Romanian economy. *Management & Marketing, 4*(4), 3–14.

Byosiere, P., & Luethge, D. J. (2008). Knowledge domains and knowledge conversion: an empirical investigation. *Journal of Knowledge Management, 12*(2), 67–78. doi:10.1108/13673270810859523

Cameron, B. H. (2008). Enterprise systems education: New directions & challenges for the future. In *Proceedings of the 2008 ACM SIGMIS CPR Conference on Computer Personnel Doctoral Consortium and Research,* (pp. 119-126). ACM Press.

Candy, P. C., & Crebert, R. G. (1991). Lifelong learning: An enduring mandate for higher education. *Higher Education Research & Development, 10*(1), 3–18. doi:10.1080/0729436910100102

Cook, S. D. N., & Brown, J. S. (1999). Bridging epistemologies: The generative dance between organizational knowledge and organizational knowing. *Organization Science, 10*(4), 381–400. doi:10.1287/orsc.10.4.381

Courte, J., & Bishop-Clark, C. (2005). Creating connections: Bringing industry and educators together. In *Proceedings of the 6th Conference on Information Technology Education,* (pp. 175-178). IEEE.

Davenport, T. H., & Prusak, L. (1998). *Working knowledge: How organizations manage what they know.* Boston, MA: Harvard Business School Press.

Davies, M., & Devlin, M. (2007). *Interdisciplinary higher education: Implications for teaching and learning.* Melbourne, Australia: The University of Melbourne.

De Freitas, S. (2008). *Serious virtual worlds: A scoping study.* Retrieved from http://www.jisc.ac.uk/media/documents/publications/seriousvirtualworldsv1.pdf

De Freitas, S. (2009, June). Serious games: Worlds of wisdom. *E-Learning Age*, 14-15.

Duan, Y., Nie, W., & Coakes, E. (2010). Identifying key factors affecting transnational knowledge transfer. *Information & Management, 47*(7-8), 356–363. doi:10.1016/j.im.2010.08.003

Evangelista, P., Esposito, E., Lauro, V., & Raffa, M. (2010). The adoption of knowledge management systems in small firms. *Electronic Journal of Knowledge Management, 8*(1), 33–42.

Fadaei, R. (2010). Technology and quality of education. *Journal of Business and Educational Leadership, 2*(1), 34–39.

Faria, A. J., Hutchinson, D., Welington, W., & Gold, S. (2009). Developments in business gaming: A review of the past 40 years. *Simulation & Gaming, 40*, 464–487. doi:10.1177/1046878108327585

Faria, A. J., & Wellington, W. (2004). A survey of simulation game users, former-users, and never-users: Simulation & gaming. *Journal of Business and Educational Leadership, 35*, 178–207.

Francisco, J. R. (2006). *Knowledge management tools supporting education*. Retrieved from http://ssrn.com/abstract=916609

Gurley, K., Wilson, D., & Jackson, P. (2010). Developing leadership skills in a virtual simulation. *Journal of Business and Educational Leadership, 2*(1), 106–115.

Harris, M., & Cullen, R. (2009). A model for curricular revision: The case of engineering. *Innovative Higher Education, 34*, 51–63. doi:10.1007/s10755-008-9090-z

Henkel, M. (2000). *Academic identities and policy change in higher education*. London, UK: Jessica Kingsley.

Hubig, L., & Jonen, A. (2006). *Hindrances, benefits and measurement of knowledge transfer in universities - Should be done more in the light of corporate social responsibility?* Retrieved from http://ssrn.com/abstract=939390

Hynie, M., Jensen, K., Johnny, M., Wedlock, J., & Phipps, D. (2011). Student internship bridge research to real world problems. *Education + Training, 53*(1), 45–56. doi:10.1108/00400911111102351

Irlbeck, S. (2002). Leadership and distance education in higher education: A US perspective. *International Review of Research in Open and Distance Learning, 3*(2). Retrieved from http://www.irrodl.org/index.php/irrodl/article/view/91/170

Jarzabek, S., & Pettersson, U. (2006). Project-driven university-industry collaboration: Modes of collaboration, outcomes, benefits, success factors. In *Proceedings of the 2006 International Workshop on Summit on Software Engineering Education*, (pp. 9-12). IEEE.

Joia, L. A., & Lemos, B. (2010). Relevant factors for tacit knowledge transfer within organizations. *Journal of Knowledge Management, 14*(3), 410–427. doi:10.1108/13673271011050139

Kember, D., Leung, D., & Ma, R. (2007). Characterizing learning environments capable of nurturing generic capabilities in higher education. *Research in Higher Education, 48*(5). doi:10.1007/s11162-006-9037-0

Kember, D., & Leung, D. Y. P. (2005b). The influence of the teaching and learning environment on the development of generic capabilities needed for a knowledge-based society. *Learning Environments Research, 8*, 245–266. doi:10.1007/s10984-005-1566-5

Kirkgoz, Y. (2009). The challenge of developing and maintaining curriculum innovation at higher education. *Procedia Social and Behavioral Sciences, 1*, 73–78. doi:10.1016/j.sbspro.2009.01.015

Kourik, J. L., & Wang, J. (2009). Reduce pressure on students and IT services via software-vendor programs and hosting. In *Proceedings of the ACM SIGUCCS Fall Conference on User Services Conference*, (pp. 75-78). ACM Press.

Laine, K., Sijde, P., Lahdeniemi, M., & Tarkkanen, J. (2008). *Higher education institutions and innovation in the knowledge society*. Paper presented at the Rectors' Conference of Finnish Universities of Applied Sciences. Helsinki, Finland. Retrieved from http://www.arene.fi/data/liitteet/115110=highereducationinstitutionsandinnovationintheknowledgesociety.pdf

Lainema, T., & Lainema, K. (2008). Advancing acquisition of business know-how: Critical learning elements. *Journal of Research on Technology in Education, 40*, 183–198.

Leckey, J. F., & McGuigan, M. A. (1997). Right tracks—Wrong rails: The development of generic skills in higher education. *Research in Higher Education, 38*(3), 365–378. doi:10.1023/A:1024902207836

Lee, N., & Horsfall, B. (2010). Accelerated learning: A study of faculty and student experiences. *Innovative Higher Education, 35*, 191–202. doi:10.1007/s10755-010-9141-0

Liyanage, C., Elhag, T., Ballal, T., & Li, Q. (2009). Knowledge communication and translation – A knowledge transfer model. *Journal of Knowledge Management, 13*(3), 118–131. doi:10.1108/13673270910962914

Longworth, N., & Davies, W. K. (1996). *Lifelong learning*. London, UK: Kogan Page.

Marlow, A., Spratt, C., & Reilly, A. (2008). Collaborative action in learning: A professional development model for educational innovation in nursing. *Nurse Education in Practice, 8*, 184–489. doi:10.1016/j.nepr.2007.07.001

McCreadie, M., Choudhurry, S., Bielec, J. A., Worona, S., & Stern, N. (2009). *The technology revolution in higher education: IT as a catalyst of change*. Paper presented at the Mid-Atlantic Regional Conferences. Durham, NC.

McNichols, D. (2010). Optimal knowledge transfer methods: A generation X perspective. *Journal of Knowledge Management, 14*(1), 24–37. doi:10.1108/13673271011015543

Messinger, P. R., Stroulia, E., Lyons, K., Bone, M., Niu, R., Smirnov, K., & Perelgut, S. (2009). Virtual worlds – Past, present, and future: New directions in social computing. *Decision Support Systems, 47*, 204–228. doi:10.1016/j.dss.2009.02.014

Murthy, K. V. B. (2007). *Re-engineering higher education - The knowledge management system*. Retrieved from http://ssrn.com/abstract=1073742

OECD. (2005). *Oslo manual: Guidelines for collecting and interpreting innovation data*. OECD.

Polanyi, M. (1962). *Personal knowledge: Towards a post-critical philosophy*. London, UK: Routledge.

Price, S., Oliver, M., Fartunova, M., Jones, C., Van der Meij, H., & Mjelstad, S. … Wasson, B. (2005). *Review of the impact of technology-enhanced learning on roles and practices in higher education*. Kaleidoscope project deliverable 30-02-01-F. Retrieved from http://hal.archives-ouvertes.fr/docs/00/19/01/47/PDF/Price-Kaleidoscope-2005.pdf

Quintas, P., Lefrere, P., & Jones, G. (1997). Knowledge management: A strategic agenda. *Long Range Planning, 30*(3), 385–391. doi:10.1016/S0024-6301(97)90252-1

Repko, A. F. (2008). *Interdisciplinary research*. Thousand Oaks, CA: Sage Publications.

Salas, E., Wildman, J. L., & Piccolo, R. F. (2009). Using simulation-based training to enhance management education. *Academy of Management Learning & Education, 8*, 559–573. doi:10.5465/AMLE.2009.47785474

Seidler-de Alwis, R., & Hartmann, E. (2008). The use of tacit knowledge within innovative companies: Knowledge management in innovative enterprises. *Journal of Knowledge Management, 12*(1), 133–147. doi:10.1108/13673270810852449

Shailer, K. (2005). *Interdisciplinarity in a disciplinary universe: A review of key issues*. Working Paper Series. Retrieved from http://academic.research.microsoft.com/Publication/4834251/interdisciplinarity-in-a-disciplinary-universe

Smith, P., & O'Neil, J. (2003). A review of action learning literature 1994-2000: Part 1: Bibliography and comments. *Journal of Workplace Learning, 15*(2), 63–69. doi:10.1108/13665620310464102

Spooner, M. (2004). Generating integration and complex understanding: Emploring the use of creative thinking tools within interdisciplinary studies. *Issues in Integrative Studies, 22*, 85–111.

Stupans, I., Scutter, S., & Pearce, K. (2010). Facilitating student learning: engagement in novel learning opportunities. *Innovative Higher Education, 35*(5), 359–366. doi:10.1007/s10755-010-9148-6

Suchan, W. K., Blair, J. R. S., Fairfax, D., Goda, B. S., Huggins, K. L., & Lemanski, M. J. (2006). Faculty development in information technology education. In *Proceedings of the 7th Conference on Information Technology Education*, (pp. 15-18). IEEE.

Suter, M. C. (2001). College faculty's transition to online teaching: From classroom space to virtual place. *Dissertation Abstracts International - A, 62*(12), 4091-4362.

Svoboda, S., & Whalen, J. (2004). Using experiential simulation to teach sustainability. *Greener Management International, 48*, 57–65.

Swain, C. (2009). Improving academic-industry collaboration for game research and education. In *Proceedings of the 4th International Conference on Foundations of Digital Games*, (pp. 191-198). IEEE.

Tait, H., & Godfrey, H. (1999). Defining and assessing competence in generic skills. *Quality in Higher Education, 5*(3), 245–253. doi:10.1080/1353832990050306

Tsoukas, H. (2005). *Complex knowledge: Studies in organizational epistemology*. Oxford, UK: Oxford University Press.

Van de Ven, A. H. (1986). Central problems in the management of innovation. *Management Science, 32*(5), 590–607. doi:10.1287/mnsc.32.5.590

Van Hoek, R., Godsell, J., & Harrison, A. (2011). Embedding "insights from industry" in supply chain programs: The role of guest lecturers. *Supply Chain Management: An International Journal, 16*(2), 142–147. doi:10.1108/13598541111115383

Wang, J., Kourik, J. L., & Maher, P. E. (2010). Introducing leading it technologies into curricula via vendor-hosted services. *Journal of Business and Educational Leadership, 2*(1), 96–105.

Webster, C. M., & Kenney, J. (2011). Embedding research activities to enhance student learning. *International Journal of Educational Management, 25*(4), 136–145. doi:10.1108/09513541111136649

Welch, J. (2007). The role of intuition in interdisciplinary insight. *Issues in Integrative Studies, 25*, 131–155.

Williams, B. (2005). Case-based learning, a review of the literature: Is there scope for educational paradigms in prehospital education? *Emergency Medicine Journal, 22*, 577–581. doi:10.1136/emj.2004.022707

Williams, R. (2008). The epistemology of knowledge and the knowledge process cycle: Beyond the objectivist vs interpretivist. *Journal of Knowledge Management, 12*(4), 72–85. doi:10.1108/13673270810884264

ADDITIONAL READING

Abramovitz, M. (1986). Catching-up, forging ahead, and falling behind. *The Journal of Economic History, 46*, 385–406. doi:10.1017/S0022050700046209

Adelman, C. (2009). *The Bologna process for U.S. eyes: Re-learning higher education in the age of convergence*. Washington, DC: Institute for Higher Education Policy.

Aghion, P., Askenazy, P., Bourlès, R., Cette, G., & Dromel, N. (2007). *Education, market rigidities and growth*. IZA Discussion Paper No. 3166. Retrieved from http://ssrn.com/abstract=1037301

Ammermüller, A., Heijke, H., & Wössmann, L. (2005). Schooling quality in eastern Europe: Educational production during transition. *Economics of Education Review, 24,* 579–599. doi:10.1016/j.econedurev.2004.08.010

Arrow, K. (1962). The economic implications of learning by doing. *The Review of Economic Studies, 29*(2), 155–173. doi:10.2307/2295952

Arrow, K., Hurwicz, L., & Uzawa, H. (1958). *Studies in linear and nonlinear programming*. Palo Alto, CA: Stanford University Press.

Barro, R. J., & Lee, J. (1993). *International comparisons of educational attainment*. Working Paper No 4349. Washington, DC: National Bureau of Economic Research.

Becker, G. S. (1975). *Human capital: A theoretical and empirical analysis* (2nd ed.). New York, NY: Columbia University Press.

Cardak, B. A. (2001). *Education choice, neoclassical growth and class structure*. Discussion Paper No. A01.07. Retrieved from http://ssrn.com/abstract=297052

Cuaresma, C. J. (2006). Convergence of educational attainment levels in the OECD: More data, more problems? *Economics of Education Review, 25,* 173–178. doi:10.1016/j.econedurev.2005.02.001

De la Croixy, D., & Monfortz, P. (1999). Education funding and regional convergence. *Journal of Population Economics, 13*(3), 403–424. doi:10.1007/s001480050144

Diebolt, C., & Jaoul-Gramare, M. (2006). Convergence of higher education and economic growth during the European construction: A contribution to the cliometrics of growth (EU-15). *Research in Comparative and International Education, 1*(1).

EACEA. (2009). *Developments in the Bologna process*. Brussels, Belgium: EACEA. *Higher Education in Europe*, 2009.

Europa. (2012). *Statistical office of the European communities*. Retrieved from http://ec.europa.eu/eurostat

European Commission. (2009). *Higher education in Europe 2009: Developments in the Bologna process*. Paris, France: European Commission.

European Higher Education Area. (1999). *The Bologna declaration*. Paris, France: European Higher Education Area.

European Higher Education Area. (2010). *Budapest-Vienna declaration on the European higher education area*. Paris, France: European Higher Education Area. Brunello, G., & Comi, S. (2000). *Education and earnings growth: Evidence from 11 European countries*. Paris, France: PURE Research Project. Cardoso, A.R., Sá, C., Portela, M., & Alexandre, F. (2007). *Demand for higher education programs: The impact of Bologna process*. CESifo Working Paper No. 2081. CESifo.

European Students Union. (2009). *Bologna with student eyes: Lifelong learning programme*. Paris, France: European Students Union.

Gill, I. S. (1989). *Technological change, education, and obsolescence of human capital: Some evidence for the U.S. Mimeo*. Unpublished.

Greiner, A., & Semmler, W. (2001). Externalities of investment, education and economic growth. *Economic Modelling, 19,* 709–727. doi:10.1016/S0264-9993(01)00076-1

Gylfason, T., & Zoega, G. (2003). *Education, social equality and economic growth: A view of the landscape*. CESifo Working Paper Series No. 876. Retrieved from http://ssrn.com/abstract=385780

Howell, D. R., & Wolff, E. N. (1992). Technical change and the demand for skills by us industries. *Cambridge Journal of Economics, 16,* 127–146.

Iancu, A. (2008). Real convergence and integration. *Romanian Journal of Economic Forecasting*, *1*, 27–33.

Koh, W. T. H., & Leung, H. M. (2003). *Education, technological progress and economic growth*. Retrieved from http://ssrn.com/abstract=637462

Kuznets, S. (1973). *Population, capital, and growth: Selected essays*. New York, NY: W.W. Norton and Company.

Pastore, F. (2007). *Employment and education policy for young people in the EU: What can new member states learn from old member states?* IZA Discussion Paper No. 3209. Retrieved from http://ssrn.com/abstract=1081648

Psacharoopoulos, G., & Layard, R. (1979). Cit. In Brunello, G., & Comi, S. (Eds.), *Education and Earnings Growth: Evidence from 11 European Countries*. Paris, France: PURE Research Project.

Şandru, I. M. D. (2008). The optimal design of the quality management concepts using mathematical modeling techniques. In *Proceedings of the 10th WSEAS International Conference on Mathematical and Computational Methods in Science and Engineering (MACMESE 2008)*, (pp. 334-339). Bucharest, Romania: WSEAS.

Schultz, T. (1961). Investment in human capital. *The American Economic Review*, *51*(1), 1–17.

Schultz, T. (1971). *Investment in human capital: The role of education and of research*. New York, NY: The Free Press.

Schultz, T. W. (1960). Capital formation by education. *The Journal of Political Economy*, *68*(6), 571–583. doi:10.1086/258393

Terry, L. S. (2006). *The Bologna process and its impact in Europe: It's so much more than degree changes*. Retrieved from http://ssrn.com/abstract=1139805

Teulings, C. N., & Van Rens, T. (2002). *Education, growth and income inequality*. CESifo Working Paper Series No. 653; Tinbergen Institute Working Paper No. 2002-001/3. Retrieved from http://ssrn.com/abstract=301175

UNESCO. (2009). *Global education digest: Comparing education statistics across the world*. Montreal, Canada: UNESCO Institute for Statistics.

Usher, A., & Cervenan, A. (2005). *Global higher education rankings, affordablity and accessibility in comparative perspective*. Washington, DC: Education Policy Institute.

Van der Ploeg, F., & Veugelers, R. (2007). *Higher education reform and the renewed Lisbon strategy: Role of member states and the European Commission*. CESifo Working Paper Series 1901. CESifo.

Voges, K., Glaser-Segura, D., Bratianu, C., & Dima, M. A. (2010). *Lessons learned: A faculty perspective of the implementation of the Bologna process in Romanian business programs & implications for US programs*. Paper presented at the Southwest 2nd Annual Southwest Teaching & Learning Conference. San Antonio, TX.

Voges, K., Glaser-Segura, D., & Dima, M. A. (2010). Challenges of Bologna process implementation in Romania. In *Proceedings of the 6th International Conference on Business Excellence*, (pp. 240-244). Braşov, Romania: Business Excellence.

Wolff, E. N. (1994). Technology, capital accumulation, and long run growth. In Fagerberg, J., von Tunzelmann, N., & Verspagen, B. (Eds.), *The Dynamics of Technology, Trade, and Growth* (pp. 53–74). London, UK: Edward Elgar Publishing Ltd.

Wolff, E. N. (2000). Human capital investment and economic growth: Exploring the cross-country evidence. *Structural Change and Economic Dynamics*, *11*, 433–472. doi:10.1016/S0954-349X(00)00030-8

KEY TERMS AND DEFINITIONS

Facilitation of Learning: Integration of learning management systems into larger lifetime personal development for cross-disciplinary work.

Innovation in Education: New techniques using technological or non-technological developments by introducing changes to teaching practices, curricula and learning activities and providing transfer of knowledge.

Interdisciplinarity: A solution to the complex problems encountered in today's world to changes in global labor markets that "require individuals who are able to frame and address new problems, employ expert thinking in a flexible manner, and communicate effectively with people who hold different perspectives on the problems at hand."

Knowledge: A mix of experience, values and information that provides a framework for evaluating and incorporating new and valuable experiences and information.

Knowledge Management in Education: A range of innovative practices and skills used by facilitators to create, generate and transfer knowledge to learners.

Sustainable Learning Environment: Interdisciplinary environment that stimulates long-life learning and continuous personal development.

University Knowledge Management: Management of change, innovation, complexity and uncertainty to create sustainable learning environment.

Chapter 18
Innovation and IT in Knowledge Management to Enhance Learning and Assess Human Capital

Livio Cricelli
University of Cassino, Italy

Michele Grimaldi
University of Cassino, Italy

Musadaq Hanandi
University of Rome, Italy

ABSTRACT

The principal aims of this chapter are to provide a comprehensive understanding of the main processes for innovative knowledge management in human capital learning and to define a theoretical model that assesses and measures the human capital value contribution to an organization's performance. The chapter aims to explain how technological advancements and innovation facilitate collaboration, support sharing of dynamic contents, and make the learning process easier and more fruitful. Finally, a summary is provided by way of a strategy map, which allows the tracking of the human capital learning process and assessment of ex-post learning performance.

1. INTRODUCTION

For years, business success rates were measured by assessing new product development, new markets, customer retention, and mass production; this manner of measurement focused only on the physical assets that the organization owned. Today, the business approach has changed vastly from that used in the past, and the most prevalent ideas about success are becoming related to how the organization thinks, what it knows, and what we can learn from that knowledge (Filstad, 2011; Argote, 2011; Ting & Lean, 2009).

DOI: 10.4018/978-1-4666-1969-2.ch018

Managers have noticed rapid advancements and change in the markets, especially now that information and communication technology have come to play a key role in creating a new form of organization, that is, the learning organization (Filstad, 2011; Argote, 2011; Sveiby, 1997; Lynn, 1998; Pulic, 1998).

The learning organization, as it has been defined in the literature, is a kind of organization through which we can develop and use new knowledge to improve the performance of our operational and human capital, by proposing a set of organizational elements that constitute the learning and knowledge creation process inside our organization.

The idea behind this kind of organization is the realization that the challenges in competitive markets are not only related to companies' tangible assets, but also to the intangible assets. As a result of this change in approach, organizations' intangible assets and knowledge are becoming the principal factors of success in today's knowledge-based economy; what an organization knows is becoming more important than what an organization owns. This is reflected by organizations today paying greater attention than ever before to their Intellectual Capital (IC), patents, trade secrets, human capital knowledge, and management experience.

Furthermore, many researchers and academics agree that there is a need to move forward in shaping the definition of IC (Bontis, 1999; Edvinsson & Malone, 1997a, 1997b; Roos, et al., 1998; Stewart, 1997; Sveiby, 1997). The majorities of the definitions previously given were mostly spin, and emerged from the term of intangible assets. The IC classification that is found in the literature refers to taxonomy, which encompasses three kinds of capital: relational, structural, and human (Youndt & Snell, 2004; Edvinsson & Sullivan, 1996; Wiig, 1997; Walsh, et al., 2008; Sharabati, et al., 2010). In this taxonomy, human capital is considered the most significant kind of capital for the organizations based on intangible assets,

for its contribution to new ideas, innovation, and knowledge sharing. With time, organizations keep investing in their human capital learning and development to guarantee a consistent flow of intangible assets among employees (Sveiby, 1997; Lynn, 1998).

Organization management has started to assign a high priority to the learning and development of their human capital as the main sources of knowledge. Moreover, interpersonal cooperation and communication between employees have been considered among the factors that utilize knowledge diffusion and allow employees to bond existing knowledge, to create new knowledge, and to solve problems.

The growing interest in learning organizations, Knowledge Management (KM), and human capital development emphasizes the strategic power of these intangible assets. Furthermore, researchers are becoming more interested in the role of higher education organizations such as universities and training institutes, and in their contributions to the development and experience of the human capital (Argote, 2011). Moreover, economists aim to understand the economic return of investments in education and training through such higher education organizations.

This chapter proposes a holistic model of KM, which identifies an operational dimension of the organization's knowledge content, while at the same time organizing the process of knowledge capturing, sharing, and codifying with the structural characteristics of the organization, to be utilized later as online content for human capital learning and development.

Finally, since organizations recognize the necessity of a strategic assessment model to evaluate the contribution of human capital as a source of added value, the chapter utilizes a new assessment tool based on the Hierarchy Assessment Index (HAI) model. This model has the capability to show a balanced image of the intangible assets of the firm, as each asset can be allotted a priority that gives the measure of its influence on performance.

The chapter is presented as follows. Section 2 discusses the efficient synchronization of people, process and Information Technology (IT) and the effectiveness of KM and the knowledge process, while Section 3 introduces the innovation of KM in education and learning. Sections 4 and 5 describe the Virtual Human Capital Development model, and define the assessment model of human capital performance by way of a strategy map. The chapter is concluded with a summary in Section 6.

2. SYNCHRONIZATION OF PEOPLE, PROCESS, AND IT

The IC taxonomy can be identified easily in today's organizations in three layers: human capital, structural capital, and relational capital. Human capital mainly concerns the contribution of people in the context of the organization. Structural capital relates to all the organizational processes, procedures, and structures. Relational capital concentrates on interactions between the organization's employees and external parties and environments, through various means of technological communication.

Therefore, the management recognizes that people, process, and IT are the most important layers in any organization.

Ultimately, the success of an organization depends not only on technical and technological innovations, but also on human capital and the organization itself. It is not enough to gather and keep information about technology, markets, organization, products, and services; they have to be used in a manner that is timely and appropriate. The above-mentioned issues highlight the significance and value of KM. The barriers in developing KM must be taken into account and the elements of the three layers ("people," "process," and "IT") have to be synchronized. The four integrated core activities of KM ("generate," "store," "distribute," and "apply") are the

synchronizing elements which link people, process and IT together. Synchronization is achieved by implementing KM tools into the education process, resulting in the improvement of certain educational process tasks related to the core KM activities, and leading to innovation. Efficient IT applications enhance existing IT tools and support these KM activities inherent to the learning process and to human capital innovation. This synchronization process of "people," "processes," and "IT" with the main core of knowledge processes will assist the organization management to understand the true relationship between the organization and KM processes, and how this association not only relates to the technological innovation of the KM System (KMS), but also concerns the contribution of human capital.

2.1 KM and the Knowledge Process Relation

Once the knowledge strategy has been clarified, the second step of a KM program regards its implementation with the definition and application of the knowledge process. The ability of integrating and applying the specialized knowledge by organization members is fundamental in creating and sustaining a competitive advantage (Grant, 1996).

Knowledge has limited value if it is not shared. KM consists of managing corporation knowledge through several systematic processes, in order to acquire, organize, apply, and renew both tacit and explicit knowledge. Several classifications of KM processes have been proposed in the literature. It is possible to integrate some of these different and relevant contributions providing a classification based on four main processes: knowledge generation, knowledge storage, and knowledge sharing and knowledge application.

The knowledge generation process assumes a fundamental and complex role in knowledge-based organizations. It comprises the creation of "new" knowledge or the acquisition/identification of knowledge through external/internal sources.

The generation process represents a pervasive and continuous process which enables companies to develop interactions by making use of their human skills, competencies, capabilities and practices.

The generated knowledge must be preserved and organized, and easily accessible. It is important that the knowledge storage process is able to maintain structure and justify knowledge, both tacit and explicit.

The knowledge sharing process concerns the diffusion and the distribution of knowledge among organization members. Knowledge sharing activities are based both on human interactive processes and on information technology infrastructures and need to be supported by the organizational culture.

Finally, the knowledge application process regards the utilization and the exploitation of previously generated, stored, and distributed knowledge. Through this process, companies can apply available knowledge in business activities in order to achieve business goals.

2.2 KM Effectiveness

Learning organizations have always sought to build upon their own past experiences and to be able to utilize their knowledge to their competitive advantage, through best practice, know-how, and lessons learned, and at the same time enhance their human capital experience and their knowledge.

Thus, the learning process takes place to improve the accumulated knowledge available to the organization's database, and to amplify the value of these intangible assets, by creating innovative and new intellectual assets, distinguished in three organizational layers: human, relational, and structural. For instance, in any learning-based organizations, knowledge is created through research and development labs, brainstorming, and in-house interaction (relational capital). Then the same created knowledge is codified and stored in the knowledge database systems of the learning organization (structural capital). Once the organizational knowledge is utilized in an effective

and efficient manner, it can be applied to the employee's development and learning according to the needs of the organization and market (human capital).

In summary, KM is an effective source of organizational competitive advantage, through human capital development, new product development, and organizational innovation. KM is able to generate high business performance to achieve a market competitive position among other competitors, once it is managed effectively in accord with the three intellectual capital layers mentioned above.

3. KM INNOVATION IN EDUCATION AND LEARNING

Organizations that learn better and faster can improve their performance in competitive markets and defeat other competitors. The goal of KMS should not only be to manage all the existing knowledge inside the organization, but also to manage the knowledge required by people within the organization; in other words, to educate the human capital and enhance people's abilities and skills.

Furthermore, the innovation shift from traditional to collaborative KM has offered organizations the opportunity to create an interdisciplinary environment in which to support the learning and development of their human capital, thereby improving the performance.

3.1 From KMS to Collaborative KM

Across the literature, knowledge has been presented as information possessed in an individual's mind; in simple terms, personalized information (which may or may not be new, unique, useful, or accurate) related to facts, procedures, concepts, interpretations, ideas, observations, and/or judgments.

Today, organizations need to manage this knowledge efficiently in order to succeed and to improve their performance over competitors in challenging markets. In particular, they need to develop precise plans and to provide employees with managerial guidelines, in order to make available the knowledge of the organization. Indeed, their success is strictly connected with the integration of tangible and intangible resources, organizational functions, and core processes and technologies. Furthermore, the IT literature has contributed greatly to the field of KM, but there is much more to KM than technology alone; as discussed in Section 2, KM is a business process dealing with people, process, and IT.

The spread of information and communication technology has increased the ability of firm to store, share and generate knowledge, thus accelerating the emergence of a new economic, organizational and technological context, termed the "knowledge-based economy." Furthermore, in order to achieve a competitive position, it is crucial to understand how value creation processes and business goals can be realized and combined; however, simply identifying the availability of innovative technology does not always lead to effective KM.

According to Bloodgood and Salisbury (2001), information technology applications enable a firm to have a simple selection and internalization process only after having defined and codified roles and interpretative procedures. It appears that there is no direct correlation between information technology investments and KM performance: business policies and practices are, rather, enabled by the strategic integration of information technology tools, business processes, and human capital.

Every organization has resources that can be transformed into capabilities, such as the know-how that can be considered tacit knowledge. The purpose of KM is to create, collect, and convert individual knowledge into organizational knowledge (Horie & Ikawa, 2011). Nonaka (1998) presented a dynamic theory of KM which suggests that both explicit and tacit knowledge interact to generate a process of creating new organizational knowledge.

3.2 Human Capital Development: Why, What, and How?

It has become known that as the business world becomes increasingly competitive and unstable, companies and organizations are searching to increase their competitive advantage among market players at any cost, by turning to more innovative sources through human capital development.

Considering the evolution from Human Capital Management (HCM) to Human Capital Development (HCD), several definitions that have been widely published consider HCM as a major management activity. HCD usually includes a broader range of activities to develop the personnel inside organizations, such as career development, Training and Development (T&D), knowledge creation and capturing, as well as the development of the organization. On the one hand, the changes in the definitions of HCM have not been significant; on the other, some definitions of HCD have made an important conceptual shift away from the process of training or organizational development, towards a focus on outcomes in terms of the impact of HCD on people, organizations, community and the nation.

Moreover, the concept of HCD has been introduced as a set of internally consistent processes and practices created and carried out to ensure that the organization's human capital contributes to the creation process of innovative competence, more efficient market performance and market positioning.

Furthermore, many researchers have viewed HCD practices as a set of techniques utilized by organizations to develop their human capital and gain expertise that will influence the performance of the organization, thus making them active as knowledge creators, generators and producers, and able to sustain a competitive advantage.

3.3 The University's Role in Human Capital Learning and Development

Human capital learning and development through universities is not a new phenomenon. It was present in different civilizations, from Greek Academies and Roman Ludi (Latin for Play Schools) to Islamic Mosques. All these great civilizations understood the importance of such institutions for the development and learning of their human capital, whether it related to battle techniques, irrigation systems, scientific inventions or even the moral and civic responsibilities toward the society and the state.

Universities, by their nature, are learning-based organizations, where knowledge is delivered to the student through the teaching process. Students acquired this knowledge through the learning process, and the knowledge is created and shared through research labs and publications.

Since the time of these ancient civilizations, universities around the world have played a significant role in the development and training of HC (Kwon, 2011; Rahmah, 1996). The process of HC development through education is a great tool for increasing the HC stock of a nation, and is still the source supplying the HC for the nation's economic development (Chew & Lee, 1995), especially in the economical transitions to the new knowledge economy (Kwon, 2011; Anuar-Zaini, 2000). Many economists considered universities as highly profitable future investments, especially in supplying trained and developed HC in several sectors. Moreover, since the managements of organizations always seek to increase their competitive advantage among market players, they have to turn to more innovative sources to develop their HC (Horie & Ikawa, 2011). This can be reached by implementing various collaboration strategies with the universities, whether by specific courses and curriculum development, by exploring new procedures to improve new or existing products, or by customizing their own masters' degrees, according to their needs.

3.4 Human Capital Learning

Web learning and the knowledge-sharing phenomenon has received major international attention from governments and even worldwide institutions. Web learning relies upon technology and electronic processes. This form of learning has given rise to what is known as virtual education or Virtual Human Capital Development (VHCD), which is education and development training conducted online, as opposed to traditional time- and space-bound human capital development in an age of obscurity, chaos and change; the world is obscure as the reality is not known, chaotic because the outcomes are never certain, and is changing in that what may be true today may be entirely the opposite tomorrow.

In the past, many researchers introduced Virtual Human Capital Management (VHCM) in different patterns by which it was considered as an application of IT for both networking and supporting at least two individuals or collective actors in their shared performance of human capital activities. Lepak et al. (1998) defined the VHCM as a kind of characterized network structure based on partnership, using information technology as a carrier, to help organizations access, develop, and utilize human capital.

Instead, McWhorter et al. (2008) introduced the Virtual Human Capital Development (VHCD) as "a process for developing and/or unleashing human expertise through T&D and organization development by utilizing a technology-enabled environment for the purpose of improving performance."

3.5 The Role of KM Systems in Human Capital Learning

The KM System (KMS) as an IT-based system was developed to support and enhance organizational processes of knowledge creation, storage/retrieval, transfer, and application. With the growing attention that the importance of KM is receiving in organizations, many may start developing KMS in order to offer various benefits that facilitate KM activities, but Hahn and Subramani (2000) recommend that during the development of KMS, an organization should pay attention to various issues and challenges related to using IT to support KM.

Most of the traditional KMSs merely focus on capturing an enterprise's knowledge and storing and organizing it in the enterprise's database. However, the purpose of KMSs was not only to make information available, but also to make sure it would be shared and leveraged in an enterprise context and between users. Therefore, focusing only on half of this equation does not provide any advantage for the development of human capital. The result is that the KMS acts like a cyberspace: full of an immense amount of information and data, but still not yet leveraged. The VHCD model could be considered as the new generation KMS, or at least a more mature version.

4. THE VIRTUAL HUMAN CAPITAL DEVELOPMENT (VHCD)

The HCD model presented here is a new approach of utilizing the captured knowledge and information inside the organizational environment (from top management and external expertise to knowledge worker and human capital), and of applying this knowledge to dynamic online training content, to be used in developing and enhancing human capital as a competitive advantage (Hanandi & Grimaldi, 2010).

Moreover, the proposed model should focus on providing the human capital with the skills needed and driving their performance to confront and solve any future problems, by capturing the knowledge during interaction activities between users and reusing it to produce dynamic e-content for the purpose of training and development, while at the same adding value for the competitive advantage

of the enterprise; Figure 1 and Figure 2 illustrate the interaction between the users.

Figure 1 indicates the interaction relation across the factors in the VHCD model. These factors depend on a number of processes and activities presented as the following:

- **Human Resource Development:** This actor playing an important role in authoring the T&D e-content for the training purpose, updating it with the new captured knowledge to enhance the user's competences, monitoring the user progress, performance assessment, and selecting the right T&D material according to the users and enterprise needs.

- **Top Management:** The managers have been always concerning about their employee's performance and their adding value to the company competiveness, this model facilitate them the opportunity to engage and participate in sharing their knowledge through different social activities, such as chat, forums, blog, and in-class training workshop and sessions with their employee; furthermore, they are also interested in evaluating their employees performance progress and their contribution to the organization intangible assets.

- **External Experts:** In this part, we are referring to the case where most of the organization always seeking to hair external expertise's for in-house training and development for their employees, therefore, this model is proposing to capture these explicit knowledge during the In-house training engagements and interacting, and to reutilized it in creating the T&D e-content, in this way the organizations start to build their own codified knowledge database, that could be accessed in the future by the organization members.

Figure 1. The interaction between the model users within the organization environment

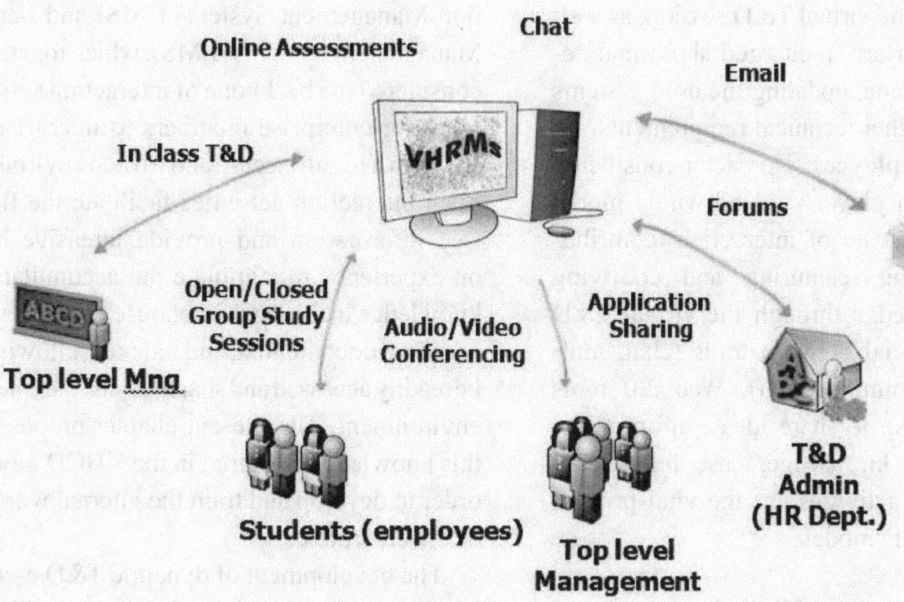

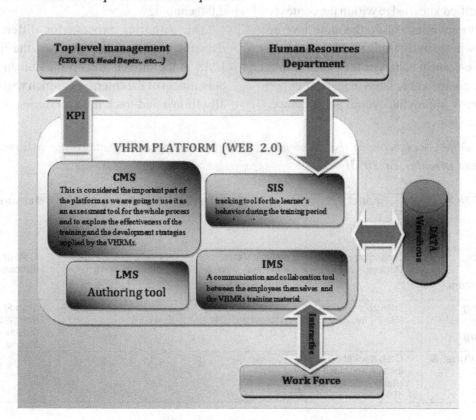

Figure 2. The VHCD conceptual model components

- **System Administrator:** These actors tasks contain the tracking of the user's interacting during the virtual T&D session, as well as this actor are in-charged about maintenance, upgrade, updating the used systems and any further technical requirements.
- **Users / Employees:** This actor considered as the main player's in the whole model where their way of interaction, contribution, sharing, capturing and codifying new knowledge through the virtual T&D courses, social network tools (chat, multimedia communication), Web 2.0 tools (wiki, blogs), to share ideas, information, experience, knowledge, case failure/success, these activities are the vital process of the VHCD model.

4.1 The Conceptual Model

The VHCD model utilizes the knowledge captured from the interaction between enterprise members and the codified knowledge within the context of the enterprise environment. Furthermore, leverage of this knowledge by dynamic training and development of e-content enhances the human capital skill base, competence, knowledge and experiences, thereby improving overall performance.

The proposed model (Figure 3) facilitates these activities via the use of Web 2.0 tools, Information Management Systems (IMS) and Learning Management Systems (LMS), which together are considered the backbone of interaction activities, allowing enterprise members to interact extensively in a highly secure and trusted environment. Such interaction activities facilitate the flow of free information and provide intensive hands-on experience to stimulate the accumulation of knowledge in the data warehouse, where it will be codified, documented, and indexed, allowing it to be readily accessed and shared inside the enterprise environment. The present chapter proposes that this knowledge is shared in the VHCD model, in order to develop and train the internal workforce of the enterprise.

The development of dynamic T&D e-content is dependent on the knowledge accumulated in the data warehouse after it has been created, shared, and captured during interaction activities between employees inside the enterprise, thanks to Web 2.0 technology.

The authoring process for different T&D dynamic objects will depend on the integrated LMS in the model, and on the human resource department of the enterprise, which will additionally follow and track the user during interaction

Figure 3. Differences between the financial valuation, value measurement, value assessment, and measurement (Andrieseen, 2003)

WHY \ HOW > ?	Financial Valuation	Value Measurement	Value Assessment	Measurement
Improving Internal Management	· Technology factor (Khoury, 1994)	· Holistic Value Approach (Pike & Roos, 2000)	· Intellectual Capital Benchmarking System (Viedma, 2001)	· IC Audit (Brooking, 1996)
Improving External Reporting	· Intangible Capital (Gu & Lev, 2002)	· Value Chain Scoreboard (Lev, 2001)		· Skandia Navigator (Edvinsson & Malone, 1997)
Transactional & Statutory Motives	· Cost, market & income approach (Reilly & Schweihs, 1999)			

activities, through the Student Information System (SIS) which will in turn work as a tracking and user feedback tool.

The Competency Management System (CMS) plays the role of the intelligent self-evaluation and grade reporting system for the competencies that have been earned during the T&D course, steering competence development and managing unstructured competence (tacit knowledge). Moreover, the CMS will provide the VHCD administrators with information on the competencies earned by the employees, and how these competencies influence the work of the enterprise and directly provide a competitive advantage in an environment in which there is a growing need for a highly qualified human capital.

The VHCD model consists of various learning technologies with different relationships (Table 1), which serve and support international enterprises through the process of capturing and sharing dynamic knowledge objects, which in turn could be created through a continuous dialogue between tacit and explicit knowledge. This dialogue would be utilized for the purpose of HCD, creating a competitive advantage both for the organization and for its employees. Furthermore, the contribution to the development of empirical research by the domain of VHCD aims to clarify the relationship between VHCD and KM orientation. This chapter contributes a better understanding of the degree of adoption of such a model in enterprises, international companies, and governments, paving the way for future comparative studies, which have the potential to take other sectors, such as health and education, into consideration.

4.2 Traditional KMS vs VHCD

It is important that an organization understands the difference between the VHCD model and current KMS. This section compares the KMS and VHCD, and Table 2 summarizes this comparison.

The comparison is based on Connectivity, Content, Community, Culture, Capacity, Business Strategy, and Business Impact. These seven criteria highlight the differences between traditional KMS and the VHCD model, and why the VHCD model could be considered as the next generation KMS. Therefore, this chapter considers the VHCD model as a candidate to replace the traditional KMS, as an innovative technological solution for human capital development, imparting significant benefits to the financial performance of the organization.

However, organizations have different processes and structures, reflecting their own unique identity. Consequently, for better implementation of the VHCD model, an organization should consider the following aspects:

- **Management:** The management process should be changed as a primary step, by changing and creating new values, organizational culture, beliefs, and behaviors inside the enterprise for both management and employees.
- **Technology readiness:** This aspect considers the existence of the relevant technology solutions and tools, as well as the availability of specific competencies and skills of the people using this technology. Usually, this is determined by assessing existing IT infrastructure and strategies.
- **Knowledge and communication:** These aspects are necessary to the transition process, and relate to communication models and the way that knowledge is shared and exchanged in the platforms and technology of the enterprise.

5. EVALUATION AND ASSESSMENT

This section will analyze and discuss the importance of human capital assessment for the organization to measure the business impact of the performance of their human capital, and for the

Table 1. The VHCD model stakeholder relationships

Actor Name	Abbreviation	Role	Relationship with
Learning Management System	LMS	T&D e-content authoring role	HRM, DW, U
Information management system	IMS	Communication and collaboration Role	U,LMS, SIS, Web2.0, CMS
Student Information system	SIS	Dynamic user feedback tool	HRM, U, TM
Web 2.0	Web.2.0	Dynamic environment for interaction between the user through web2.0 tools	IMS, LMS, U, DW
Competency Management System	CMS	Intelligent self-evaluation for the competency earned from the proposed T&D e-content.	HRM, TM
Enterprise Environment	EE	Where K create, share, capture and retrieved as a T&D e-content	HRM, DW
Data Ware house	DW	Codifying and accumulating the captured knowledge for T&D purpose.	HRM, U
Human Resource Management	HRM	The VHRD model administrative for the e-content development for the users	LMS, U, DW, TM
Top management/Stock holders	TM	TM affect or be affected by the attainment of organizational model.(earning retunes, profits, competitive advantage)	KPI, CMS, WEB2.0
Users / Employees	U	End User of the VHRD Model	VHRD Model
Key Performance Indictors	KPI	Measurement tool for the	TM, HRM
Virtual Human Resource Development	VHRD	Human resource development and training	All

Table 2. VHCD model comparisons among traditional KMS

Compression	Traditional KMS	VHCD model
Connectivity	Online/intranet	Online/ intranet
Content	Out-dated, irrelevant, ill-structured	Utilized according to the business requirement/ employees need/ updated with the new knowledge captured
Community	Management not involved/ organization internal environment	Management involved / external expertise / organization environment
Culture	Contract Sharing Knowledge (forced without motivation)	Sharing for development and earning new experiences/ Management commitment through their participation
Capacity	Online interaction	In-class interaction/online interaction /external expertise
Business strategy	Traditional KMS taken as a short project and non long term project/ Unalignment between the Knowledge managed & the strategy goals.	VHCD aligning between the Knowledge managed and the strategy goals of the organization.
Business Impact	Deficulyies in defining the business impact	Knowledge evaluated according to performance. Measurement of ROI and the achievements of the employee's performance.

management to understand how their organization's human assets are performing.

5.1 Intellectual Assets Assessment

Organization management in different sectors considers intellectual assets as important strategic assets, constituting the source of competitive advantages, financial performance, and market value. Intellectual capital assessment is still under exploration and a general and recognized methodology has not yet been defined (Zack, 1999; Johansson, et al., 2001; Andreou, et al., 2007). With regard to intellectual capital, numerous evaluation models have been proposed. However, the wide variety of these models is instantly clear. Most of them rely on different techniques and approaches for solving various problems related to intellectual capital assessment (Figure 3), such as the 'Why' x 'How' matrix (Figure 4) regarding the current assessment methods by Andriessen (2004). Thus, it becomes a necessity for companies to find a single suitable and flexible approach to meet their needs to move forward with intellectual capital evaluation, thus avoiding having to rely on numerous different approaches for every problem that may arise in future.

Furthermore, experience has demonstrated that, in addition to listing and classifying companies' intangible assets, it is necessary to determine the characteristics which influence companies'

performance and their positive and negative trends, such as human capital, which has been identified as playing an important role in creating and sustaining the value of the organization's intellectual capital.

Since a firm's intangible asset development is strictly related to its competitive strategy, Zack (1999) recognized the importance of adopting a strategy reflecting the management's decision on how to respond to external reality. To do this, managerial perceptions should shape the way knowledge resources are used, and should be valued as an intangible asset to the organization. Thus, managers' opinions and experiences should be taken into account for the achievement of the desired performance not only with regard to the actual state of the company's performance, but also with regard to its development over time. Reasonably, the choice of intangible assets to be developed by an organization is strictly dependent on its capability to make this choice fit for the business strategy of the company (Johansson, et al., 2001); equally, it is relevant to understand on which specific areas the organization needs to focus and which knowledge assets of human capital need to be leveraged within each specific area (Andreou, et al., 2007).

Additionally, four scenarios have been discussed earlier by Andriessen (2003) regarding the differences between financial valuation, value measurement, value assessment, and measurement

Figure 4. The "why" x "how" matrix (Andriessen, 2004)

Scenario.1: IC Measurement	Scenario.2: IC Financial Valuation
A numerical scale reflects the usefulness or desirability, with observed characteristics variables at hand.	The numerical scale reflects the usefulness or desirability, and the money unit used on this value scale.
Scenario.3: IC Value Measurement	Scenario.4: IC Value Assessment
A numerical value scale reflects the usefulness or desirability, but without any Money units used on the value scale, but the value can translate into observed criteria.	A numerical value scale reflects the usefulness or desirability, but without any money unit on the value scale, and without any observable criteria.

(Figure 5). The proposed model considers the third scenario as the most suitable to support managers with a unique method for their IC assessment, by reflecting usefulness and desirability, without monetary and financial indicators, but through qualitative and subjective perspectives.

5.2 The HAI as New Human Capital Assessment Model

The Hierarchical Assessment Index (HAI) model is based on the previous study by Grimaldi and Cricelli (2009). The HAI classifies all the intangible assets in successive levels so that each of them directly influences the performance measurement (Figure 5). The model has the capability to show a balanced image of the intangible assets of the

firm, as each asset can be allotted a priority that gives the measure of the influence on the performance. The definition of these priorities is based on a process that assembles managers' thoughts and experiences through the Analytic Hierarchy Process (AHP; Saaty, 1980).

5.3 HAI Taxonomy: The Value Drivers

The first level of the hierarchical structure encompasses the organization's goals and, therefore, holds the highest degree of significance. This global value includes all of the second level elements (value drivers), which specify contents and meaning of the company's goal; the tangible and intangible assets referring to each element of the second level are grouped into the elements of the

Figure 5. The HAI hierarchy structure

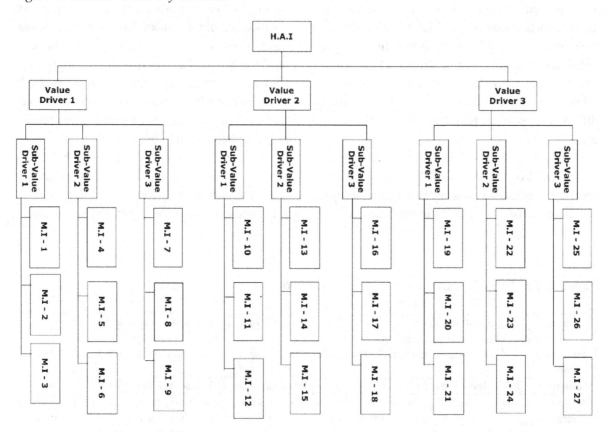

third level (characteristics); at the last level, the measurement indicators are provided.

5.4 The HAI Assessment Process

The assessment process begins with the determination of the numerical value of each of the selected measurement indicators, placed at the last level of the hierarchy. A quantitative value, which expresses the measure of its performance (m_{ijk}), is associated with every measurement indicator, where:

- i value refers to the value driver and runs from 1 to 3 (human capital; organizational capital; relational capital)
- j value refers to the 3 characteristics of each value driver, and also runs from 1 to 3 (stability; efficiency; growth)
- k value is the measurement indicator that relates to each value driver and to each characteristic; it runs from 1 to the total number of the selected indicators.

Moreover, in case of qualitative measures, the values of the measure of the performance "m_{ijk}" are turned into the values of the desired performance "$p_{ii'jk}$," which accounts for the temporal trend and for managers' expectations.

In the following step of the process, a qualitative value, which expresses its degree of importance (priority) with regard to the totality of the assets in achieving the company prefixed goals, is associated with every measurement indicator: "w_{ijk}." To do this, the AHP is used to determine the degree of importance of each element of the hierarchical structure and to calculate its overall priority. In order to establish the priorities of the elements in the hierarchy, the elements are compared pair-wise against the forefather element. This comparison is performed using the AHP comparison scale (Saaty, 1980), which expresses comparisons verbally, and these verbal

comparisons are then represented numerically. In particular, the pair-wise comparison process starts at the top of the hierarchy to select the value driver with the highest priority. Then, at the level immediately below, the priorities of the value drivers are divided by the weighting process among their descendant, and so on. To obtain the set of overall priorities of the hierarchy elements, all the results of the pair-wise comparison need to be synthesized. The overall priority of an element is the degree of importance of that element with regard to all the other elements in the hierarchical structure, and represents its significance with respect to the whole of the company performance.

Therefore, the overall priority of every measurement indicator is expressed by x_{ijk}, where the indexes i, j, and k are the same as for the value range and connotation of the quantitative value m_{ijk}.

Regarding the qualitative value of measurement indicators (x_{ijk}), it is worth bearing in mind that each value is expressed as a percentage and that their total sum is unitary.

In the process of calculating the HAI, which is based on the combination of all the measures of indicators (m_{ijk}) with their overall priorities (x_{ijk}), it is necessary to take into account both the temporal variations of m_{ijk} and the managers' expectations for its improvement. To fulfill this objective, it is once again necessary to make use of the AHP, but in a different application from that previously implemented. A pair-wise comparison is performed among three elements for each measurement indicator:

- The value of the performance calculated for the time period "T" (P_T);
- The value of the performance calculated for the time period immediately preceding the time period "T," that is "T-1" (P_{T-1});
- The desired performance ($P_{Desired}$).

The three element matrix of the pair-wise comparison is represented in Table 3. The three values are derived as follows: $P_{(T-1;T)}$ is the numerical ratio between the value of the performance of the indicator calculated for the time period "T" (P_T) and that calculated for the time period "T-1"; $P_{(T-1;\ Desired)}$ is inferred from the opinion of the manager about his expectation for the value of that indicator ($P_{Desired}$); $P_{(T;\ Desired)}$ is determined by simply substituting one relation into the other, so obtaining a numerical value. This particular procedure helps to avoid the inconsistency that could emerge from the fact that one of the three terms of comparison derives from subjective considerations ($P_{Desired}$) and, also, that some measurement indicators derive from qualitative data.

By means of the same procedure as the one used to find the priorities of the pair-wise comparison matrix, the normalized values of the priorities for each of P_T, P_{T-1}, and $P_{Desired}$ are obtained. The priority of P_T is the weight of the performance of the measurement indicator, calculated for the time period "T" with respect to its correspondent value for "T-1" and to its desired performance.

Reiterating the aforementioned procedure for each of the indicators supplies an evaluation of performance (p_{ijk}), where the indexes i, j, and k are the same as for the value range and connotation of the quantitative value x_{ijk}.

For each indicator, the value of p_{ijk} is comprised between 0 and 0.5. This follows from the fact that the sum of the three weights of P_T, P_{T-1}, and $P_{Desired}$ must be unitary and that the value of $P_{Desired}$ must be higher than those of P_T and P_{T-1}, as a consequence of managers' expectations. It is demonstrable that the weights of P_T and P_{T-1} cannot assume values that are either negative or higher than 0.5.

At this point, for each indicator, it is possible to combine the weights of the performance (p_{ijk}) with their overall priorities (x_{ijk}). The sum of the products of p_{ijk} and x_{ijk} of each measurement indicator results in a unique index, the HAI:

Table 3. The pair-wise comparison matrix of each measurement indicator

	P_{T-1}	P_T	$P_{Desired}$
P_{T-1}	1	$P_{(T-1;\ T)}$	$P_{(T-1;\ Desired)}$
P_T		1	$P_{(T;\ Desired)}$
$P_{Desired}$			1

$$HAI = \sum_i \sum_j \sum_k x_{ijk} \cdot p_{ijk}$$

The value of HAI is comprised between 0 and 0.5, in consequence of the fact that every p_{ijk} cannot assume a value which is either negative or higher that 0.5 and that every x_{ijk} cannot assume a value either negative or higher than 1. Indeed, the closer value of the HAI to 0.5, which is the maximum value that HAI can assume, the more advantageous the utilization of the available assets by the company. On the other hand, the margin of divergence from 0.5 will indicate the measure of the relevance of corrective strategies.

In addition, a sectional analysis can be performed on successful or unsuccessful actions at every level of the structure. It is possible, in fact, to focus the attention on the performance and on the weights of the indicators for each value driver, separately.

5.5 Human Capital Assessment Implementation

Having understood the suggested models, it is now logical to design and advise a strategy and pathway that will allow the organization to assess their human capital development process and the benefits they gain by applying the VHCD model.

Moreover, the management will be able to evaluate the human capital learning process inside the organization, in different interdisciplinary environments, according to the analyzed results of the proposed human capital assessment model.

The following steps define the assessment process for the organization's human capital, starting with defining the HAI goal for the assessment process, which, in our case, should be the human capital performance; subsequently, we move toward setting up value drivers for human capital learning.

The value drivers selected in this chapter are as follows: stability; efficiency; growth. These characteristics refer to specific aspects of each value driver by means of properly defined performance indicators.

Stability represents the endowment of the company in terms of material and immaterial talents and capabilities examined at a precise time ("As-Is" condition).

Efficiency is intended as the capacity of obtaining the desired performance by means of the available tangible and intangible assets.

Growth answers the demand for controlling company development and the positive trend of its continuous improvement. The analysis of growth studies the "To-Be" condition of the variables.

Furthermore, the organizations must additionally define their measurement indicators, which align with the chosen value drivers in the previous step. Measurement indicators vary from one organization to another and depend on the typology of the industry and on the dimension of the firm. The measurement indicators could be identified by reviewing what the management wants to know about their human capital, including employee turnover, employee awareness or motivations, new ideas and innovation from employees, saving from employees implemented suggestions, investment in training, new skills, and employee satisfaction, education, competencies and experience.

Once the HAI hierarchy is set up, the pair-wise comparison can be undertaken. In the final step, once we obtain the numerical weights for each one of the measurement indicators, we are able to compare the impact of the VHCD model on the organization's performance, and to compare these results with the past performance of the organization.

It is highly recommended to conduct an HAI assessment for the organization's human capital performance before the VHCD model is implemented, in order to evaluate the performance both before and after the integration of the VHCD model, so that organizations will be able to evaluate thoroughly the difference that the implementation has made to their human capital

6. DISCUSSION AND CONCLUSION

It is clear that organizations understand the importance of their human capital, treating it as an asset rather than an expense, and that the importance of investing in their human capital is understood better now than previously. It is particularly pertinent in today's knowledge economy, where market competitive strength is sustained by what an organization knows rather than what an organization owns. For this reason, organizations refer to their employees as human capital when their financial and performance impact is appreciated.

Furthermore, universities today play a significant role in the human capital development process, starting from the early stages of the individual's life, through graduate studies and on to specific professional courses, to enhance the human capital career path through knowledge, experience, and innovation.

In general, the process of human capital development has evolved from very primitive to highly advanced and technologically-based methods; such evolution is necessary in order to adapt to the current and future requirements and challenges of the knowledge economy. It can be said that in service-based or product-based organizations, the human capitals strongly influences all the activities of organization in terms of innovation, new product development, and performance improvement. New models and systems have evolved since the integration of technology in the field of human capital management, and the benefits are evident at all levels.

This chapter has provided an explanation for the advantages of VHCD with an oriented human capital assessment model that is highly flexible in terms of measurement and evaluations.

Moreover, we have explained the obstacles and solutions, which derive from the implementation of KMS in learning processes and in the human capital assessment model. They can be summarized in three main points: Firstly, during the human capital learning process, relevant knowledge requires an efficient innovative KM approach to prevent duplication and to ensure its knowledge is relevant, current, and useful. Secondly, in many cases in the development of performance measurement frameworks, human capital knowledge is not always considered. Thirdly, most of the relevant knowledge inside organizations is not targeted effectively, and there is often either information overload, or a lack of access to important information. This situation requires an efficient innovative KM approach, such as the proposed VHCD model, for managing and linking knowledge and information to prevent duplication and to ensure that the knowledge is relevant, current and useful to the human capital learning process.

Finally, this chapter presents a roadmap illustrating the transition from current processes of human capital assessment and development to the advanced processes previously provided. Without doubt, as with any other business process of human capital assessment and development, the main motivators and goals are increased productivity, improved efficiency and effectiveness, reduced costs, and minimized waste of resources. The idea of VCHD and HAI as a proof of concept of virtual human capital development and assessment processes for today's organizations illustrates the possibility, feasibility, and great potential for such projects that can be applied by any traditional or new-born organization around the world.

REFERENCES

Andreou, A. N., Green, A., & Stankosky, M. (2007). A framework of intangible valuation areas and antecedents. *Journal of Intellectual Capital*, *8*(1), 52–75. doi:10.1108/14691930710715060

Andriessen, D. (2003). IC valuation and measurement- Why and how? *PMA IC Research Symposium*. Retrieved Nov 2006 from http://www.weightlesswealth.com/Publications%20and%20downloads_files%5CPaper%20Andriessen%20PMA%202003.pdf

Andriessen, D. (2004). *Making sense of intellectual capital – Designing a method for the valuation of intangibles*. Amsterdam, The Netherlands: Elsevier Butterworth-Heninemann.

Argote, L. (2011). Organizational learning research: Past, present and future. *Management Learning*, *42*(4), 439–446. doi:10.1177/1350507611408217

Bontis, N. (1999). Managing organizational knowledge by diagnosing intellectual capital: Framing and advancing the state of the field. *International Journal of Technology Management*, *18*(6), 433–462. doi:10.1504/IJTM.1999.002780

Brooking, A. (1996). *Intellectual capital: Core asset for the third millennium*. London, UK: International Thomson Business Press.

Edvinsson, L., & Malone, M. S. (1997a). *Intellectual capital: Realizing your company's true value by finding its hidden brainpower*. New York, NY: Harper Business.

Edvinsson, L., & Malone, M. S. (1997b). *Intellectual capital, the proven way to establish your company's real value by measuring its hidden brainpower*. London, UK: Judy Piatkus.

Edvinsson, L., & Sullivan, P. H. (1996). Developing a model for managing intellectual capital. *European Management Journal*, *14*(4), 356–364. doi:10.1016/0263-2373(96)00022-9

Filstad, C. (2011). Organizational commitment through organizational socialization tactics. *Journal of Workplace Learning, 23*(6), 376–390. doi:10.1108/13665621111154395

Grant, R. M. (1996). Toward a knowledge-based theory of the firm. *Strategic Management Journal, 17*, 109–122.

Grimaldi, M., & Cricelli, L. (2009). Intangible asset contribution to company performance: The hierarchical assessment index. *Vine, 39*(1), 40–54. doi:10.1108/03055720910962434

Hahn, J., & Subramani, M. R. (2000). A framework of knowledge management systems: Issues and challenges for theory and practice. In *Proceedings of the 21st International Conference on Information Systems*, (pp. 302-312). IEEE.

Hanandi, M., & Grimaldi, M. (2010). Internal organizational and collaborative knowledge management: A virtual HRD model based on Web 2.0. *The International Journal of Advanced Computer Science & Applications, 1*(4), 11–19.

Horie, N., & Ikawa, Y. (2011). Knowledge integration in a product development organization accompanied by M&A: A case study of a precision device manufacturer. In *Proceedings of the Technology Management in the Energy Smart World (PICMET)*, (pp. 1-8). PICMET.

Johansson, U., Martensson, M., & Skoog, M. (2001). Measuring to understand intangible performance drivers. *European Accounting Review, 10*(3), 407–437.

Khoury, S. (1994). *Valuing intellectual properties. Internal Paper*. Midland, MI: The Dow Chemical Company.

Kwon, K.-S. (2011). The co-evolution of universities' academic research and knowledge-transfer activities: The case of South Korea. *Science & Public Policy, 38*(6), 493–503. doi:10.3152/030234211X12960315267930

Lepak, D. P., & Snell, S. A. (1998). Virtual HR: Strategic human resource management in the 21st century. *Human Resource Management Review, 8*(3), 215–234. doi:10.1016/S1053-4822(98)90003-1

Lev, B. (2001). *Intangibles: Management, measurement and reporting*. Washington, DC: The Brookings Institution.

Lynn, B. (1998). Intellectual capital. *CMA Magazine, 72*(1), 10–15.

McWhorter. Mancuso, & Hurt. (2008). *Adult learning in a virtual environment*. Retrieved from http://www.slideshare.net/rochell/adult-learning-in-a-virtual-environment-ahrd-2008

Nonaka, I. (1998). *The knowledge-creating company*. Boston, MA: Harvard Business School Press.

Pike, S., & Roos, G. (2000). Intellectual capital measurement and holistic value approach (HVA). *Works Institute Journal, 42*.

Pulic, A. (1998). *Measuring the performance of intellectual potential in knowledge economy*. Paper presented at the 2nd World Congress on Measuring and Managing Intellectual Capital. Hamilton, Canada.

Reilly, R., & Schweihs, R. (1999). *Valuing intangible assets*. New York, NY: McGraw-Hill.

Roos, G., Roos, J., Dragonetti, N., & Edvinsson, L. (1998). *Intellectual capital: Navigating in the new business landscape*. New York, NY: New York University Press.

Saaty, T. L. (1980). *The analytic hierarchy process*. New York, NY: McGraw-Hill.

Salisbury, M. W., & Plass, J. L. (2001). Design and development of a web-based knowledge management system. *Journal of Interactive Instruction Development, 14*, 23–29.

Sharabati, A. A. A., Jawad, S. N., & Bontis, N. (2010). Intellectual capital and business performance in the pharmaceutical sector of Jordan. *Journal of Management Decision, 48*(1), 105–131. doi:10.1108/00251741011014481

Stewart, T. A. (1997). *Intellectual capital: The new wealth of organizations*. New York, NY: Doubleday.

Sveiby, K. (1997). *The new organizational wealth: Managing and measuring knowledge based assets*. San Francisco, CA: Berrett-Koehler.

Ting, W. K. I., & Lean, H. H. (2009). Intellectual capital performance of financial institutions in Malaysia. *Journal of Intellectual Capital, 10*(4), 588–599. doi:10.1108/14691930910996661

Walsh, K., Enz, C. A., & Canina, L. (2008). The impact of strategic orientation on intellectual capital investments in customer service firms. *Journal of Service Research, 10*(4), 300–317. doi:10.1177/1094670508314285

Wiig, K. M. (1997). Knowledge management: An introduction and perspective. *Journal of Knowledge Management, 1*(1), 6–14. doi:10.1108/13673279710800682

Youndt, M. A., & Snell, S. A. (2004). Human resource management, intellectual capital, and organizational performance. *Journal of Managerial Issues, 16*(3), 337–360.

Zack, M. H. (1999). Managing codified knowledge. *Sloan Management Review, 40*(4), 45–58.

ADDITIONAL READING

Bratianu, C. (2004). The learning paradox and the university. *Journal of Applied Quantitative Methods, 2*(4).

Daum, J. (2001). *Interview with Leif Edvinsson: Intellectual capital: The new wealth of corporations*. The New Economy Analyst Report. Retrieved from http://www.juergendaum.com/news/11_13_2001.htm

Edvinsson, L. (1997). Developing intellectual capital at Skandia. *Long Range Planning, 30*(3), 366–373. doi:10.1016/S0024-6301(97)90248-X

Edvinsson, L., & Malone, M. S. (1997a). *Intellectual capital: Realizing your company's true value by finding its hidden brainpower*. New York, NY: Harper Business.

Edvinsson, L., & Malone, M. S. (1997b). *Intellectual capital, the proven way to establish your company's real value by measuring its hidden brainpower*. London, UK: Judy Piatkus.

Grimaldi, M., & Cricelli, L. (2009). Intangible asset contribution to company performance: The hierarchical assessment index. *Vine, 39*(1), 40–54. doi:10.1108/03055720910962434

Hanandi, M., & Grimaldi, M. (2010). Internal organizational and collaborative knowledge management: A virtual HRD model based on Web 2.0. *The International Journal of Advanced Computer Science & Applications, 1*(4), 11–19.

Thomas, R. J., Cheese, P., & Bento, J. M. (2003). *Research Note Human capital development*. Retrieved from http://info.su-goo.com/TW/Ebook/%E9%9B%BB%E5%-AD%90%E6%9B%B8%E7%B1%8D/%E9-%81%8B%E4%BD%9C%E7%AE%A1%-E7%90%86/%E5%9F%83%E6%A3%AE-%E5%93%B2%20-%20Human%20Capital%20Development.pdf

Chapter 19
Knowledge Management in Practice:
Using Wikis to Facilitate Project-Based Learning

Fiona Masterson
National University of Galway, Ireland

ABSTRACT

Knowledge is created when individuals come together to solve a problem. Project-based learning focuses on solving problems. One aspect of the work of a 21st century design engineer is the requirement to work remotely on design projects. Engineers coming together to design a product face the problem of working remotely, collaborating, creating, and sharing knowledge. This chapter explores the use of wikis in a product design and development class at an Irish university. This chapter begins by giving an introduction to wikis and their use in education. The design project exercise and assessment process is described. The results of a study are provided that indicate that the vast majority of students found wikis to be a good tool for project collaboration. Wikis were found to be an excellent knowledge management tool that facilitates project-based learning.

INTRODUCTION

Project-based learning is regarded as the best pedagogical approach for teaching product design and development. Design education courses should prepare students for scenarios which mimic those faced by design engineers in industry (Clough, 2005). One aspect of the work of a 21st century de-sign engineer is the requirement to work remotely on design projects (Gupta, Denny, O'Toole, & Bondade, 2011; Hertel, Geister, & Konradt, 2005; Jarvenpaa & Leidner, 1999; Martins, Gilson, & Maynard, 2004). Today's design teams frequently consist of engineers who are not in the same building, country or perhaps continent (Jarvenpaa & Leidner, 1999; Martins, et al., 2004). They need

DOI: 10.4018/978-1-4666-1969-2.ch019

therefore to have knowledge of technologies that facilitate collaborative work (Endean, et al., 2008). Organisations are using a number of Web 2.0 technologies, including wikis to facilitate this need for collaboration (Standing & Kiniti, 2011). To give students an opportunity to use such a technology a wiki was infused throughout a National University of Ireland, Galway engineering design project. The wiki was used to increase the emphasis on technological and "soft" skills, in addition to academic content (Blumenfeld, et al., 1991). The students in the product design and development class used the wiki to document the entire spectrum of the design process, from idea generation to prototype design. An investigation of the use of wikis in a product design and development class has not being published previously; this study aims to address this research gap.

The main objective of the chapter is to describe the use of wikis as a knowledge management tool in project-based learning. Additional objectives are to:

- Provide an introduction to the Web 2.0 technology wiki
- Describe the use of wikis as a knowledge management tool
- Describe the use of wikis in education
- Provide examples of studies that describe the use of wikis in engineering design education
- Outline some common problems experienced when using wikis in an education setting
- Describe how a wiki was used in a product design and development class in an Irish University
- Outline future research directions

To summarise, the wiki was chosen for the design class for two reasons; firstly to introduce the students to a technology that facilitates collaborative work and secondly to increase the emphasis on technological and "soft" skills, in addition to academic content. The remainder of this chapter gives the reader an understanding of a practitioner experience of using wikis in a classroom setting.

BACKGROUND: WHAT IS A WIKI?

Web 2.0 is the term used to describe a variety of websites and applications that allow users to create and share information or material. A central feature of the technology is that it allows people to create, share, communicate, and collaborate (Richardson, 2009). Web 2.0 differs from other types of websites, as it does not require any Web design or publishing skills to participate. Examples of Web 2.0 technologies include wikis, discussion forums, blogs, Twitter, and Facebook.

The □rst wiki, WikiWikiWeb, was developed by Ward Cunningham in 1994 (Leuf & Cunningham, 2001). Wiki is the Hawaiian word for "quick." Cunningham's objective was to develop a platform on the Internet for software programmers that could be used to share a program code easily and rapidly. It was hoped that this platform would enable the possibility for seamless collaborative work on program codes. Given that the same program code can be edited by many people, the software must automatically track changes made in documents as well as the complete history of a document (Ebersbach, Glaser, & Heigl, 2004). From the initial use of a wiki by software programmers it is now used by anyone who wishes to work collaboratively on a website. Since the mid-1990s wikis have been used in businesses and educational institutions promote sharing and collaborative creation of Web content (Ebersbach, Glaser, & Heigl, 2005; Leuf & Cunningham, 2001). The popularity of wikis is largely due to the rise in popularity of Wikipedia, the well-known wiki-based on-line encyclopaedia.

Let us consider one of the most popular alternative Web 2.0 technologies, blogs, and see how they differ from wikis. Blogs allow an author to make a series of diary-like posts online that can include text, images, audio and video (Churchill, 2011). Blogs also allow those who read the posts to make comments. Blog entries are made in a journal style and displayed in reversed chronological order. Wikis on the other hand are a collaborative tool that allows many people to create and edit online documents or Web pages and allow linking amongst pages. Blogs and wikis share some common traits: they are both Web- and HTML-based; both their content is user-generated, and they both allow users to comment on the content. Wikis are better than blogs at archiving information for easy access. They are also better at gathering information from a group of people. Blogs do have some advantages over wikis, however. Most notably, they are better at starting and maintaining a dialog between the publisher and reader. It is up to the teacher to determine the objective of using the learning technology and to determine what tool is most suitable. In this case, the ability to collaborate was a key reason for choosing to use the wiki tool in the design class.

WIKI AS A KNOWLEDGE MANAGEMENT TOOL

The creation and sharing of knowledge in engineering design includes both explicit and tacit knowledge (Nonaka, 1994). Design engineers solve problems, interact with other designers, generate ideas, and communicate their thoughts (Cross & Clayburn Cross, 1995). Wikis are cited as being a knowledge management tool (Hasan & Pfaff, 2006; Raman, Ryan, & Olfman, 2005). They can be used to create, store and share knowledge. All of these activities generate new knowledge that must be captured. The use of wikis by design engineers in industry has shown that wikis can support collaborative design activities. Let us look further at how this can be achieved using wikis.

Knowledge Creation

Wikis encourage incremental knowledge creation; when a page is created the content can be incomplete or incorrect since additional collaborators can edit and add more information to the page (Wagner & Bolloju, 2005). The contributors to the site can create new pages or modify existing ones, with optional access control to set limits on authorship (Tapscott & Williams, 2006). The ability to create hyperlinks to other websites illustrates the incremental way knowledge is created in a wiki (Wagner, 2004).

Knowledge Storage

Since wikis are a centralised resource on the Web, they support a decentralised group of users that need access to a single knowledge repository. Wikis act therefore as a knowledge repository (Wagner & Bolloju, 2005). Different types of knowledge can be stored on the wiki pages including links to external websites, different types of files (for example video and audio files).

Knowledge Sharing

A wikis principal objective is to provide a platform for collaboration and to facilitate the exchange of information within and between teams or individuals (Leuf & Cunningham, 2001). Wikis allow distributed teams to write and edit documents collaboratively over the Internet in a shared online workspace. Once information is added to a wiki, it can be viewed at any time. The wikis can be accessed anywhere in the world through the Internet. As wikis are Web applications, they can be viewed from almost anywhere, as the http protocol used to transfer the information is allowed through most network firewalls.

Given what was outlined above, it is clear that wikis can effectively serve as a knowledge management tool by acting as a platform to create, store and share knowledge.

THE USE OF WIKIS IN EDUCATION

The potential for wikis in education has been explored in a number of articles and books (Karasavvidis, 2010; Richardson, 2009; West & West, 2009). Wikis are viewed as a means to combine students' knowledge in a collaborative authoring project (Parker & Chao, 2007). As a result of several contributors adding material, a wiki can develop and expand and can therefore address pedagogical objectives such as student involvement, group activity, peer and tutor review. Wikis permit students to work together in a collaborative space, with the evolution of the work observable to all participating students of the wiki, and to the tutor or teacher, at any time (Endean, et al., 2008). This visibility and sense of creativity and progress can be highly motivating (Wheeler, Yeomans, & Wheeler, 2008). Students, teachers and tutors can provide feedback on the work, and help to improve it (Lundin, 2008).

Wikis can be saved so that future students can review work done on previous wikis. They therefore offer an effective way for students, and their teachers, to maintain a repository of learning resources (Wodehouse, et al., 2010). Students can build on the knowledge created by students in previous years.

A number of studies investigate the adoption of wikis in a wide variety of higher education settings. Hulbert Williams (2010) explored the use of wikis in a postgraduate psychology research methods module. (Hulbert-Williams, 2010). Results indicated that the students enjoyed the wiki task and perceived educational benefit from it. However, the content of the wikis created suggested that the instructions given to the students may not have been clear enough and in particular that student s were unsure of what the nature and purpose of a wiki is. The use of wikis in nursing education has also being explored (Ciesielka, 2008). In the Ciesielka (2008) students worked in teams, and collected data for their project and posted that information on the wiki. The students found the wiki as a useful tool for group work and to support online communication with team members. The students continued to contribute to the wiki even after grades were assigned. Minocha, Petre, and Roberts (2008) describe the use of wikis in software engineering (Minocha, Petre, & Roberts, 2008). They found that the strength of a wiki, as a collaborative authoring tool, is to facilitate the learning of course concepts.

It has also been found that there are certain usability aspects of wikis that can mar a positive student experience, which we will explore in greater detail later in the chapter. Wikis have also being used in tourism education (Benckendorff, 2008). Overall, the students in the Benckendorff (2008) study had a positive experience with using the wiki. Students acknowledged the convenience of being able to work on their wiki 'any time, any place.'

Wikis in Design Education

Design is more and more seen as a social process that involves communication and collaboration among participants (Boujut & Tiger, 2002; Bucciarelli, 2002; Hietikko & Rajaniemi, 2000; Maier, et al., 2008). Effective communication and collaboration tools are therefore necessary to support the design process (Citera, et al., 1995). A number of studies have being published that describe the use of wikis in design education. One such study describes the use of wikis at the University of Karlsruhe in Germany. Students in a product development course used a wiki as a repository for design documentation. The wiki's purpose was to serve as an aid in "sharing and distributing knowledge, using knowledge, and preserving knowledge" (Albert, et al., 2007). The study focused mainly on the use of the wiki for knowledge management. The study found that wikis are suitable for storing and sharing the documentation created during the product development processes. A similar study at the University of Strathclyde in Scotland focused specifically on the sharing of information and resources in a design course. The study found that students preferred to browse the wiki structure to find information rather than to use keyword searches (Grierson, Nicol, Littlejohn, & Wodehouse, 2004).

In another study Chen et al. (2005) looked at how the use of wikis in a project-based engineering design course can have a positive effect on students' knowledge and skills at Stanford university (Chen, et al., 2005). The results of the study confirmed that wikis assisted students to become more alert to their design skills, demonstrating the aptness of wikis as tools for design education. Saleh and McKinnon (2009) describe a case study of the use of a wiki in a mine design class at the Queen's University in Canada (Saleh & McKinnon, 2009). Results showed that the students learned more when using the wiki tool.

Wodehouse et al. (2004) presented a study of third year design engineering students who were using a particular wiki engine, TikiWiki, for solving a rapid design task (Wodehouse, et al., 2004). The results from the study were mixed. On the one hand, results showed that using the wiki helped students to generate product concepts. The researchers found that the teams who interacted more with stored information in the wiki achieved better results in the design project. The study also found, however, that transferring concept information into the digital domain was identified as a disadvantage that caused additional effort for the students. The authors also hypothised that an improved understanding of information management in design processes may serve to improve the effectiveness of wikis for design education.

PROBLEMS IDENTIFIED WITH WIKIS

The use of this knowledge management tool is not problem free (Karasavvidis, 2010). Problems with the technical operation of the wiki tool have being cited in the literature (Lundin, 2008; Wheeler, Yeomans, & Wheeler, 2008). If wiki pages are not initially structured by the tutor or teacher students have found this to be problematic (Lundin, 2008). Students do not always welcome the use of wikis (Rick & Guzdial, 2006). Rick and Guzdial (2006) describe how students preferred not to use a wiki and therefore to accept a lower grade than if they used the wiki. Students in another class did not see the benefit of a wiki as a collaborative tool (Elgort, Smith, & Toland, 2008). Limited participation by students is another problem that is experienced when wikis are used (Carr, Morrison, Cox, & Deacon, 2007; Cole, 2009). Some students also find wikis formal, and prefer the interactive and community features of a forum (Hemmi, Bayne, & Land, 2009).

Vratulis and Dobson (2008) discovered that students may not all be able to play an equal role in making contributions to a wiki (Vratulis & Dobson, 2008). As in other forms of group work, some students overshadow others, which can result in the end product not being representative of all students' perspectives. These issues can be particularly problematic in a wiki because of the lack of clear ownership of contributions, and the facility for users to change each others' contributions. This can cause irritation for some students, who may feel that their own work is no longer represented in the wiki. Even if participation is reasonably equal, some students may still feel uncomfortable with the prospect of modifying each others' work (Hemmi, Bayne, & Land, 2009).

To summaries, the literature review revealed that wikis are used in a variety of educational settings. While the majority of use cases have reported positive results a number of challenges have been identified.

The next section of the chapter will give an account of the experiences of a practitioner using wikis in a design class.

CASE STUDY: USE OF WIKI IN A PRODUCT DESIGN AND DEVELOPMENT CLASS

This section describes the experience of using a wiki in a Product Design and Development course at the National University of Ireland, Galway. The purpose of the study was to provide an exploratory analysis of student attitudes toward the use of wikis in a product design and development class. The specific aims of the study are to examine student's views about their experience of using the wiki.

Course Background

Setting

A wiki was implemented in a module entitled "Product Design and Development" in the National University of Galway, Ireland. It is a project-based course augmented by lectures. The course was taken by third year Industrial Engineering and Masters in Applied Science students. The assessment of this course was based on a project undertaken by the students throughout the module. The project was worth 100% of the final grade for the course. The objective of the project was to design a new product following the product development process discussed in the lectures. The students created a prototype of their new product and presented that prototype as a final product. The Product Design and Development course covered all major steps of the product design process, including:

- New product development processes
- Planning product development projects
- Identifying customer needs
- Developing and writing product specifications
- Methodologies for generating product concept
- How to select the final product concept

- Methods to test concepts
- Design for manufacture
- Prototyping methodologies
- Design for environment
- Patents and intellectual property

An objective of the course was for students to gain practical experience in applying design principles, theories, and problem-solving methodologies to the design of a physical product. Another objective of the course was for students develop skills for working in teams and for problem solving.

Profile of Participants

Seventeen students participated in the course: five were undergraduate third-year industrial engineering students (4 male, 1 female) and twelve were postgraduate students (10 male and 2 female). Their mean age was 25 (range 21 to 50). Two postgraduate students (male) took the module via distance learning. They worked on the projects by themselves. The class met weekly for two hours over 12 weeks.

Project Brief

In the first lecture, student groups were given an open project brief: "Assume you work within a company with a strong focus on selling and marketing to college students. Your senior management has asked your team to develop a new product to address a product category in the college student market." The students formed groups of 2-3 students. The distance-learning students worked on the projects by themselves. Project deliverables (the quantifiable goods or services that will be provided upon the completion of a project) were allocated in class on Mondays. Each task corresponded to a step in the design process. The project deliverables were as follows:

- Generation of five market opportunities consistent with the project mission statement
- Generation of a needs analysis where the customer needs are translated into product requirements
- Concepts generation, rationalise decisions and the selection of a winning concept to move forward with by testing the ideas with users
- Generation of a concept prototype
- Design of a concept testing plan and test the concept
- Determine the selling price of the concept
- A ten minute presentation of the product idea to an expert panel

Assessment Criteria

The project was assessed against the following criteria:

- The understanding and analysis of the design context deliverables undertaken, and a demonstration that theory is understood.
- The completion of each project deliverable.
- The quality of the work completed.
- The quality and feasibility of recommendations made.
- The feasibility of recommendations made.

Implementation of the Wiki in the Design Class

The Learning Management System (LMS) Blackboard was used for the course. This LMS is used across the National University of Ireland, Galway campus. The Product Design and Development course had its own Blackboard site. The Blackboard site was maintained by the lecturer. The module's blackboard site contained the lecture slides delivered in class, design case studies, links to design websites and other material that would be of interest to students taking the course. There

is a wiki plugin feature in Blackboard that create pages that include all the functions of a wiki, such as managing who can see and edit content and keeping track of what changes have been made. The lecturer used this feature to create the wikis for the class. The lecturer was available outside of classroom hours to discuss any queries the students might have regarding their design project. An engineering technician was also available to students to advise or assist the students with their projects. One of the university's learning technologists was also available to the students if they had any technical issues or queries regarding the use of their wikis.

Wiki Design and Structure

On the first day of class, the learning technologists gave the students an overview on how to use wikis and provided them with a wiki guide. The wiki guide provided information on the purpose of the wiki, how to create a wiki page, how to edit the wiki, how to add a hyperlink to a wiki page and how to see the revision history. For each new design task students had to create a wiki page. The students addressed the deliverable(s) of each task by documenting their assignment on their wiki. They also had one wiki page that they could use as a group workspace. When the project was completed, each group had created 8 new wiki pages corresponding to the eight project deliverables assigned as part of the project. This need for structure in the wiki design was determined necessary by the lecturer in order to ensure that all of the students knew of the project expectations. Figure 1 is an illustration of the wiki structure.

There are three levels to the wiki structure as shown in Figure 1:

- **Home Page:** The first level contains an overview of the assignment and links to each of the team wikis.
- **Individual Wiki Team Home Pages:** The third level contains links to the team's indi-

vidual wiki pages. Each wiki page contains the material that addresses each of the project deliverables.

- **Individual Wiki Team's Team Page and Deliverables Pages:** The third level contained a team workspace wiki page. This is where the teams could use for whatever purpose they wanted to. They could use it for example to document brainstorming activities or to record team meeting minutes. The content of this page was not assessed or graded by the lecturer. The individual project deliverable pages (seven in total) was where the students answered there assignment questions.

As technical writing skills are an essential skill for a design engineer the students were required to structure their wiki pages in a set format. The headings that they had to include in their wiki page for each task were:

- Executive Summary
- Table of Contents
- List of Tables and/or Illustrations
- Introduction Section
- Results
- Conclusion and Recommendations
- References

Figure 1. Wiki structure

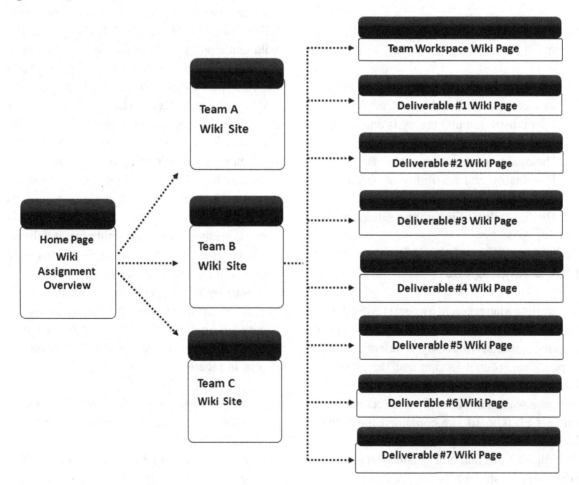

Figure 2 is an illustration of the one of students completed wiki pages.

Participants' Experience of Wikis

Data Gathering Methods

In order to study the attitudes of the students when using the wiki, data was collected from a number of sources. Data collected included online observations of the development of the wiki pages, individual semi-structured interviews, interview transcripts, and researcher notes. To investigate the experience of the students, a survey consisting of 14 questions including three open response questions was administered. The questions were developed to evaluate the student's experience of using the wiki in the course.

The key themes that emerged in the students' responses were technical difficulties with using a wiki, issues of working in teams, the benefits of using a wiki to support collaborative work and the benefits of wikis as distance learning tools.

Technical Difficulties and Wikis

The principal disadvantages identified in using the wiki were technology related issues. Virtually all of the respondents experienced technical difficulties with using the new technology, particularly at the beginning of the project. Only one student in the class had used a wiki before. It was therefore a new technology for the majority of the class. The first technology challenge was that the wiki site within Blackboard went down for 3 days before the first project deliverable was due. As soon as the lecturer learned of this issue she extended the due date for the first project deliverable. This initial false start caused apprehension.

Another technology issue that a number of students experienced were problems with Internet connectivity in their homes. One student said that

Figure 2. Example of a complete wiki page

Executive Summary

This wiki contains the report on market opportunities and customer need and documents the methodology, results and conclusions of that analysis. Several interviews were undertaken within a mature student target group and research was performed to find articles which had been written by students detailing the challenges they faced. The raw data gained from these sources has been compiled into both existing market opportunities and a hierarchical list of customer needs from which new products can be based. A particular focus was set on those who had rentered further education as a result of recently losing employment as it was felt that this was a growing customer base.

The conclusions were that the main needs of mature and reskilling students revolve around time management and a mission statement was generated from this. From this mission statement a list of product needs were fed into a final refined mission statement.

Contents

1. List of Tables and/or Illustrations
2. Introduction
3. Methods and Design Approach
4. Results
5. Conclusion and Recommendations

List of tables and/or Illustrations

Hierarchical table of needs............................Results section

Introduction

Recent events in Ireland have seen a massive increase in unemployment, with levels set to top 500,000 people. As a significant number of these have sought out retraining it si felt that this group represents a new emerging demographic in the student market.

With this in mind, interviews were held with individuals who have recently lost employment and now find themselves as students once more. These have been used in an attempt to create a breakdown of customer needs which can later be turned into product

Print (w/ comments)

Page Stats
Views: 54
Edits: 37
Contributors: 2
Comments: 0

Page Contributors

Search
Search

Site Navigation
1. Home Page - Wiki Assignment Overview
2. Wiki Help
3 Group Work Space
Deliverable 1 - Customer Needs
Deliverable 2 - Concept Generation
Deliverable 3 - Concept Selection
Deliverable 4 - Concept Prototype
Deliverable 5 - Concept testing outline
Deliverable 6 - Results of Concept Testing
Deliverable 7 - Team Presentation

Toolbox
Page List
Export Site

Privacy

"some wiki pages crashed a lot when used from home." One student could not access the wiki from their home, as they did not have an Internet connection in it. They could only access the wiki from either using an Internet cafe or on a campus computer.

Another problem that students experienced was the incapability of some external file formats with the wiki tool in Blackboard. One of the deliverables of the project was a product concept drawing. This drawing could be done using different drawing packages. The students experienced problems with up-loading the design drawings from different design packages into the wiki. One student noted that it was "not easy to upload all the required drawings." When these issues were brought to the attention of the lecturer, she directed them to submit a hardcopy of the drawings that they could not be uploaded to the site.

The Benefits of using a Wiki to Support Collaborative Work

In spite of the technical difficulties with using the wiki the students noted some considerable benefits. All students were glad that they had been exposed to wikis through the product design and development class. When asked about the advantages of using the wiki they identified that it helped them work with students that were based in different locations, so they did not have to be physically in the same location to work. One student said "Great tool for working with others on projects that are not based in the same location." All of the students identified this as a key advantage of the wiki. They did not need to have as frequent face-to-face meetings, as they could use the team workspace to post messages to their team members. They highlighted that they could work on their project from outside of the college. One student said that he frequently "Could work from home." They found that the wiki offered flexibility in that they could work on it anywhere as long as they had an Internet connection.

The Benefits of Wikis as Distance Learning Tools

The distance-learning students found it particularly good. The distance-learning students said that they felt a "constant connection" with the lecturer even though they had never met. One of the distance-learning students stated, "As a distance-learning student I relied heavily on the wiki to engage with my lecturer and ensure I could keep up with the rest of the class. The wiki was simple, useable and user friendly. I would very much like to see it used again."

The students felt working through the wiki gave them a good experience of the design process. One student said, "The project provided me with a practical experience that otherwise I would not have gained just by reading a book." The students felt that the way the design project was aligned with the wiki structure helped then get a better understanding about how the product development process is structured.

The Lecturer's Experience of the Wiki

The lecturer had never used a wiki before. As she had support from a learning technologist, she never felt alone in using the wiki. In the interview at the end of the project, the course tutor concurred with student views on the usefulness of the new technology. She found the quality of student work was often of a high standard. The tutor has saved the wiki pages and will make them available for classes in the future, in order to show future students how previous students approached the project's task. She said that the wiki allowed her to easily keep a repository of design projects. In particular, she liked the way she could dip in and out in real time to track the progress of the students "I could monitor students' progress in real time. I had access to a full history of team member contributions." After the students submitted each deliverable, the lecturer reviewed and graded it and left feedback on the bottom of the wiki page.

The lecturer also felt that the use of a wiki was a time-intensive process. At the beginning of the course, the initial setting up of the team wikis was time consuming. It took time to learn how to set up the wiki pages and structure the project deliverables so they aligned with the wiki structure. After a few weeks, this process became easier. Based on her experience, the lecturer recommends that a wiki that it be first used with a small number of students in order to gain experience before being implemented with larger classes.

The case study also showed that students may not like to collaborate because individuals do not contribute equally. Using a wiki provides a solution to these issues as well. All wiki programs provide an activity report. The activity report provides a full accounting for all changes, additions, and comments made by each individual. This activity report can be used to objectively evaluate a student's level of participation and hold each student accountable for the amount of effort they contributed to a project.

In summary the lessons learned from implementing the wiki in the product design and development class are as follows:

- Poor Internet connectivity in student's homes can cause problems.
- The lecturer/teacher should be aware that there are some file formats that may be incompatible with the wiki and he/she should make provisions for this.
- Wikis help students work with others based in different locations.
- Wikis offer flexibility; students can work from anywhere as long as they had an Internet connection.
- Wiks are particularly beneficial to distance learning students.
- The lecturer felt that she had a better oversight of the class; she could dip in and out

in real time to track the progress of the students.
- The lecturer could monitor team members' participation in the project easily through the wikis history page.
- Use a small number of students when implementing a wiki in a class for the first time, in order to gain experience before being implemented with larger classes.

There are other possible research directions concerning the use of wikis in education, the next section will endeavour to suggest some of them.

FUTURE RESEARCH DIRECTIONS

The use of wikis in education is a growing phenomenon. There are a number of potential areas for future research. One such area might be how wikis can be leveraged to facilitate and promote students' problem solving skills in design projects. Another might be to dig deeper into the specific skills, both technical and organisational, that are required to maximize the benefit of using wikis in project-based assignments. Another area of potential interest is the methodology employed by students when developing and crafting the knowledge that makes up a wiki page.

Combining technologies, such desktop sharing programs, VOIP (Voice-Over-IP), communication software, and wikis to enhance the experience of students when working on a project is a potential area of interest.

In addition to the aforementioned areas, a specific investigation into the use of wikis by distance learning students might also be warranted. The course structure and content of distance learning courses is a good fit for the communication and collaboration abilities provided by Wikis.

These are just initial samples of potential areas of investigation for researching the use of wikis in education. The possibilities are constantly growing and evolving, as new technologies, both complimentary and disruptive, are developed each year.

CONCLUSION

The results of the study indeed show that if wikis are used for teaching project design and development they have are beneficial. Some issues did arise with using wikis but overall the experience was positive.

On a few occasions technical difficulties were experienced by the students when they were using the wiki. They were mainly related to connectivity issues, Blackboard down time and the inability to upload some files into the wiki. To give a full list of the types of problems that may occur with wikis and how they can be dealt with is beyond the scope of this chapter but a few suggestions may assist to avert any potential crisis. Firstly, the teacher should be aware that computer technology is never totally reliable. The problems that occur may be of minor nature technically, but the consequences may still be serious in terms of functionality. Most problems that occurred in this case were minor in nature. Being prepared for the fact that technical problems may occur will enable the teacher to deal with issues when they happen. Being prepared means that the teacher should have a back-up plan. When, for example in this case, the wiki went down, the lecturer extended the project deliverable due date. Technical problems will happen and the important thing is not to panic and to be adaptable, for example, sometimes rearranging the original course plan might be necessary. Clearly, it would be beneficial to have technical support at hand to help with such problems. In this case, a learning technologist was available to the lecturer for assistance if any technical issues arose with the wiki.

The ability to collaborate easily on the project was seen as a key advantage of the wiki. It afforded students the ability to work with one another without regard to time or location. This is a benefit because many of today's students may not live in close proximity to one another or the university, they may work, and/or they may have families to attend to. Students reported that difficulty coordinating schedules is a key reason students prefer not to collaborate with each other. The students who were taking the course as a distance-learning module found the wiki particularly beneficial.

The wiki was shown to be an effective knowledge management tool. Students were able to create new knowledge easily. The structured layout of each wiki page as set out as a project requirement ensured that the knowledge created was in a structured format. This facilitated easy review of the wiki content by both students and lecturers. Wikis offered a suitable platform for storing project knowledge. Students could document all required information into the wiki page, and link to sources outside of the wiki, e.g. hyperlinks to websites. One of the reasons the lecturer liked the wiki was that she could build a knowledge repository of projects for future students to review when they start working on their projects. The knowledge storage facility is therefore another benefit of using wikis.

There are lots of collaboration tools available on the Internet (blogs, discussion forms, Google docs) but wikis, remain one of the simplest ways of creating large, shared information repositories. As other studies have shown students have found wikis to be beneficial when working on collaborative projects (Hulbert-Williams, 2010; Mirk, Burkiewicz, & Komperda, 2010). Wikis are not perfect, of course. Without a bit of thought and initial structure put into the wiki, the pages can become cumbersome and navigation is not as intuitive as it could be. The wiki was found to encourage student engagement in the projects and improve the instructor's ability to observe and to facilitate timely feedback. Overall, it was a positive experience and would be recommended for future project-based assignments.

ACKNOWLEDGMENT

The author would like to thank Colin Shine for his careful review of this chapter and for his constructive comments. The author would also like to thank Paul Gormley for the support he gave in implementing the wiki in the Product Design and Development class. Thanks also to Dr. Kathryn Cormican for her support of the use of wikis in the Product Design and Development class.

REFERENCES

Albert, A., Tobias, D., Moritz, D., Claudia, E., Mirko, M., & Christian, S. (2007). *Wikis as a cooperation and communication platform within product development*. Paper presented at International Conference on Engineering Design. Paris, France.

Benckendorff, P. (2008). Using wikis to enhance the creative collaboration and knowledge management skills of tourism students. In *Proceedings of CAUTHE 2008: Tourism and Hospitality Research, Training and Practice*, (p. 588). CAUTHE.

Blumenfeld, P. C., Soloway, E., Marx, R. W., Krajcik, J. S., Guzdial, M., & Palincsar, A. (1991). Motivating project-based learning: Sustaining the doing, supporting the learning. *Educational Psychologist, 26*(3/4), 369–398.

Boujut, J. F., & Tiger, H. (2002). A socio-technical research method for analysing and instrumenting the design activity. *Journal of Desert Research, 2*(2).

Bucciarelli, L. L. (2002). Between thought and object in engineering design. *Design Studies, 23*(3), 219–231. doi:10.1016/S0142-694X(01)00035-7

Carr, T., Morrison, A., Cox, G., & Deacon, A. (2007). Weathering wikis: Net-based learning meets political science in a South African university. *Computers and Composition, 24*(3), 266–284. doi:10.1016/j.compcom.2007.06.001

Chen, H. L., Cannon, D., Gabrio, J., Leifer, L., Toye, G., & Bailey, T. (2005). *Using wikis and weblogs to support reflective learning in an introductory engineering design course*. Paper presented at the American Society for Engineering Education Annual Conference & Exposition. Portland, OR.

Churchill, D. (2011). Web 2.0 in education: A study of the explorative use of blogs with a postgraduate class. *Innovations in Education and Teaching International, 48*(2), 149–158. doi:10.1080/1470 3297.2011.564009

Ciesielka, D. (2008). Using a wiki to meet graduate nursing education competencies in collaboration and community health. *The Journal of Nursing Education, 47*(10), 473–476. doi:10.3928/01484834-20081001-02

Citera, M., McNeese, M. D., Brown, C. E., Selvaraj, J. A., Zaff, B. S., & Whitaker, R. D. (1995). Fitting information systems to collaborating design teams. *Journal of the American Society for Information Science American Society for Information Science, 46*(7), 551–559. doi:10.1002/(SICI)1097-4571(199508)46:7<551::AID-ASI8>3.0.CO;2-1

Clough, G. (2005). *Educating the engineer of 2020: Adapting engineering education to the new century*. Washington, DC: National Academy Press.

Cole, M. (2009). Using wiki technology to support student engagement: Lessons from the trenches. *Computers & Education, 52*(1), 141–146. doi:10.1016/j.compedu.2008.07.003

Cross, N., & Clayburn Cross, A. (1995). Observations of teamwork and social processes in design. *Design Studies, 16*(2), 143–170. doi:10.1016/0142-694X(94)00007-Z

Ebersbach, A., Glaser, M., & Heigl, R. (2005). *Wiki: Web collaboration*. Dordrecht, The Netherlands: Springer-Verlag Berlin.

Elgort, I., Smith, A. G., & Toland, J. (2008). Is wiki an effective platform for group course work? *Educational Technology, 24*(2), 195–210.

Endean, M., Weidmann, G., Armstrong, A., Moffat, J., Nixon, T., & Reuben, B. (2008). Team project work for distance learners in engineering–Challenges and benefits. *Engineering Education: Journal of the Higher Education Academy Engineering Subject Centre, 3*(2), 11–20.

Grierson, H., Nicol, D., Littlejohn, A., & Wodehouse, A. (2004). *Structuring and sharing information resources to support concept development and design learning*. Paper presented at the Network Learning Conference. Exeter, UK.

Gupta, A., Denny, N. T., O'Toole, K., & Bondade, R. (2011). Global software development using the 24-hour knowledge factory paradigm. *International Journal of Computer Applications in Technology, 40*(3), 191–202. doi:10.1504/IJCAT.2011.039140

Hasan, H., & Pfaff, C. (2006). *Overcoming organisational resistance to using wiki technology for knowledge management*. Paper presented at the 10th Pacic Asia Conference on Information Systems. Kuala Lumpur, Malaysia.

Hemmi, A., Bayne, S., & Land, R. (2009). The appropriation and repurposing of social technologies in higher education. *Journal of Computer Assisted Learning, 25*(1), 19–30. doi:10.1111/j.1365-2729.2008.00306.x

Hertel, G., Geister, S., & Konradt, U. (2005). Managing virtual teams: A review of current empirical research. *Human Resource Management Review, 15*(1), 69–95. doi:10.1016/j.hrmr.2005.01.002

Hietikko, E., & Rajaniemi, E. (2000). Visualized data-tool to improve communication in distributed product development projects. *Journal of Engineering Design, 11*(1), 95–101. doi:10.1080/095448200261207

Hulbert-Williams, N. J. (2010). Facilitating collaborative learning using online wikis: Evaluation of their application within postgraduate psychology teaching. *Psychology Learning & Teaching, 9*(1), 45–51. doi:10.2304/plat.2010.9.1.45

Jarvenpaa, S. L., & Leidner, D. E. (1999). Communication and trust in global virtual teams. *Organization Science, 10*(6), 791–815. doi:10.1287/orsc.10.6.791

Karasavvidis, I. (2010). Wiki uses in higher education: Exploring barriers to successful implementation. *Interactive Learning Environments, 18*(3). doi:10.1080/10494820.2010.500514

Leuf, B., & Cunningham, W. (2001). *The wiki way: Quick collaboration on the web*. Boston, MA: Addison-Wesley.

Lundin, R. W. (2008). Teaching with wikis: Toward a networked pedagogy. *Computers and Composition, 25*(4), 432–448. doi:10.1016/j.compcom.2008.06.001

Maier, A. M., Kreimeyer, M., Hepperle, C., Eckert, C. M., Lindemann, U., & Clarkson, P. J. (2008). Exploration of correlations between factors influencing communication in complex product development. *Concurrent Engineering, 16*(1), 37. doi:10.1177/1063293X07084638

Martins, L. L., Gilson, L. L., & Maynard, M. T. (2004). Virtual teams: What do we know and where do we go from here? *Journal of Management, 30*(6), 805. doi:10.1016/j.jm.2004.05.002

Minocha, S., Petre, M., & Roberts, D. (2008). Using wikis to simulate distributed requirements development in a software engineering course. *International Journal of Engineering Education, 24*(4), 689–704.

Mirk, S. M., Burkiewicz, J. S., & Komperda, K. E. (2010). Student perception of a wiki in a pharmacy elective course. *Currents in Pharmacy Teaching and Learning, 2*(2), 72–78. doi:10.1016/j.cptl.2010.01.002

Nonaka, I. (1994). A dynamic theory of organizational knowledge creation. *Organization Science, 5*(1), 14–37. doi:10.1287/orsc.5.1.14

Parker, K. R., & Chao, J. T. (2007). Wikis as a teaching tool. *Interdisciplinary Journal of Knowledge and Learning Objects, 3*, 16.

Raman, M., Ryan, T., & Olfman, L. (2005). Designing knowledge management systems for teaching and learning with wiki technology. *Journal of Information Systems Education, 16*(3), 311.

Richardson, W. (2009). *Blogs, wikis, podcasts, and other powerful web tools for classrooms* (2nd ed.). Thousand Oaks, CA: Corwin Press.

Rick, J., & Guzdial, M. (2006). Situating CoWeb: A scholarship of application. *International Journal of Computer-Supported Collaborative Learning, 1*(1), 89–115. doi:10.1007/s11412-006-6842-6

Saleh, N., & McKinnon, S. (2009). *MineWiki: The use of wiki technology as a tool in a senior mine design course.* Paper presented at the 6th Canadian Design Engineering Network (CDEN) Annual Conference. Hamilton, Canada.

Standing, C., & Kiniti, S. (2011). How can organizations use wikis for innovation? *Technovation, 31*(7), 287–295. doi:10.1016/j.technovation.2011.02.005

Tapscott, D., & Williams, A. (2006). *Wikinomics: How mass collaboration changes everything.* New York, NY: Penguin Group Publishers.

Vratulis, V., & Dobson, T. M. (2008). Social negotiations in a wiki environment: A case study with pre service teachers. *Educational Media International, 45*(4), 285–294. doi:10.1080/09523980802571531

Wagner, C., & Bolloju, N. (2005). Supporting knowledge management in organizations with conversational technologies: Discussion forums, weblogs, and wikis. *Journal of Database Management, 16*(2).

West, J. A., & West, M. L. (2009). *Using wikis for online collaboration: The power of the read-write web.* San Francisco, CA: Jossey-Bass Inc Pub.

Wheeler, S., Yeomans, P., & Wheeler, D. (2008). The good, the bad and the wiki: Evaluating student generated content for collaborative learning. *British Journal of Educational Technology, 39*(6), 987–995. doi:10.1111/j.1467-8535.2007.00799.x

Wodehouse, A., Grierson, H., Ion, W., Juster, N., Lynn, A., & Stone, A. (2004). *TikiWiki: A tool to support engineering design students in concept generation.* Paper presented at the International Engineering and Product Design Education Conference. Delft, The Netherlands.

Wodehouse, A. J., Grierson, H. J., Breslin, C., Eris, O., Ion, W. J., & Leifer, L. J. (2010). A framework for design engineering education in a global context. *Artificial Intelligence for Engineering Design, Analysis and Manufacturing, 24*(3), 367–378. doi:10.1017/S0890060410000259

ADDITIONAL READING

Barr, T. F., Dixon, A. L., & Gassenheimer, J. B. (2005). Exploring the "lone wolf" phenomenon in student teams. *Journal of Marketing Education, 27*(1), 81. doi:10.1177/0273475304273459

Benckendorff, P. (2009). Evaluating wikis as an assessment tool for developing collaboration and knowledge management skills. *Journal of Hospitality and Tourism Management, 16*(1), 102–112. doi:10.1375/jhtm.16.1.102

Bonk, C. J. (2009). *The world is open: How web technology is revolutionizing education.* San Francisco, CA: Wiley.

Borgman, C. L., Abelson, H., Dirks, L., Johnson, R., Koedinger, K. R., & Linn, M. C. (2008). *Fostering learning in the networked world: The cyberlearning opportunity and challenge, a 21st century agenda for the national science foundation.* Washington, DC: NSF.

Bucciarelli, L. L. (2002). Between thought and object in engineering design. *Design Studies, 23*(3), 219–231. doi:10.1016/S0142-694X(01)00035-7

Chatfield, T. B. (2009). *The complete guide to wikis: How to set up, use, and benefit from wikis for teachers, business professionals, families, and friends.* Ocala, FL: Atlantic Pub Co.

de Eyto, A., Mc Mahon, M., Hadfield, M., & Hutchings, M. (2008). Strategies for developing sustainable design practice for students and SME professionals. *European Journal of Engineering Education.* Retrieved from http://eprints.bournemouth.ac.uk/10693/1/deEyto_McMahon__Hadfield_Hutchings_EJEE_(2).pdf

Gibson, I. S. (2003). From solo-run to mainstream thinking: Project-based learning in engineering design. *European Journal of Engineering Education, 28*(3), 331–337. doi:10.1080/0304379031000108768

Grace, T. P. L. (2009). Wikis as a knowledge management tool. *Journal of Knowledge Management, 13*(4), 64–74. doi:10.1108/13673270910971833

Hazari, S., North, A., & Moreland, D. (2009). Investigating pedagogical value of wiki technology. *Journal of Information Systems Education, 20*(2), 187–198.

Johri, A., & Olds, B. (2011). Situated engineering learning: Bridging engineering education research and the learning sciences. *Journal of Engineering Education, 100*(1), 151–185.

Mader, S. (2008). *Wikipatterns.* New York, NY: Wiley.

McKay, A., & Raffo, D. (2007). Project-based learning: A case study in sustainable design. *International Journal of Engineering Education, 23*(6), 1096–1115.

Mindel, J. L., & Verma, S. (2006). Wikis for teaching and learning. *Communications of the Association for Information Systems, 18*(1), 1.

Moursund, D., Boss, S., Krauss, J., Polman, J., Ronis, D., & Warlick, D. (2002). *Project-based learning: Using information technology.* Worthington, OH: Linworth Publishing.

Okudan, G. E., & Zappe, S. E. (2006). Teaching product design to non-engineers: A review of experience, opportunities and problems. *Technovation, 26*(11), 1287–1293. doi:10.1016/j.technovation.2005.10.009

Palmer, S., & Hall, W. (2011). An evaluation of a project-based learning initiative in engineering education. *European Journal of Engineering Education, 36*(4), 357–365. doi:10.1080/03043797.2011.593095

Prince, M. J., & Felder, R. M. (2006). Inductive teaching and learning methods: Definitions, comparisons, and research bases. *Journal of Engineering Education, 95*(2), 123–138.

Raman, M., Ryan, T., & Olfman, L. (2005). Designing knowledge management systems for teaching and learning with wiki technology. *Journal of Information Systems Education, 16*(3), 311.

Rosenberg, M. J. (2001). *E-learning: Strategies for delivering knowledge in the digital age* (*Vol. 9*). New York, NY: McGraw-Hill.

Sallis, E., & Jones, G. (2002). *Knowledge management in education: Enhancing learning & education*. London, UK: Routledge.

Schaffert, S. (2006). Ikewiki: A semantic wiki for collaborative knowledge management. In *Proceedings of the 1st International Workshop on Semantic Technologies in Collaborative Applications (STICA)*. STICA.

Sibley, J., & Parmelee, D. X. (2008). Knowledge is no longer enough: Enhancing professional education with team based learning. *New Directions for Teaching and Learning, 116*, 41–53. doi:10.1002/tl.332

Turnbull, M., Littlejohn, A., & Allan, M. (2010). Creativity and collaborative learning and teaching strategies in the design disciplines. *Industry and Higher Education, 24*(2), 127–133. doi:10.5367/000000010791191029

KEY TERMS AND DEFINITIONS

Learning Management System (LMS): A Learning Management System is a software package that enables the management and delivery of learning content and resources to students via a Web browser.

Project Deliverable: Any item produced as the outcome of a project. Deliverables must be tangible and verifiable.

Project-Based Learning: Project-based learning begins with an assignment to carry out one or more tasks that lead to the production of a final product. The culmination of the product is a written and/or oral presentation.

Web 2.0: The term used to describe a variety of websites and application that allow users to create and share information or material.

Wiki: A wiki is a website that allows the creation and editing of a Web page via a Web browser.

Compilation of References

Ackoff, R. L. (1989). From data to wisdom. *Journal of Applied Systems Analysis*, *16*(1), 3–9.

Agrawal, A. (2001). University-to-industry knowledge transfer: Literature review and unanswered questions. *International Journal of Management Reviews*, *3*(4), 285–302. doi:10.1111/1468-2370.00069

Agrawal, A., & Henderson, R. M. (2002). Putting patents in context: Exploring knowledge transfer from MIT. *Management Science*, *48*(1), 44–60. doi:10.1287/mnsc.48.1.44.14279

Ahmed, P. K., Lim, K. K., & Zairi, M. (1999). Measurement practice for knowledge management. *Journal of Workplace Learning: Employee Counseling Today*, *11*, 304–311.

Ahuja, G., & Katila, R. (2001). Technological acquisitions and the innovation performance of acquiring firms: A longitudinal study. *Strategic Management Journal*, *22*, 197–220. doi:10.1002/smj.157

Ahuja, G., & Lampert, C. (2001). Entrepreneurship in the large corporation: A longitudinal study of how established firms create breakthrough inventions. *Strategic Management Journal*, *22*, 521–543. doi:10.1002/smj.176 doi:10.1002/smj.176

Akgun, A. E., Byrne, J. C., Lynn, G. S., & Keskin, H. (2007). Team stressors, management support, and project and process outcomes in new development projects. *Techinnovation*, *27*(10), 628–639. doi:10.1016/j.technovation.2007.02.008

Akkermans, H. (2008). *Organizational climate as an intervening variable between leadership behaviour and innovative productivity: An exploratory study*. Retrieved 15 May, 2011, from http:77www.s-d.be/assets/Thesissen-HR-Award-2009/HUBrusselHnsAkkermans.pdf

Al-Alawi, A. I., Al-Marzooqi, N. Y., & Mohammed, Y. F. (2007). Organizational culture and knowledge sharing: Critical success factors. *Journal of Knowledge Management*, *11*(2), 22–42. doi:10.1108/13673270710738898

Alavi, M., & Leidner, D. E. (1999). Knowledge management systems: Issues, challenges, and benefits. *Communications of the Association for Information Systems*, *1*(7), 1–37.

Alavi, M., & Leidner, D. E. (2001). Review: Knowledge management and knowledge management systems: Conceptual foundations and research issues. *Management Information Systems Quarterly*, *25*(1), 107–136. doi:10.2307/3250961

Alazmi, M., & Zairi, M. (2003). Knowledge management critical success factors. *Total Quality Management*, *14*(2), 199–204. doi:10.1080/1478336032000051386

Albert, A., Tobias, D., Moritz, D., Claudia, E., Mirko, M., & Christian, S. (2007). *Wikis as a cooperation and communication platform within product development*. Paper presented at International Conference on Engineering Design. Paris, France.

Albrecht, W. (2002, March-April). Accounting education on the edge. *BizEd*, 41-45.

Albrecht, C. C., Romney, M., Lowry, P. B., & Moody, G. (2009). The IS core: An integration of the core IS courses. *Journal of Information Systems Education*, *20*(4), 451–468.

Alferoff, C., & Knights, D. (2009). Making and mending your nets: Managing relevance, participation and uncertainty in academic-practitioner knowledge networks. *British Journal of Management, 20*(18), 125–140. doi:10.1111/j.1467-8551.2007.00556.x

Alford, K. L., Carter, C. A., Ragsdale, D. J., Ressler, E. K., & Reynolds, C. W. (2004). Specification and managed development of information technology curricula. In *Proceedings of the 5th Conference on Information Technology Education*, (pp. 261-266). IEEE.

Allam, C. (2008). *Creative activity and its impact on student learning – Issues of implementation learning and teaching services*. Sheffield, UK: University of Sheffield.

Allee, V. (1997). *The knowledge evolution: Expanding organizational intelligence*. Newton, MA: Butterworth-Heinemann.

Altmeyer, D., & Georg, S. (2002). *Die bedeutung von wissensmanagement für unternehmen*. Aachen, Germany: Shaker Verlag.

Alvesson, M. (2001). Knowledge work: Ambiguity, image and identity. *Human Relations, 54*(7), 863–886. doi:10.1177/0018726701547004

Alvesson, M. (2004). *Knowledge work and knowledge-intensive firms*. Oxford, UK: Oxford University Press.

Alvesson, M., & Kärreman, D. (2001). Odd couple: Making sense of the curious concept of knowledge management. *Journal of Management Studies, 38*(7), 995–1018. doi:10.1111/1467-6486.00269

Alvesson, M., Kärreman, D., & Swan, J. (2002). Departures from knowledge and/or management in knowledge management. *Management Communication Quarterly, 16*(2), 282–291. doi:10.1177/089331802237242

Alwis, R. S., & Hartmann, E. (2008). The use of tacit knowledge within innovative companies: Knowledge management in innovative enterprises. *Journal of Knowledge Management, 12*(1), 133–147. doi:10.1108/13673270810852449

Amabile, T. M. (1988). A model of creativity and innovation in organizations. In B. M. Staw & L. Cummings (Eds.), *Research in Organizational Behavior* (Vol. 10). Greenwich, CT: JAI Press.

Amabile, T. M. (1996). *Creativity in context*. Oxford, UK: Westview.

Amabile, T. M. (1983). *The social psychology of creativity*. New York, NY: Basic Books. doi:10.1007/978-1-4612-5533-8

Amabile, T. M. (1993). Motivational synergy: Toward new conceptualization of intrinsic and extrinsic motivation in the workplace. *Human Resource Management Review, 3*(3), 185–201. doi:10.1016/1053-4822(93)90012-S doi:10.1016/1053-4822(93)90012-S

Amabile, T. M., Conti, R., Coon, H., Lazenby, J., & Herron, M. (1996). Assessing the work environment for creativity. *Academy of Management Journal, 39*, 1154–1184. doi:10.2307/256995 doi:10.2307/256995

Amabile, T. M., & Gryskiewicz, N. D. (1989). The creative environment scales: Work environment inventory. *Creativity Research Journal, 2*, 231–253. doi:10.1080/10400418909534321

Amabile, T. M., Schatzel, E. A., Moneta, G. B., & Kramer, S. J. (2004). Leader behaviors and the work environment for creativity: Perceived leader support. *The Leadership Quarterly, 15*(1), 5–32. doi:10.1016/j.leaqua.2003.12.003 doi:10.1016/j.leaqua.2003.12.003

Ambrosini, V., Bowman, C., & Collier, N. (2009). Dynamic capabilities: An exploration of how firms renew their resource base. *British Journal of Management, 20*(S1), S9–S24. doi:10.1111/j.1467-8551.2008.00610.x

Amidon, D. (1997). *Innovation strategy for the knowledge economy: The ken awakening*. Boston, MA: Butterworth-Heinemann.

Amidon, D. M. (2003). *The innovation superhighway*. Amsterdam, The Netherlands: Butterworth-Heinemann.

Anatan, L. (2007). Innovation as core competencies: The role of knowledge and organizational learning in knowledge-based competition era. *Jurnal Manajemen, 9*(2), 87–99.

Anderson, P. H., & Lawton, L. (2009). Business simulations and cognitive learning. *Simulation & Gaming, 40*, 193–216. doi:10.1177/1046878108321624

Andreou, A. N., Green, A., & Stankosky, M. (2007). A framework of intangible valuation areas and antecedents. *Journal of Intellectual Capital*, 8(1), 52–75. doi:10.1108/14691930710715060

Andreou, A. N., Green, A., & Stankosky, M. (2007). A framework of intangible valuation areas and antecedents. *Journal of Intellectual Capital*, 8, 52–75. doi:10.1108/14691930710715060

Andriessen, D. (2003). IC valuation and measurement-Why and how? *PMA IC Research Symposium*. Retrieved Nov 2006 from http://www.weightlesswealth.com/Publications%20and%20downloads_files%5CPaper%20Andriessen%20PMA%202003.pdf

Andriessen, D. (2004). *Making sense of intellectual capital – Designing a method for the valuation of intangibles*. Amsterdam, The Netherlands: Elsevier Butterworth-Heninemann.

Andriessen, D. G. (2008). Stuff or love? How metaphors direct our efforts to manage knowledge in organisations. *Knowledge Management Research & Practice*, 6, 5–12. doi:10.1057/palgrave.kmrp.8500169

Ankiewicz, P. J., & De Swardt, A. E. (2002). *Aspects to be taken into account when compiling a learning programme to support effective facilitation of technology education*. Paper presented at the National Conference for Technology Teachers. Durban, South Africa.

Antonacopoulou, E., & Easterby-Smith, M. (2005). *Dynamic capabilities and organizational learning: Advanced institute of* management research paper no. 014. Retrieved 14/08/2010 from http://papers.ssrn.com/sol3/papers.cfm?abstract_id=1306958

APC.org. (2005). *Internet & ICTs for social justice and development news*. Retrieved from http://www.apc.org/english/news/index.shtml?x=5038198

Aranson, Z. H., Reilly, R. R., & Lynn, G. S. (2006). The impact of leader personality on new product development teamwork and performance: The moderating role of uncertainty. *Journal of Engineering and Technology Management*, 23(3), 221–247. doi:10.1016/j.jengtecman.2006.06.003

Argote, L. (2011). Organizational learning research: Past, present and future. *Management Learning*, 42(4), 439–446. doi:10.1177/1350507611408217

Argote, L., Beckman, S., & Epple, D. (1990). The persistence and transfer of learning in industrial settings. *Management Science*, 36, 1750–1763. doi:10.1287/mnsc.36.2.140

Argote, L., & Ingram, P. (2000). Knowledge transfer: A basis for competitive advantage in firms. *Organizational Behavior and Human Decision Processes*, 82(1), 150–169. doi:10.1006/obhd.2000.2893

Arguello, J., Butler, B., Joyce, E., Kraut, R., Ling, K. S., & Wang, X. (2006). Talk to me: Foundations for successful individual-Group interactions in online communities. In *Proceedings of CHI 2006*. ACM Press.

Argyris, C., & Schon, D. A. (1978). *Organizational learning: A theory of action perspective*. Reading, MA: Addison-Wesley Publishing.

Armitage, I. (2010). Fundamo: Providing a mobile platform. *African Business Review*. Retrieved 10 July 2010, from http://www.technology-digital.com/company-reports/fundamo

Arora, R. (2002). Implementing KM: A balanced scorecard approach. *Journal of Knowledge Management*, 6(3), 240–249. doi:10.1108/13673270210434340

Arrington, M., & Schonfeld, E. (2008). *The real twitter usage numbers*. Retrieved from http://www.techcrunch.com/2008/04/29/end-of-speculation-the-reral-twitter-usage-numbers/

Arthur, W. B. (1996). Increasing returns and the new world of business. *Harvard Business Review*, 74(4), 100–109.

Arvanitis, S., Kubli, U., & Woerter, M. (2008). University-industry knowledge and technology transfer in Switzerland: What university scientists think about co-operation with private enterprises. *Research Policy*, 37, 1865–1883. doi:10.1016/j.respol.2008.07.005

Atkinson, P. (1995). *Medical talk and medical work*. Thousand Oaks, CA: Sage Publications.

Audretsch, D. B. (2006). *Entrepreneurship, innovation and economic growth*. Northampton, MA: Edward Elgar Publishing Limited. doi:10.1093/acprof:oso/9780195183511.001.0001doi:10.1093/acprof:oso/9780195183511.001.0001

Auernhammer, K., Leslie, A., Neumann, M., & Lettice, F. (2003). Creation of innovation by knowledge management – A case study of a learning software organisation. In *Proceedings of WM 2003: Professionelles Wissesmanagement - Erfahrungen und Visionen*, (pp. 53-57). WM.

Austin Free-Net. (2012). *Blogging!* Retrieved from http://www.austinfree.net/curricula/blogging_curriculum.html

Autio, E., Sapienza, H. J., & Almeida, J. G. (2000). Effects of age at entry, knowledge intensity, and imitability on international growth. *Organization Science, 43*(5), 909–924.

AUTM. (2012). *The association of university technology managers website*. Retrieved from http://www.autm.net

Avelini Holjevac, I. (2002). *Upravljanje kvalitetom u turizmu i hotelskoj industriji*. Opatija, Croatia: Fakultet za Menadžment u Turizmu i Ugostiteljstvu.

Axup, J. (2012). *Mobile community design*. Retrieved from http://www.mobilecommunitydesign.com/pages/faq.html

Badran, I. (2007). Enhancing creativity and innovation in engineering education. *European Journal of Engineering Education, 32*(5), 573–585. doi:10.1080/03043790701433061

Bahtijarević Šiber, F. (1999). *Management ljudskih potencijala*. Zagreb, Croatia: Golden Marketing.

Baldrige National Quality Program. (2007). *Criteria for performance excellence*. Gaithersburg, MD: Baldrige National Quality Program.

Bandura, A. (1977). *Social learning theory*. Englewood Cliffs, NJ: Prentice-Hall.

Barkema, H. G., & Vermeulen, F. (1998). International expansion through start-up or acquisition: A learning perspective. *Academy of Management Journal, 41*(1), 7–26. doi:10.2307/256894

Barnett, H. G. (1953). *Innovation: The basis of cultural change*. New York, NY: McGraw-Hill.

Barney, J. B. (1991). Firm resources and sustained competitive advantage. *Journal of Management, 17*(1), 99–120. doi:10.1177/014920639101700108

Barron, F. (1988). Putting creativity to work. In R. J. Sternberg (Ed.), *The Nature of Creativity: Contemporary Psychological Perspectives*. New York, NY: Cambridge University Press.

Barron, F., & Harrington, D. (1981). Creativity, intelligence, and personality. *Annual Review of Psychology, 32*, 439–476. doi:10.1146/annurev.ps.32.020181.002255 doi:10.1146/annurev.ps.32.020181.002255

Barsh, Capozzi, & Davidson. (2008). Leadership and innovation. *McKinsey Quarterly*. Retrieved from http://www.mckinseyquarterly.com/Leadership_and_innovation_2089

Bartlett, S. J. (2008). *The abnormal psychology of creativity and the pathology of normality*. Retrieved June 20, 2011, from http://www.mendeley.com/research/abnormal-psychology-creativity-pathology-normality/# Basadur, M., & Gelade, G. (2006). The role of knowledge management in the innovation process. *Creativity and Innovation Management, 15*(1), 45- 62.

Bartlett, C., & Goshal, S. (1989). *Managing across borders: The transnational solution*. Boston, MA: Harvard Business School Press.

Basdekis, I., Klironomos, I., Antona, M., & Stephanidis, C. (2006). *Online communities for all: The role of design for all in the formation and support of inclusive online communities*. Paper presented at the International Design for All Conference 2006. Rovaniemi, Finland.

Bates, T. (2000). *Managing technological change: Strategies for college and university leaders*. San Francisco, CA: Jossey-Bass.

Baum, J. R. (2003*). Entrepreneurs' start-up cognitions and behaviours: Dreams, surprises, shortages, and fast zigzags*. Paper presented at the Babson-Kauffman Entrepreneurship Research Conference. Wellesley, MA.

Baum, J. R., & Locke, E. A. (2004). The relationship of entrepreneurial traits, skill, and motivation to subsequent venture growth. *The Journal of Applied Psychology, 89*(4), 587–598. doi:10.1037/0021-9010.89.4.587

Baxter, W. T. (1971). *Depreciation.* London, UK: Sweet & Maxwell.

Beazley, H. (2003*). Knowledge continuity: The new competitive advantage.* Retrieved April 13, 2010, from http://www.asaecenter.org/PublicationsResources/EUArticle.cfm?ItemNumber=11836

Beazley, H., Boenisch, J., & Harden, D. (2002). *Continuity management: Preserving corporate knowledge and productivity when employees leave.* New York, NY: Wiley.

Becker, B., & Gerhart, B. (1996). The impact of human resource management on organizational performance: Progress and prospects. *Academy of Management Journal, 39*(4), 779–801. doi:10.2307/256712

Becker, G. S. (1993). *Human capital: A theoretical and empirical analysis, with special reference to education* (3rd ed.). Chicago, IL: The University of Chicago Press.

Beckman, T. (1997). *A methodology for knowledge management.* Paper presented at the AI and Soft Computing Conference. Banff, Canada.

Beenen, G., Ling, K., Wang, X., Chang, K., Resnick, P., & Kraut, R. E. (2004). *Using social psychology to motivate contributions to online communities.* Retrieved from http://www.si.umich.edu/~presnick/papers/cscw04preprint.pdf

Behrens, T. R., & Gray, D. O. (2001). Unintended consequences of cooperative research: Impact of industry sponsorship on climate for academic freedom and other graduate student outcome. *Research Policy, 30*(2), 179–199. doi:10.1016/S0048-7333(99)00112-2

Beijerse, R. (1999). Questions in knowledge management: Defining and conceptualizing a phenomenon. *Journal of Knowledge Management, 3*(2), 94–110. doi:10.1108/13673279910275512

Bell, B. S., Kanar, A. M., & Kozlowski, S. W. (2008). Current issues and future directions in simulation-based training in North America. *International Journal of Human Resource Management, 19*, 1416–1434. doi:10.1080/09585190802200173

Ben Aharon, N. (2000). *Policy for innovation and creativity in traditional industry.* Jerusalem, Israel: Jerusalem Institute for Israel Study.

Benckendorff, P. (2008). Using wikis to enhance the creative collaboration and knowledge management skills of tourism students. In *Proceedings of CAUTHE 2008: Tourism and Hospitality Research, Training and Practice,* (p. 588). CAUTHE.

Bender, S., & Fish, A. (2000). The transfer of knowledge and the retention of expertise: The continuing need for global assignments. *Journal of Knowledge Management, 4*(2), 125–137. doi:10.1108/13673270010372251

Berardi, F. (2009). *The soul at work: From alienation to autonomy.* Los Angeles, CA: Semiotext(e).

Berardi, F. (2007). Technology and knowledge in a universe on indetermination. *SubStance, 36*(1), 57–74. doi:10.1353/sub.2007.0000

Bercovitz, J., & Feldman, M. (2006). Entrepreneurial universities and technology transfer: A conceptual framework for understanding knowledge-based economic development. *The Journal of Technology Transfer, 31*(1), 175–188. doi:10.1007/s10961-005-5029-z

Bereiter, C., Scardamalia, M., Cassells, C., & Hewitt, J. (1997). Postmodernism, knowledge building, and elementary science. *The Elementary School Journal, 97,* 329–340. doi:10.1086/461869

Bergan, S. (2009). Presentación. In Alonso, L. E., Fernández Rodríguez, C. J., & Nyssen, J. M. (Eds.), *El Debate Sobre las Competencias: Una Investigación Qualitativa en Torno a la Educacíon Superior y el Mercado de Trabajo en España.* Madrid, Spain: ANECA.

Berlyne, D. (1967). Arousal and reinforcement. In D. Levine (Ed.), *Nebraska Symposium on Motivation.* Lincoln, NE: University of Nebraska Press.

Besterfield, D. H., Besterfiell-Michna, C., Besterfield, G. H., & Besterfield-Sacre, M. (1999). *Total quality management.* Upper Saddle River, NJ: Prentice Hall.

Bettis, R. A., & Prahalad, C. K. (1995). The dominant logic: Retrospective and extension. *Strategic Management Journal, 16*(1), 5–14. doi:10.1002/smj.4250160104

Bhardwaj, M., & Monin, J. (2006). Tacit to explicit: an interplay shaping organization knowledge. *Journal of Knowledge Management, 10*(3), 72–85. doi:10.1108/13673270610670867

Bhatt, G. D. (2000). Organizing knowledge in the knowledge development cycle. *Journal of Knowledge Management, 4*(1), 15–26. doi:10.1108/13673270010315371

Bierly, P., & Daly, P. (2002). Aligning human resource management practices and knowledge strategies. In Choo, C. W., & Bontis, N. (Eds.), *The Strategic Management of Intellectual Capital and Organizational Knowledge* (pp. 277–295). Oxford, UK: Oxford University Press.

Bijker, W. E., & Luciano, D. A. (Eds.). (2009). *Handbook on the socialization of scientific and technological research social sciences and European research capacities (SS-ERC) project*. Geneva, Switzerland: FP6.

Bilodeau, E. (2003). *Using communities of practice to enhance student learning: Examples and issues*. Retrieved from http://www.coolweblog.com/bilodeau/docs/2003-10-01-cop-enhancing-student-learning.pdf

Biloslavo, R., & Trnavčevič, A. (2007). Knowledge management audit in a higher educational institution: A case study. *Knowledge and Process Management, 14*(4), 275–286. doi:10.1002/kpm.293

Bishir, J. W., & Drewes, D. W. (1970). *Mathematics in the behavioural and social sciences*. New York, NY: Harcourt, Brace & World Inc.

Bis, R. (2009). Financing innovation: A project finance approach to funding patentable innovation. *Intellectual Property & Technology Law Journal, 21*(11), 23–45.

Blackler, F. (1995). Knowledge, knowledge work and organizations: An overview and interpretation. *Organization Studies, 16*(6), 1021–1046. doi:10.1177/017084069501600605

Blair, M. M. (2005). Closing the theory gap: How the economic theory of property rights can help bring "stakeholders" back into theories of the firm. *Journal of Management and Government, 9*, 33–39. Retrieved from http://www.springerlink.com/content/p744646n5qw22h66/ doi:10.1007/s10997-005-1566-y

Blair, M. M., & Wallman, S. M. (2001). *Unseen wealth: Report of the Brookings task force on intangibles*. Washington, DC: Brookings Institution Press.

Blumberg, P. (2009). Maximizing learning through course alignment and experience with different types of knowledge. *Innovative Higher Education, 34*, 93–103. doi:10.1007/s10755-009-9095-2

Blumenfeld, P. C., Soloway, E., Marx, R. W., Krajcik, J. S., Guzdial, M., & Palincsar, A. (1991). Motivating project-based learning: Sustaining the doing, supporting the learning. *Educational Psychologist, 26*(3/4), 369–398.

Blumenthal, D., Gluck, M., Louis, K. S., Stoto, M. A., & Wise, D. (1986). University-industry research relationships in biotechnology - Implications for the university. *Science, 232*(4756), 1361–1366. doi:10.1126/science.3715452

Boden, M. (1998). Creativity and artificial intelligence. *Artificial Intelligence, 103*(1-2), 347–356. doi:10.1016/S0004-3702(98)00055-1 doi:10.1016/S0004-3702(98)00055-1

Boisot, M. H. (1998). *Knowledge assets: Securing competitive advantage in the information economy*. Oxford, UK: Oxford University Press.

Boix-Mansilla, V. (2010). *MYP guide to interdisciplinary teaching and learning*. Wales, UK: International Baccalaureate.

Bolton, E. B. (1980). A conceptual analysis of the mentor relationship in the career development of women. *Adult Education, 30*, 195–207. doi:10.1177/074171368003000401

Bonaccorsi, A., & Piccaluga, A. (1994). A theoretical framework for the evaluation of university-industry relationships. *R & D Management, 24*(3), 229–247. doi:10.1111/j.1467-9310.1994.tb00876.x

Bonner, D. (2000). *Leading knowledge management and learning*. Alexandria, VA: American Society of Training & Development.

Bontis, N. (1998). Intellectual capital: An exploratory study that develops measures and models. *Management Decision, 36*(2), 63–76. doi:10.1108/00251749810204142

Bontis, N. (1999). Managing organizational knowledge by diagnosing intellectual capital: Framing and advancing the state of the field. *International Journal of Technology Management, 18*(6), 433–462. doi:10.1504/IJTM.1999.002780

Bontis, N. (1999). The knowledge toolbox: A review of the tools available to measure and manage intangible resources. *European Management Journal, 17*, 391–402. doi:10.1016/S0263-2373(99)00019-5

Borg, E. A. (2001). Knowledge, information and intellectual property: Implications for marketing relationships. *Technovation, 21*(8), 515–524. doi:10.1016/S0166-4972(00)00066-3

Boswell, W. R., & Bondreau, J. W. (2001). How leading companies create, measure and achieve strategic results through 'line of sight'. *Measurement Decision, 39*(10), 851–859. doi:10.1108/EUM0000000006525

Botkin, J., Elmandjira, M., & Malitza, M. (1979). *No limits to learning: Bridging the human gap: Report to the club of Rome*. New York, NY: Pergamon Press.

Boujut, J. F., & Tiger, H. (2002). A socio-technical research method for analysing and instrumenting the design activity. *Journal of Desert Research, 2*(2).

Bower, J. L., & Christensen, C. M. (1995). Disruptive technologies: Catching the wave. *Harvard Business Review*. Retrieved from http://www.cc.gatech.edu/~spencer/courses/ethics/misc/bower.pdf

Bratianu, C. (2004, May). Entrepreneurial dimensions in the Romanian higher education: Letters from the Black Sea. *International Journal of the Black Sea Universities Network*, 34-37.

Bratianu, C., & Vasilache, S. (2009). Implementing innovation and knowledge management in the Romanian economy. In *Proceedings of the Fourth International KMO Conference*. Taipei, Taiwan: KMO.

Brătianu, C., & Lefter, V. (2001). *Management strategic universitar*. Bucureşti, Romania: Editura Rao.

Bratianu, C., & Vasilache, S. (2009). Implementing innovation and knowledge management in the Romanian economy. *Management & Marketing, 4*(4), 3–14.

Brennan, L. (2005). *Integrating work base learning into higher education: A guide to good practice*. Boston, MA: University Vocational Awards Council.

Brooking, A. (1996). *Intellectual capital: Core asset for the third millennium*. London, UK: International Thomson Business Press.

Brooks, H. (1982). *Social and technological innovation*. New York, NY: Pergamon Press.

Brown, J., & Duguid, P. (1992). *Stolen knowledge: Educational technology publications*. Retrieved from http://tech-head.com/learning.htm

Brown, S., & Eisenhardt, K. (1998). *Competing on the edge: Strategy as structured chaos*. Boston, MA: Harvard Business School Press.

Brown, J. S., Collins, A., & Duguid, P. (1989). Situated cognition and the culture of learning. *Educational Researcher, 18*(1), 32–42.

Brown, J. S., & Duguid, P. (1991). Organizational learning and communities-of-practice: Toward a unified view of working, learning and innovation. *Organization Science, 2*(1), 40–57. doi:10.1287/orsc.2.1.40

Brown, J. S., & Duguid, P. (1998). Organizing knowledge. *California Management Review, 40*(3), 90–111.

Brunner, J. J. (2009). Prólogo. In Alonso, L. E., Fernández Rodríguez, C. J., & Nyssen, J. M. (Eds.), *El Debate Sobre las Competencias: Una Investigación Qualitativa en Torno a la Educacíon Superior y el Mercado de Trabajo en España*. Madrid, Spain: ANECA.

Bruno, D., Frederick, A. S., Gary, A. M., & Michael, M. (2005). Learning to build a car: An empirical investigation of organizational learning. *Journal of Management Studies, 42*(2), 387–416. doi:10.1111/j.1467-6486.2005.00501.x

Bucciarelli, L. L. (2002). Between thought and object in engineering design. *Design Studies, 23*(3), 219–231. doi:10.1016/S0142-694X(01)00035-7

Buckley, S. B. (2009). *Knowledge sharing through communities of practice at institutions of higher education*. Johannesburg, South Africa: University of Johannesburg.

Buckley, S., & Du Toit, A. (2010). Academics leave your ivory tower: Form communities of practice. *Educational Studies, 36*(5), 493–503. doi:10.1080/03055690903425532

Butler, T., Heavin, C., & O'Donovan, F. (2007). A theoretical model and framework for understanding knowledge management system implementation. *Journal of Organizational and End User Computing, 19*(4), 1–21. doi:10.4018/joeuc.2007100101

Byosiere, P., & Luethge, D. J. (2008). Knowledge domains and knowledge conversion: an empirical investigation. *Journal of Knowledge Management, 12*(2), 67–78. doi:10.1108/13673270810859523

Caballero, F. G., Piñeiro, G. P., & García-Pintos, A. (2008). Las prácticas en empresas en la universidad española? Cómo son los centros universitários más involucrados? In Neira, (Eds.), *Investigaciones de Economía de la Educación*. Madrid, Spain: AEDE.

Cabrera, À., & Cabreta, E. F. (2002). Knowledge-sharing dilemmas. *Organization Studies, 23*(5), 687–710. doi:10.1177/0170840602235001

Cabrilo, S. (2008). *Researching indicators of intellectual capital within organization.* Unpublished Doctorial Dissertation. Novi Sad, Serbia: University of Novi Sad.

Cabrilo, S. (2009). IC-based inter-industry variety in Serbia. In C. Stam & D. Andriessen (Eds.), *1st European Conference on Intellectual Capital,* (pp. 104-114). Haarlem, The Netherlands: Academic Publishing Limited.

Cabrilo, S., & Grubic-Nesic, L. (2010). A strategic model for intellectual capital reporting: Study of service industry in Serbia. In S. C. Serrano Fernandes Rodrigues (Ed.), *2nd European Conference on Intellectual Capital,* (pp. 161-170). Lisbon, Portugal: Academic Publishing Limited.

Cameron, B. H. (2008). Enterprise systems education: New directions & challenges for the future. In *Proceedings of the 2008 ACM SIGMIS CPR Conference on Computer Personnel Doctoral Consortium and Research,* (pp. 119-126). ACM Press.

Candy, P. C., & Crebert, R. G. (1991). Lifelong learning: An enduring mandate for higher education. *Higher Education Research & Development, 10*(1), 3–18. doi:10.1080/0729436910100102

Canoy, M., Carvalho, G., Hammarlund, C., Hubert, A., Lerais, F., & Melich, A. (2006). Investing in youth: From childhood to adulthood. *Bureau of European Policy Advisers*. Retrieved 11 October 2006 from http://ec.europa.eu/dgs/policy_advisers/publications/index_en.htm

Carayanis, E. (1999). Fostering synergies between information technology and managerial and organizational cognition: The role of knowledge management. *Technovation, 19*, 219–231. doi:10.1016/S0166-4972(98)00101-1

Carayol, N. (2003). Objectives, agreements and matching in science-industry collaborations: Reassembling the pieces of the puzzle. *Research Policy, 32*(6), 887–908. doi:10.1016/S0048-7333(02)00108-7

Cardon, M. (2008). Is passion contagious? The transference of entrepreneurial passion to employees. *Human Resource Management Review, 18*, 77–86. doi:10.1016/j.hrmr.2008.04.001

Carney, A. (2003). *Factors in instructional design: Training versus education*. Retrieved from http://www.uic.edu/depts/accc/itl/conf2003/usetech2enhance/carney2.pdf

Carr, N. (2010). *The shallows: What the internet is doing to our brains*. New York, NY: W.W Norton & Company.

Carr, T., Morrison, A., Cox, G., & Deacon, A. (2007). Weathering wikis: Net-based learning meets political science in a South African university. *Computers and Composition, 24*(3), 266–284. doi:10.1016/j.compcom.2007.06.001

Castells, M. (1996). *The rise of the network society: The information age: Economy, society and culture*. Oxford, UK: Blackwell.

Cavagnoli, D. (2011). A conceptual framework for innovation: An application to human resource management policies in Australia. *Innovation: Management. Policy & Practice, 13*(1), 111–125. doi:10.5172/impp.2011.13.1.111

Cavan, S. (2007). *Networking with other parties – Developing strategic partnerships*. Paper presented at the International Conference in Educator Lifelong Learning, Kwazulu-Natal Education. Durban, South Africa.

Cavusgil, S., Calantone, R., & Zhao, Y. (2003). Tacit knowledge transfer and firm innovation capability. *Journal of Business and Industrial Marketing, 18*(1), 6–21. doi:10.1108/08858620310458615

Chapman, C. S. (1997). Reflections on a contingent view of accounting. *Accounting, Organizations and Society, 22*(2), 189–205. doi:10.1016/S0361-3682(97)00001-9

Chase, R. L. (1997). The knowledge-based organization: An international survey. *Journal of Knowledge Management, 1*(1), 38–49. doi:10.1108/EUM0000000004578

Chaudhuri, S., & Ghosh, R. (2011). Reverse mentoring: A social exchange tool for keeping the boomers engaged and millennials committed. *Human Resource Development Review*. Retrieved October 30, 2011 from http://hrd.sagepub.com/content/early/2011/08/20/1534484311417562

Chen, H. L., Cannon, D., Gabrio, J., Leifer, L., Toye, G., & Bailey, T. (2005). *Using wikis and weblogs to support reflective learning in an introductory engineering design course.* Paper presented at the American Society for Engineering Education Annual Conference & Exposition. Portland, OR.

Cheong, R., & Tsui, E. (2010). Exploring the linkages between personal knowledge management and organizational learning. In Pauleen, D., & Gorman, G. E. (Eds.), *Personal Knowledege Management* (pp. 189–227). Surrey, UK: Gower.

Chesbrough, H. (2003). The new business logic of open innovation. *Strategy & Innovation, 1*(2), 11–15.

Chesbrough, H., West, J., & Vanhaverbeke, W. (2006). *Open innovation: Researching a new paradigm.* Oxford, UK: Oxford University Press.

Choi, S. Y., Lee, H., & Yoo, Y. (2010). The impact of information technology and tran active memory systems on knowledge sharing, application, and team performance: A field study. *Management Information Systems Quarterly, 34*(4), 855–870.

Christensen, C. (1997). *The innovators dilemma: When new technologies cause great firms to fail.* Boston, MA: Harvard Business School Press.

Chuang, L. (2005). An empirical study of the construction of measuring model for organizational innovation in Taiwanese high-tech enterprises. *The Journal of American Academy of Business, 9*(2), 299–304.

Churchill, D. (2011). Web 2.0 in education: A study of the explorative use of blogs with a postgraduate class. *Innovations in Education and Teaching International, 48*(2), 149–158. doi:10.1080/14703297.2011.564009

Ciborra, C., & Andreu, R. (2001). Sharing knowledge across boundaries. *Journal of Information Technology, 16*(2), 73–81. doi:10.1080/02683960110055103

Ciesielka, D. (2008). Using a wiki to meet graduate nursing education competencies in collaboration and community health. *The Journal of Nursing Education, 47*(10), 473–476. doi:10.3928/01484834-20081001-02

Citera, M., McNeese, M. D., Brown, C. E., Selvaraj, J. A., Zaff, B. S., & Whitaker, R. D. (1995). Fitting information systems to collaborating design teams. *Journal of the American Society for Information Science American Society for Information Science, 46*(7), 551–559. doi:10.1002/(SICI)1097-4571(199508)46:7<551::AID-ASI8>3.0.CO;2-1

Clark, B. R. (1983). *The higher education system: Academic Organization in cross-cultural perspective.* London, UK: University of California Press.

Clark, B. R. (1998). *Creating entrepreneurial universities: Organizational pathways of transformation.* New York, NY: Pergamon.

Claver, E., & Tari, J. J. (2003). Levels of quality management in certified firms. *Total Quality Management and Business Excellence, 14*(9), 981–998. doi:10.1080/1478336032000151439

Clough, G. (2005). *Educating the engineer of 2020: Adapting engineering education to the new century.* Washington, DC: National Academy Press.

Coff, R. W. (1997). Human assets and management dilemmas: Coping with the hazards on the road to resource-based theory. *Academy of Management Review, 22*(2), 374–402.

Cohen, W. M. (2008). Knowledge and teaching. *Oxford Review of Education, 34*(3), 357–378. doi:10.1080/03054980802116972

Cohen, W. M., & Levinthal, D. A. (1990). Absorptive capacity: A new perspective on learning and innovation. *Administrative Science Quarterly, 35*, 128–152. doi:10.2307/2393553

Cohen, W. M., Nelson, R. R., & Walsh, J. P. (2002). Links and impacts: The influence of public research on industrial R&D. *Management Science, 48*(1), 1–23. doi:10.1287/mnsc.48.1.1.14273

Cohen, W., & Levinthal, D. (1990). Absorptive capacity: A new perspective on learning and innovation. *Administrative Science Quarterly, 35*, 128–152. doi:10.2307/2393553

Cole, M. (2009). Using wiki technology to support student engagement: Lessons from the trenches. *Computers & Education, 52*(1), 141–146. doi:10.1016/j.compedu.2008.07.003

Collins, A., Hawkins, J., & Carver, S. (1991). A cognitive apprenticeship for disadvantaged students. In Means, B. (Ed.), *Teaching Advanced Skills to Disadvantaged Students* (pp. 216–243). San Francisco, CA: Jossey-Bass.

Collins, C., & Clerk, K. (2004). Strategic human resource practices, top management team social networks and firm performance: The role of human resource practices in creating organizational competitive advantage. *Academy of Management Journal, 46*, 740–751. doi:10.2307/30040665

Collins, H. M. (1993). The structure of knowledge. *Social Research, 60*(1), 95–116.

Collinson, C., & Parcell, G. (2005). *Learning to fly – Practical KM from leading and learning organizations.* Oxford, UK: Capstone Publishing Limited.

Collison, C., & Parcel, G. (2005). *Knowledge management.* Brno, Czech Republic: Computer Press.

Commun, I. T. (2006). *Getting started with blogging software.* Retrieved from http://www.communit.info/index.php?option=com_content&task=view&id=779&Itemid=60

Conley, C. A., & Zheng, W. (2009). Factors critical to knowledge management success. *Advances in Developing Human Resources, 11*(3), 334–348. doi:10.1177/1523422309338159

Conner, K. R. (1991). A historical comparison of the resource-based theory and five schools of thought within industrial organization economics: Do we have a new theory of the firm? *Journal of Management, 17*(1), 121–154. doi:10.1177/014920639101700109

Cook, S. D. N., & Brown, J. S. (1999). Bridging epistemologies: The generative dance between organizational knowledge and organizational knowing. *Organization Science, 10*(4), 381–400. doi:10.1287/orsc.10.4.381

Cooper, R. (1993). *Winning at new products: Accelerating the process from idea to launch.* Reading, MA: Perseus Books.

Cortada, J. W., & Woods, J. A. (Eds.). (1999). *The knowledge management yearbook: 1999-2000.* Boston, MA: Butterworth-Heinemann.

Cortada, J. W., & Woods, J. A. (Eds.). (2000). *The knowledge management yearbook: 2000-2001.* Boston, MA: Butterworth-Heinemann.

Costa, C., Benham, G., Reinhardt, W., & Sillaots, M. (2008). *Microblogging in technology enhanced learning: A use-case inspection of PPE summer school 2008.* Retrieved from ftp.informatik.rwth-aachen.de/Publications/CEUR-WS/Vol-382/paper3.pdf

Courte, J., & Bishop-Clark, C. (2005). Creating connections: Bringing industry and educators together. In *Proceedings of the 6th Conference on Information Technology Education,* (pp. 175-178). IEEE.

Črnjar, K. (2010). *Strategija upravljanja znanjem u funkciji konkurentnosti hotelske industrije.* Doctoral Dissertation. Rijeka, Croatia: Sveučilište u Rijeci.

Črnjar, K. (2005). Faktori produktivnosti rada u hotelskoj indistriji Hrvatske. *Tourism and Hospitality Management, 11*(1), 251–265.

Črnjar, M., & Črnjar, K. (2009). *Menadžment održivog razvoja: Ekonomija, ekologija, zaštita okoliša.* Opatija, Croatia: Fakultet za Menadžment u Turizmu i Ugostiteljstvu.

Cross, N., & Clayburn Cross, A. (1995). Observations of teamwork and social processes in design. *Design Studies, 16*(2), 143–170. doi:10.1016/0142-694X(94)00007-Z

Cross, R., & Cummings, J. N. (2004). Tie and network correlates of individual performance in knowledge-intensive work. *Academy of Management Journal, 47*(6), 928–937. doi:10.2307/20159632

Cruywagen, M. (2010). *Knowledge-centric capabilities: A configurational approach.* Unpublished Doctotal Dissertation. Stellenbosch, South Africa: University of Stellenbosch.

Cruywagen, M., Swart, J., & Gevers, W. (2008). One size does not fit all – Towards a typology of knowledge-centric organizations. *Electronic Journal of Knowledge Management, 6*(2), 101–110.

Csikszentmihalyi, M. (1988). Society, culture and person: A systems view of creativity. In R. J. Sternberg (Ed.), *The Nature of Creativity: Contemporary Psychological Perspectives*. New York, NY: Cambridge University Press.

Csikszentmihalyi, M. (1996). *Creativity: Flow and the psychology of discovery and invention*. New York, NY: Harper Perennial.

Csikszentmihalyi, M. (1998). *Finding flow: The psychology of engagement with everyday life*. New York, NY: Perseus Books Group.

Cyert, R. M., & March, J. G. (1963). *Behavioral theory of the firm*. Malden, MA: Blackwell Publishers.

Daconta, M., Obrst, L., & Smith, K. (2003). *The semantic web*. New York, NY: Wiley Publishing.

Dahlbom, B., & Mathiassen, L. (1993). *Computers in context: The philosophy and practice of system design*. Oxford, UK: Blackwell Publishers.

Dalkir, K. (2005). *Knowledge management in theory and practice*. Burlington, VT: Elsevier.

Dall'Alba, G., & Sandberg, J. (2006). Unveiling professional development: A critical review of stage models. *American Educational Research, 76*(3), 383–412.

Damanpour, F. (1990). Innovation effectiveness, adoption and organizational performance. In M. West & J. Farr (Eds.), *Innovation and Creativity at Work* (pp. 125–141). Chichester, UK: Wiley.

Damanpour, F., & Evan, W. M. (1984). Organizational innovation and performance: The problem of organizational lag. *Administrative Science Quarterly, 29*(3), 329–409. doi:10.2307/2393031

Damanpour, F., Szabat, K. A., & Evan, W. M. (1989). The relationship between types of innovation and organizational performance. *Journal of Management Studies, 26*(6), 587–601. doi:10.1111/j.1467-6486.1989.tb00746.x

Dammers, E. (1999). *Innovation and learning- Knowledge management and rural innovation*. The Hague, The Netherlands: NRLO. EIT website. (2009). *The European institute of innovation and technology*. Retrieved from http://eit.europa.eu/home.html

Daneels, E. (2003). Tight-loose coupling with customers: The enactment of a customer orientation. *Strategic Management Journal, 24*(6), 559–576. doi:10.1002/smj.319

Darling, L. A. W. (1985). 'Mentors' and 'mentoring'. *The Journal of Nursing Administration, 15*(3), 42–43.

Darr, E. D., Argote, L., & Epple, D. (1995). The acquisition, transfer and depreciation of knowledge in service organizations: Productivity in franchises. *Management Science, 41*(11), 1650–1713. doi:10.1287/mnsc.41.11.1750

Dasborough, M. T., & Ashkanasy, N. M. (2002). Emotion and attribution of intentionality in leader–member relationships. *The Leadership Quarterly, 13*, 615–634. doi:10.1016/S1048-9843(02)00147-9

Davenport, T. H., Prusak, L., & Strong, B. (2008). Business insight (A special report): Organization: Putting ideas to work: Knowledge management can make a difference – But it needs to be more pragmatic. *Wall Street Journal*, p. R11.

Davenport, T., & Prusak, L. (1997). *Information ecology: Mastering the information and knowledge environment*. Oxford, UK: Oxford University Press.

Davenport, T., & Prusak, L. (1998). *Working knowledge: How organizations manage what they know*. Boston, MA: Harvard Business School Press.

Davenport, T. (2010). Personal knowledge management and knowledge worker capabilities. In Pauleen, D., & Gorman, G. E. (Eds.), *Personal Knowledge Management* (pp. 167–188). Surrey, UK: Gower.

Davies, J., & Ryan, M. (2011). Vocational education in the 20th and 21st centuries. *Management Services, 55*(2), 31–36.

Davies, M., & Devlin, M. (2007). *Interdisciplinary higher education: Implications for teaching and learning*. Melbourne, Australia: The University of Melbourne.

De Bono, E. (1990). *Lateral thinking for management*. London, UK: Penguin Books.

De Freitas, S. (2008). *Serious virtual worlds: A scoping study*. Retrieved from http://www.jisc.ac.uk/media/documents/publications/seriousvirtualworldsv1.pdf

De Freitas, S. (2009, June). Serious games: Worlds of wisdom. *E-Learning Age*, 14-15.

de Wit, H. (2002). *Internationalisation of higher education in the United States of America and Europe*. New York, NY: Greenwood.

Dearden, L., McGranahan, L., & Sianesi, B. (2004). The role of credit constraints in educational choices: Evidence from NCDS and BCS70. *Centre for the Economics of Education*. Retrieved from http://cee.lse.ac.uk/ceedps//ceedp48.pdf

deBono, E. (1976). *Lateral thinking for management*. New York, NY: American Management Association.

Deci, E., & Ryan, R. (1985). *Intrinsic motivation and self-determination in human behavior*. New York, NY: Plenum Press.

Demarest, M. (1997). Understanding knowledge management. *Long Range Planning*, *30*(3), 374–384. doi:10.1016/S0024-6301(97)90250-8

Desouza, K. C., & Awazu, Y. (2006). Knowledge management at SMEs: 5 peculiarities. *Journal of Knowledge Management*, *10*(1), 32–43. doi:10.1108/13673270610650085

Despres, C. (2011). *Leading issues in knowledge management research*. Reading, UK: Academic Publishing International.

D'Este, P., & Patel, P. (2007). University-industry linkages in the UK: What are the factors determining the variety of interactions with industry? *Research Policy*, *36*(9), 1295–1313. doi:10.1016/j.respol.2007.05.002

Diefenbach, T. (2006). Intangible resources: A categorical system of knowledge and other intangible assets. *Journal of Intellectual Capital*, 7, 406–420. Retrieved from http://www.emeraldinsight.com/Insight/ViewContentServlet?Filename=/published/emeraldfulltextarticle/pdf/2500070308.pdfdoi:10.1108/14691930610681483

Diehl, A., Grabill, J. T., & Hart-Davidson, W. (2008). Grassroots: Supporting the knowledge work of everydaylLife. *Technical Communication Quarterly*, *17*(4), 413–434. doi:10.1080/10572250802324937

Dierickx, I., & Cool, K. (1989). Asset stock accumulation and sustainability of competitive advantage. *Management Science*, *35*(12), 1504–1511. doi:10.1287/mnsc.35.12.1504

Dixon, N. (2000). *Common knowledge*. Boston, MA: Harvard Business School Press.

Dobija, M. (1998). How to place human resources into the balance sheet. *Journal of Human Resource Costing and Accounting*, *3*(1), 83–92. doi:10.1108/eb029044

Dobre, R. (2005). *Inovacije, tehnološke promjene i strategije*. Šibenik, Croatia: Školska knjiga.

Dodd, J. L., & Chen, S. (1997). Economic value added (EVA super TM): An empirical examination of a new corporate performance measure. *Journal of Managerial Issues*, *9*, 318–333.

Dodd, S. C. (1955). Diffusion is predictable: Testing probability models for laws of interaction. *American Sociological Review*, *20*(4), 392–401. doi:10.2307/2092736

Dosi, G., Nelson, R. R., & Winter, S. G. (2000). Introduction: The nature and dynamics of organizational capabilities. In Dosi, G., Nelson, R. R., & Winter, S. G. (Eds.), *The Nature and Dynamics of Organizational Capabilities*. Oxford, UK: Oxford University Press. doi:10.1093/0199248540.003.0001

Douglas, T., & Seely-Brown, J. (2011). *A new culture of learning: Cultivating the imagination for a world of constant change*. New York, NY: CreateSpace.

Doz, Y., & Prahalad, C. (1991). Managing MNC's: A search for a new paradigm. *Strategic Management Journal*, *12*(5), 145–164. doi:10.1002/smj.4250120911

Drazin, R., Glynn, M. A., & Kazanjian, R. K. (1999). Multilevel theorizing about creativity in organizations: A sense making perspective. *Academy of Management Review*, *24*, 286–307.

Drucker, P. (1993). *Post-capitalist society*. New York, NY: HarperCollins.

Drucker, P. (1985). Creating strategies of innovation. *Strategy and Leadership*, *13*(6), 8–45. doi:10.1108/eb054121

Drucker, P. (1985). The discipline of innovation. *Harvard Business Review*, *5*(6), 25–45.

Drucker, P. (1993). *Innovation and entrepreneurship.* Prague, Czech Republic: Management Press.

Drucker, P. (1993). *Post-capitalist society.* Oxford, UK: Butterworth Heinemann.

Drucker, P. (1998). Management's new paradigms. *Forbes, 162*(7), 152–177.

Drucker, P. (1999). Managing oneself. *Harvard Business Review, 77*(2), 65–74.

Drucker, P. (2000). *Age of discontinuity: Guidelines to our changing society* (3rd ed.). New York, NY: Harper and Row.

Drucker, P. (2000). Knowledge work. *Executive Excellence, 17*(4), 11–12.

Drucker, P. F. (1985). *Innovation and entrepreneurship: Practice and principle.* New York, NY: Harper Business.

DTI. (2001). *Creating value from your intangible assets.* Retrieved from http://www.exinfm.com/pdffiles/intangible_assets.pdf

Duan, Y., Nie, W., & Coakes, E. (2010). Identifying key factors affecting transnational knowledge transfer. *Information & Management, 47*(7-8), 356–363. doi:10.1016/j.im.2010.08.003

Duffy, T., & Cunningham, D. (1996). *Constructivism: Implications for the design and delivery of instruction. Handbook of Research for Educational Telecommunications and Technology* (pp. 170–198). New York, NY: Macmillan.

Dufour, Y., & Steane, P. (2007). Implementing knowledge management: A more robust model. *Journal of Knowledge Management, 11*(6), 66–80. doi:10.1108/13673270710832172

Duke, S., Makey, P., & Kiras, N. (1999). *Knowledge management 1999 report series.* Hull, UK: Butler Group.

Dyck, B., Starke, F. A., Mischke, G. A., & Mauws, M. (2005). Learning to build a car: An empirical investigation of organizational learning. *Journal of Management Studies, 42*(2), 387–416. doi:10.1111/j.1467-6486.2005.00501.x

DZS. (2009a). *Državni zavod za statistiku: Turizam u 2009.* Retroeved frp, http://www.dzs.hr/Hrv_Eng/publication/2010/SI-1408.pdf

DZS. (2009b). *Državni zavod za statistiku: Ugostiteljstvo u 2009.* Retrieved from http://www.dzs.hr/Hrv_Eng/publication/2010/SI-1427.pdf

Easterby-Smith, M., & Lyles, M. A. (2003). Introduction: Watersheds of organizational learning and knowledge management. In Easterby-Smith, M., & Lyles, M. A. (Eds.), *The Blackwell Handbook of Organizational Learning and Knowledge* (pp. 1–15). Oxford, UK: Blackwell Publishers.

Easterby-Smith, M., & Prieto, I. (2009). Dynamic capabilities and knowledge management: An integrative role for learning. *British Journal of Management, 19*(3), 235–249. doi:10.1111/j.1467-8551.2007.00543.x

Ebersbach, A., Glaser, M., & Heigl, R. (2005). *Wiki: Web collaboration.* Dordrecht, The Netherlands: Springer-Verlag Berlin.

Edmonds, E., & Candy, L. (2002). Creativity, art practical and knowledge. *Communications of the ACM Special Sections on Creativity and Interface, 45*(10), 91–95.

Edvinsson, L. (2000). Some perspectives on intangibles and intellectual capital. *Journal of Intellectual Capital, 1*, 12–16. doi:10.1108/14691930010371618

Edvinsson, L., & Malone, M. (1997). *Intellectual capital: Realizing your company's true value by finding its hidden brainpower.* New York, NY: Harper Collins.

Edvinsson, L., & Malone, M. S. (1997a). *Intellectual capital: Realizing your company's true value by finding its hidden brainpower.* New York, NY: Harper Business.

Edvinsson, L., & Malone, M. S. (1997b). *Intellectual capital, the proven way to establish your company's real value by measuring its hidden brainpower.* London, UK: Judy Piatkus.

Edvinsson, L., & Sullivan, P. H. (1996). Developing a model for managing intellectual capital. *European Management Journal, 14*(4), 356–364. doi:10.1016/0263-2373(96)00022-9

EFQM. (2009). *EFQM transition guide.* Brussels, Belgium: EFQM.

Eisenhardt, K. M. (1989). Building theories from case study research. *Strategic Management Journal, 14*(4), 532–549.

Eisenhardt, K. M., & Martin, J. (2000). Dynamic capabilities: What are they? *Strategic Management Journal, 21*(10-11), 1105–1121. doi:10.1002/1097-0266(200010/11)21:10/11<1105::AID-SMJ133>3.0.CO;2-E

Eisenhardt, K. M., & Santos, F. M. (2002). Knowledge-based view : A new theory of strategy? In Pettigrew, A., Thomas, H., & Whittington, R. (Eds.), *Handbook of Strategy and Management*. Thousand Oaks, CA: Sage Publications Inc.doi:10.4135/9781848608313.n7

Elenurm, T. (2007). Entrepreneurial knowledge sharing about business opportunities in virtual networks. In B. Martins & D. Remenyi (Eds.), *Proceedings of the 8th European Conference on Knowledge Management,* (pp. 285-290). Reading, UK: Academic Conferences.

Elenurm, T. (2008). Applying cross-cultural student teams for supporting international networking of Estonian enterprises. *Baltic Journal of Management, 3*(2), 145–158. doi:10.1108/17465260810875488

Elenurm, T. (2010). Knowledge as open space. *Electronic Journal of Knowledge Management, 8*(2), 181–266.

Elenurm, T., Ennulo, J., & Laar, J. (2007). Structures of motivation and entrepreneurial orientation in students as the basis for differentiated approaches in developing human resources for future business initiatives. *EBS Review, 23*(2), 50–61.

Elgort, I., Smith, A. G., & Toland, J. (2008). Is wiki an effective platform for group course work? *Educational Technology, 24*(2), 195–210.

Elkin-Koren, N. (2007). *The ramifications of technology transfer based on intellectual property licensing*. Haifa, Israel: S. Neaman Institute.

Endean, M., Weidmann, G., Armstrong, A., Moffat, J., Nixon, T., & Reuben, B. (2008). Team project work for distance learners in engineering–Challenges and benefits. *Engineering Education: Journal of the Higher Education Academy Engineering Subject Centre, 3*(2), 11–20.

Ercan, T. (2010). Towards virtualization: A competitive business continuity. *African Journal of Business Management, 4*(10), 2164–2173.

Ericsson, K. A. (1996). The acquisition of expert performance: An introduction to some of the issues. In Ericsson, K. A. (Ed.), *The Road to Excellence: The Acquisition of Expert Performance in the Arts and Sciences, Sports, and Games* (pp. 1–50). Hillsdale, NJ: Lawrence Erlbaum Associates.

Etzkowitz, H. (1998). The norms of entrepreneurial science: Cognitive effects of the new university-industry linkages. *Research Policy, 27*(8), 823–833. doi:10.1016/S0048-7333(98)00093-6

Etzkowitz, H. (2002). *The rise of the entrepreneurial university*. New York, NY: Science Policy Institute. doi:10.4324/9780203216675

Etzkowitz, H. (2003). Research groups as 'quasi-firms': The invention of the entrepreneurial university. *Research Policy, 32*(1), 109–121. doi:10.1016/S0048-7333(02)00009-4

Etzkowitz, H., & Leydesdorff, L. (2000). The dynamics of innovation: From national systems and 'mode two' to a triple helix of university, industry and government relations. *Research Policy, 29*(22), 109–123. doi:10.1016/S0048-7333(99)00055-4

Europe. (2012). *Smart growth*. Retrieved April 15, 2011, from http://ec.europa.eu/europe2020/priorities/smart-growth/index_en.htm

European Commission. (2005). *A study on returns of various types of investment in education and training*. Retrieved from http://www.londecon.co.uk/le/publications/pdf/invest05_en.pdf

European Policy Brief. (2009). *INGINEUS -Impact of networks, globalization, and their interaction with EU strategies*. Geneva, Switzerland: European Research Area.

Evangelista, P., Esposito, E., Lauro, V., & Raffa, M. (2010). The adoption of knowledge management systems in small firms. *Electronic Journal of Knowledge Management, 8*(1), 33–42.

Fadaei, R. (2010). Technology and quality of education. *Journal of Business and Educational Leadership, 2*(1), 34–39.

Fahey, L., & Prusak, L. (1998). The eleven deadliest sins of knowledge management. *California Management Review, 40*(3), 265–276.

Faraj, S., & Sproull, L. (2000). Coordinating expertise in software development teams. *Management Science, 46*(12), 1554–1568. doi:10.1287/mnsc.46.12.1554.12072

Faria, A. J., Hutchinson, D., Welington, W., & Gold, S. (2009). Developments in business gaming: A review of the past 40 years. *Simulation & Gaming, 40*, 464–487. doi:10.1177/1046878108327585

Faria, A. J., & Wellington, W. (2004). A survey of simulation game users, former-users, and never-users: Simulation & gaming. *Journal of Business and Educational Leadership, 35*, 178–207.

Farjoun, M. (2010). Beyond dualism: Stability and change as a duality. *Academy of Management Review, 35*(2), 202–225. doi:10.5465/AMR.2010.48463331

Farok, J. (Ed.). (2001). *Valuation of intangible assets in global operations.* Westport, CT: Quorum Books.

Faucher, J.-B. P. L., Everett, A. M., & Lawson, R. (2008). Reconstituting knowledge management. *Journal of Knowledge Management, 12*(3), 3–16. doi:10.1108/13673270810875822

Felin, T., Zenger, T. R., & Tomsik, J. (2009). The knowledge economy, emerging organizational forms, missing micro foundations, and key considerations for managing human capital. *Human Resource Management, 48*(4), 555–570. doi:10.1002/hrm.20299

Feller, I. (1990). Universities as engines of R&D-based economic growth: They think they can. *Research Policy, 19*(4), 335–348. doi:10.1016/0048-7333(90)90017-Z

Field, A. (2005). *Discovering statistics using SPSS* (2nd ed.). Thousand Oaks, CA: Sage Publications.

Filstad, C. (2011). Organizational commitment through organizational socialization tactics. *Journal of Workplace Learning, 23*(6), 376–390. doi:10.1108/13665621111154395

FINA. (2010). *Financijski pokazatelji za sve poduzetnike: Sve djelatnosti i razred I 55109.* Rijeka, Croatia: FINA.

Fincham, R., & Clark, T. (2009). Introduction to point counterpoint on rigour and relevance in management studies: Can we bridge the rigour relevance gap. *Journal of Management Studies, 46*(3), 510–515. doi:10.1111/j.1467-6486.2009.00834.x

Finerty, T. (1997). Integrating learning and knowledge infrastructure. *Journal of Knowledge Management, 1*(2), 98–104. doi:10.1108/EUM0000000004584

Fiol, C. M., & Lyles, M. A. (1985). Organizational learning. *Academy of Management Review, 10*(4), 803–813.

Firestone, J. M. (2001). Key issues in knowledge management. *Knowledge and Innovation: Journal of the KMCI, 1*(3), 8–38.

Fitz-Enz, J. (1995). *How to measure human resources management* (2nd ed.). New York, NY: McGraw-Hill.

Flamholtz, E. G. (1985). *Human resource accounting* (2nd ed.). San Francisco, CA: Jossey-Bass.

Flignor, P., & Orozco, D. (2012). *Intangible assets and intellectual property valuation: A multidisciplinary perspective.* Retrieved from http://www.wipo.int/sme/en/documents/ip_valuation.htm#legal

Forbes, T. (2008). Valuing customers. *Database Marketing and Customer Strategy Management.* Retrieved from http://www.intangiblebusiness.us/store/data/files/389-Valuing_Customers_Thayne_Forbes_Database_of_Customer_Marketing_January_2008.pdf

Foss, N. J., & Christensen, J. F. (2001). A market-process approach to corporate coherence. *Managerial and Decision Economics, 22*, 213–226. doi:10.1002/mde.1012

Francisco, J. R. (2006). *Knowledge management tools supporting education.* Retrieved from http://ssrn.com/abstract=916609

Freire, P. (2001). *Pedagogia de autonomia: Saberes necessários à prática educative* (19th ed.). Rio de Janeiro, Brazil: Páz e Terra.

Friedman, T. L. (2006). *The world is flat: A brief history of the twenty-first century.* New York, NY: Farrar, Straus and Giroux.

Frigda, N. H. (1988). The laws of emotion. *The American Psychologist, 43*, 349–358. doi:10.1037/0003-066X.43.5.349

Fundamo. (2011). *Fundamo enterprise platform.* Retrieved 23 June, 2011, from http://www.fundamo.com

Furubotn, E. G., & Pejovich, S. (1974). Introduction: The new property rights literature. In Furubtn, E. G., & Pejovich, S. (Eds.), *The Economics of Property Rights*. Cambridge, MA: Ballinger Publishing Company.

Gardner, H. (1993). *Creating minds*. New York, NY: Basic Books.

Gardner, H. (1999, November 5). Multiple intelligences. *Atlantic Monthly*.

Gartner. (2009). *Hype cycle for consumer mobile applications, 2009*. Washington, DC: Gartner.

Garvin, D. A. (1998). The processes of organization and management. *Sloan Management Review, 39*(4), 33–50.

Geiger, A. H. (1992). Measures for mentors. *Training & Development, 46*(2), 65–67.

Geng, Q., Townley, C., Huang, K., & Zhang, J. (2005). Comparative knowledge management: A pilot study of Chinese and American universities. *Journal of the American Society for Information Science and Technology, 56*(10), 1031–1044. doi:10.1002/asi.20194

George, J. M. (2000). Emotions and leadership: The role of emotional intelligence. *Human Relations, 53*, 1027–1055. doi:10.1177/0018726700538001

Geuna, A., & Muscio, A. (2008). *The governance of university knowledge transfer*. SPRU Electronic Working Paper Series, Paper no. 173. SPRU.

Gherardi, S. (2000). Practice based theorizing on learning and knowing in organisations. *Organization, 7*(2), 211–233. doi:10.1177/135050840072001

Gherardi, S. (2009). Guest editorial: Knowing and learning in practice-based studies: An introduction. *The Learning Organization, 16*(5), 352–359. doi:10.1108/09696470910974144

Ghosh, T., Yates, J., & Orlikowski, W. J. (2004, October). *Using communication norms for coordination evidence from a distributed team*. Retrieved October 20, 2011, from http://seeit.mit.edu/Publications/Orlikowski_Comm_Coordination_8-05_REVISED.pdf

Gibbert, M., Ruigrok, W., & Wicki, B. (2008). What passes as a rigorous case study? *Strategic Management Journal, 29*(13), 1465–1474. doi:10.1002/smj.722

Gibbons, M. (2008). *Why is knowledge translation important: Grounding the conversation*. Retrieved from http://www.ncddr.org/kt/products/focus/focus21

Gibson, D. (2001). Paper. In *Proceedings of the 34th Annual Hawaii International Conference on System Sciences (HICSS-34)*. HICSS.

Giddens, A. (1984). *The constitution of society-Outlines of the theory of structure*. Cambridge, UK: Polity Press.

Giligen, P. W. (2007). *The ideal technology incubator workshop in Warsaw, Poland*. Retrieved from http://science24.com/resources/paper/9512/NST2B_Gilgen.P.pdf

Gill, A. (2009). Knowledge management initiatives at a small university. *International Journal of Educational Management, 23*(7), 604–616. doi:10.1108/09513540910990834

Gizir, S., & Simsek, H. (2005). Communication in an academic context. *Higher Education, 50*(2), 197–221. doi:10.1007/s10734-004-6349-x

Glaser, B., & Bero, L. (2005). Attitudes of academic and clinical researchers toward financial ties in research: A systematic review. *Science and Engineering Ethics, 11*(4), 553–573. doi:10.1007/s11948-005-0026-z

Globerson, A., Globerson, S., & Frampton, J. (1991). *You can't manage what you don't measure*. Aldershot, UK: Avebury.

Gloor, P. (2006). *Swarm creativity: Competitive advantage through collaborative innovative networks*. Oxford, UK: Oxford University Press.

Glow, J. (2010). *What problem are we really trying to solve?* In N. Paine & E. Masie (Eds.), *Learning Perspectives 2010*. Retrieved July 28, 2011 from http://www.learning2010.com/ebook

Goh, S. C. (2002). Managing effective knowledge transfer: An integrative framework and some practice implications. *Journal of Knowledge Management, 6*(1), 23–30. doi:10.1108/13673270210417664

Goldfarb, B., & Henrekson, M. (2003). Bottom-up versus top-down policies towards the commercialization of university intellectual property. *Research Policy, 4*(32), 639–658. doi:10.1016/S0048-7333(02)00034-3

Gold, J., Thorpe, R., Woodall, J., & Sadler-Smith, E. (2007). Continuing professional development in the legal profession: A practice based perspective. *Management Learning, 38*(2), 235–250. doi:10.1177/1350507607075777

Goleman, D. (1998). *Working with emotional intelligence.* London, UK: Bloomsbury Publishing.

Gomezelj Omerzel, D., Biloslavo, R., & Trnavčevič, A. (2010). *Management znanja v visokošolskih zavodih.* Koper, Slovenija: Univerza na Primorskem, Fakulteta za management Koper.

Gordon, W. (1971). *The metaphorical way.* Cambridge, MA: Porpoise Books.

Gordon, W. (1956). Operational approach to creativity. *Harvard Business Review, 34*, 41–51.

Government of Croatia. (2009). *Croatian qualifications framework.* Zagreb, Croatia: Government of the Republic of Croatia, Ministry of Science, Education, and Sports.

Granovetter, M. (1974). *Getting a job: A study of contacts and careers.* Chicago, IL: The University of Chicago Press.

Grant, R. (1996). Towards a knowledge-based theory of the firm. *Strategic Management Journal, 17*, 109–122.

Grant, R. M. (1996). Prospering in dynamically-cometitive environments: Organizational capability as knowledge integration. *Organization Science, 7*(4), 375–387. doi:10.1287/orsc.7.4.375

Grant, R. M. (1996). Toward a knowledge-based theory of the firm. *Strategic Management Journal, 17*, 109–117.

Grant, R. M. (1997). The knowledge-based view of the firm: Implications for management practice. *Long Range Planning, 30*(3), 450–454. doi:10.1016/S0024-6301(97)00025-3

Gray, C. (2006). Absorptive capacity, knowledge management and innovation in entrepreneurial small firms. *International Journal of Entrepreneurial Behaviour & Research, 12*(6), 345–360. doi:10.1108/13552550610710144

Grierson, H., Nicol, D., Littlejohn, A., & Wodehouse, A. (2004). *Structuring and sharing information resources to support concept development and design learning.* Paper presented at the Network Learning Conference. Exeter, UK.

Grigorenko, E. L., & Sternberg, R. J. (2001). Analytical, creative, and practical intelligence as predictors of self–reported adaptive functioning: A case study in Russia. *Intelligence, 29*, 57–73. doi:10.1016/S0160-2896(00)00043-X

Grimaldi, M., & Cricelli, L. (2009). Intangible asset contribution to company performance: The hierarchical assessment index. *Vine, 39*(1), 40–54. doi:10.1108/03055720910962434

Grover, V., & Davenport, T. H. (2001). General perspectives on knowledge management: Fostering a research agenda. *Journal of Management Information Systems, 18*(1), 5–21.

Grubic-Nesic, L. (2005). *Razvoj ljudskih resursa.* [Development of human resources]. Novi Sad, Serbia: AB Print.

Guilford, J. P. (1950). Creativity research: Past, present, and future. *The American Psychologist, 5*, 444–454. doi:10.1037/h0063487

Gupta, A. K., & Govindarajan, V. (2000). Knowledge management's social dimension: Lessons from Nucor steel. *Sloan Management Review, 41*(1), 71–80.

Gupta, A., Denny, N. T., O'Toole, K., & Bondade, R. (2011). Global software development using the 24-hour knowledge factory paradigm. *International Journal of Computer Applications in Technology, 40*(3), 191–202. doi:10.1504/IJCAT.2011.039140

Gurley, K., Wilson, D., & Jackson, P. (2010). Developing leadership skills in a virtual simulation. *Journal of Business and Educational Leadership, 2*(1), 106–115.

Gurteen, D. (2006). *The gurteen perspective.* Retrieved from http://www.ikmagazine.com/display.asp?articleid=AE03F1CA-F94B-4BD5-9BE9-0CB68079CB6F

Gurteen, D. (1998). Knowledge, creativity and innovation. *Journal of Knowledge Management, 2*(1), 5–13. doi:10.1108/13673279810800744

Guthrie, J. (2001). High involvement practices, turnover and productivity. *Academy of Management Journal, 44*, 180–190. doi:10.2307/3069345

Haas, M. R., & Hansen, M. T. (2007). Different knowledge, different benefits: Towards a productivity perspective on knowledge sharing in organizations. *Strategic Management Journal, 28*, 1133–1153. doi:10.1002/smj.631

Hackbarth, G. (1998). The impact of organizational memory on IT systems. In E. Hoadley & I. Benbasat (Eds.), *Proceedings of the Fourth Americas Conference on Information Systems*, (pp. 588-590). ACIS.

Hackman, J., & Oldham, G. (1980). *Work redesign*. Reading, MA: Addison-Wesley.

Hahn, J., & Subramani, M. R. (2000). A framework of knowledge management systems: Issues and challenges for theory and practice. In *Proceedings of the 21st International Conference on Information Systems*, (pp. 302-312). IEEE.

Hall, M. (2006). Knowledge management and the limits of knowledge codification. *Journal of Knowledge Management, 10*(3), 117–126. doi:10.1108/13673270610670894

Hall, R. (1992). The strategic analysis of intangible resources. *Strategic Management Journal, 13*, 135–144. doi:10.1002/smj.4250130205

Hall, R. (1993). A framework for linking intangible resources and capabilities to sustainable competitive advantage. *Strategic Management Journal, 14*, 607–618. doi:10.1002/smj.4250140804

Hall, R., & Andriani, P. (2002). Managing knowledge for innovation. *Long Range Planning, 35*, 29–48. doi:10.1016/S0024-6301(02)00019-5

Hameyer, U., & Strittmatter, A. (2001). Wissensmanagement – Die neue Selbstverständlichkeit. *Journal für Schulentwicklung, 1*, 4–5.

Hanandi, M., & Grimaldi, M. (2010). Internal organizational and collaborative knowledge management: A virtual HRD model based on Web 2.0. *The International Journal of Advanced Computer Science & Applications, 1*(4), 11–19.

Handy, C. (1996, December). Intelligence – Capitalism's most potent asset. *HR Monthly*, 8–11.

Haneda, M. (1997). Second language learning in a 'community of practice': A case study of adult Japanese learners. *Canadian Modern Language Review, 54*(1), 11–27. doi:10.3138/cmlr.54.1.11

Hansen, M. T., & Nohria, N. (2004). How to build collaborative advantage. *MIT Sloan Management Review, 46*(1), 22–30.

Hansen, M. T., Nohria, N., & Tierney, T. (1999, March-April). What's your strategy for managing knowledge? *Harvard Business Review*, 106–116.

Hargadon, A. B. (1998). Firms as knowledge brokers: Lessons in pursuing continuous innovation. *California Management Review, 40*, 209–227.

Harlow, H. (2008). The effects of tacit knowledge on a firm's performance. *Journal of Knowledge Management, 12*(1), 148–163. doi:10.1108/13673270810852458

Harrington, D., & Kearney, A. (2010). The business school in transition: New opportunities in management development, knowledge transfer and knowledge creation. *Journal of European Industrial Training, 35*(2), 116–134. doi:10.1108/03090591111109334

Harris, M., & Cullen, R. (2009). A model for curricular revision: The case of engineering. *Innovative Higher Education, 34*, 51–63. doi:10.1007/s10755-008-9090-z

Harrison, R., & Kessels, J. (2004). *Human resource development in a knowledge economy*. Basingstoke, UK: Palgrave Macmillan.

Harung, H. S. (1996). A world-leading learning organization: A case study of Tomra Systems, Oslo, Norway. *The Learning Organization, 3*(4), 22–34. doi:10.1108/09696479610126716

Harvard Business School. (2009). *Annual report 2009*. Retrieved from http://www.hbs.edu/about/annualreport/2009/download2009/annual-2009.pdf

Hasan, H., & Pfaff, C. (2006). *Overcoming organisational resistance to using wiki technology for knowledge management*. Paper presented at the 10th Pacic Asia Conference on Information Systems. Kuala Lumpur, Malaysia.

Hatakenaka, S. (2005). *Development of third stream activities lessons from international experience*. New York, NY: Higher Education Policy Institute.

Hauschildt, J. (1993). *Innovationsmanagement*. München, Germany: Vahlen.

Hauser, J., & Katz, G. (1998). Metrics: You are what you measure. *European Management Journal, 16*(5), 517–528. doi:10.1016/S0263-2373(98)00029-2

Hautala, J. (2011). International academic knowledge creation and ba: A case study from Finland. *Knowledge Management Research & Practice, 9*, 4–16. doi:10.1057/kmrp.2010.23

Hay, K. E. (1993). Legitimate peripheral participation, instructionism, and constructivism: Whose situation is it anyway? *Educational Technology, 33*(3), 33–38.

Heaton, L., & Taylor, J. R. (2002). Knowledge management and professional work: A communication perspective on the knowledge-based organization. *Management Communication Quarterly, 16*(2), 210–236. doi:10.1177/089331802237235

Hedlund, G. (1994). A model of knowledge management and the N-form corporation. *Strategic Management Journal, 15*, 73–90. doi:10.1002/smj.4250151006

Helfat, C. E., Finkelstein, S., Mitchell, W., Peteraf, M. A., Singh, H., & Teece, D. J. (2007). *Dynamic capabilities: Understanding strategic change in organisations*. Oxford, UK: Blackwell Publishing.

Helfat, C. E., & Peteraf, M. A. (2003). The dynamic resource-based view: Capability lifecycles. *Strategic Management Journal, 24*(10), 997–1010. doi:10.1002/smj.332

Hemmi, A., Bayne, S., & Land, R. (2009). The appropriation and repurposing of social technologies in higher education. *Journal of Computer Assisted Learning, 25*(1), 19–30. doi:10.1111/j.1365-2729.2008.00306.x

Hendry, J., & Seidl, D. (2003). The structure and significance of strategic episodes: Social systems theory and the routine practices of strategic change. *Journal of Management Studies, 40*(1), 175–196. doi:10.1111/1467-6486.00008

Henkel, M. (2000). *Academic identities and policy change in higher education*. London, UK: Jessica Kingsley.

Herbane, B. (2010). The evolution of business kontinuity management: A historical review of practices nad drives. *Business History, 52*(6), 978–1002. doi:10.1080/00076791.2010.511185

Herschel, R. T., Nemati, H., & Steiger, D. (2001). Tacit to explicit knowledge conversion: knowledge protocols. *Journal of Knowledge Management, 5*(1), 107–116. doi:10.1108/13673270110384455

Hertel, G., Geister, S., & Konradt, U. (2005). Managing virtual teams: A review of current empirical research. *Human Resource Management Review, 15*(1), 69–95. doi:10.1016/j.hrmr.2005.01.002

Herzberg, F., Mausner, B., & Snyderman, B. (1959). *The motivation to work* (2nd ed.). New York, NY: Wiley.

Hietikko, E., & Rajaniemi, E. (2000). Visualized data-tool to improve communication in distributed product development projects. *Journal of Engineering Design, 11*(1), 95–101. doi:10.1080/095448200261207

Hodgkinson, G. P., & Rousseau, D. (2009). Bridging the rigour relevance gap in management studies: Its already happening. *Journal of Management Studies, 46*(3), 534–546. doi:10.1111/j.1467-6486.2009.00832.x

Hoegl, M., Ernst, H., & Proserpio, P. (2007). How teamwork matters more as team member dispersion increases? *Journal of Product Innovation Management, 24*(2), 156–165. doi:10.1111/j.1540-5885.2007.00240.x

Hofstede, G. (2001). *Culture's consequences: Comparing values, behaviours, institutions and organizations across cultures* (2nd ed.). Thousand Oaks, CA: Sage Publications.

Hofstede, G., Hofstede, G. J., & Minkov, M. (2010). *Cultures and organizations: Software of the mind: Intercultural cooperation and its importance for survival*. New York, NY: McGraw-Hill.

Hogarth, R. M., Michaud, C., Doz, Y., & Van der Heyden, L. (1991). *Longevity of business firms: A four-stage framework for analysis*. Unpublished Manuscript.

Holsappie, C. (1987). *Knowledge management organization and the information society*. London, UK: Taylor & Francis.

Holtham, C., Ward, V., & Bohn, M. (2002). *Slow knowledge: The importance of in team debriefing and in individual learning*. Unpublished. Retrieved 18/7/2011 from http://www2.warwick.ac.uk/fac/soc/wbs/conf/olkc/archive/oklc3/papers/id246.pdf

Holtman, C., & Courtney, N. (1998). The executive learning ladder: A knowledge creation process grounded in the strategic information systems domain. In E. Hoadley & I. Benbasat (Eds.), *Proceedings of the Fourth Americas Conference on Information Systems*, (pp. 594-597). Baltimore, MD: ACIS.

Hong, H. O., Chen, F. C., Chai, C. S., & Chan, W. C. (2010). Teacher-education students' views about knowledge building theory and practice. *Instructional Science Journal*. Retrieved from http://www.cl.ncu.edu.tw/papers/ChenFC/Teachereducation%20students%27views%20about%20knowledge.pdf

Honig, B. (2004). Entrepreneurship education: Toward ad model of contingency-based business planning. *Academy of Management Learning & Education, 3*(3), 258–273. doi:10.5465/AMLE.2004.14242112

Hope, S. (2010). Symposium: Teaching creativity, creativity, content, and policy. *Arts Education Policy Review, 111*, 39–47. doi:10.1080/10632910903455736

Ho, R. (2006). *Handbook of univariate and multivariate data analysis and interpretation with SPSS*. New York, NY: Taylor & Francis Group. doi:10.1201/9781420011111

Horie, N., & Ikawa, Y. (2011). Knowledge integration in a product development organization accompanied by M&A: A case study of a precision device manufacturer. In *Proceedings of the Technology Management in the Energy Smart World (PICMET)*, (pp. 1-8). PICMET.

Horovitz, E., & Brodeth, D. (2008). *Israel 2028 vision and social-economic strategy in the global world*. Jerusalem, Israel: US-Israel Science and Technology Foundation.

Howells, J. (1996). Tacit knowledge, innovation and technology transfer. *Technology Analysis and Strategic Management, 8*(2), 91–106. doi:10.1080/09537329608524237

Hubig, L., & Jonen, A. (2006). *Hindrances, benefits and measurement of knowledge transfer in universities - Should be done more in the light of corporate social responsibility?* Retrieved from http://ssrn.com/abstract=939390

Hulbert-Williams, N. J. (2010). Facilitating collaborative learning using online wikis: Evaluation of their application within postgraduate psychology teaching. *Psychology Learning & Teaching, 9*(1), 45–51. doi:10.2304/plat.2010.9.1.45

Hung, D., & Nichani, M. (2002). Bringing communities of practice into schools: Implications for instructional technologies from Vygotskian perspectives. *International Journal of Instructional Media, 29*(2), 171–184.

Hurley, R., & Hult, T. (1988). Innovation, market orientation, and organizational learning: An integration and empirical examination. *Journal of Marketing, 62*, 42–54. doi:10.2307/1251742

Huysman, M., Creemers, M., & Derksen, D. (1998). Learning from the environment: Exploring the relation between organizational learning, knowledge management and information/communication technology. In E. Hoadley & I. Benbasat (Eds.), *Proceedings of the Fourth Americas Conference on Information Systems*, (pp. 598-600). Baltimore, MD: ACIS.

Hynie, M., Jensen, K., Johnny, M., Wedlock, J., & Phipps, D. (2011). Student internship bridge research to real world problems. *Education + Training, 53*(1), 45–56. doi:10.1108/00400911111102351

Iansiti, M., & Clark, K. B. (1994). Integration and dynamic capability: Evidence from product development in automobiles and mainframe computers. *Industrial and Corporate Change, 3*(3), 557–605. doi:10.1093/icc/3.3.557

IDRC. (2012a). *Part 1: Getting set up*. Retrieved from http://www.idrc.ca/en/ev-31833-201-1-DO_TOPIC.html

IDRC. (2012b). *Part 2: Working together*. Retrieved from http://www.idrc.ca/en/ev-31838-201-1-DO_TOPIC.html

IDRC. (2012c). *Part 3: Resources*. Retrieved from http://www.idrc.ca/en/ev-31839-201-1-DO_TOPIC.html

IFAC. (1998). *The measurement and management of intellectual capital: An introduction*. New York, NY: IFAC Publishing.

Imai, K. (1991). *Globalization and cross-border networks of Japanese firms*. Paper presented to Japan in a Global Economy Conference. Stockholm, Sweden.

INGINEUS. (2011). Impact of networks, globalisation, and their interaction with EU strategies, 2009-2011. Retrieved from http://www.ingineus.eu/getpage.aspx?id=1&sec=1

Inkpen, A., & Dikur, I. (1998). Knowledge management processes and international joint ventures. *Organization Science*, *9*(4), 454–468. doi:10.1287/orsc.9.4.454

Investopedia. (2009). *Intangible asset*. Retrieved from http://investopedia.com/terms/i/intangibleasset.asp

Irlbeck, S. (2002). Leadership and distance education in higher education: A US perspective. *International Review of Research in Open and Distance Learning*, *3*(2). Retrieved from http://www.irrodl.org/index.php/irrodl/article/view/91/170

ISO. (2000). *Quality management systems – Requirements*. Geneva, Switzerland: ISO. *ISO, 9000*, 2000.

Itami, H. (1984). Invisible resources and their accumulation for corporate growth. *Hitotsubahi Journal of Commerce & Management*, *19*, 20–39.

Ivari, J., & Linger, H. (1999). Knowledge work as collaborative work: A situated activity theory view. In *Proceedings of the Thirty-Second Annual Hawaii International Conference on Systems Sciences*. Los Alamitos, CA: IEEE Press.

Jackson, S. E., May, K. E., & Whitney, K. (1992). Understanding the dynamics of diversity in decision-making teams. In *Diversity in the Workplace: Human Resources Initiatives*. New York, NY: Guiford Press.

Jacobs, D. (1999). *The knowledge offensive: Smart competition in the knowledge economy*. Deventer, The Netherlands: Samson.

Jakovljevic, M. (2002). *An instructional model for teaching complex thinking through web page design*. Unpublished Doctoral Dissertation. Johannesburg, South Africa: Rand Afrikaans University.

Jakovljevic, M. (2007). *CPTD report. Unpublished article*. Johannesburg, South Africa: University of Johannesburg.

James, M., & Rykert, L. (1998). *From workplace to workspace: Using Email lists to work together*. IDRC Publications.

Jansen, W., Steenbakkers, W., & Jagers, H. (2007). *New business models for the knowledge economy*. New York, NY: Gower Publisher.

Jarvenpaa, S. L., & Leidner, D. E. (1999). Communication and trust in global virtual teams. *Organization Science*, *10*(6), 791–815. doi:10.1287/orsc.10.6.791

Jarzabek, S., & Pettersson, U. (2006). Project-driven university-industry collaboration: Modes of collaboration, outcomes, benefits, success factors. In *Proceedings of the 2006 International Workshop on Summit on Software Engineering Education*, (pp. 9-12). IEEE.

Jasimuddin, S. M. (2008). A holistic view of knowledge management strategy. *Journal of Knowledge Management*, *12*(2), 57–66. doi:10.1108/13673270810859514

Jasimuddin, S. M., Klein, J. H., & Connell, C. (2005). The paradox of using tacit and explicit knowledge: Strategies to face dilemmas. *Management Decision*, *43*(1), 102–112. doi:10.1108/00251740510572515

Jirásek, J. A. (2004). *Duel of the brains*. Prague, Czech Republic: Alfa Publishing.

Johannesson, C. (2006). *University strategies for knowledge transfer and commercialization - An overview based on peer reviews at 24 Swedish universities. Vinnova Report 17*. Vinnova.

Johansson, U., Martensson, M., & Skoog, M. (2001). Measuring to understand intangible performance drivers. *European Accounting Review*, *10*(3), 407–437.

Johnson, B. (1992). Institutional learning. In Lundvall, B.-A. (Ed.), *National Systems of Innovation – Towards a Theory of Innovation and Interactive Learning* (pp. 23–44). London, UK: Pinter Publishers.

Johnson, G., Melin, L., & Whittington, R. (2003). Guest editors' introduction micro strategy and strategizing : Towards an activity-based view. *Journal of Management Studies*, *40*, 3–22. doi:10.1111/1467-6486.t01-2-00002

Johnson, P. S. (1975). *The economic invention and innovation*. London, UK: Martin Robertson & Company.

Joia, L. A., & Lemos, B. (2010). Relevant factors for tacit knowledge transfer within organizations. *Journal of Knowledge Management*, *14*(3), 410–427. doi:10.1108/13673271011050139

Jones, Q., & Grandhi, S. A. (2005). *Supporting proximate communities with P3-systems: Technology for connecting people-to-people-to-geographical-places*. In M. Wilber (Ed.), *The Interaction Society: Practice, Theories and Supportive Technologies*, (pp. 215-224). Hershey, PA: IGI Global.

Jones, R. (2003). Measuring the benefits of knowledge management at the financial services authority: A case study. *Journal of Information Science, 29*(6), 475–487. doi:10.1177/0165551503296005

Junnarkar, B., & Brown, C. V. (1997). Re-assessing the enabling role of information technology in KM. *Journal of Knowledge Management, 1*(2), 142–148. doi:10.1108/EUM0000000004589

Kakabadse, N. K., Kakabadse, A., & Kouzmin, A. (2003). Reviewing the knowledge management literature: Towards a taxonomy. *Journal of Knowledge Management, 7*(4), 75–91. doi:10.1108/13673270310492967

Kanji, G. K. (2002). *Measuring business excellence*. London, UK: Routledge-Taylor Francis Group.

Kaplan, R. S., & Norton, D. P. (1996). *The balanced scorecard: From strategy to action*. Boston, MA: Harvard Business School Press.

Kaplan, R. S., & Norton, D. P. (1996). *Translating strategy into action: The balanced scorecard*. Boston, MA: Harvard Business School Press.

Kaplan, R. S., Norton, D. P., & Rugelsjoen, B. (2010). Managing alliances with the balanced scorecard. *Harvard Business Review*, 114–120.

Karasavvidis, I. (2010). Wiki uses in higher education: Exploring barriers to successful implementation. *Interactive Learning Environments, 18*(3). doi:10.1080/10494820.2010.500514

Keengwe, J. (2010). Fostering cross cultural competence in preservice teachers through multicultural education experiences. *Early Childhood Education Journal, 38*(3), 197–204. doi:10.1007/s10643-010-0401-5

Kelly, G. A. (1955). *The psychology of personal constructs*. New York, NY: Norton.

Kember, D., & Leung, D. Y. P. (2005b). The influence of the teaching and learning environment on the development of generic capabilities needed for a knowledge-based society. *Learning Environments Research, 8*, 245–266. doi:10.1007/s10984-005-1566-5

Kember, D., Leung, D., & Ma, R. (2007). Characterizing learning environments capable of nurturing generic capabilities in higher education. *Research in Higher Education, 48*(5). doi:10.1007/s11162-006-9037-0

Kerr, N. L. (1989). Illusions of efficacy: The effects of group size on perceived efficacy in social dilemmas. *Journal of Experimental Social Psychology, 25*(4), 287–313. doi:10.1016/0022-1031(89)90024-3

Kessels, J. (1996). Knowledge productivity and the corporate curriculum. In J. Schreinemakers (Ed.), *Knowledge Management: Organization Competence and Methodology: Advances in Knowledge Management* (Vol. 1, pp. 168–174). Wurzburg, Germany: Ergon.

Kessels, J. (2001). Learning in organisations: A corporate curriculum for the knowledge economy. *Futures, 33*, 497–506. doi:10.1016/S0016-3287(00)00093-8

Kessler, I., & Purcell, J. (1992). Performance-related pay: Objectives and application. *Human Resource Management Journal, 2*(3), 16–33. doi:10.1111/j.1748-8583.1992.tb00258.x

Khoury, S. (1994). *Valuing intellectual properties. Internal Paper*. Midland, MI: The Dow Chemical Company.

Kidwell, J. J., Vander Linde, K. M., & Johnson, S. L. (2000). Applying corporate knowledge management practices in higher education. *EDUCAUSE Quarterly, 23*(4), 28–33.

Kiernan, M. J. (1995). *Get innovative or get dead! Building competitive companies for the 21st century*. Vancouver, Canada: Douglas & McIntyre.

Kieser, A., & Leiner, L. (2009). Why the rigour relevance gap in management research is unbridgeable. *Journal of Management Studies, 46*(3), 516–533. doi:10.1111/j.1467-6486.2009.00831.x

King, W. R. (2006). Knowledge transfer. In D. G. Schwartz (Ed.), *Encyclopedia of Knowledge Management* (pp. 538–543). Hershey, PA: IGI Global. doi:10.4018/978-1-59140-573-3.ch070doi:10.4018/978-1-59140-573-3.ch070

Kirchhoff, D. (2001). Wissensmanagement ist mehr als das Umgehen mit Informationen. *Journal für Schulentwicklung, 1*, 36–41.

Kirkgoz, Y. (2009). The challenge of developing and maintaining curriculum innovation at higher education. *Procedia Social and Behavioral Sciences, 1*, 73–78. doi:10.1016/j.sbspro.2009.01.015

Kitzinger, J. (1995). Introducing focus groups. *British Medical Journal, 311*(29), 299–302. doi:10.1136/bmj.311.7000.299

Kleiman, P. (2008). Towards transformation: Conceptions of creativity in higher education. *Educational Media International, 45*(3), 177–194.

Klopčič, J. (2006). *Pomen organizacijskega učenja v sodobni organizaciji.* Specialistično delo, Univerza v Ljubljani: Ekonomska fakulteta.

Knight, P. (2002). *The idea of a creative curriculum.* Retrieved February 4, 2011, from http://www.palatine.ac.uk/files/999.pdf

Kogut, B., & Zander, U. (1992). Knowledge of the firm, combinative capabilities, and the replication of technology. *Organization Science, 3*(3), 383–397. doi:10.1287/orsc.3.3.383

Kok, A. (2007). Intellectual capital management as part of knowledge management initiatives at institutions of higher education. *Journal of Knowledge Management, 5*(2), 181–192.

Kolb, A. Y., & Kolb, D. A. (2005). Learning styles and learning spaces: Enhancing experiential learning in higher education. *Academy of Management Learning & Education, 4*(2), 193–212. doi:10.5465/AMLE.2005.17268566

Kolb, D. G. (2008). Exploring the connectivity metaphor: Attributes dimensions and duality. *Organization Studies, 29*(1), 127–144. doi:10.1177/0170840607084574

Kollock, P., & Smith, M. (1999). *Communities in cyberspace.* London, UK: Routledge.

Kontic, L., & Cabrilo, S. (2009). A strategic model for measuring intellectual capital in Serbian industrial enterprises. *Economic Annals, 65*(183), 89–117. doi:10.2298/EKA0983089K

Kontzer, T. (2001). Management legend: Trust never goes out of style. *Information Week.* Retrieved 05/07/2011 from http://www.informationweek.com/news/6507112

Korac-Kakabadse, M., Korac-Kakabadse, A., & Kouzim, A. (2001). Leadership renewal: Towards the philosophy of wisdom. *International Review of Administrative Sciences, 67*(2), 207–227. doi:10.1177/0020852301672002

Košturiak, J., & Chal', J. (2008). *Innovation your competitive advantage!* Brno, Czech Republic: Computer Press.

Kourik, J. L., & Wang, J. (2009). Reduce pressure on students and IT services via software-vendor programs and hosting. In *Proceedings of the ACM SIGUCCS Fall Conference on User Services Conference,* (pp. 75-78). ACM Press.

KPMG. (2000). *Knowledge management research report 2000.* KPMG Consulting. Retrieved April 5, 2011, from http://www.providersedge.com/docs/km_articles/KPMG_KM_Research_Report_2000.pdf

Krimsky, S. (2003). *Science in the private interest: Has the lure of profits corrupted the virtue of biomedical research?* Lanham, UK: Rowman & Littlefield.

Kucza, T. (2001). *Knowlegde management process model.* Retrieved July 25, 2011, from http://www.vtt.fi/inf/pdf/publications/2001/P455.pdf

Kulkarni, U. R., Ravindran, S., & Freeze, R. (2007). A knowledge management success model: Theoretical development and empirical validation. *Journal of Management Information Systems, 23*(3), 309–347. doi:10.2753/MIS0742-1222230311

Kumar, J. (2004). *Transition from production-based to knowledge-based economy: An overview.* Retrieved from http://www.apo-tokyo.org/00e-books/IS-02_Training-KnowledgeWorkers.htm

Kwon, K.-S. (2011). The co-evolution of universities' academic research and knowledge-transfer activities: The case of South Korea. *Science & Public Policy, 38*(6), 493–503. doi:10.3152/030234211X12960315267930

Lachkovics, A., Metz, T., Goldberg, E., Alluri, K., & Quek, P. (2006). *Innovative use of internet-based collaboration tools and methods in an institutional context.* Retrieved from http://www.col.org/pcf3/Papers/PDFs/Lachkovics_etal_Alluri.pdf

Lach, S., & Schankerman, M. (2008). Incentives and invention in universities. *The Rand Journal of Economics*, *39*(2), 403–433. doi:10.1111/j.0741-6261.2008.00020.x

Laine, K., Sijde, P., Lahdeniemi, M., & Tarkkanen, J. (2008). *Higher education institutions and innovation in the knowledge society.* Paper presented at the Rectors' Conference of Finnish Universities of Applied Sciences. Helsinki, Finland. Retrieved from http://www.arene.fi/data/liitteet/115110=highereducationinstitutionsandinnovationintheknowledgesociety.pdf

Lainema, T., & Lainema, K. (2008). Advancing acquisition of business know-how: Critical learning elements. *Journal of Research on Technology in Education, 40*, 183–198.

Lam, A. (2000). Tacit knowledge, organizational learning and societal institutions: An integrated framework. *Organization Studies, 21*(3), 487–513. doi:10.1177/0170840600213001

Lam, A., & Lambermont-Ford, J. (2010). Knowledge sharing in organisational contexts: A motivation based perspective. *Journal of Knowledge Management, 14*(1), 51–66. doi:10.1108/13673271011015561

Lambert, R. (2003). *Lambert review of university-business collaboration.* London, UK: HM Treasury.

Lane, P. J., Koka, B. R., & Pathak, S. (2006). The reification of absorptive capacity: A critical review and rejuvenation of the construct. *Academy of Management Review, 31*(4), 833–863. doi:10.5465/AMR.2006.22527456

Lane, P. J., & Lubatkin, M. (1998). Relative absorptive capacity and interorganizational learning. *Strategic Management Journal, 19*, 461–478. doi:10.1002/(SICI)1097-0266(199805)19:5<461::AID-SMJ953>3.0.CO;2-L

Laursen, K., & Foss, N. (2003). New human resource management practices, complementarities and the impact on innovation performance. *Cambridge Journal of Economics, 27*, 243–263. doi:10.1093/cje/27.2.243

Lave, J., & Wenger, E. (1991). *Situated learning: Legitimate peripheral participation.* New York, NY: Cambridge University Press.

Lazaric, N., & Marengo, L. (2000). Towards a characterization of assets and knowledge created in technological agreements: Some evidence from the automobile robotics sector. *Industrial and Corporate Change, 9*, 53–86. doi:10.1093/icc/9.1.53

Lazar, J. R., Tsao, R., & Preece, J. (1999). One foot in cyberspace and the other on the ground: A case study of analysis and design issues in a hybrid virtual and physical community. *WebNet Journal: Internet Technologies. Applications and Issues, 1*(3), 49–57.

Leckey, J. F., & McGuigan, M. A. (1997). Right tracks—Wrong rails: The development of generic skills in higher education. *Research in Higher Education, 38*(3), 365–378. doi:10.1023/A:1024902207836

Lee, J. (2001). The impact of knowledge sharing, organizational capability and partnership quality on IS outsourcing success. *Information & Management, 38*(5), 323–335. doi:10.1016/S0378-7206(00)00074-4

Lee, N., & Horsfall, B. (2010). Accelerated learning: A study of faculty and student experiences. *Innovative Higher Education, 35*, 191–202. doi:10.1007/s10755-010-9141-0

Lee, Y. S. (1996). Technology transfer and the research university: A search for the boundaries of university-industry collaboration. *Research Policy, 25*(6), 843–863. doi:10.1016/0048-7333(95)00857-8

Lee, Y. S. (2000). The sustainability of university-industry research collaboration: An empirical assessment. *The Journal of Technology Transfer, 25*(2), 111–133. doi:10.1023/A:1007895322042

LeFever, L. (2006). *Wikis described in plain English.* Retrieved from http://www.commoncraft.com/archives/000644.html

Leinwand, P., & Mainardi, C. (2011). *the essential advantage: how to win with a capabilities-driven strategy.* Cambridge, MA: Harvard Business Review Press.

Leitch, C. (2007). An action research approach to entrepreneurship. In Neergard, H., & Ulhøi, J. P. (Eds.), *Handbook of Qualitative Research Methods in Entrepreneurship* (pp. 144–169). Cheltenham, UK: Edward Elgar.

Lengnick-Hall, M. L., & Lengnick-Hall, C. A. (2002). *Human resource management in the knowledge economy*. San Francisco, CA: Berrett-Koehle Publishers.

Leonard, D., & Sensiper, S. (2002). The role of tacit knowledge in group innovation. In N. Bontis & C. W. Choo (Eds.), *The Strategic Management of Intellectual Capital and Organizational Knowledge* (pp. 485–499). Oxford, UK: Oxford University Press. doi:10.1142/978 9814295505_0013doi:10.1142/9789814295505_0013

Leonard-Barton, D. (1995). *Wellsprings of knowledge: Building and sustaining the sources of innovation*. Boston, MA: Harvard Business School Press.

Leonard-Barton, D. (1998). Implementation as mutual adaptation of technology and organization. *Research Policy*, *17*, 251–267. doi:10.1016/0048-7333(88)90006-6

Leonard, D., & Sensiper, S. (1998). The role of tacit knowledge in group innovation. *California Management Review*, *40*(3), 112–125.

Lepak, D. P., & Snell, S. A. (1998). Virtual HR: Strategic human resource management in the 21st century. *Human Resource Management Review*, *8*(3), 215–234. doi:10.1016/S1053-4822(98)90003-1

Leuf, B., & Cunningham, W. (2001). *The wiki way: Quick collaboration on the web*. Boston, MA: Addison-Wesley.

Lev, B. (2001). *Intangibles: Management, measurement and reporting*. Washington, DC: Brooking Institute Press.

Levinthal, D. A., & March, J. G. (1993). The myopia of learning. *Strategic Management Journal*, *14*(8), 95–112. doi:10.1002/smj.4250141009

Levitt, B., & March, J. G. (1988). Organizational learning. *Annual Review of Sociology*, *14*, 319–340. doi:10.1146/annurev.so.14.080188.001535

Levitt, T. (1963, May-June). Creativity is not enough. *Harvard Business Review*, 3–10.

Lewis, D., & Allan, B. (2005). *Virtual learning communities: A guide for practitioners*. London, UK: Open University Press.

Liebeskind, J. P. (1996). Knowledge, strategy, and the theory of the firm. *Strategic Management Journal*, *17*, 93–107.

Liebowitz, J., & Chen, Y. (2003). Knowledge sharing proficiencies: The key to knowledge management. In Holsapple, C. W. (Ed.), *Handbook on Knowledge Management 1: Knowledge Matters* (pp. 409–424). Berlin, Germany: Springer.

Link, A., Siegel, D., & Bozeman, B. (2007). An empirical analysis of the propensity of academics to engage in informal university technology transfer. *Industrial and Corporate Change*, *4*(16), 641–655. doi:10.1093/icc/dtm020

Litke, H.-D. (1995). *Projektmanagement: Methoden, techniken, verhaltensweisen*. München, Germany: Hanser.

Liu, A. (2004). *The laws of cool: Knowledge work and the culture of information*. Chicago, IL: The University of Chicago Press.

Liu, T. L. (2007). Knowledge transfer: Past research and future directions. *Business Review (Federal Reserve Bank of Philadelphia)*, *7*(1), 273–281.

Liyanage, C., Elhag, T., Ballal, T., & Li, Q. (2009). Knowledge communication and translation – A knowledge transfer model. *Journal of Knowledge Management*, *13*(3), 118–131. doi:10.1108/13673270910962914

Llorens, F., & Capdeferro, N. (2011). Facebook's potential for collaborative e-learning. *Revista de Universidad y Sociedad del Conocimiento*, *8*(2), 197–210.

Long, L. N., & Schweitzer, S. J. (2004). *Information and knowledge transfer through archival journals and on-line communities*. Retrieved from http://www.personal.psu.edu/lnl/papers/aiaa2004_1264.pdf

Longworth, N., & Davies, W. K. (1996). *Lifelong learning*. London, UK: Kogan Page.

Lowendahl, B. (1997). *Strategic management of professional service firms*. Copenhagen, Denmark: Handelshojskolens Forlag.

Lubart, T. I. (2001). Models of the creative process: Past, present, and future. *Creativity Research Journal, 13*, 295–308. doi:10.1207/S15326934CRJ1334_07

Lubatkin, M., Florin, J., & Lane, P. (2001). Learning together and apart: A model of reciprocal interfirm learning. *Human Relations, 54*(10), 1353–1382.

Lumpkin, G. T., & Dess, G. G. (1996). Clarifying the entrepreneurial orientation construct and linking it to performance. *Academy of Management Review, 21*(1), 135–172.

Lundin, R. W. (2008). Teaching with wikis: Toward a networked pedagogy. *Computers and Composition, 25*(4), 432–448. doi:10.1016/j.compcom.2008.06.001

Lundvall, B. A., & Johnson, B. (1994). The learning economy. *Journal of Industry Studies, 1*, 22–42. doi:10.1080/13662719400000002

Lynn, B. (1998). Intellectual capital. *CMA Magazine, 72*(1), 10–15.

MacDuffie, J. (1995). Human resource bundles and manufacturing performance. *Industrial & Labor Relations Review, 48*(2), 197–221. doi:10.2307/2524483

Machlup, F. (1981). *Knowledge and knowledge production*. Princeton, NJ: Princeton University Press.

MacKenzie, S. B., Podsakoff, N. P., & Rich, G. A. (2001). Transformational and transactional leadership and salesperson performance. *Journal of the Academy of Marketing Science, 29*(2), 115–134. doi:10.1177/03079459994506

MacKinnon, D. (1971). Creativity and transliminal experience. *The Journal of Creative Behavior, 5*, 227–241. doi:10.1002/j.2162-6057.1971.tb00893.x

Maier, A. M., Kreimeyer, M., Hepperle, C., Eckert, C. M., Lindemann, U., & Clarkson, P. J. (2008). Exploration of correlations between factors influencing communication in complex product development. *Concurrent Engineering, 16*(1), 37. doi:10.1177/1063293X07084638

Major, E., & Cordey-Hayes, M. (2000). Knowledge translation: a new perspective on knowledge transfer and foresight. *Foresight, 2*(4), 411–423. doi:10.1108/14636680010802762

Malhotra, Y. (2000). *Knowledge management and virtual organizations*. Hershey, PA: IGI Global. doi:10.4018/978-1-87828-973-5

Management Consulting, K. P. M. G. (1998). *Case Study: Building a platform for corporate knowledge*. New York, NY: KPMG Management Consulting.

Mansfield, E. (1995). Academic research underlying industrial innovations: Sources, characteristics, and financing. *The Review of Economics and Statistics, 77*(1), 55–65. doi:10.2307/2109992

March, J. G. (1991). Exploration and exploitation in organizational learning. *Organization Science, 2*(1), 71–87. doi:10.1287/orsc.2.1.71

Marengo, L. (1994). *Structure, competence and learning in an adaptive model of the firm. Papers in Economics and Evolution no. 9203*. Freiburg, Germany: European Study Group for Evolutionary Economics.

Marlow, A., Spratt, C., & Reilly, A. (2008). Collaborative action in learning: A professional development model for educational innovation in nursing. *Nurse Education in Practice, 8*, 184–489. doi:10.1016/j.nepr.2007.07.001

Marquardt, M. J. (1996). *Building the learning organization: A systems approach to quantum improvement and global success*. New York, NY: McGraw-Hill.

Marqués, D. P., & Simón, F. J. G. (2006). The effect of knowledge management practices on firm performance. *Journal of Knowledge Management, 10*(3), 143–156. doi:10.1108/13673270610670911

Marr, B., Gupta, O., Pike, S., & Roos, G. (2003). Intellectual capital and knowledge management effectiveness. *Management Decision, 1*(8), 771–781. doi:10.1108/00251740310496288

Marshall, N. (2008). Cognitive and practice based theories of organizational knowledge and learning: Incompatible or complementary. *Management Learning, 39*(4), 413–435. doi:10.1177/1350507608093712

Martensson, M. (2000). A critical review of knowledge management as a management tool. *Journal of Knowledge Management, 4*(3), 204–216. doi:10.1108/13673270010350002

Martin, B. (2000). Knowledge management within the context of management: An evolving relationship. *Singapore Management Review*, *22*(2), 17–36.

Martin, K., & Bourke, J. (2009). *Integrated talent management: Improving business results through visibility and alignment*. Boston, MA: Aberdeen Group.

Martinka, V. (2006). *Inovacije članak: Praksa inoviranja*. Retrieved July 2011, from http://www.quantum21.net

Martins, P. S. (2004). *Firm-level social returns to education*. IZA Discussion Paper, 1382. Retrieved from http://www.econstor.eu/bitstream/10419/20678/1/dp1382.pdf

Martins, L. L., Gilson, L. L., & Maynard, M. T. (2004). Virtual teams: What do we know and where do we go from here? *Journal of Management*, *30*(6), 805. doi:10.1016/j.jm.2004.05.002

Mascha, M. F. (2001). The effect of task complexity and expert system type on the acquisition of procedural knowledge: Some new evidence. *International Journal of Accounting Information Systems*, *2*(2), 103–124. doi:10.1016/S1467-0895(01)00016-1

Matos, F., Lopes, A., Rodrigues, S., & Matos, N. (2010). Why intellectual capital management accreditation is a tool for organizational development? *Electronic Journal of Knowledge Management*, *8*(2), 235–244.

Matsuo, M., & Kusumi, T. (2002). Salesperson's procedural knowledge, experience and performance: An empirical study in Japan. *European Journal of Marketing*, *36*(7/8), 840–854. doi:10.1108/03090560210430836

Mayer, J. D., Salovey, P., & Caruso, D. (2000). Models of emotional intelligence. In Sternberg, R. (Ed.), *Handbook of Human Intelligence* (pp. 396–420). New York, NY: Cambridge University Press.

McAdam, R., & McCreedy, S. (1999). A critical review of knowledge management models. *The Learning Organization*, *6*(3), 91–100. doi:10.1108/09696479910270416

McCarthy, J. (2009). Utilising Facebook: Immersing generation-Y students into first year university. *Ergo*, *1*(2), 39–49.

McCreadie, M., Choudhurry, S., Bielec, J. A., Worona, S., & Stern, N. (2009). *The technology revolution in higher education: IT as a catalyst of change*. Paper presented at the Mid-Atlantic Regional Conferences. Durham, NC.

McDermott, R. (2000). *Learning across teams: The role of communities of practice in team organisations*. Retrieved from http://home.att.net/~discon/KM/Learning.pdf

McDonald, L. (2006). *Fundamo awarded technology leadership award*. Retrieved 15 July, 2010, from http://www.cbr.co.za/news.aspx?pklnewsid=22202

McElroy, M. W. (2000). Integrating complexity theory, knowledge management and organizational learning. *Journal of Knowledge Management*, *4*(3), 195–203. doi:10.1108/13673270010377652

McGoldrick, C. (2002). Creativity and curriculum design: What academics think? York, UK: LTSN Generic Centre. Retrieved May 2011, from http://www.palatine.ac.uk/files/1038.pdf

McGrath, R. (2001). Exploratory learning, innovative capacity and managerial oversight. *Academy of Management Journal*, *44*, 118–131. doi:10.2307/3069340

McGuinness, M. (2011). *RSS creativity, routines, systems, spontaneity*. Retrieved 10 August 2011, from http://the99percent.com/tips/6127/rss-creativity-routines-systems-spontaneity

McKelvey, M., & Holmén, M. (Eds.). (2009). *Learning to compete in European universities: From social institution to knowledge business*. Cheltenham, UK: Edward Elgar.

Mckeown, M. (2008). *The truth about innovation*. Upper Saddle River, NJ: Pearson.

McLean, J. E. (2005, June/July). ICT and knowledge management. *British Journal of Administrative Management*, 17–18.

McLuhan, M. (1962). *The Gutenberg galaxy*. London, UK: Routledge & Kegan Paul.

McNabb, D. E. (2007). *Knowledge management in the public sector: A blueprint for innovation in government*. New York, NY: M.E. Sharpe, Inc.

McNichols, D. (2010). Optimal knowledge transfer methods: A generation X perspective. *Journal of Knowledge Management, 14*(1), 24–37. doi:10.1108/13673271011015543

McWhorter. Mancuso, & Hurt. (2008). *Adult learning in a virtual environment.* Retrieved from http://www.slideshare.net/rochell/adult-learning-in-a-virtual-environment-ahrd-2008

Meeker, M. (1969). *The structure of intellect: Its interpretation and uses.* Columbus, OH: Charles E. Merrill Publishing Company.

Mende, J. (2006). *Using inference trees to detect reasoning errors in expository reports.* Paper presented at the Teaching and Learning Conference, CLTD. Johannesburg, South Africa.

Merriam, S. (1983). Mentors and protégés: A critical review of the literature. *Adult Education Quarterly, 33*(3), 161–173.

Merriam, S. B. (2009). *Qualitative research: A guide to design and implementation.* San Francisco, CA: Jossey-Bass.

Meso, P., & Smith, R. (2000). A resource-based view of organizational knowledge management systems. *Journal of Knowledge Management, 4*(3), 224–234. doi:10.1108/13673270010350020

Messinger, P. R., Stroulia, E., Lyons, K., Bone, M., Niu, R., Smirnov, K., & Perelgut, S. (2009). Virtual worlds – Past, present, and future: New directions in social computing. *Decision Support Systems, 47*, 204–228. doi:10.1016/j.dss.2009.02.014

Metcalfe, A. S. (2006). The political economy of knowledge management in higher education. In Metcalfe, A. S. (Ed.), *Knowledge Management and Higher Education: A Critical Analysis* (pp. 1–20). Hershey, PA: IGI Global. doi:10.4018/978-1-59140-509-2.ch001

Meyer-Krahmer, F., & Schmoch, U. (1998). Science-based technologies: University-industry interactions in four fields. *Research Policy, 27*(8), 835–851. doi:10.1016/S0048-7333(98)00094-8

Middlehurst, R., Goreham, H., & Woodfield, S. (2009). Why research leadership in higher education? Exploring contributions from the UK's leadership foundation for higher education. *Leadership, 5*(3), 311–329. doi:10.1177/1742715009337763

Miller, D., & Friesen, P. H. (1980). Momentum and revolution in organizational adaptation. *Academy of Management Journal, 23*, 591–614. doi:10.2307/255551

Minocha, S., Petre, M., & Roberts, D. (2008). Using wikis to simulate distributed requirements development in a software engineering course. *International Journal of Engineering Education, 24*(4), 689–704.

Minonne, C. (2007). *Towards an integrative approach for managing implicit and explicit knowledge: An exploratory study in Switzerland.* Unpublished Doctoral Dissertation. Adelaide, Australia: University of South Australia.

Minonne, C. (2008, November-December). Wissensmanagement: Wie lautet das erfolgsrezept. *Wissensmanagement Magazin*, 48-49.

Minonne, C. (2009). *Strategic knowledge management: An integrative approach.* Saarbrücken, Germany: SVH Verlag.

Minonne, C., & Turner, G. (2009). Evaluating knowledge management performance. *Electronic Journal of Knowledge Management, 7*(5), 583–592.

Mintzberg, H. (2004). *Managers, not MBAs: A hard look at the soft practice of managing and management development.* San Francisco, CA: Berrett-Koehler.

Mirk, S. M., Burkiewicz, J. S., & Komperda, K. E. (2010). Student perception of a wiki in a pharmacy elective course. *Currents in Pharmacy Teaching and Learning, 2*(2), 72–78. doi:10.1016/j.cptl.2010.01.002

Mitev, N., & Venters, W. (2009). Reflexive evaluation of an academic industry research collaboration: Can mode two research be achieved? *Journal of Management Studies, 46*(5), 733–754. doi:10.1111/j.1467-6486.2009.00846.x

Mlčoch, J. (2002). *Innovation and organizational productivity.* Prague, Czech Republic: Linde.

Moffet, S., McAdam, R., & Parkinson, S. (2002). Developing a model for technology and cultural factors in knowledge management: A factor analysis. *Knowledge and Process Management, 9*(4), 237–255. doi:10.1002/kpm.152

Mooradian, N. (2005). Tacit knowledge: Philosophical roots and role in KM. *Journal of Knowledge Management, 9*(6), 104–113. doi:10.1108/13673270510629990

Moos, B., Beimborn, D., Wagner, H.-T., & Weitzel, T. (2010). *Knowledge management systems, absorptive capacity, and innovation success*. Unpublished. Retrieved 06/08/2011 from http://is2.lse.ac.uk/asp/aspecis/20110149.pdf

Morgenson, F. P., Reider, M. H., & Campion, M. A. (2005). Selecting individuals in team settings: The importance of social skills, personality characteristics and team performance. *Personnel Psychology, 58*, 583–611. doi:10.1111/j.1744-6570.2005.655.x

Morrison, A., & Johnston, B. (2006). Personal creativity for entrepreneurship: Teaching and learning strategies. *Active Learning in Higher Education, 4*, 145–158. doi:10.1177/1469787403004002003

Morrow, N. M. (2001). Knowledge management: An introduction. In M. E. Williams (Ed.), *Annual Review of Information Science and Technology (ARIST), 35*, 381-422.

Mostert, N. (2007). Diversity of the mind as the key to successful creativity at Unilever. *Creativity and Innovation Management, 16*(1), 93–100. doi:10.1111/j.1467-8691.2007.00422.x

Mouritsen, J., Bukh, P., Larsen, H., & Johansen, M. (2002). Developing and managing knowledge through intellectual capital statements. *Journal of Intellectual Capital, 3*(1), 10–29. doi:10.1108/14691930210412818

Mowery, D. C., & Nelson, R. R. (Eds.). (2004). *Ivory tower and industrial innovation: University-industry technology before and after the Bayh-Dole act*. Palo Alto, CA: Stanford University Press.

Mowery, D. C., & Sampat, B. N. (2005). The Bayh-Dole act of 1980 and university–industry technology transfer: A model for other OECD governments? *The Journal of Technology Transfer, 30*(1/2), 115–127.

Murthy, K. V. B. (2007). *Re-engineering higher education - The knowledge management system*. Retrieved from http://ssrn.com/abstract=1073742

Myers, P. S. (1996). *Knowledge management and organizational design*. Boston, MA: Butterworth-Heinemann.

Nahapiet, J., & Ghoshal, S. (1998). Social capital, intellectual capital and the organizational advantage. *Academy of Management Review, 23*, 242–266.

Nanda, A. (1996). Resources, capabilities, and competencies. In Moingeon, B., & Edmonson, A. (Eds.), *Organizational Learning and Competitive Advantage* (pp. 93–120). London, UK: Sage. doi:10.4135/9781446250228.n6

Ndonzuau, F., Pirnay, F., & Surlemont, B. (2002). A stage model of academic spin-off creation. *Technovation, 22*, 281–289. doi:10.1016/S0166-4972(01)00019-0

Neely, A. (2002). *Business performance measurement*. London, UK: Economist Books. doi:10.1017/CBO9780511753695

Nelson, R. R. (2004). The market economy, and the scientific commons. *Research Policy, 33*(3), 455–471. doi:10.1016/j.respol.2003.09.008

Nelson, R. R., & Winter, S. G. (1982). *An evolutionary theory of economic change*. Cambridge, MA: Harvard University Press.

Neo, B. S., & Chen, G. (2007). *Dynamic governance: Embedding culture, capabilities and change in Singapore*. Singapore: World Scientific. doi:10.1142/9789812771919

Newell, G., Scarbrough, H., Bresnen, M., Edelman, L., & Swan, J. (2000). Sharing knowledge across projects: Limits to ICT led projects review. *Management Learning Practices, 37*, 167–185. doi:10.1177/1350507606063441

Newell, S., David, G., & Chand, D. (2007). An analysis of trust among globally distributed work teams in and organisational setting. *Knowledge and Process Management, 14*(3), 158–168. doi:10.1002/kpm.284

Nickols, F. W. (2000). The knowledge in knowledge management. In Cortada, J. W., & Woods, J. A. (Eds.), *The Knowledge Management Yearbook 2000-2001* (pp. 12–21). Boston, MA: Butterworth-Heinemann.

Noble, D. F. (1977). *America by design: Science, technology, and the rise of 37 corporate capitalism*. New York, NY: Knopf.

Nonaka, I., & Takeuchi, H. (1995). *The knowledge creating company: How Japanese companies create the dynamics of innovation*. Oxford, UK: Oxford University Press.

Nonaka, I. (1991). The knowledge-creating economy. *Harvard Business Review*, *69*(6), 96–104.

Nonaka, I. (1994). A dynamic theory of organizational knowledge creation. *Organization Science*, *5*(1), 14–37. doi:10.1287/orsc.5.1.14

Nonaka, I. (1994). A dynamic theory of organizational knowledge creation. *Organization Science*, *5*(1), 14–37. doi:10.1287/orsc.5.1.14

Nonaka, I. (2007). The knowledge-creating company. *Harvard Business Review*, *85*(7/8), 162–171.

Nonaka, I., & Konno, N. (1998). The concept of "ba": Building a foundation for knowledge creation. *California Management Review*, *40*(3), 673–684.

Nonaka, I., & Peltokorpi, V. (2006). Objectivity and subjectivity in knowledge management: A review of top twenty articles. *Knowledge and Process Management*, *13*(2), 73–82. doi:10.1002/kpm.251

Nonaka, I., & Takeuchi, H. (1995). *The knowledge creating company: How Japanese companies create the dynamics of innovation*. Oxford, UK: Oxford University Press.

Nonaka, I., Toyama, R., & Hirata, T. (2008). *Managing flow: A process theory of the knowledge-based firm*. Hampshire, UK: Palgrave Macmillan Ltd.

Nonaka, I., Toyama, R., & Konno, N. (2000). SECI, ba and leadership: A unified model of dynamic knowledge creation. *Long Range Planning*, *33*(4), 4–34.

Nonaka, I., Toyama, R., & Nagata, A. (2000). A firm as a knowledge-creating entity: A new perspective on the theory of the firm. *Industrial and Corporate Change*, *9*(1), 1–20. doi:10.1093/icc/9.1.1

Nonaka, I., & von Krogh, G. (2009). Tacit knowledge and knowledge conversion: Controversy and advancement in organizational knowledge creation theory. *Organization Science*, *20*(3), 635–652. doi:10.1287/orsc.1080.0412

North, K., & Hornung, T. (2003). The benefits of knowledge management - Results of the German award "knowledge manager 2002". *Journal of Universal Computer Science*, *9*(6), 463–471.

NSF. (2007). *Knowledge transfer activities in connection with nanoscale science and engineering. Final Report*. Washington, DC: National Science Foundation.

O'Dell, C. (1998). *If only we knew what we know: The transfer of internal knowledge and best practice*. New York, NY: The Free Press.

O'Leonard, K. (2009). *Bersin & associates 2009 talent management factbook: Executive summary*. Retrieved April 20, 2011, from http://www.bersin.com/uploadedFiles/052909_ES_TMFactbook2009_KOL_Final.pdf

Oakland, J. S. (1995). *Total quality management - The route to improving performance*. Oxford, UK: Elsevier Butteworth Heinemann Ltd. Oakland, J. S. (2003). *Total quality management-Text with cases*. Oxford, UK: Elsevier Butteworth-Heinemann Ltd.

O'Dell, C., & Grayson, C. J. Jr. (1999). Knowledge transfer: Discover your value proposition. *Strategy and Leadership*, *27*(2), 10–15. doi:10.1108/eb054630

OECD Directorate for Education. (2007). *Research and knowledge management*. Retrieved from http://www.oecd.org/about/0,3347,en_2649_39263301_1_1_1_1_1,00.html

OECD. (1996). *Measuring what people know: Human capital accounting for the knowledge economy*. Paris, France: OECD Publishing.

OECD. (2005). *Oslo manual: Guidelines for collecting and interpreting innovation data*. OECD.

OECD. (2007). *Higher education and region: Globally competitive locally engaged*. OECD Publication.

OECD. (2007). *Innovation and growth: Rational for an innovation strategy*. OECD Publication.

OECD. (2008a). *Science, technology and industry outlook*. Paris, France: OECD.

OECD. (2008b). *Higher education to 2030: Demography (Vol. 1)*. Paris, France: OECD.

OECD. (2009). *The OECD innovation strategy: An interim report*. Paris, France: OECD.

Oldham, G. R., & Cummings, A. (1996). Employee creativity: Personal and contextual factors at work. *Academy of Management Journal, 39*(3), 607–634. doi:10.2307/256657

Orlikowski, W. J. (1992). The duality of technology: Rethinking the concept of technology in organizations. *Organization Science, 3*(3), 398–427. doi:10.1287/orsc.3.3.398

Orlikowski, W. J. (2007). Sociomaterial practices: Exploring technology at work. *Organization Studies, 28*(9), 1435–1448. doi:10.1177/0170840607081138

Orr, D. W. (1996). Slow knowledge. *Conservation Biology, 10*(3), 699–702. doi:10.1046/j.1523-1739.1996.10030699.x

Osborn, A. (1953). *Applied imagination*. New York, NY: Charles Scribner.

Osguthorpe, R. T., & Graham, C. R. (2003). Blended learning environments, definitions and directions. *The Quarterly Review of Distance Education, 4*(3), 227–233.

Overseas Development Institute. (2009). *Helping researchers become policy entrepreneur*. London, UK: Overseas Development Institute.

Owen, H. (2008). *Open space technology: A user's guide* (3rd ed.). San Francisco, CA: Berrett-Koehler.

Owen-Smith, J., & Powell, W. W. (2003). To patent or not: Faculty decisions and institutional success at technology transfer. *The Journal of Technology Transfer, 26*(1), 99–114. doi:10.1023/A:1007892413701

Panckhurst, R. (2008). *Communities of practice: Using the open web as a collaborative learning platform*. Retrieved from http://halshs.archives-ouvertes.fr/hal-00291874/

Paquet, S. (2002). *Personal knowledge publishing and its uses in research*. Retrieved from http://weblogs.com/0110772/stories/2002/10/03/

Parker, K. R., & Chao, J. T. (2007). Wikis as a teaching tool. *Interdisciplinary Journal of Knowledge and Learning Objects, 3*, 16.

Parkhe, A. (1993). Strategic alliances structuring: A game theoretic and transaction cost examination of infirm cooperation. *Academy of Management Journal, 38*(4), 794–829. doi:10.2307/256759

Pascale, R. T., Millemann, M., & Gioja, L. (2000). *Surfing the edge of chaos*. New York, NY: Random House.

Patterson, G. (2001). The applicability of institutional goals to the university. *Journal of Higher Education Policy and Management, 23*(2), 159–169. doi:10.1080/13600800120088652

Pearlson, K. E., & Saunders, C. S. (2004). *Managing and using information systems: A strategic approach*. New York, NY: John Wiley and Sons.

Pelgrum, W. J. (2001). Obstacles to the integration of ICT in education: Results from a worldwide educational assessment. *Computers & Education, 37*, 163–178. doi:10.1016/S0360-1315(01)00045-8

Pena, I. (2002). Knowledge networks as part of an integrated knowledge management approach. *Journal of Knowledge Management, 6*(5), 469–478. doi:10.1108/13673270210450423

Penrose, E. T. (1959). *The theory of the growth of the firm*. New York, NY: John Wiley.

Perkmann, M., & Walsh, K. (2007). University-industry relationships and open innovation: Towards a research agenda. *International Journal of Management Reviews, 9*(4), 259–280. doi:10.1111/j.1468-2370.2007.00225.x

Perkmann, M., & Walsh, K. (2008). Engaging the scholar: Three forms of academic consulting and their impact on universities and industry. *Research Policy, 37*(10), 1884–1891. doi:10.1016/j.respol.2008.07.009

Perry, M. (2002). *Knowledge management processes in university*. M.A Thesis. Tel Aviv, Israel: Tel Aviv University.

Perry, M., & Shoham, S. (2007). *Knowledge management as a mechanism for large-scale technological and organizational change management in Israeli Universities*. Unpublished.

Petrides, L., & Nguyen, L. (2006). Knowledge management trends: Challenges and opportunities for education institutions. In Metcalfe, A. S. (Ed.), *Knowledge Management and Higher Education: A Critical Analysis* (pp. 21–33). Hershey, PA: IGI Global. doi:10.4018/978-1-59140-509-2.ch002

Pfeffer, J. (1997). Pitfalls on the road to measurement: The dangerous liaison of human resources with the ideas of accounting and finance. *Human Resource Management, 36*(3), 357–365. doi:10.1002/(SICI)1099-050X(199723)36:3<357::AID-HRM7>3.0.CO;2-V

Pfeffer, J. (1998). Six dangerous myths about pay. *Harvard Business Review, 76*(3), 108–119.

Pfeffer, J., & Sutton, R. (2000). *The knowing-doing gap.* Boston, MA: Harvard Business School Press.

Pfleeger, S., & Merty, N. (1995). Executive mentoring: What makes it work? *Communications of the American Academy of Management, 38*(1), 63–73.

Piccoli, G., Ahmad, R., & Ives, B. (2000). Knowledge management in academia: A proposed framework. *Information Technology Management, 1,* 229–245. doi:10.1023/A:1019129226227

Pike, S., & Roos, G. (2000). Intellectual capital measurement and holistic value approach (HVA). *Works Institute Journal, 42.*

Pitra, Z. (1997). *The role of innovations in business strategy.* Prague, Czech Republic: Grada Publishing.

Polanyi, M. (1966). *The tacit dimension.* New York, NY: Doubleday.

Polanyi, M. (1958). *Personal knowledge: Towards a post-critical philosophy.* London, UK: Routledge and Kegan Paul Ltd.

Polanyi, M. (1966). *The tacit dimension.* Garden City, NY: Doubleday & Company, Inc.

Polanyi, M. (1975). Personal knowledge. In Polanyi, M., & Prosch, H. (Eds.), *Meaning* (pp. 22–45). Chicago, IL: University of Chicago Press.

Polyani, M. (1969). *Knowing and being.* London, UK: Routledge and Kogan Paul Ltd.

Powell, W. W., & Snellman, K. (2004). The knowledge economy. *Annual Review of Sociology, 30,* 199–220. doi:10.1146/annurev.soc.29.010202.100037

Prahalad, C. K., & Bettis, R. A. (1986). The dominant logic: A new linkage between diversity and performance. *Strategic Management Journal, 7*(6), 485–501. doi:10.1002/smj.4250070602

Prahalad, C. K., & Hamel, G. (1990, May-June). The core competence of the corporation. *Harvard Business Review,* 79–91.

Preece, J. (2000). *Online communities: Designing usability, supporting sociability.* New York, NY: John Wiley & Sons, Inc.

Preece, J., Maloney-Krichmar, D., & Abras, C. (2003). History and emergence of online communities. In Wellman, B. (Ed.), *Encyclopedia of Community.* Thousand Oaks, CA: Sage.

Prester, J. (2010). *Management of innovations.* Zagreb, Croatia: Sinergija, nakladništvo, d o.o.

Price, S., Oliver, M., Fartunova, M., Jones, C., Van der Meij, H., & Mjelstad, S. … Wasson, B. (2005). *Review of the impact of technology-enhanced learning on roles and practices in higher education.* Kaleidoscope project deliverable 30-02-01-F. Retrieved from http://hal.archives-ouvertes.fr/docs/00/19/01/47/PDF/Price-Kaleidoscope-2005.pdf

Probst, G., Raub, S., & Romhardt, K. (1999). *Wissen managen: Wie unternehmen ihre wertvollste ressource optimal nutzen.* Frankfurt, Germany: FAZ.

Probst, G., Raub, S., & Romhardt, K. (1999). *Managing knowledge: Building blocks for success.* New York, NY: John Wiley & Sons.

Prusak, L., & Granefield, J. (2010). Managing your own knowledge: A personal perspective. In Pauleen, D., & Gorman, G. E. (Eds.), *Personal Knowledege Management* (pp. 99–113). Surrey, UK: Gower.

Pulic, A. (1998). *Measuring the performance of intellectual potential in knowledge economy.* Paper presented at the 2nd World Congress on Measuring and Managing Intellectual Capital. Hamilton, Canada.

Puxty, A. G. (1993). *The social and organizational context of management accounting.* London, UK: Academic Press.

Pyöriä, P. (2005). The concept of knowledge work revisited. *Journal of Knowledge Management, 9*(3), 116–127. doi:10.1108/13673270510602818

Quinn, J. B. (1992). *Intelligent enterprise: A knowledge and service based paradigm for industry.* New York, NY: The Free Press.

Quinn, J. B., Anderson, P., & Finkelstein, S. (1996). Managing professional intellect: Making the most of the best. *Harvard Business Review, 74*(2), 71–80.

Quintas, P., Lefrere, P., & Jones, G. (1997). Knowledge management: A strategic agenda. *Long Range Planning, 30*(3), 385–391. doi:10.1016/S0024-6301(97)90252-1

Rahe, M. (2009). Subjectivity and cognition in knowledge management. *Journal of Knowledge Management, 13*(3), 102–117. doi:10.1108/13673270910962905

Ramanathan, K., Seth, A., & Thomas, H. (2001). The value of new knowledge-based intangible assets: An examination of in the global pharmaceutical industry. In Forak, J. (Ed.), *Valuation of Intangible Assets in Global Operations.* Westport, CT: Quorum Books.

Raman, M., Ryan, T., & Olfman, L. (2005). Designing knowledge management systems for teaching and learning with wiki technology. *Journal of Information Systems Education, 16*(3), 311.

Rank, J., Pace, V. L., & Frese, M. (2004). Three avenues for future research on creativity, innovation, and initiative. *Applied Psychology: An International Review, 53*, 518–528. doi:10.1111/j.1464-0597.2004.00185.x

Rapoport, A., Bornstein, G., & Erev, I. (1989). Intergroup competition for public goods: Effects of unequal resources and relative group size. *Journal of Personality and Social Psychology, 56*(5), 748–756. doi:10.1037/0022-3514.56.5.748

Ratha, D. (2011). Worldwide remittance flows updated to $483 billion for 2011. *People Move (World Bank).* Retrieved 7 December, 2011, from http://blogs.worldbank.org/peoplemove/worldwide-remittance-flows-updated-to-483-billion-for-2011

Reber, A. (1989). Implicit learning and tacit knowledge. *Journal of Experimental Psychology, 118*(3), 219–235.

Reilly, R., & Schweihs, R. (1999). *Valuing intangible assets.* New York, NY: McGraw-Hill.

Repko, A. F. (2008). *Interdisciplinary research.* Thousand Oaks, CA: Sage Publications.

Report, D. (2007). *Dearing.* Retrieved May 2011, from http://www.bbc.co.uk/news/special//politics97/news/07/0723

Research, A. B. I. (2007). *Social communities go mobile: 174 million members forecasted by 2011.* Retrieved from http://www.abiresearch.com/abiprdisplay.jsp?pressid=780

Revans, R. (1980). *Action learning.* London, UK: Blond & Briggs.

Rheingold, H. (2003). Mobile virtual communities. *The Feature.* Retrieved from http://www.thefeaturearchives.com/topic/Culture/Mobile_Virtual_Communities.html

Ricarda. (2007). *Intellectual capital reporting for regional cluster and networking initiatives: Developing and application of a methodology.* Ricarda.

Richardson, W. (2009). *Blogs, wikis, podcasts, and other powerful web tools for classrooms* (2nd ed.). Thousand Oaks, CA: Corwin Press.

Rick, J., & Guzdial, M. (2006). Situating CoWeb: A scholarship of application. *International Journal of Computer-Supported Collaborative Learning, 1*(1), 89–115. doi:10.1007/s11412-006-6842-6

Rix, G., & Lièvre, P. (2008). Towards a codification of practical knowledge. *Knowledge Management Research & Practice, 6*(3), 225–232. doi:10.1057/kmrp.2008.13

Roberts, E. (2007). Managing invention and innovation. *Research Technology Management, 50*, 35–54.

Roberts, J. (2000). From know-how to show-how? Questioning the role of information and communication technologies in knowledge transfer. *Technology Analysis and Strategic Management, 12*(4), 429–443. doi:10.1080/713698499

Robinson, R. B. (1982). The importance of "outsiders" in small firm strategic planning. *Academy of Management Journal, 25*(1), 80–93. doi:10.2307/256025

Rodgers, W. (2003). Measurement and reporting of knowledge-based assets. *Journal of Intellectual Capital, 4,* 181–190. doi:10.1108/14691930310472802

Roehl, H. (2000). *Instrumente der wissensorganization.* Wiesbaden, Germany: Gabler.

Roos, G., & Roos, J. (1997). Measuring your company's intellectual performance. *Long Range Planning, 30,* 413–426. doi:10.1016/S0024-6301(97)90260-0

Roos, G., Roos, J., Dragonetti, N., & Edvinsson, L. (1998). *Intellectual capital: Navigating in the new business landscape.* New York, NY: New York University Press.

Roos, J., & von Krogh, G. (2002). The new language lab – Parts 1 and 2. In Little, S., Quintas, P., & Ray, P. (Eds.), *Managing Knowledge: An Essential Reader.* London, UK: Sage.

Rosell, C., & Agrawal, A. (2009). Have university knowledge flows narrowed? Evidence from patent data. *Research Policy, 38*(1), 1–13. doi:10.1016/j.respol.2008.07.014

Roslender, R., & Dyson, J. R. (1992). Accounting for the worth of employees: A new look at an old problem. *The British Accounting Review, 24*(4), 311–329. doi:10.1016/S0890-8389(05)80040-X

Rothenberg, A., & Hausman, C. R. (1976). *The creativity question.* Durham, NC: Duke University Press.

Rowley, J. (2000). From learning organisation to knowledge entrepreneur. *Journal of Knowledge Management, 4*(1), 7–15. doi:10.1108/13673270010315362

Rowley, J. (2006). Where is the wisdom that we have lost in knowledge? *The Journal of Documentation, 62*(2), 251–270. doi:10.1108/00220410610653322

Rüdiger, M., & Vanini, S. (1998). Das tacit knowledge phänomen und seine implikationen für das innovationsmanagement. *DBW, 58*(4), 467–480.

Russell, J. A., & Barrett, L. F. (1999). Core affect, prototypical emotional episodes, and other things called emotion: Dissecting the elephant. *Journal of Personality and Social Psychology, 76*(5), 805–819. doi:10.1037/0022-3514.76.5.805

Saaty, T. L. (1980). *The analytic hierarchy process.* New York, NY: McGraw-Hill.

Sabar Ben Yehoshua, N. (1990). *The qualitative research.* Givataim, Israel: Massada.

Sackman, S. A., Flamholtz, E. G., & Bullen, M. L. (1989). Human resource accounting: A state of the art review. *Journal of Accounting Literature, 8,* 235–264.

Sainsbury, L. (2007). *Race to the top: Sainsbury review of science and innovation.* London, UK: HM Treasury.

Šajeva, S. (2010). The analysis of key elements of socio-technical knowledge management system. *Ekonomika IR Vadyba, 15,* 765–775.

Salas, E., Wildman, J. L., & Piccolo, R. F. (2009). Using simulation-based training to enhance management education. *Academy of Management Learning & Education, 8,* 559–573. doi:10.5465/AMLE.2009.47785474

Saldaña, J. (2009). *The coding manual for qualitative researchers.* Thousand Oaks, CA: Sage Publications.

Saleh, N., & McKinnon, S. (2009). *MineWiki: The use of wiki technology as a tool in a senior mine design course.* Paper presented at the 6th Canadian Design Engineering Network (CDEN) Annual Conference. Hamilton, Canada.

Salisbury, M. W., & Plass, J. L. (2001). Design and development of a web-based knowledge management system. *Journal of Interactive Instruction Development, 14,* 23–29.

Salvato, C. (2003). The role of micro-strategies in the engineering of firm evolution. *Journal of Management Studies, 40*(1), 83–108. doi:10.1111/1467-6486.t01-2-00005

Sanderlands, L. E., & Stablein, R. E. (1987). The concept of organization mind. In Bachrach, S., & DiTomaso, N. (Eds.), *Research in the Sociology of Organization* (*Vol. 5,* pp. 135–162). Greenwich, CT: JAI Press.

Santoro, M., & Bierly, P. E. (2006). Facilitators of knowledge transfer in university-industry collaborations: A knowledge-based perspective. *IEEE Transactions on Engineering Management, 53*(4), 495–507. doi:10.1109/TEM.2006.883707

Santoro, M., & Gopalakrishnan, S. (2000). The institutionalization of knowledge transfer activities within industry–university collaborative ventures. *Journal of Engineering and Technology Management, 17*, 299–319. doi:10.1016/S0923-4748(00)00027-8

Sarvary, M. (1999). Knowledge management and competition in the consulting industry. *California Management Review, 41*, 95–108.

Satterfield, B. (2006). *Exploring the world of wikis: Collaborative Web sites organize information, encourage participation.* Retrieved from http://www.techsoup.org/learningcenter/webbuilding/

Scarborough, H., & Knights, D. (2009). *In search of relevance.* Organisation Studies.

Scarborough, H. (2008). *The evolution of business knowledge.* Oxford, UK: Oxford University Press.

Scarbrough, H. (2003). Knowledge management, HRM and the innovation process. *International Journal of Manpower, 24*(5), 501–516. doi:10.1108/01437720310491053

Scarbrough, H., Swan, J., & Preston, J. (1999). *Knowledge management: A literature review.* London, UK: Institute of Personnel and Development.

Scardamalia, M., & Bereiter, C. (2003). Knowledge building. In Guthrie, J. W. (Ed.), *Encyclopedia of Education* (2nd ed., pp. 1370–1373). New York, NY: Macmillan Reference.

Schacter, D. L. (1996). *Searching for memory: The brain, the mind, and the past.* New York, NY: Basic Books.

Schartinger, D., Rammer, C., Fischer, M. M., & Fröhlich, J. (2002). Knowledge interactions between universities and industry in Austria: Sectoral patterns and determinants. *Research Policy, 31*(3), 303–328. doi:10.1016/S0048-7333(01)00111-1

Schienstock, G. (2011). Path dependency and path creation: Continuity vs. fundamental change in national economies. *Journal of Future Studies, 12*(4), 63–67.

Schonstrom, M. (2005). Creating knowledge networks: Lessons from practice. *Journal of Knowledge Management, 9*(6), 17–29. doi:10.1108/13673270510629936

Schoonhoven, C., Eisenhardt, K., & Lyman, K. (1990). Speeding products to market: Waiting time to first product introduction in new firms. *Administrative Science Quarterly, 35*, 177–207. doi:10.2307/2393555

Schumpeter, J. A. (1934). *The theory of economic development: An inquiry into profits, capital, credit, interest, and the business cycle* (Opie, R., Trans.). Cambridge, MA: Harvard University Press.

Schumpeter, J. A. (1961). *Theory of economic development.* Oxford, UK: Oxford University Press.

Schwartz, M. F., & Woods, D. C. M. (1993). Discovering shared interests among people using graph analysis. *Communications of the ACM, 36*(8), 78–89. doi:10.1145/163381.163402

Scott, S. G., & Bruce, R. A. (1994). Determinants of innovative behaviour: A path model of individual innovation in the workplace. *Academy of Management Journal, 37*, 580–607. doi:10.2307/256701

Seeley-Brown, J., & Solomon-Gray, E. (1995). *The people are the company.* Retrieved from http://www.fastcompany.com

Seeley-Brown, J., & Duquid, P. (2000). *The social life of information.* Boston, MA: Harvard Business Press.

Seidler-de Alwis, R., Hartmann, E., & Gemünden, H. (2004). *The role of tacit knowledge in innovation management.* Competitive Paper submitted to the 20th Annual IMP Conference. Copenhagen, Denmark.

Seidler-de Alwis, R., & Hartmann, E. (2008). The use of tacit knowledge within innovative companies: Knowledge management in innovative enterprises. *Journal of Knowledge Management, 12*(1), 133–147. doi:10.1108/13673270810852449

Senge, P. (1990). *The fifth discipline: The art nd practice of the learning organization.* New York, NY: Doubleday.

Senge, P. M. (2000). The academy as learning community: Contradiction in terms or realizable future? In Lucas, A. F. (Ed.), *Leading Academic Change: Essential Roles for Department Chairs* (pp. 215–245). San Francisco, CA: Jossey-Bass.

Senor, D., & Singer, S. (2009). *Start-up nation: The story of Israel's economic miracle.* New York, NY: Hachette Book Group.

Serban, A. M., & Luan, J. (Eds.). (2002). *Knowledge management: Building a competitive advantage in higher education.* San Francisco, CA: Jossey Bass.

Seufert, A., Krogh, G. V., & Bach, A. (1999). Towards knowledge networking. *Journal of Knowledge Management, 3*(3), 180–190. doi:10.1108/13673279910288608

Shailer, K. (2005). *Interdisciplinarity in a disciplinary universe: A review of key issues.* Working Paper Series. Retrieved from http://academic.research.microsoft.com/Publication/4834251/interdisciplinarity-in-a-disciplinary-universe

Shane, S. A. (2004). *Academic entrepreneurship: University spinoffs and wealth creation.* Cheltenham, UK: Edward Elgar.

Sharabati, A. A. A., Jawad, S. N., & Bontis, N. (2010). Intellectual capital and business performance in the pharmaceutical sector of Jordan. *Journal of Management Decision, 48*(1), 105–131. doi:10.1108/00251741011014481

Sharimllah Devi, R., Chong, S. C., & Lin, B. (2007). Organizational culture and KM processes from the perspective of an institution of higher learning. *Inernational Journal of Management in Education, 1*(1/2), 57–79. doi:10.1504/IJMIE.2007.014377

Sharp, J. (1997). *Key hypotheses in supporting communities of practice.* Retrieved from http://www.tfriend.com/hypothesis.html

Sher, P. J., & Lee, V. C. (2004). Information technology as a facilitator for enhancing dynamic capabilities through knowledge management. *Information & Management, 41*(8), 933–945. doi:10.1016/j.im.2003.06.004

Shipton, H., Fay, D., West, M., Patterson, M., & Birdi, K. (2005). Managing peopple to promote innovation. *Creativity and Innovation Management, 14*(2), 118–128. doi:10.1111/j.1467-8691.2005.00332.x

Shubik, M. (1975). *Games for society, business, and war: Toward a theory of gaming.* New York, NY: Elsevier.

Siegel, D. S., Wright, M., & Lockett, A. (2007). The rise of entrepreneurial activity at universities: Organizational and societal implications. *Industrial and Corporate Change, 16*(4), 489–504. doi:10.1093/icc/dtm015

Simonetti, J. L., Ariss, S., & Martinez, J. (1999). Through the top with mentoring. *Business Horizons, 42*(6), 56–63. doi:10.1016/S0007-6813(99)80039-1

Simonin, B. L. (1999). Ambiguity and the process of knowledge transfer in strategic alliances. *Strategic Management Journal, 20*(7), 595–623. doi:10.1002/(SICI)1097-0266(199907)20:7<595::AID-SMJ47>3.0.CO;2-5

Sinha, K. K., & Van de Ven, A. H. (2005). Designing work within and between organizations. *Organization Science, 16*(4), 389–408. doi:10.1287/orsc.1050.0130

Skoko, H. (2000). *Upravljanje kvalitetom.* Zagreb, Croatia: Sinergija.

Skyrme, D. J., et al. (2010). *Knowledge management: Approaches and policies.* Retrieved June 1, 2010, from http://www.skyme.com

Slaughter, S., & Leslie, L. L. (1997). *Academic capitalism: Politics, policies and the entrepreneurial university.* Baltimore, MD: Johns Hopkins University Press.

Smith, G. F. (1998). Idea-generation techniques: A formulary of active ingredients. *The Journal of Creative Behavior, 32*(2), 107–133. doi:10.1002/j.2162-6057.1998.tb00810.x

Smith, P., & O'Neil, J. (2003). A review of action learning literature 1994-2000: Part 1: Bibliography and comments. *Journal of Workplace Learning, 15*(2), 63–69. doi:10.1108/13665620310464102

Snowden, D. (1998). The ecology of a sustainable knowledge management program. *Knowledge Management, 1*(6).

Snowden, D. (2005). From atomism to networks in social systems. *The Learning Organization, 12*(6), 552–562. doi:10.1108/09696470510626757

Snowden, D. J. (1999). The paradox of story: Simplicity and complexity in strategy. *Journal of Strategy and Scenario Planning, 1*(5), 24–32.

Soliman, F., & Spooner, K. (2000). Strategies for implementing knowledge management: Role of human resource management. *Journal of Knowledge Management, 4*(4), 337–345. doi:10.1108/13673270010379894

Song, J., Almeida, P., & Wu, G. (2003). Learning by hiring: When is mobility more likely to facilitate interfirm knowledge transfer? *Organization Science, 49*, 351–365.

Spender, J. (1996). Competitive advantage from tacit knowledge? Unpacking the concept and its strategic implications. In B. Mosingeon & A. Edmondson (Eds.), *Organizational Learning and Competitive Advantage* (pp. 56–73). London, UK: Sage Publications. doi:10.4135/9781446250228.n4doi:10.4135/9781446250228.n4

Spender, J. C. (1992). Strategy theorizing: Expanding the agenda. In Shrivastava, P., Huff, A., & Dutton, J. (Eds.), *Advances in Strategic Management* (pp. 3–32). Greenwich, CT: JAI Press.

Spender, J. C. (1996a). Making knowledge the basis of a dynamic theory of the firm. *Strategic Management Journal, 17*, 45–62.

Spender, J. C. (1996b). Organizational knowledge, learning and memory: Three concepts in search of a theory. *Journal of Organizational Change Management, 9*, 63–78. doi:10.1108/09534819610156813

Spooner, M. (2004). Generating integration and complex understanding: Emploring the use of creative thinking tools within interdisciplinary studies. *Issues in Integrative Studies, 22*, 85–111.

Spring, M. (2003). Knowledge management in extended operations networks. *Journal of Knowledge Management, 7*(4), 29–37. doi:10.1108/13673270310492921

Srića, V. (1992). *Upravljanje kreativnošću*. Zagreb, Croatia: Školska knjiga.

Srikanthan, G., & Dalrymple, J. F. (2002). Developing a holistic model for quality in higher education. *Quality in Higher Education, 8*(2), 215–224. doi:10.1080/1353832022000031656

Stachová, K., & Stacho, Z. (2010). Organisations operating in Slovakia are aware of the need to focus on "innovative organisation", but they have problems to practically adopt it. In *TOIOTARITY: Knowledge Using is Service Management* (pp. 65–76). Warszawa, Poland: Publisher Institute Wydawniczy PTM.

Stam, C. (2007). *Knowledge productivity: Designing and testing a method to diagnose knowledge productivity and plan for enhancement*. Haarlem, The Netherlands: Christiaan Stam.

Stam, C. (2009). *Knowledge and the ageing employee: A research agenda*. Haarlem, The Netherlands: Holland University of Applied Sciences.

Standing, C., & Kiniti, S. (2011). How can organizations use wikis for innovation? *Technovation, 31*(7), 287–295. doi:10.1016/j.technovation.2011.02.005

Starbuck, W. H. (1992). Learning by knowledge-intensive firms. *Journal of Management Studies, 29*(6), 713–740. doi:10.1111/j.1467-6486.1992.tb00686.x

Starbuck, W., & Hedberg, B. (1977). Saving an organization from a stagnating environment. In Thorelli, H. (Ed.), *Strategy + Structure = Performance* (pp. 249–258). Bloomington, IN: University Press.

Starovic, D., & Marr, B. (2003). *Understanding corporate value: Managing and reporting intellectual capital*. London, UK: Chartered Institute of Management Accountants.

Stein, S. J., McRobbie, C. J., & Ginns, I. (1999). *A model for the professional development of teachers in design and technology*. Paper presented at the Annual Conference of the Australian Association for Research in Education, New Zealand Association for Research in Education. Melbourne, Australia.

Steinkellner, P. F., & Czerny, E. J. (2010). *Educating managers for a paradox world – Duality and paradoxes in management*. Paper presented at the International Conference on Management Learning Management Makes the World Go Around. Vienna, Austria.

Stephan, P. E. (2001). Educational implications of university-industry technology transfer. *The Journal of Technology Transfer, 26*, 199–205. doi:10.1023/A:1011164806068

Sternberg, R., & Lubart, T. (1995). *Defying the crowd*. New York, NY: Free Press.

Sternberg, R. J. (2006). The nature of creativity. *Creativity Research Journal, 18*(1), 87–98. doi:10.1207/s15326934crj1801_10

Sternberg, R. J., & Lubart, T. I. (1991). An investment theory of creativity and its development. *Human Development, 34*(1), 1–31. doi:10.1159/000277029

Sternberg, R. J., & Lubart, T. I. (1999). The concepts of creativity: Prospects and paradigms. In Sternberg, R. J. (Ed.), *The Handbook of Creativity* (pp. 3–15). Cambridge, UK: Cambridge University Press.

Sternberg, R., & Lubart, T. (1996). Investing in creativity. *The American Psychologist, 51*(7), 677–688. doi:10.1037/0003-066X.51.7.677

Stewart, T. (1997). *Intellectual capital: The new wealth of organizations*. New York, NY: DoubleDay.

Stover, M. (2004). Making tacit knowledge explicit. *RSR. Reference Services Review, 32*(2), 164–173. doi:10.1108/00907320410537685

STRIKE. (2012). *Website.* Retrieved from http://www.cost.esf.org/index.php?id=1095

Struyven, K., & De Meyst, M. (2010). Competence-based teacher education: Illusion or reality? An assessment of the implementation status in Flanders from teachers' and students' points of view. *Teaching and Teacher Education, 26*(8), 1495–1510. doi:10.1016/j.tate.2010.05.006

Stupans, I., Scutter, S., & Pearce, K. (2010). Facilitating student learning: engagement in novel learning opportunities. *Innovative Higher Education, 35*(5), 359–366. doi:10.1007/s10755-010-9148-6

Styre, A. (2003). Knowledge management beyond codification: Knowing as practice/concept. *Journal of Knowledge Management, 7*(5), 32–40. doi:10.1108/13673270310505368

Suchan, W. K., Blair, J. R. S., Fairfax, D., Goda, B. S., Huggins, K. L., & Lemanski, M. J. (2006). Faculty development in information technology education. In *Proceedings of the 7th Conference on Information Technology Education*, (pp. 15-18). IEEE.

Sullivan, P. H. (1998). *Profiting from intellectual capital: Extracting value from innovation*. New York, NY: Wiley.

Suter, M. C. (2001). College faculty's transition to online teaching: From classroom space to virtual place. *Dissertation Abstracts International - A, 62*(12), 4091-4362.

Sveiby, K. (1997). *The new organizational wealth: Managing and measuring knowledge-based assets*. San Francisco, CA: Berrett-Koehler.

Sveiby, K.-E. (2010). *Methods for measuring intangible assets*. Retrieved July 25, 2011, from http://www.sveiby.com/articles/IntangibleMethods.htm

Sveiby, K.-E. (2001). A knowledge-based theory of the firm to guide in strategy formulation. *Journal of Intellectual Capital, 2*(4), 344–358. doi:10.1108/14691930110409651

Švejda, P. (2007). *Business innovation*. Prague, Czech Republic: Association of Business Innovation.

Svensson, G., & Wood, G. (2007). Are university students really customers? When illusion may lead to delusion for all! *International Journal of Educational Management, 21*(1), 17–28. doi:10.1108/09513540710716795

Svoboda, R. (2006). *Inovacije: Inovativnost - uvažavanje kreativnosti svih zaposlenika*. Retrieved December 2006, from http://www.quantum21.net

Svoboda, S., & Whalen, J. (2004). Using experiential simulation to teach sustainability. *Greener Management International, 48*, 57–65.

Swain, C. (2009). Improving academic-industry collaboration for game research and education. In *Proceedings of the 4th International Conference on Foundations of Digital Games*, (pp. 191-198). IEEE.

Swan, J., & Scarbrough, H. (2001). Knowledge management: Concepts and controversies. *Journal of Management Studies, 38*, 913–921. doi:10.1111/1467-6486.00265

Swap, W., Leonard, D., Shields, M., & Abrams, L. (2001). Using mentoring and storytelling to transfer knowledge in the workplace. *Journal of Management Information Systems, 18*(1), 95–114.

Syed-Ikhsan, S. O. S., & Rowland, F. (2004). Knowledge management in a public organization: A study on the relationship between organizational elements and the performance of knowledge transfer. *Journal of Knowledge Management, 8*(2), 95–111. doi:10.1108/13673270410529145

Szulanski, G. (1996). Exploring internal stickiness: Impediments to the transfer of best practices within the firm. *Strategic Management Journal, 22,* 27–44.

Tadmor, Z. (2003). *The triad research university model or a post 20th century research university model. Haifa, Israel: The S. Neaman Institute of Advance Studies in Science and Technology. European Commission. (2007). Towards a European research area science.* Paris, France: European Commission.

Tait, H., & Godfrey, H. (1999). Defining and assessing competence in generic skills. *Quality in Higher Education, 5*(3), 245–253. doi:10.1080/1353832990050306

Takeuchi, H. (1998). Beyond knowledge management: Lessons from Japan. *Monash Mt-Eliza Business Journal, 1*(1), 21–30.

Talukdar, A. (2008). *What is intellectual capital: And why it should be measured.* Founder, Czech Republic: Attainix Consulting.

Tapscott, D. (2009). *Grown up digital.* New York, NY: McGraw-Hill.

Tapscott, D., & Williams, A. (2006). *Wikinomics: How mass collaboration changes everything.* New York, NY: Penguin Group Publishers.

Taylor, C. (1975). *Perspectives on creativity.* Chicago, IL: Aldine.

Taylor, J. (2004). Toward a strategy for internationalisation: Lessons and practice from four universities. *Journal of Studies in International Education, 8*(2), 149–171. doi:10.1177/1028315303260827

Technion Innovation Center. (2012). *Website.* Retrieved from http://ieinnov.technion.ac.il/wps/portal/InnovationCenter/Home/!ut/p/c5/04_SB8K8xLLM9MS-SzPy8xBz9CP0os3hnd0cPE3MfAwODAF8DAyM-3H0OvgNBQIwMvM_1wkA48Kkwg8gY4g-KOBvp9Hfm6qfkF2dpqjo6IiADRPfgM!/dl3/d3/L2dBISEvZ0FBIS9nQSEh/

Teece, D. J. (1998). Research directions for knowledge management. *California Management Review, 40*(3), 289–292.

Teece, D. J. (2000). *Managing intellectual capital.* Oxford, UK: Oxford University Press.

Teece, D. J. (2007). Explicating dynamic capabilities: The nature and microfoundations of (sustainable) enterprise performance. *Strategic Management Journal, 28,* 1319–1350. doi:10.1002/smj.640

Teece, D. J., & Pisano, G. (1994). The dynamic capabilities of firms: An introduction. *Industrial and Corporate Change, 3*(3), 537–556. doi:10.1093/icc/3.3.537-a

Teece, D. J., Pisano, G., & Shuen, A. (1997). Dynamic capabilities and strategic management. *Strategic Management Journal, 18*(7), 509–533. doi:10.1002/(SICI)1097-0266(199708)18:7<509::AID-SMJ882>3.0.CO;2-Z

Teece, D. J., Rumelt, R., Dosi, G., & Winter, S. (1994). Understanding corporate coherence: Theory and evidence. *Journal of Economic Behavior & Organization, 23*(1), 1–30. doi:10.1016/0167-2681(94)90094-9

Teichler, U. (2004). The changing debate on internationalisation of higher education. *Higher Education, 48,* 5–26. doi:10.1023/B:HIGH.0000033771.69078.41

Tenkasi, R. V., & Boland, R. J. (1996). Exploring knowledge diversity in knowledge intensive firms: A new role for information systems. *Journal of Organizational Change Management, 9*(1), 79–91. doi:10.1108/09534819610107330

Tenner, A. R., & DeToro, I. J. (1992). *Total quality management-Three steps to continuous improvement. Reading, MA: Addison-Wsley Publishing Company, Inc. Deming Prize Committee. (2007). The guide for the deming application prize.* Tokyo, Japan: The Deming Prize Committee.

Thiessen, M. S. W., Hindriks, P. H. J., & Essers, C. (2007). Research and development knowledge transfer across national cultures. In Pauleen, D. (Ed.), *Cross-Cultural Perspectives of Knowledge Management* (pp. 219–243). Westport, CT: Libraries Unlimited.

Thomas, H. (Ed.). (1997). *The unit of activity: Towards an alternative to the theories of the firm, strategy, structure and style.* Copenhagen, Denmark: Wiley.

Tidd, J., Bessant, J., & Pavitt, K. (1997). *Managing Innovation: Integrating technological, market and organisational change.* Chichester, UK: John Wiley and Sons Ltd.

Tidd, J., & Bessant,, J. (2009). *Managing innovation.* West Sussex, UK: John Wiley & Sons.

Tierney, P., Farmer, S. M., & Graen, G. B. (1999). An examination of leadership and employee creativity: The relevance of traits and relationships. *Personnel Psychology*, *52*, 591–620. doi:10.1111/j.1744-6570.1999.tb00173.x

Tijssen, R. J. W. (2004). Is the commercialization of scientific research affecting the production of public knowledge? Global trends in the output of corporate research articles. *Research Policy*, *33*, 709–733. doi:10.1016/j.respol.2003.11.002

Ting, W. K. I., & Lean, H. H. (2009). Intellectual capital performance of financial institutions in Malaysia. *Journal of Intellectual Capital*, *10*(4), 588–599. doi:10.1108/14691930910996661

Tippins, M. J. (2003). Implementing knowledge management in academia: Teaching the teachers. *International Journal of Educational Management*, *17*(7), 339–345. doi:10.1108/09513540310501021

Tissen, R., Andriessen, D., & Deprezz, F. L. (1998). *Value-based knowledge management*. Amsterdam, The Netherlands: Addison Wesley Longman.

Todorova, G., & Durisin, B. (2007, September). The concept and the reconceptualization of absorptive capacity: Recognizing the value. *Academy of Management Review*.

Toffler, A. (1980). *The third wave*. New York, NY: Morrow.

Tovar, J. J. (2010). How to measure innovation? New evidence of the technology growth linkage. *UK Research in Economics*, *64*, 81–96.

Trott, P. (1998). *Innovation management and new product development*. Harlow, UK: Pearson Education.

Tsai, W. (2001). Knowledge transfer in intraorganizational networks: Effects of network position and absorptive capacity on business unit innovation and performance. *Academy of Management Journal*, *44*, 996–1004. doi:10.2307/3069443

Tseng, S.-M. (2008). The effects of information technology on knowledge management systems. *Expert Systems with Applications*, *35*(1-2), 150–160. doi:10.1016/j.eswa.2007.06.011

Tsoukas, H. (1996). The firm as a distributed knowledge system: A constructionist approach. *Strategic Management Journal*, *17*, 11–25.

Tsoukas, H. (2002). Introduction: Knowledge-based perspectives on organizations: Situated knowledge, novelty, and communities of practice. *Management Learning*, *33*(4), 419–426. doi:10.1177/1350507602334001

Tsoukas, H. (2005). *Complex knowledge: Studies in organizational epistemology*. Oxford, UK: Oxford University Press.

Tsoukas, H. (2009). A dialogical approach to the creation of new knowledge in organizations. *Organization Science*, *20*(6), 941–957. doi:10.1287/orsc.1090.0435

Tsoukas, H., & Mylonopoulos, N. (2004). *Organizations as knowledge systems: Knowledge, learning and dynamic capabilities*. London, UK: Palgrave Macmillan.

Tull, J., & Dumay, J. (2007). Does IC management 'make a difference'? A critical case study application of structuration theory. *Electronic Journal of Knowledge Management*, *5*(4), 515–526.

Tuomi, I. (1999). Data is more than knowledge: Implications of the reversed hierarchy for knowledge management and organizational memory. In *Proceedings of the Thirty-Second Annual Hawaii International Conference on Systems Sciences*. Los Alamitos, CA: IEEE Computer Society Press.

Tuomi, I. (1999). *Corporate knowledge: Theory and practice of intelligent organizations*. Helsinki, Finland: Metaxis.

Tuomi, I. (2002). The future of knowledge management. *Lifelong Learning in Europe*, *7*(2), 69–79.

Tureková, H., & Mičieta, B. (2003). *Innovative management*. Žilina, Slovakia: EDIS.

Turner, G. (1996). Human resource accounting: Whim or wisdom? *Journal of Human Resource Costing and Accounting*, *1*(1), 63–73. doi:10.1108/eb029023

Turner, G. (2000). Using human resource accounting to bring balance to the balanced scorecard. *Journal of Human Resource Costing and Accounting*, *5*(2), 31–44. doi:10.1108/eb029067

Turner, G. (2005). Accounting for human resources: Quo vadis? *International Journal of Environmental, Cultural. Economic and Social Sustainability*, *1*(3), 11–17.

Turner, G., & Jackson-Cox, J. (2002). If management requires measurement how may we cope with knowledge? *Singapore Management Review, 24*(3), 101–111.

Tyler, J. R., Wilkinson, D. M., & Huberman. (2012). *Email as spectroscopy: Automated discovery of community structure within organisations.* Retrieved from http://www.hpl.hp.com/research/idl/papers/email/email.pdf

UNESCO. (2002). *Medium-term strategy: Contribution to peace and human development in an era of globalization through education, the sciences, culture and communication, 2002-2007.* Paris, France: UNESCO.

Uzzi, B., Amaral, L. A., & Reed-Tsochas, F. (2007). Small-world networks and management science research: A review. *European Management Review, 4,* 77–91. doi:10.1057/palgrave.emr.1500078

Vallas, S. P., & Kleinman, L. (2008). Contradiction, convergence and the knowledge economy: The confluence of academic and commercial biotechnology. *Socio-economic Review, 6*(2), 283–311. doi:10.1093/ser/mwl035

Van de Ven, A. H. (1986). Central problems in the management of innovation. *Management Science, 32*(5), 590–607. doi:10.1287/mnsc.32.5.590

Van de Ven, A., & Johnson, P. (2006). Knowledge for theory and practice. *Academy of Management Review, 31*(4), 802–821. doi:10.5465/AMR.2006.22527385

Van den Bosch, F. A., Volberda, H. W., & de Boer, M. (1999). Coevolution of firm absorptive capacity and knowledge environment : Organizational forms and combinative capabilities. *Organization Science, 10*(5), 551–568. doi:10.1287/orsc.10.5.551

Van Hoek, R., Godsell, J., & Harrison, A. (2011). Embedding "insights from industry" in supply chain programs: The role of guest lecturers. *Supply Chain Management: An International Journal, 16*(2), 142–147. doi:10.1108/13598541111115383

Varey, R. J. (2005). Informational and communicational explanations of corporations as interaction systems. In Wiberg, M. (Ed.), *The Interaction Society: Practice, Theories and Supportive Technologies.* Hershey, PA: IGI Global. doi:10.4018/978-1-59140-530-6.ch006

Vera, D., & Crossan, M. (2003). Organizational learning and knowledge management: Toward an integrative framework. In Easterby-Smith, M., & Lyles, M. A. (Eds.), *The Blackwell Handbook of Organizational Learning and Knowledge* (pp. 122–142). Oxford, UK: Blackwell Publishers.

Vinig, T., & Rijsbergen, P. (2008). *Determinants of university technology transfer - Comparative study of US, Europe, and Australian universities.* Retrieved from http://ssrn.com/abstract=1324601

von Hippel, E. (1986). Lead users: A source of novel product concepts. *Management Science, 32*(7), 791–805. doi:10.1287/mnsc.32.7.791

von Krogh, G. (1998). Care in knowledge creation. *California Management Review, 40*(3), 133–153.

von Krogh, G., Ichijo, K., & Nonaka, I. (2000). *Enabling knowledge creation: How to unlock the mystery of tacit knowledge and release the power of innovation.* Oxford, UK: Oxford University Press.

Von Krogh, G., Roos, J., & Klein, D. (Eds.). (1998). *Knowing firms: Understanding, managing, and measuring knowledge.* London, UK: Sage Publications.

Vratulis, V., & Dobson, T. M. (2008). Social negotiations in a wiki environment: A case study with pre service teachers. *Educational Media International, 45*(4), 285–294. doi:10.1080/09523980802571531

Vrtodušić Hrgović, A. M. (2010). *Upravljanje potpunom kvalitetom i poslovna izvrsnost u hotelskoj industriji Hrvatske. Doctoral Disseration.* Rijeka, Croatia: Sveučilište u Rijeci.

Vujić, V., Črnjar, K., & Maškarin, H. (2009). *Knowledge and education of human resources in the Croatian hospitality industry.* Paper presented at the 4th International Scientific Conference: Planning for the Future, Learning from the Past. Rhodes Island, Greece.

Wagner, C., & Bolloju, N. (2005). Supporting knowledge management in organizations with conversational technologies: Discussion forums, weblogs, and wikis. *Journal of Database Management, 16*(2).

Wallas, G. (1926). *The art of thought.* New York, NY: Harcourt.

Walsh, J. P., & Ungson, G. R. (1991). Organizational memory. *Academy of Management Review*, *16*(1), 57–91.

Walsh, K., Enz, C. A., & Canina, L. (2008). The impact of strategic orientation on intellectual capital investments in customer service firms. *Journal of Service Research*, *10*(4), 300–317. doi:10.1177/1094670508314285

Wang, J., Kourik, J. L., & Maher, P. E. (2010). Introducing leading it technologies into curricula via vendor-hosted services. *Journal of Business and Educational Leadership*, *2*(1), 96–105.

Wang, S., & Noe, R. (2010). Knowledge sharing: A review and direction for future research. *Human Resource Management Review*, *20*, 115–131. doi:10.1016/j.hrmr.2009.10.001

Ward, L. F. (1968). *Dynamic sociology 2*. New York, NY: Johnson Reprint Corporation.

WB. (2010). *Innovation policy: A guide for developing countries*. Washington, DC: The World Bank.

Webster, C. M., & Kenney, J. (2011). Embedding research activities to enhance student learning. *International Journal of Educational Management*, *25*(4), 136–145. doi:10.1108/09513541111136649

Weggeman, M. (1997). *Knowledge management: Design and management of knowledge intensive organizations*. Schiedam, The Netherlands: Scriptum.

Weggeman, M. (2000). *Knowledge management in practice*. Schiedam, The Netherlands: Scriptum.

Weick, K., & Roberts, K. (1993). Collective mind in organizations: Heedful interrelating on flight decks. *Administrative Science Quarterly*, *38*(3), 357–381. doi:10.2307/2393372

Weisberg, R. (1999). Creativity and knowledge: A challenge to theories. In R. Sternberg (Ed.), *Handbook of Creativity* (pp. 226–250). Cambridge, UK: Cambridge University Press.

Weisberg, R. W. (1986). *Creativity genius and other myths*. New York, NY: Freman.

Welch, J. (2007). The role of intuition in interdisciplinary insight. *Issues in Integrative Studies*, *25*, 131–155.

Wellman, B. (2002). Designing the Internet for a networked society: Little boxes, globalisation and networked individualism. *Communications of the ACM*, *45*(5), 91–96. doi:10.1145/506218.506221

Wenger, E. (2001). *Supporting communities of practice: A survey of community-oriented technologies*. Retrieved from http://www.ewenger.com/theory/communities_of_practice_intro.htm

Wenger, E., White, N., Smith, J. D., & Rowe, K. (2005). *Technology for communities*. Retrieved from http://www.technologyforcommunities.com

Wenger, E. (1998). *Communities of practice: Learning, meaning and identity*. Cambridge, UK: Cambridge University Press.

Wenger, E. C., McDermott, R., & Snyder, W. (2007). *Cultivating communities of practice: A guide to managing knowledge*. Boston, MA: Harvard Business School Press.

Wenger, E. C., & Snyder, W. M. (2000). Communities of practice: The organizational frontier. *Harvard Business Review*, *78*(1), 139–145.

Werner, R., Ankiewicz, P. J., De Swardt, E., & Jakovljevic, M. (2012). *A theoretical framework for continuing professional teacher development (CPTD)*. Johannesburg, South Africa: University of Johannesburg.

West, M., & Farr, J. (1990). *Innovation and creativity at work: Psychologocal and organizational strategies*. Chichester, UK: John Wiley.

West, J. A., & West, M. L. (2009). *Using wikis for online collaboration: The power of the read-write web*. San Francisco, CA: Jossey-Bass Inc Pub.

West, M. A. (2003). Innovation implementation in work teams. In Paulus, P. B., & Nijstad, B. A. (Eds.), *Group Creativity*. Oxford, UK: Oxford University Press. doi:10.1093/acprof:oso/9780195147308.003.0012

West, M., Hirst, G., Richter, A., & Shipton, H. (2004). Twelve steps to heaven: Successfully managing change through developing innovative teams. *European Journal of Work and Organizational Psychology*, *13*, 269–299. doi:10.1080/13594320444000092

Wheeler, S., Yeomans, P., & Wheeler, D. (2008). The good, the bad and the wiki: Evaluating student generated content for collaborative learning. *British Journal of Educational Technology*, *39*(6), 987–995. doi:10.1111/j.1467-8535.2007.00799.x

White, N. (2006). *Blogs and community – Launching a new paradigm for online community?* Retrieved from http://kt.flexiblelearning.net.au

White, R. (1959). Motivation reconsidered: The concept of competence. *Psychological Review*, *66*(5), 297–333. doi:10.1037/h0040934

Whittaker, S., & Sidner, C. (1996). Email overload: Exploring personal information management of email. In *Proceedings of CHI 1996*, (pp. 276-283). ACM Press.

Wickramasinghe, N. (2006). Knowledge creation. In D. G. Schwartz (Ed.), *Encyclopedia of Knowledge Management* (pp. 326–335). Hershey, PA: IGI Global. doi:10.4018/978-1-59140-573-3.ch043doi:10.4018/978-1-59140-573-3.ch043

Wiig, K. M. (1993). *Knowledge management foundations: Thinking about thinking: How people and organizations create, represent, and use knowledge*. Arlington, TX: Schema Press.

Wiig, K. M. (1997). Integrating intellectual capital and knowledge management. *Long Range Planning*, *30*(3), 399–405. doi:10.1016/S0024-6301(97)90256-9

Wiig, K. M. (1997). Knowledge management: An introduction and perspective. *Journal of Knowledge Management*, *1*(1), 6–14. doi:10.1108/13673279710800682

Wiig, K. M. (1997). Knowledge management: Where did it come from and where will it go? *Expert Systems with Applications*, *13*(1), 1–14. doi:10.1016/S0957-4174(97)00018-3

Wiig, K. M. (1999). What future knowledge management users may expect. *Journal of Knowledge Management*, *3*(2), 155–165. doi:10.1108/13673279910275611

Wikibooks. (2008). *Online learning communities and communities of practice*. Retrieved from http://en.wikibooks.org/wiki/Online_Learning_Communities_and_Communities_of_Practice

Wild, M. (1999). The anatomy of practice in the use of mailing lists: A case study. *Australian Journal of Educational Technology*, *15*(2), 117–135.

Wild, R., & Griggs, K. (2008). A model of information technology opportunities for facilitating the practice of knowledge management. *The Journal of Information and Knowledge Management Systems*, *38*(4), 490–506.

Willem, A., & Scarborough, H. (2006). Social capital and political bias in knowledge sharing: An exploratory study. *Human Relations*, *59*(10), 1343–1370. doi:10.1177/0018726706071527

Williams, B. (2005). Case-based learning, a review of the literature: Is there scope for educational paradigms in prehospital education? *Emergency Medicine Journal*, *22*, 577–581. doi:10.1136/emj.2004.022707

Williams, R. (2008). The epistemology of knowledge and the knowledge process cycle: Beyond the objectivist vs interpretivist. *Journal of Knowledge Management*, *12*(4), 72–85. doi:10.1108/13673270810884264

Willke, H. (1998). *Systemisches wissensmanagement*. Stuttgart, Germany: Lucius & Lucius.

Wilson, T. D. (2002). The nonsense of "knowledge management". *Information Research, 8*(1).

Wilson, O. (1998). Knowledge management: Putting a good idea to work. *Managing Information*, *5*(2), 31–33.

Wilson, T. D. (2005). The nonsense of knowledge management revisited. In Maceviciute, E., & Wilson, T. D. (Eds.), *Introducing Information Management: An Information Research Reader* (pp. 151–164). London, UK: Facet Publishing.

Wind, J., & Main, J. (1999). *Diving change*. New York, NY: The Free Press.

Winter, S. G. (1996). Organizing for continuous improvement: Evolutionary theory meets the quality revolution. In Cohen, M. D., & Sproull, L. S. (Eds.), *Organizational Learning* (pp. 460–483). Thousand Oaka, CA: Sage Publications.

Winterton, J. Delamare - Le Deist, F., & Stringfellow, E. (2005). *Typology of knowledge, skills, and competences: Clarification of the concept and prototype.* Retrieved June 13, 2011, from http://www.ecotec.com/europeaninventory/publications/method/cedefop_typology.pdf

Wodehouse, A., Grierson, H., Ion, W., Juster, N., Lynn, A., & Stone, A. (2004). *TikiWiki: A tool to support engineering design students in concept generation.* Paper presented at the International Engineering and Product Design Education Conference. Delft, The Netherlands.

Wodehouse, A. J., Grierson, H. J., Breslin, C., Eris, O., Ion, W. J., & Leifer, L. J. (2010). A framework for design engineering education in a global context. *Artificial Intelligence for Engineering Design, Analysis and Manufacturing, 24*(3), 367–378. doi:10.1017/S0890060410000259

Wolfe, J., Naylor, T., & Drueke, J. (2010). The role of the academic reference librarian in the learning commons. *DigitalCommons@University of Nebraska – Lincoln, 50*(2), 107-113. Retrieved October 28, 2011 from http://digitalcommons.unl.edu/libraryscience/221

Wong, N. W. (2009). Paper. *Journal of Business Continuity & Emergency Planning, 4*(1), 62–68.

Woodman, R., Sawyer, R., & Griffin, W. (1993). Toward a theory of organizational creativity. *Academy of Management Review, 18*(2), 293–321.

Wood, S. (1996). High commitment management and payment systems. *Journal of Management Studies, 33,* 53–77. doi:10.1111/j.1467-6486.1996.tb00798.x

World Bank. (2007). *Building knowledge economies, advanced strategies for development.* Washington, DC: The World Bank.

Worldbank.org. (2012). *Communities of practice, questions and answers.* Retrieved from http://siteresources.worldbank.org/WBI/Resources/CoP_QA.pdf

Wright, M., Clarysse, B., Lockett, A., & Knockaert, M. (2008). Mid-range universities' linkages with industry: Knowledge types and the role of intermediaries. *Research Policy, 37,* 1205–1223. doi:10.1016/j.respol.2008.04.021

Xu, J., & Quaddus, M. (2005). From rhetoric towards a model of practical knowledge management systems. *Journal of Management Development, 24*(4), 291–319. doi:10.1108/02621710510591325

Yeo, R. K. (2005). Revisiting the roots of learning organization: A synthesis of the learning organization literature. *The Learning Organization, 12*(4), 368–382. doi:10.1108/09696470510599145

Yin, R. K. (2003). *Case study research design and methods* (3rd ed.). Thousand Oaks, CA: Sage Publishing.

Youndt, M. A., & Snell, S. A. (2004). Human resource management, intellectual capital, and organizational performance. *Journal of Managerial Issues, 16*(3), 337–360.

Young, R. (2005). Knowledge management - Back to basic principles. *Knowledge-management-online.com.* Retrieved April 5, 2010, from http://www.knowledge-management-online.com/knowledge-management-back-to-basic-principles.html

Yusuf, S. (2008). Intermediating knowledge exchange between universities and businesses. *Research Policy, 37,* 1167–1174. doi:10.1016/j.respol.2008.04.011

Yusuf, S. (2009). From creativity to innovation. *Technology in Society, 31*(1), 1–8. doi:10.1016/j.techsoc.2008.10.007

Zack, M. (1998). What knowledge problems can information technology help to solve. In E. Hoadley & I. Benbasat (Eds.), *Proceedings of the Fourth Americas Conferences on Information Systems,* (pp. 644-646). Baltimore, MD: ACIS.

Zack, M. H. (1999). Developing a knowledge strategy. *California Management Review, 41*(3), 125–145.

Zack, M. H. (1999). Managing codified knowledge. *Sloan Management Review, 40*(4), 45–58.

Zahra, S. A., & George, G. (2002). Absorptive capacity: A review, reconceptualization, and extension. *Academy of Management Review, 27*(2), 185–203.

Zerhouni, E. (2003). The NIH roadmap. *Science, 302*(5642), 63–72. doi:10.1126/science.1091867

Zhang, H., Xu, S. J., & Malter, A. J. (2010). Managing knowledge for innovation: The role of cooperation, competition and alliance nationality. *Journal of International Marketing, 18*(4), 74–94. doi:10.1509/jimk.18.4.74

Zhang, X. M., & Bartol, K. M. (2010). Linking empowering leadership and employee creativity: The influence of psychological empowerment, intrinsic motivation, and creative process engagement. *Academy of Management Journal*, *53*(1), 107–128. doi:10.5465/AMJ.2010.48037118

Zhou, J., & George, J. M. (2003). Awakening employee creativity: The role of leader emotional intelligence. *The Leadership Quarterly*, *14*, 545–568. doi:10.1016/S1048-9843(03)00051-1

Zollo, M., & Winter, S. G. (2002). Deliberate learning and the evolution of dynamic capabilities. *Organization Science*, *13*(3), 339–351. doi:10.1287/orsc.13.3.339.2780

About the Contributors

Sheryl Buckley is an Associate Professor in the School of Computing at the University of South Africa (UNISA). She holds a Primary Teacher's Diploma, Further Diploma in Education, National Diploma in Computer Practice, BEd in Computer-Based Education, Med in Computer-Based Education, Postgraduate diploma in Information Management, and DLitt et Phil in Information Science. Sheryl previously taught at a high school and at a technical college for 10 years, respectively. Sheryl has been teaching, researching, practicing, and supervising students engaged in research at both doctoral and masters level for more than 25 years. Sheryl is a member of the Computer Society of South Africa and an Examiner for the Gauteng Department of Education. In addition, she is a peer reviewer for local, national, and international conferences and journals.

Maria Jakovljevic is currently an Associate Professor in the Department of Economics at the University of Zadar, Croatia. She was an academic staff member at the University of the Witwatersrand and the University of Johannesburg. She has been teaching, researching and supervising students in various business colleges and educational institutions over the past 22 years. Maria has initiated international educational and business collaborations between universities and institutions in Croatia and South Africa. She has authored and managed a number of winning innovative R & D projects. She led the Commission for Quality Assurance at the Department of Economics, University of Zadar. Maria is the Editor-in-Chief of the journal, *Oeconomica Jadertina*, at the University of Zadar. She is a member of the Publishing body at the University of Zadar. She has undergone extensive training at various prestigious banking and SMEs companies in South Africa in Project Management and Software Engineering fields. She has been a highly active peer reviewer for international journals and conferences as well as an invited speaker and presenter.

* * *

Alina Mihaela Dima is Associate Professor at the Bucharest Academy of Economic Studies, School of Business Administration, and Director of UNESCO Chair for Business Administration. She earned a PhD. in Economics in 2007 with a specialization in International Business and Economics. The main fields of interest are: international business, competition policy, European integration, and higher education. She coordinated two national projects related to competition policy and higher education in Europe, and she is a member of the scientific board of the journal *Management and Marketing*, indexed in international databases (Cabell's, Index Copernicus, CEEOL, EBSCO, RePEc, DOAJ, Ulrich, and ProQuest). She has presented various papers at international conferences in Europe and USA, and she is an active member of different international associations.

Roberto Biloslavo is a Professor of Management at the University of Primorska, Faculty of Management. His research work is focused on management and leadership, knowledge management, strategic management, and sustainable development. In the last four years, he was a Vice-Rector for Academic Affairs at the University of Primorska. Besides teaching and researching, he consults to different domestic and international companies about vision and mission statement development, knowledge management, and leadership improvement.

Sladjana Cabrilo holds a PhD in Industrial Engineering and Engineering Management and a M.Sc. in Electrical Engineering from the University of Novi Sad (Serbia). Her major areas are Knowledge Management (KM), Intellectual Capital (IC), innovation, and change management. Her experience includes participation in numerous scientific and industry-related projects, publishing many scientific articles and papers, and lectures and presentations worldwide. Some of these were held at the George Washington University (Washington DC, USA), the World Bank (Paris), and the Global Forum (Washington DC, USA). She is a member of the New Club of Paris, Committee Member of the European Conference on Intellectual Capital, and a Member of the IC Group at the Regional Chamber of Commerce (Serbia).

Livio Cricelli works as an Associate Professor in Industrial Engineering in the Faculty of Engineering at the University of Cassino. He graduated in Aeronautical Engineering from the University Federico II of Naples and received his PhD in Industrial Engineering from the University of Rome Tor Vergata. He is the author and co-author of several scientific papers presented at national and international conferences or published on national and international reviews. His research interests include issues related to business management and strategy.

Kristina Črnjar, PhD, was born in 1976 and is an Assistant Professor of the Department for Knowledge management at the Faculty of Tourism and Hospitality Management in Opatija, University of Rijeka, Croatia. She earned her Master degree in 2006 and her PhD in 2010. "Knowledge Management in the Function of Sustainable Tourism Development in Primorsko-Goranska County" and "Knowledge Management Strategy in Increasing the Competitive Ability of the Hotel Industry" are the titles of her Master and PhD theses, respectively. She has participated in many international exchange programs and projects. She took part in the yearlong program "JOSZEF Program for Young Management in Middle and East Europe" at Wirtschaftuniversitat Vienna, Austria, and a yearlong program of student exchange in Florida, USA. She was a researcher in the projects: "Management of Knowledge and Personnel in Tourism as a Feature of Croatian Identity," "New Knowledge and Development in Croatian Hospitality Management," "Master Plan of Tourism Development in Primorsko-Goranska County," etc. Her fields of interest are knowledge management, HRM, and education for sustainable tourism.

Marié Cruywagen is a researcher specializing in knowledge management, strategy management, and information technology. Her research focus is on the nature of a knowledge-centric capability and its contribution to an organisation's long-term competitiveness. She has more than 15 years of experience in the information technology industry as a business analyst and business architect. Her consulting business, Connaissance Solutions, specializes in business analysis and knowledge-centric solutions. She completed both her MBA and PhD at the University of Stellenbosch Business School (USB) in South Africa and is a member of the Business Architects Association (BAA).

Tiit Elenurm is Head of the Entrepreneurship Department at the Estonian Business School. He earned his Ph. D. in 1980 for the dissertation "Management of the Process of Implementation of New Organizational Structures." He is the author of more than 110 research publications. He acquired entrepreneurial experience in 1990s as the main owner of EM-International, a training and consulting company. The vision of Tiit Elenurm is to develop synergy between knowledge management and entrepreneurship training, consulting, and research activities in entrepreneurship. The research interests of Tiit Elenurm include knowledge management, change management, international transfer of management knowledge, and developing cross-cultural fluency of SMEs for growing through international business. He tries to link virtual learning communities with using case studies, self-assessment tools, and team projects that enhance innovative learning.

Wim Gevers is the Associate Director of the University of Stellenbosch Business School (USB) in South Africa. He was trained as a civil engineer, and after seven years in the consulting engineering industry, he joined the USB, where he completed his PhD in Finance. His current teaching responsibility at the USB is in Decision Analysis, where he focuses on modeling for decision support. He is a fellow and past president of ORSSA, the Operations Research Society of South Africa.

Apostolos (Paul) Giannakopoulos was born in Greece, Pyrgos Ilias, and after matriculating, his parents immigrated to South Africa, where he received his B.Sc degree majoring in Mathematics, Applied Mathematics, and Physics. After his diploma in Machine Design, he worked as a designer for more than ten years. After graduating, he turned to education in 1980. He has since obtained a diploma in Higher Education and Computer Science, B.Ed and M.Ed, and he is currently busy with his Ph.D. He has taught in high schools, teachers training colleges, and at the present university since 1990. A few years back, he developed a passion about knowledge management, and since then, he has tried to "knock some sense" into management styles by using his mathematical pragmatic logic. He is a believer of pragmatism driven by mathematico-logical passion, giving rise to what he calls "a psycho-pragmatic" approach to everything. He has presented his creative ideas to a number of international and national conferences on mathematics, information technology, and knowledge management. He has also written mathematics textbooks and co-authored others.

Katjuša Gorela is a Research Assistant at the Faculty of Management, University of Primorska (Slovenia). She graduated in Political Science – Public Administration at the Faculty of Social Sciences and in Italian Language and Literature at the the Faculty of Arts, University of Ljubljana (Slovenia). She is currently a Ph.D. student at the Faculty of Education, University of Primorska. She focuses her research interests on knowledge management.

Michele Grimaldi received his first-class honor degree and a Master in Industrial Engineering. He received his Doctorate in Industrial and Management Engineering from the University of Rome Tor

Vergata. He is an Assistant Professor at the Faculty of Engineering of the University of Cassino (Italy). He teaches MBA and Undergraduate courses on the Economics of Industrial Systems and Knowledge Management. He has published several papers in international journals and conference proceedings. His current research field is focused on knowledge management strategies and intellectual capital assessment.

Leposava Grubic-Nesic holds PhD from the University of Novi Sad, Novi Sad-Serbia. Her major areas include human resource management, leadership and work motivation. She has published few books and numerous scientific articles. She participates in numerous industry-related projects related to the development of human capital in working processes. She is the Head of the Department for Human Resources Management at the Faculty of Technical Sciences (Industrial Engineering and Management) in Novi Sad (Serbia).

Musadaq Hanandi is a PhD candidate in the University of Rome Tor Vergata, Italy. He holds a Master degree in e-Business Management from the e-Business Management School – ISUFI – University of Lecce, Italy, and a Bachelor degree in Accounting from the Yarmouk University, Jordan. His primary research interests are intellectual capital and knowledge management, business performance evaluation, business process improvement models, and frameworks.

Ivanka Avelini Holjevac, Ph.D., Full Professor, has been on the Faculty of Tourism and Hospitality Management in Opatija, University of Rijeka, since 1976. Prof. Avelini Holjevac has built a specialization for controlling and total quality management abroad (France, Botswana, USA) and has published 280 scientific and expert papers in domestic and international publications and several books (mainly on controlling and total quality management in the tourism and hospitality industry). In 1998, Prof. Avelini Holjevac received the Lifetime Achievement Award from the City of Opatija, in 1999 a National Award for Science, in 2003, the "Antun Štifanić" Award from the Croatian National Tourist Board, in 2005, the Award for Education and Science from the University of Rijeka, and in 2006, a Lifetime Achievement Award from the Croatian Society for Quality. Prof. Avelini Holjevac is a member of the AIEST, Scientific Council of Tourism, at the Croatian Academy of Science and Arts, CHRIE, ATLAS, IHRA, Croatian Society of Quality Managers, Croatian Controller Association, and the International Inner Wheel Club (Rotary Club).

Ana-Marija Vrtodušić Hrgović, PhD, was born on 1971 and is an Assistant Professor of the Department for Quality and Controlling at the Faculty of Tourism and Hospitality Management in Opatija, University of Rijeka, Croatia. In 2003, she finished her postgraduate study with the Master thesis, "Quality Management and Business Results in the Hotel Industry," and in 2010, her Doctoral study with the PhD thesis, "Total Quality Management and Business Excellence in the Croatian Hotel Industry." Her previous job experience is in the field of auditing. Her work specializes in the field of controlling and quality management (CEEPUS scholarship at the Wirtscaftsünivesität Wien – Institut für Tourismus und Frezietwirtschaft, Quality Management Development Program - ISO 9001:2008 Quality System Auditing). She is actively participating as a researcher in the following projects: "Management of Business Results in the Croatian Hotel Industry," "Models and Standards of Quality and Business Excellence for the Hotel Industry," and "Personnel Standards." She is a member of the Croatian Society of Quality Managers and Croatian Controller Association.

Martina Königová holds a M.Sc. in the field of Economics and Management and a Ph.D. in Management granted by the Czech University of Life Sciences in Prague. Since 2005, she has been a member of the Department of Management of the Faculty of Economics and Management of the Czech University of Life Sciences in Prague. She lectures on Human Resource Management and Crisis Management as well as leads Bachelor and diploma theses. She is a main researcher and a co-researcher of several significant projects. The main areas of her research cover human resource management, risk management, and crisis management.

Ana Martins has submitted a PhD in Intellectual Capital Management and Organisational Sustainability; she has a Postgraduate diploma in Management and BA Hons in Communication Science. She is currently a Lecturer at Xi'an Jiaotong-Liverpool University, in the Department of Business, Economics, and Management. Her research areas are: leadership and emotional intelligence and strategic HRM and knowledge management. She is an associate reviewer of various international academic journals.

Isabel Martins has submitted a PhD in Human Capital and Knowledge Management. She has a Postgraduate diploma in Management, a MA in Communication Science, and a BA Hons. in Communication Science. Currently, she is a Consultant in Strategic Knowledge Management. Her research areas are: HRM and knowledge management, intellectual capital—developing human capital and tacit knowledge in high performance working organizations and learning organizations. She is an associate reviewer of various international academic journals.

Fiona Masterson, B.Sc., M.App.Sc., is a Researcher at the National University of Ireland, Galway. She has twelve years industry experience as a senior quality engineer in a number of multinational corporations. She is currently working on her Doctorate of Biomedical Engineering. Her thesis focuses on the successful commercialisation and regulation of innovative medical technologies. Fiona has delivered a wide range of courses at undergraduate and postgraduate level including product design and development, operations engineering, project management, quality management, innovation, and entrepreneurship. She has a particular research interest in the use of innovative learning technologies in education.

Sari Metso has a MSc. (Econ.) and is a Postgraduate Student of Knowledge Management in the School of Business at Lappeenranta University of Technology, Finland. Her research focus is on knowledge management and professional skills learning. She has several years of experience developing and planning vocational education.

Clemente Minonne is a Management Advisor, Researcher, and Senior Lecturer in the School of Management and Law at the Zurich University of Applied Sciences, where he is also the Director of the Center for Knowledge and Information Management. He concentrates on the topics of strategic, process, knowledge, and information management. Dr Minonne has more than 21 years of business experience and has held senior business and project management positions in multinational companies including Hewlett-Packard, Zurich Financial Services, and Ascom Telecommunications, as well as in several management consulting organisations. Using an inductive approach in his Doctoral research, he investigated managers' perceptions regarding an "integrative" (synchronised) approach to managing knowledge and information in support of organisational processes. Dr. Minonne lives in Switzerland and speaks fluent Italian, German, and English.

Ezra Ondari-Okemwa's interest in research lies in knowledge management in its broadest terms. Within the broader field of knowledge management, he has research interests in organizational learning, knowledge management in government-owned organizations in sub-Saharan Africa, knowledge production through scholarly publishing, management of indigenous knowledge systems, open access as a publishing mode of enhancing knowledge production, and distribution of knowledge in the sub-Saharan Africa region. He also has research interests in knowledge management education in departments of library and information science in institutions of higher learning in South Africa.

Orlando Petiz Pereira holds a PhD in Economic and Business Sciences. He is an Assistant Professor at the University of Minho, School of Economics and Management, Department of Economics, Portugal. His research areas are innovation and knowledge economics, economics of the firm and human resources, labour and education economics, management and economics of competitiveness and creativity, social economics, and entrepreneurship.

Milly Perry has been employed since 1999 with The Open University of Israel, holding management positions. Through her positions, as well as her PhD. on Information Science and Knowledge Management (Bar-Ilan University, Israel) and Post Doc periods, Dr. Perry has gained strong expertise in higher education knowledge management and ICT change management. She was a member of the steering committee of Israel's National Science Council, a member of The World Bank Knowledge-Management Research and Policy GDN, and serves as an external expert at the OECD IMHE, The European-Mediterranean University policy forum, and a Board Director at the European Association for Research managers and Administrators (EARMA). Dr. Perry served as the initiator and facilitator of aKadeMya, (CoP for managers and scholars implementing knowledge management in higher education) a member of the editorial committee of *The Israeli KM* book, a Chief Knowledge Officer of the Israeli Knowledge Managers' Association, and a management committee member of the European Network for Science and Technology Research in a Knowledge-Based Economy (STRIKE). Dr. Perry is a member of several scientific committees and a speaker at KM conferences worldwide.

Juani Swart specializes in knowledge management and the management of knowledge workers. She is Head of the Organization Studies group and Director of the Work and Employment Research Centre (WERC), which has world-class expertise in knowledge, change and leadership. Her research is focused on the management of knowledge in professional services firms. This research develops an understanding of the transfer of human capital into intellectual capital, thereby linking the intellectual capital, HRM, and performance debates. She has published widely in the area of people management in knowledge intensive firms, intellectual capital structures, and systems approaches to knowledge management.

John Tull, held CEO, regional MD, and SVP roles in his 25 years of technology business across Asia before applying that experience to entrepreneurship development in developing economies. Since 2009, he has worked extensively in Rwanda, Kenya, Tanzania, and Mozambique to create and implement industry transformation programs in agriculture-related businesses by applying an "inclusive" social investor approach. John is the founder of Inclusive Capital, a capability effectiveness consultancy focused on Africa and Asia. Inclusive Capital identifies three interacting forms of organisational capital (financial, intellectual, and social, and calls them the "Capital Triple Play") that combine to create the adaptive strategic capabilities essential to delivering sustainable value in uncertain environments. John is a graduate of Johns Hopkins University, has published academic papers on intellectual capital and strategic change management, authored numerous practitioner articles, and is returning to part-time PhD completion at the University of Sydney.

Geoff Turner is the Executive Director of the European Centre of Knowledge Management Research, which is hosted by the University of Nicosia, Cyprus, where he is an Associate Professor in Accounting. He holds a BA in Accountancy and an MBA and PhD in Accounting. Prior to embarking on an academic career, Geoff was a practicing financial manager in Australia, holding senior positions at various times in British Aerospace, Avery Dennison, and TI Automotive Systems. Since then, and for more than 20 years, he has been researching, teaching, practicing, and advising internationally in the fields of accounting, financial management, and performance measurement, as well as supervising students engaged in research at both Doctoral and Masters level. In addition, he is the Editor of the *Electronic Journal of Knowledge Management*, a member of the executive committee for a number of European and international conferences, and Treasurer of the Cyprus Cricket Association.

Hana Urbancova graduated in 2008 with a Master's degree in the field of Business and Business Administration at the Faculty of Economics and Management at the Czech University of Life Sciences in Prague, where she continues her Ph.D. studies in the field of Management. In her Ph.D. studies, she focuses on Knowledge Management and Knowledge Continuity Management. In her pedagogical and scientific-research work, she focuses mainly on the area of Strategic Management. She is a researcher and co-researcher of several projects and grants and regularly publishes the results of her work in scientific journals and at conferences.

Index

A

absorptive capacity (ACAP) 277
abstracting 354
accelerated learning 353
avatar 349

B

Balanced Scorecard 54, 120, 126, 128, 154, 156-157, 169-171, 173, 244-246, 266
Bio-KM 141
Blackboard 391
blogs 322, 386
Bottom-up approach 23, 47
bulletin boards 330
Business Continuity Management (BCM) 255
business simulations 349

C

capacity 302
Centre for Corporate Innovation and Development in Catalonia (CIDEM) 54
collective mind 89, 106, 230
Communities of Practice (CoPs) 38, 316-317
competence 240
Computer-Mediated Communication (CMC) 317
conceptual knowledge 98
conferencing systems 330
contagion model 165
Continuous Professional Teacher Development (CPTD) framework 68
creativity 69, 211
Creativity, Invention, and Innovation (CII) 66
CroSA project 68, 72, 75, 79, 81, 87

D

discussion lists 333
Domain Knowledge 149, 159-164, 166
dynamic capability approach 299

E

Economic Value Added (EVA) 244-245
education 242
email 325
embedded knowledge 4, 99, 355
embodied knowledge 4, 195
embrained knowledge 4
encoded knowledge 4, 6
encultured knowledge 4
Entrepreneurial Projects 79, 87
European Institute of Innovation and Technology (EIT) 38
explicit knowledge 210

F

Facebook 322
factual knowledge 98
FEXIS programme 97
first generation KM 275
Ford 237

G

gatekeepers 108, 118, 120
Giddens' Structuration Theory 285
global village 115, 118, 126, 161

H

Hierarchy Assessment Index (HAI) model 367
Higher Educational Institutions (HEIs) 1
Higher Education (HE) 339